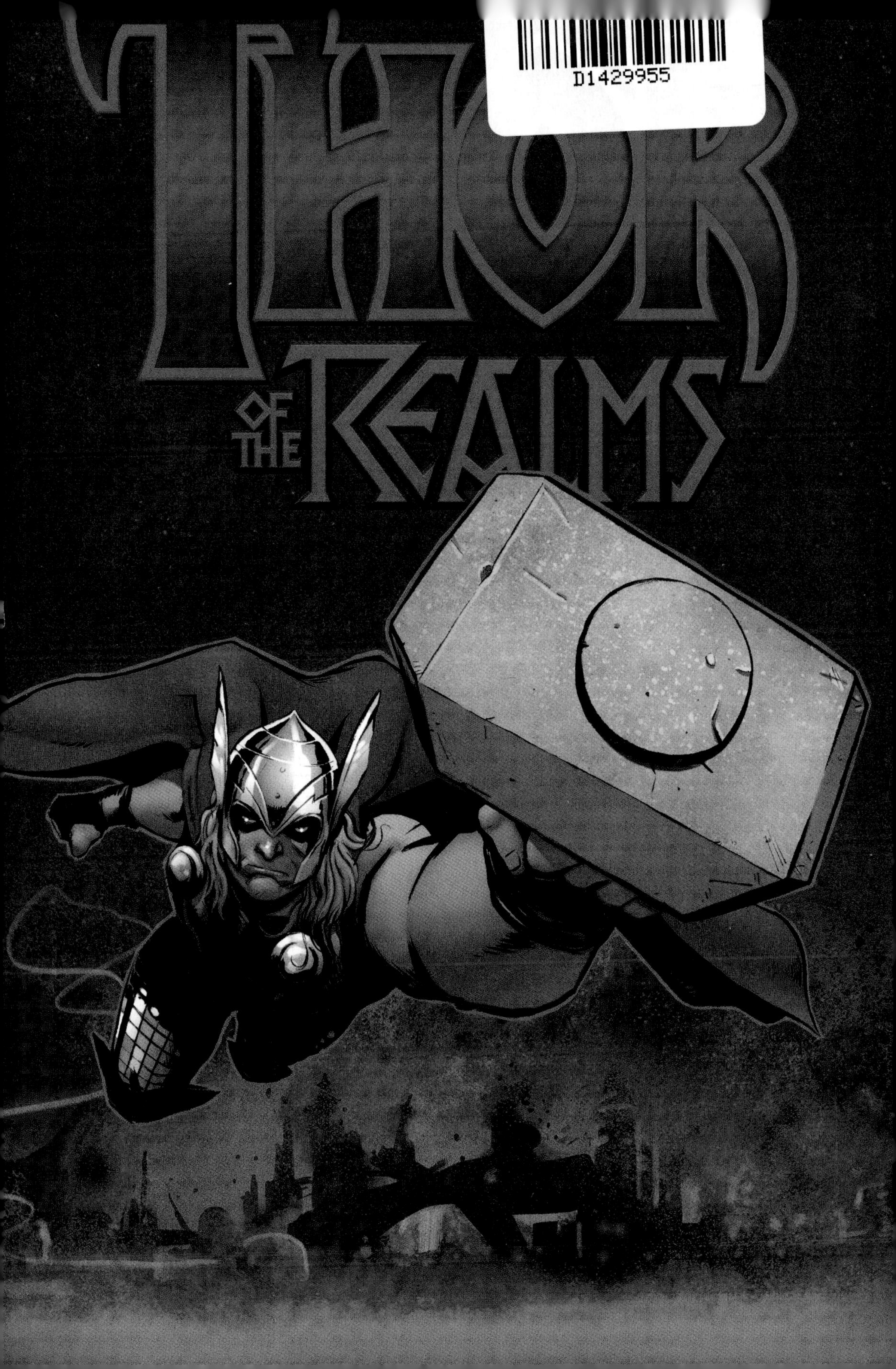
THOR
OF THE REALMS

**ASSISTANT EDITORS:** HOWARD MACKIE, ALEJANDRO ARBONA, CHARLES BEACHAM & JON MOISAN WITH MARC SIRY

**EDITORS:** STAN LEE, LEN WEIN, MARK GRUENWALD, WARREN SIMONS & WIL MOSS WITH RALPH MACCHIO

**EXECUTIVE EDITOR (Mighty Thor #12):** TOM BREVOORT

COLLECTION EDITOR: **MARK D. BEAZLEY**
ASSISTANT EDITOR **CAITLIN O'CONNELL**
ASSOCIATE MANAGING EDITOR: **KATERI WOODY**
ASSOCIATE MANAGER, DIGITAL ASSETS: **JOE HOCHSTEIN**
MASTERWORKS EDITOR: **CORY SEDLMEIER**
SENIOR EDITOR, SPECIAL PROJECTS: **JENNIFER GRÜNWALD**
VP PRODUCTION & SPECIAL PROJECTS: **JEFF YOUNGQUIST**
RESEARCH: **JESS HARROLD**
LAYOUT: **JEPH YORK**

PRODUCTION: **SALENA MAHINA**
BOOK DESIGNER: **STACIE ZUCKER**

SVP PRINT, SALES & MARKETING: **DAVID GABRIEL**
DIRECTOR, LICENSED PUBLISHING: **SVEN LARSEN**
EDITOR IN CHIEF: **C.B. CEBULSKI**
CHIEF CREATIVE OFFICER: **JOE QUESADA**
PRESIDENT: **DAN BUCKLEY**
EXECUTIVE PRODUCER: **ALAN FINE**

THOR CREATED BY **STAN LEE, LARRY LIEBER & JACK KIRBY**

THOR OF THE REALMS. Contains material originally published in magazine form as THOR (1966) #157, #159, #233-234, #347-349 and #400; THOR (2007) #12; THOR: THE TRIAL OF THOR; MIGHTY THOR #12; ORIGINAL SIN #5.1; and JOURNEY INTO MYSTERY #97. First printing 2019. ISBN 978-1-302-91838-5. Published by MARVEL WORLDWIDE, INC., a subsidiary of MARVEL ENTERTAINMENT, LLC. OFFICE OF PUBLICATION: 135 West 50th Street, New York, NY 10020. © 2019 MARVEL. No similarity between any of the names, characters, persons, and/or institutions in this magazine with those of any living or dead person or institution is intended, and any such similarity which may exist is purely coincidental. **Printed in the U.S.A.** DAN BUCKLEY, President, Marvel Entertainment; JOHN NEE, Publisher; JOE QUESADA, Chief Creative Officer; TOM BREVOORT, SVP of Publishing; DAVID BOGART, Associate Publisher & SVP of Talent Affairs; DAVID GABRIEL, SVP of Sales & Marketing, Publishing; JEFF YOUNGQUIST, VP of Production & Special Projects; DAN CARR, Executive Director of Publishing Technology; ALEX MORALES, Director of Publishing Operations; DAN EDINGTON, Managing Editor; SUSAN CRESPI, Production Manager; STAN LEE, Chairman Emeritus. For information regarding advertising in Marvel Comics or on Marvel.com, please contact Vit DeBellis, Custom Solutions & Integrated Advertising Manager, at vdebellis@marvel.com. For Marvel subscription inquiries, please call 888-511-5480. Manufactured between 5/31/2019 and 7/2/2019 by LSC COMMUNICATIONS INC., KENDALLVILLE, IN, USA.

10 9 8 7 6 5 4 3 2 1

# THOR OF THE REALMS

**JOURNEY INTO MYSTERY #97** – YGGDRASIL THE WORLD-TREE

WRITER: STAN LEE PENCILER: JACK KIRBY INKER: GEORGE ROUSSOS LETTERER: ART SIMEK COVER ART: JACK KIRBY

**THOR #157** – ASGARD
**THOR #159** – NIFFLEHEIM

WRITER: STAN LEE PENCILER: JACK KIRBY INKER: VINCE COLLETTA LETTERER: SAM ROSEN COVER ART: JACK KIRBY

**THOR #233-234** – MIDGARD

WRITER: GERRY CONWAY PENCILER: JOHN BUSCEMA INKERS: CHIC STONE & JOE SINNOTT
COLORIST: PETRA GOLDBERG LETTERERS: ART SIMEK & JOHN COSTANZA COVER ART: GIL KANE

**THOR #347-348** – SVARTALFHEIM
**THOR #349** – MUSPELHEIM

WRITER & PENCILER: WALTER SIMONSON INKERS: WALTER SIMONSON & BOB WIACEK
COLORISTS: STEVE OLIFF & OLYOPTICS 2.0 AFTER CHRISTIE SCHEELE LETTERER: JOHN WORKMAN
COVER ART: WALTER SIMONSON, STEVE OLIFF & OLYOPTICS 2.0

**THOR #400** – ALFHEIM

WRITER: RANDALL FRENZ ARTIST: CHARLES VESS COLORIST: CHRISTIE SCHEELE LETTERER: MICHAEL HEISLER
COVER ART: RON FRENZ & BRETT BREEDING

**THOR (2007) #12** – JOTUNHEIM

WRITER: J. MICHAEL STRACZYNSKI PENCILER: OLIVIER COIPEL INKER: MARK MORALES COLORIST: LAURA MARTIN
LETTERER: CHRIS ELIOPOULOS COVER ART: OLIVIER COIPEL, MARK MORALES & LAURA MARTIN

**THOR: THE TRIAL OF THOR** – VANAHEIM

WRITER: PETER MILLIGAN ARTIST: CARY NORD COLORIST: CHRISTINA STRAIN LETTERER: VC's JOE CARAMAGNA
COVER ART: CARY NORD & CHRISTINA STRAIN

**MIGHTY THOR #12** – NIDAVELLIR

WRITER: JASON AARON ARTIST: RUSSELL DAUTERMAN (PAGES 1-4 & 19-20)
COLORIST: MATTHEW WILSON (PAGES 1-4 & 19-20) ART & COLOR: FRAZER IRVING (PAGES 5-18) LETTERER: VC's JOE SABINO
COVER ART: RUSSELL DAUTERMAN & MATTHEW WILSON

**ORIGINAL SIN #5.1** – HEVEN

PLOTTERS: JASON AARON & AL EWING SCRIPTER: AL EWING ARTIST: LEE GARBETT (PAGES 1-17 & 20)

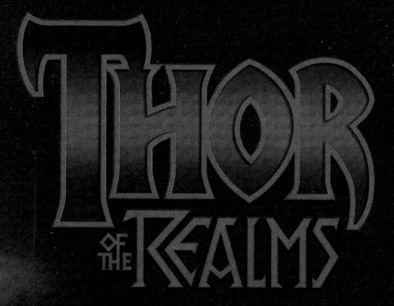

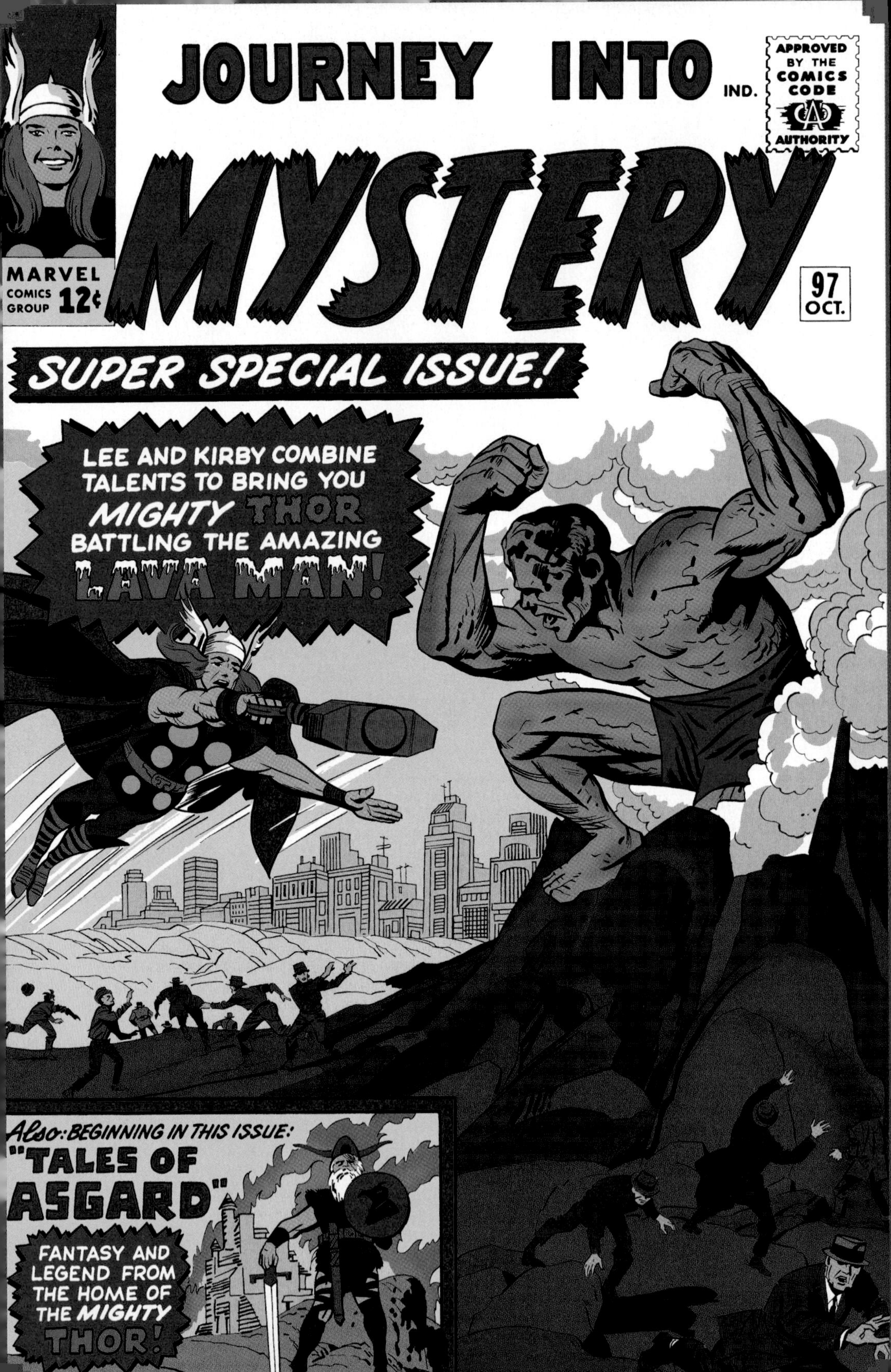
JOURNEY INTO MYSTERY
IND.
APPROVED BY THE COMICS CODE AUTHORITY
MARVEL COMICS GROUP 12¢
97 OCT.
SUPER SPECIAL ISSUE!
LEE AND KIRBY COMBINE TALENTS TO BRING YOU MIGHTY THOR BATTLING THE AMAZING LAVA MAN!
Also: BEGINNING IN THIS ISSUE: "TALES OF ASGARD"
FANTASY AND LEGEND FROM THE HOME OF THE MIGHTY THOR!

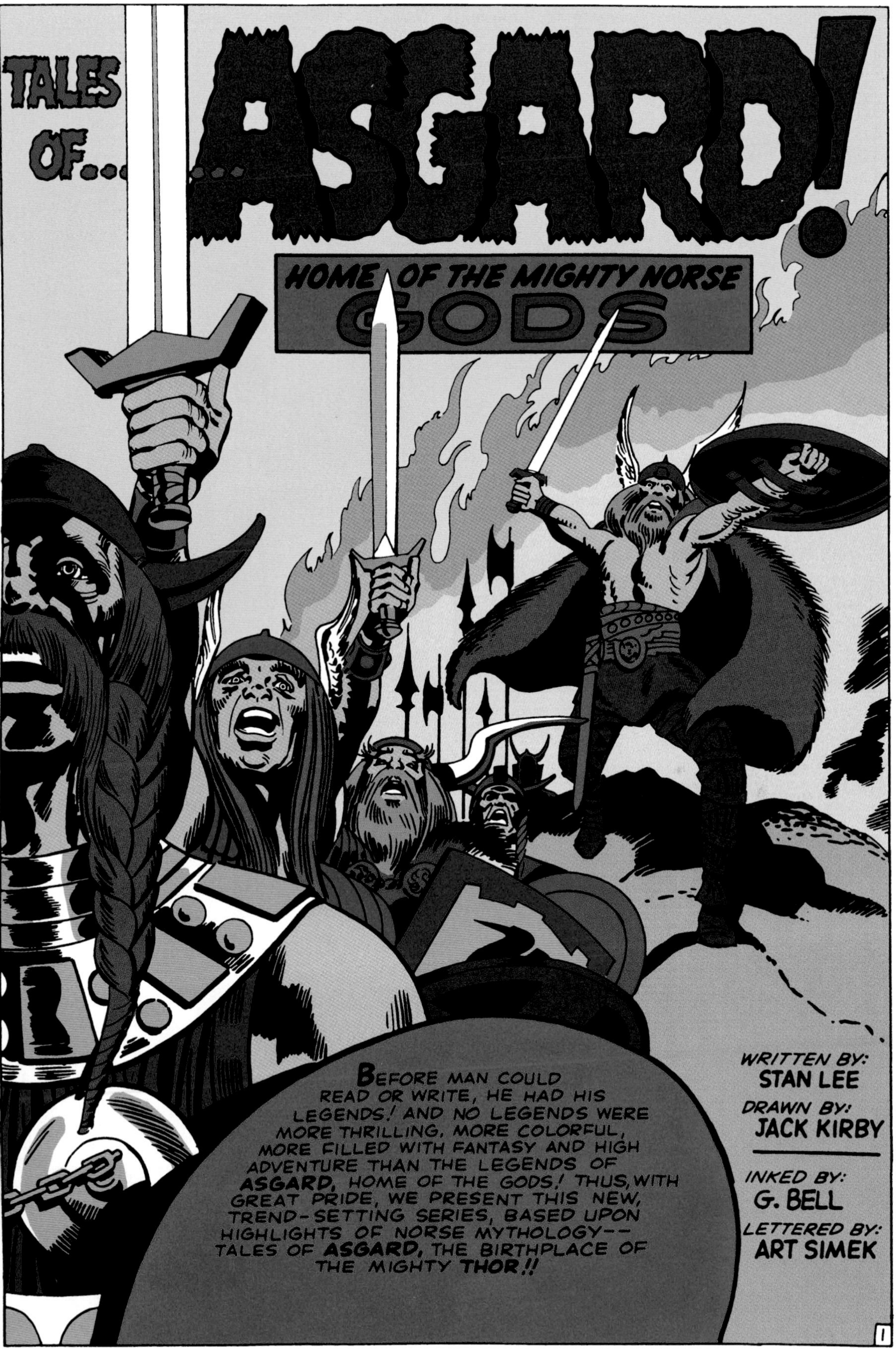
TALES OF... ...ASGARD!
HOME OF THE MIGHTY NORSE GODS
BEFORE MAN COULD READ OR WRITE, HE HAD HIS LEGENDS! AND NO LEGENDS WERE MORE THRILLING, MORE COLORFUL, MORE FILLED WITH FANTASY AND HIGH ADVENTURE THAN THE LEGENDS OF ASGARD, HOME OF THE GODS! THUS, WITH GREAT PRIDE, WE PRESENT THIS NEW, TREND-SETTING SERIES, BASED UPON HIGHLIGHTS OF NORSE MYTHOLOGY-- TALES OF ASGARD, THE BIRTHPLACE OF THE MIGHTY THOR!!
WRITTEN BY: STAN LEE
DRAWN BY: JACK KIRBY
INKED BY: G. BELL
LETTERED BY: ART SIMEK
1

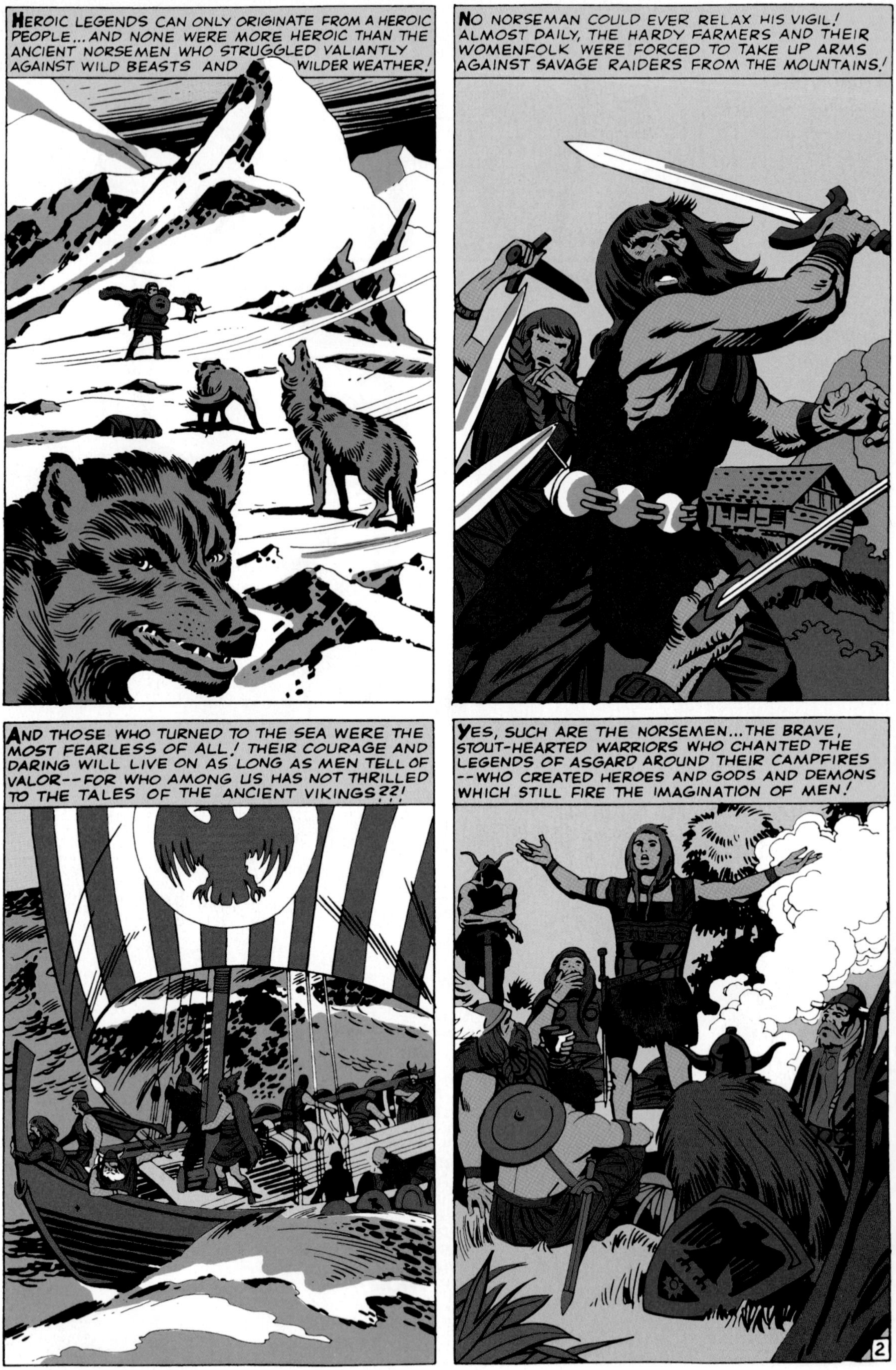
HEROIC LEGENDS CAN ONLY ORIGINATE FROM A HEROIC PEOPLE... AND NONE WERE MORE HEROIC THAN THE ANCIENT NORSEMEN WHO STRUGGLED VALIANTLY AGAINST WILD BEASTS AND WILDER WEATHER!
NO NORSEMAN COULD EVER RELAX HIS VIGIL! ALMOST DAILY, THE HARDY FARMERS AND THEIR WOMENFOLK WERE FORCED TO TAKE UP ARMS AGAINST SAVAGE RAIDERS FROM THE MOUNTAINS!
AND THOSE WHO TURNED TO THE SEA WERE THE MOST FEARLESS OF ALL! THEIR COURAGE AND DARING WILL LIVE ON AS LONG AS MEN TELL OF VALOR--FOR WHO AMONG US HAS NOT THRILLED TO THE TALES OF THE ANCIENT VIKINGS??!
YES, SUCH ARE THE NORSEMEN...THE BRAVE, STOUT-HEARTED WARRIORS WHO CHANTED THE LEGENDS OF ASGARD AROUND THEIR CAMPFIRES --WHO CREATED HEROES AND GODS AND DEMONS WHICH STILL FIRE THE IMAGINATION OF MEN!
2

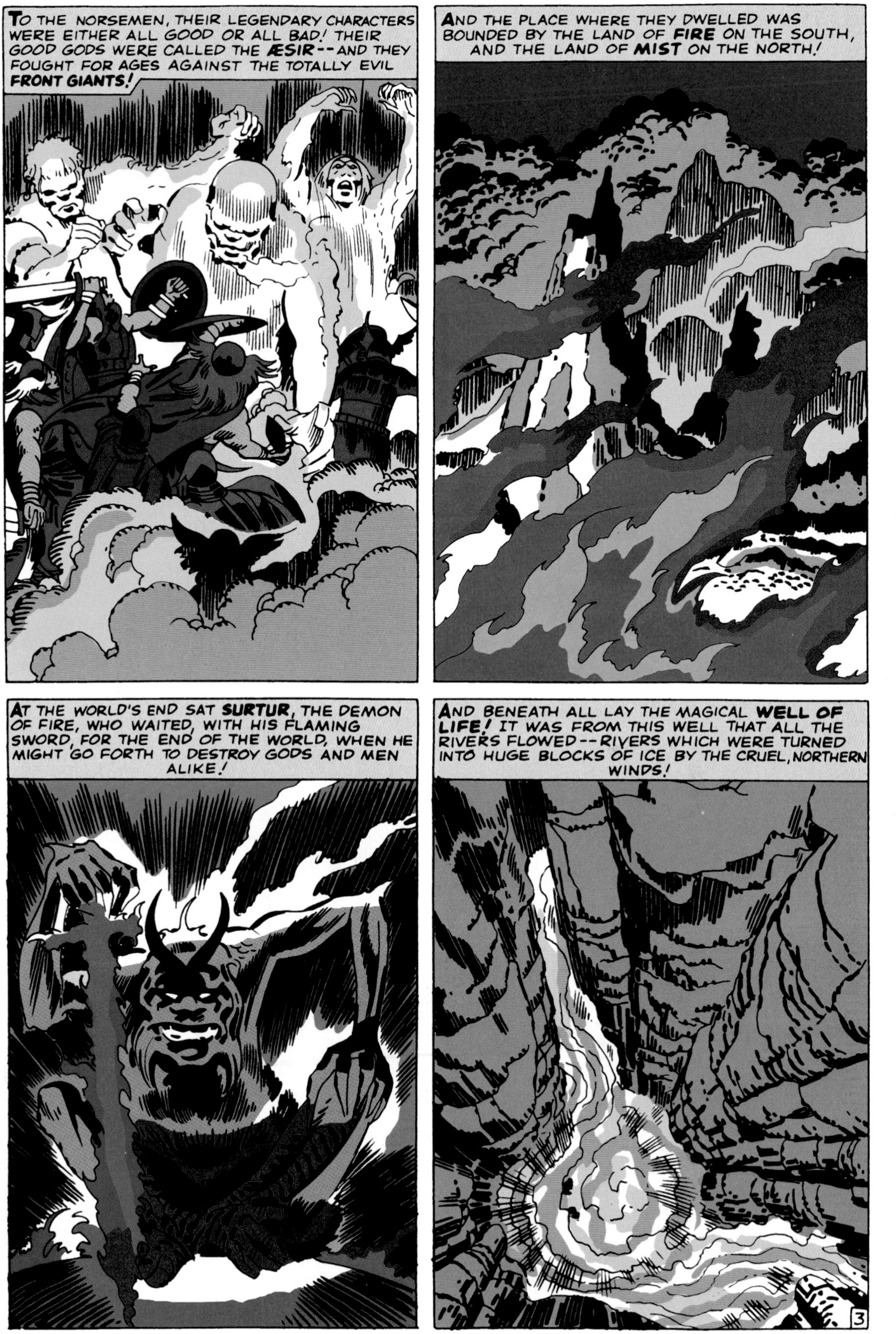

TO THE NORSEMEN, THEIR LEGENDARY CHARACTERS WERE EITHER ALL GOOD OR ALL BAD! THEIR GOOD GODS WERE CALLED THE ÆSIR--AND THEY FOUGHT FOR AGES AGAINST THE TOTALLY EVIL FRONT GIANTS!
AND THE PLACE WHERE THEY DWELLED WAS BOUNDED BY THE LAND OF FIRE ON THE SOUTH, AND THE LAND OF MIST ON THE NORTH!
AT THE WORLD'S END SAT SURTUR, THE DEMON OF FIRE, WHO WAITED, WITH HIS FLAMING SWORD, FOR THE END OF THE WORLD, WHEN HE MIGHT GO FORTH TO DESTROY GODS AND MEN ALIKE!
AND BENEATH ALL LAY THE MAGICAL WELL OF LIFE! IT WAS FROM THIS WELL THAT ALL THE RIVERS FLOWED--RIVERS WHICH WERE TURNED INTO HUGE BLOCKS OF ICE BY THE CRUEL, NORTHERN WINDS!
3

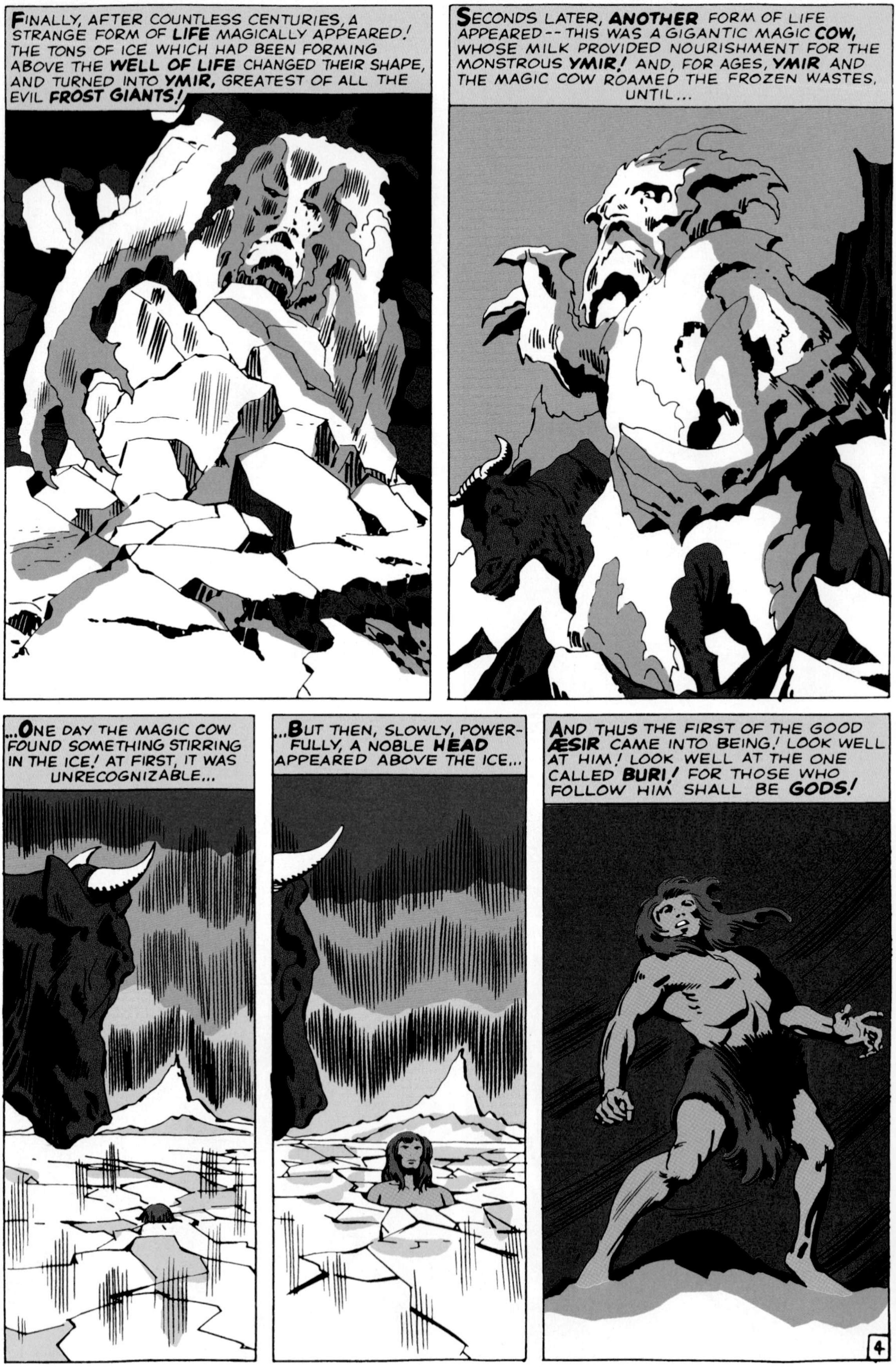
FINALLY, AFTER COUNTLESS CENTURIES, A STRANGE FORM OF LIFE MAGICALLY APPEARED! THE TONS OF ICE WHICH HAD BEEN FORMING ABOVE THE WELL OF LIFE CHANGED THEIR SHAPE, AND TURNED INTO YMIR, GREATEST OF ALL THE EVIL FROST GIANTS!
SECONDS LATER, ANOTHER FORM OF LIFE APPEARED -- THIS WAS A GIGANTIC MAGIC COW, WHOSE MILK PROVIDED NOURISHMENT FOR THE MONSTROUS YMIR! AND, FOR AGES, YMIR AND THE MAGIC COW ROAMED THE FROZEN WASTES, UNTIL...
...ONE DAY THE MAGIC COW FOUND SOMETHING STIRRING IN THE ICE! AT FIRST, IT WAS UNRECOGNIZABLE...
...BUT THEN, SLOWLY, POWERFULLY, A NOBLE HEAD APPEARED ABOVE THE ICE...
AND THUS THE FIRST OF THE GOOD ÆSIR CAME INTO BEING! LOOK WELL AT HIM! LOOK WELL AT THE ONE CALLED BURI! FOR THOSE WHO FOLLOW HIM SHALL BE GODS!
4

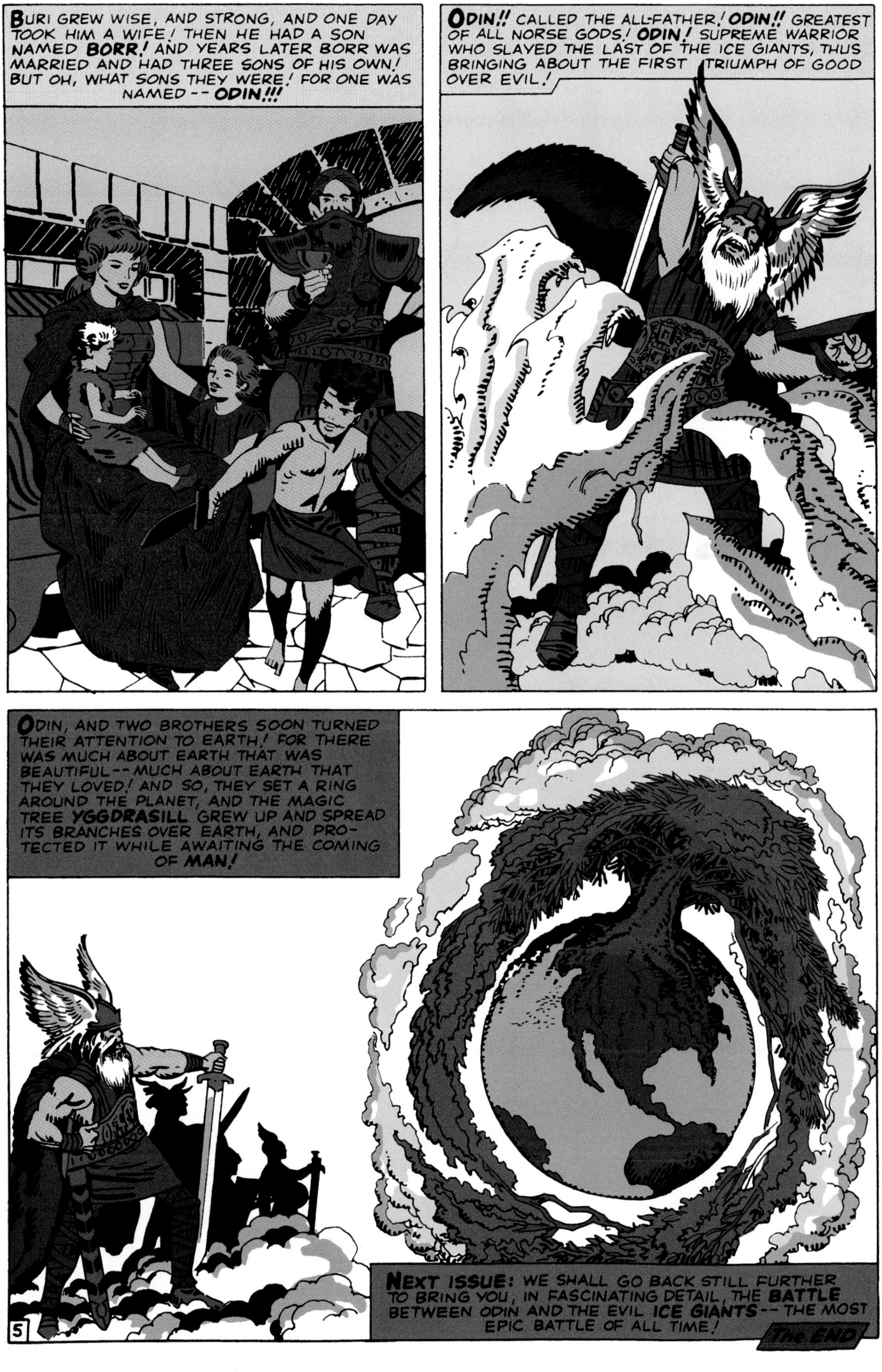
BURI GREW WISE, AND STRONG, AND ONE DAY TOOK HIM A WIFE! THEN HE HAD A SON NAMED BORR! AND YEARS LATER BORR WAS MARRIED AND HAD THREE SONS OF HIS OWN! BUT OH, WHAT SONS THEY WERE! FOR ONE WAS NAMED--ODIN!!!
ODIN!! CALLED THE ALL-FATHER! ODIN!! GREATEST OF ALL NORSE GODS! ODIN! SUPREME WARRIOR WHO SLAYED THE LAST OF THE ICE GIANTS, THUS BRINGING ABOUT THE FIRST TRIUMPH OF GOOD OVER EVIL!
ODIN, AND TWO BROTHERS SOON TURNED THEIR ATTENTION TO EARTH! FOR THERE WAS MUCH ABOUT EARTH THAT WAS BEAUTIFUL--MUCH ABOUT EARTH THAT THEY LOVED! AND SO, THEY SET A RING AROUND THE PLANET, AND THE MAGIC TREE YGGDRASILL GREW UP AND SPREAD ITS BRANCHES OVER EARTH, AND PROTECTED IT WHILE AWAITING THE COMING OF MAN!
5
NEXT ISSUE: WE SHALL GO BACK STILL FURTHER TO BRING YOU, IN FASCINATING DETAIL, THE BATTLE BETWEEN ODIN AND THE EVIL ICE GIANTS--THE MOST EPIC BATTLE OF ALL TIME!
The END

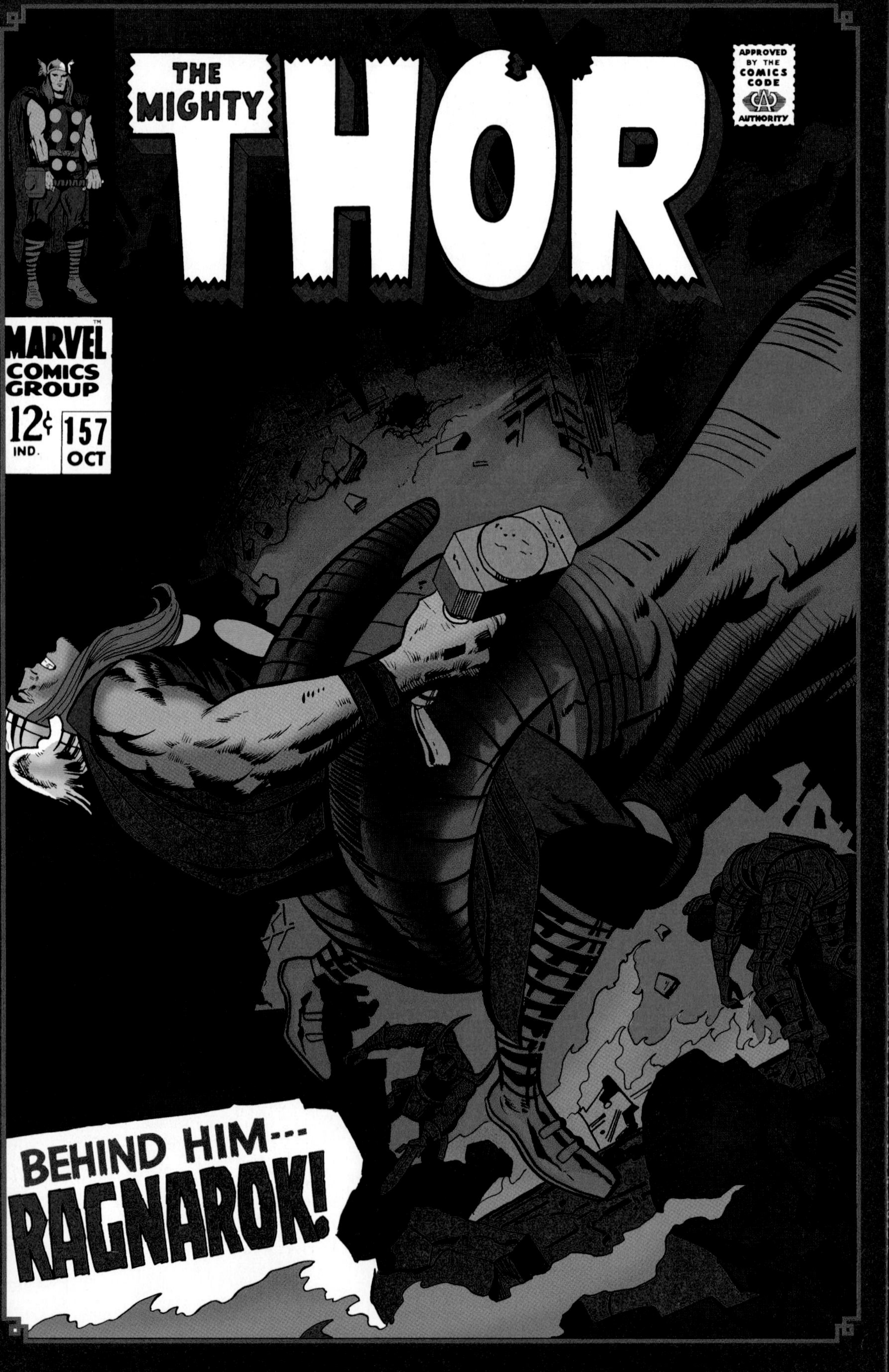
THE MIGHTY
THOR
APPROVED BY THE COMICS CODE AUTHORITY
MARVEL COMICS GROUP
12¢ IND.
157 OCT
BEHIND HIM---
RAGNAROK!

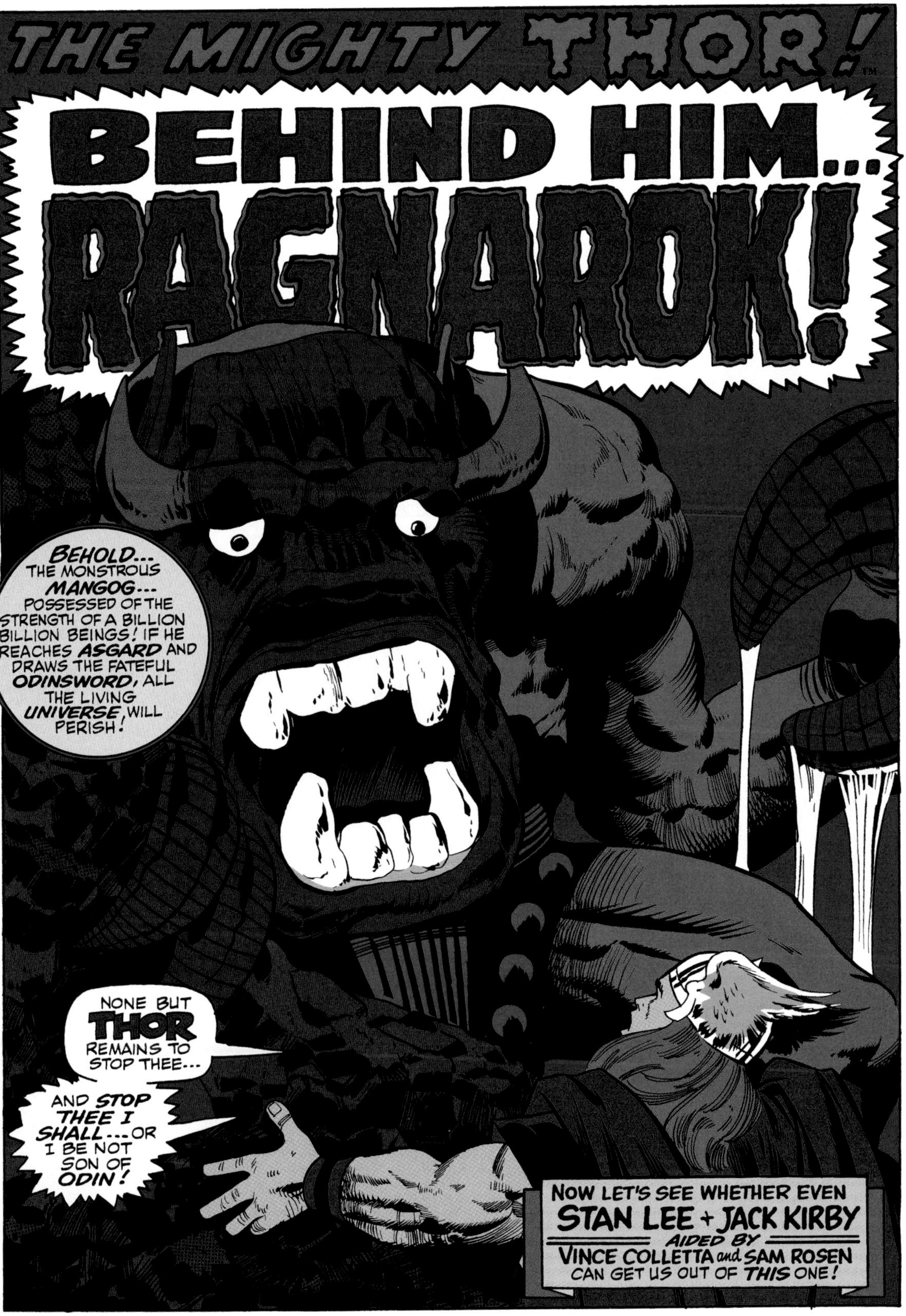
THE MIGHTY THOR!
BEHIND HIM... RAGNAROK!
BEHOLD... THE MONSTROUS MANGOG... POSSESSED OF THE STRENGTH OF A BILLION BILLION BEINGS! IF HE REACHES ASGARD AND DRAWS THE FATEFUL ODINSWORD, ALL THE LIVING UNIVERSE WILL PERISH!
NONE BUT THOR REMAINS TO STOP THEE...
AND STOP THEE I SHALL...OR I BE NOT SON OF ODIN!
NOW LET'S SEE WHETHER EVEN STAN LEE + JACK KIRBY AIDED BY VINCE COLLETTA and SAM ROSEN CAN GET US OUT OF THIS ONE!

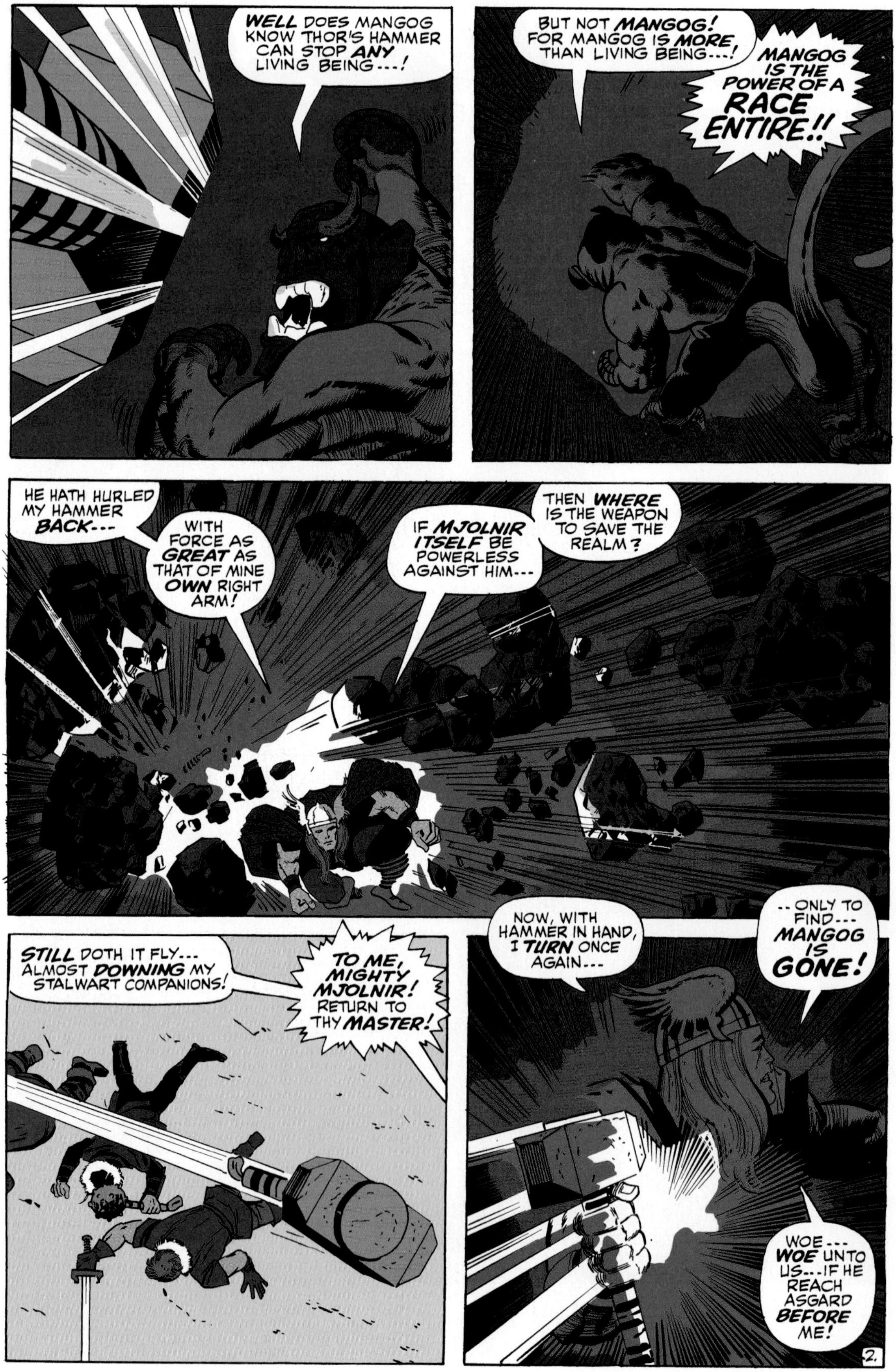
WELL DOES MANGOG KNOW THOR'S HAMMER CAN STOP ANY LIVING BEING---!
BUT NOT MANGOG! FOR MANGOG IS MORE, THAN LIVING BEING---!
MANGOG IS THE POWER OF A RACE ENTIRE!!
HE HATH HURLED MY HAMMER BACK---
WITH FORCE AS GREAT AS THAT OF MINE OWN RIGHT ARM!
IF MJOLNIR ITSELF BE POWERLESS AGAINST HIM---
THEN WHERE IS THE WEAPON TO SAVE THE REALM?
STILL DOTH IT FLY--- ALMOST DOWNING MY STALWART COMPANIONS!
TO ME, MIGHTY MJOLNIR! RETURN TO THY MASTER!
NOW, WITH HAMMER IN HAND, I TURN ONCE AGAIN---
--ONLY TO FIND--- MANGOG IS GONE!
WOE--- WOE UNTO US---IF HE REACH ASGARD BEFORE ME!
2.

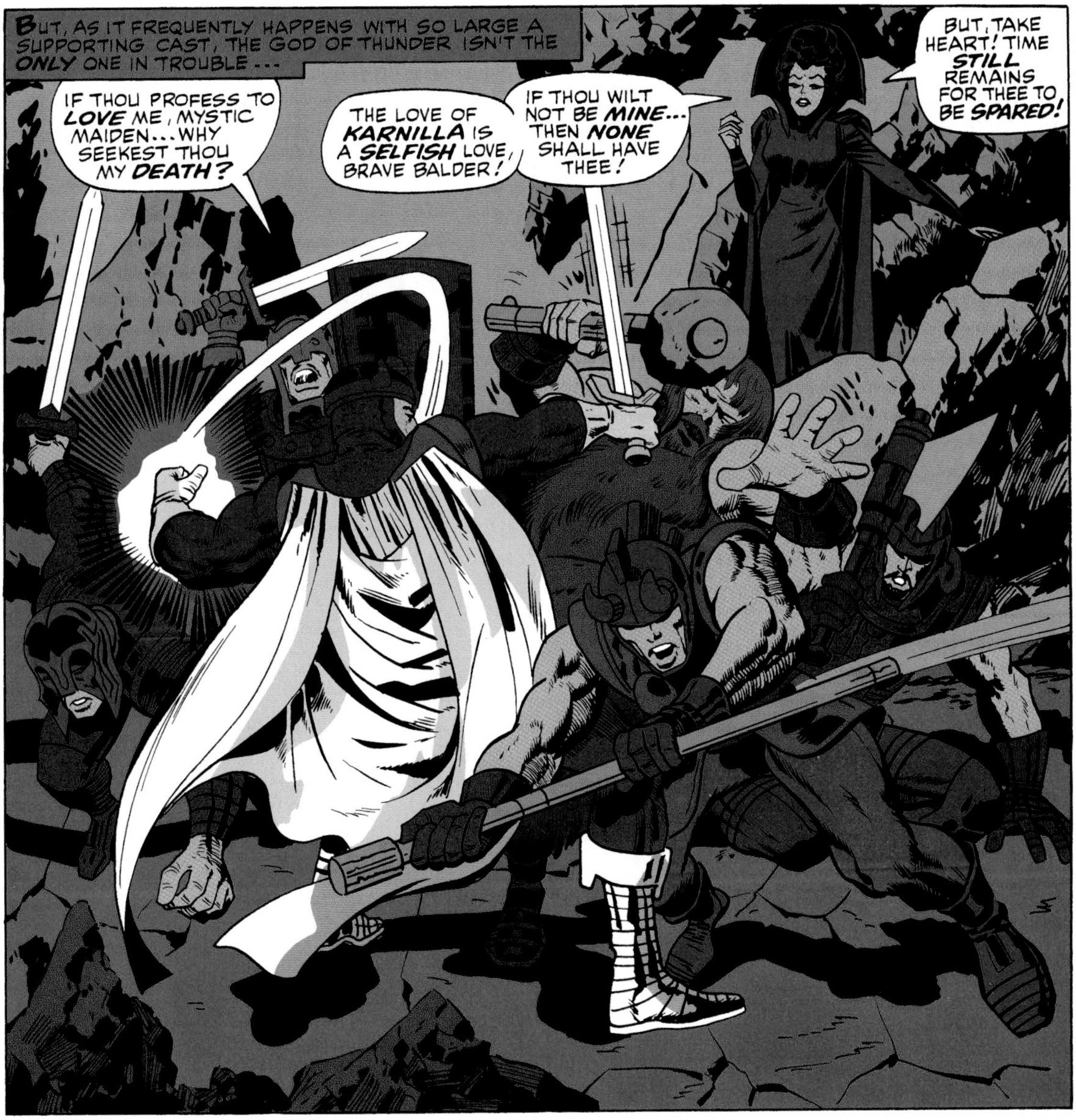

But, as it frequently happens with so large a supporting cast, the God of Thunder isn't the only one in trouble...
If thou profess to love me, Mystic Maiden... why seekest thou my death?
The love of Karnilla is a selfish love, brave Balder!
If thou wilt not be mine... then none shall have thee!
But, take heart! Time still remains for thee to be spared!

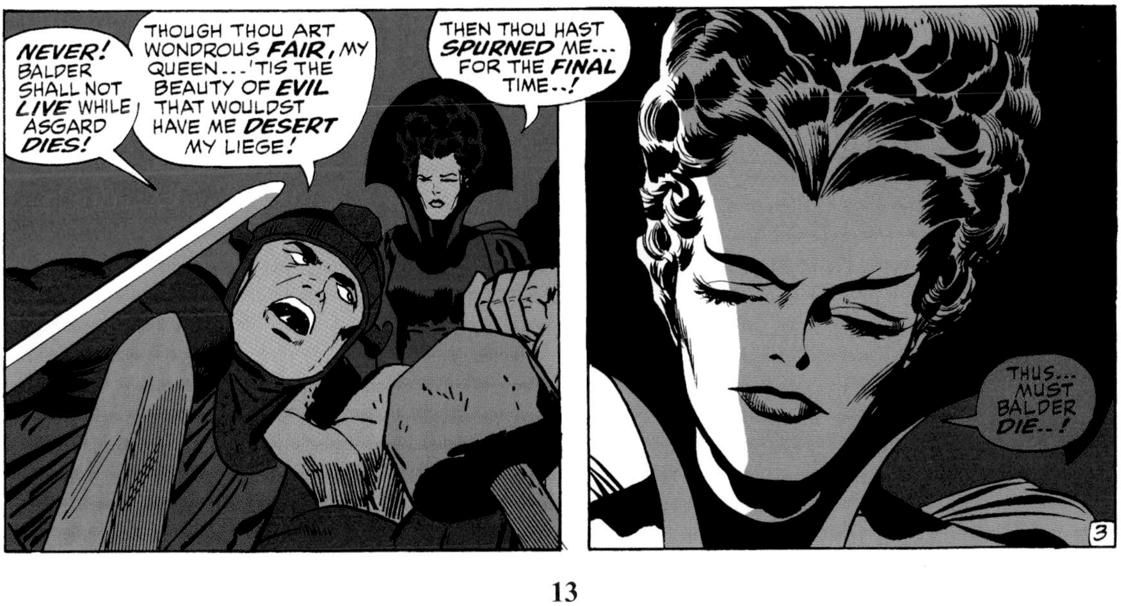

Never! Balder shall not live while Asgard dies!
Though thou art wondrous fair, my queen... 'tis the beauty of evil that wouldst have me desert my liege!
Then thou hast spurned me... for the final time..!
Thus... must Balder die..!
3

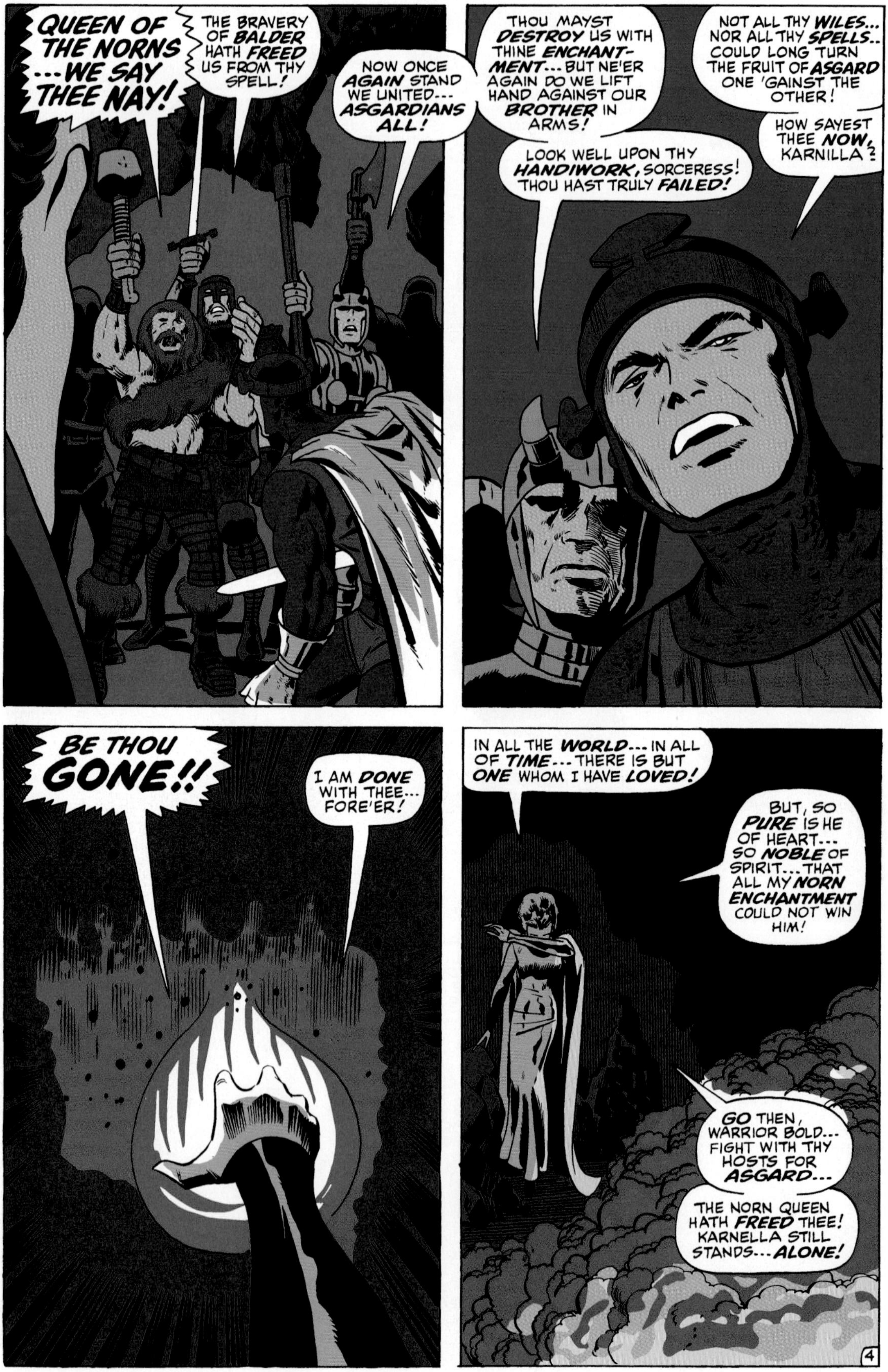
QUEEN OF THE NORNS ...WE SAY THEE NAY!
THE BRAVERY OF BALDER HATH FREED US FROM THY SPELL!
NOW ONCE AGAIN STAND WE UNITED--- ASGARDIANS ALL!
THOU MAYST DESTROY US WITH THINE ENCHANTMENT... BUT NE'ER AGAIN DO WE LIFT HAND AGAINST OUR BROTHER IN ARMS!
NOT ALL THY WILES... NOR ALL THY SPELLS.. COULD LONG TURN THE FRUIT OF ASGARD ONE 'GAINST THE OTHER!
LOOK WELL UPON THY HANDIWORK, SORCERESS! THOU HAST TRULY FAILED!
HOW SAYEST THEE NOW, KARNILLA?
BE THOU GONE!!
I AM DONE WITH THEE... FORE'ER!
IN ALL THE WORLD--- IN ALL OF TIME--- THERE IS BUT ONE WHOM I HAVE LOVED!
BUT, SO PURE IS HE OF HEART--- SO NOBLE OF SPIRIT... THAT ALL MY NORN ENCHANTMENT COULD NOT WIN HIM!
GO THEN, WARRIOR BOLD... FIGHT WITH THY HOSTS FOR ASGARD...
THE NORN QUEEN HATH FREED THEE! KARNELLA STILL STANDS--- ALONE!
4

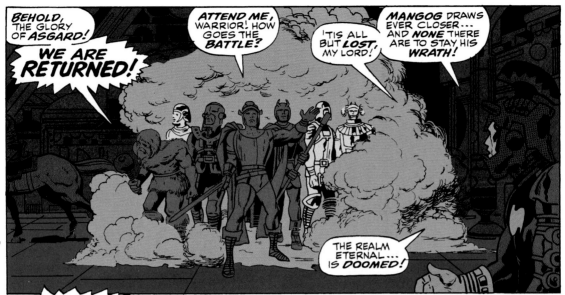

BEHOLD, THE GLORY OF *ASGARD!*

WE ARE *RETURNED!*

ATTEND ME, WARRIOR! HOW GOES THE *BATTLE?*

'TIS ALL BUT *LOST,* MY LORD!

*MANGOG* DRAWS EVER CLOSER... AND *NONE* THERE ARE TO STAY HIS *WRATH!*

THE REALM ETERNAL... IS *DOOMED!*

NOT WHILST AN ASGARDIAN *LIVES!*

TAKE ARMS, ONE AND ALL!! WE FIGHT TILL WE *FALL!*

DIRECTLY AHEAD... LIES *ASGARD!*

NOW, AT LAST, SHALL *MANGOG* AVENGE A BILLION BILLION *DEATHS!*

AS EFFORTLESSLY AS I SHATTER YON *MOUNTAIN*... SO SHALL I SHATTER THE *WORLD* ABOUT ME!

EVEN *NOW,* THEIR SOULS ARE FILLED WITH *FEAR*... WITH DARK AND HAUNTING *DREAD*...

FOR THEY KNOW *FULL WELL* THAT ODIN AND ALL HIS REALM---ARE *DOOMED!*

5

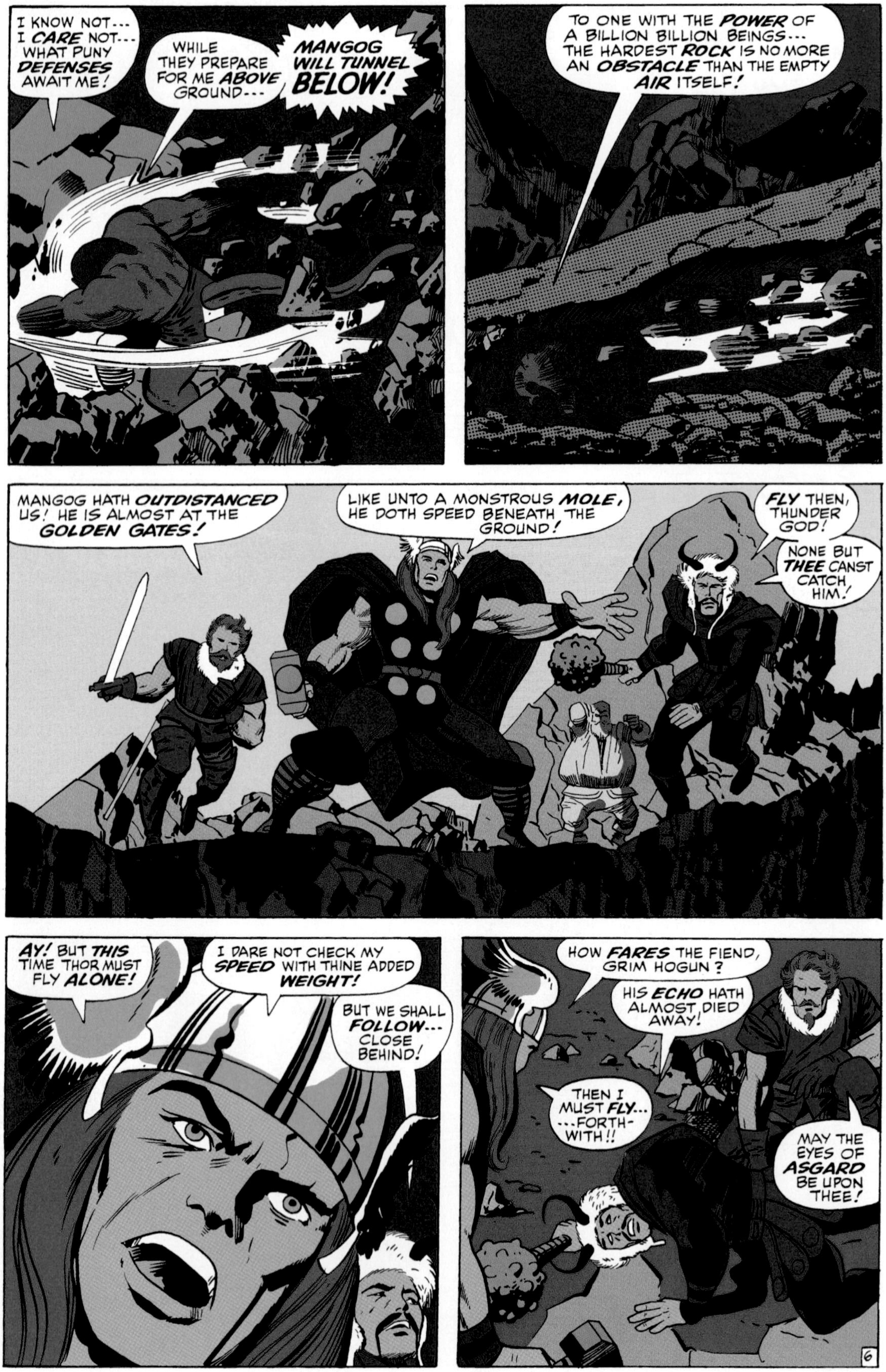
I KNOW NOT--- I CARE NOT--- WHAT PUNY DEFENSES AWAIT ME!
WHILE THEY PREPARE FOR ME ABOVE GROUND---
MANGOG WILL TUNNEL BELOW!
TO ONE WITH THE POWER OF A BILLION BILLION BEINGS--- THE HARDEST ROCK IS NO MORE AN OBSTACLE THAN THE EMPTY AIR ITSELF!
MANGOG HATH OUTDISTANCED US! HE IS ALMOST AT THE GOLDEN GATES!
LIKE UNTO A MONSTROUS MOLE, HE DOTH SPEED BENEATH THE GROUND!
FLY THEN, THUNDER GOD!
NONE BUT THEE CANST CATCH HIM!
AY! BUT THIS TIME THOR MUST FLY ALONE!
I DARE NOT CHECK MY SPEED WITH THINE ADDED WEIGHT!
BUT WE SHALL FOLLOW--- CLOSE BEHIND!
HOW FARES THE FIEND, GRIM HOGUN?
HIS ECHO HATH ALMOST DIED AWAY!
THEN I MUST FLY--- ---FORTH-WITH!!
MAY THE EYES OF ASGARD BE UPON THEE!
6

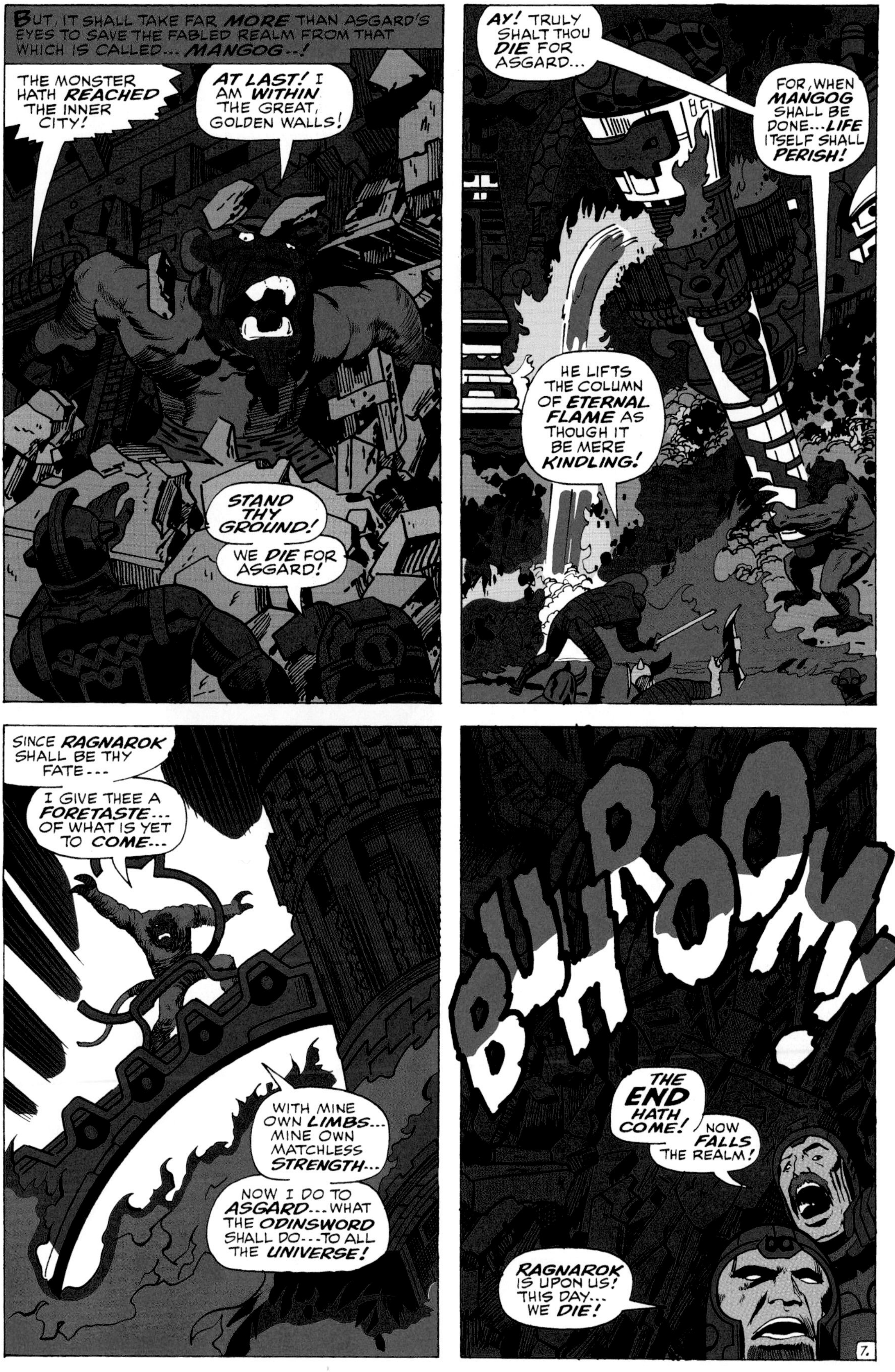

BUT, IT SHALL TAKE FAR MORE THAN ASGARD'S EYES TO SAVE THE FABLED REALM FROM THAT WHICH IS CALLED... MANGOG--!
THE MONSTER HATH REACHED THE INNER CITY!
AT LAST! I AM WITHIN THE GREAT, GOLDEN WALLS!
STAND THY GROUND!
WE DIE FOR ASGARD!
AY! TRULY SHALT THOU DIE FOR ASGARD...
FOR, WHEN MANGOG SHALL BE DONE... LIFE ITSELF SHALL PERISH!
HE LIFTS THE COLUMN OF ETERNAL FLAME AS THOUGH IT BE MERE KINDLING!
SINCE RAGNAROK SHALL BE THY FATE---
I GIVE THEE A FORETASTE... OF WHAT IS YET TO COME...
WITH MINE OWN LIMBS... MINE OWN MATCHLESS STRENGTH...
NOW I DO TO ASGARD--- WHAT THE ODINSWORD SHALL DO---TO ALL THE UNIVERSE!
BUROOM!!
THE END HATH COME!
NOW FALLS THE REALM!
RAGNAROK IS UPON US! THIS DAY... WE DIE!
7.

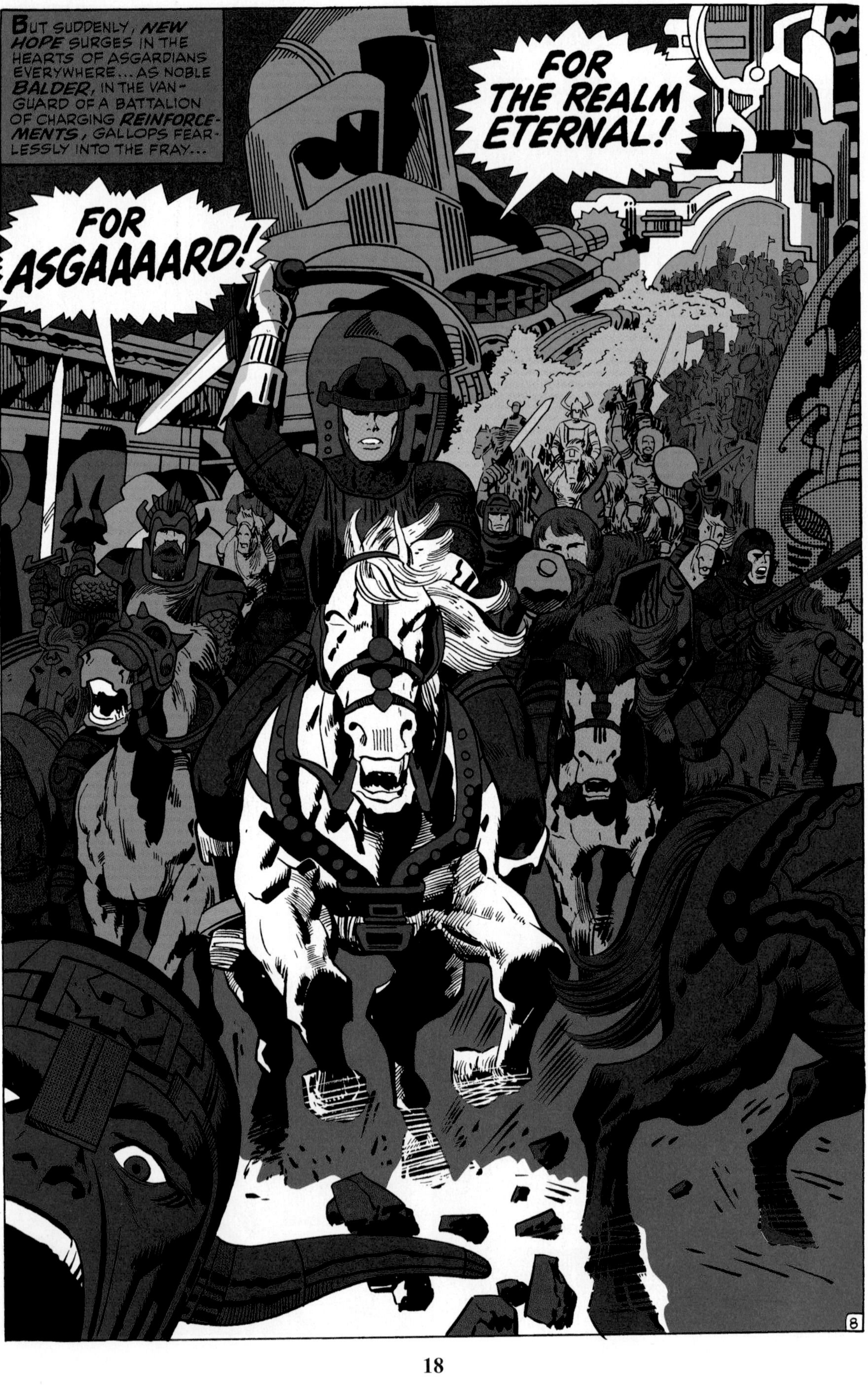
BUT SUDDENLY, NEW HOPE SURGES IN THE HEARTS OF ASGARDIANS EVERYWHERE... AS NOBLE BALDER, IN THE VAN-GUARD OF A BATTALION OF CHARGING REINFORCE-MENTS, GALLOPS FEAR-LESSLY INTO THE FRAY...
FOR THE REALM ETERNAL!
FOR ASGAAAARD!
8

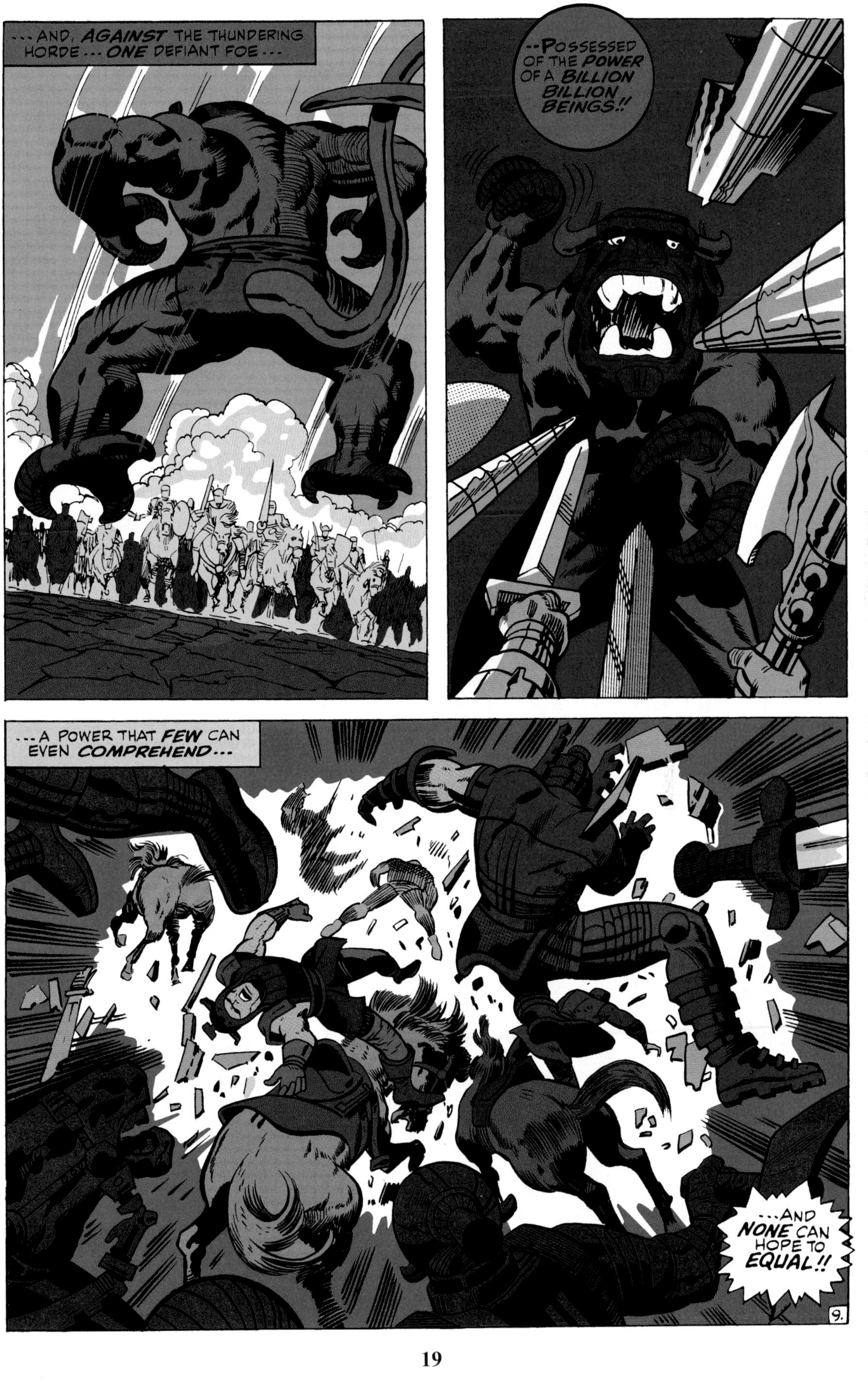
...AND, AGAINST THE THUNDERING HORDE...ONE DEFIANT FOE...
--POSSESSED OF THE POWER OF A BILLION BILLION BEINGS!!
...A POWER THAT FEW CAN EVEN COMPREHEND...
...AND NONE CAN HOPE TO EQUAL!!
9.

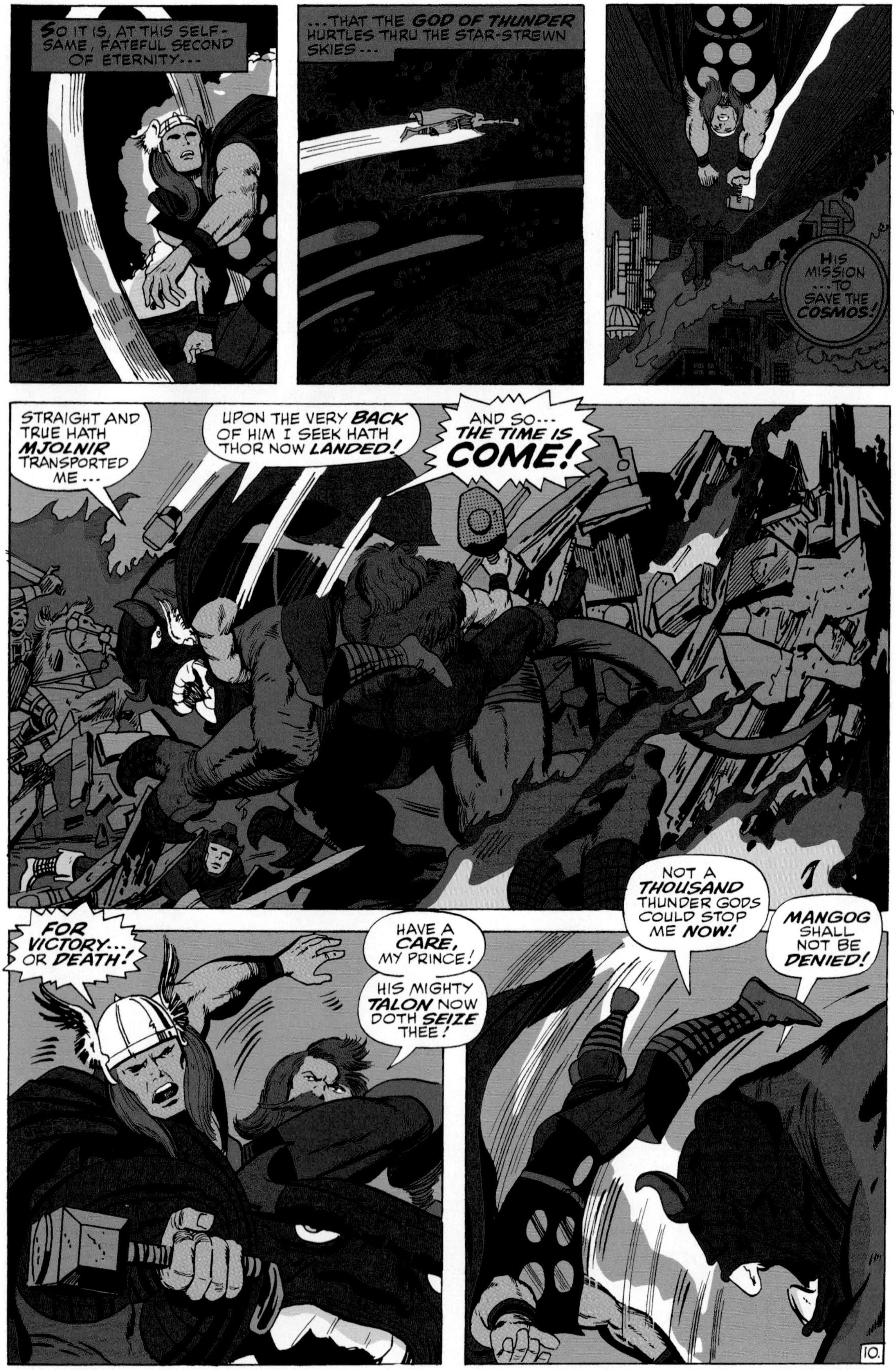

SO IT IS, AT THIS SELF-SAME, FATEFUL SECOND OF ETERNITY...
...THAT THE GOD OF THUNDER HURTLES THRU THE STAR-STREWN SKIES...
HIS MISSION ...TO SAVE THE COSMOS!
STRAIGHT AND TRUE HATH MJOLNIR TRANSPORTED ME...
UPON THE VERY BACK OF HIM I SEEK HATH THOR NOW LANDED!
AND SO... THE TIME IS COME!
FOR VICTORY... OR DEATH!
HAVE A CARE, MY PRINCE!
HIS MIGHTY TALON NOW DOTH SEIZE THEE!
NOT A THOUSAND THUNDER GODS COULD STOP ME NOW!
MANGOG SHALL NOT BE DENIED!
10.

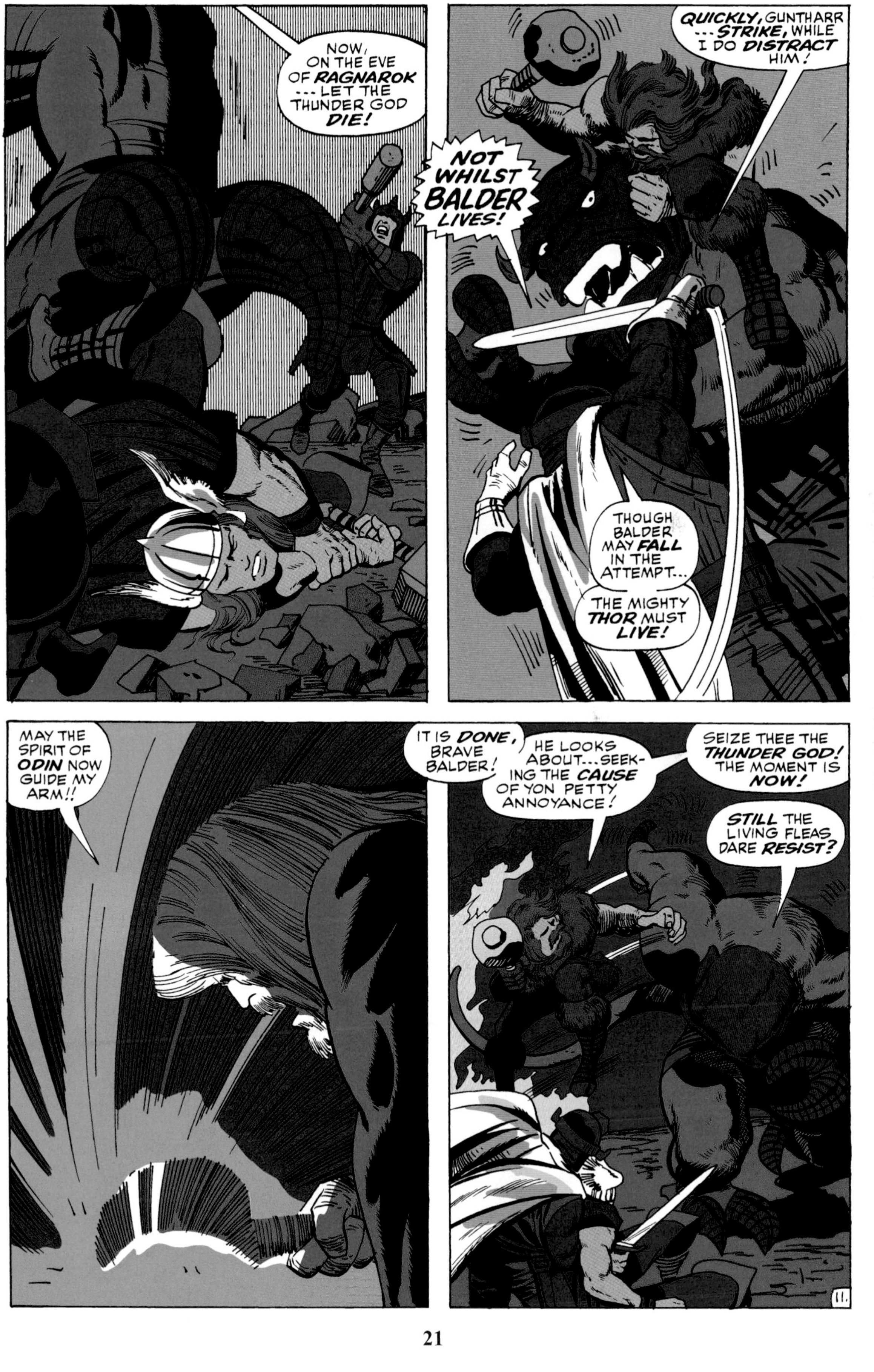
NOW, ON THE EVE OF RAGNAROK --- LET THE THUNDER GOD DIE!
QUICKLY, GUNTHARR --- STRIKE, WHILE I DO DISTRACT HIM!
NOT WHILST BALDER LIVES!
THOUGH BALDER MAY FALL IN THE ATTEMPT...
THE MIGHTY THOR MUST LIVE!
MAY THE SPIRIT OF ODIN NOW GUIDE MY ARM!!
IT IS DONE, BRAVE BALDER!
HE LOOKS ABOUT... SEEK-ING THE CAUSE OF YON PETTY ANNOYANCE!
SEIZE THEE THE THUNDER GOD! THE MOMENT IS NOW!
STILL THE LIVING FLEAS DARE RESIST?
11.

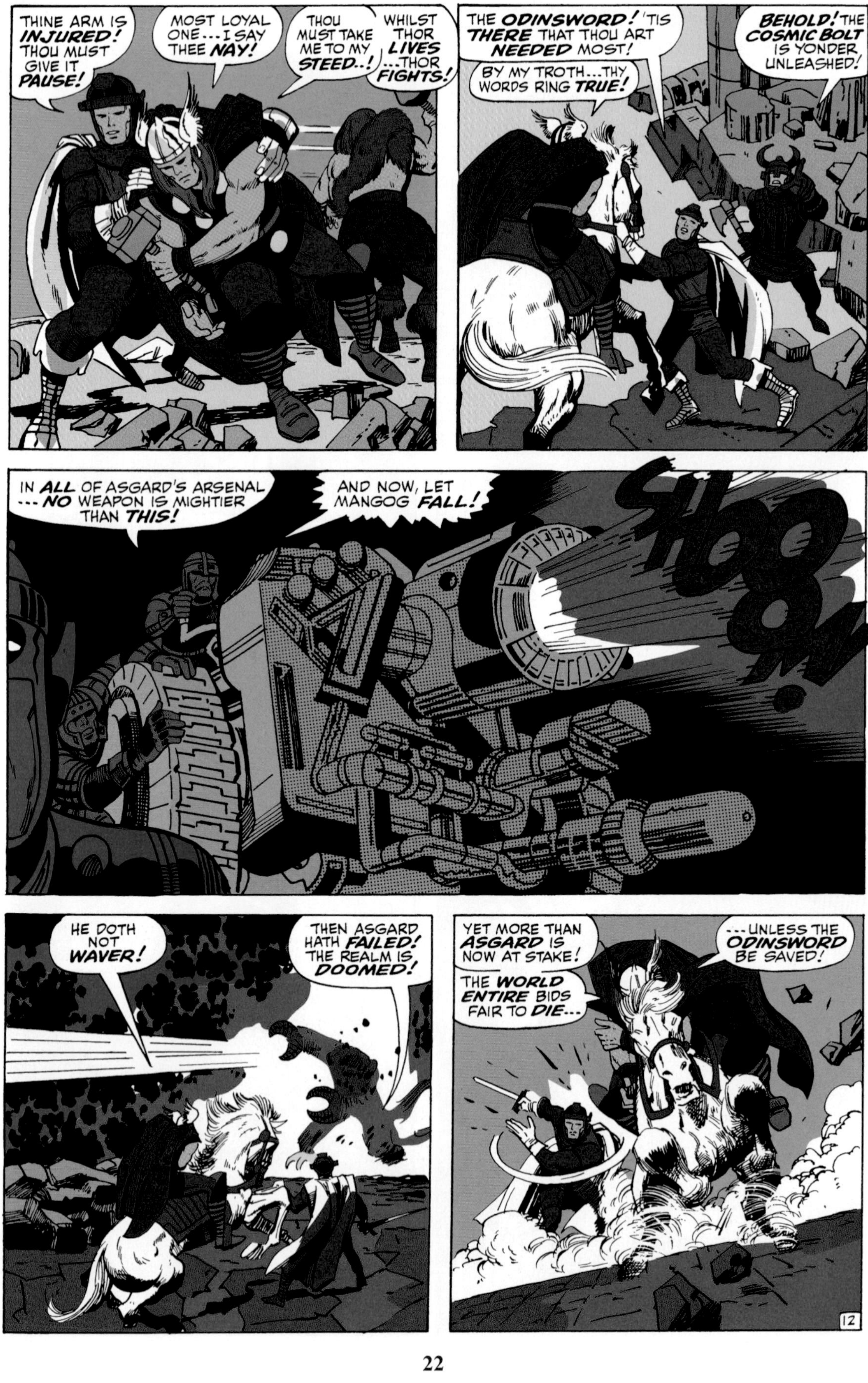
THINE ARM IS INJURED! THOU MUST GIVE IT PAUSE!
MOST LOYAL ONE... I SAY THEE NAY!
THOU MUST TAKE ME TO MY STEED..!
WHILST THOR LIVES ...THOR FIGHTS!
THE ODINSWORD! 'TIS THERE THAT THOU ART NEEDED MOST!
BY MY TROTH...THY WORDS RING TRUE!
BEHOLD! THE COSMIC BOLT IS YONDER UNLEASHED!
IN ALL OF ASGARD'S ARSENAL ---NO WEAPON IS MIGHTIER THAN THIS!
AND NOW, LET MANGOG FALL!
SHOOOOM!
HE DOTH NOT WAVER!
THEN ASGARD HATH FAILED! THE REALM IS DOOMED!
YET MORE THAN ASGARD IS NOW AT STAKE!
THE WORLD ENTIRE BIDS FAIR TO DIE...
---UNLESS THE ODINSWORD BE SAVED!
12

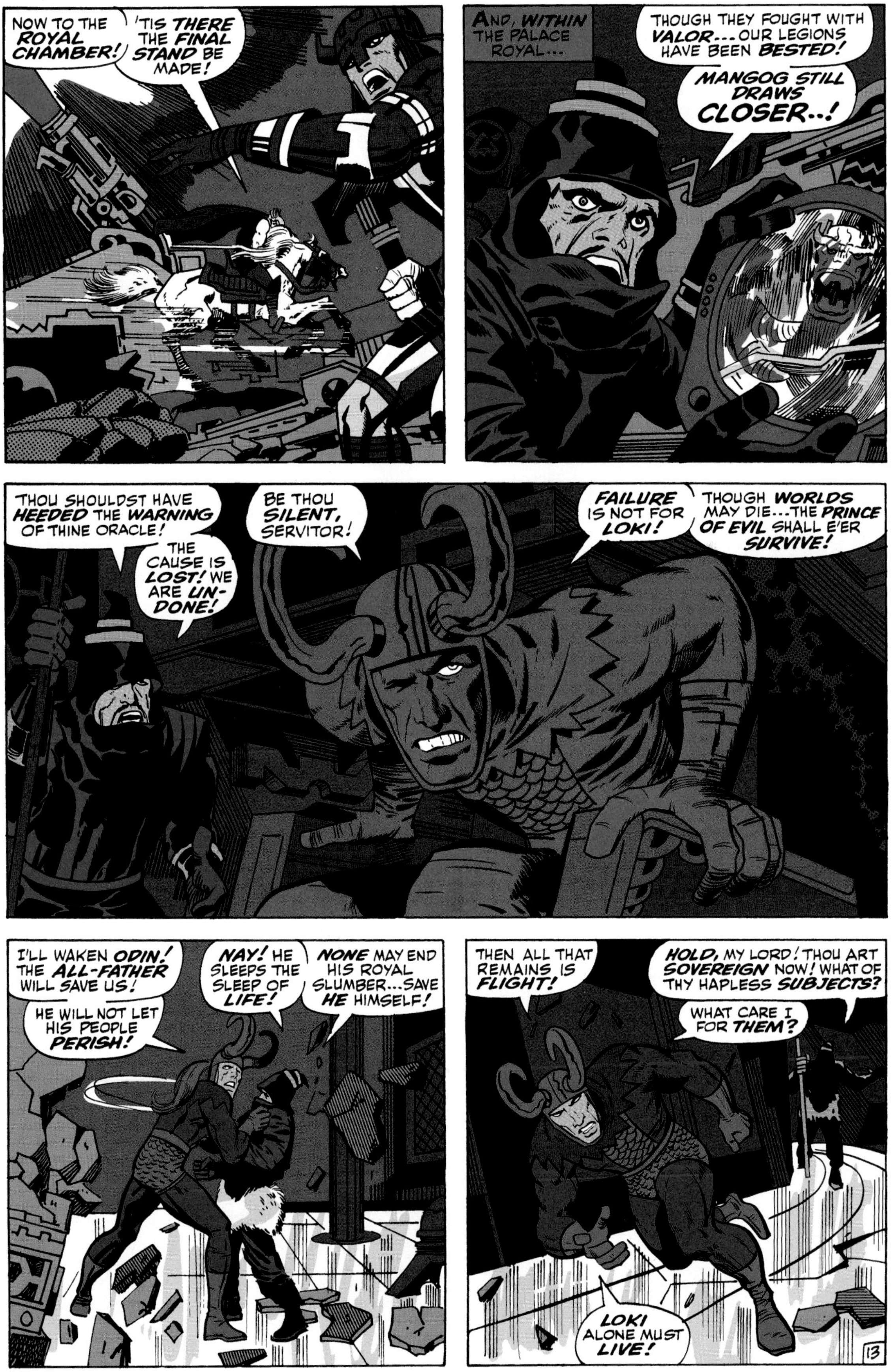
NOW TO THE ROYAL CHAMBER!
'TIS THERE THE FINAL STAND BE MADE!
AND, WITHIN THE PALACE ROYAL...
THOUGH THEY FOUGHT WITH VALOR... OUR LEGIONS HAVE BEEN BESTED!
MANGOG STILL DRAWS CLOSER..!
THOU SHOULDST HAVE HEEDED THE WARNING OF THINE ORACLE!
THE CAUSE IS LOST! WE ARE UN-DONE!
BE THOU SILENT, SERVITOR!
FAILURE IS NOT FOR LOKI!
THOUGH WORLDS MAY DIE...THE PRINCE OF EVIL SHALL E'ER SURVIVE!
I'LL WAKEN ODIN! THE ALL-FATHER WILL SAVE US!
HE WILL NOT LET HIS PEOPLE PERISH!
NAY! HE SLEEPS THE SLEEP OF LIFE!
NONE MAY END HIS ROYAL SLUMBER...SAVE HE HIMSELF!
THEN ALL THAT REMAINS IS FLIGHT!
HOLD, MY LORD! THOU ART SOVEREIGN NOW! WHAT OF THY HAPLESS SUBJECTS?
WHAT CARE I FOR THEM?
LOKI ALONE MUST LIVE!
13

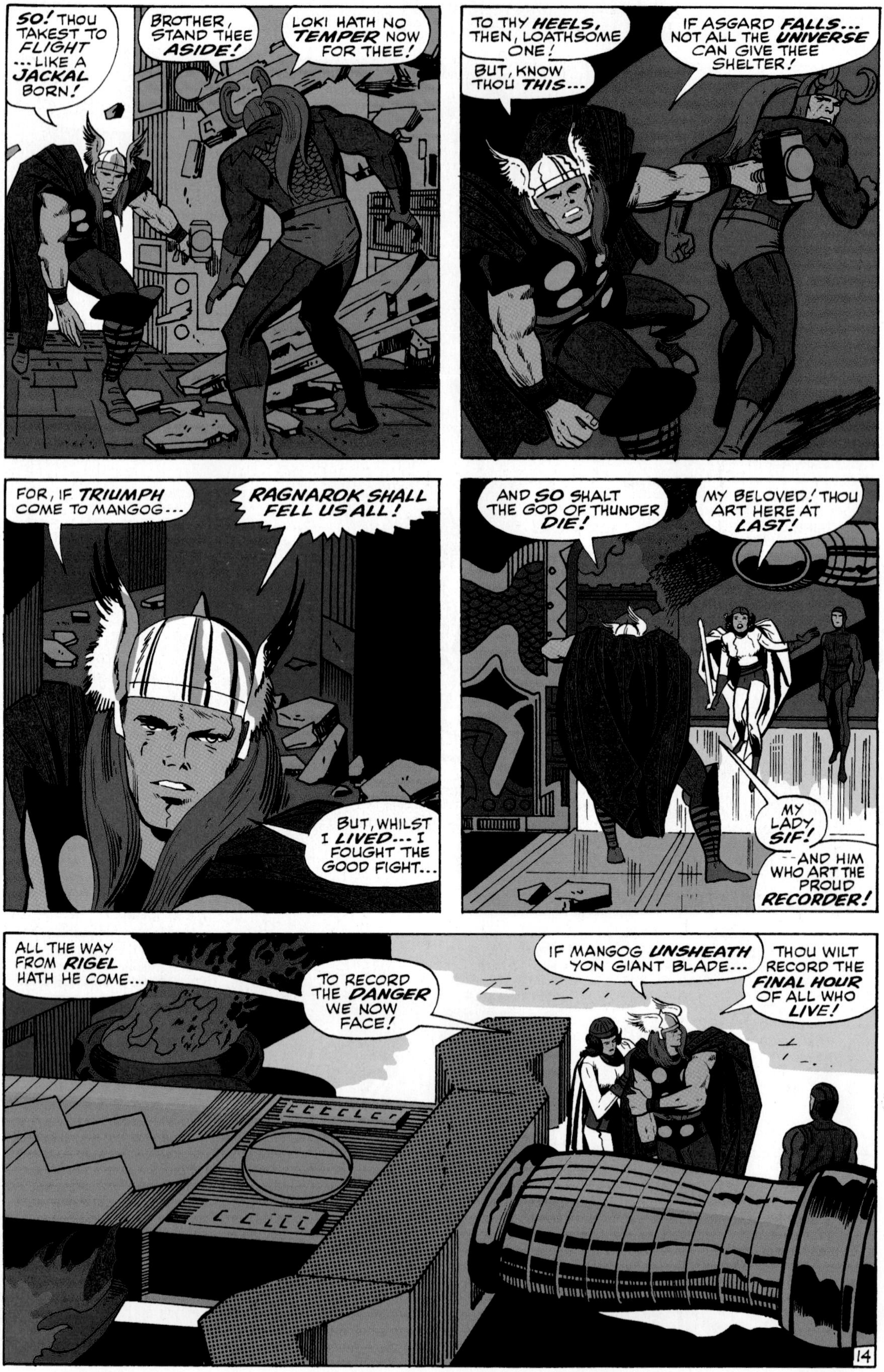
SO! THOU TAKEST TO FLIGHT ...LIKE A JACKAL BORN!
BROTHER, STAND THEE ASIDE!
LOKI HATH NO TEMPER NOW FOR THEE!
TO THY HEELS, THEN, LOATHSOME ONE!
BUT, KNOW THOU THIS...
IF ASGARD FALLS... NOT ALL THE UNIVERSE CAN GIVE THEE SHELTER!
FOR, IF TRIUMPH COME TO MANGOG...
RAGNAROK SHALL FELL US ALL!
BUT, WHILST I LIVED... I FOUGHT THE GOOD FIGHT...
AND SO SHALT THE GOD OF THUNDER DIE!
MY BELOVED! THOU ART HERE AT LAST!
MY LADY SIF!
--AND HIM WHO ART THE PROUD RECORDER!
ALL THE WAY FROM RIGEL HATH HE COME...
TO RECORD THE DANGER WE NOW FACE!
IF MANGOG UNSHEATH YON GIANT BLADE...
THOU WILT RECORD THE FINAL HOUR OF ALL WHO LIVE!
14

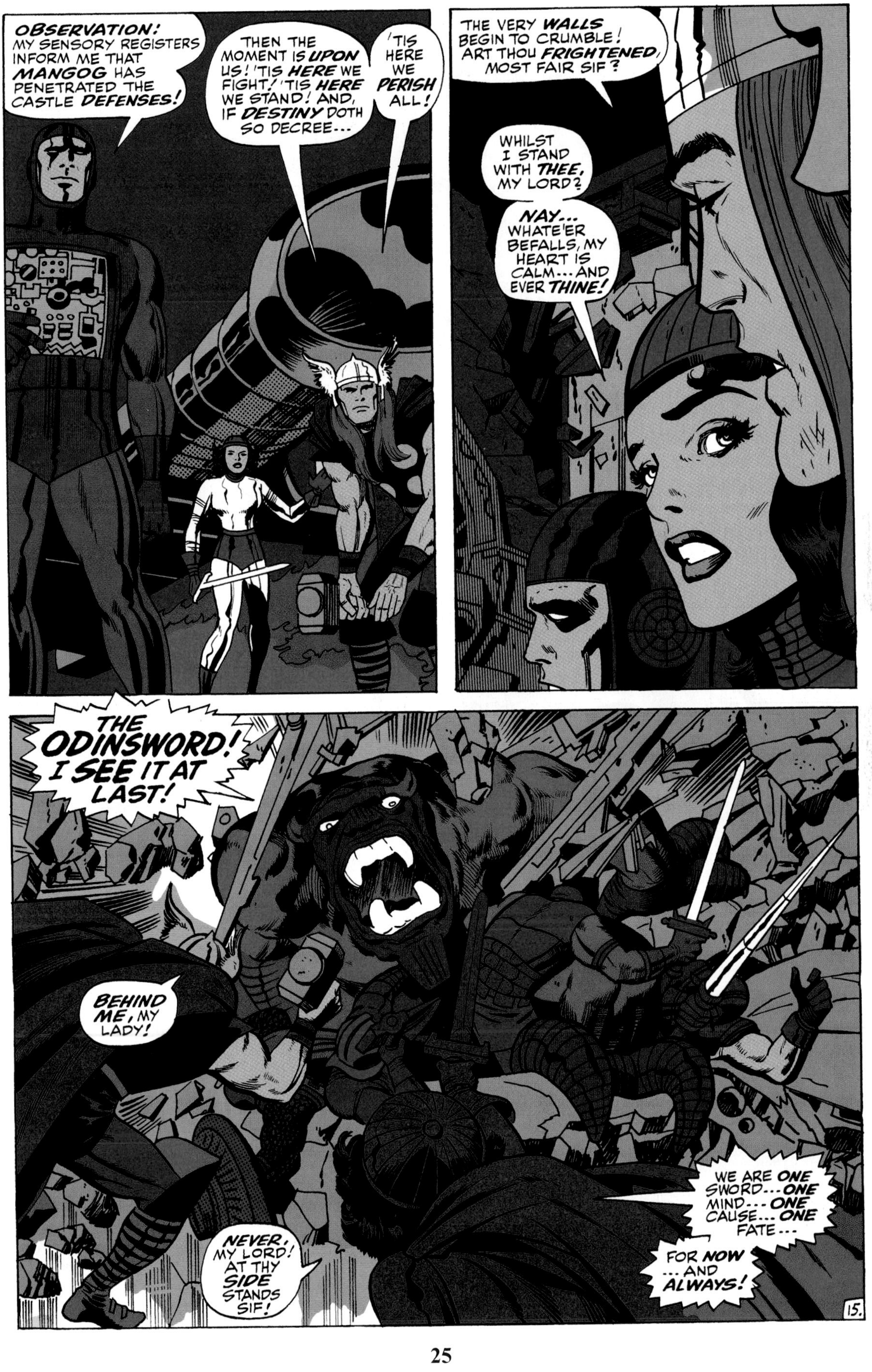
OBSERVATION: MY SENSORY REGISTERS INFORM ME THAT MANGOG HAS PENETRATED THE CASTLE DEFENSES!
THEN THE MOMENT IS UPON US! 'TIS HERE WE FIGHT! 'TIS HERE WE STAND! AND, IF DESTINY DOTH SO DECREE...
'TIS HERE WE PERISH ALL!
THE VERY WALLS BEGIN TO CRUMBLE! ART THOU FRIGHTENED, MOST FAIR SIF?
WHILST I STAND WITH THEE, MY LORD?
NAY... WHATE'ER BEFALLS, MY HEART IS CALM... AND EVER THINE!
THE ODINSWORD! I SEE IT AT LAST!
BEHIND ME, MY LADY!
NEVER, MY LORD! AT THY SIDE STANDS SIF!
WE ARE ONE SWORD... ONE MIND... ONE CAUSE... ONE FATE...
FOR NOW ... AND ALWAYS!
15.

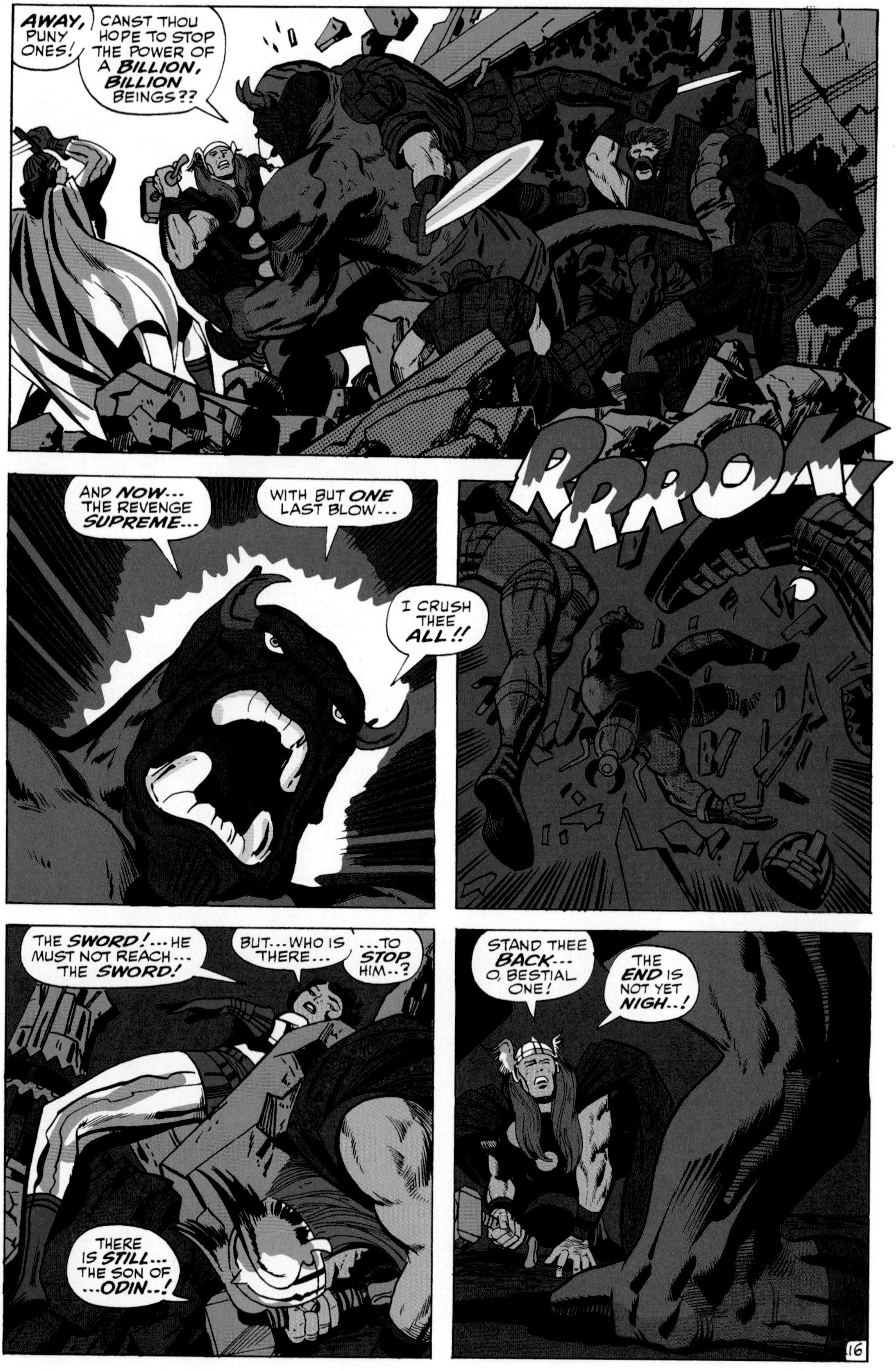
AWAY, PUNY ONES!
CANST THOU HOPE TO STOP THE POWER OF A BILLION, BILLION BEINGS??
AND NOW... THE REVENGE SUPREME...
WITH BUT ONE LAST BLOW...
I CRUSH THEE ALL!!
RRROK
THE SWORD!... HE MUST NOT REACH... THE SWORD!
BUT... WHO IS THERE...
...TO STOP HIM...?
THERE IS STILL... THE SON OF ...ODIN..!
STAND THEE BACK... O, BESTIAL ONE!
THE END IS NOT YET NIGH..!
16

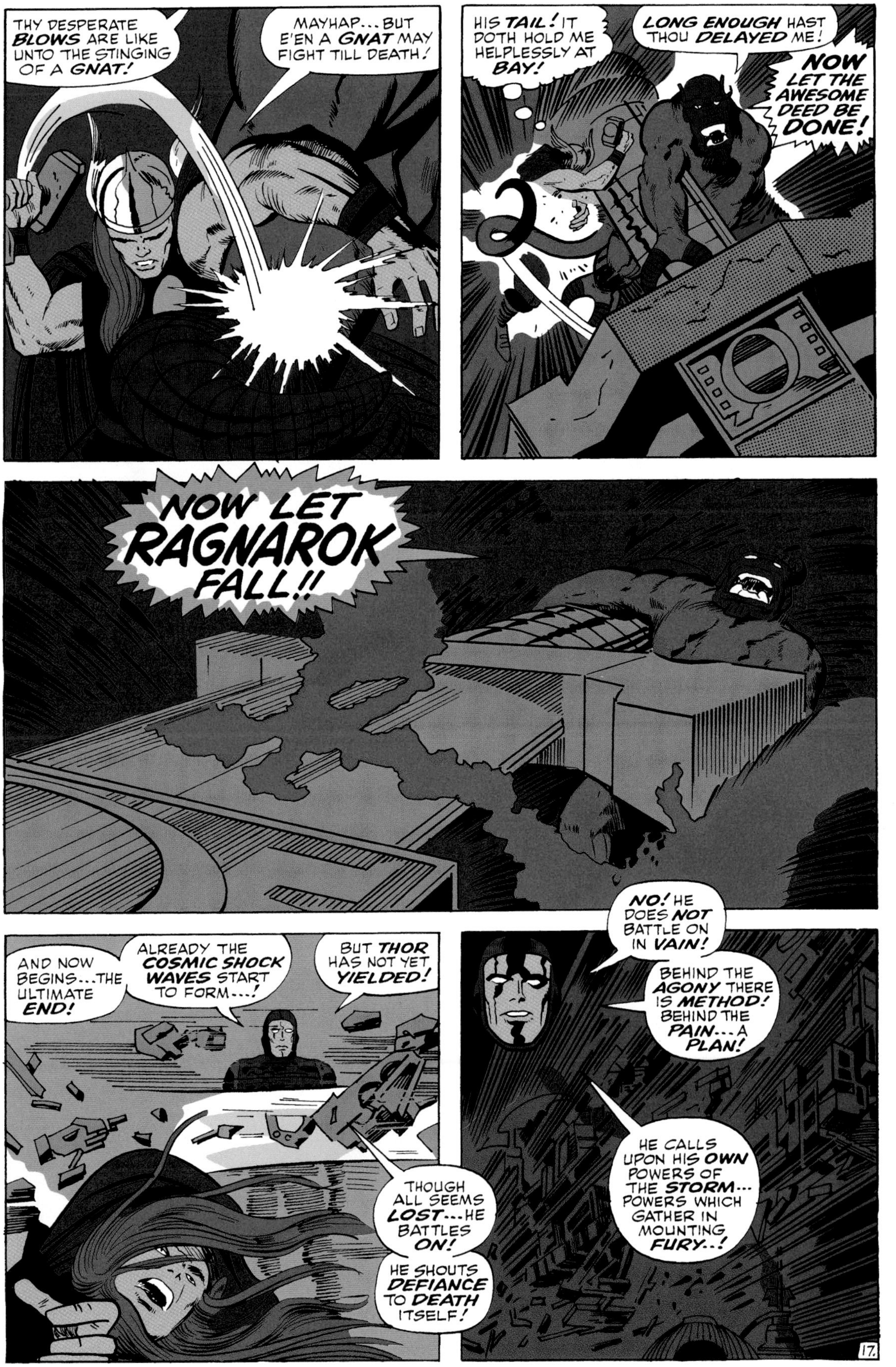
THY DESPERATE BLOWS ARE LIKE UNTO THE STINGING OF A GNAT!
MAYHAP... BUT E'EN A GNAT MAY FIGHT TILL DEATH!
HIS TAIL! IT DOTH HOLD ME HELPLESSLY AT BAY!
LONG ENOUGH HAST THOU DELAYED ME!
NOW LET THE AWESOME DEED BE DONE!
NOW LET RAGNAROK FALL!!
AND NOW BEGINS... THE ULTIMATE END!
ALREADY THE COSMIC SHOCK WAVES START TO FORM...!
BUT THOR HAS NOT YET YIELDED!
THOUGH ALL SEEMS LOST... HE BATTLES ON!
HE SHOUTS DEFIANCE TO DEATH ITSELF!
NO! HE DOES NOT BATTLE ON IN VAIN!
BEHIND THE AGONY THERE IS METHOD! BEHIND THE PAIN... A PLAN!
HE CALLS UPON HIS OWN POWERS OF THE STORM... POWERS WHICH GATHER IN MOUNTING FURY..!
17.

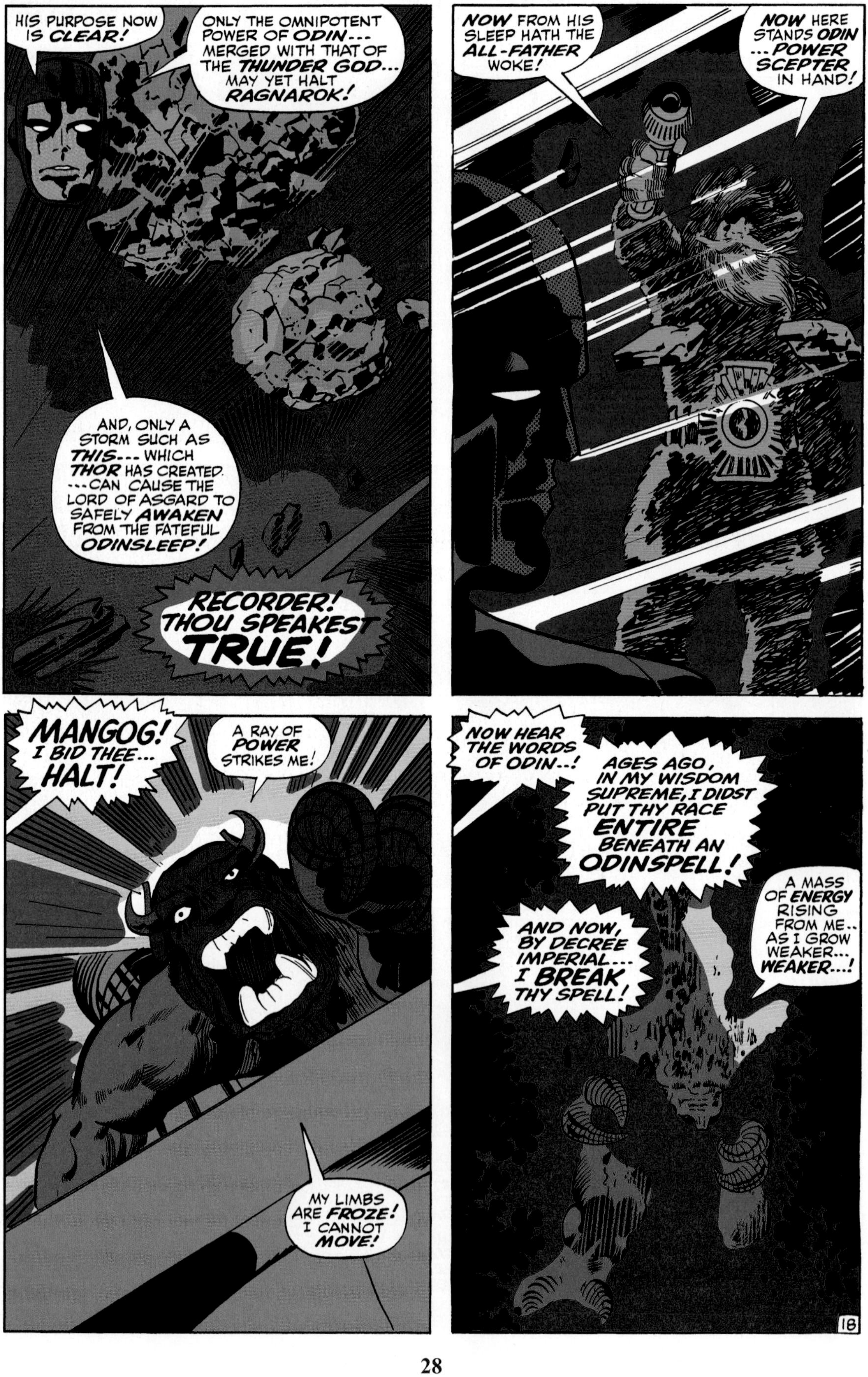
HIS PURPOSE NOW IS CLEAR!
ONLY THE OMNIPOTENT POWER OF ODIN--- MERGED WITH THAT OF THE THUNDER GOD... MAY YET HALT RAGNAROK!
AND, ONLY A STORM SUCH AS THIS--- WHICH THOR HAS CREATED ---CAN CAUSE THE LORD OF ASGARD TO SAFELY AWAKEN FROM THE FATEFUL ODINSLEEP!
RECORDER! THOU SPEAKEST TRUE!
NOW FROM HIS SLEEP HATH THE ALL-FATHER WOKE!
NOW HERE STANDS ODIN ...POWER SCEPTER IN HAND!
MANGOG! I BID THEE... HALT!
A RAY OF POWER STRIKES ME!
MY LIMBS ARE FROZE! I CANNOT MOVE!
NOW HEAR THE WORDS OF ODIN--!
AGES AGO, IN MY WISDOM SUPREME, I DIDST PUT THY RACE ENTIRE BENEATH AN ODINSPELL!
A MASS OF ENERGY RISING FROM ME.. AS I GROW WEAKER... WEAKER...!
AND NOW, BY DECREE IMPERIAL... I BREAK THY SPELL!
18

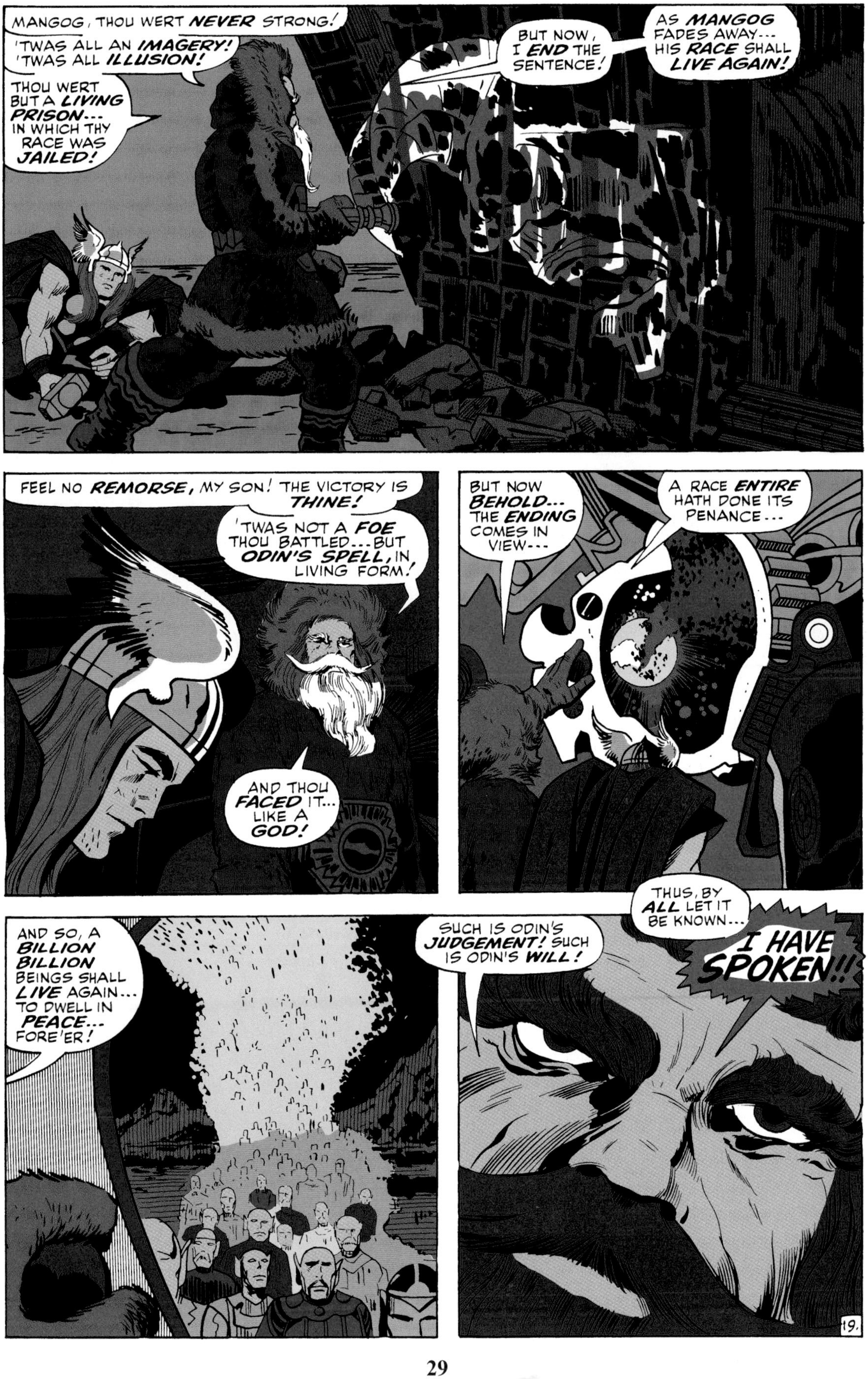
MANGOG, THOU WERT NEVER STRONG!
'TWAS ALL AN IMAGERY! 'TWAS ALL ILLUSION!
THOU WERT BUT A LIVING PRISON... IN WHICH THY RACE WAS JAILED!
BUT NOW, I END THE SENTENCE!
AS MANGOG FADES AWAY... HIS RACE SHALL LIVE AGAIN!
FEEL NO REMORSE, MY SON! THE VICTORY IS THINE!
'TWAS NOT A FOE THOU BATTLED... BUT ODIN'S SPELL, IN LIVING FORM!
AND THOU FACED IT... LIKE A GOD!
BUT NOW BEHOLD... THE ENDING COMES IN VIEW---
A RACE ENTIRE HATH DONE ITS PENANCE...
AND SO, A BILLION BILLION BEINGS SHALL LIVE AGAIN... TO DWELL IN PEACE... FORE'ER!
SUCH IS ODIN'S JUDGEMENT! SUCH IS ODIN'S WILL!
THUS, BY ALL LET IT BE KNOWN...
I HAVE SPOKEN!!
19.

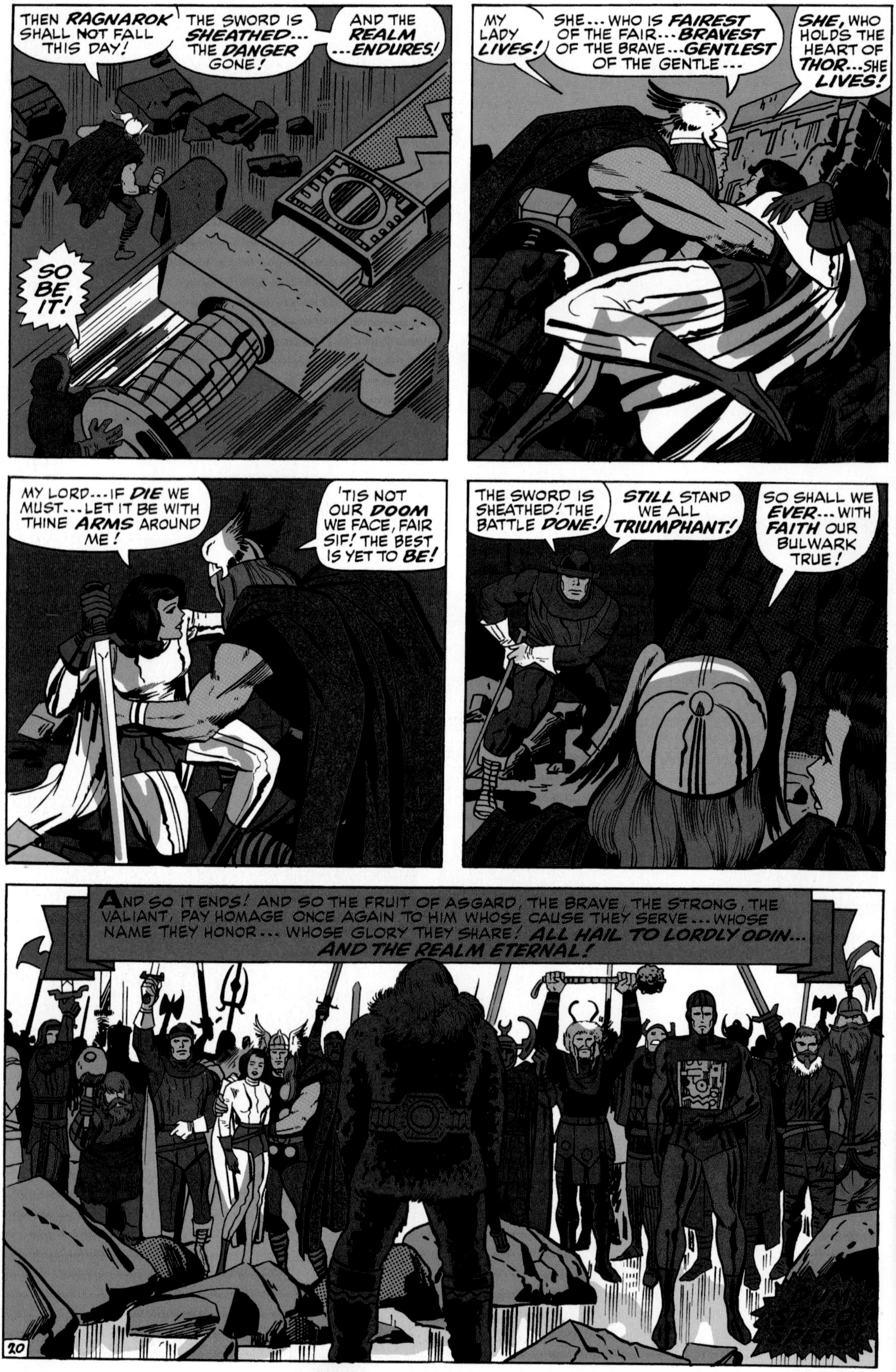
THEN RAGNAROK SHALL NOT FALL THIS DAY!
THE SWORD IS SHEATHED... THE DANGER GONE!
AND THE REALM ...ENDURES!
SO BE IT!
MY LADY LIVES!
SHE... WHO IS FAIREST OF THE FAIR... BRAVEST OF THE BRAVE... GENTLEST OF THE GENTLE...
SHE, WHO HOLDS THE HEART OF THOR... SHE LIVES!
MY LORD... IF DIE WE MUST... LET IT BE WITH THINE ARMS AROUND ME!
'TIS NOT OUR DOOM WE FACE, FAIR SIF! THE BEST IS YET TO BE!
THE SWORD IS SHEATHED! THE BATTLE DONE!
STILL STAND WE ALL TRIUMPHANT!
SO SHALL WE EVER... WITH FAITH OUR BULWARK TRUE!
AND SO IT ENDS! AND SO THE FRUIT OF ASGARD, THE BRAVE, THE STRONG, THE VALIANT, PAY HOMAGE ONCE AGAIN TO HIM WHOSE CAUSE THEY SERVE... WHOSE NAME THEY HONOR... WHOSE GLORY THEY SHARE! ALL HAIL TO LORDLY ODIN... AND THE REALM ETERNAL!
20

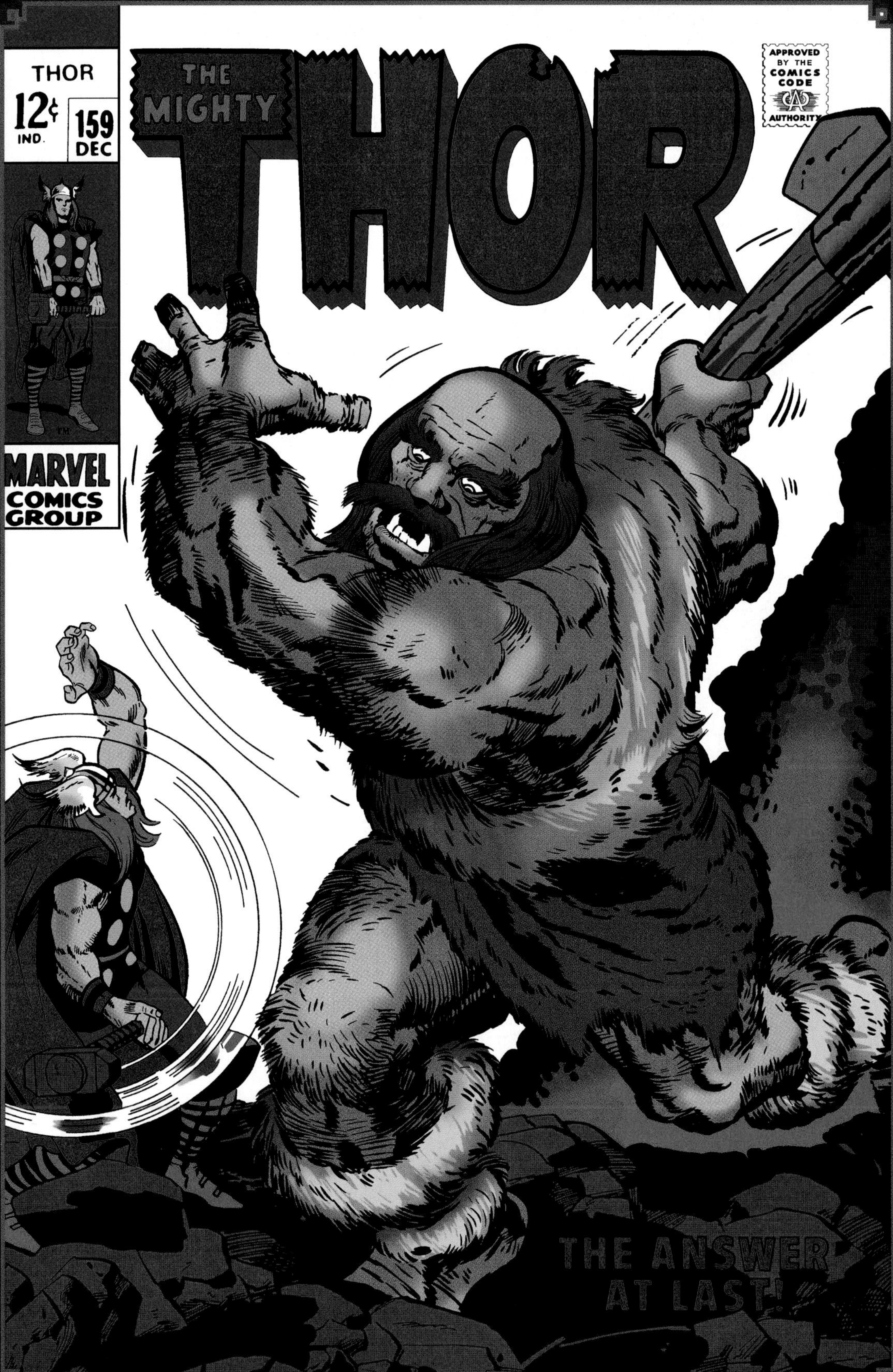
THOR
12¢
IND.
159
DEC
MARVEL
COMICS
GROUP
THE MIGHTY
THOR
APPROVED BY THE COMICS CODE AUTHORITY
THE ANSWER AT LAST!

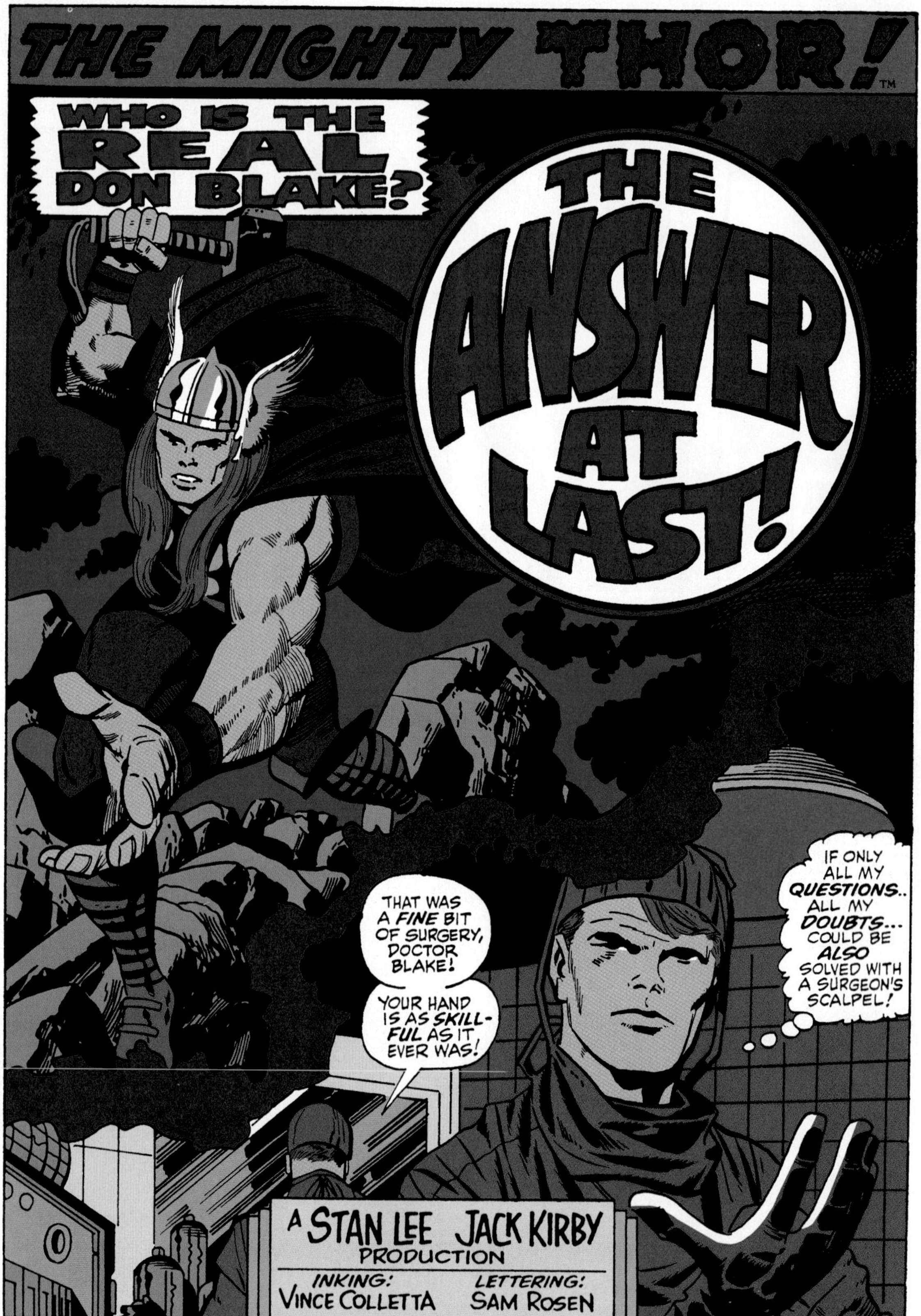
THE MIGHTY THOR!™
WHO IS THE REAL DON BLAKE?
THE ANSWER AT LAST!
THAT WAS A FINE BIT OF SURGERY, DOCTOR BLAKE!
YOUR HAND IS AS SKILL-FUL AS IT EVER WAS!
IF ONLY ALL MY QUESTIONS.. ALL MY DOUBTS... COULD BE ALSO SOLVED WITH A SURGEON'S SCALPEL!
A STAN LEE JACK KIRBY PRODUCTION
INKING: VINCE COLLETTA
LETTERING: SAM ROSEN

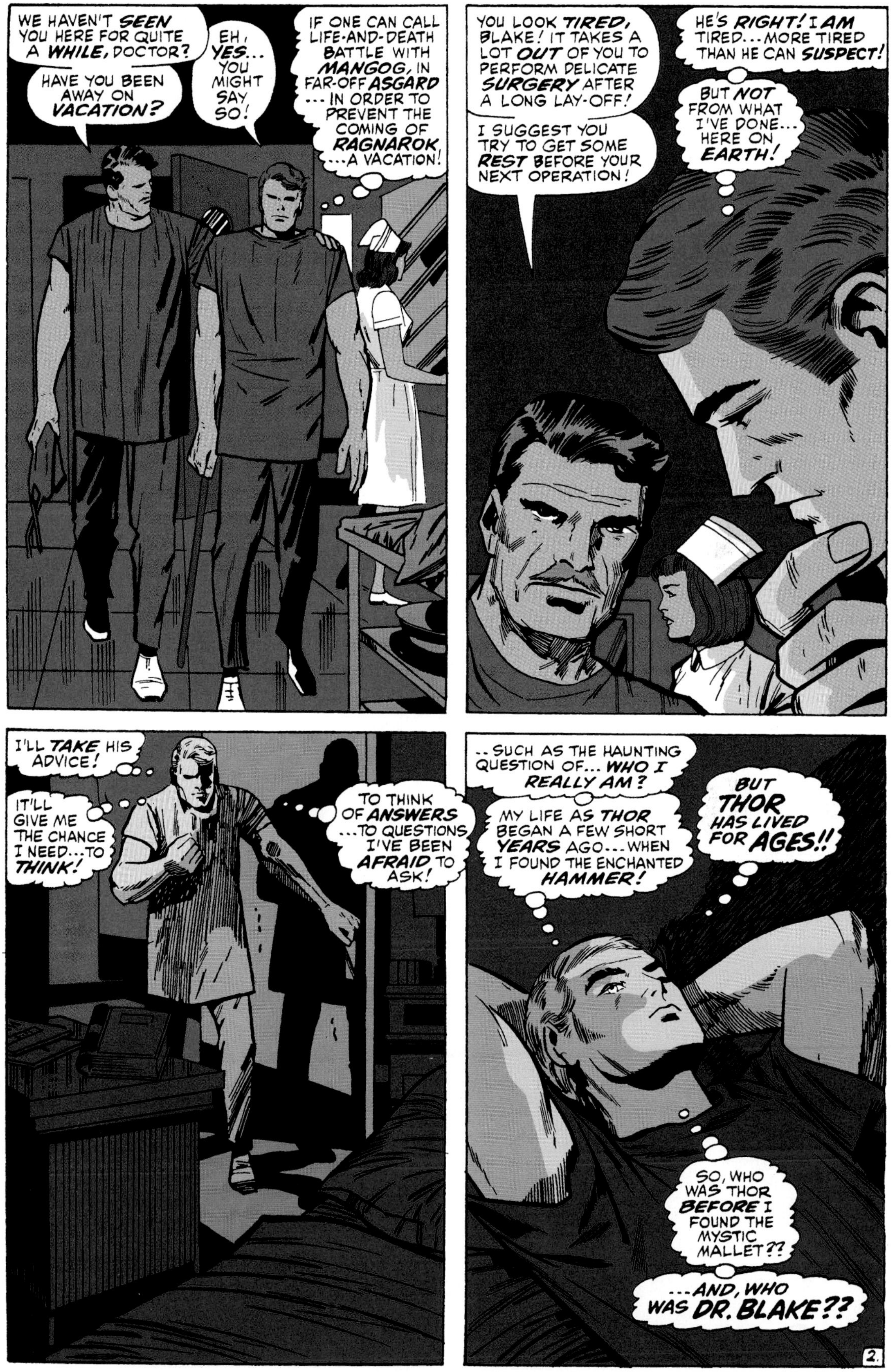
WE HAVEN'T SEEN YOU HERE FOR QUITE A WHILE, DOCTOR?
HAVE YOU BEEN AWAY ON VACATION?
EH, YES... YOU MIGHT SAY SO!
IF ONE CAN CALL LIFE-AND-DEATH BATTLE WITH MANGOG, IN FAR-OFF ASGARD ... IN ORDER TO PREVENT THE COMING OF RAGNAROK ...A VACATION!
YOU LOOK TIRED, BLAKE! IT TAKES A LOT OUT OF YOU TO PERFORM DELICATE SURGERY AFTER A LONG LAY-OFF!
I SUGGEST YOU TRY TO GET SOME REST BEFORE YOUR NEXT OPERATION!
HE'S RIGHT! I AM TIRED... MORE TIRED THAN HE CAN SUSPECT!
BUT NOT FROM WHAT I'VE DONE... HERE ON EARTH!
I'LL TAKE HIS ADVICE!
IT'LL GIVE ME THE CHANCE I NEED... TO THINK!
TO THINK OF ANSWERS ...TO QUESTIONS I'VE BEEN AFRAID TO ASK!
..SUCH AS THE HAUNTING QUESTION OF... WHO I REALLY AM?
MY LIFE AS THOR BEGAN A FEW SHORT YEARS AGO... WHEN I FOUND THE ENCHANTED HAMMER!
BUT THOR HAS LIVED FOR AGES!!
SO, WHO WAS THOR BEFORE I FOUND THE MYSTIC MALLET??
...AND, WHO WAS DR. BLAKE??
2.

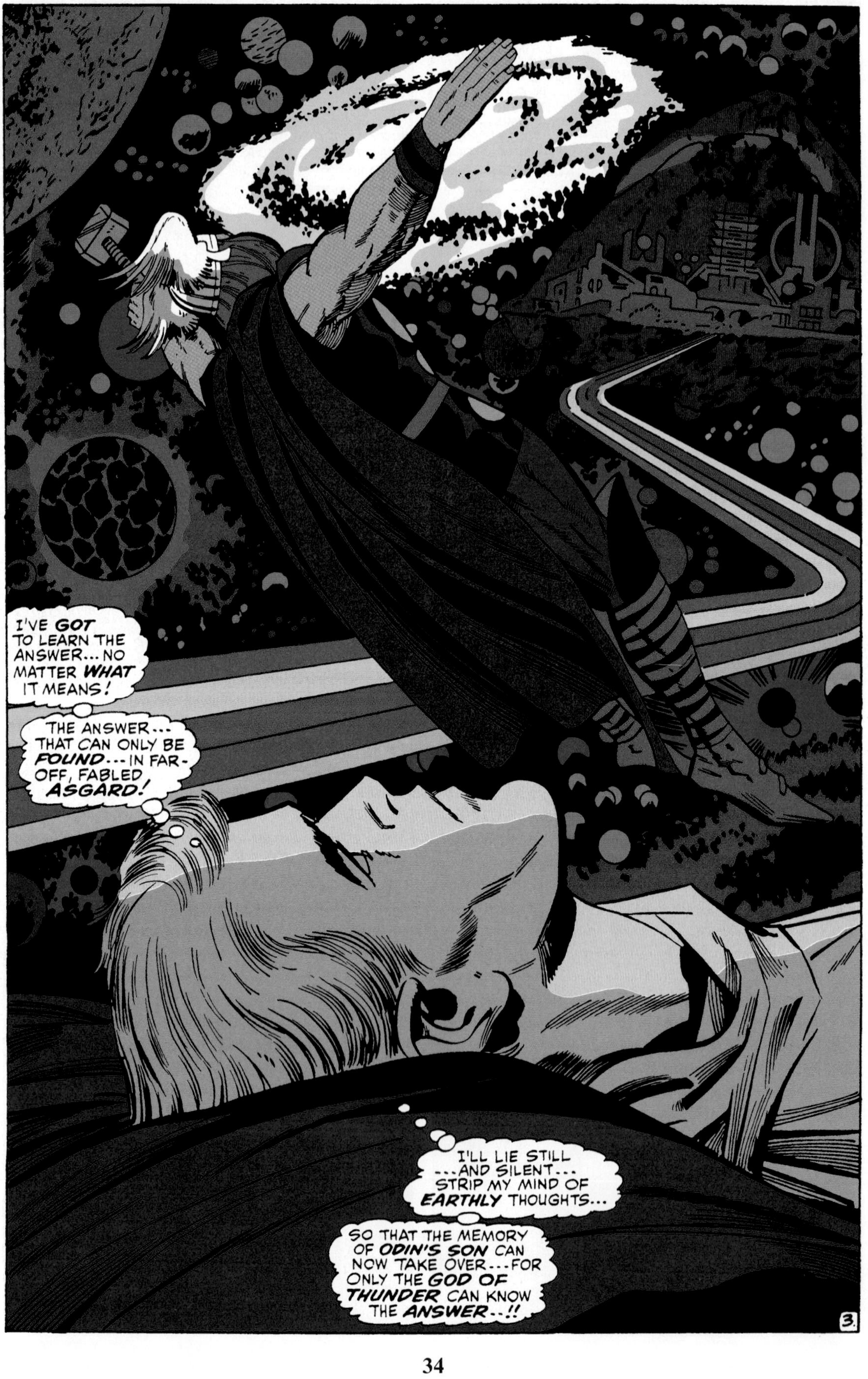
I'VE GOT TO LEARN THE ANSWER... NO MATTER WHAT IT MEANS!
THE ANSWER... THAT CAN ONLY BE FOUND... IN FAR-OFF, FABLED ASGARD!
I'LL LIE STILL ...AND SILENT... STRIP MY MIND OF EARTHLY THOUGHTS...
SO THAT THE MEMORY OF ODIN'S SON CAN NOW TAKE OVER...FOR ONLY THE GOD OF THUNDER CAN KNOW THE ANSWER--!!
3.

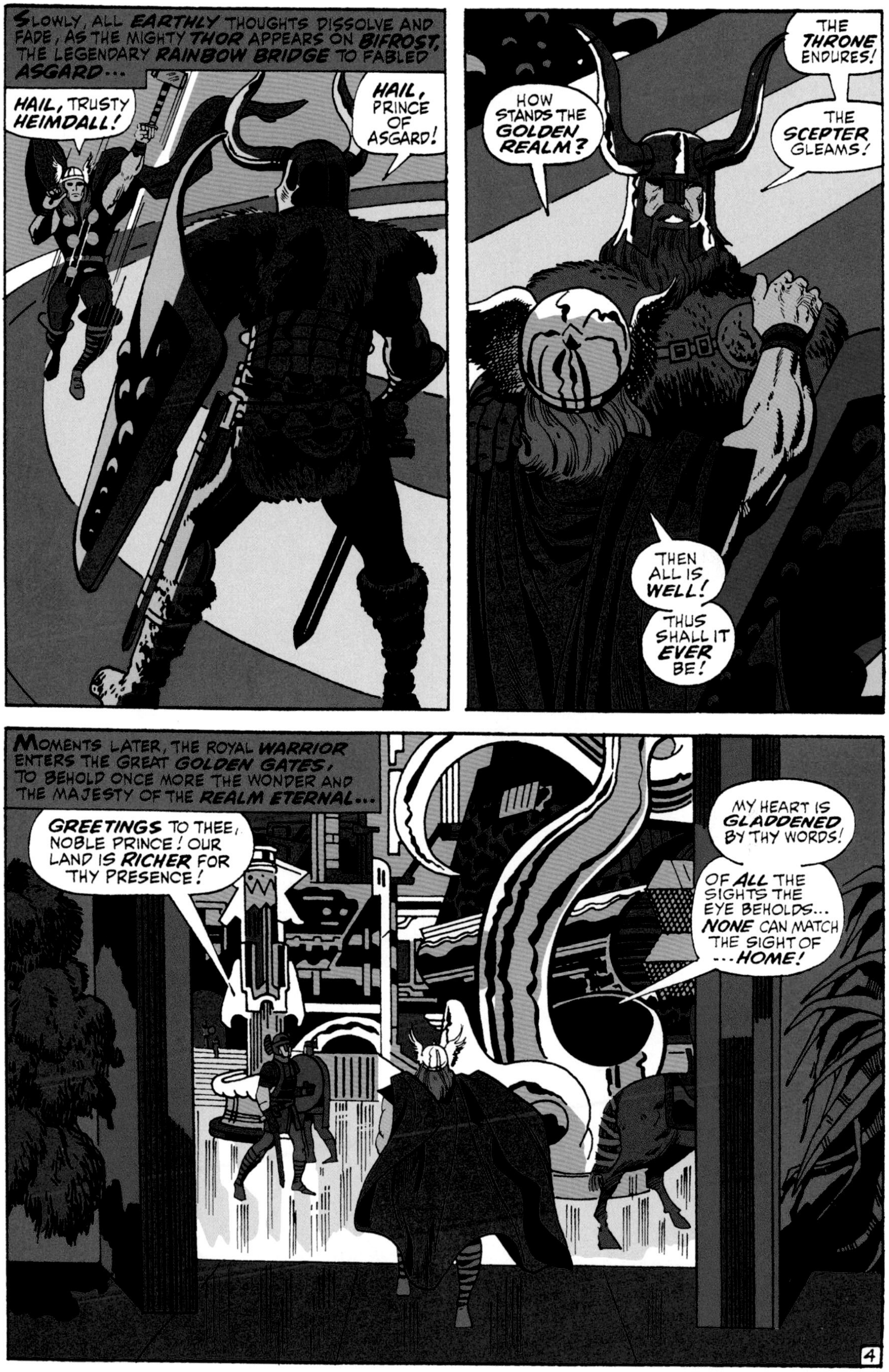
SLOWLY, ALL EARTHLY THOUGHTS DISSOLVE AND FADE, AS THE MIGHTY THOR APPEARS ON BIFROST, THE LEGENDARY RAINBOW BRIDGE TO FABLED ASGARD...
HAIL, TRUSTY HEIMDALL!
HAIL, PRINCE OF ASGARD!
HOW STANDS THE GOLDEN REALM?
THE THRONE ENDURES!
THE SCEPTER GLEAMS!
THEN ALL IS WELL!
THUS SHALL IT EVER BE!
MOMENTS LATER, THE ROYAL WARRIOR ENTERS THE GREAT GOLDEN GATES, TO BEHOLD ONCE MORE THE WONDER AND THE MAJESTY OF THE REALM ETERNAL...
GREETINGS TO THEE, NOBLE PRINCE! OUR LAND IS RICHER FOR THY PRESENCE!
MY HEART IS GLADDENED BY THY WORDS!
OF ALL THE SIGHTS THE EYE BEHOLDS... NONE CAN MATCH THE SIGHT OF ...HOME!
4

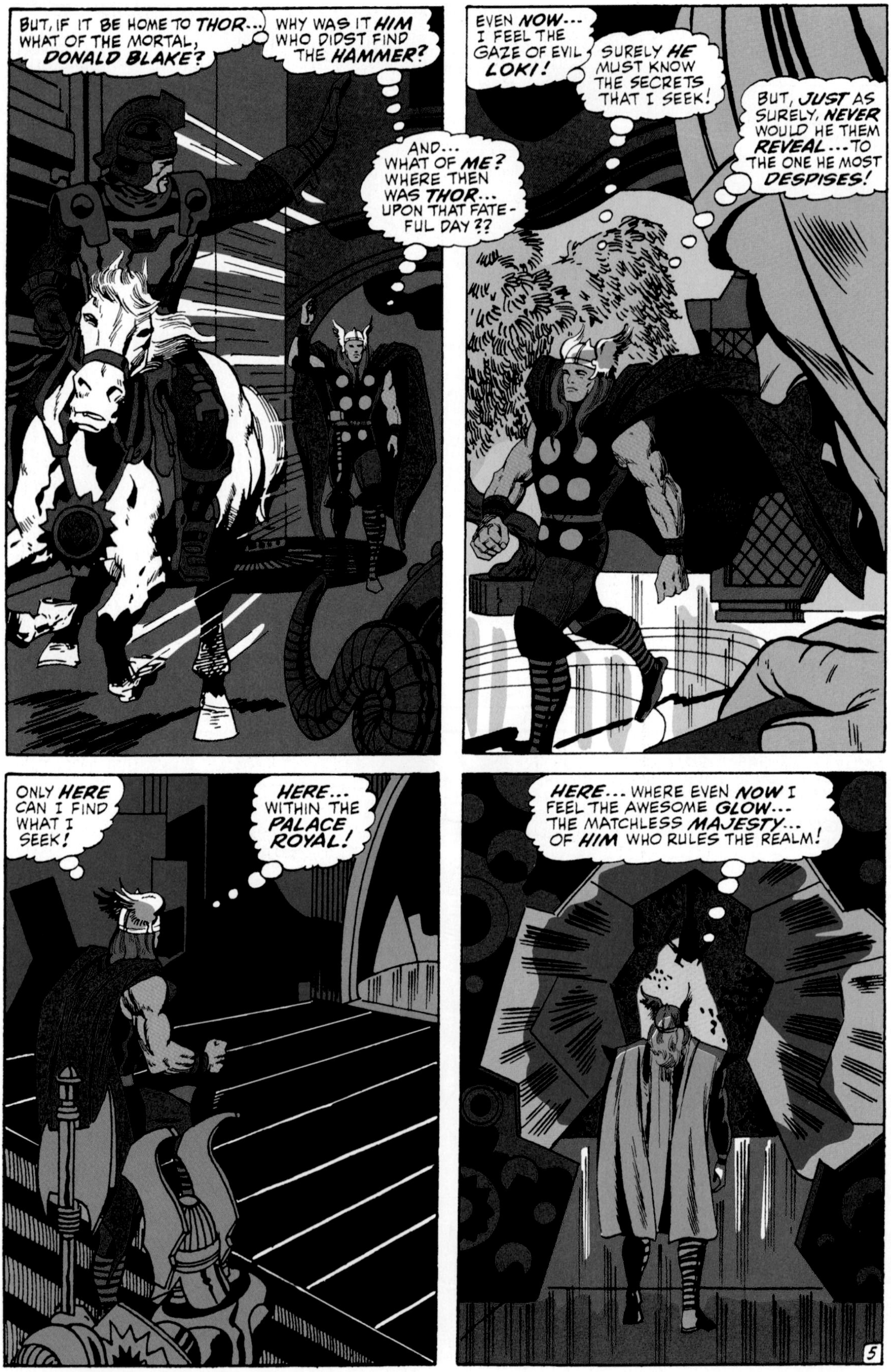
BUT, IF IT BE HOME TO THOR... WHAT OF THE MORTAL, DONALD BLAKE?
WHY WAS IT HIM WHO DIDST FIND THE HAMMER?
AND... WHAT OF ME? WHERE THEN WAS THOR... UPON THAT FATE-FUL DAY??
EVEN NOW... I FEEL THE GAZE OF EVIL LOKI!
SURELY HE MUST KNOW THE SECRETS THAT I SEEK!
BUT, JUST AS SURELY, NEVER WOULD HE THEM REVEAL... TO THE ONE HE MOST DESPISES!
ONLY HERE CAN I FIND WHAT I SEEK!
HERE... WITHIN THE PALACE ROYAL!
HERE... WHERE EVEN NOW I FEEL THE AWESOME GLOW... THE MATCHLESS MAJESTY... OF HIM WHO RULES THE REALM!
5

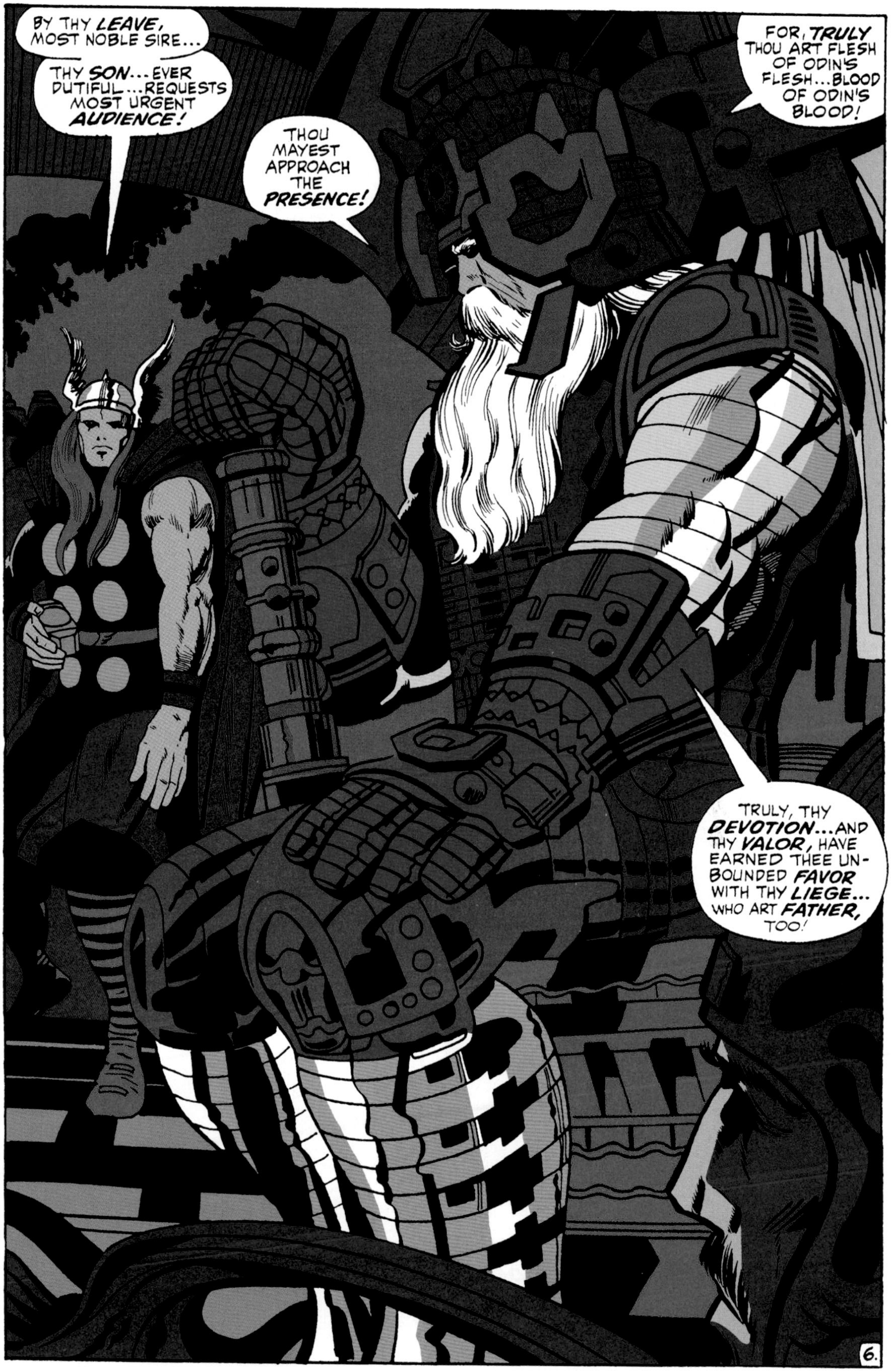
BY THY LEAVE, MOST NOBLE SIRE...
THY SON... EVER DUTIFUL... REQUESTS MOST URGENT AUDIENCE!
THOU MAYEST APPROACH THE PRESENCE!
FOR, TRULY THOU ART FLESH OF ODIN'S FLESH... BLOOD OF ODIN'S BLOOD!
TRULY, THY DEVOTION... AND THY VALOR, HAVE EARNED THEE UN-BOUNDED FAVOR WITH THY LIEGE... WHO ART FATHER, TOO!
6.

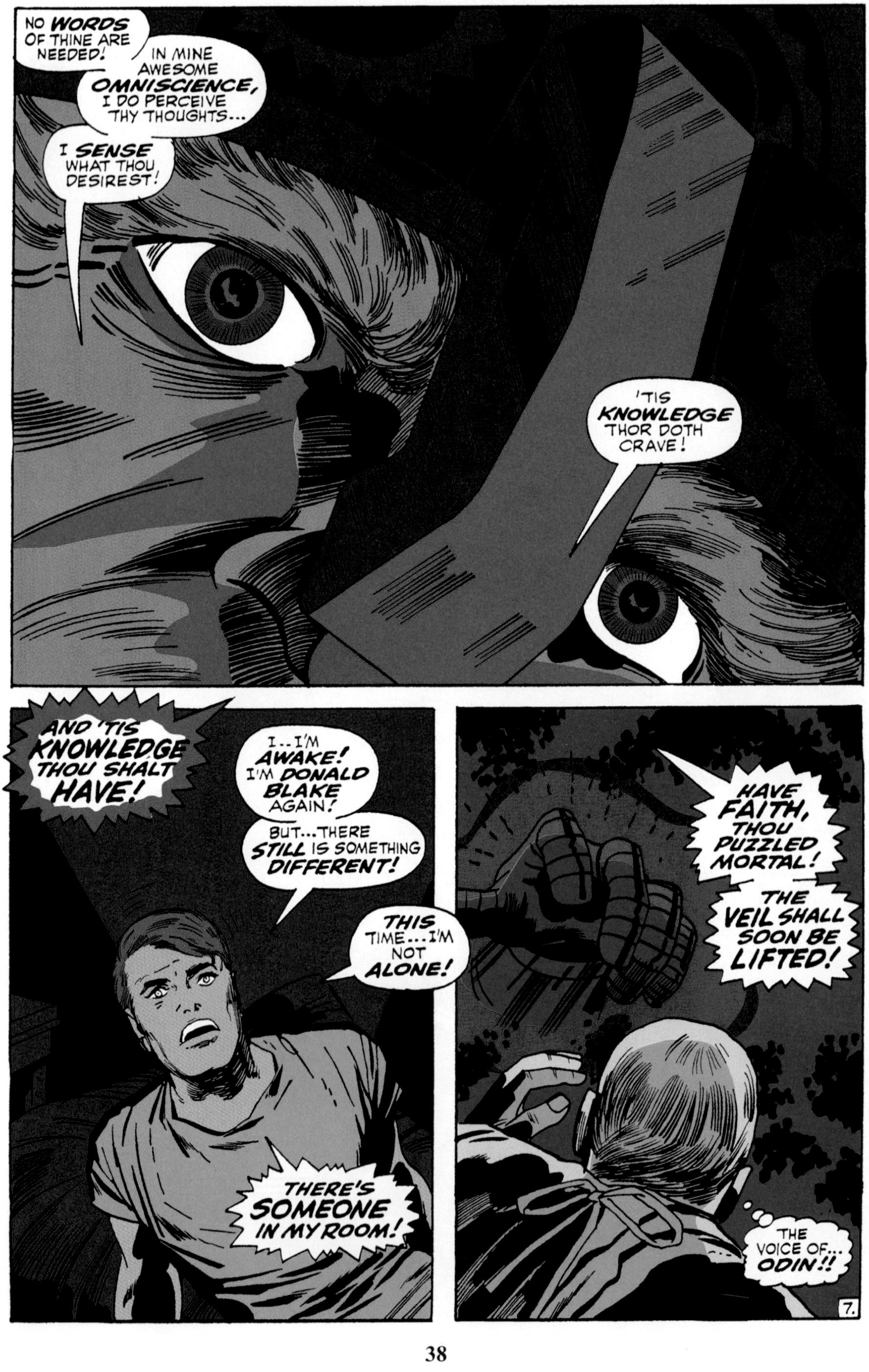
NO WORDS OF THINE ARE NEEDED!
IN MINE AWESOME OMNISCIENCE, I DO PERCEIVE THY THOUGHTS...
I SENSE WHAT THOU DESIREST!
'TIS KNOWLEDGE THOR DOTH CRAVE!
AND 'TIS KNOWLEDGE THOU SHALT HAVE!
I..I'M AWAKE! I'M DONALD BLAKE AGAIN!
BUT...THERE STILL IS SOMETHING DIFFERENT!
THIS TIME...I'M NOT ALONE!
THERE'S SOMEONE IN MY ROOM!
HAVE FAITH, THOU PUZZLED MORTAL!
THE VEIL SHALL SOON BE LIFTED!
THE VOICE OF... ODIN!!
7.

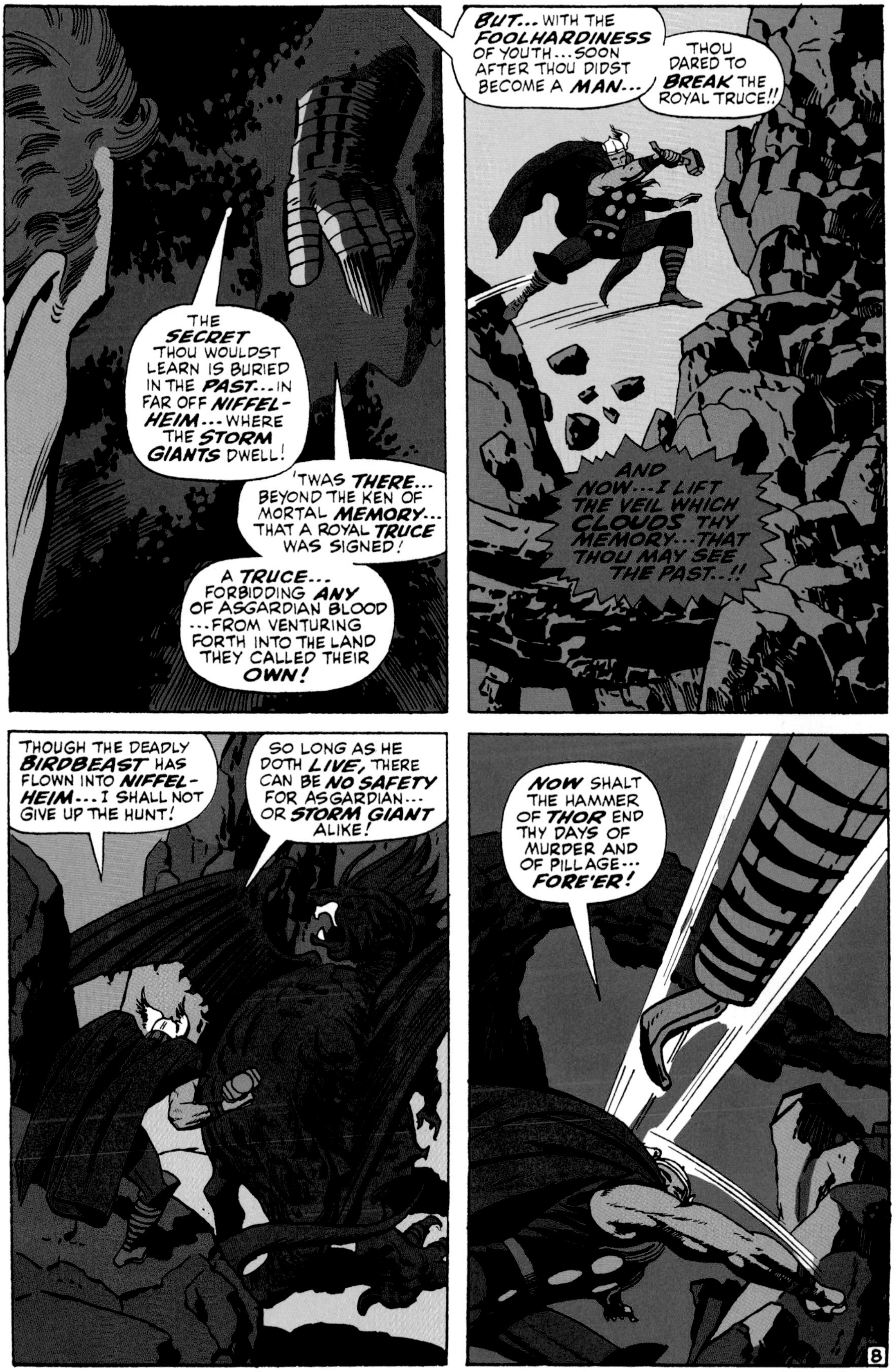
THE SECRET THOU WOULDST LEARN IS BURIED IN THE PAST... IN FAR OFF NIFFELHEIM... WHERE THE STORM GIANTS DWELL!
'TWAS THERE... BEYOND THE KEN OF MORTAL MEMORY... THAT A ROYAL TRUCE WAS SIGNED!
A TRUCE... FORBIDDING ANY OF ASGARDIAN BLOOD ...FROM VENTURING FORTH INTO THE LAND THEY CALLED THEIR OWN!
BUT... WITH THE FOOLHARDINESS OF YOUTH... SOON AFTER THOU DIDST BECOME A MAN...
THOU DARED TO BREAK THE ROYAL TRUCE!!
AND NOW... I LIFT THE VEIL WHICH CLOUDS THY MEMORY... THAT THOU MAY SEE THE PAST..!!
THOUGH THE DEADLY BIRDBEAST HAS FLOWN INTO NIFFELHEIM... I SHALL NOT GIVE UP THE HUNT!
SO LONG AS HE DOTH LIVE, THERE CAN BE NO SAFETY FOR ASGARDIAN... OR STORM GIANT ALIKE!
NOW SHALT THE HAMMER OF THOR END THY DAYS OF MURDER AND OF PILLAGE... FORE'ER!
8

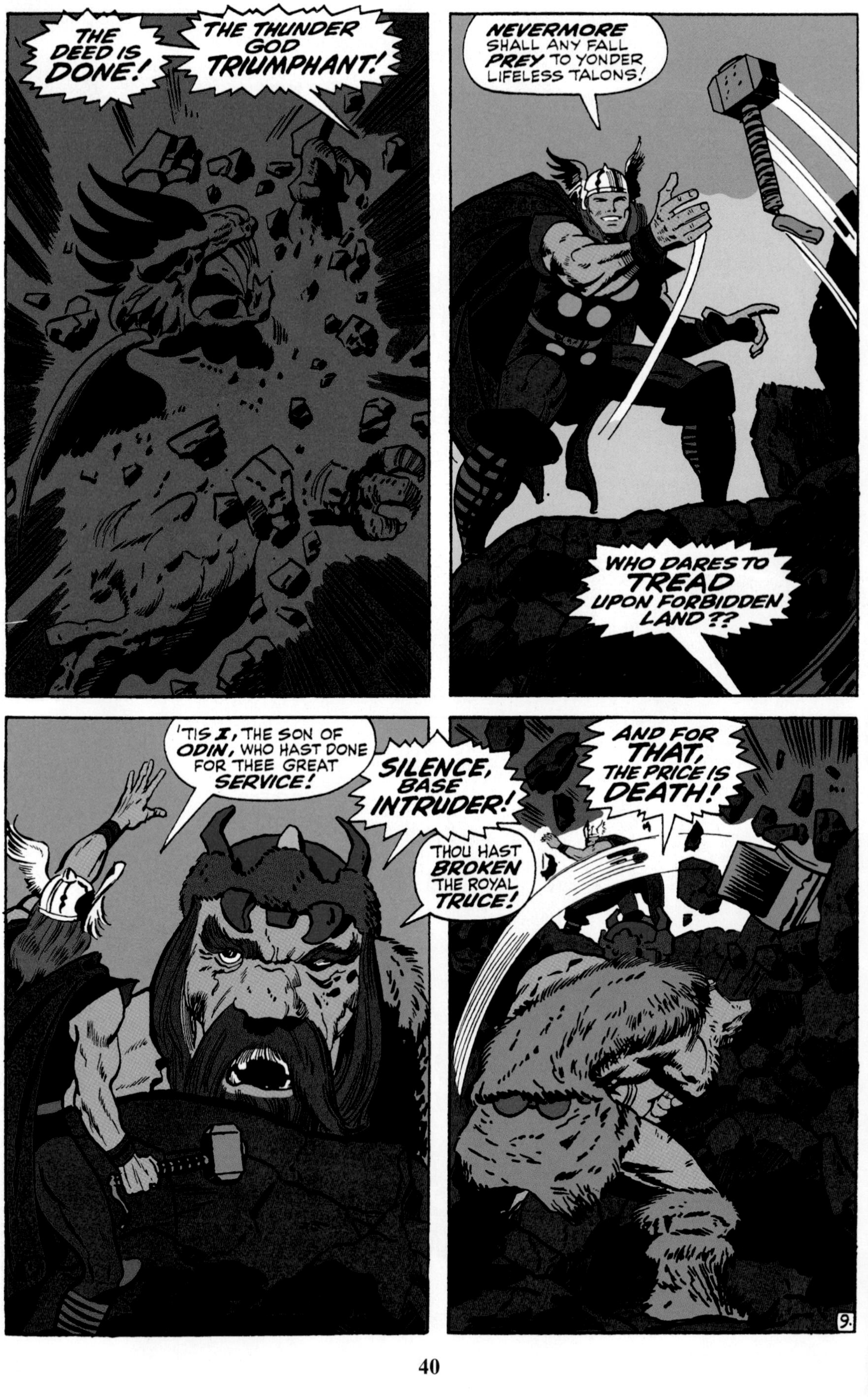
THE DEED IS DONE!
THE THUNDER GOD TRIUMPHANT!
NEVERMORE SHALL ANY FALL PREY TO YONDER LIFELESS TALONS!
WHO DARES TO TREAD UPON FORBIDDEN LAND??
'TIS I, THE SON OF ODIN, WHO HAST DONE FOR THEE GREAT SERVICE!
SILENCE, BASE INTRUDER!
THOU HAST BROKEN THE ROYAL TRUCE!
AND FOR THAT, THE PRICE IS DEATH!
9.

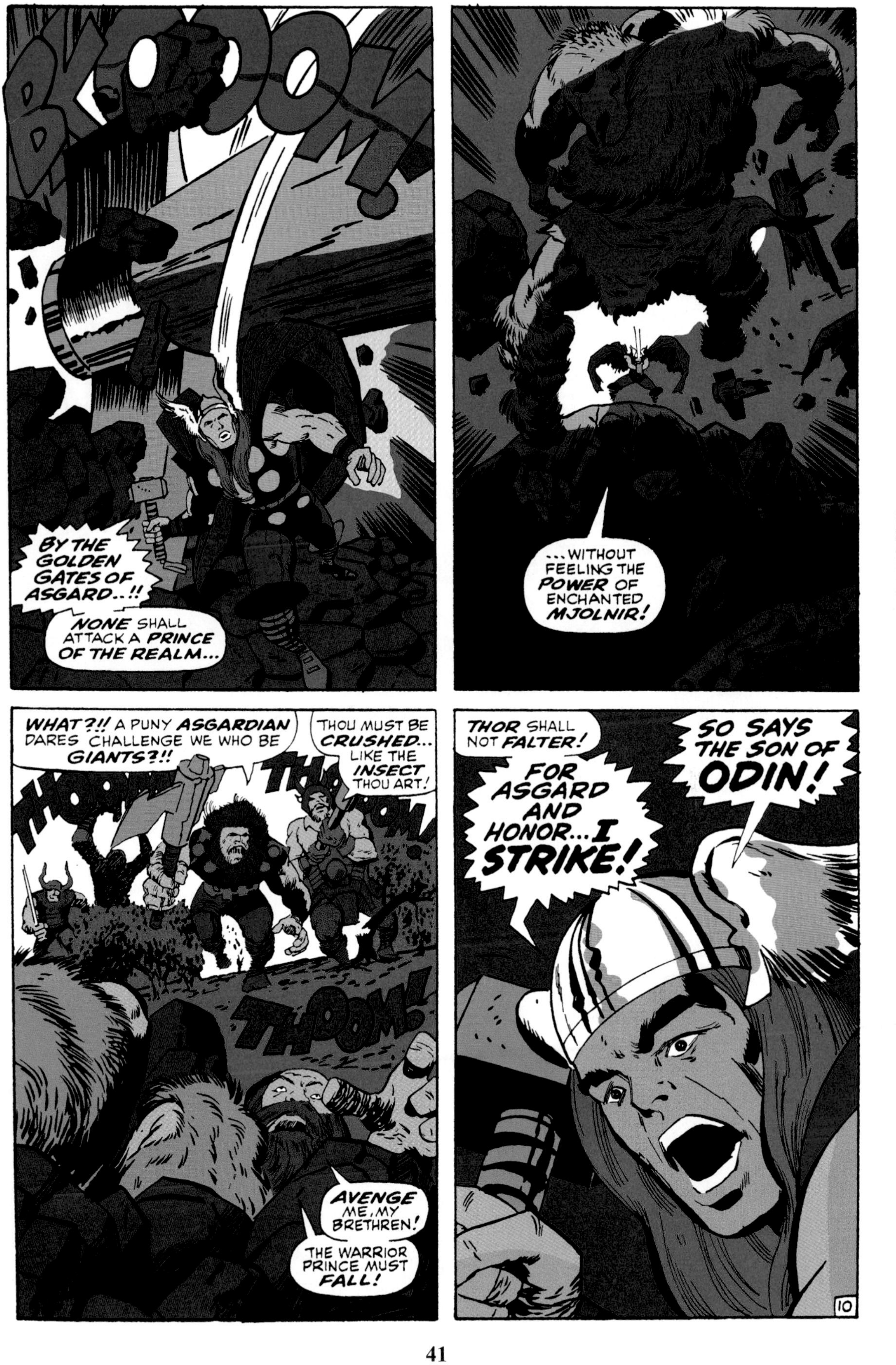
BKOOOM!
BY THE GOLDEN GATES OF ASGARD..!!
NONE SHALL ATTACK A PRINCE OF THE REALM...
...WITHOUT FEELING THE POWER OF ENCHANTED MJOLNIR!
WHAT?!! A PUNY ASGARDIAN DARES CHALLENGE WE WHO BE GIANTS?!!
THOU MUST BE CRUSHED... LIKE THE INSECT THOU ART!
THOOM!
AVENGE ME, MY BRETHREN!
THE WARRIOR PRINCE MUST FALL!
THOR SHALL NOT FALTER!
FOR ASGARD AND HONOR...I STRIKE!
SO SAYS THE SON OF ODIN!
10

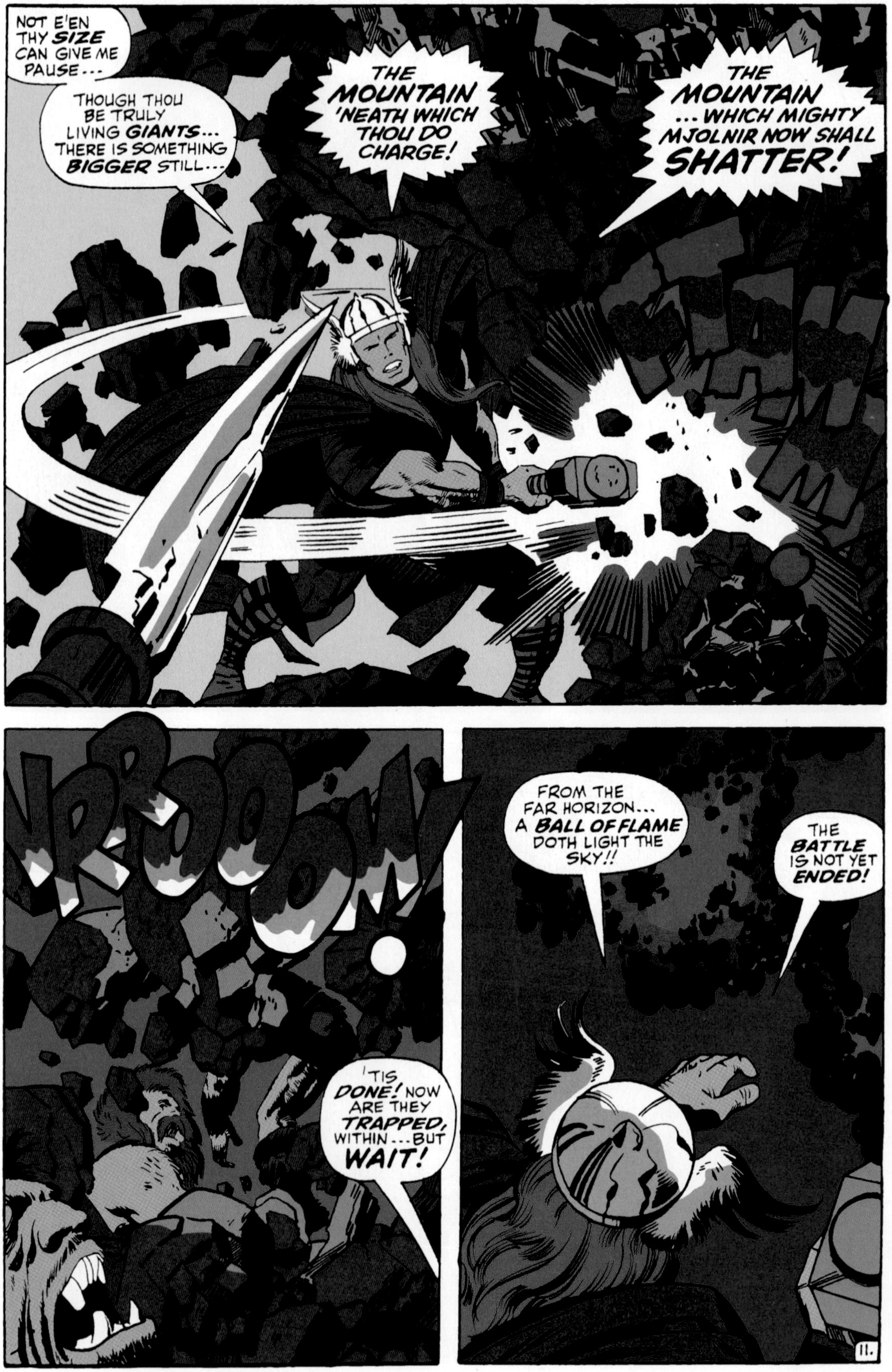
NOT E'EN THY SIZE CAN GIVE ME PAUSE...
THOUGH THOU BE TRULY LIVING GIANTS... THERE IS SOMETHING BIGGER STILL...
THE MOUNTAIN 'NEATH WHICH THOU DO CHARGE!
THE MOUNTAIN ...WHICH MIGHTY MJOLNIR NOW SHALL SHATTER!
'TIS DONE! NOW ARE THEY TRAPPED, WITHIN...BUT WAIT!
FROM THE FAR HORIZON... A BALL OF FLAME DOTH LIGHT THE SKY!!
THE BATTLE IS NOT YET ENDED!
11.

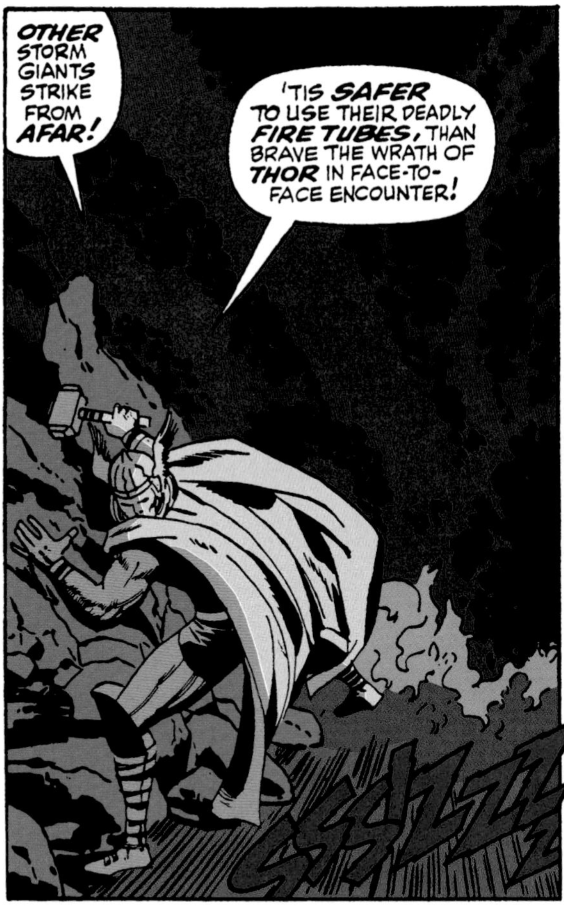
OTHER STORM GIANTS STRIKE FROM AFAR!
'TIS SAFER TO USE THEIR DEADLY FIRE TUBES, THAN BRAVE THE WRATH OF THOR IN FACE-TO-FACE ENCOUNTER!
SSSZZZZ

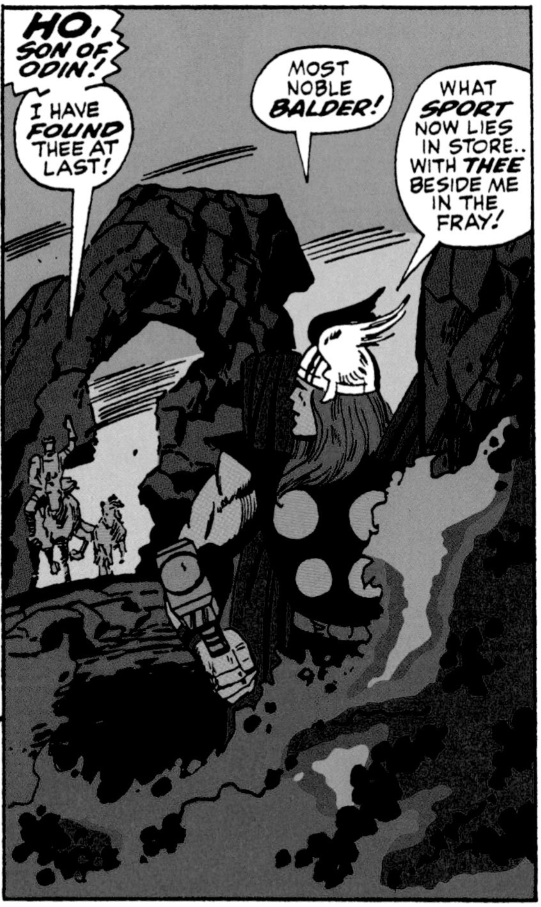
HO, SON OF ODIN!
I HAVE FOUND THEE AT LAST!
MOST NOBLE BALDER!
WHAT SPORT NOW LIES IN STORE.. WITH THEE BESIDE ME IN THE FRAY!

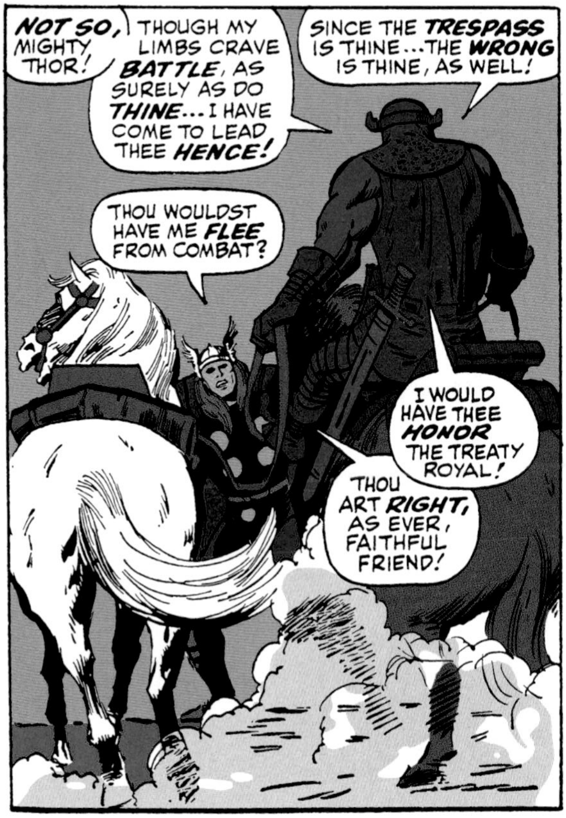
NOT SO, MIGHTY THOR!
THOUGH MY LIMBS CRAVE BATTLE, AS SURELY AS DO THINE... I HAVE COME TO LEAD THEE HENCE!
SINCE THE TRESPASS IS THINE... THE WRONG IS THINE, AS WELL!
THOU WOULDST HAVE ME FLEE FROM COMBAT?
I WOULD HAVE THEE HONOR THE TREATY ROYAL!
THOU ART RIGHT, AS EVER, FAITHFUL FRIEND!

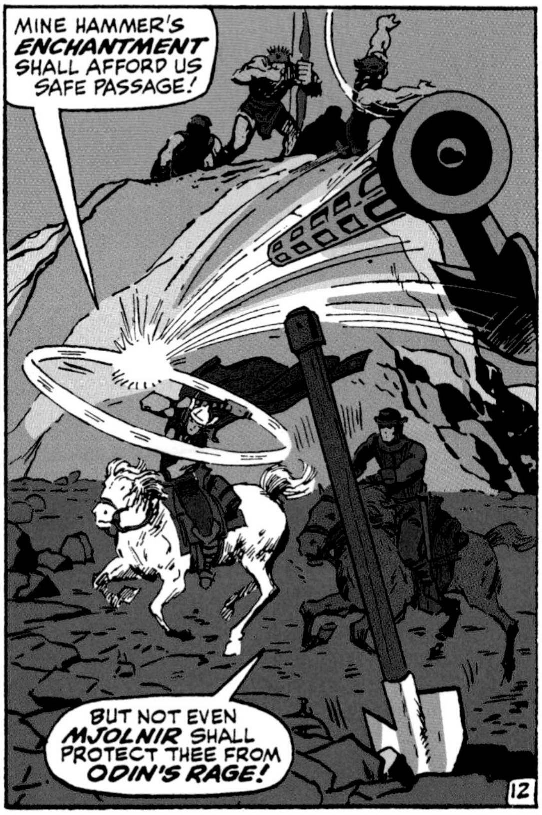
MINE HAMMER'S ENCHANTMENT SHALL AFFORD US SAFE PASSAGE!
BUT NOT EVEN MJOLNIR SHALL PROTECT THEE FROM ODIN'S RAGE!
12

YOU HAVE SHOWN THAT THOR WAS *YOUNG*... *HEADSTRONG*... SUPREMELY *CONFIDENT* OF HIS OWN GODLIKE *POWER!*

BUT, WHAT HAS THAT TO DO WITH *ME?*

CANST THOU NOT *SEE?* THY FATE... AND *HIS*... ARE *ONE AND THE SAME!*

BUT *STILL* YOU SPEAK IN RIDDLES!

HOW DID *I* ENTER THE PICTURE? AND WHERE WAS *HE?* WHERE WAS THE *ORIGINAL* THOR, WHEN I CAME ON THE SCENE??

ONLY *YOU* CAN TELL ME... FOR I HAVE *NO MEMORY* OF THOSE EVENTS!

*AYE!* 'TIS AS ODIN *PLANNED* IT!

'TWAS NOT *SEEMLY* FOR THEE TO *KNOW*... TILL *NOW!*

THEREFORE, CLEAR THY *MIND* OF EVERY THOUGHT... AS I TAKE THEE TO THE *PAST* ONCE MORE...!

FOR THOU MUST *RETURN* TO ASGARD... TO THE MEMORY OF YON *LUSTY*, BRAWLING ERA..!

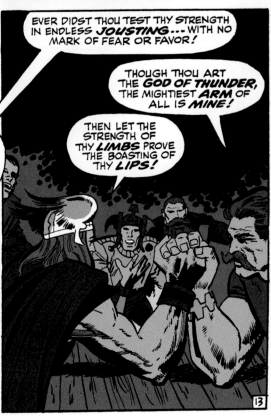

EVER DIDST THOU TEST THY STRENGTH IN ENDLESS *JOUSTING*... WITH NO MARK OF FEAR OR FAVOR!

THOUGH THOU ART THE *GOD OF THUNDER*, THE MIGHTIEST *ARM* OF ALL IS *MINE!*

THEN LET THE STRENGTH OF THY *LIMBS* PROVE THE BOASTING OF THY *LIPS!*

13

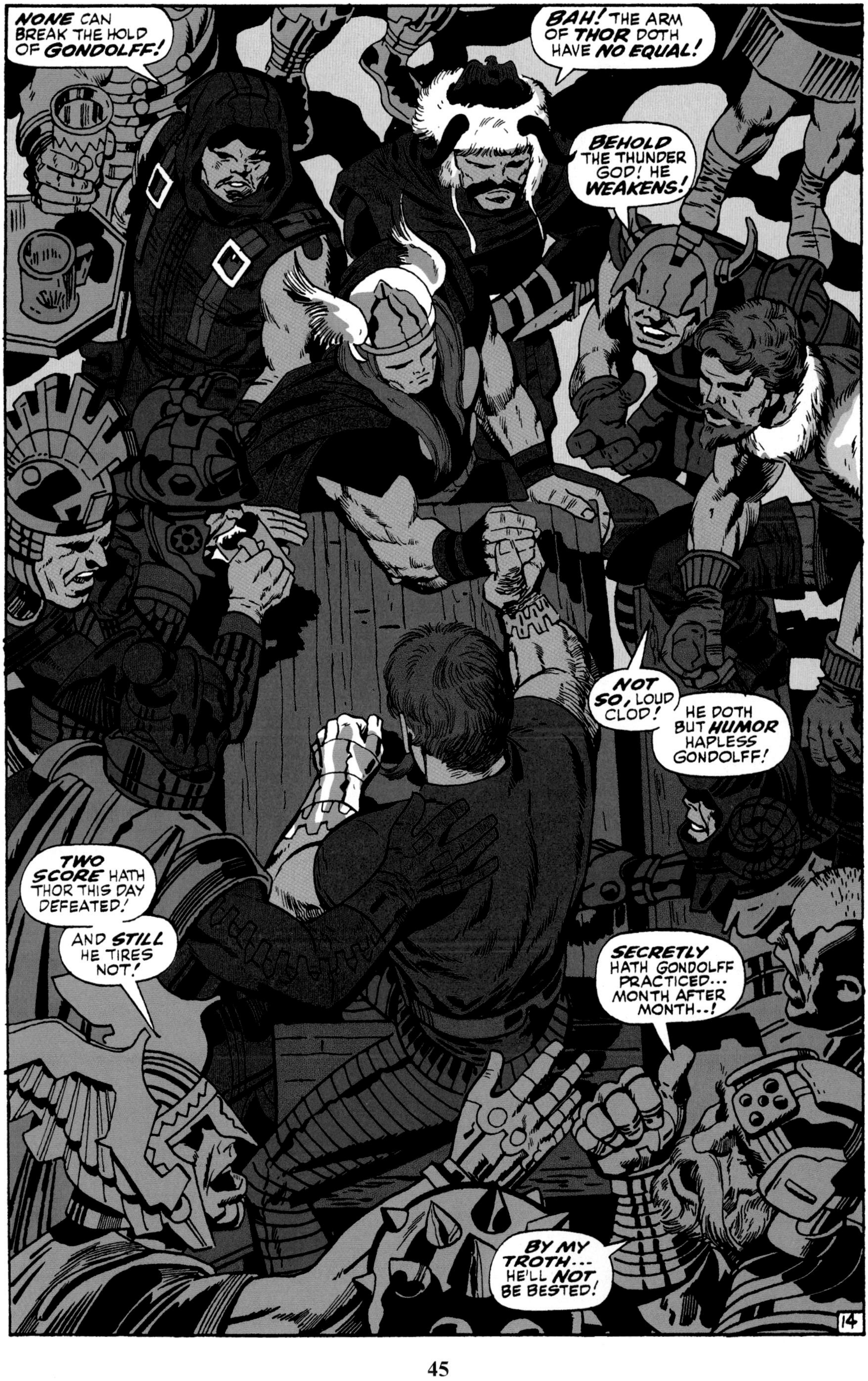
NONE CAN BREAK THE HOLD OF GONDOLFF!
BAH! THE ARM OF THOR DOTH HAVE NO EQUAL!
BEHOLD THE THUNDER GOD! HE WEAKENS!
NOT SO, LOUD CLOD!
HE DOTH BUT HUMOR HAPLESS GONDOLFF!
TWO SCORE HATH THOR THIS DAY DEFEATED!
AND STILL HE TIRES NOT!
SECRETLY HATH GONDOLFF PRACTICED... MONTH AFTER MONTH..!
BY MY TROTH... HE'LL NOT BE BESTED!
14

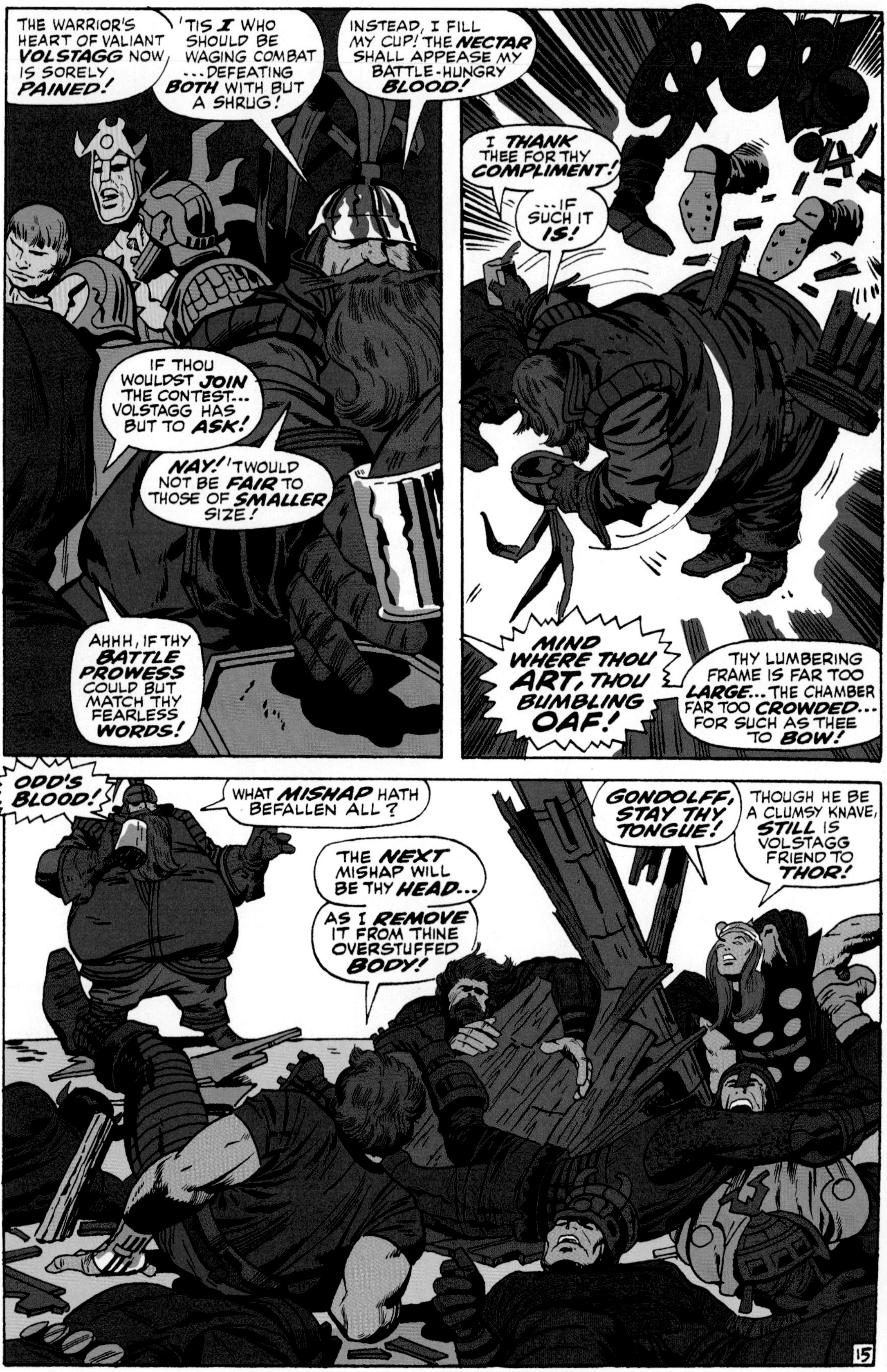
THE WARRIOR'S HEART OF VALIANT VOLSTAGG NOW IS SORELY PAINED!
'TIS I WHO SHOULD BE WAGING COMBAT ...DEFEATING BOTH WITH BUT A SHRUG!
INSTEAD, I FILL MY CUP! THE NECTAR SHALL APPEASE MY BATTLE-HUNGRY BLOOD!
IF THOU WOULDST JOIN THE CONTEST... VOLSTAGG HAS BUT TO ASK!
NAY! 'TWOULD NOT BE FAIR TO THOSE OF SMALLER SIZE!
AHHH, IF THY BATTLE PROWESS COULD BUT MATCH THY FEARLESS WORDS!
I THANK THEE FOR THY COMPLIMENT!
...IF SUCH IT IS!
MIND WHERE THOU ART, THOU BUMBLING OAF!
THY LUMBERING FRAME IS FAR TOO LARGE... THE CHAMBER FAR TOO CROWDED... FOR SUCH AS THEE TO BOW!
ODD'S BLOOD!
WHAT MISHAP HATH BEFALLEN ALL?
THE NEXT MISHAP WILL BE THY HEAD...
AS I REMOVE IT FROM THINE OVERSTUFFED BODY!
GONDOLFF, STAY THY TONGUE!
THOUGH HE BE A CLUMSY KNAVE, STILL IS VOLSTAGG FRIEND TO THOR!
15

THEN 'TIS AS I **SUSPECTED!**

WHEN THOU DIDST SEE THAT **GONDOLFF** HAD THEE **BEATEN...** THOU SIGNALLED **VOLSTAGG,** TO **END** THE CONTEST!

BUT **NOW** HATH THE GOD OF THUNDER **O'ER-STEPPED** HIMSELF!

BY LAW OF **ASGARD...** NOW MUST THOU **ADMIT** THY BASE **DECEPTION!**

I CALL THEE **LIAR!**

THE VICTORY WAS **MINE!** I DID BUT **TOY** WITH THEE!

THEN, LET OUR **STEEL** DECIDE!

I HAVE COMRADES **A'PLENTY** TO STRIKE FOR **GONDOLFF!**

**THOR** HATH BUT **FEW...**

BUT WE BE **MORE** THAN ENOW! FOR, WE BE **HOGUN THE GRIM...**

AND **FANDRAL THE DASHING...**

...AND VOLUMINOUS **VOLSTAGG,** WHOSE VERY **NAME** MAKES ARMIES **TREMBLE!**

WHILST **THOU** DO BATTLE **YONDER...**

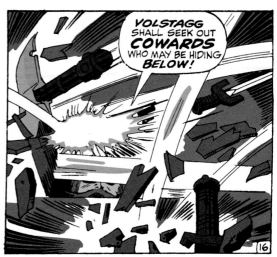

**VOLSTAGG** SHALL SEEK OUT **COWARDS** WHO MAY BE HIDING **BELOW!**

16

47

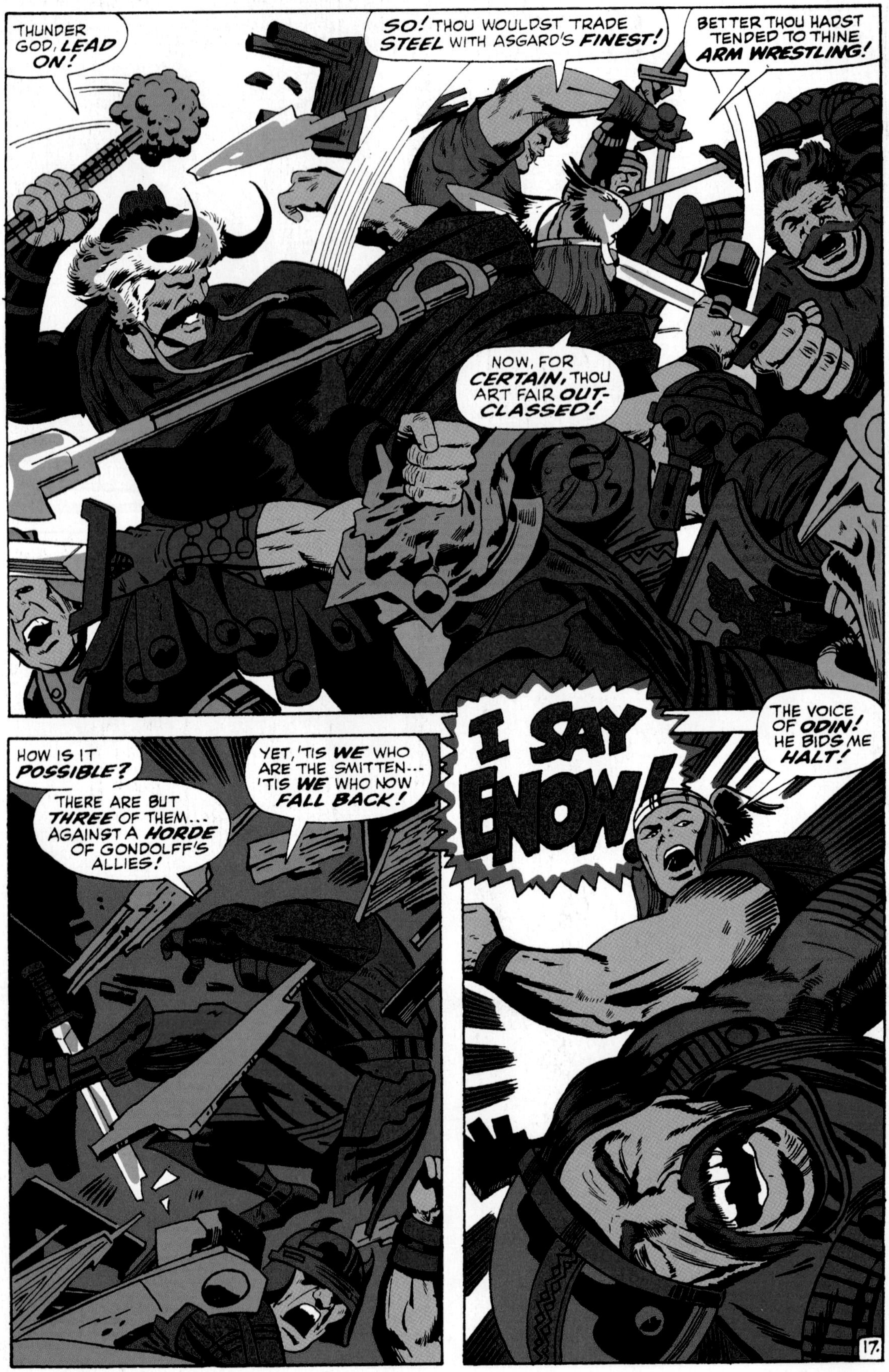
THUNDER GOD, LEAD ON!
SO! THOU WOULDST TRADE STEEL WITH ASGARD'S FINEST!
BETTER THOU HADST TENDED TO THINE ARM WRESTLING!
NOW, FOR CERTAIN, THOU ART FAIR OUT-CLASSED!
HOW IS IT POSSIBLE?
THERE ARE BUT THREE OF THEM... AGAINST A HORDE OF GONDOLFF'S ALLIES!
YET, 'TIS WE WHO ARE THE SMITTEN... 'TIS WE WHO NOW FALL BACK!
I SAY ENOW!
THE VOICE OF ODIN! HE BIDS ME HALT!
17.

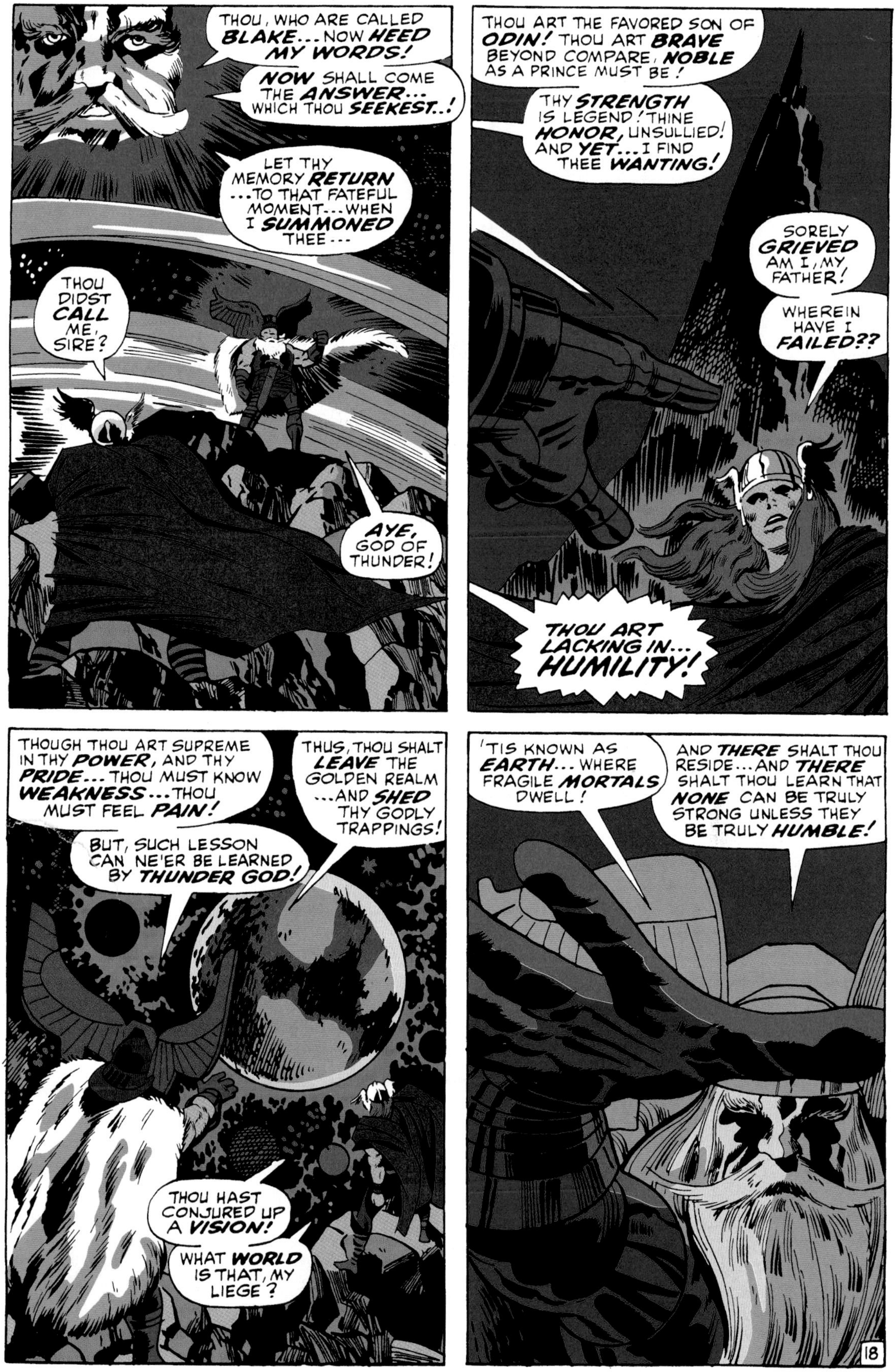
THOU, WHO ARE CALLED BLAKE... NOW HEED MY WORDS!
NOW SHALL COME THE ANSWER... WHICH THOU SEEKEST..!
LET THY MEMORY RETURN ...TO THAT FATEFUL MOMENT...WHEN I SUMMONED THEE---
THOU DIDST CALL ME, SIRE?
AYE, GOD OF THUNDER!
THOU ART THE FAVORED SON OF ODIN! THOU ART BRAVE BEYOND COMPARE, NOBLE AS A PRINCE MUST BE!
THY STRENGTH IS LEGEND! THINE HONOR, UNSULLIED! AND YET...I FIND THEE WANTING!
SORELY GRIEVED AM I, MY FATHER!
WHEREIN HAVE I FAILED??
THOU ART LACKING IN... HUMILITY!
THOUGH THOU ART SUPREME IN THY POWER, AND THY PRIDE... THOU MUST KNOW WEAKNESS...THOU MUST FEEL PAIN!
BUT, SUCH LESSON CAN NE'ER BE LEARNED BY THUNDER GOD!
THUS, THOU SHALT LEAVE THE GOLDEN REALM ...AND SHED THY GODLY TRAPPINGS!
THOU HAST CONJURED UP A VISION!
WHAT WORLD IS THAT, MY LIEGE?
'TIS KNOWN AS EARTH... WHERE FRAGILE MORTALS DWELL!
AND THERE SHALT THOU RESIDE...AND THERE SHALT THOU LEARN THAT NONE CAN BE TRULY STRONG UNLESS THEY BE TRULY HUMBLE!
18

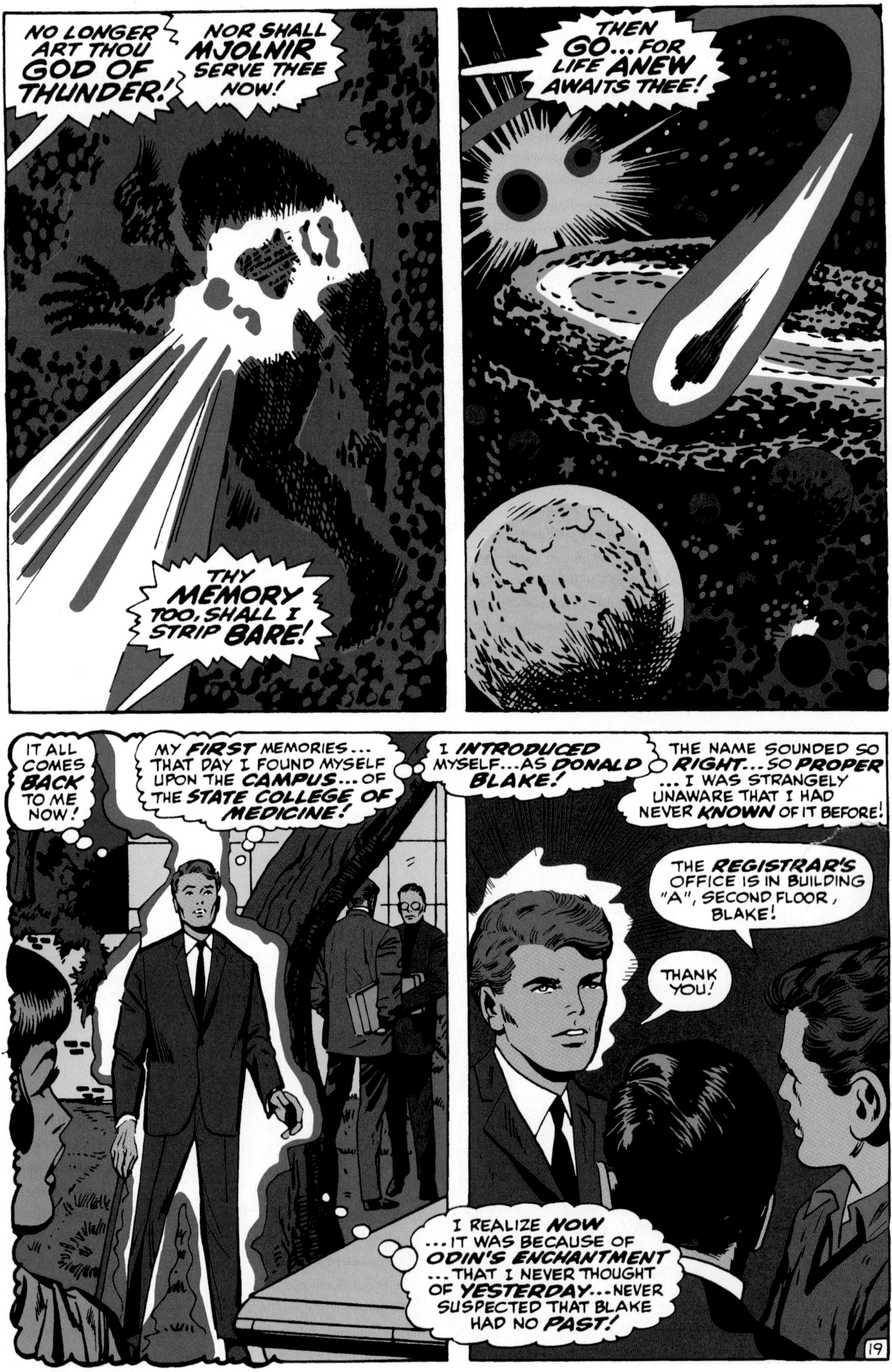
NO LONGER ART THOU GOD OF THUNDER!
NOR SHALL MJOLNIR SERVE THEE NOW!
THY MEMORY TOO, SHALL I STRIP BARE!
THEN GO... FOR LIFE ANEW AWAITS THEE!
IT ALL COMES BACK TO ME NOW!
MY FIRST MEMORIES... THAT DAY I FOUND MYSELF UPON THE CAMPUS... OF THE STATE COLLEGE OF MEDICINE!
I INTRODUCED MYSELF... AS DONALD BLAKE!
THE NAME SOUNDED SO RIGHT... SO PROPER ... I WAS STRANGELY UNAWARE THAT I HAD NEVER KNOWN OF IT BEFORE!
THE REGISTRAR'S OFFICE IS IN BUILDING "A", SECOND FLOOR, BLAKE!
THANK YOU!
I REALIZE NOW ... IT WAS BECAUSE OF ODIN'S ENCHANTMENT ... THAT I NEVER THOUGHT OF YESTERDAY... NEVER SUSPECTED THAT BLAKE HAD NO PAST!
19

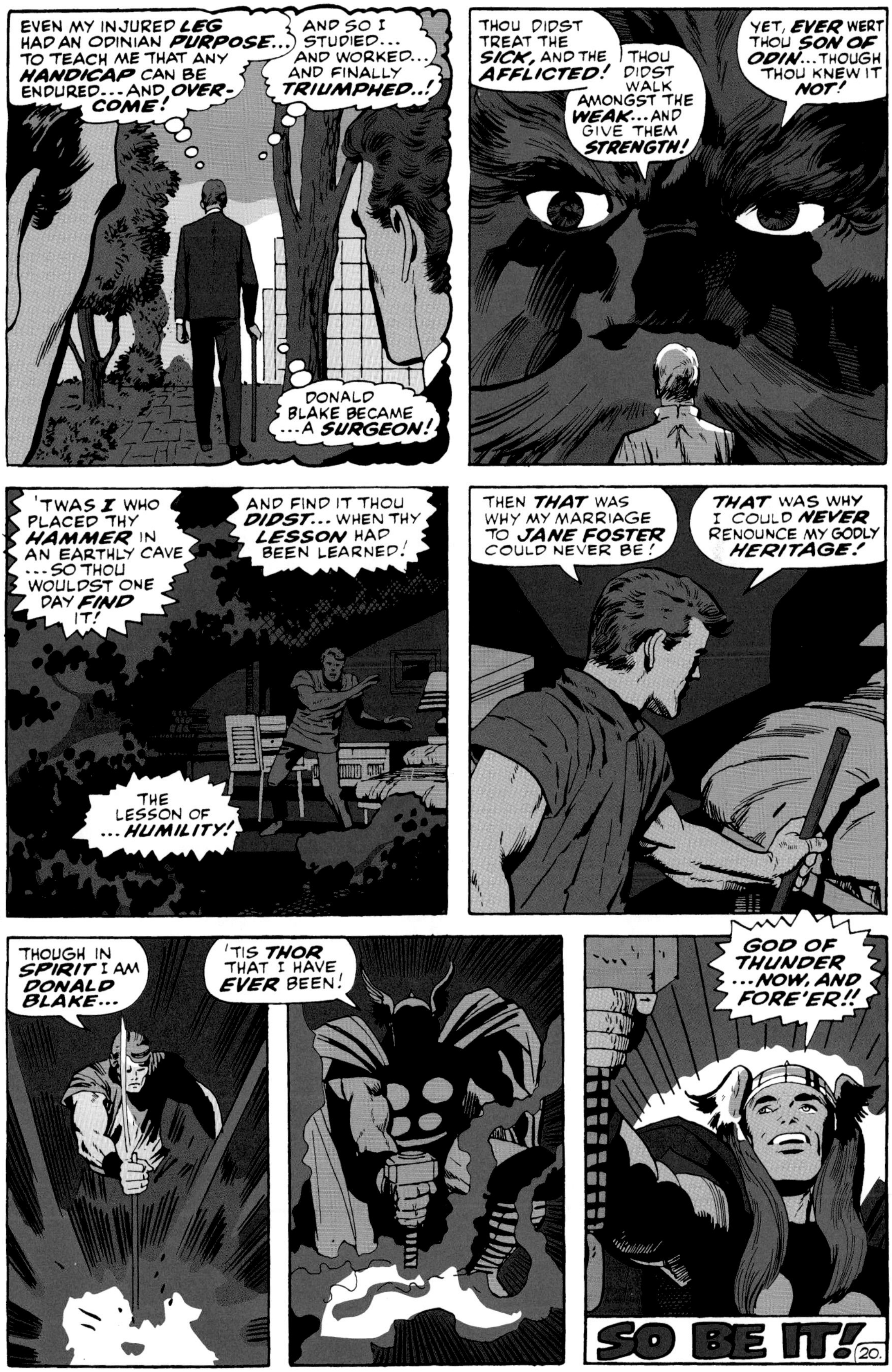
EVEN MY INJURED LEG HAD AN ODINIAN PURPOSE... TO TEACH ME THAT ANY HANDICAP CAN BE ENDURED... AND OVERCOME!
AND SO I STUDIED... AND WORKED... AND FINALLY TRIUMPHED..!
DONALD BLAKE BECAME ...A SURGEON!
THOU DIDST TREAT THE SICK, AND THE AFFLICTED!
THOU DIDST WALK AMONGST THE WEAK... AND GIVE THEM STRENGTH!
YET, EVER WERT THOU SON OF ODIN... THOUGH THOU KNEW IT NOT!
'TWAS I WHO PLACED THY HAMMER IN AN EARTHLY CAVE ...SO THOU WOULDST ONE DAY FIND IT!
AND FIND IT THOU DIDST... WHEN THY LESSON HAD BEEN LEARNED!
THE LESSON OF ...HUMILITY!
THEN THAT WAS WHY MY MARRIAGE TO JANE FOSTER COULD NEVER BE!
THAT WAS WHY I COULD NEVER RENOUNCE MY GODLY HERITAGE!
THOUGH IN SPIRIT I AM DONALD BLAKE...
'TIS THOR THAT I HAVE EVER BEEN!
GOD OF THUNDER ...NOW, AND FORE'ER!!
SO BE IT!
20.

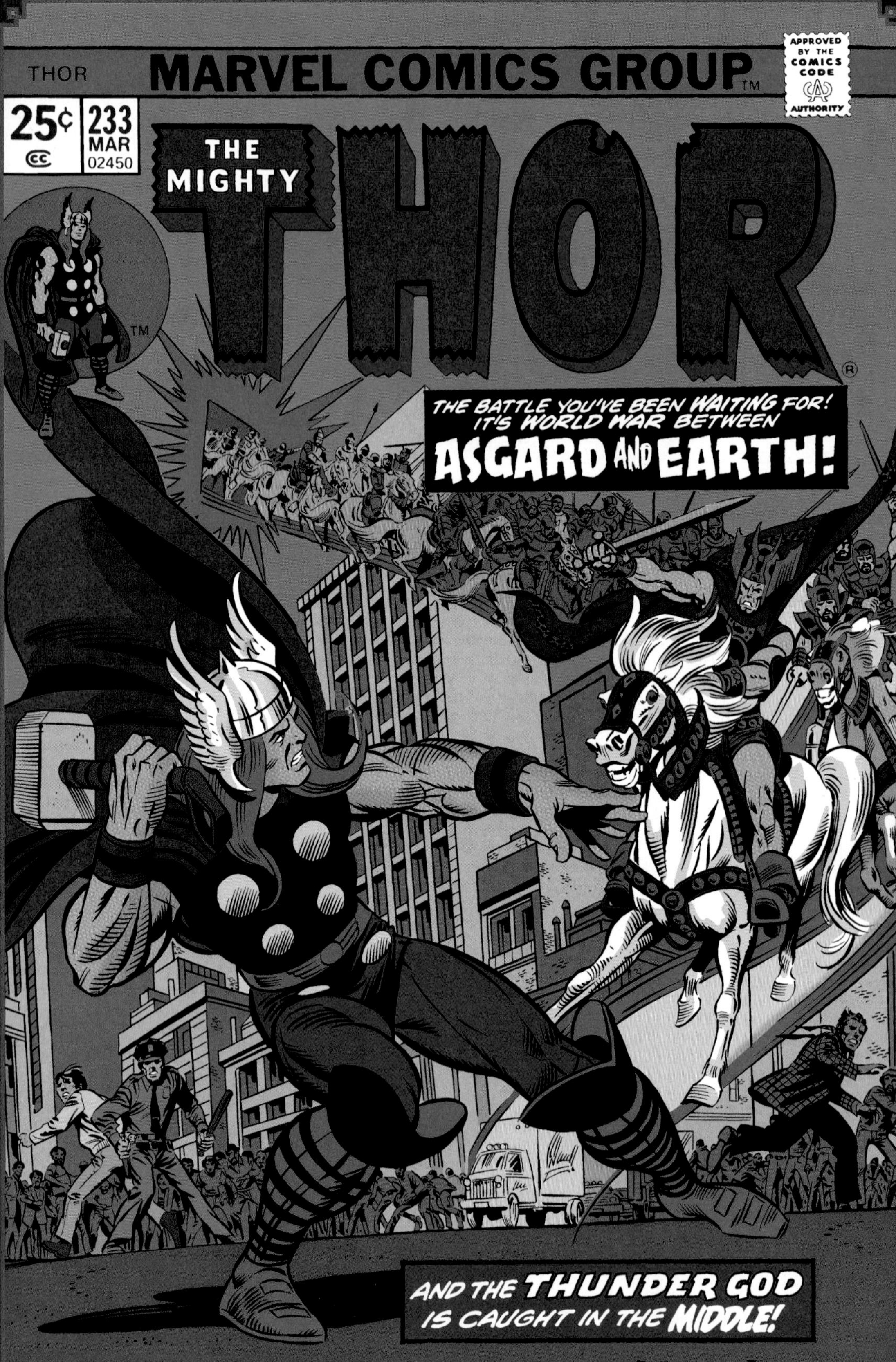
THOR
MARVEL COMICS GROUP
APPROVED BY THE COMICS CODE AUTHORITY
25¢
233 MAR 02450
THE MIGHTY THOR
THE BATTLE YOU'VE BEEN WAITING FOR! IT'S WORLD WAR BETWEEN ASGARD AND EARTH!
AND THE THUNDER GOD IS CAUGHT IN THE MIDDLE!

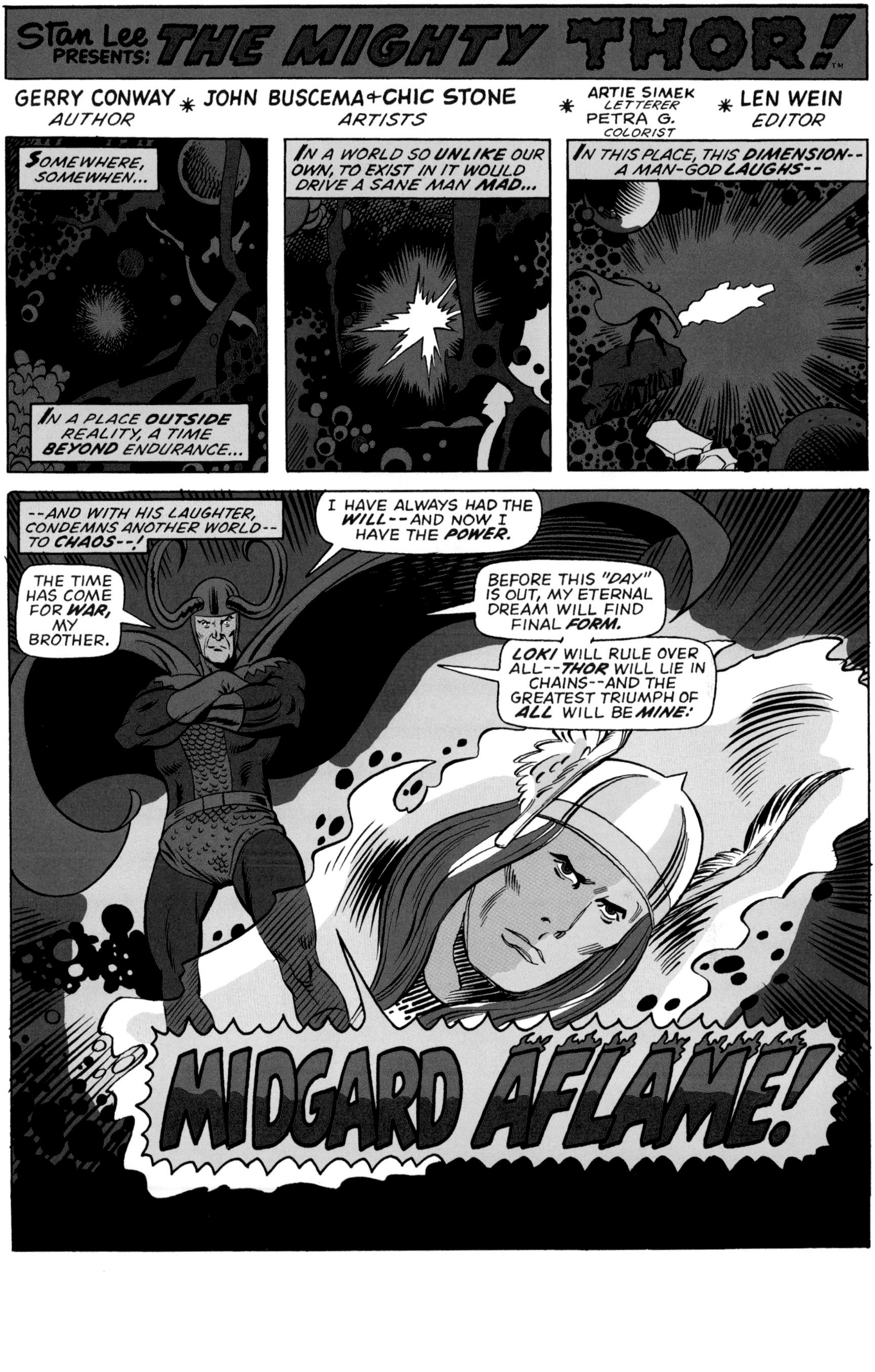
Stan Lee PRESENTS: THE MIGHTY THOR!
GERRY CONWAY AUTHOR
JOHN BUSCEMA + CHIC STONE ARTISTS
ARTIE SIMEK LETTERER
PETRA G. COLORIST
LEN WEIN EDITOR
SOMEWHERE, SOMEWHEN...
IN A PLACE OUTSIDE REALITY, A TIME BEYOND ENDURANCE...
IN A WORLD SO UNLIKE OUR OWN, TO EXIST IN IT WOULD DRIVE A SANE MAN MAD...
IN THIS PLACE, THIS DIMENSION-- A MAN-GOD LAUGHS--
--AND WITH HIS LAUGHTER, CONDEMNS ANOTHER WORLD-- TO CHAOS--!
I HAVE ALWAYS HAD THE WILL--AND NOW I HAVE THE POWER.
THE TIME HAS COME FOR WAR, MY BROTHER.
BEFORE THIS "DAY" IS OUT, MY ETERNAL DREAM WILL FIND FINAL FORM.
LOKI WILL RULE OVER ALL--THOR WILL LIE IN CHAINS--AND THE GREATEST TRIUMPH OF ALL WILL BE MINE!
MIDGARD AFLAME!

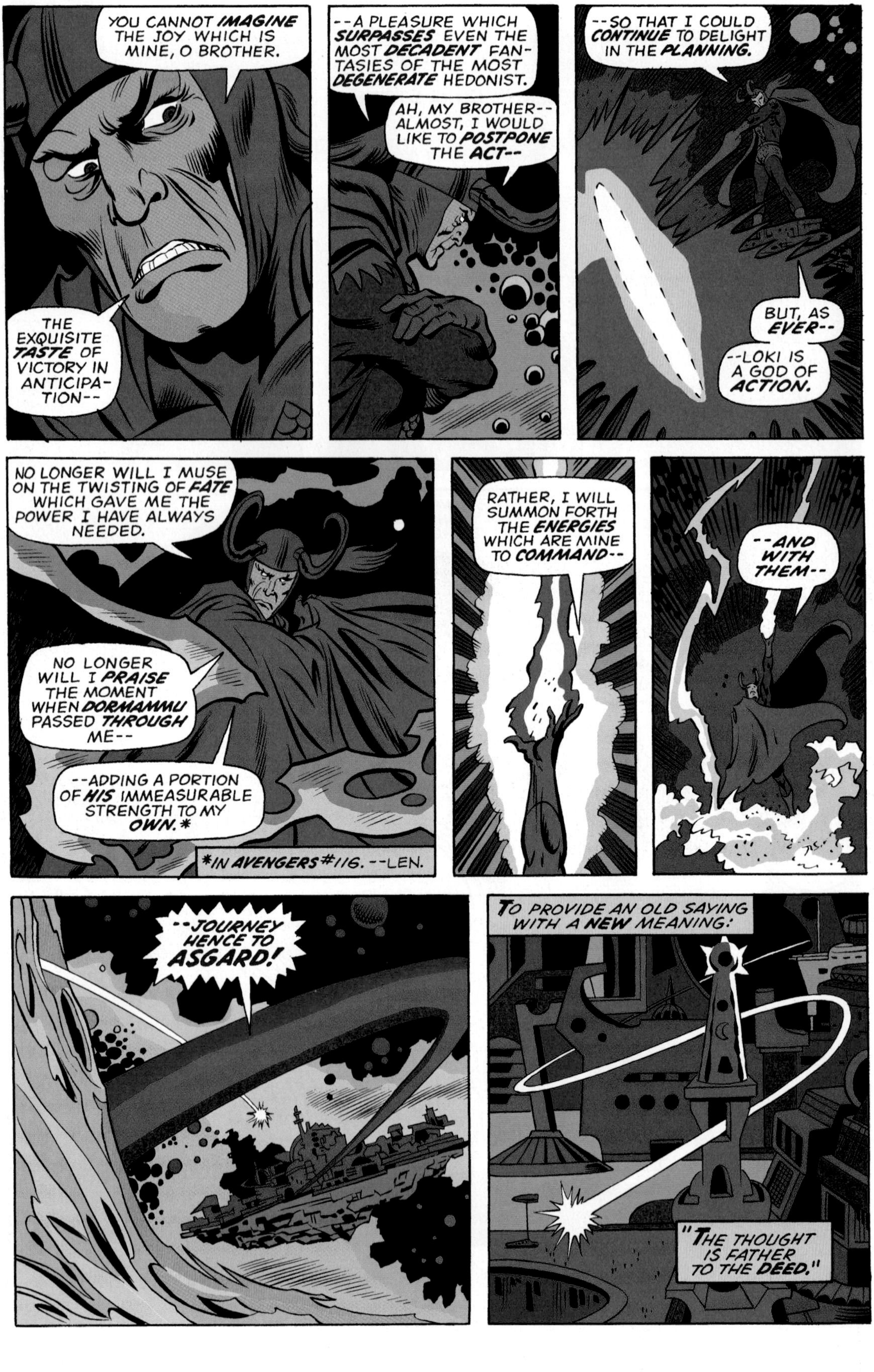
YOU CANNOT IMAGINE THE JOY WHICH IS MINE, O BROTHER.
THE EXQUISITE TASTE OF VICTORY IN ANTICIPA- TION--
--A PLEASURE WHICH SURPASSES EVEN THE MOST DECADENT FAN- TASIES OF THE MOST DEGENERATE HEDONIST.
AH, MY BROTHER-- ALMOST, I WOULD LIKE TO POSTPONE THE ACT--
--SO THAT I COULD CONTINUE TO DELIGHT IN THE PLANNING.
BUT, AS EVER--
--LOKI IS A GOD OF ACTION.
NO LONGER WILL I MUSE ON THE TWISTING OF FATE WHICH GAVE ME THE POWER I HAVE ALWAYS NEEDED.
NO LONGER WILL I PRAISE THE MOMENT WHEN DORMAMMU PASSED THROUGH ME--
--ADDING A PORTION OF HIS IMMEASURABLE STRENGTH TO MY OWN.*
*IN AVENGERS #116. --LEN.
RATHER, I WILL SUMMON FORTH THE ENERGIES WHICH ARE MINE TO COMMAND--
--AND WITH THEM--
--JOURNEY HENCE TO ASGARD!
TO PROVIDE AN OLD SAYING WITH A NEW MEANING:
"THE THOUGHT IS FATHER TO THE DEED."

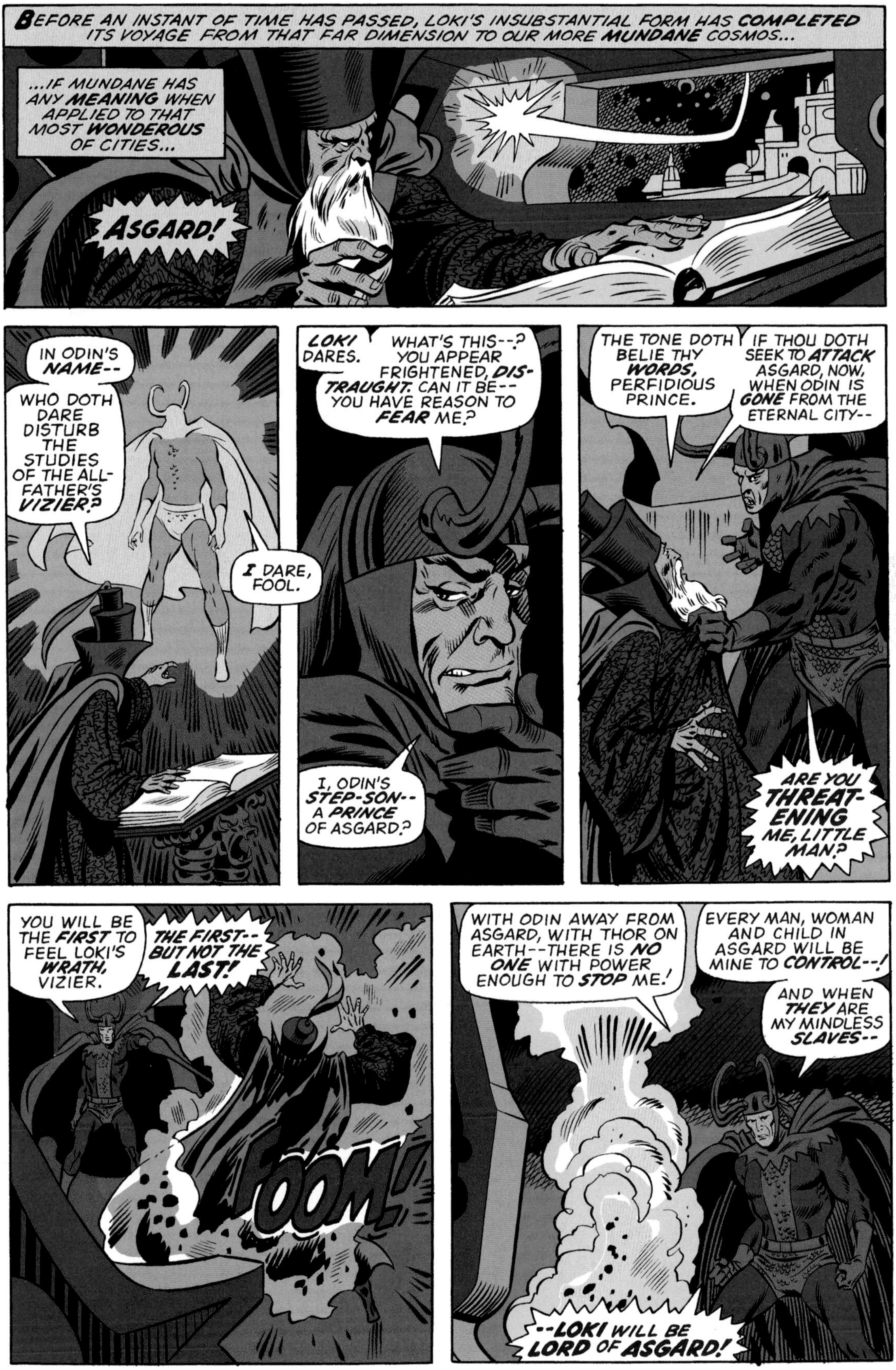
BEFORE AN INSTANT OF TIME HAS PASSED, LOKI'S INSUBSTANTIAL FORM HAS COMPLETED ITS VOYAGE FROM THAT FAR DIMENSION TO OUR MORE MUNDANE COSMOS...
...IF MUNDANE HAS ANY MEANING WHEN APPLIED TO THAT MOST WONDEROUS OF CITIES...
ASGARD!
IN ODIN'S NAME--
WHO DOTH DARE DISTURB THE STUDIES OF THE ALL-FATHER'S VIZIER?
I DARE, FOOL.
LOKI DARES.
WHAT'S THIS--? YOU APPEAR FRIGHTENED, DISTRAUGHT. CAN IT BE--YOU HAVE REASON TO FEAR ME?
I, ODIN'S STEP-SON--A PRINCE OF ASGARD?
THE TONE DOTH BELIE THY WORDS, PERFIDIOUS PRINCE.
IF THOU DOTH SEEK TO ATTACK ASGARD, NOW, WHEN ODIN IS GONE FROM THE ETERNAL CITY--
ARE YOU THREATENING ME, LITTLE MAN?
YOU WILL BE THE FIRST TO FEEL LOKI'S WRATH, VIZIER.
THE FIRST--BUT NOT THE LAST!
FOOM!
WITH ODIN AWAY FROM ASGARD, WITH THOR ON EARTH--THERE IS NO ONE WITH POWER ENOUGH TO STOP ME.!
EVERY MAN, WOMAN AND CHILD IN ASGARD WILL BE MINE TO CONTROL--!
AND WHEN THEY ARE MY MINDLESS SLAVES--
--LOKI WILL BE LORD OF ASGARD!

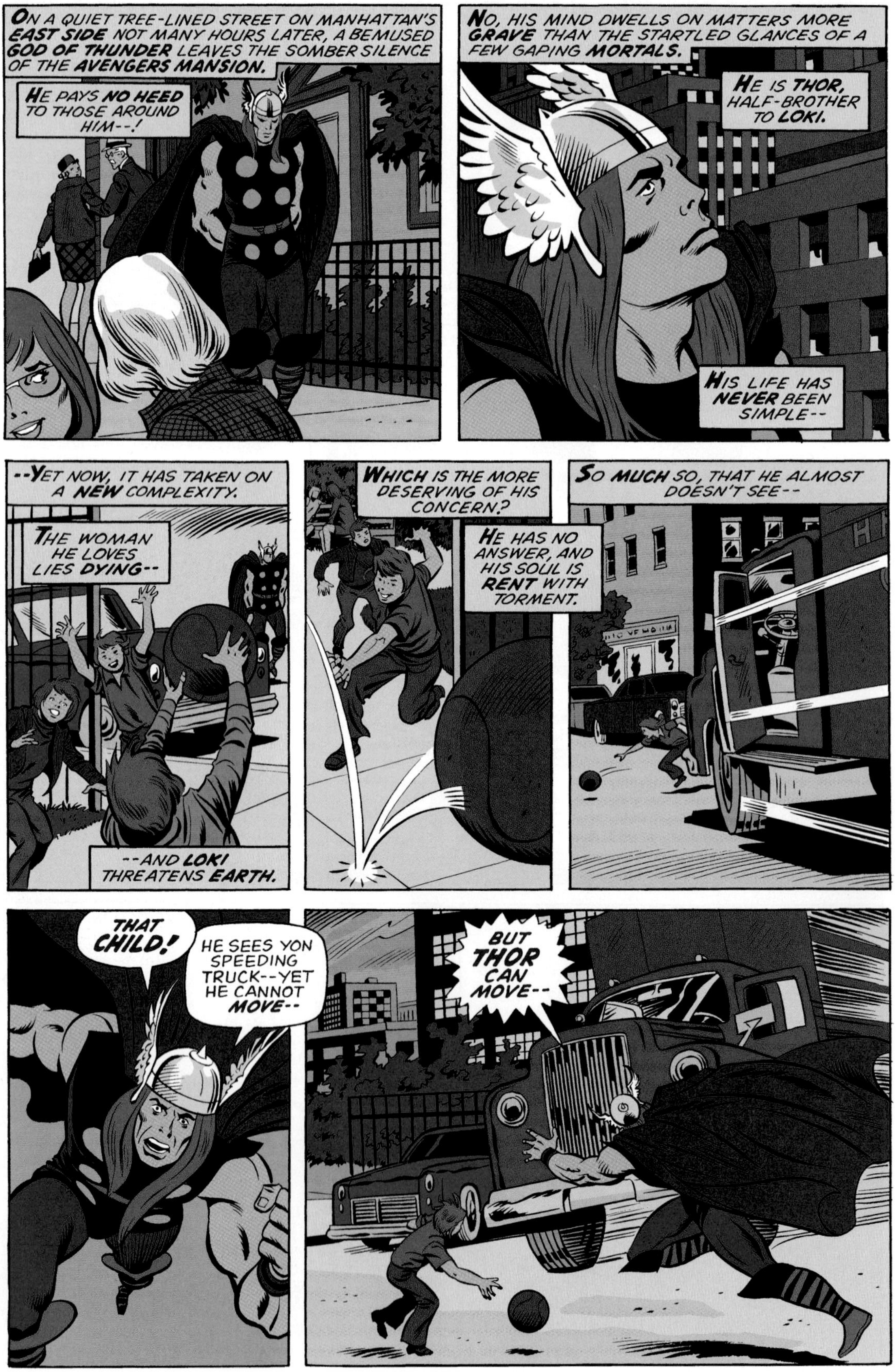
ON A QUIET TREE-LINED STREET ON MANHATTAN'S EAST SIDE NOT MANY HOURS LATER, A BEMUSED GOD OF THUNDER LEAVES THE SOMBER SILENCE OF THE AVENGERS MANSION.
HE PAYS NO HEED TO THOSE AROUND HIM--!
NO, HIS MIND DWELLS ON MATTERS MORE GRAVE THAN THE STARTLED GLANCES OF A FEW GAPING MORTALS.
HE IS THOR, HALF-BROTHER TO LOKI.
HIS LIFE HAS NEVER BEEN SIMPLE--
--YET NOW, IT HAS TAKEN ON A NEW COMPLEXITY.
THE WOMAN HE LOVES LIES DYING--
--AND LOKI THREATENS EARTH.
WHICH IS THE MORE DESERVING OF HIS CONCERN?
HE HAS NO ANSWER, AND HIS SOUL IS RENT WITH TORMENT.
SO MUCH SO, THAT HE ALMOST DOESN'T SEE--
THAT CHILD!
HE SEES YON SPEEDING TRUCK--YET HE CANNOT MOVE--
BUT THOR CAN MOVE--

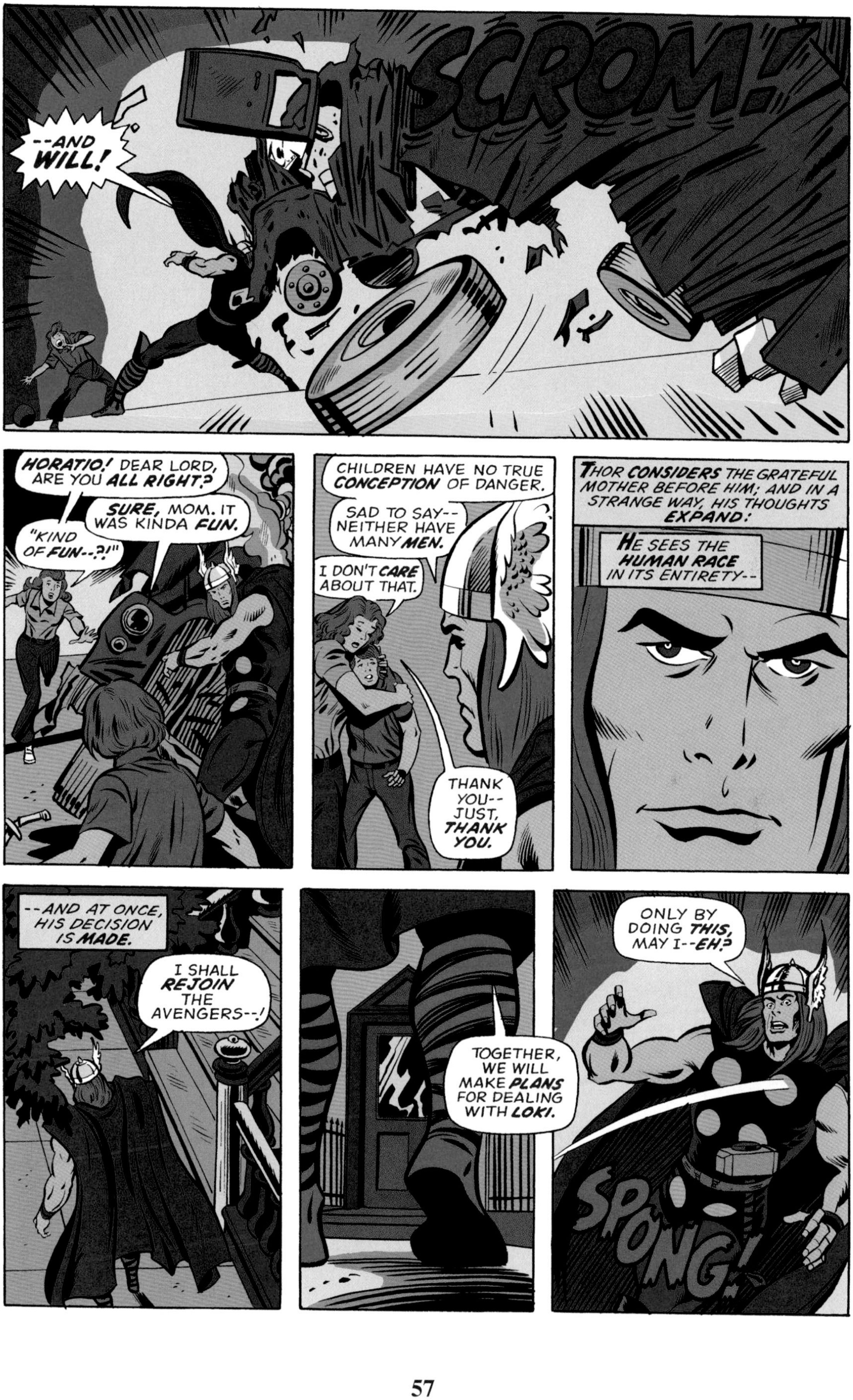
--AND WILL!
SCROM!
HORATIO! DEAR LORD, ARE YOU ALL RIGHT?
SURE, MOM. IT WAS KINDA FUN.
"KIND OF FUN--?!"
CHILDREN HAVE NO TRUE CONCEPTION OF DANGER.
SAD TO SAY-- NEITHER HAVE MANY MEN.
I DON'T CARE ABOUT THAT.
THANK YOU-- JUST, THANK YOU.
THOR CONSIDERS THE GRATEFUL MOTHER BEFORE HIM; AND IN A STRANGE WAY, HIS THOUGHTS EXPAND:
HE SEES THE HUMAN RACE IN ITS ENTIRETY--
--AND AT ONCE, HIS DECISION IS MADE.
I SHALL REJOIN THE AVENGERS--!
TOGETHER, WE WILL MAKE PLANS FOR DEALING WITH LOKI.
ONLY BY DOING THIS, MAY I--EH?
SPONG!

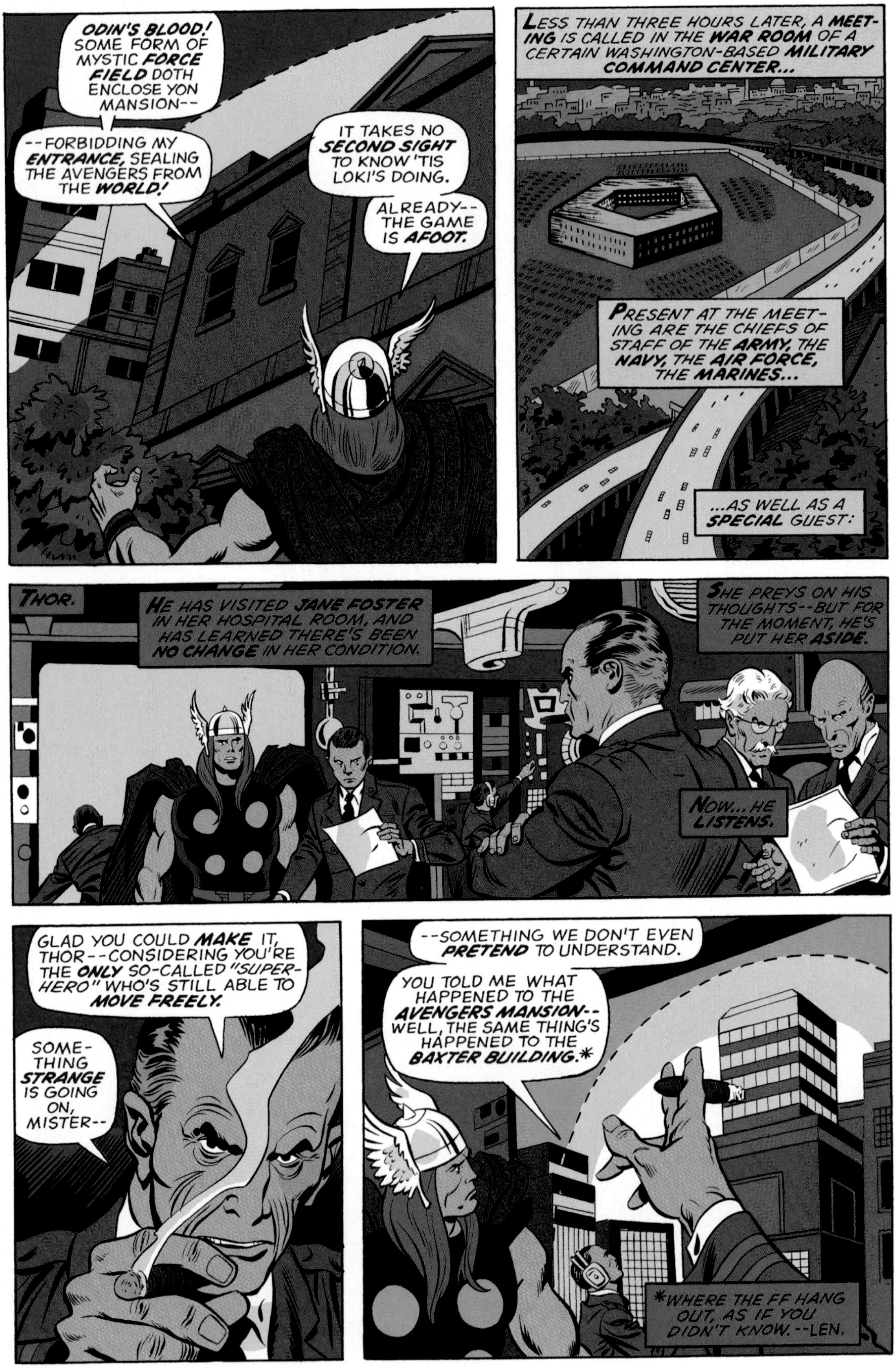

ODIN'S BLOOD! SOME FORM OF MYSTIC FORCE FIELD DOTH ENCLOSE YON MANSION--
--FORBIDDING MY ENTRANCE, SEALING THE AVENGERS FROM THE WORLD!
IT TAKES NO SECOND SIGHT TO KNOW 'TIS LOKI'S DOING.
ALREADY-- THE GAME IS AFOOT.
LESS THAN THREE HOURS LATER, A MEETING IS CALLED IN THE WAR ROOM OF A CERTAIN WASHINGTON-BASED MILITARY COMMAND CENTER...
PRESENT AT THE MEETING ARE THE CHIEFS OF STAFF OF THE ARMY, THE NAVY, THE AIR FORCE, THE MARINES...
...AS WELL AS A SPECIAL GUEST:
THOR.
HE HAS VISITED JANE FOSTER IN HER HOSPITAL ROOM, AND HAS LEARNED THERE'S BEEN NO CHANGE IN HER CONDITION.
SHE PREYS ON HIS THOUGHTS--BUT FOR THE MOMENT, HE'S PUT HER ASIDE.
NOW... HE LISTENS.
GLAD YOU COULD MAKE IT, THOR--CONSIDERING YOU'RE THE ONLY SO-CALLED "SUPER-HERO" WHO'S STILL ABLE TO MOVE FREELY.
SOME-THING STRANGE IS GOING ON, MISTER--
--SOMETHING WE DON'T EVEN PRETEND TO UNDERSTAND.
YOU TOLD ME WHAT HAPPENED TO THE AVENGERS MANSION-- WELL, THE SAME THING'S HAPPENED TO THE BAXTER BUILDING.*
*WHERE THE FF HANG OUT, AS IF YOU DIDN'T KNOW. --LEN.

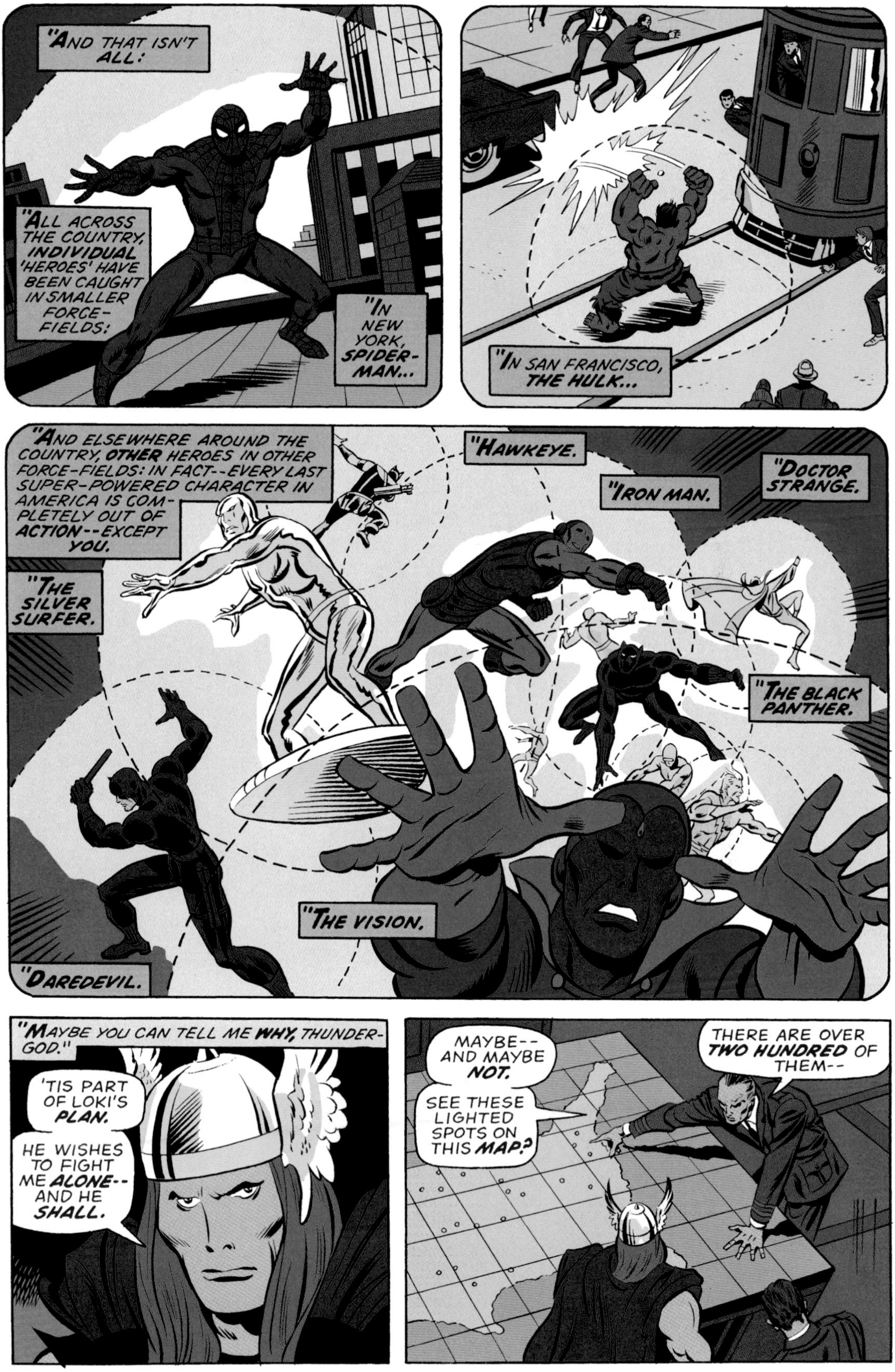
"AND THAT ISN'T ALL:
"ALL ACROSS THE COUNTRY, INDIVIDUAL 'HEROES' HAVE BEEN CAUGHT IN SMALLER FORCE-FIELDS:
"IN NEW YORK, SPIDER-MAN...
"IN SAN FRANCISCO, THE HULK...
"AND ELSEWHERE AROUND THE COUNTRY, OTHER HEROES IN OTHER FORCE-FIELDS: IN FACT--EVERY LAST SUPER-POWERED CHARACTER IN AMERICA IS COMPLETELY OUT OF ACTION--EXCEPT YOU.
"HAWKEYE.
"IRON MAN.
"DOCTOR STRANGE.
"THE SILVER SURFER.
"THE BLACK PANTHER.
"THE VISION.
"DAREDEVIL.
"MAYBE YOU CAN TELL ME WHY, THUNDER-GOD."
'TIS PART OF LOKI'S PLAN.
HE WISHES TO FIGHT ME ALONE--AND HE SHALL.
MAYBE--AND MAYBE NOT.
SEE THESE LIGHTED SPOTS ON THIS MAP?
THERE ARE OVER TWO HUNDRED OF THEM--

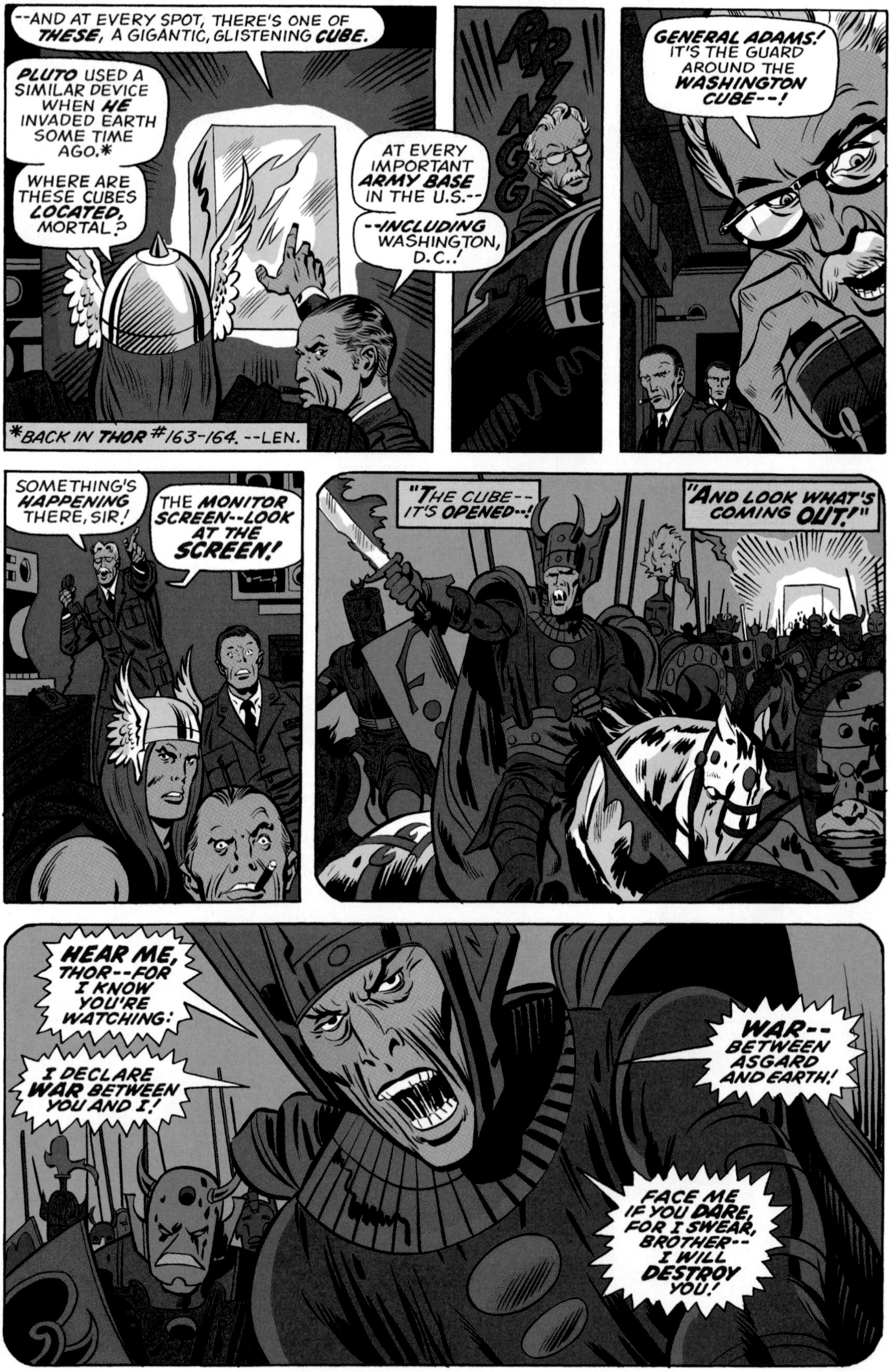
--AND AT EVERY SPOT, THERE'S ONE OF THESE, A GIGANTIC, GLISTENING CUBE.
PLUTO USED A SIMILAR DEVICE WHEN HE INVADED EARTH SOME TIME AGO.*
WHERE ARE THESE CUBES LOCATED, MORTAL?
AT EVERY IMPORTANT ARMY BASE IN THE U.S.--
--INCLUDING WASHINGTON, D.C.!
*BACK IN THOR #163-164. --LEN.
RRRINNGG
GENERAL ADAMS! IT'S THE GUARD AROUND THE WASHINGTON CUBE--!
SOMETHING'S HAPPENING THERE, SIR!
THE MONITOR SCREEN--LOOK AT THE SCREEN!
"THE CUBE-- IT'S OPENED--!
"AND LOOK WHAT'S COMING OUT!"
HEAR ME, THOR--FOR I KNOW YOU'RE WATCHING:
I DECLARE WAR BETWEEN YOU AND I!
WAR-- BETWEEN ASGARD AND EARTH!
FACE ME IF YOU DARE, FOR I SWEAR, BROTHER-- I WILL DESTROY YOU!

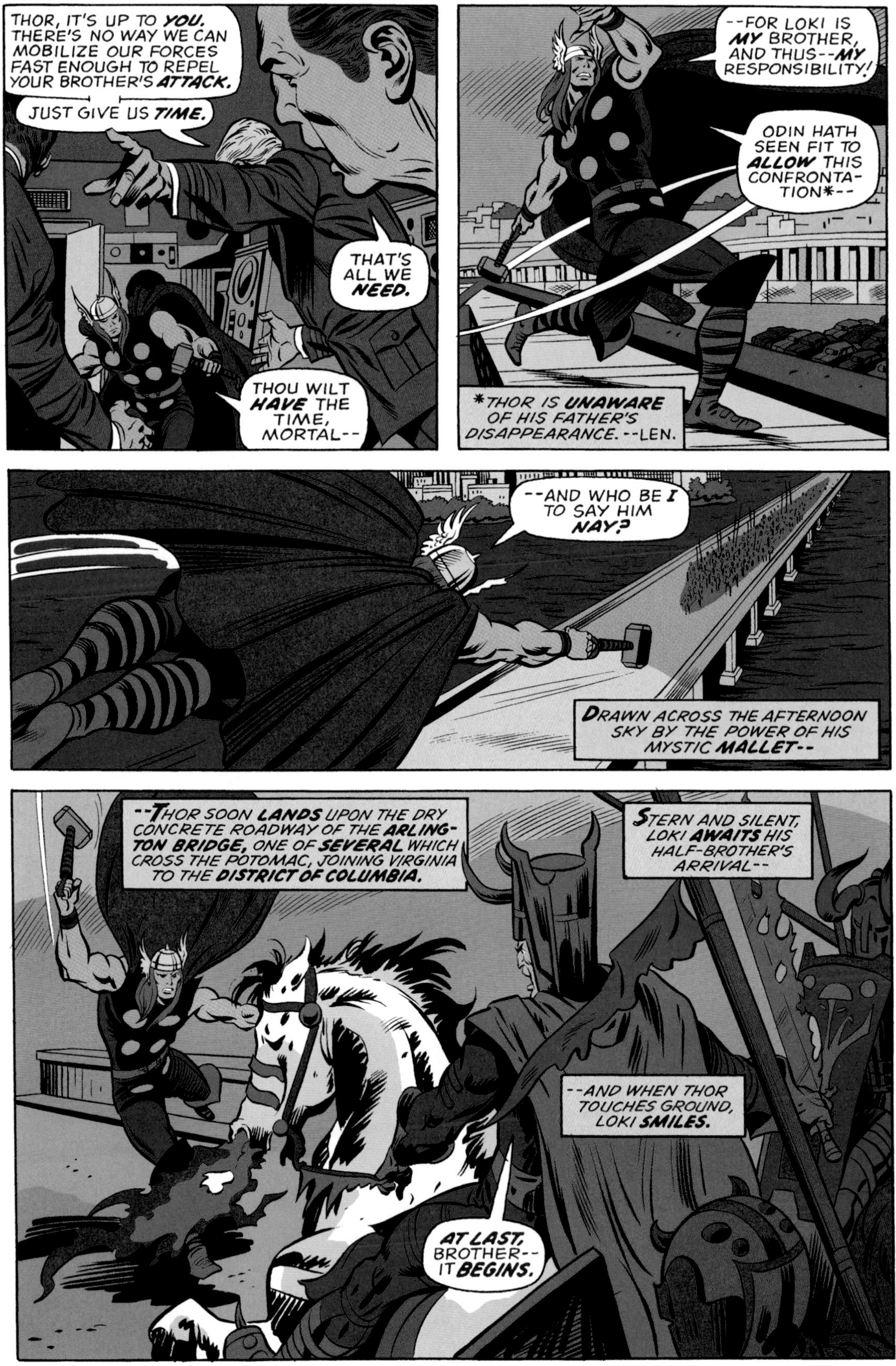
THOR, IT'S UP TO YOU. THERE'S NO WAY WE CAN MOBILIZE OUR FORCES FAST ENOUGH TO REPEL YOUR BROTHER'S ATTACK.
JUST GIVE US TIME.
THAT'S ALL WE NEED.
THOU WILT HAVE THE TIME, MORTAL--
--FOR LOKI IS MY BROTHER, AND THUS--MY RESPONSIBILITY!
ODIN HATH SEEN FIT TO ALLOW THIS CONFRONTATION*--
*THOR IS UNAWARE OF HIS FATHER'S DISAPPEARANCE. --LEN.
--AND WHO BE I TO SAY HIM NAY?
DRAWN ACROSS THE AFTERNOON SKY BY THE POWER OF HIS MYSTIC MALLET--
--THOR SOON LANDS UPON THE DRY CONCRETE ROADWAY OF THE ARLINGTON BRIDGE, ONE OF SEVERAL WHICH CROSS THE POTOMAC, JOINING VIRGINIA TO THE DISTRICT OF COLUMBIA.
STERN AND SILENT, LOKI AWAITS HIS HALF-BROTHER'S ARRIVAL--
--AND WHEN THOR TOUCHES GROUND, LOKI SMILES.
AT LAST, BROTHER-- IT BEGINS.

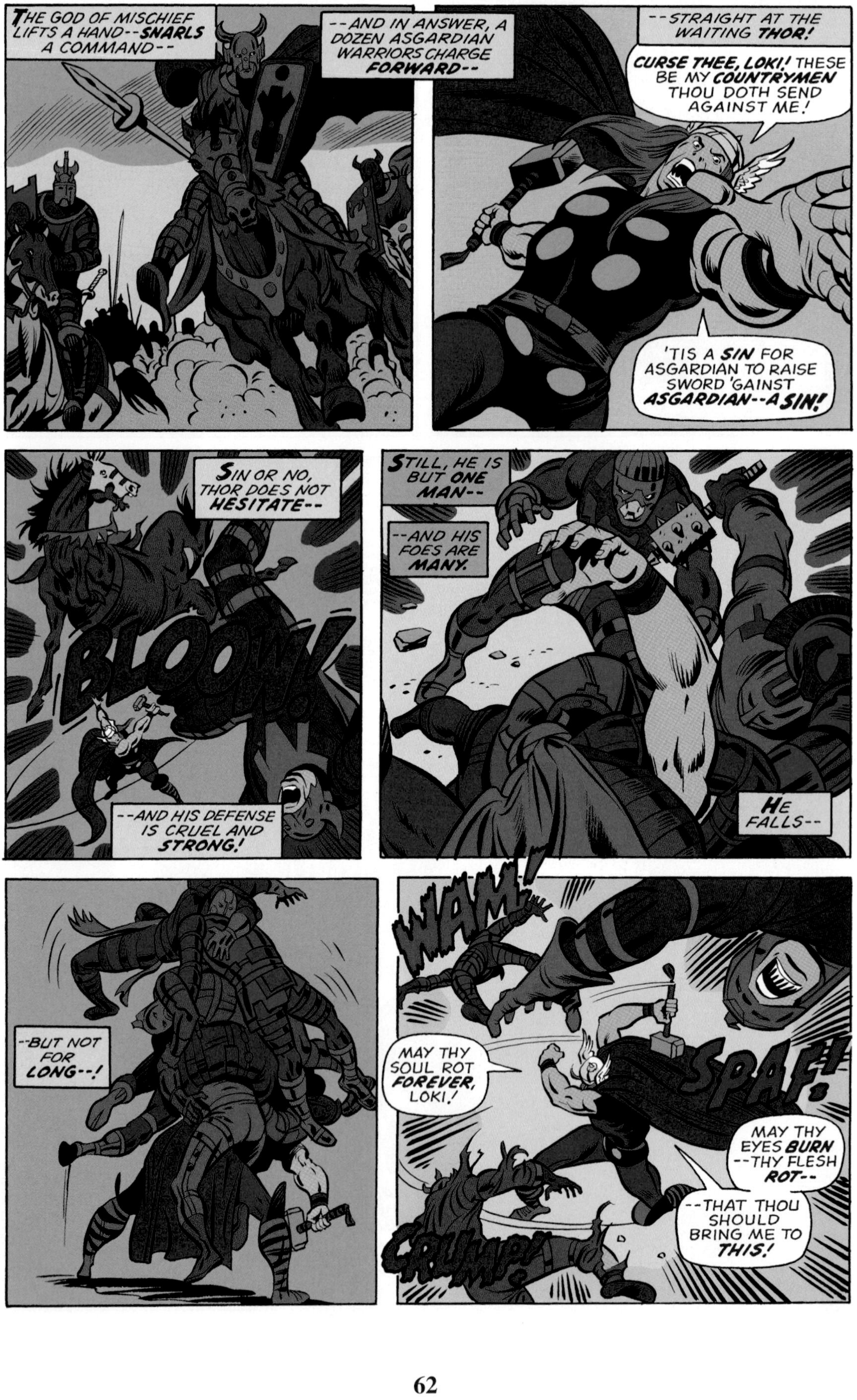
THE GOD OF MISCHIEF LIFTS A HAND--SNARLS A COMMAND--
--AND IN ANSWER, A DOZEN ASGARDIAN WARRIORS CHARGE FORWARD--
--STRAIGHT AT THE WAITING THOR!
CURSE THEE, LOKI! THESE BE MY COUNTRYMEN THOU DOTH SEND AGAINST ME!
'TIS A SIN FOR ASGARDIAN TO RAISE SWORD 'GAINST ASGARDIAN--A SIN!
SIN OR NO, THOR DOES NOT HESITATE--
--AND HIS DEFENSE IS CRUEL AND STRONG!
STILL, HE IS BUT ONE MAN--
--AND HIS FOES ARE MANY.
HE FALLS--
--BUT NOT FOR LONG--!
WAM!
MAY THY SOUL ROT FOREVER, LOKI!
SPAF!
MAY THY EYES BURN --THY FLESH ROT--
--THAT THOU SHOULD BRING ME TO THIS!

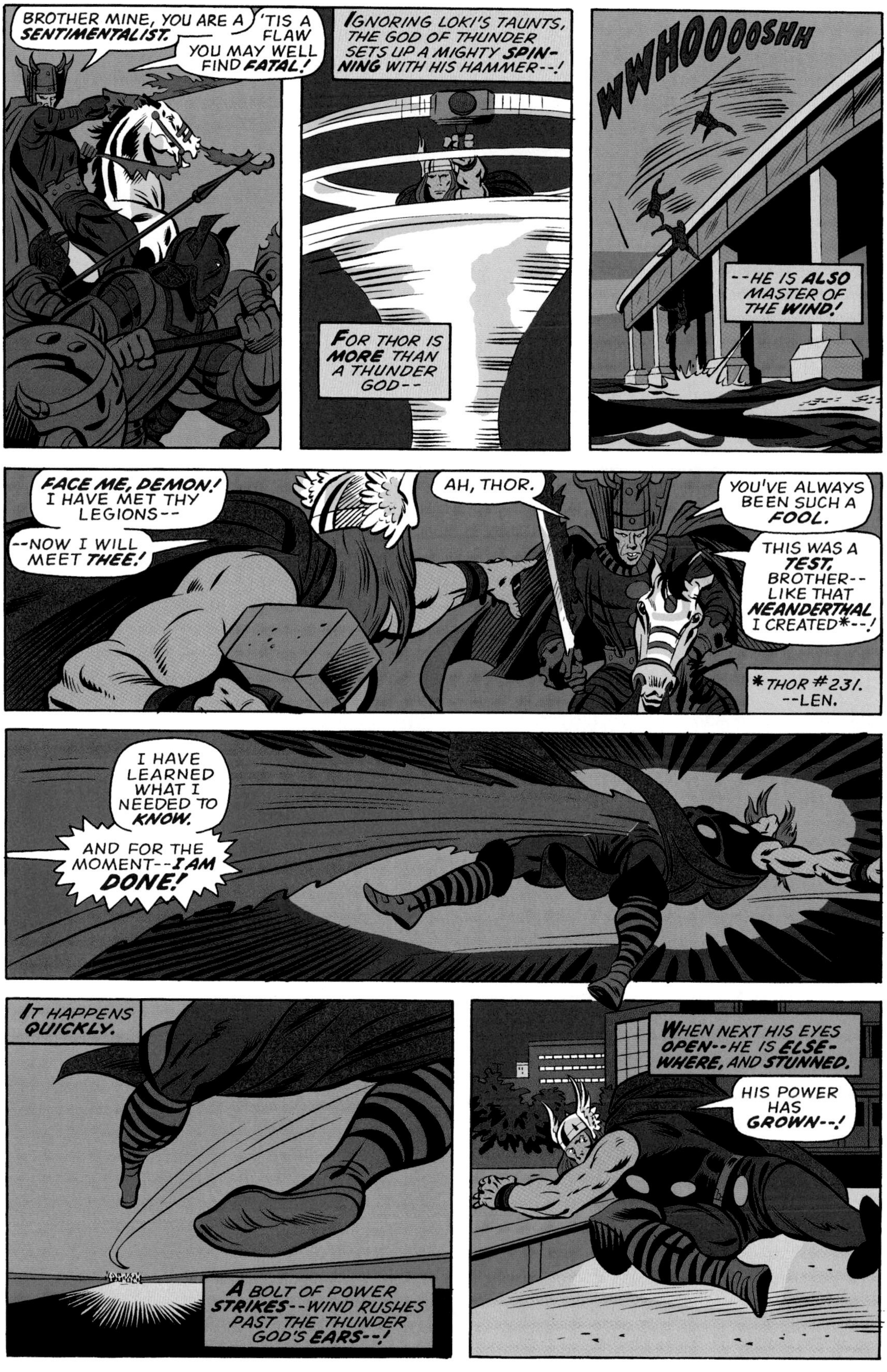

BROTHER MINE, YOU ARE A SENTIMENTALIST.
'TIS A FLAW YOU MAY WELL FIND FATAL!
IGNORING LOKI'S TAUNTS, THE GOD OF THUNDER SETS UP A MIGHTY SPINNING WITH HIS HAMMER--!
FOR THOR IS MORE THAN A THUNDER GOD--
WWHOOOOOSHH
--HE IS ALSO MASTER OF THE WIND!
FACE ME, DEMON! I HAVE MET THY LEGIONS--
--NOW I WILL MEET THEE!
AH, THOR.
YOU'VE ALWAYS BEEN SUCH A FOOL.
THIS WAS A TEST, BROTHER-- LIKE THAT NEANDERTHAL I CREATED*--!
*THOR #231. --LEN.
I HAVE LEARNED WHAT I NEEDED TO KNOW.
AND FOR THE MOMENT--I AM DONE!
IT HAPPENS QUICKLY.
A BOLT OF POWER STRIKES--WIND RUSHES PAST THE THUNDER GOD'S EARS--!
WHEN NEXT HIS EYES OPEN--HE IS ELSEWHERE, AND STUNNED.
HIS POWER HAS GROWN--!

SOMEHOW HE IS **STRONGER** THAN E'ER BEFORE--HIS VOICE HAS **CHANGED**, HIS EYES HOLD MORE **MADNESS** THAN EVEN A MADMAN'S MIND COULD **CONTAIN**--!

YOU'RE SAYING HE'S PRETTY **TOUGH.**

RIGHT?

WHO--?

THE NAME'S **SAWYER,** SON. **GENERAL SAM SAWYER.**

THE BRASS ASKED ME TO TAKE **COMMAND** OF OUR **DEFENSIVE FORCES**--

--AND IN A WAY, I GUESS THAT INCLUDES **YOU.**

14 ST. BRIDGE ENTRANCE

THAT'S **THEM** OVER THERE.

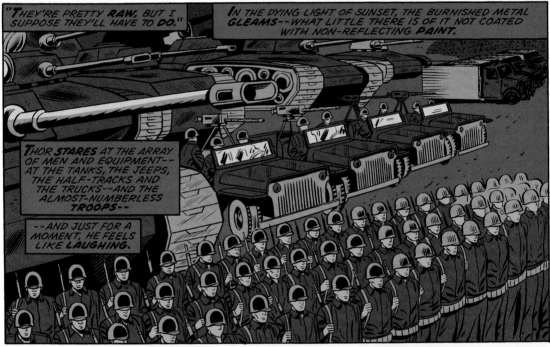

"THEY'RE PRETTY **RAW**, BUT I SUPPOSE THEY'LL HAVE TO **DO**."

IN THE DYING LIGHT OF SUNSET, THE BURNISHED METAL **GLEAMS**--WHAT LITTLE THERE IS OF IT NOT COATED WITH NON-REFLECTING **PAINT.**

THOR **STARES** AT THE ARRAY OF MEN AND EQUIPMENT-- AT THE TANKS, THE JEEPS, THE HALF-TRACKS AND THE TRUCKS--AND THE ALMOST-NUMBERLESS **TROOPS**--

--AND JUST FOR A MOMENT, HE FEELS LIKE **LAUGHING.**

**SORRY** BUNCH OF GOLDBRICKS, AREN'T THEY?

WELL-- THAT'S THE **ARMY,** SON. IT'S ALL WE'VE **GOT.**

NOW LISTEN: I'VE GOT A **PLAN.**

THE GENERAL SPEAKS **QUICKLY.** THE GOD OF THUNDER **NODS.**

THEN, AS THE SUN BEGINS TO **MELT** THE HORIZON--

THOR **TURNS**--

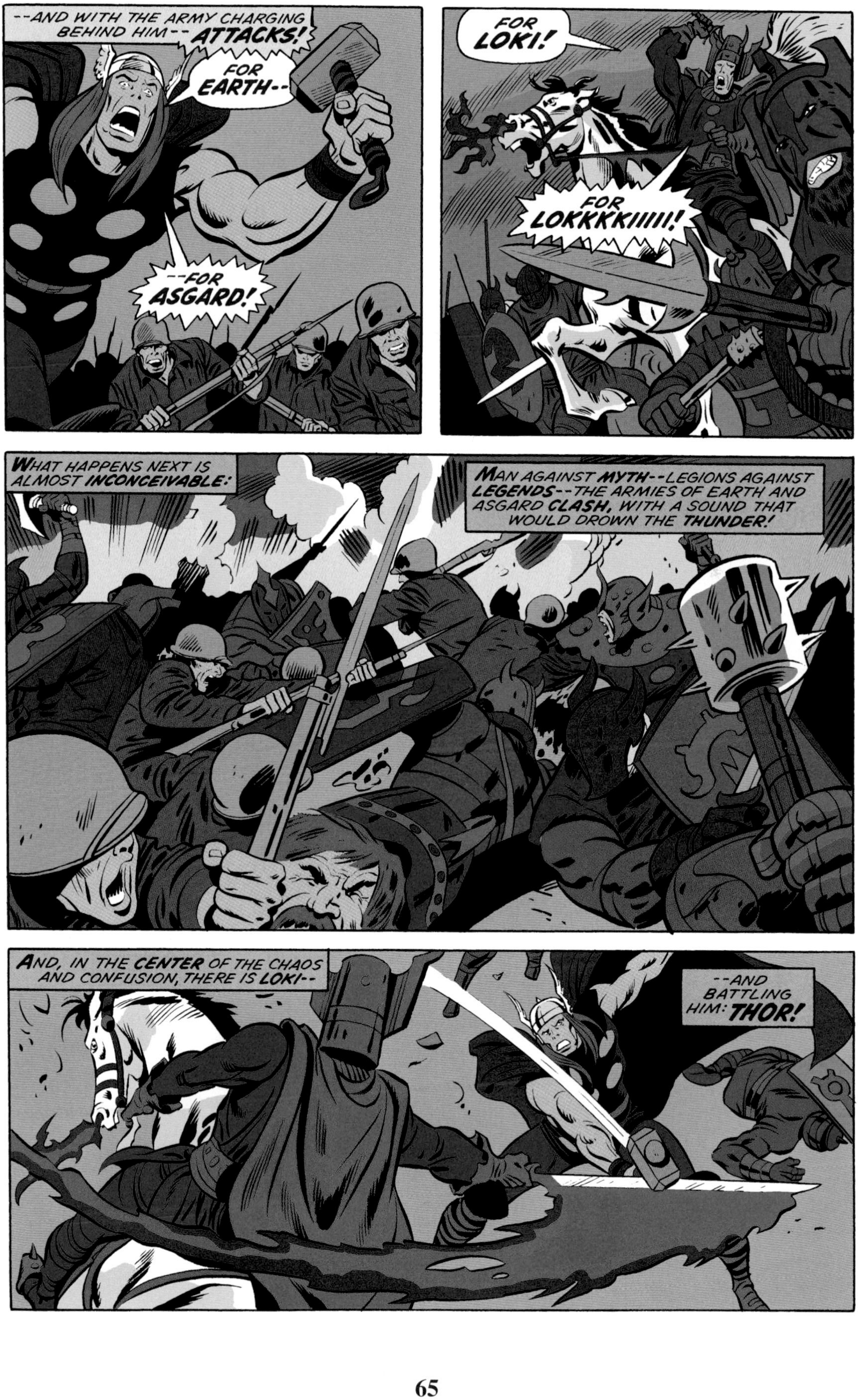
--AND WITH THE ARMY CHARGING BEHIND HIM-- ATTACKS!
FOR EARTH--
--FOR ASGARD!
FOR LOKI!
FOR LOKKKKIIIII!
WHAT HAPPENS NEXT IS ALMOST INCONCEIVABLE:
MAN AGAINST MYTH--LEGIONS AGAINST LEGENDS--THE ARMIES OF EARTH AND ASGARD CLASH, WITH A SOUND THAT WOULD DROWN THE THUNDER!
AND, IN THE CENTER OF THE CHAOS AND CONFUSION, THERE IS LOKI--
--AND BATTLING HIM: THOR!

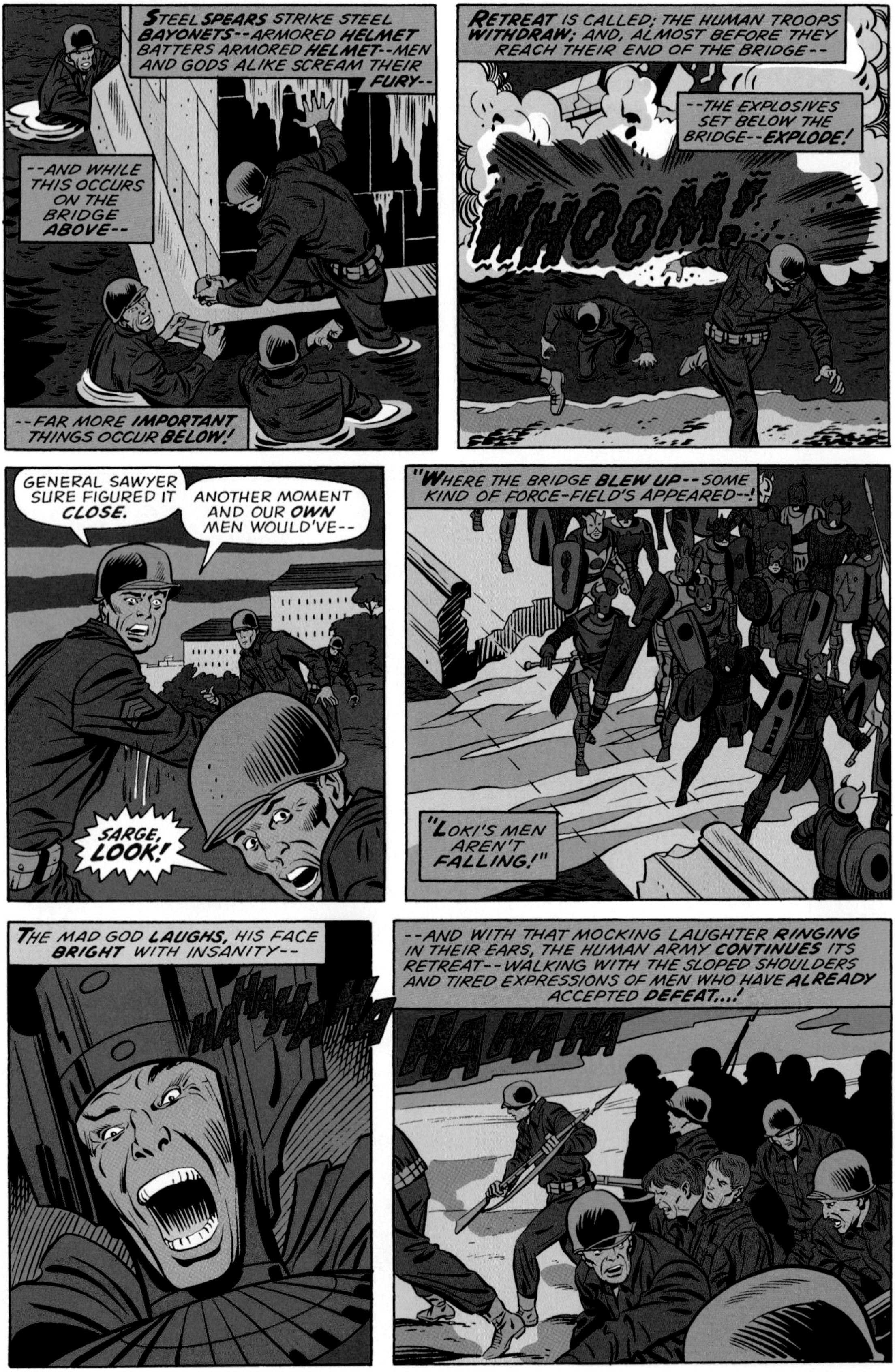
STEEL SPEARS STRIKE STEEL BAYONETS--ARMORED HELMET BATTERS ARMORED HELMET--MEN AND GODS ALIKE SCREAM THEIR FURY--
--AND WHILE THIS OCCURS ON THE BRIDGE ABOVE--
--FAR MORE IMPORTANT THINGS OCCUR BELOW!
RETREAT IS CALLED; THE HUMAN TROOPS WITHDRAW; AND, ALMOST BEFORE THEY REACH THEIR END OF THE BRIDGE--
--THE EXPLOSIVES SET BELOW THE BRIDGE--EXPLODE!
WHOOM!
GENERAL SAWYER SURE FIGURED IT CLOSE.
ANOTHER MOMENT AND OUR OWN MEN WOULD'VE--
SARGE, LOOK!
"WHERE THE BRIDGE BLEW UP--SOME KIND OF FORCE-FIELD'S APPEARED--!
"LOKI'S MEN AREN'T FALLING!"
THE MAD GOD LAUGHS, HIS FACE BRIGHT WITH INSANITY--
HA HA HA HA HA
--AND WITH THAT MOCKING LAUGHTER RINGING IN THEIR EARS, THE HUMAN ARMY CONTINUES ITS RETREAT--WALKING WITH THE SLOPED SHOULDERS AND TIRED EXPRESSIONS OF MEN WHO HAVE ALREADY ACCEPTED DEFEAT...!
HA HA HA HA

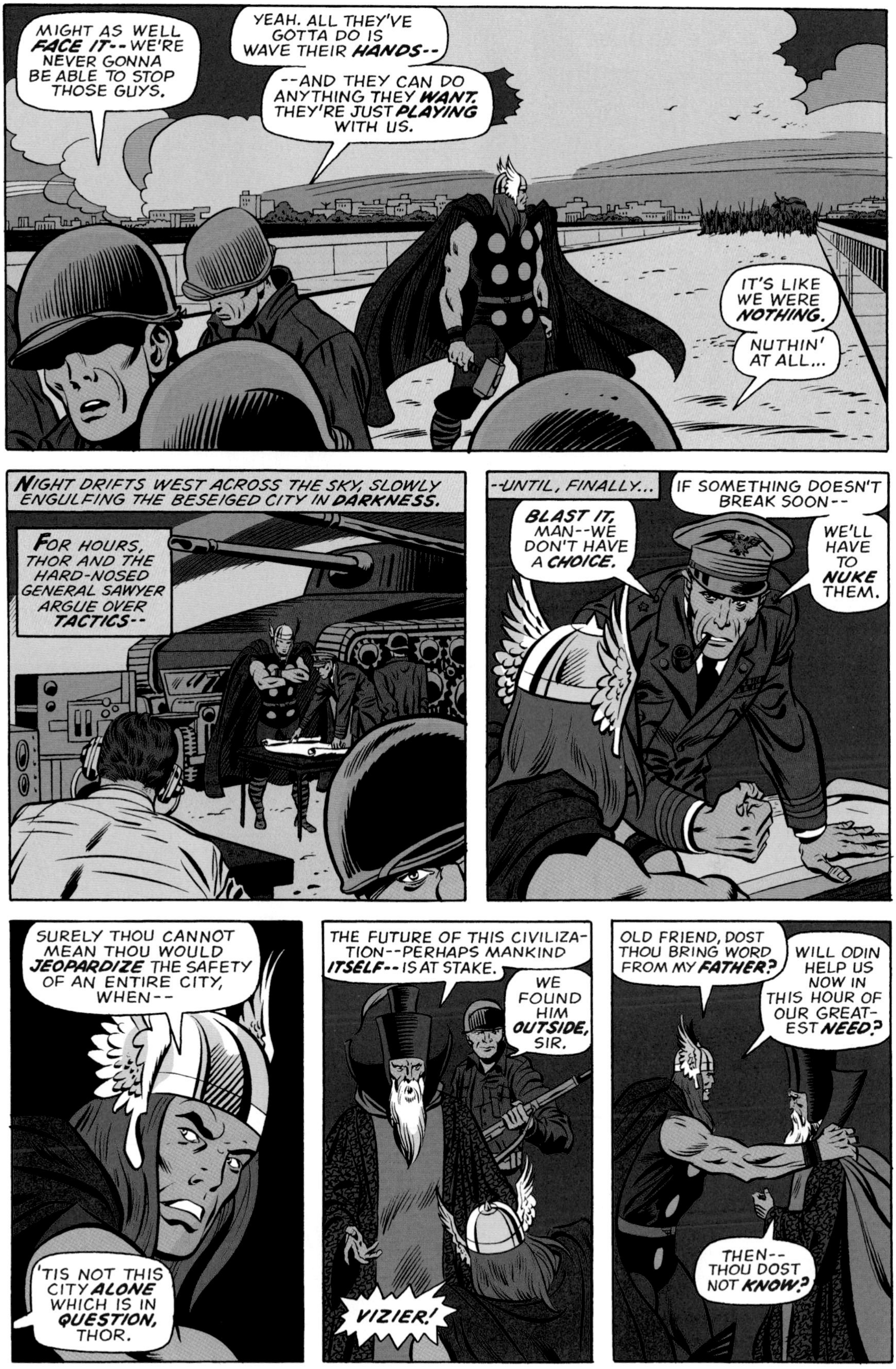
MIGHT AS WELL FACE IT--WE'RE NEVER GONNA BE ABLE TO STOP THOSE GUYS.
YEAH. ALL THEY'VE GOTTA DO IS WAVE THEIR HANDS--
--AND THEY CAN DO ANYTHING THEY WANT. THEY'RE JUST PLAYING WITH US.
IT'S LIKE WE WERE NOTHING.
NUTHIN' AT ALL...
NIGHT DRIFTS WEST ACROSS THE SKY, SLOWLY ENGULFING THE BESEIGED CITY IN DARKNESS.
FOR HOURS, THOR AND THE HARD-NOSED GENERAL SAWYER ARGUE OVER TACTICS--
--UNTIL, FINALLY...
IF SOMETHING DOESN'T BREAK SOON--
WE'LL HAVE TO NUKE THEM.
BLAST IT, MAN--WE DON'T HAVE A CHOICE.
SURELY THOU CANNOT MEAN THOU WOULD JEOPARDIZE THE SAFETY OF AN ENTIRE CITY, WHEN--
'TIS NOT THIS CITY ALONE WHICH IS IN QUESTION, THOR.
THE FUTURE OF THIS CIVILIZATION--PERHAPS MANKIND ITSELF--IS AT STAKE.
WE FOUND HIM OUTSIDE, SIR.
VIZIER!
OLD FRIEND, DOST THOU BRING WORD FROM MY FATHER?
WILL ODIN HELP US NOW IN THIS HOUR OF OUR GREATEST NEED?
THEN--THOU DOST NOT KNOW?

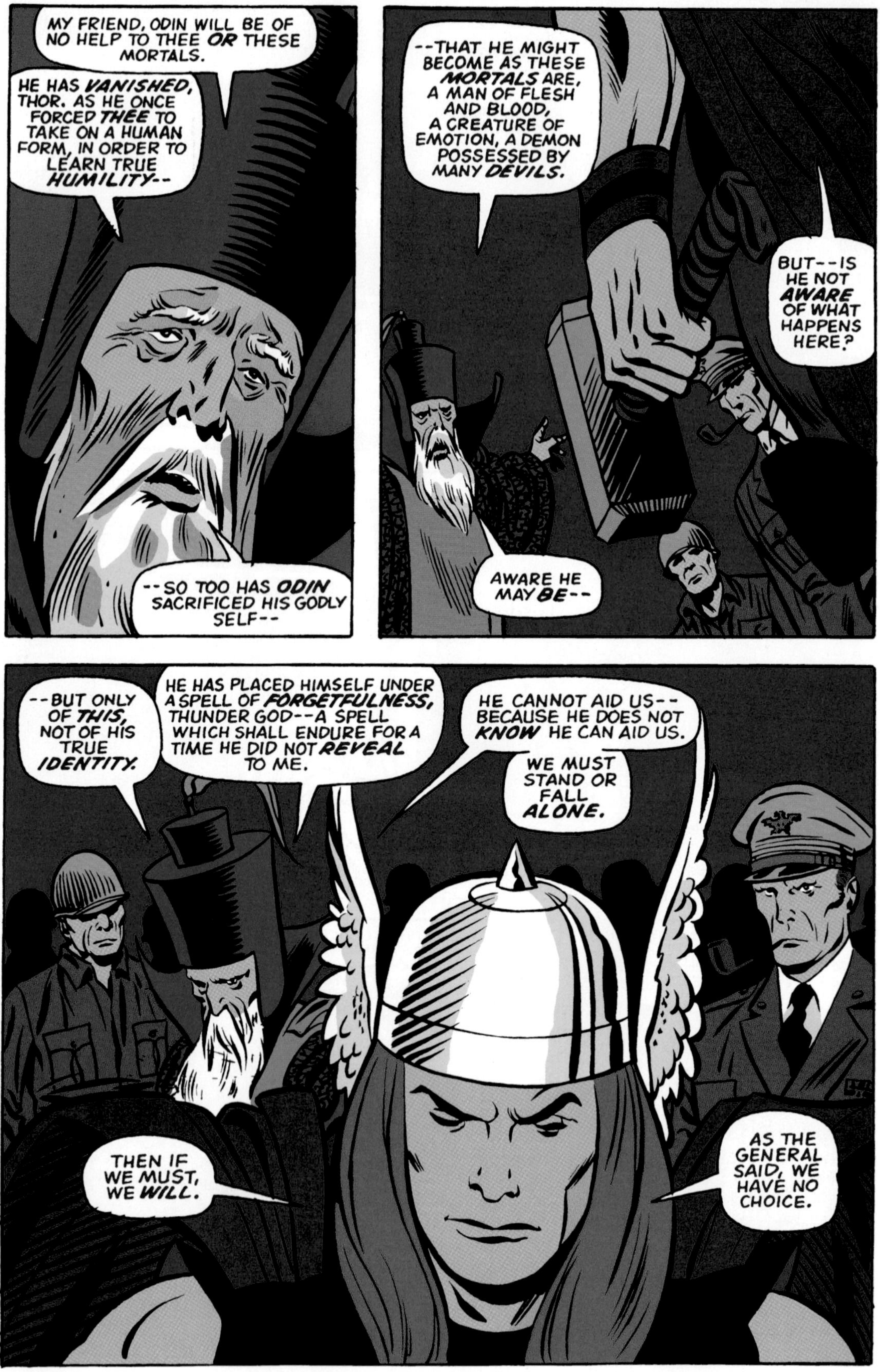
MY FRIEND, ODIN WILL BE OF NO HELP TO THEE OR THESE MORTALS.
HE HAS VANISHED, THOR. AS HE ONCE FORCED THEE TO TAKE ON A HUMAN FORM, IN ORDER TO LEARN TRUE HUMILITY--
--SO TOO HAS ODIN SACRIFICED HIS GODLY SELF--
--THAT HE MIGHT BECOME AS THESE MORTALS ARE, A MAN OF FLESH AND BLOOD, A CREATURE OF EMOTION, A DEMON POSSESSED BY MANY DEVILS.
BUT--IS HE NOT AWARE OF WHAT HAPPENS HERE?
AWARE HE MAY BE--
--BUT ONLY OF THIS, NOT OF HIS TRUE IDENTITY.
HE HAS PLACED HIMSELF UNDER A SPELL OF FORGETFULNESS, THUNDER GOD--A SPELL WHICH SHALL ENDURE FOR A TIME HE DID NOT REVEAL TO ME.
HE CANNOT AID US--BECAUSE HE DOES NOT KNOW HE CAN AID US.
WE MUST STAND OR FALL ALONE.
THEN IF WE MUST, WE WILL.
AS THE GENERAL SAID, WE HAVE NO CHOICE.

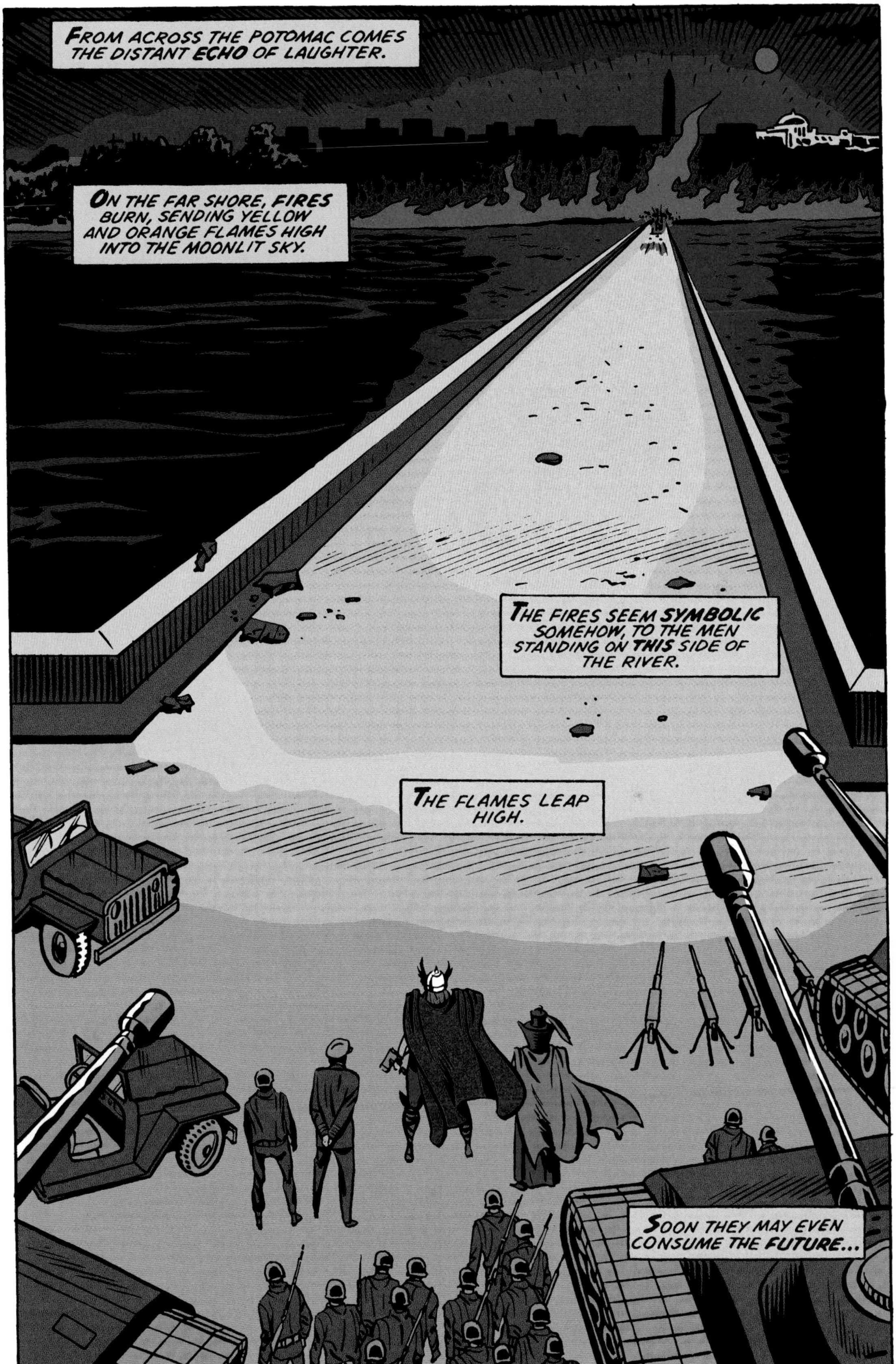

FROM ACROSS THE POTOMAC COMES THE DISTANT ECHO OF LAUGHTER.
ON THE FAR SHORE, FIRES BURN, SENDING YELLOW AND ORANGE FLAMES HIGH INTO THE MOONLIT SKY.
THE FIRES SEEM SYMBOLIC SOMEHOW, TO THE MEN STANDING ON THIS SIDE OF THE RIVER.
THE FLAMES LEAP HIGH.
SOON THEY MAY EVEN CONSUME THE FUTURE...

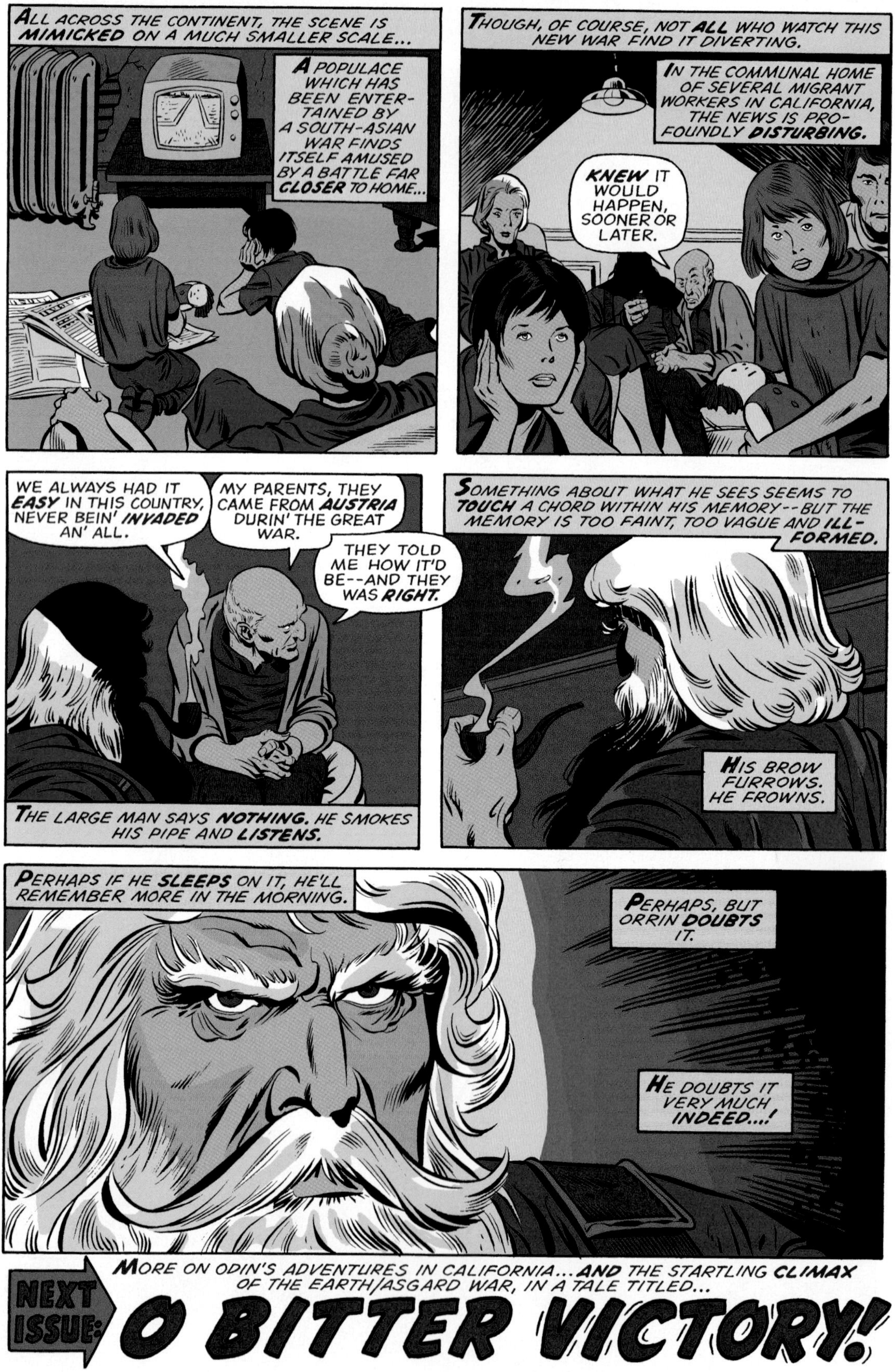
ALL ACROSS THE CONTINENT, THE SCENE IS MIMICKED ON A MUCH SMALLER SCALE...
A POPULACE WHICH HAS BEEN ENTERTAINED BY A SOUTH-ASIAN WAR FINDS ITSELF AMUSED BY A BATTLE FAR CLOSER TO HOME...
THOUGH, OF COURSE, NOT ALL WHO WATCH THIS NEW WAR FIND IT DIVERTING.
IN THE COMMUNAL HOME OF SEVERAL MIGRANT WORKERS IN CALIFORNIA, THE NEWS IS PROFOUNDLY DISTURBING.
KNEW IT WOULD HAPPEN, SOONER OR LATER.
WE ALWAYS HAD IT EASY IN THIS COUNTRY, NEVER BEIN' INVADED AN' ALL.
MY PARENTS, THEY CAME FROM AUSTRIA DURIN' THE GREAT WAR.
THEY TOLD ME HOW IT'D BE--AND THEY WAS RIGHT.
THE LARGE MAN SAYS NOTHING. HE SMOKES HIS PIPE AND LISTENS.
SOMETHING ABOUT WHAT HE SEES SEEMS TO TOUCH A CHORD WITHIN HIS MEMORY--BUT THE MEMORY IS TOO FAINT, TOO VAGUE AND ILL-FORMED.
HIS BROW FURROWS. HE FROWNS.
PERHAPS IF HE SLEEPS ON IT, HE'LL REMEMBER MORE IN THE MORNING.
PERHAPS, BUT ORRIN DOUBTS IT.
HE DOUBTS IT VERY MUCH INDEED...!
MORE ON ODIN'S ADVENTURES IN CALIFORNIA... AND THE STARTLING CLIMAX OF THE EARTH/ASGARD WAR, IN A TALE TITLED...
NEXT ISSUE:
O BITTER VICTORY!

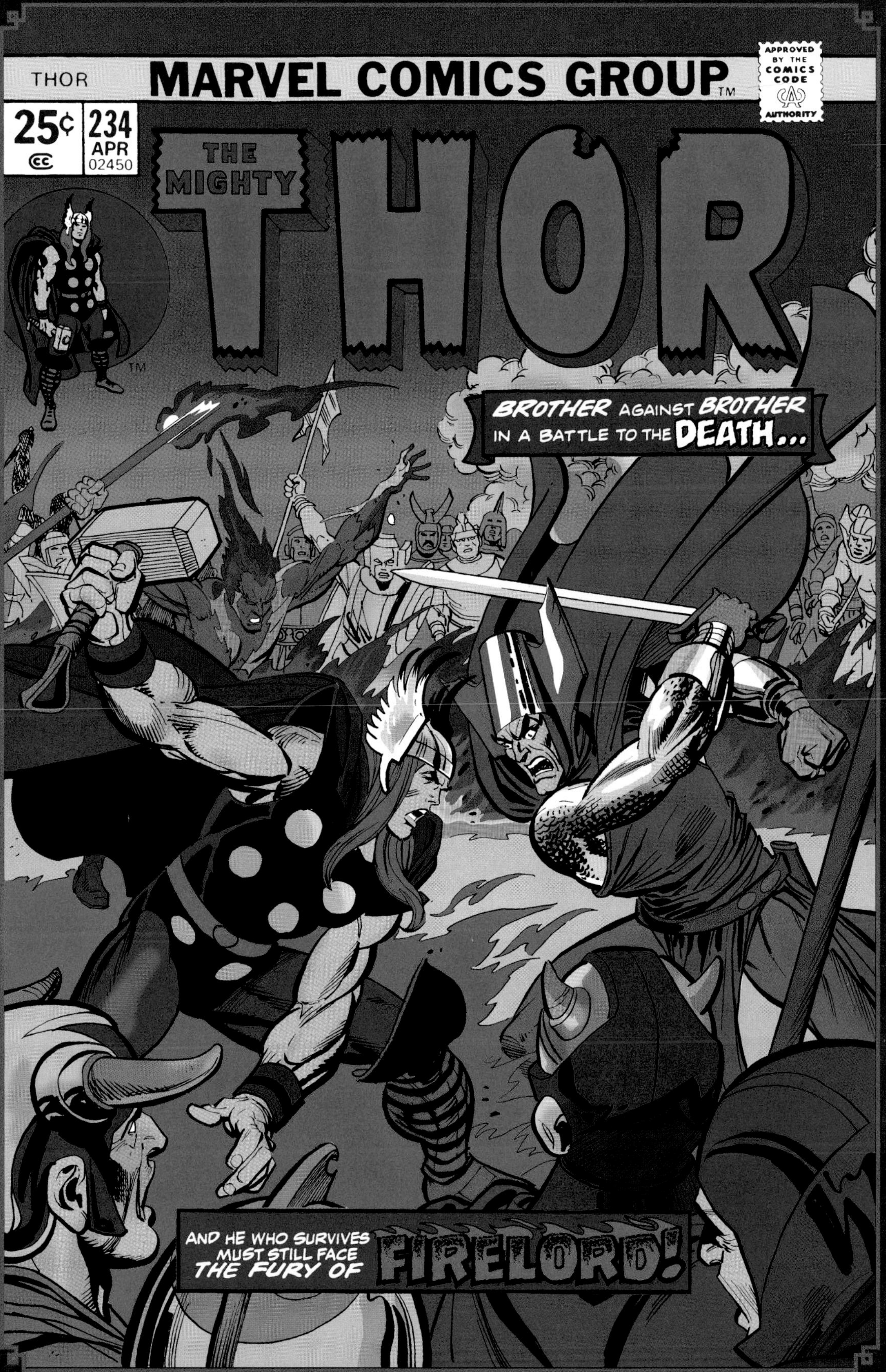

THOR
MARVEL COMICS GROUP
APPROVED BY THE COMICS CODE AUTHORITY
25¢
234 APR 02450
THE MIGHTY THOR
BROTHER AGAINST BROTHER IN A BATTLE TO THE DEATH...
AND HE WHO SURVIVES MUST STILL FACE THE FURY OF FIRELORD!

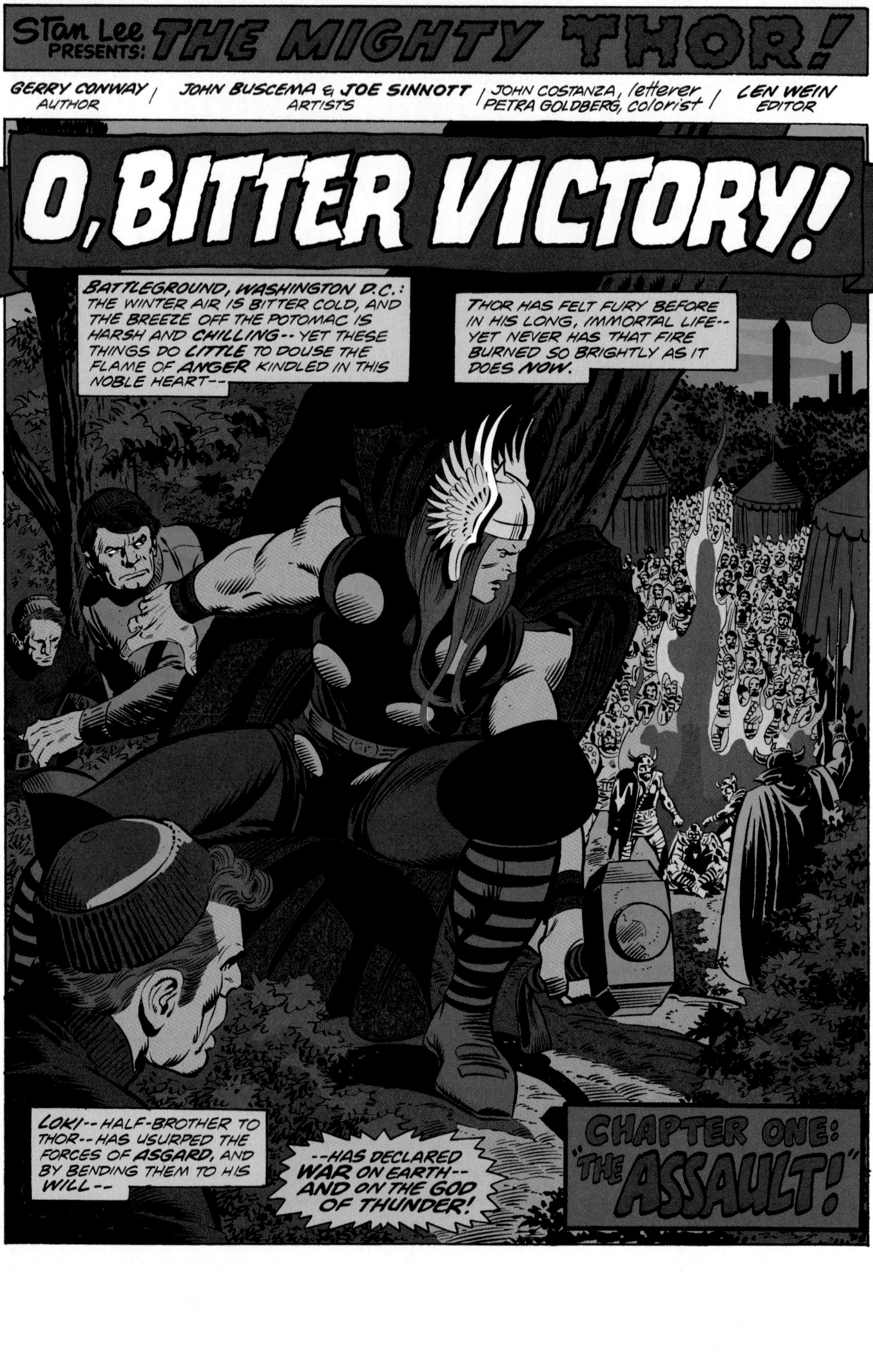

Stan Lee PRESENTS: THE MIGHTY THOR!
GERRY CONWAY / AUTHOR
JOHN BUSCEMA & JOE SINNOTT / ARTISTS
JOHN COSTANZA, letterer / PETRA GOLDBERG, colorist
LEN WEIN / EDITOR
O, BITTER VICTORY!
BATTLEGROUND, WASHINGTON D.C.: THE WINTER AIR IS BITTER COLD, AND THE BREEZE OFF THE POTOMAC IS HARSH AND CHILLING-- YET THESE THINGS DO LITTLE TO DOUSE THE FLAME OF ANGER KINDLED IN THIS NOBLE HEART--
THOR HAS FELT FURY BEFORE IN HIS LONG, IMMORTAL LIFE-- YET NEVER HAS THAT FIRE BURNED SO BRIGHTLY AS IT DOES NOW.
LOKI--HALF-BROTHER TO THOR--HAS USURPED THE FORCES OF ASGARD, AND BY BENDING THEM TO HIS WILL--
--HAS DECLARED WAR ON EARTH-- AND ON THE GOD OF THUNDER!
CHAPTER ONE: "THE ASSAULT!"

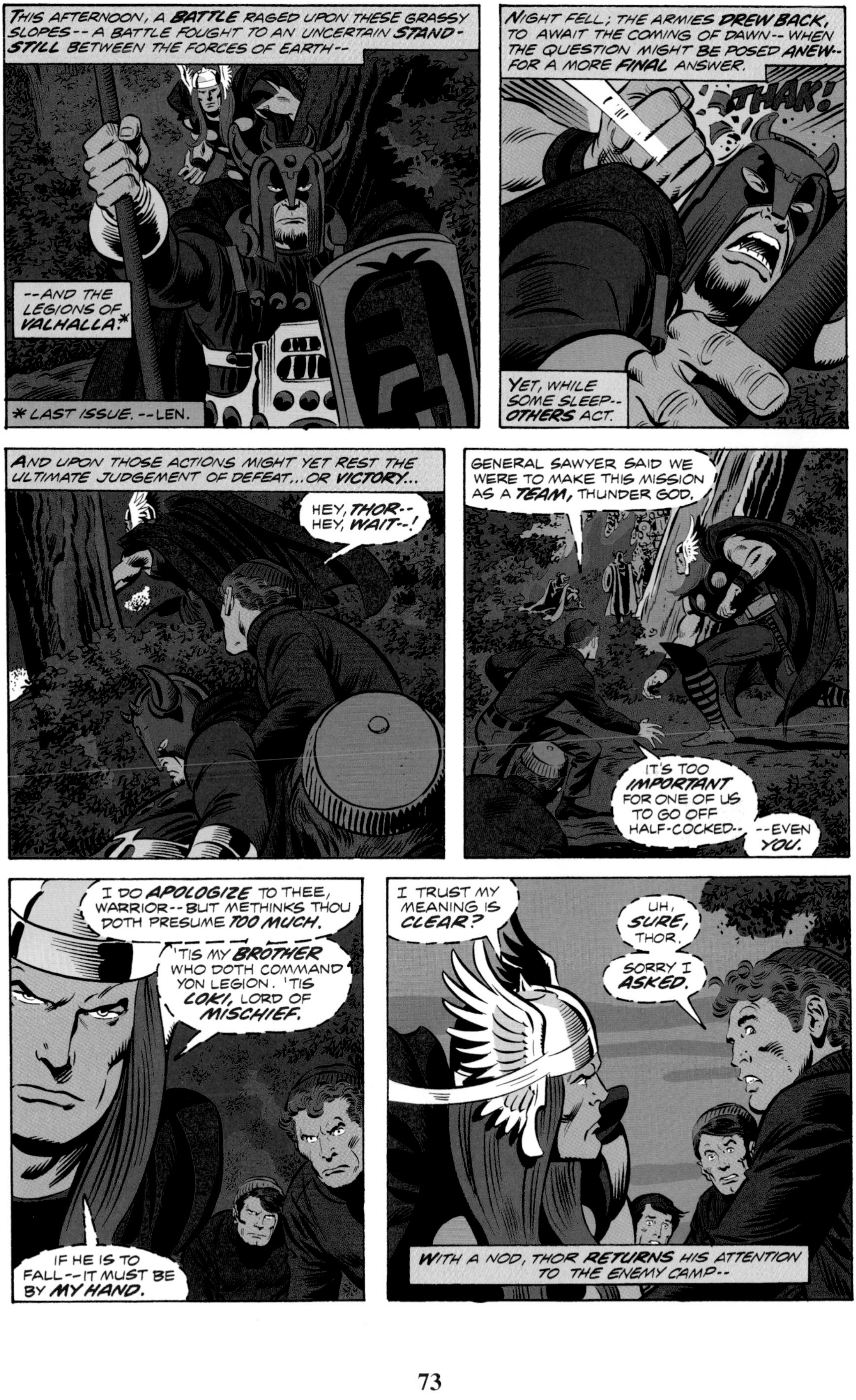
THIS AFTERNOON, A BATTLE RAGED UPON THESE GRASSY SLOPES-- A BATTLE FOUGHT TO AN UNCERTAIN STAND-STILL BETWEEN THE FORCES OF EARTH--
--AND THE LEGIONS OF VALHALLA!*
* LAST ISSUE. --LEN.
NIGHT FELL; THE ARMIES DREW BACK, TO AWAIT THE COMING OF DAWN-- WHEN THE QUESTION MIGHT BE POSED ANEW-- FOR A MORE FINAL ANSWER.
THAK!
YET, WHILE SOME SLEEP-- OTHERS ACT.
AND UPON THOSE ACTIONS MIGHT YET REST THE ULTIMATE JUDGEMENT OF DEFEAT...OR VICTORY...
HEY, THOR-- HEY, WAIT--!
GENERAL SAWYER SAID WE WERE TO MAKE THIS MISSION AS A TEAM, THUNDER GOD.
IT'S TOO IMPORTANT FOR ONE OF US TO GO OFF HALF-COCKED--
--EVEN YOU.
I DO APOLOGIZE TO THEE, WARRIOR-- BUT METHINKS THOU DOTH PRESUME TOO MUCH.
'TIS MY BROTHER WHO DOTH COMMAND YON LEGION. 'TIS LOKI, LORD OF MISCHIEF.
IF HE IS TO FALL--IT MUST BE BY MY HAND.
I TRUST MY MEANING IS CLEAR?
UH, SURE, THOR.
SORRY I ASKED.
WITH A NOD, THOR RETURNS HIS ATTENTION TO THE ENEMY CAMP--

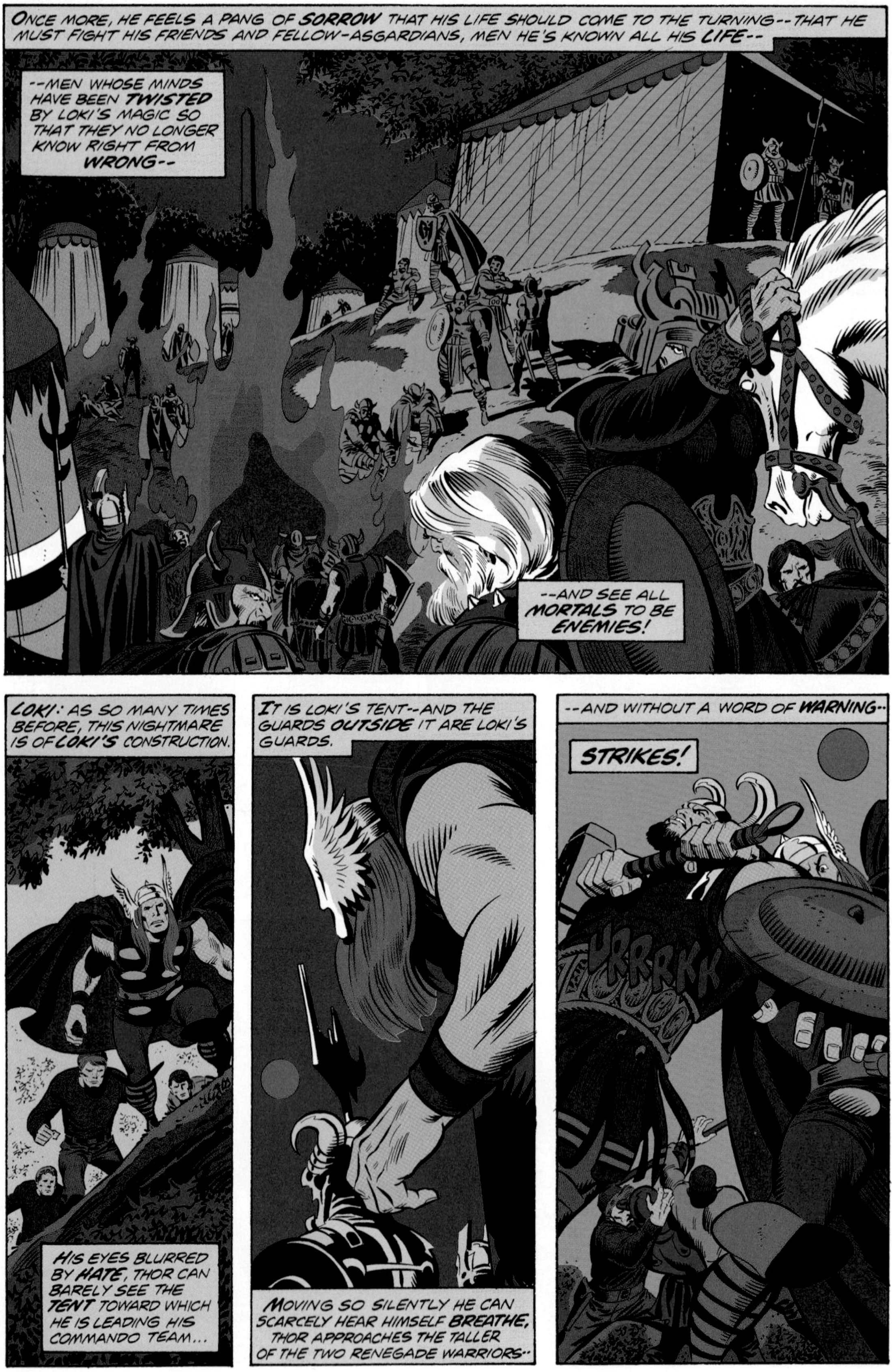
ONCE MORE, HE FEELS A PANG OF SORROW THAT HIS LIFE SHOULD COME TO THE TURNING--THAT HE MUST FIGHT HIS FRIENDS AND FELLOW-ASGARDIANS, MEN HE'S KNOWN ALL HIS LIFE--
--MEN WHOSE MINDS HAVE BEEN TWISTED BY LOKI'S MAGIC SO THAT THEY NO LONGER KNOW RIGHT FROM WRONG--
--AND SEE ALL MORTALS TO BE ENEMIES!
LOKI: AS SO MANY TIMES BEFORE, THIS NIGHTMARE IS OF LOKI'S CONSTRUCTION.
HIS EYES BLURRED BY HATE, THOR CAN BARELY SEE THE TENT TOWARD WHICH HE IS LEADING HIS COMMANDO TEAM...
IT IS LOKI'S TENT--AND THE GUARDS OUTSIDE IT ARE LOKI'S GUARDS.
MOVING SO SILENTLY HE CAN SCARCELY HEAR HIMSELF BREATHE, THOR APPROACHES THE TALLER OF THE TWO RENEGADE WARRIORS--
--AND WITHOUT A WORD OF WARNING--
STRIKES!
URRRKK

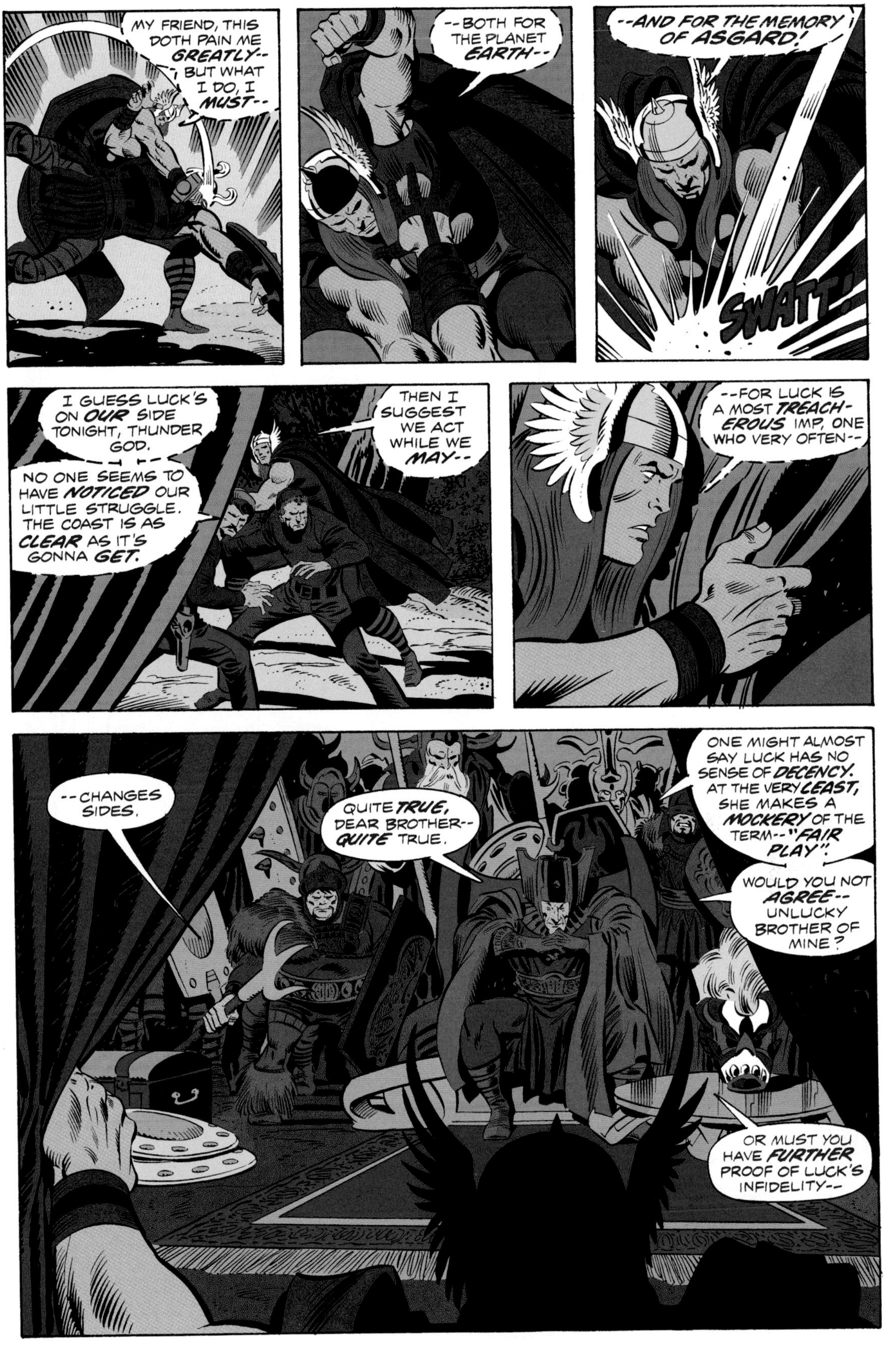
MY FRIEND, THIS DOTH PAIN ME GREATLY-- BUT WHAT I DO, I MUST--
--BOTH FOR THE PLANET EARTH--
--AND FOR THE MEMORY OF ASGARD!
SWATT!
I GUESS LUCK'S ON OUR SIDE TONIGHT, THUNDER GOD.
NO ONE SEEMS TO HAVE NOTICED OUR LITTLE STRUGGLE. THE COAST IS AS CLEAR AS IT'S GONNA GET.
THEN I SUGGEST WE ACT WHILE WE MAY--
--FOR LUCK IS A MOST TREACHEROUS IMP, ONE WHO VERY OFTEN--
--CHANGES SIDES.
QUITE TRUE, DEAR BROTHER-- QUITE TRUE.
ONE MIGHT ALMOST SAY LUCK HAS NO SENSE OF DECENCY. AT THE VERY LEAST, SHE MAKES A MOCKERY OF THE TERM--"FAIR PLAY".
WOULD YOU NOT AGREE-- UNLUCKY BROTHER OF MINE?
OR MUST YOU HAVE FURTHER PROOF OF LUCK'S INFIDELITY--

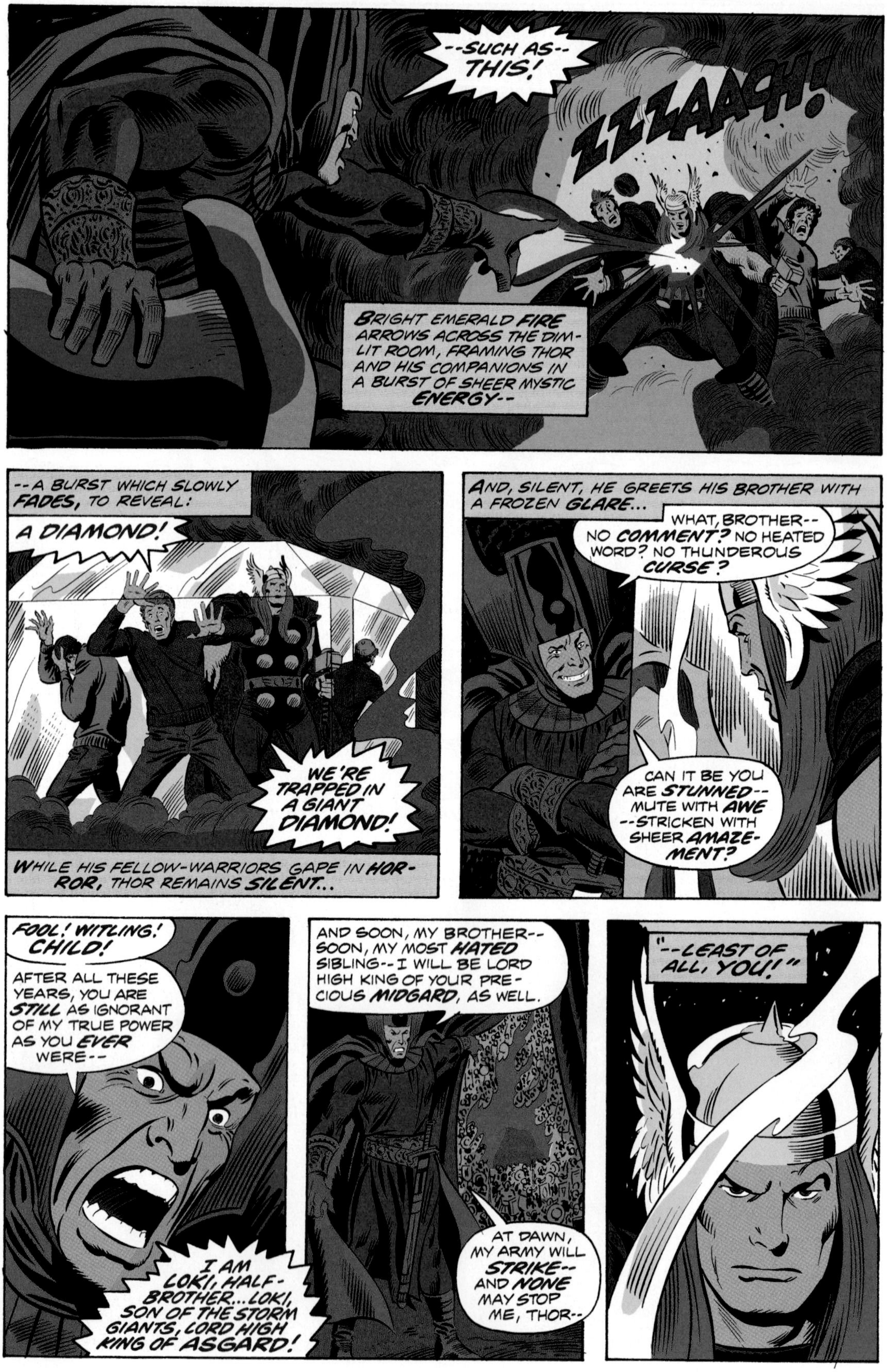
--SUCH AS-- THIS!
ZZZAACH!
BRIGHT EMERALD FIRE ARROWS ACROSS THE DIM-LIT ROOM, FRAMING THOR AND HIS COMPANIONS IN A BURST OF SHEER MYSTIC ENERGY--
--A BURST WHICH SLOWLY FADES, TO REVEAL:
A DIAMOND!
WE'RE TRAPPED IN A GIANT DIAMOND!
WHILE HIS FELLOW-WARRIORS GAPE IN HORROR, THOR REMAINS SILENT...
AND, SILENT, HE GREETS HIS BROTHER WITH A FROZEN GLARE...
WHAT, BROTHER-- NO COMMENT? NO HEATED WORD? NO THUNDEROUS CURSE?
CAN IT BE YOU ARE STUNNED-- MUTE WITH AWE --STRICKEN WITH SHEER AMAZEMENT?
FOOL! WITLING! CHILD!
AFTER ALL THESE YEARS, YOU ARE STILL AS IGNORANT OF MY TRUE POWER AS YOU EVER WERE--
I AM LOKI, HALF-BROTHER...LOKI, SON OF THE STORM GIANTS, LORD HIGH KING OF ASGARD!
AND SOON, MY BROTHER-- SOON, MY MOST HATED SIBLING--I WILL BE LORD HIGH KING OF YOUR PRECIOUS MIDGARD, AS WELL.
AT DAWN, MY ARMY WILL STRIKE-- AND NONE MAY STOP ME, THOR--
"--LEAST OF ALL, YOU!"

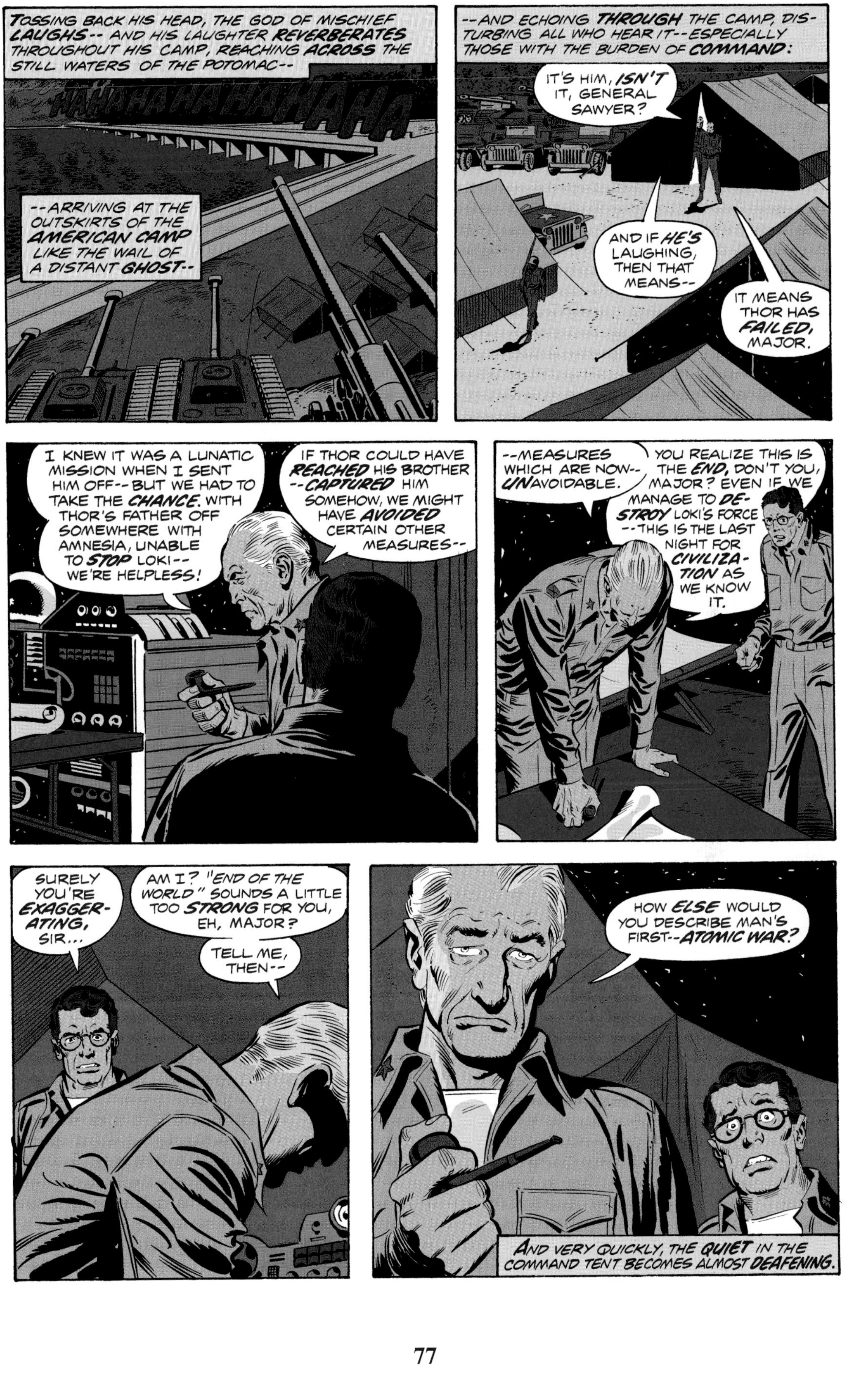
TOSSING BACK HIS HEAD, THE GOD OF MISCHIEF LAUGHS-- AND HIS LAUGHTER REVERBERATES THROUGHOUT HIS CAMP, REACHING ACROSS THE STILL WATERS OF THE POTOMAC--
--ARRIVING AT THE OUTSKIRTS OF THE AMERICAN CAMP LIKE THE WAIL OF A DISTANT GHOST--
--AND ECHOING THROUGH THE CAMP, DISTURBING ALL WHO HEAR IT--ESPECIALLY THOSE WITH THE BURDEN OF COMMAND:
IT'S HIM, ISN'T IT, GENERAL SAWYER?
AND IF HE'S LAUGHING, THEN THAT MEANS--
IT MEANS THOR HAS FAILED, MAJOR.
I KNEW IT WAS A LUNATIC MISSION WHEN I SENT HIM OFF--BUT WE HAD TO TAKE THE CHANCE. WITH THOR'S FATHER OFF SOMEWHERE WITH AMNESIA, UNABLE TO STOP LOKI-- WE'RE HELPLESS!
IF THOR COULD HAVE REACHED HIS BROTHER --CAPTURED HIM SOMEHOW, WE MIGHT HAVE AVOIDED CERTAIN OTHER MEASURES--
--MEASURES WHICH ARE NOW-- UNAVOIDABLE.
YOU REALIZE THIS IS THE END, DON'T YOU, MAJOR? EVEN IF WE MANAGE TO DESTROY LOKI'S FORCE --THIS IS THE LAST NIGHT FOR CIVILIZATION AS WE KNOW IT.
SURELY YOU'RE EXAGGERATING, SIR...
AM I? "END OF THE WORLD" SOUNDS A LITTLE TOO STRONG FOR YOU, EH, MAJOR?
TELL ME, THEN--
HOW ELSE WOULD YOU DESCRIBE MAN'S FIRST--ATOMIC WAR?
AND VERY QUICKLY, THE QUIET IN THE COMMAND TENT BECOMES ALMOST DEAFENING.

# CHAPTER TWO: "DECISION AT DAWN!"

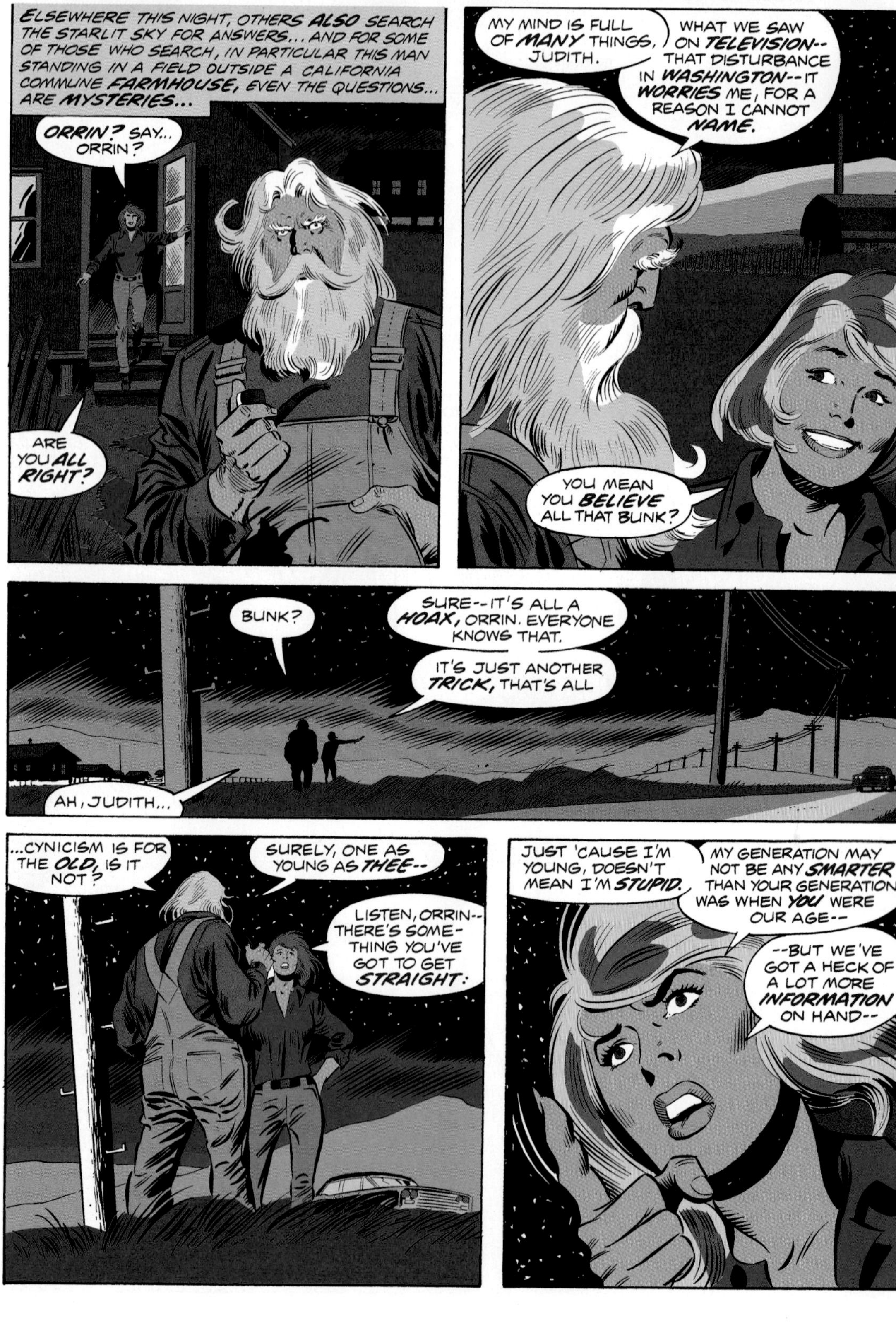

ELSEWHERE THIS NIGHT, OTHERS ALSO SEARCH THE STARLIT SKY FOR ANSWERS... AND FOR SOME OF THOSE WHO SEARCH, IN PARTICULAR THIS MAN STANDING IN A FIELD OUTSIDE A CALIFORNIA COMMUNE FARMHOUSE, EVEN THE QUESTIONS... ARE MYSTERIES...
ORRIN? SAY... ORRIN?
ARE YOU ALL RIGHT?
MY MIND IS FULL OF MANY THINGS, JUDITH.
WHAT WE SAW ON TELEVISION-- THAT DISTURBANCE IN WASHINGTON-- IT WORRIES ME, FOR A REASON I CANNOT NAME.
YOU MEAN YOU BELIEVE ALL THAT BUNK?
BUNK?
SURE-- IT'S ALL A HOAX, ORRIN. EVERYONE KNOWS THAT.
IT'S JUST ANOTHER TRICK, THAT'S ALL
AH, JUDITH...
...CYNICISM IS FOR THE OLD, IS IT NOT?
SURELY, ONE AS YOUNG AS THEE--
LISTEN, ORRIN-- THERE'S SOME-THING YOU'VE GOT TO GET STRAIGHT:
JUST 'CAUSE I'M YOUNG, DOESN'T MEAN I'M STUPID.
MY GENERATION MAY NOT BE ANY SMARTER THAN YOUR GENERATION WAS WHEN YOU WERE OUR AGE--
--BUT WE'VE GOT A HECK OF A LOT MORE INFORMATION ON HAND--

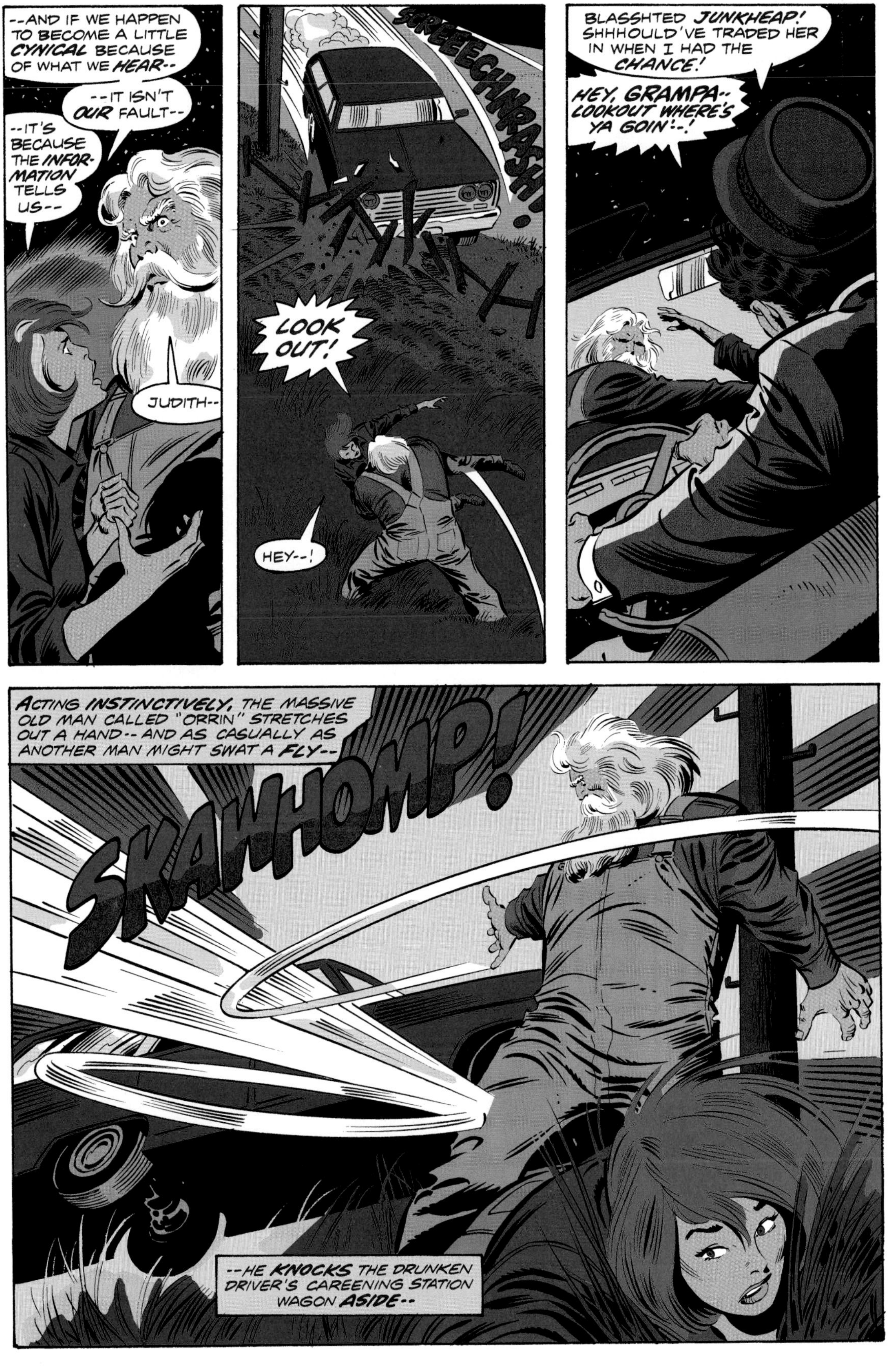
--AND IF WE HAPPEN TO BECOME A LITTLE CYNICAL BECAUSE OF WHAT WE HEAR--
--IT ISN'T OUR FAULT--
--IT'S BECAUSE THE INFORMATION TELLS US--
JUDITH--
SCREEECHNRASH!
LOOK OUT!
HEY--!
BLASSHTED JUNKHEAP! SHHHOULD'VE TRADED HER IN WHEN I HAD THE CHANCE!
HEY, GRAMPA-- LOOKOUT WHERE'S YA GOIN'--!
ACTING INSTINCTIVELY, THE MASSIVE OLD MAN CALLED "ORRIN" STRETCHES OUT A HAND-- AND AS CASUALLY AS ANOTHER MAN MIGHT SWAT A FLY--
SKAWHOMP!
--HE KNOCKS THE DRUNKEN DRIVER'S CAREENING STATION WAGON ASIDE--

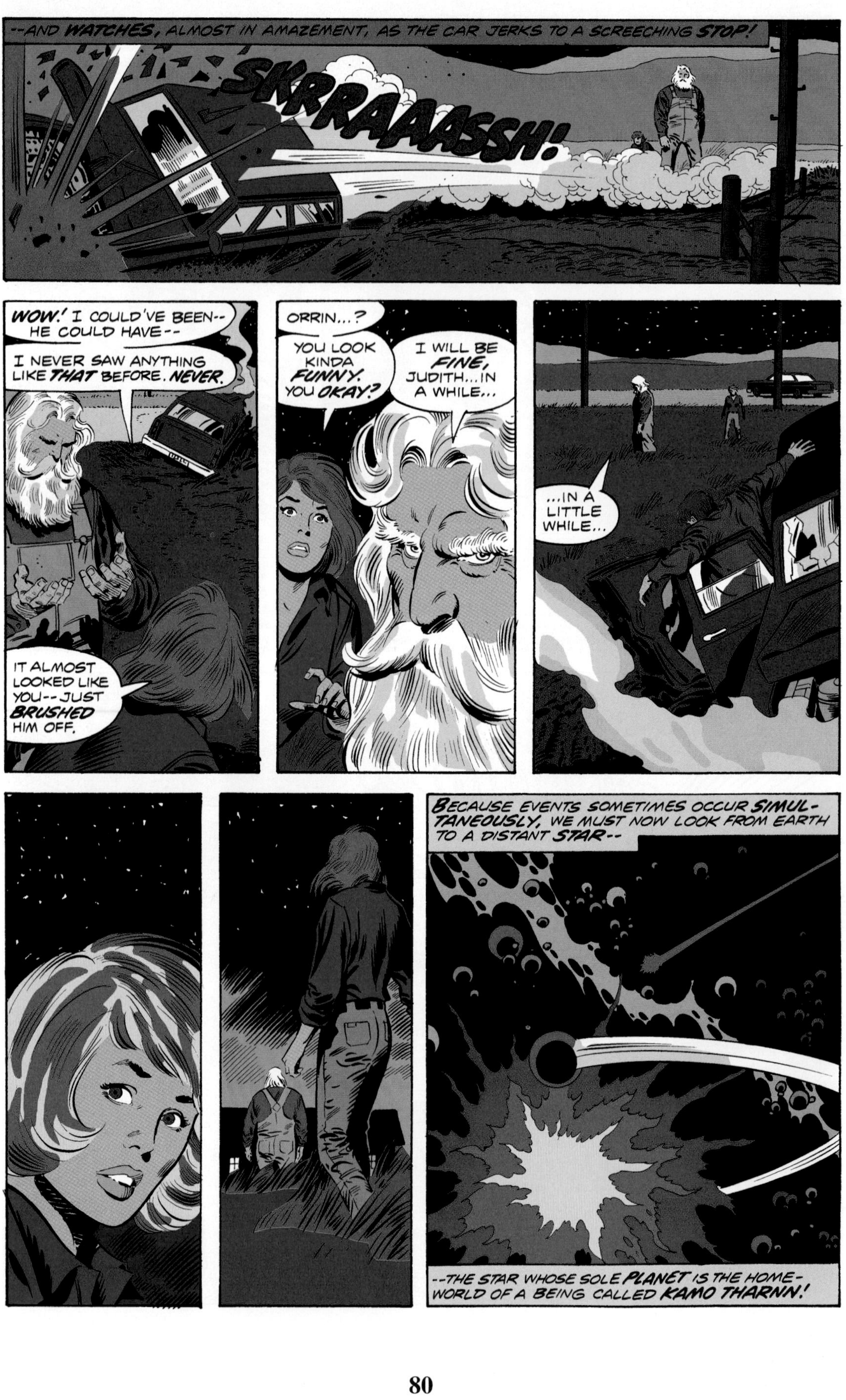
--AND WATCHES, ALMOST IN AMAZEMENT, AS THE CAR JERKS TO A SCREECHING STOP!
SKRRAAAASSH!
WOW! I COULD'VE BEEN-- HE COULD HAVE--
I NEVER SAW ANYTHING LIKE THAT BEFORE. NEVER.
IT ALMOST LOOKED LIKE YOU--JUST BRUSHED HIM OFF.
ORRIN...?
YOU LOOK KINDA FUNNY. YOU OKAY?
I WILL BE FINE, JUDITH...IN A WHILE...
...IN A LITTLE WHILE...
BECAUSE EVENTS SOMETIMES OCCUR SIMULTANEOUSLY, WE MUST NOW LOOK FROM EARTH TO A DISTANT STAR--
--THE STAR WHOSE SOLE PLANET IS THE HOME-WORLD OF A BEING CALLED KAMO THARNN!

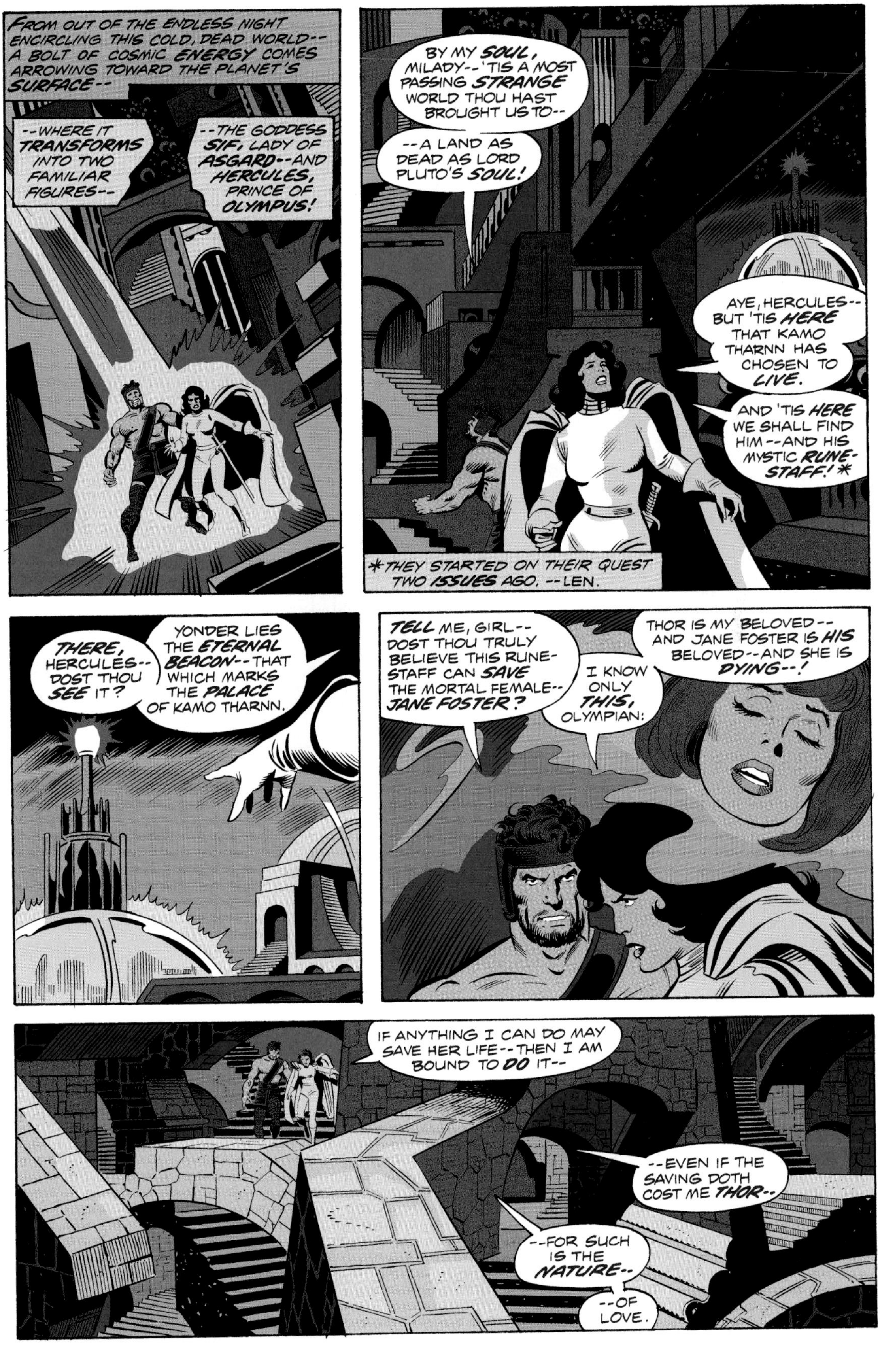
FROM OUT OF THE ENDLESS NIGHT ENCIRCLING THIS COLD, DEAD WORLD-- A BOLT OF COSMIC ENERGY COMES ARROWING TOWARD THE PLANET'S SURFACE--
--WHERE IT TRANSFORMS INTO TWO FAMILIAR FIGURES--
--THE GODDESS SIF, LADY OF ASGARD--AND HERCULES, PRINCE OF OLYMPUS!
BY MY SOUL, MILADY--'TIS A MOST PASSING STRANGE WORLD THOU HAST BROUGHT US TO--
--A LAND AS DEAD AS LORD PLUTO'S SOUL!
AYE, HERCULES-- BUT 'TIS HERE THAT KAMO THARNN HAS CHOSEN TO LIVE.
AND 'TIS HERE WE SHALL FIND HIM--AND HIS MYSTIC RUNE-STAFF! *
* THEY STARTED ON THEIR QUEST TWO ISSUES AGO. --LEN.
THERE, HERCULES-- DOST THOU SEE IT?
YONDER LIES THE ETERNAL BEACON--THAT WHICH MARKS THE PALACE OF KAMO THARNN.
TELL ME, GIRL-- DOST THOU TRULY BELIEVE THIS RUNE-STAFF CAN SAVE THE MORTAL FEMALE-- JANE FOSTER?
I KNOW ONLY THIS, OLYMPIAN:
THOR IS MY BELOVED-- AND JANE FOSTER IS HIS BELOVED--AND SHE IS DYING--!
IF ANYTHING I CAN DO MAY SAVE HER LIFE--THEN I AM BOUND TO DO IT--
--EVEN IF THE SAVING DOTH COST ME THOR--
--FOR SUCH IS THE NATURE--
--OF LOVE.

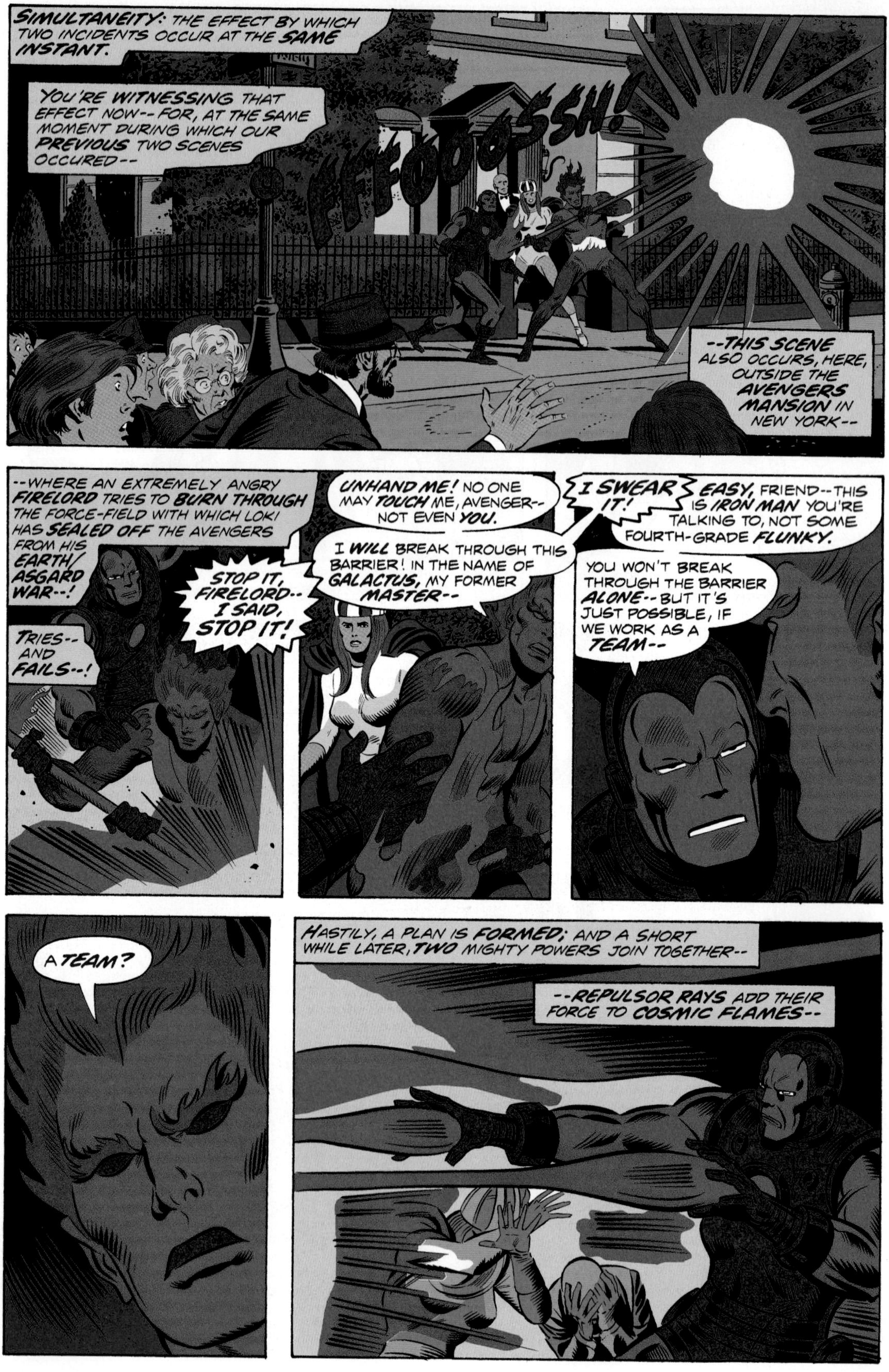
SIMULTANEITY: THE EFFECT BY WHICH TWO INCIDENTS OCCUR AT THE SAME INSTANT.
YOU'RE WITNESSING THAT EFFECT NOW-- FOR, AT THE SAME MOMENT DURING WHICH OUR PREVIOUS TWO SCENES OCCURED--
FFFOOOSSSH!
--THIS SCENE ALSO OCCURS, HERE, OUTSIDE THE AVENGERS MANSION IN NEW YORK--
--WHERE AN EXTREMELY ANGRY FIRELORD TRIES TO BURN THROUGH THE FORCE-FIELD WITH WHICH LOKI HAS SEALED OFF THE AVENGERS FROM HIS EARTH/ASGARD WAR--!
TRIES-- AND FAILS--!
STOP IT, FIRELORD-- I SAID, STOP IT!
UNHAND ME! NO ONE MAY TOUCH ME, AVENGER-- NOT EVEN YOU.
I WILL BREAK THROUGH THIS BARRIER! IN THE NAME OF GALACTUS, MY FORMER MASTER--
I SWEAR IT!
EASY, FRIEND-- THIS IS IRON MAN YOU'RE TALKING TO, NOT SOME FOURTH-GRADE FLUNKY.
YOU WON'T BREAK THROUGH THE BARRIER ALONE-- BUT IT'S JUST POSSIBLE, IF WE WORK AS A TEAM--
A TEAM?
HASTILY, A PLAN IS FORMED; AND A SHORT WHILE LATER, TWO MIGHTY POWERS JOIN TOGETHER--
--REPULSOR RAYS ADD THEIR FORCE TO COSMIC FLAMES--

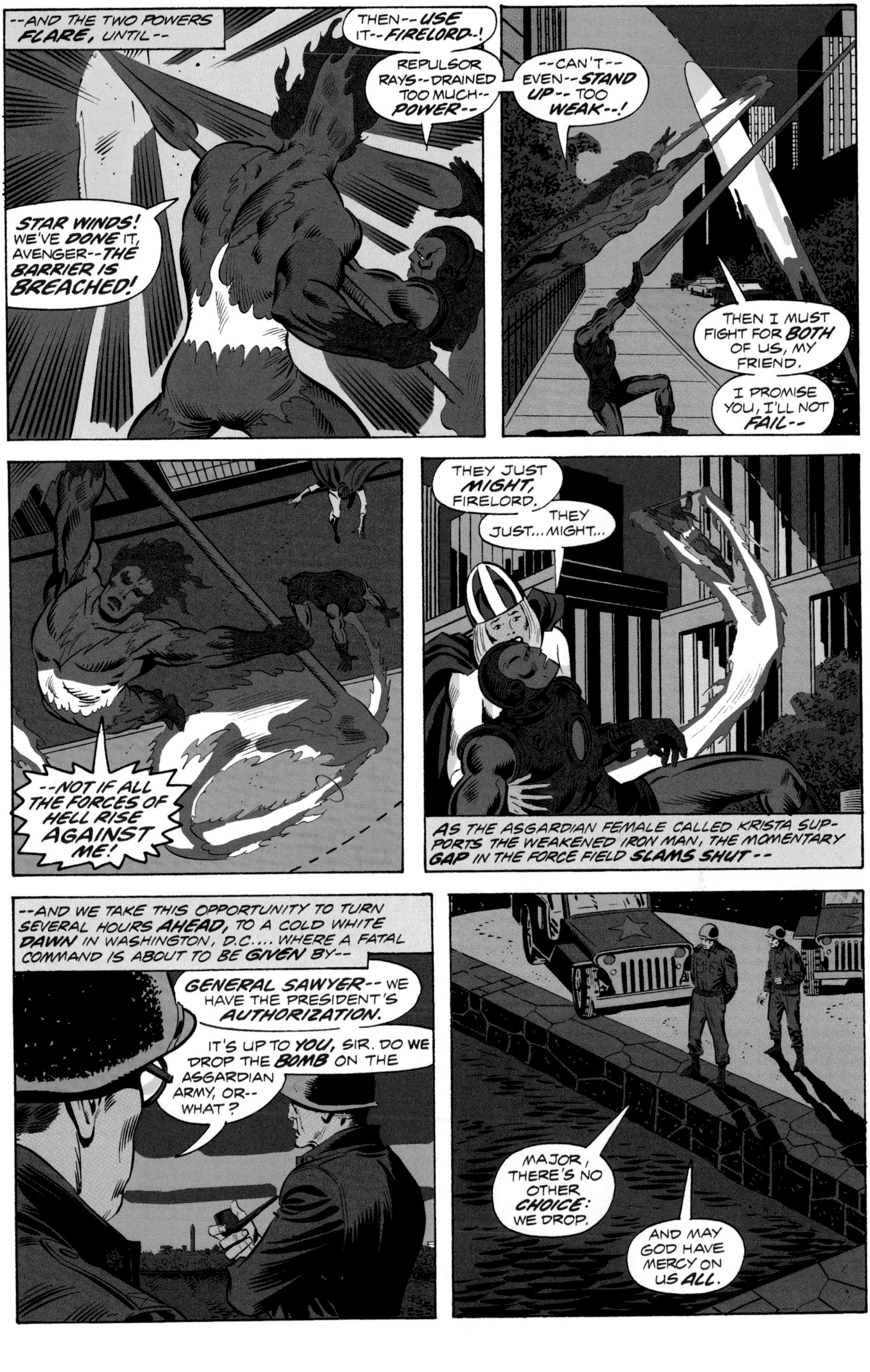

--AND THE TWO POWERS FLARE, UNTIL--
THEN--USE IT--FIRELORD-!
REPULSOR RAYS--DRAINED TOO MUCH--POWER--
--CAN'T--EVEN--STAND UP--TOO WEAK--!
STAR WINDS! WE'VE DONE IT, AVENGER--THE BARRIER IS BREACHED!
THEN I MUST FIGHT FOR BOTH OF US, MY FRIEND.
I PROMISE YOU, I'LL NOT FAIL--
--NOT IF ALL THE FORCES OF HELL RISE AGAINST ME!
THEY JUST MIGHT, FIRELORD.
THEY JUST... MIGHT...
AS THE ASGARDIAN FEMALE CALLED KRISTA SUPPORTS THE WEAKENED IRON MAN, THE MOMENTARY GAP IN THE FORCE FIELD SLAMS SHUT--
--AND WE TAKE THIS OPPORTUNITY TO TURN SEVERAL HOURS AHEAD, TO A COLD WHITE DAWN IN WASHINGTON, D.C.... WHERE A FATAL COMMAND IS ABOUT TO BE GIVEN BY--
GENERAL SAWYER--WE HAVE THE PRESIDENT'S AUTHORIZATION.
IT'S UP TO YOU, SIR. DO WE DROP THE BOMB ON THE ASGARDIAN ARMY, OR--WHAT?
MAJOR, THERE'S NO OTHER CHOICE: WE DROP.
AND MAY GOD HAVE MERCY ON US ALL.

# CHAPTER THREE: "SIXTY SECONDS TO DIE!"

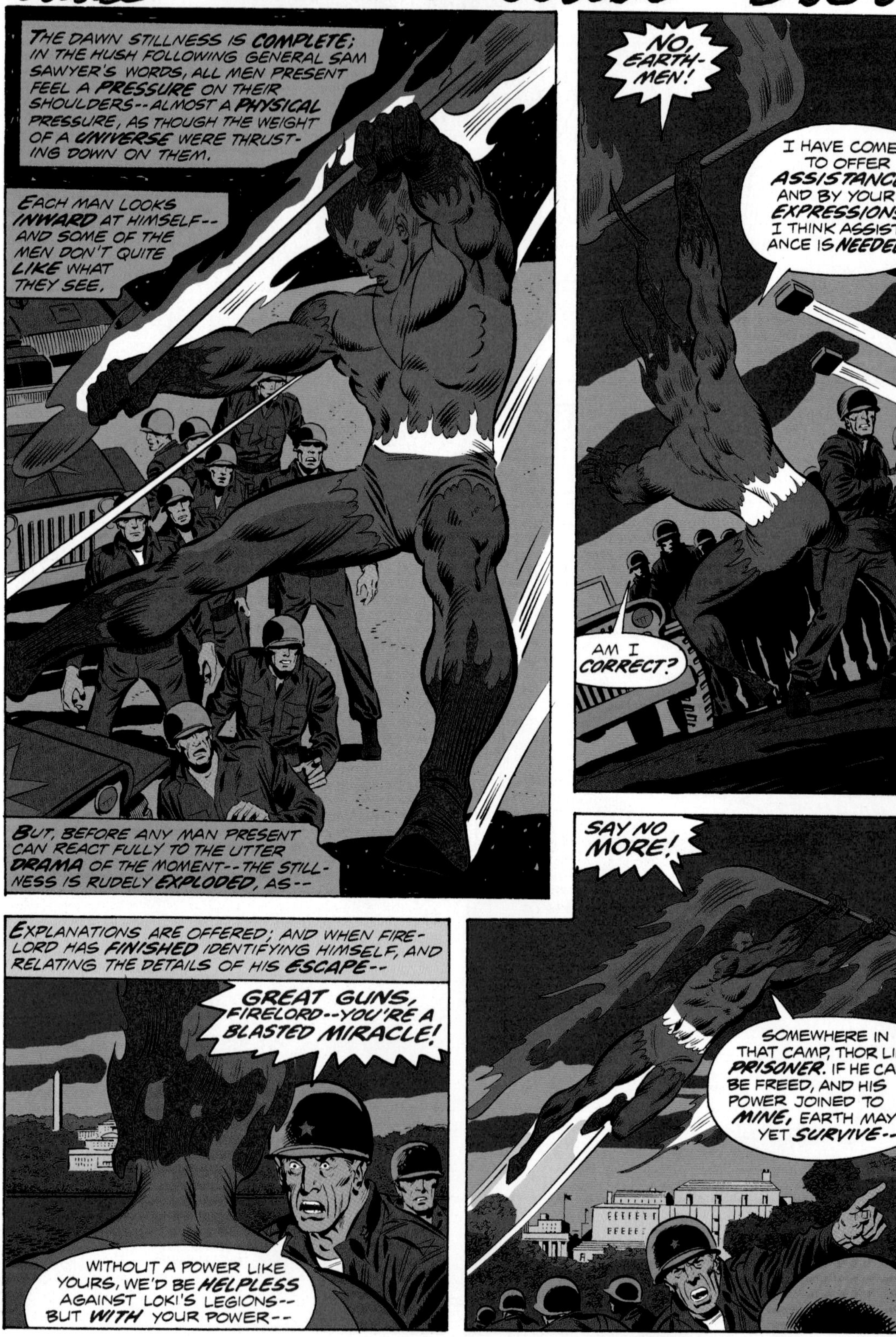

THE DAWN STILLNESS IS COMPLETE; IN THE HUSH FOLLOWING GENERAL SAM SAWYER'S WORDS, ALL MEN PRESENT FEEL A PRESSURE ON THEIR SHOULDERS--ALMOST A PHYSICAL PRESSURE, AS THOUGH THE WEIGHT OF A UNIVERSE WERE THRUSTING DOWN ON THEM.
EACH MAN LOOKS INWARD AT HIMSELF--AND SOME OF THE MEN DON'T QUITE LIKE WHAT THEY SEE.
BUT, BEFORE ANY MAN PRESENT CAN REACT FULLY TO THE UTTER DRAMA OF THE MOMENT--THE STILLNESS IS RUDELY EXPLODED, AS--
NO, EARTHMEN!
I HAVE COME TO OFFER ASSISTANCE--AND BY YOUR EXPRESSIONS--I THINK ASSISTANCE IS NEEDED.
AM I CORRECT?
EXPLANATIONS ARE OFFERED; AND WHEN FIRELORD HAS FINISHED IDENTIFYING HIMSELF, AND RELATING THE DETAILS OF HIS ESCAPE--
GREAT GUNS, FIRELORD--YOU'RE A BLASTED MIRACLE!
WITHOUT A POWER LIKE YOURS, WE'D BE HELPLESS AGAINST LOKI'S LEGIONS--BUT WITH YOUR POWER--
SAY NO MORE!
SOMEWHERE IN THAT CAMP, THOR LIES PRISONER. IF HE CAN BE FREED, AND HIS POWER JOINED TO MINE, EARTH MAY YET SURVIVE--

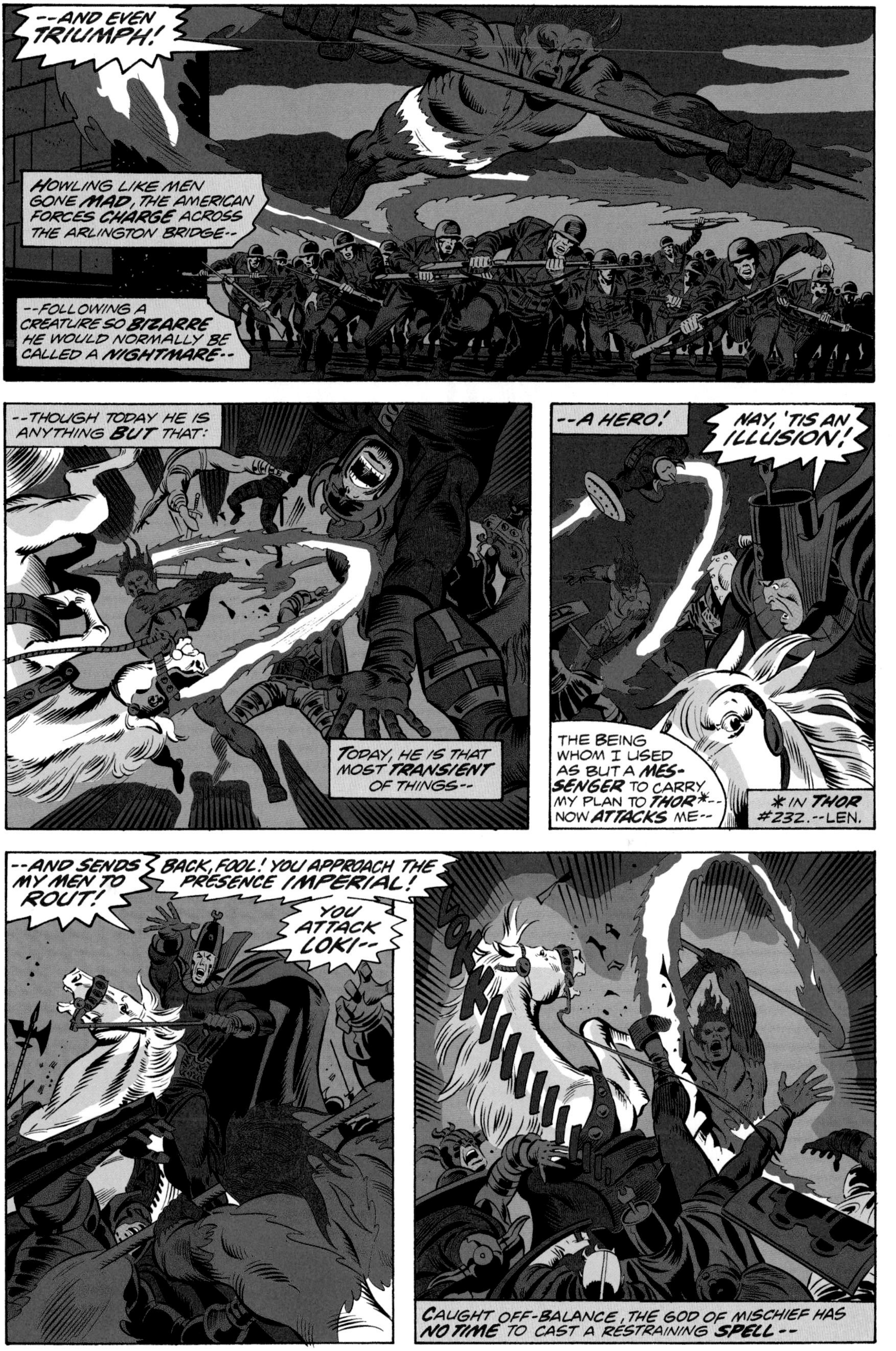
--AND EVEN TRIUMPH!
HOWLING LIKE MEN GONE MAD, THE AMERICAN FORCES CHARGE ACROSS THE ARLINGTON BRIDGE--
--FOLLOWING A CREATURE SO BIZARRE HE WOULD NORMALLY BE CALLED A NIGHTMARE--
--THOUGH TODAY HE IS ANYTHING BUT THAT:
TODAY, HE IS THAT MOST TRANSIENT OF THINGS--
--A HERO!
NAY, 'TIS AN ILLUSION!
THE BEING WHOM I USED AS BUT A MES-SENGER TO CARRY MY PLAN TO THOR*--NOW ATTACKS ME--
*IN THOR #232.--LEN.
--AND SENDS MY MEN TO ROUT!
BACK, FOOL! YOU APPROACH THE PRESENCE IMPERIAL!
YOU ATTACK LOKI--
KIIIIIIII
CAUGHT OFF-BALANCE, THE GOD OF MISCHIEF HAS NO TIME TO CAST A RESTRAINING SPELL--

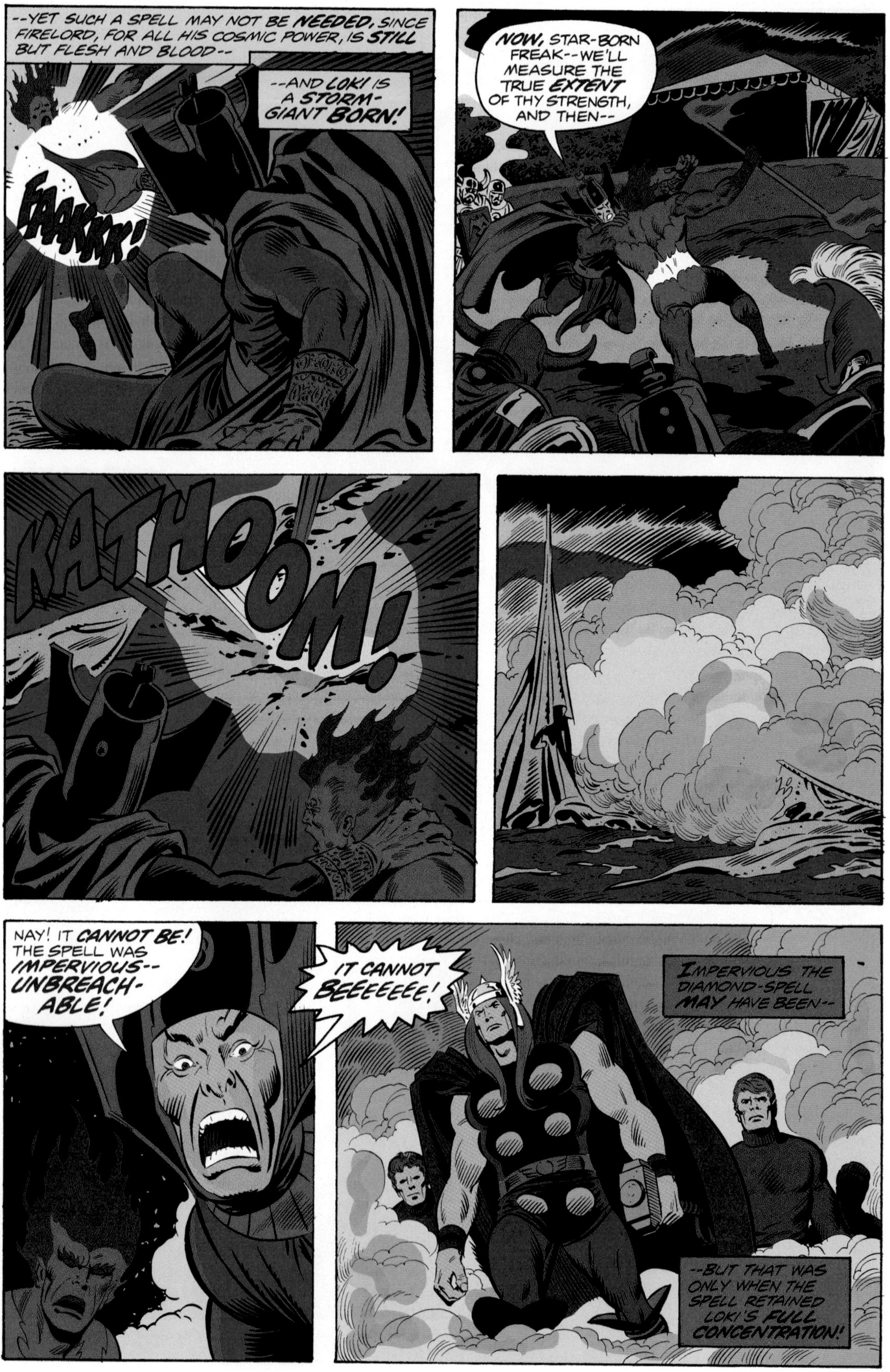

--YET SUCH A SPELL MAY NOT BE NEEDED, SINCE FIRELORD, FOR ALL HIS COSMIC POWER, IS STILL BUT FLESH AND BLOOD--
--AND LOKI IS A STORM-GIANT BORN!
FAAKKKK!
NOW, STAR-BORN FREAK--WE'LL MEASURE THE TRUE EXTENT OF THY STRENGTH, AND THEN--
KATHOOOM!
NAY! IT CANNOT BE! THE SPELL WAS IMPERVIOUS--UNBREACH-ABLE!
IT CANNOT BEEEEEEE!
IMPERVIOUS THE DIAMOND-SPELL MAY HAVE BEEN--
--BUT THAT WAS ONLY WHEN THE SPELL RETAINED LOKI'S FULL CONCENTRATION!

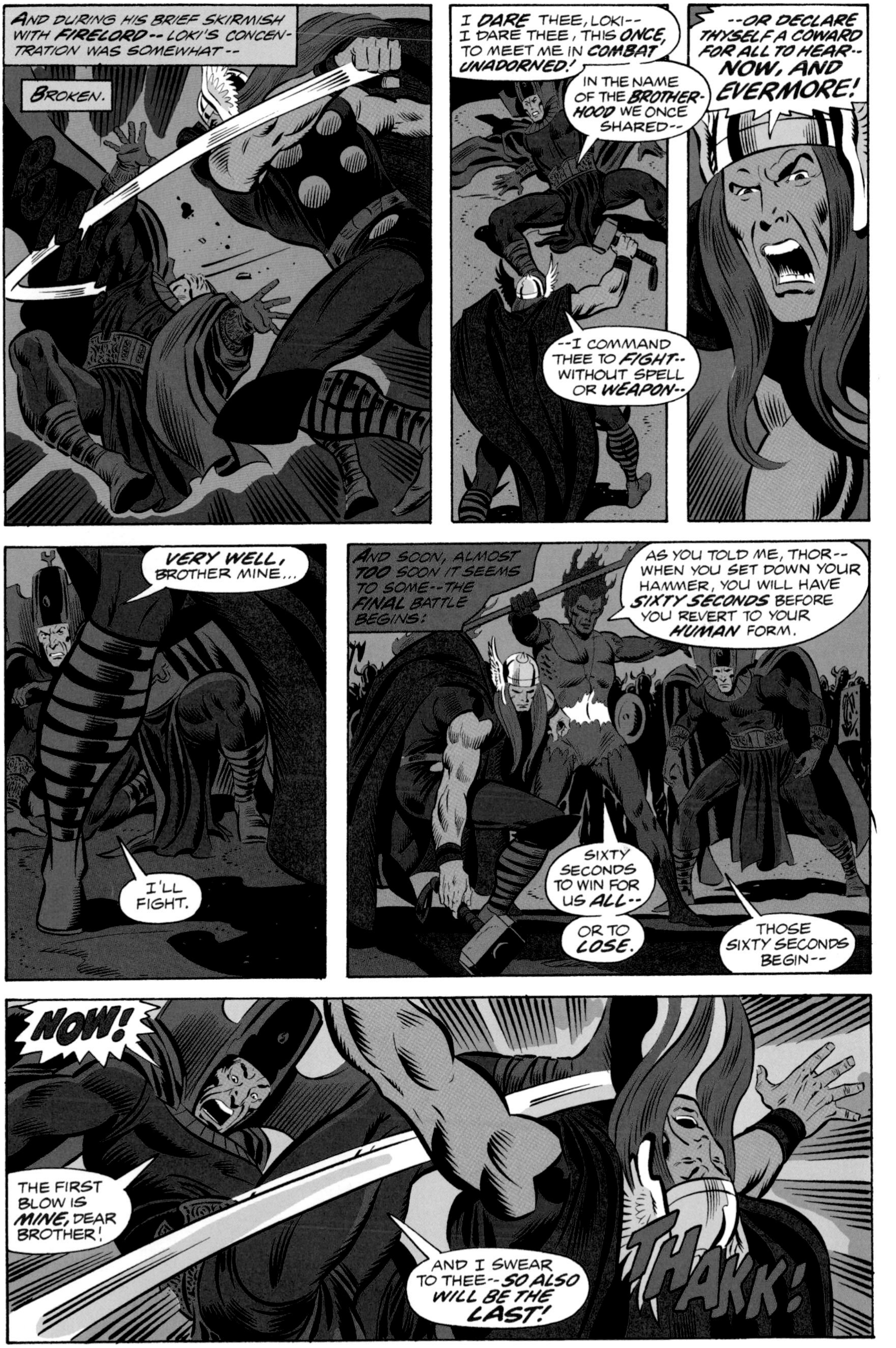
AND DURING HIS BRIEF SKIRMISH WITH FIRELORD -- LOKI'S CONCENTRATION WAS SOMEWHAT --
BROKEN.
I DARE THEE, LOKI-- I DARE THEE, THIS ONCE, TO MEET ME IN COMBAT UNADORNED!
IN THE NAME OF THE BROTHERHOOD WE ONCE SHARED--
--I COMMAND THEE TO FIGHT-- WITHOUT SPELL OR WEAPON--
--OR DECLARE THYSELF A COWARD FOR ALL TO HEAR-- NOW, AND EVERMORE!
VERY WELL, BROTHER MINE...
I'LL FIGHT.
AND SOON, ALMOST TOO SOON IT SEEMS TO SOME--THE FINAL BATTLE BEGINS:
AS YOU TOLD ME, THOR-- WHEN YOU SET DOWN YOUR HAMMER, YOU WILL HAVE SIXTY SECONDS BEFORE YOU REVERT TO YOUR HUMAN FORM.
SIXTY SECONDS TO WIN FOR US ALL--
OR TO LOSE.
THOSE SIXTY SECONDS BEGIN--
NOW!
THE FIRST BLOW IS MINE, DEAR BROTHER!
AND I SWEAR TO THEE--SO ALSO WILL BE THE LAST!
THAKK!

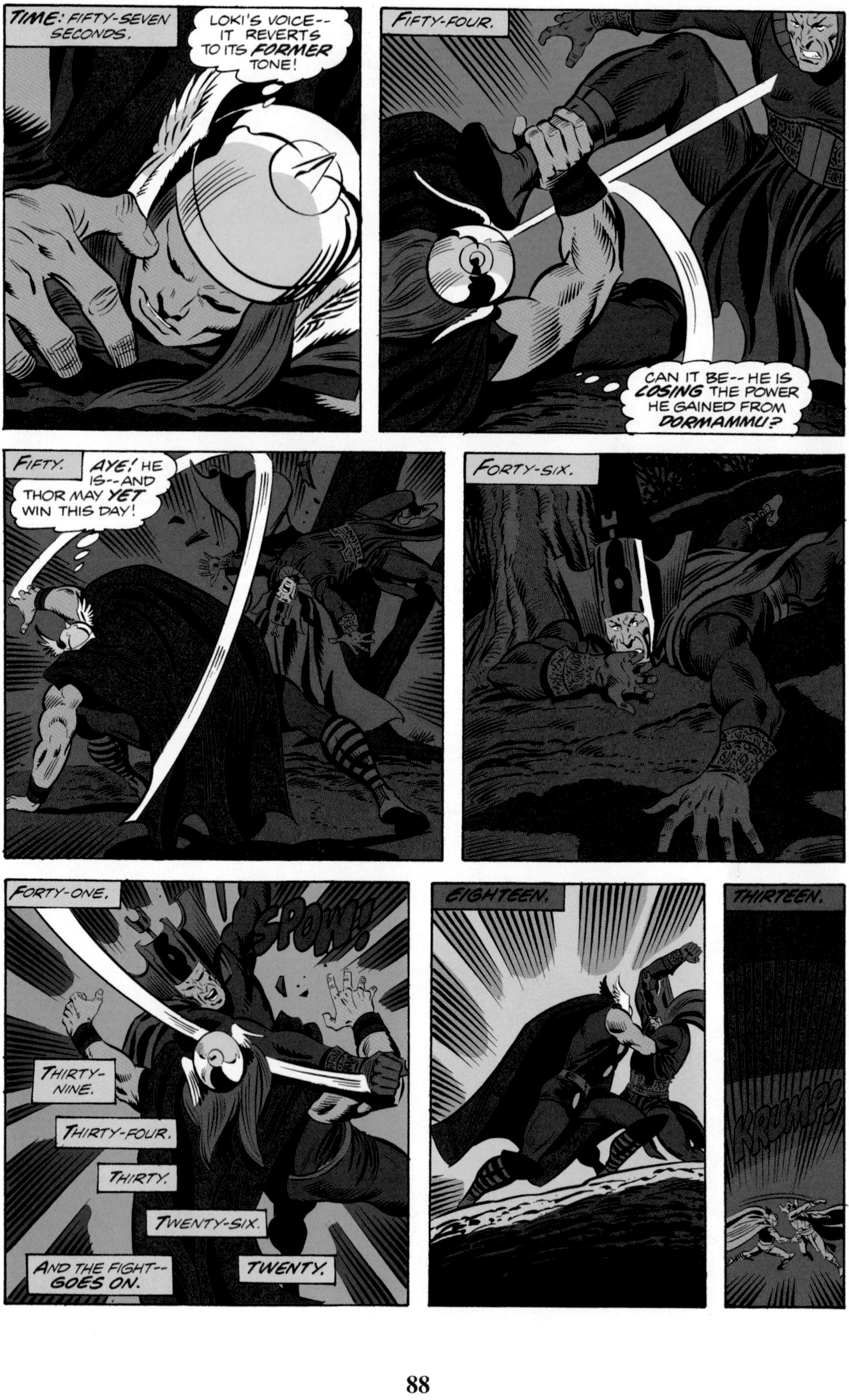
TIME: FIFTY-SEVEN SECONDS.
LOKI'S VOICE-- IT REVERTS TO ITS FORMER TONE!
FIFTY-FOUR.
CAN IT BE-- HE IS LOSING THE POWER HE GAINED FROM DORMAMMU?
FIFTY.
AYE! HE IS--AND THOR MAY YET WIN THIS DAY!
FORTY-SIX.
FORTY-ONE.
SPOW!!
THIRTY-NINE.
THIRTY-FOUR.
THIRTY.
TWENTY-SIX.
AND THE FIGHT-- GOES ON.
TWENTY.
EIGHTEEN.
THIRTEEN.
KRUMP!

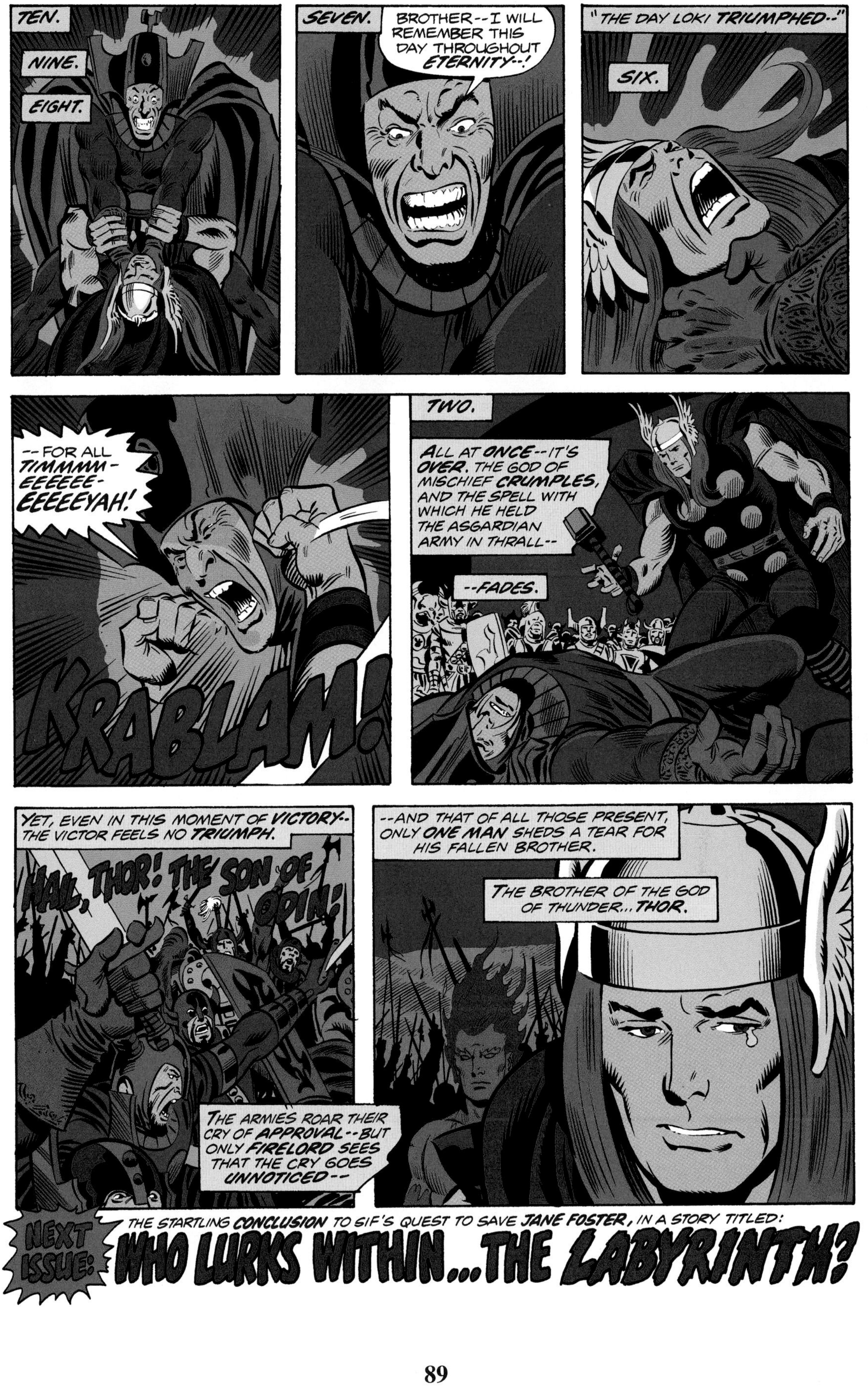
TEN.
NINE.
EIGHT.
SEVEN.
BROTHER--I WILL REMEMBER THIS DAY THROUGHOUT ETERNITY--!
"THE DAY LOKI TRIUMPHED--"
SIX.
--FOR ALL TIMMMM-EEEEEE-EEEEEYAH!
KRABLAM!
TWO.
ALL AT ONCE--IT'S OVER. THE GOD OF MISCHIEF CRUMPLES, AND THE SPELL WITH WHICH HE HELD THE ASGARDIAN ARMY IN THRALL--
--FADES.
YET, EVEN IN THIS MOMENT OF VICTORY-- THE VICTOR FEELS NO TRIUMPH.
HAIL, THOR! THE SON OF ODIN!
THE ARMIES ROAR THEIR CRY OF APPROVAL--BUT ONLY FIRELORD SEES THAT THE CRY GOES UNNOTICED--
--AND THAT OF ALL THOSE PRESENT, ONLY ONE MAN SHEDS A TEAR FOR HIS FALLEN BROTHER.
THE BROTHER OF THE GOD OF THUNDER...THOR.
NEXT ISSUE:
THE STARTLING CONCLUSION TO SIF'S QUEST TO SAVE JANE FOSTER, IN A STORY TITLED:
WHO LURKS WITHIN...THE LABYRINTH?

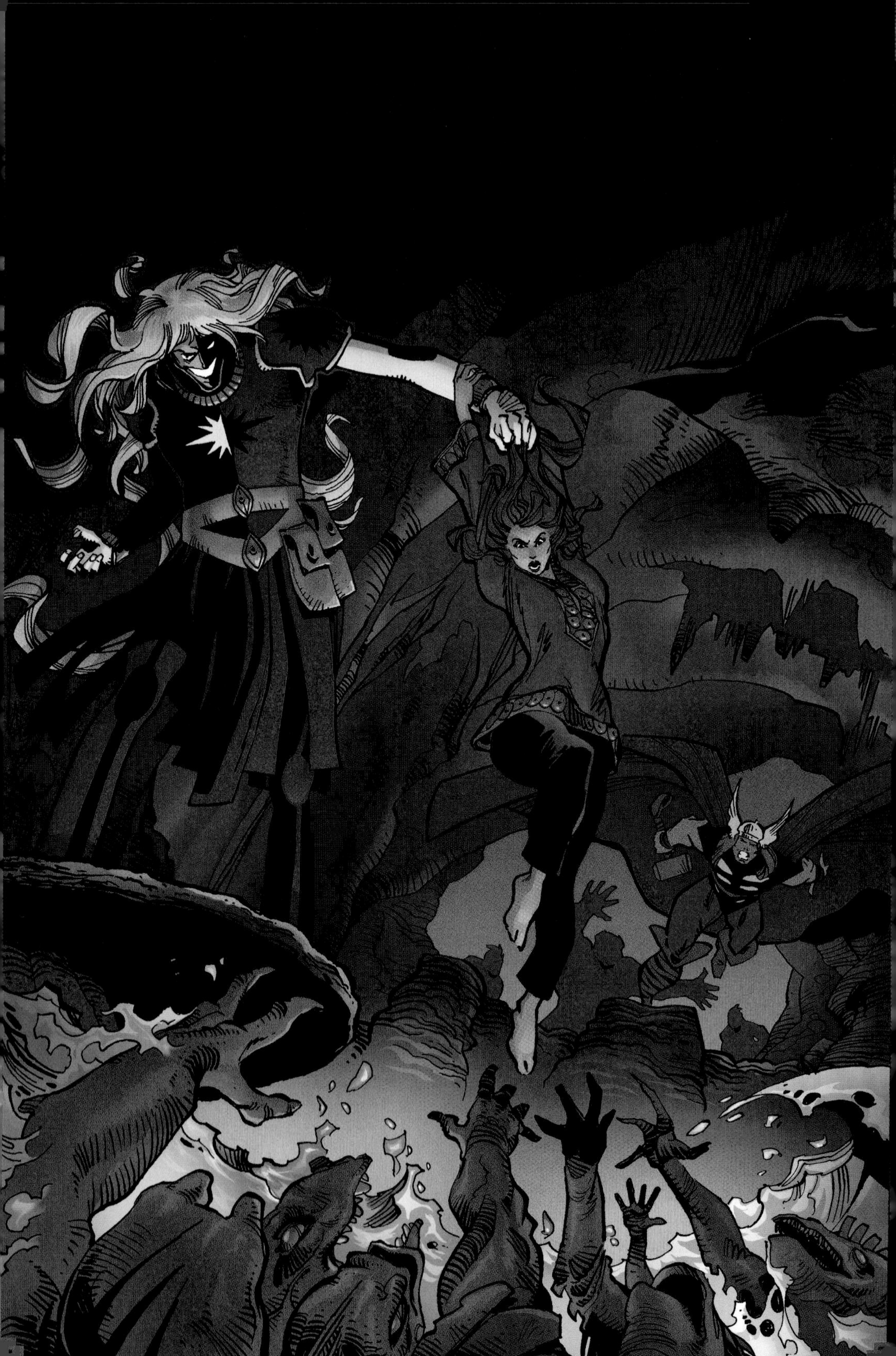

STAN LEE PRESENTS: the MIGHTY THOR®

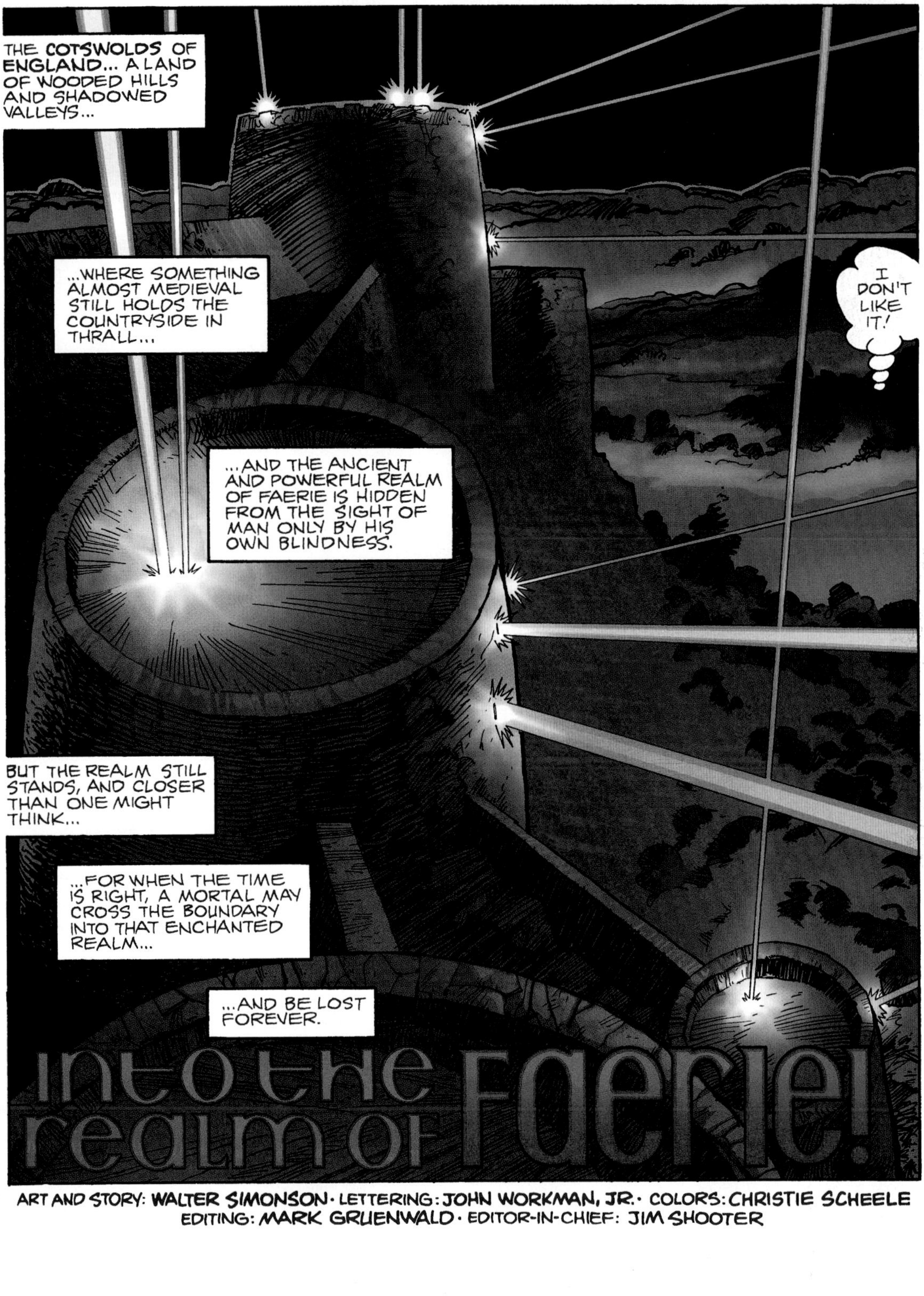
THE COTSWOLDS OF ENGLAND... A LAND OF WOODED HILLS AND SHADOWED VALLEYS...
...WHERE SOMETHING ALMOST MEDIEVAL STILL HOLDS THE COUNTRYSIDE IN THRALL...
I DON'T LIKE IT!
...AND THE ANCIENT AND POWERFUL REALM OF FAERIE IS HIDDEN FROM THE SIGHT OF MAN ONLY BY HIS OWN BLINDNESS.
BUT THE REALM STILL STANDS, AND CLOSER THAN ONE MIGHT THINK...
...FOR WHEN THE TIME IS RIGHT, A MORTAL MAY CROSS THE BOUNDARY INTO THAT ENCHANTED REALM...
...AND BE LOST FOREVER.
INTO THE REALM OF FAERIE!

ART AND STORY: WALTER SIMONSON · LETTERING: JOHN WORKMAN, JR. · COLORS: CHRISTIE SCHEELE
EDITING: MARK GRUENWALD · EDITOR-IN-CHIEF: JIM SHOOTER

I'VE CARRIED A STEEL PLATE AROUND IN MY HEAD SINCE KOREA WHEN I STUCK MY HEAD IN A DUMFOOL PLACE WITHOUT LOOKING!

...BUT I FEEL JUST LIKE I'M STARING INTO THAT ENEMY PILLBOX AGAIN.

AND MAYBE THERE'S NOTHING BUT A DESERTED CASTLE UP THERE...

I WISH THOR WERE HERE.

I'M WORRIED ABOUT HIM. EVER SINCE HE DRANK THAT STUFF BACK IN NEW YORK, HE SEEMS A LITTLE SCATTERED.

AND NOW I'M STUCK WITH THE CASKET OF ANCIENT WINTERS IN A KNAPSACK...

...TRYING HARD TO FIGURE OUT HOW TO LOCATE SOME BLASTED ELVES OR SOMETHING!

NOW, BROTHERS! STRIKE HIM DOWN!

I'VE FOUND THEM!

WHOCK!

KLOP!

UGH!

A MORTAL! AND SO CLOSE TO OUR FASTNESS!

YET HE IS **NOT** ONE OF OUR SLAVES, A FAERIE MORTAL, FOR HE DID NOT SEE US.

HOW FORTUNATE THAT WE ARE INVISIBLE TO SUCH FOOLS UNLESS THEIR EYES ARE ANOINTED WITH THE **OIL OF VISION.**

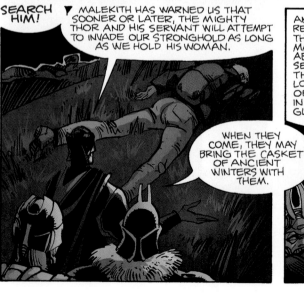

SEARCH HIM!

MALEKITH HAS WARNED US THAT SOONER OR LATER, THE MIGHTY THOR AND HIS SERVANT WILL ATTEMPT TO INVADE OUR STRONGHOLD AS LONG AS WE HOLD HIS WOMAN.

AND WHEN WE HAVE RECOVERED IT, THEN SHALL MALEKITH BE ABLE TO SERVE THE LORD OF FIRE IN HIS GLORY.

WHEN THEY COME, THEY MAY BRING THE CASKET OF ANCIENT WINTERS WITH THEM.

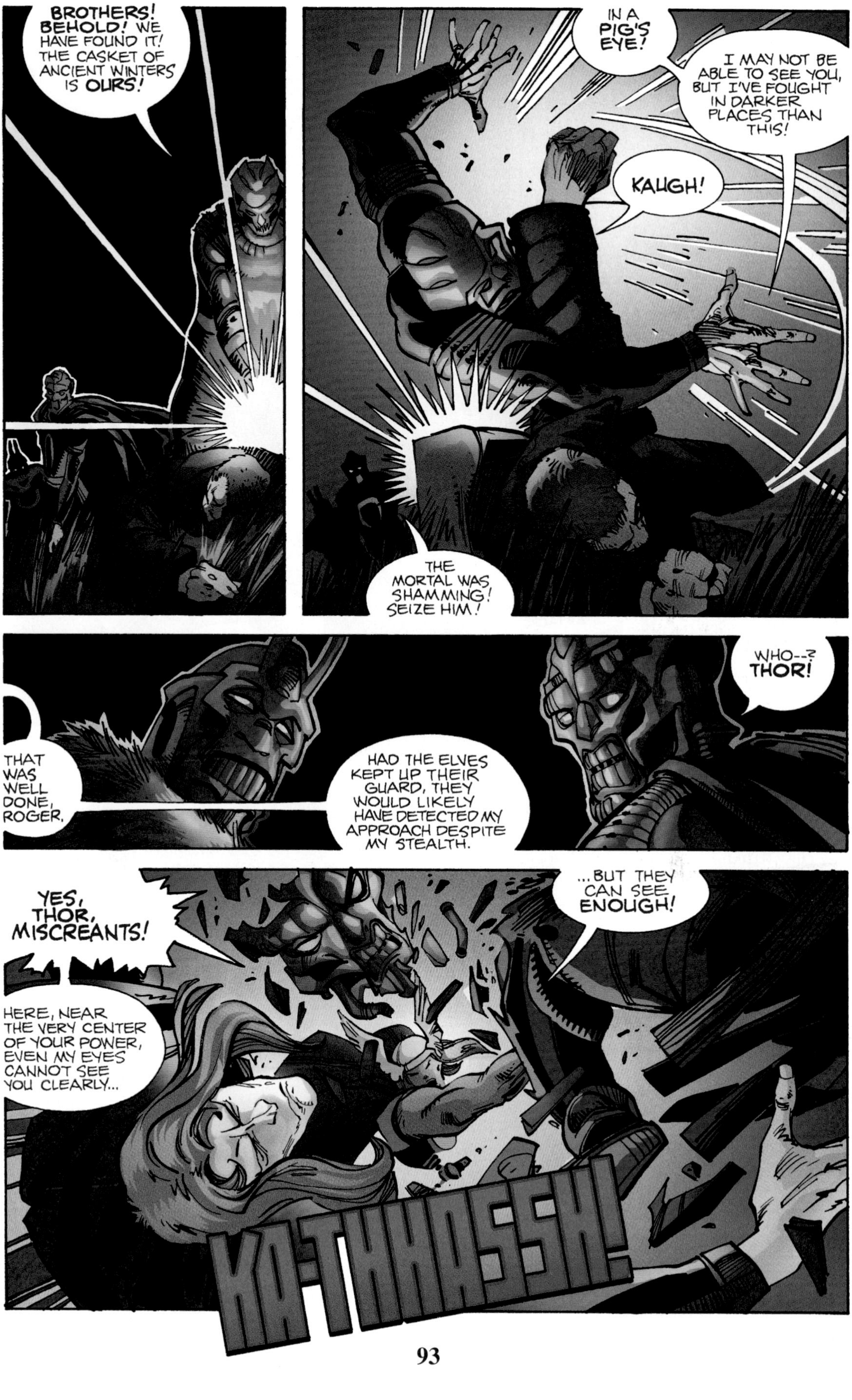
BROTHERS! BEHOLD! WE HAVE FOUND IT! THE CASKET OF ANCIENT WINTERS IS OURS!
IN A PIG'S EYE!
I MAY NOT BE ABLE TO SEE YOU, BUT I'VE FOUGHT IN DARKER PLACES THAN THIS!
KAUGH!
THE MORTAL WAS SHAMMING! SEIZE HIM!
WHO--? THOR!
THAT WAS WELL DONE, ROGER.
HAD THE ELVES KEPT UP THEIR GUARD, THEY WOULD LIKELY HAVE DETECTED MY APPROACH DESPITE MY STEALTH.
YES, THOR, MISCREANTS!
HERE, NEAR THE VERY CENTER OF YOUR POWER, EVEN MY EYES CANNOT SEE YOU CLEARLY...
...BUT THEY CAN SEE ENOUGH!
KA-THHASSH!

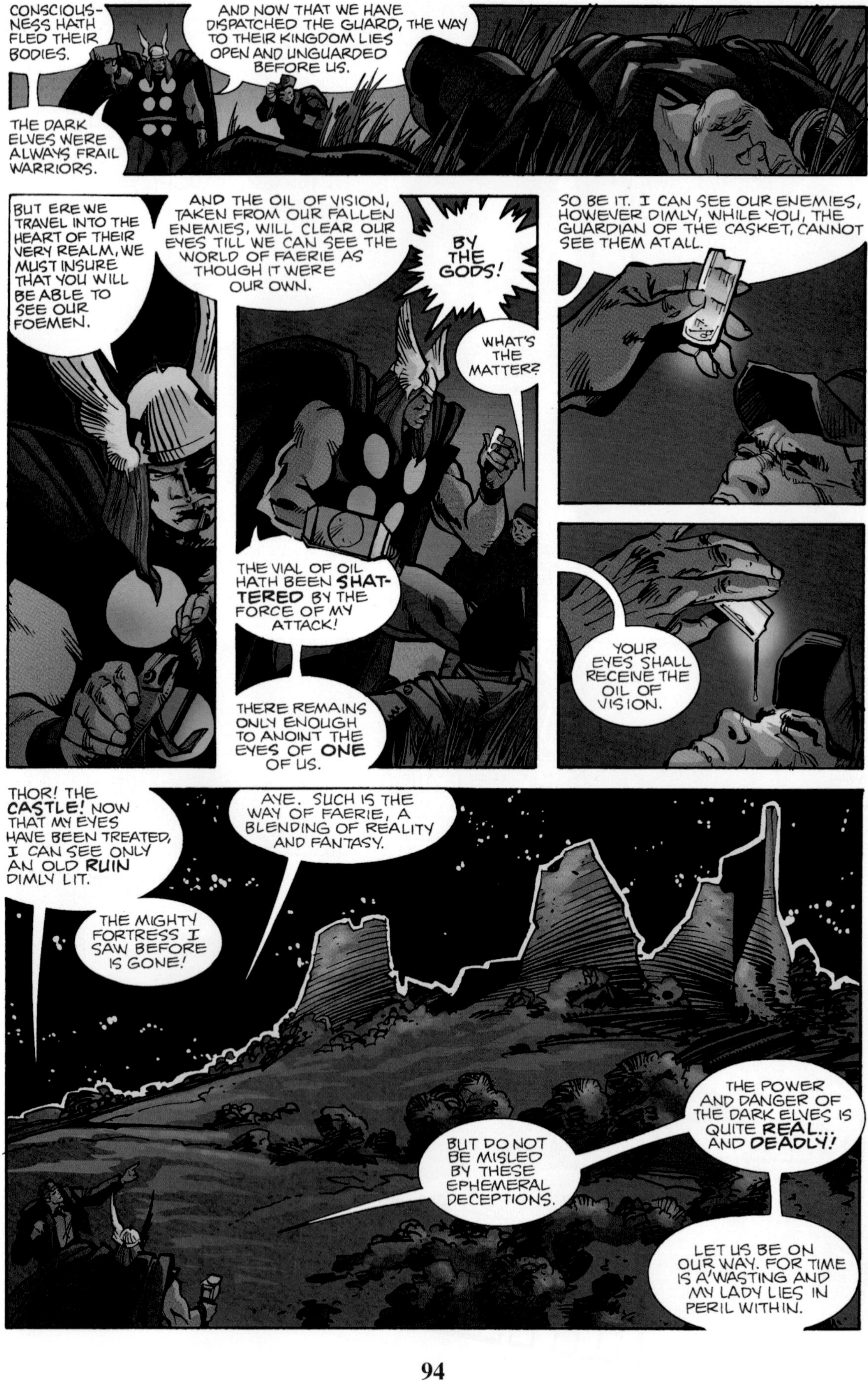
CONSCIOUSNESS HATH FLED THEIR BODIES.
THE DARK ELVES WERE ALWAYS FRAIL WARRIORS.
AND NOW THAT WE HAVE DISPATCHED THE GUARD, THE WAY TO THEIR KINGDOM LIES OPEN AND UNGUARDED BEFORE US.
BUT ERE WE TRAVEL INTO THE HEART OF THEIR VERY REALM, WE MUST INSURE THAT YOU WILL BE ABLE TO SEE OUR FOEMEN.
AND THE OIL OF VISION, TAKEN FROM OUR FALLEN ENEMIES, WILL CLEAR OUR EYES TILL WE CAN SEE THE WORLD OF FAERIE AS THOUGH IT WERE OUR OWN.
BY THE GODS!
WHAT'S THE MATTER?
THE VIAL OF OIL HATH BEEN SHATTERED BY THE FORCE OF MY ATTACK!
THERE REMAINS ONLY ENOUGH TO ANOINT THE EYES OF ONE OF US.
SO BE IT. I CAN SEE OUR ENEMIES, HOWEVER DIMLY, WHILE YOU, THE GUARDIAN OF THE CASKET, CANNOT SEE THEM AT ALL.
YOUR EYES SHALL RECEIVE THE OIL OF VISION.
THOR! THE CASTLE! NOW THAT MY EYES HAVE BEEN TREATED, I CAN SEE ONLY AN OLD RUIN DIMLY LIT.
THE MIGHTY FORTRESS I SAW BEFORE IS GONE!
AYE. SUCH IS THE WAY OF FAERIE, A BLENDING OF REALITY AND FANTASY.
BUT DO NOT BE MISLED BY THESE EPHEMERAL DECEPTIONS.
THE POWER AND DANGER OF THE DARK ELVES IS QUITE REAL... AND DEADLY!
LET US BE ON OUR WAY. FOR TIME IS A'WASTING AND MY LADY LIES IN PERIL WITHIN.

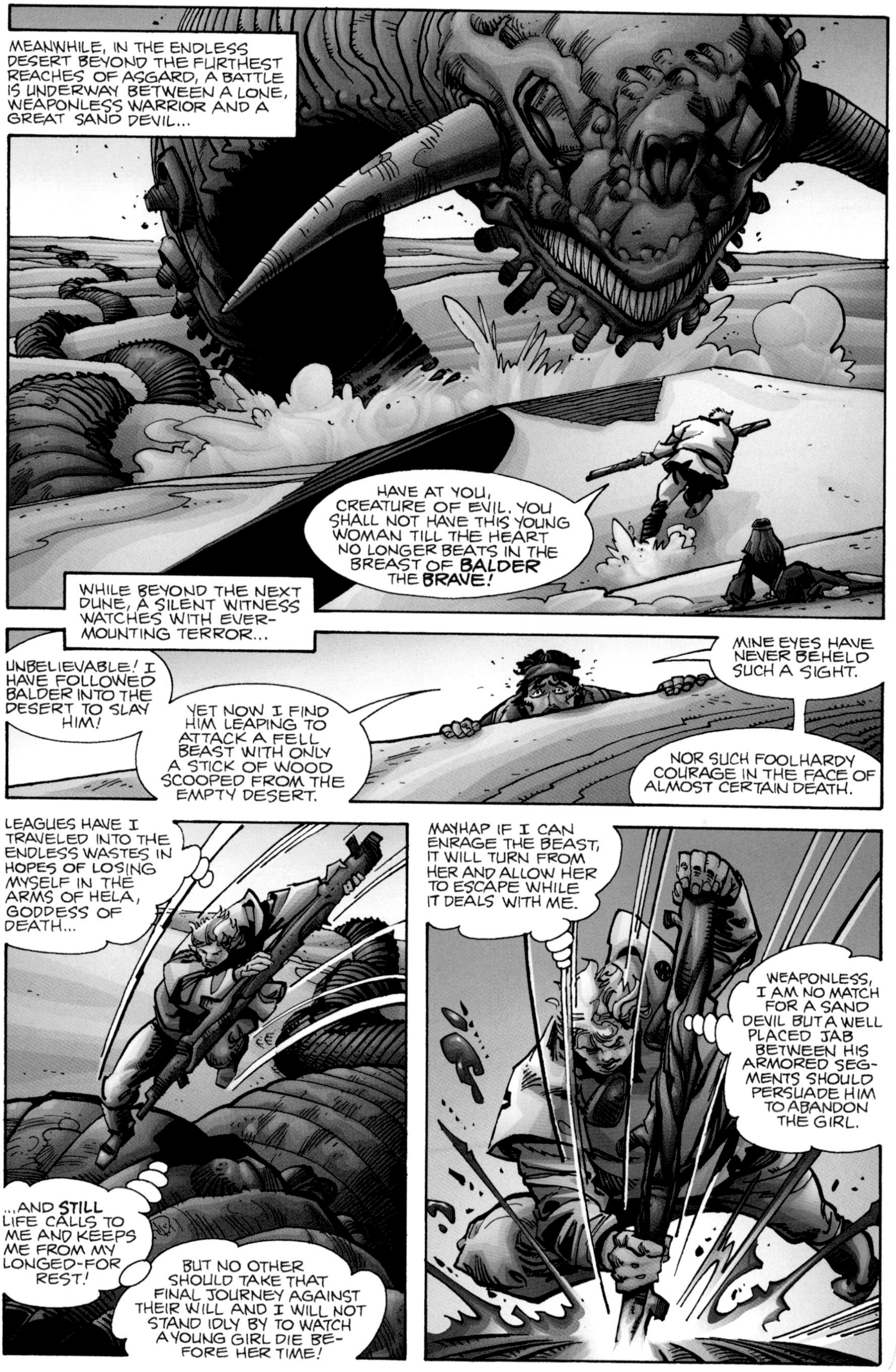
MEANWHILE, IN THE ENDLESS DESERT BEYOND THE FURTHEST REACHES OF ASGARD, A BATTLE IS UNDERWAY BETWEEN A LONE, WEAPONLESS WARRIOR AND A GREAT SAND DEVIL...
HAVE AT YOU, CREATURE OF EVIL. YOU SHALL NOT HAVE THIS YOUNG WOMAN TILL THE HEART NO LONGER BEATS IN THE BREAST OF BALDER THE BRAVE!
WHILE BEYOND THE NEXT DUNE, A SILENT WITNESS WATCHES WITH EVER-MOUNTING TERROR...
UNBELIEVABLE! I HAVE FOLLOWED BALDER INTO THE DESERT TO SLAY HIM!
YET NOW I FIND HIM LEAPING TO ATTACK A FELL BEAST WITH ONLY A STICK OF WOOD SCOOPED FROM THE EMPTY DESERT.
MINE EYES HAVE NEVER BEHELD SUCH A SIGHT.
NOR SUCH FOOLHARDY COURAGE IN THE FACE OF ALMOST CERTAIN DEATH.
LEAGUES HAVE I TRAVELED INTO THE ENDLESS WASTES IN HOPES OF LOSING MYSELF IN THE ARMS OF HELA, GODDESS OF DEATH...
...AND STILL LIFE CALLS TO ME AND KEEPS ME FROM MY LONGED-FOR REST!
BUT NO OTHER SHOULD TAKE THAT FINAL JOURNEY AGAINST THEIR WILL AND I WILL NOT STAND IDLY BY TO WATCH A YOUNG GIRL DIE BEFORE HER TIME!
MAYHAP IF I CAN ENRAGE THE BEAST, IT WILL TURN FROM HER AND ALLOW HER TO ESCAPE WHILE IT DEALS WITH ME.
WEAPONLESS, I AM NO MATCH FOR A SAND DEVIL BUT A WELL PLACED JAB BETWEEN HIS ARMORED SEGMENTS SHOULD PERSUADE HIM TO ABANDON THE GIRL.

SUCCESS! HIS MIGHTY HEAD SWINGS THIS WAY. IF THE FATES ARE WITH ME, I MAY YET--

UGGH!

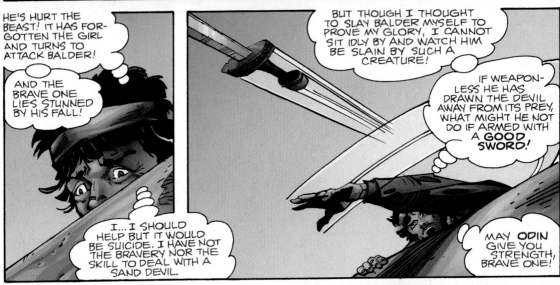

HE'S HURT THE BEAST! IT HAS FORGOTTEN THE GIRL AND TURNS TO ATTACK BALDER!

AND THE BRAVE ONE LIES STUNNED BY HIS FALL!

I... I SHOULD HELP BUT IT WOULD BE SUICIDE. I HAVE NOT THE BRAVERY NOR THE SKILL TO DEAL WITH A SAND DEVIL.

BUT THOUGH I THOUGHT TO SLAY BALDER MYSELF TO PROVE MY GLORY, I CANNOT SIT IDLY BY AND WATCH HIM BE SLAIN BY SUCH A CREATURE!

IF WEAPONLESS HE HAS DRAWN THE DEVIL AWAY FROM ITS PREY, WHAT MIGHT HE NOT DO IF ARMED WITH A GOOD SWORD!

MAY ODIN GIVE YOU STRENGTH, BRAVE ONE!

'TWOULD SEEM MY DEATH IS FINALLY AT HAND! AND THOUGH I HAVE SOUGHT IT FOR AN ETERNITY, I DO REGRET... BUT WAIT!

WHAT'S THIS BEFORE ME?

A RIGHT STRONG BLADE!

TRULY, THE FATES HAVE SMILED UPON ME THIS DAY!

THE LADY AND I MAY YET HAVE A CHANCE TO ESCAPE OUR DOOM!

FOR ASGARD AND ODIN!

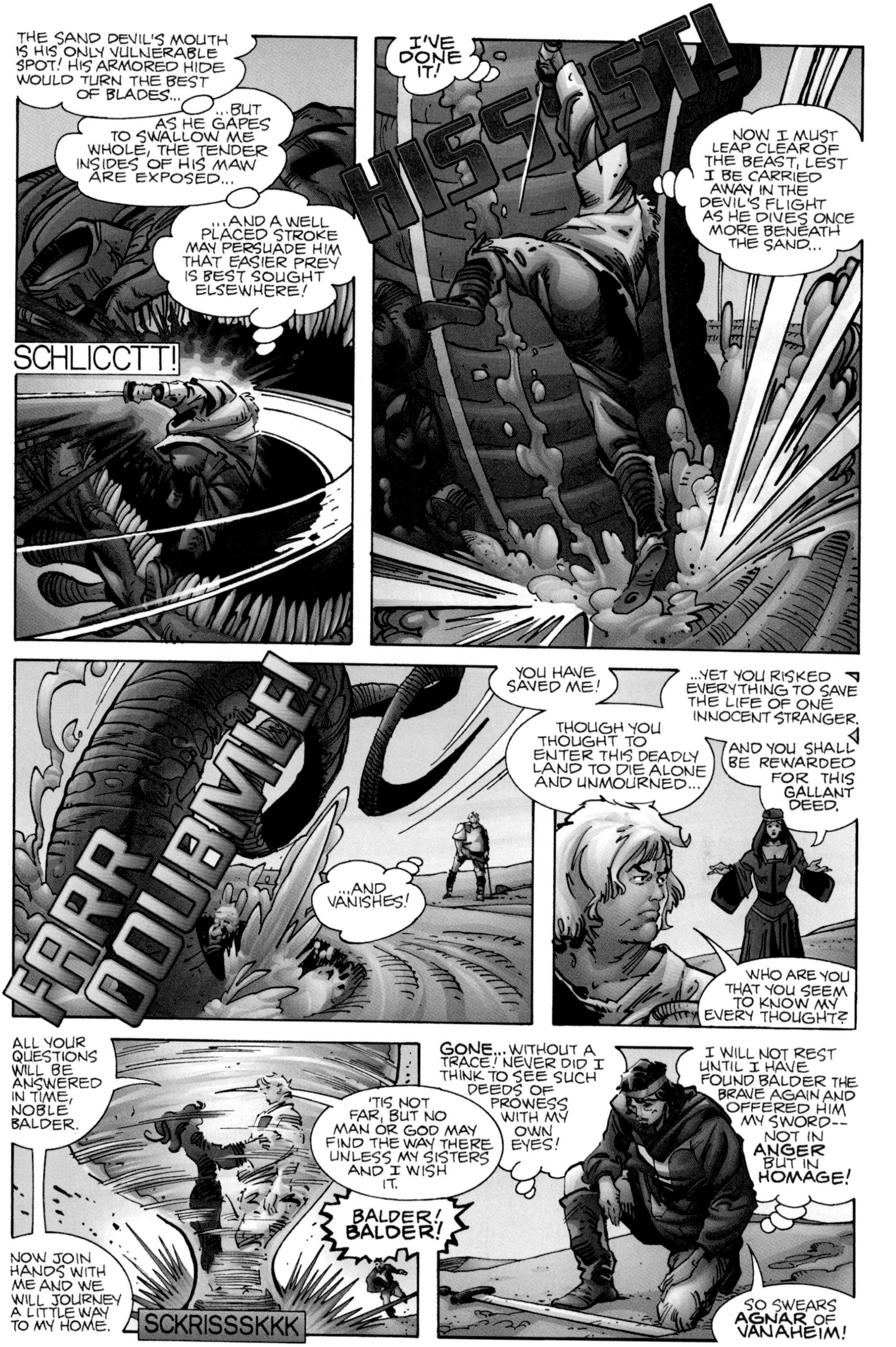
THE SAND DEVIL'S MOUTH IS HIS ONLY VULNERABLE SPOT! HIS ARMORED HIDE WOULD TURN THE BEST OF BLADES...
...BUT AS HE GAPES TO SWALLOW ME WHOLE, THE TENDER INSIDES OF HIS MAW ARE EXPOSED...
...AND A WELL PLACED STROKE MAY PERSUADE HIM THAT EASIER PREY IS BEST SOUGHT ELSEWHERE!
SCHLICCTT!
I'VE DONE IT!
HISSSST!
NOW I MUST LEAP CLEAR OF THE BEAST, LEST I BE CARRIED AWAY IN THE DEVIL'S FLIGHT AS HE DIVES ONCE MORE BENEATH THE SAND...
FARR OOUBMLE!
...AND VANISHES!
YOU HAVE SAVED ME!
THOUGH YOU THOUGHT TO ENTER THIS DEADLY LAND TO DIE ALONE AND UNMOURNED...
...YET YOU RISKED EVERYTHING TO SAVE THE LIFE OF ONE INNOCENT STRANGER.
AND YOU SHALL BE REWARDED FOR THIS GALLANT DEED.
WHO ARE YOU THAT YOU SEEM TO KNOW MY EVERY THOUGHT?
ALL YOUR QUESTIONS WILL BE ANSWERED IN TIME, NOBLE BALDER.
'TIS NOT FAR, BUT NO MAN OR GOD MAY FIND THE WAY THERE UNLESS MY SISTERS AND I WISH IT.
NOW JOIN HANDS WITH ME AND WE WILL JOURNEY A LITTLE WAY TO MY HOME.
SCKRISSSKKK
BALDER! BALDER!
GONE... WITHOUT A TRACE! NEVER DID I THINK TO SEE SUCH DEEDS OF PROWESS WITH MY OWN EYES!
I WILL NOT REST UNTIL I HAVE FOUND BALDER THE BRAVE AGAIN AND OFFERED HIM MY SWORD-- NOT IN ANGER BUT IN HOMAGE!
SO SWEARS AGNAR OF VANAHEIM!

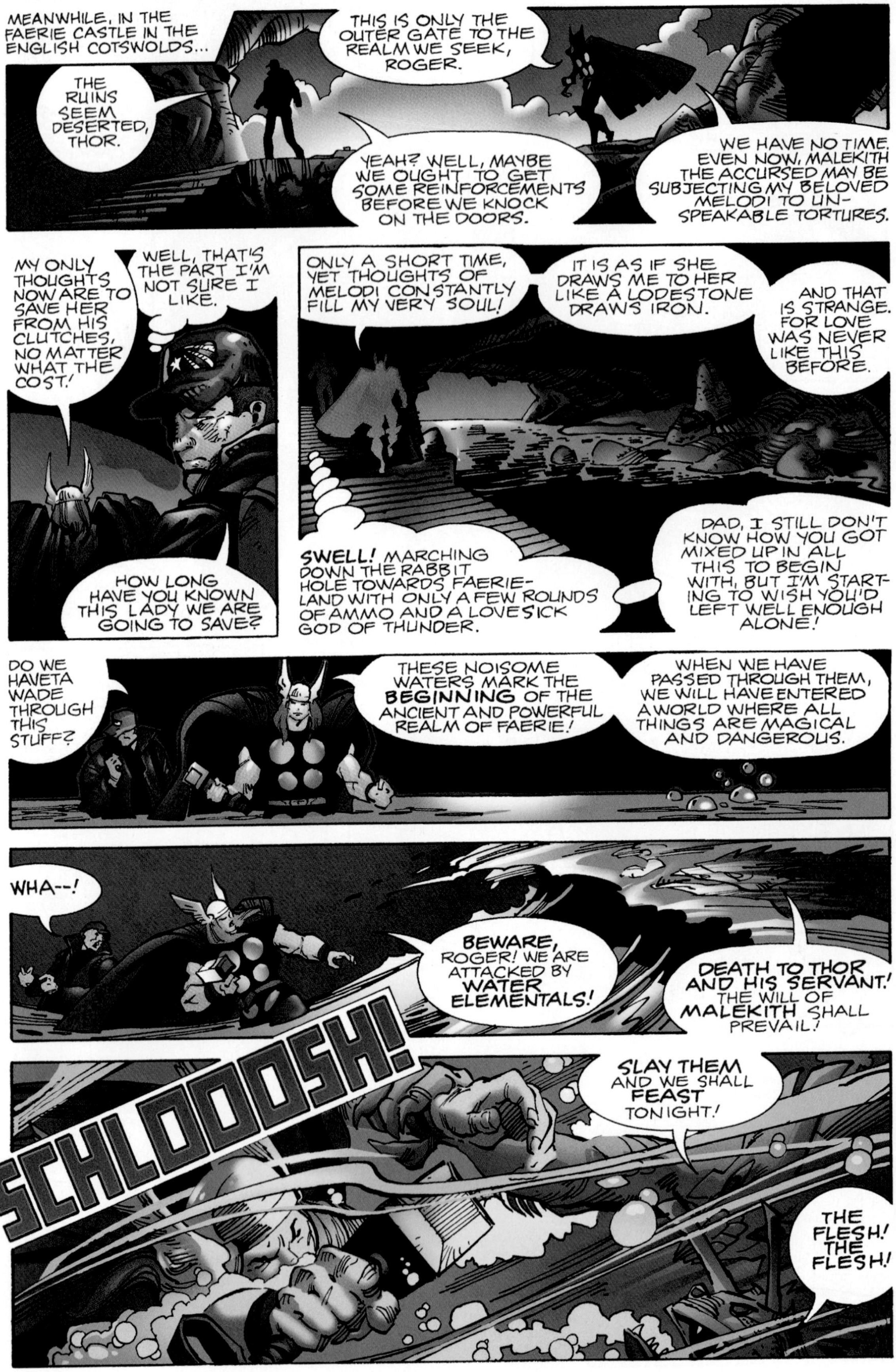
MEANWHILE, IN THE FAERIE CASTLE IN THE ENGLISH COTSWOLDS...
THE RUINS SEEM DESERTED, THOR.
THIS IS ONLY THE OUTER GATE TO THE REALM WE SEEK, ROGER.
YEAH? WELL, MAYBE WE OUGHT TO GET SOME REINFORCEMENTS BEFORE WE KNOCK ON THE DOORS.
WE HAVE NO TIME. EVEN NOW, MALEKITH THE ACCURSED MAY BE SUBJECTING MY BELOVED MELODI TO UN-SPEAKABLE TORTURES.
MY ONLY THOUGHTS NOW ARE TO SAVE HER FROM HIS CLUTCHES, NO MATTER WHAT THE COST!
WELL, THAT'S THE PART I'M NOT SURE I LIKE.
HOW LONG HAVE YOU KNOWN THIS LADY WE ARE GOING TO SAVE?
ONLY A SHORT TIME, YET THOUGHTS OF MELODI CONSTANTLY FILL MY VERY SOUL!
IT IS AS IF SHE DRAWS ME TO HER LIKE A LODESTONE DRAWS IRON.
AND THAT IS STRANGE. FOR LOVE WAS NEVER LIKE THIS BEFORE.
SWELL! MARCHING DOWN THE RABBIT HOLE TOWARDS FAERIE-LAND WITH ONLY A FEW ROUNDS OF AMMO AND A LOVESICK GOD OF THUNDER.
DAD, I STILL DON'T KNOW HOW YOU GOT MIXED UP IN ALL THIS TO BEGIN WITH, BUT I'M STARTING TO WISH YOU'D LEFT WELL ENOUGH ALONE!
DO WE HAVETA WADE THROUGH THIS STUFF?
THESE NOISOME WATERS MARK THE BEGINNING OF THE ANCIENT AND POWERFUL REALM OF FAERIE!
WHEN WE HAVE PASSED THROUGH THEM, WE WILL HAVE ENTERED A WORLD WHERE ALL THINGS ARE MAGICAL AND DANGEROUS.
WHA--!
BEWARE, ROGER! WE ARE ATTACKED BY WATER ELEMENTALS!
DEATH TO THOR AND HIS SERVANT! THE WILL OF MALEKITH SHALL PREVAIL!
SCHLOOOSH!
SLAY THEM AND WE SHALL FEAST TONIGHT!
THE FLESH! THE FLESH!

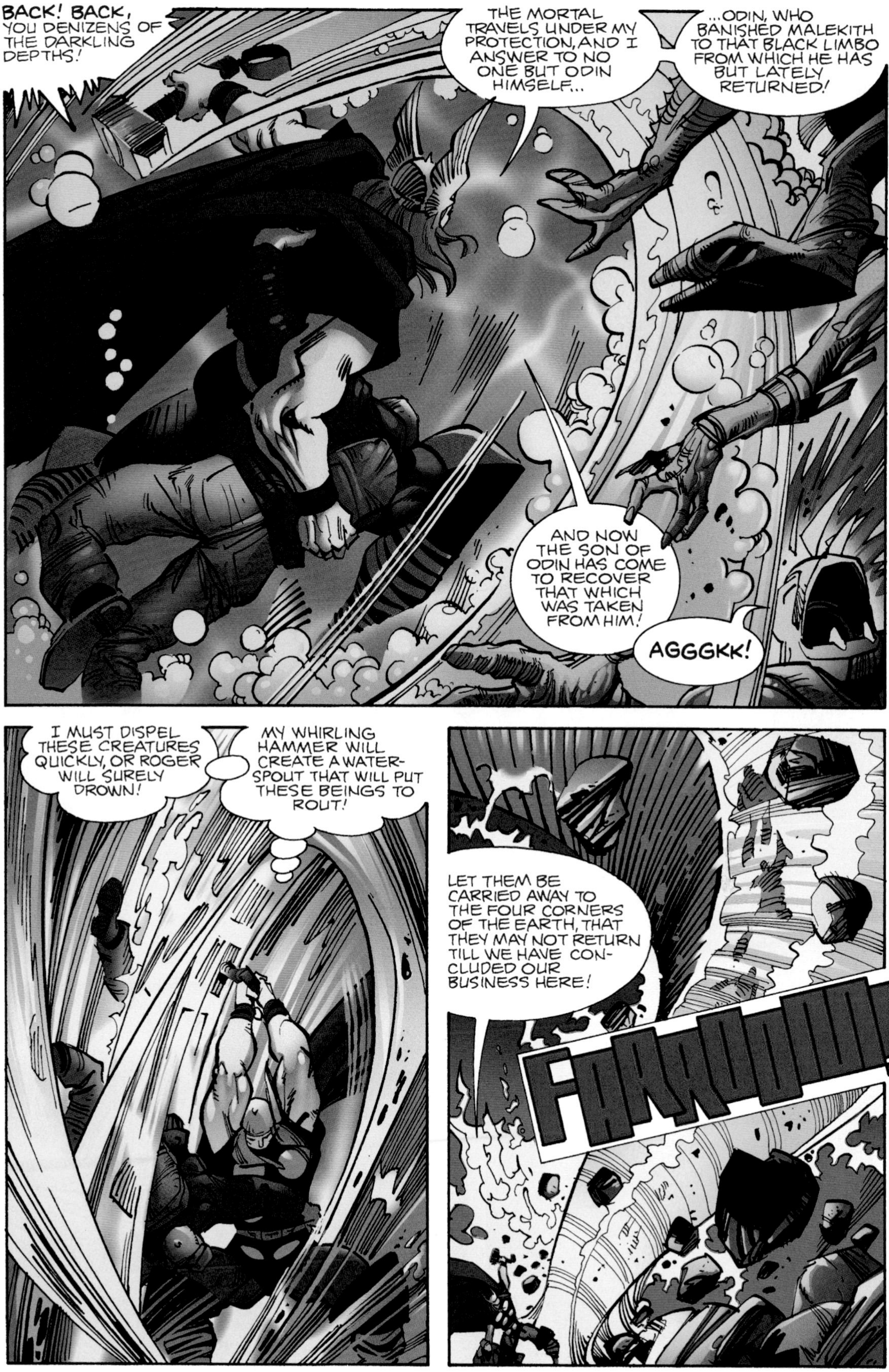
BACK! BACK, YOU DENIZENS OF THE DARKLING DEPTHS!
THE MORTAL TRAVELS UNDER MY PROTECTION, AND I ANSWER TO NO ONE BUT ODIN HIMSELF...
...ODIN, WHO BANISHED MALEKITH TO THAT BLACK LIMBO FROM WHICH HE HAS BUT LATELY RETURNED!
AND NOW THE SON OF ODIN HAS COME TO RECOVER THAT WHICH WAS TAKEN FROM HIM!
AGGGKK!
I MUST DISPEL THESE CREATURES QUICKLY, OR ROGER WILL SURELY DROWN!
MY WHIRLING HAMMER WILL CREATE A WATER-SPOUT THAT WILL PUT THESE BEINGS TO ROUT!
LET THEM BE CARRIED AWAY TO THE FOUR CORNERS OF THE EARTH, THAT THEY MAY NOT RETURN TILL WE HAVE CONCLUDED OUR BUSINESS HERE!
FARROOOM!

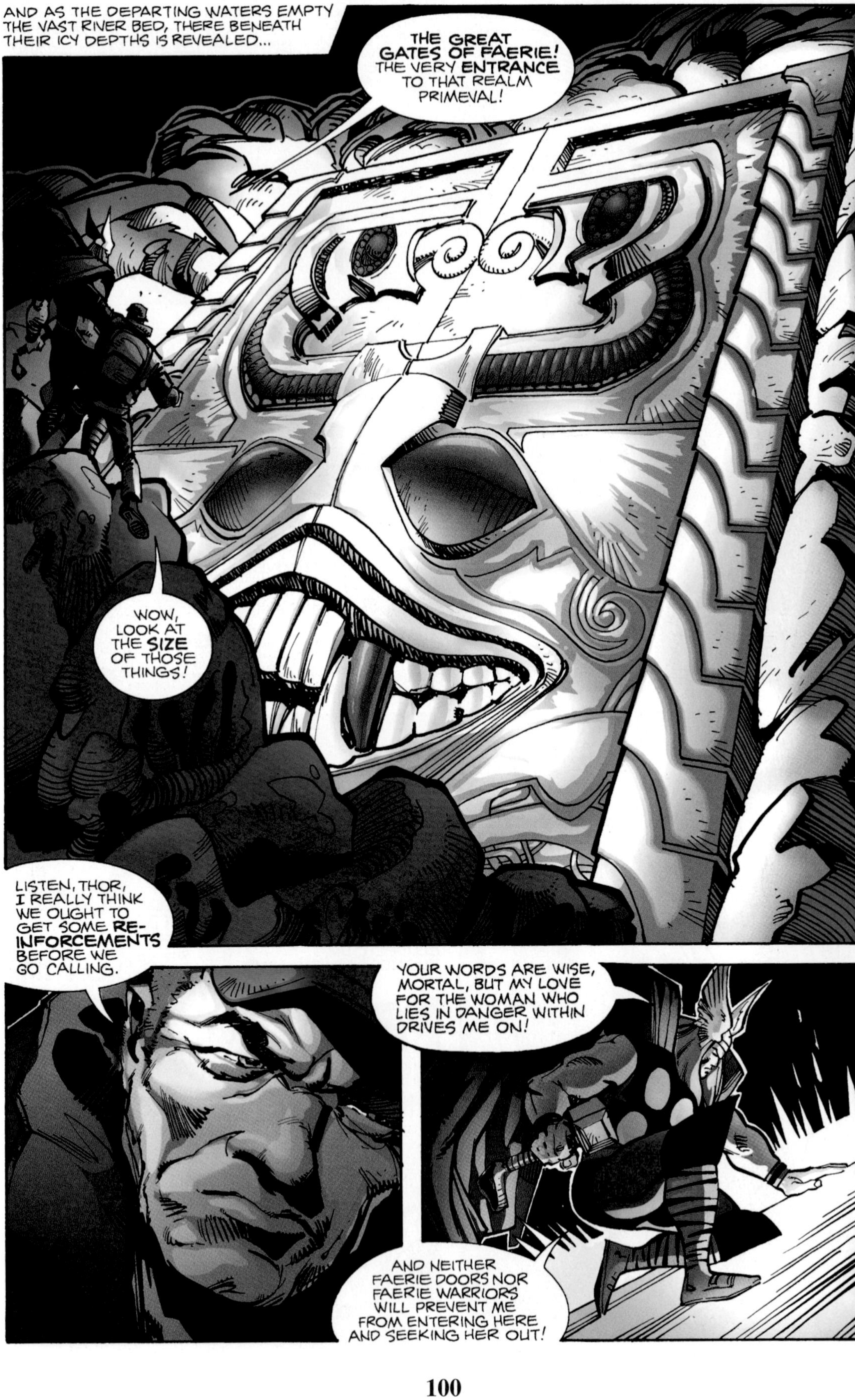
AND AS THE DEPARTING WATERS EMPTY THE VAST RIVER BED, THERE BENEATH THEIR ICY DEPTHS IS REVEALED...
THE GREAT GATES OF FAERIE! THE VERY ENTRANCE TO THAT REALM PRIMEVAL!
WOW, LOOK AT THE SIZE OF THOSE THINGS!
LISTEN, THOR, I REALLY THINK WE OUGHT TO GET SOME RE-INFORCEMENTS BEFORE WE GO CALLING.
YOUR WORDS ARE WISE, MORTAL, BUT MY LOVE FOR THE WOMAN WHO LIES IN DANGER WITHIN DRIVES ME ON!
AND NEITHER FAERIE DOORS NOR FAERIE WARRIORS WILL PREVENT ME FROM ENTERING HERE AND SEEKING HER OUT!

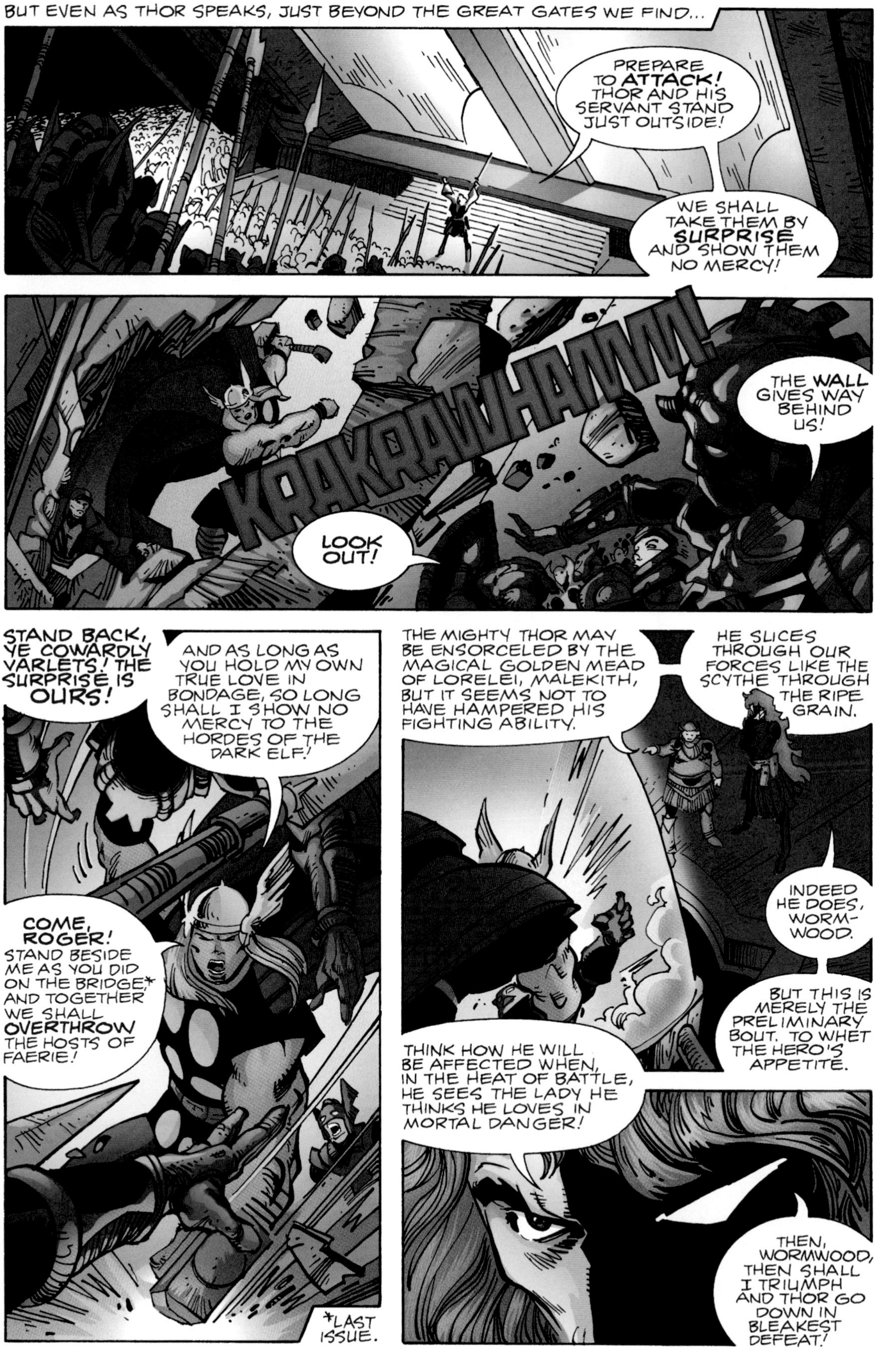

BUT EVEN AS THOR SPEAKS, JUST BEYOND THE GREAT GATES WE FIND...
PREPARE TO ATTACK! THOR AND HIS SERVANT STAND JUST OUTSIDE!
WE SHALL TAKE THEM BY SURPRISE AND SHOW THEM NO MERCY!
KRAKRAWHAMMM!
THE WALL GIVES WAY BEHIND US!
LOOK OUT!
STAND BACK, YE COWARDLY VARLETS! THE SURPRISE IS OURS!
AND AS LONG AS YOU HOLD MY OWN TRUE LOVE IN BONDAGE, SO LONG SHALL I SHOW NO MERCY TO THE HORDES OF THE DARK ELF!
COME, ROGER! STAND BESIDE ME AS YOU DID ON THE BRIDGE* AND TOGETHER WE SHALL OVERTHROW THE HOSTS OF FAERIE!
*LAST ISSUE.
THE MIGHTY THOR MAY BE ENSORCELED BY THE MAGICAL GOLDEN MEAD OF LORELEI, MALEKITH, BUT IT SEEMS NOT TO HAVE HAMPERED HIS FIGHTING ABILITY.
HE SLICES THROUGH OUR FORCES LIKE THE SCYTHE THROUGH THE RIPE GRAIN.
INDEED HE DOES, WORM-WOOD.
BUT THIS IS MERELY THE PRELIMINARY BOUT, TO WHET THE HERO'S APPETITE.
THINK HOW HE WILL BE AFFECTED WHEN, IN THE HEAT OF BATTLE, HE SEES THE LADY HE THINKS HE LOVES IN MORTAL DANGER!
THEN, WORMWOOD, THEN SHALL I TRIUMPH AND THOR GO DOWN IN BLEAKEST DEFEAT!

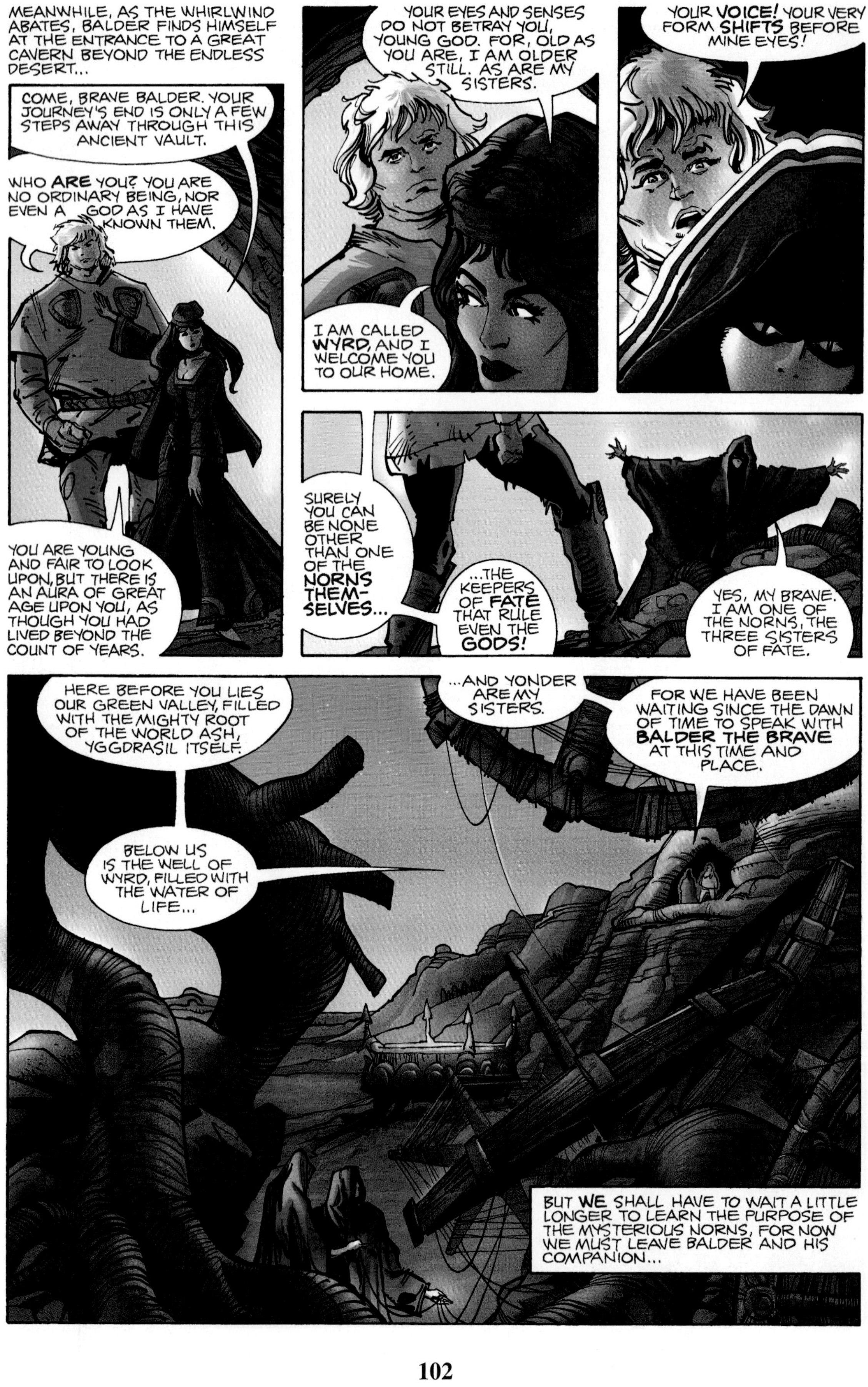
MEANWHILE, AS THE WHIRLWIND ABATES, BALDER FINDS HIMSELF AT THE ENTRANCE TO A GREAT CAVERN BEYOND THE ENDLESS DESERT...
COME, BRAVE BALDER. YOUR JOURNEY'S END IS ONLY A FEW STEPS AWAY THROUGH THIS ANCIENT VAULT.
WHO ARE YOU? YOU ARE NO ORDINARY BEING, NOR EVEN A GOD AS I HAVE KNOWN THEM.
YOU ARE YOUNG AND FAIR TO LOOK UPON, BUT THERE IS AN AURA OF GREAT AGE UPON YOU, AS THOUGH YOU HAD LIVED BEYOND THE COUNT OF YEARS.
YOUR EYES AND SENSES DO NOT BETRAY YOU, YOUNG GOD. FOR, OLD AS YOU ARE, I AM OLDER STILL. AS ARE MY SISTERS.
I AM CALLED WYRD, AND I WELCOME YOU TO OUR HOME.
YOUR VOICE! YOUR VERY FORM SHIFTS BEFORE MINE EYES!
SURELY YOU CAN BE NONE OTHER THAN ONE OF THE NORNS THEMSELVES...
...THE KEEPERS OF FATE THAT RULE EVEN THE GODS!
YES, MY BRAVE. I AM ONE OF THE NORNS, THE THREE SISTERS OF FATE.
HERE BEFORE YOU LIES OUR GREEN VALLEY, FILLED WITH THE MIGHTY ROOT OF THE WORLD ASH, YGGDRASIL ITSELF.
BELOW US IS THE WELL OF WYRD, FILLED WITH THE WATER OF LIFE...
...AND YONDER ARE MY SISTERS.
FOR WE HAVE BEEN WAITING SINCE THE DAWN OF TIME TO SPEAK WITH BALDER THE BRAVE AT THIS TIME AND PLACE.
BUT WE SHALL HAVE TO WAIT A LITTLE LONGER TO LEARN THE PURPOSE OF THE MYSTERIOUS NORNS, FOR NOW WE MUST LEAVE BALDER AND HIS COMPANION...

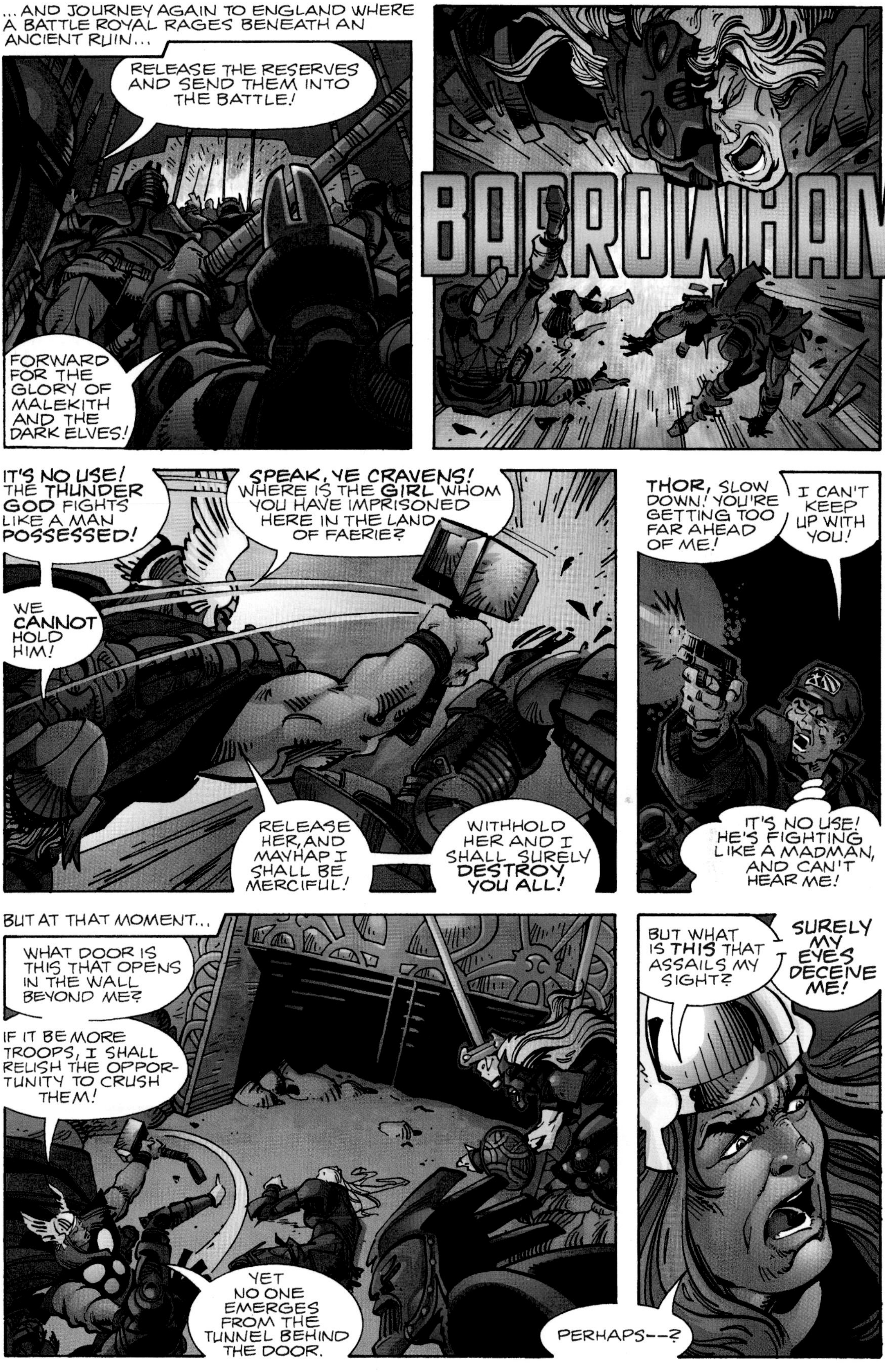
...AND JOURNEY AGAIN TO ENGLAND WHERE A BATTLE ROYAL RAGES BENEATH AN ANCIENT RUIN...
RELEASE THE RESERVES AND SEND THEM INTO THE BATTLE!
FORWARD FOR THE GLORY OF MALEKITH AND THE DARK ELVES!
BARROWHAM
IT'S NO USE! THE THUNDER GOD FIGHTS LIKE A MAN POSSESSED!
SPEAK, YE CRAVENS! WHERE IS THE GIRL WHOM YOU HAVE IMPRISONED HERE IN THE LAND OF FAERIE?
WE CANNOT HOLD HIM!
RELEASE HER, AND MAYHAP I SHALL BE MERCIFUL!
WITHHOLD HER AND I SHALL SURELY DESTROY YOU ALL!
THOR, SLOW DOWN! YOU'RE GETTING TOO FAR AHEAD OF ME!
I CAN'T KEEP UP WITH YOU!
IT'S NO USE! HE'S FIGHTING LIKE A MADMAN, AND CAN'T HEAR ME!
BUT AT THAT MOMENT...
WHAT DOOR IS THIS THAT OPENS IN THE WALL BEYOND ME?
IF IT BE MORE TROOPS, I SHALL RELISH THE OPPORTUNITY TO CRUSH THEM!
YET NO ONE EMERGES FROM THE TUNNEL BEHIND THE DOOR.
BUT WHAT IS THIS THAT ASSAILS MY SIGHT?
SURELY MY EYES DECEIVE ME!
PERHAPS--?

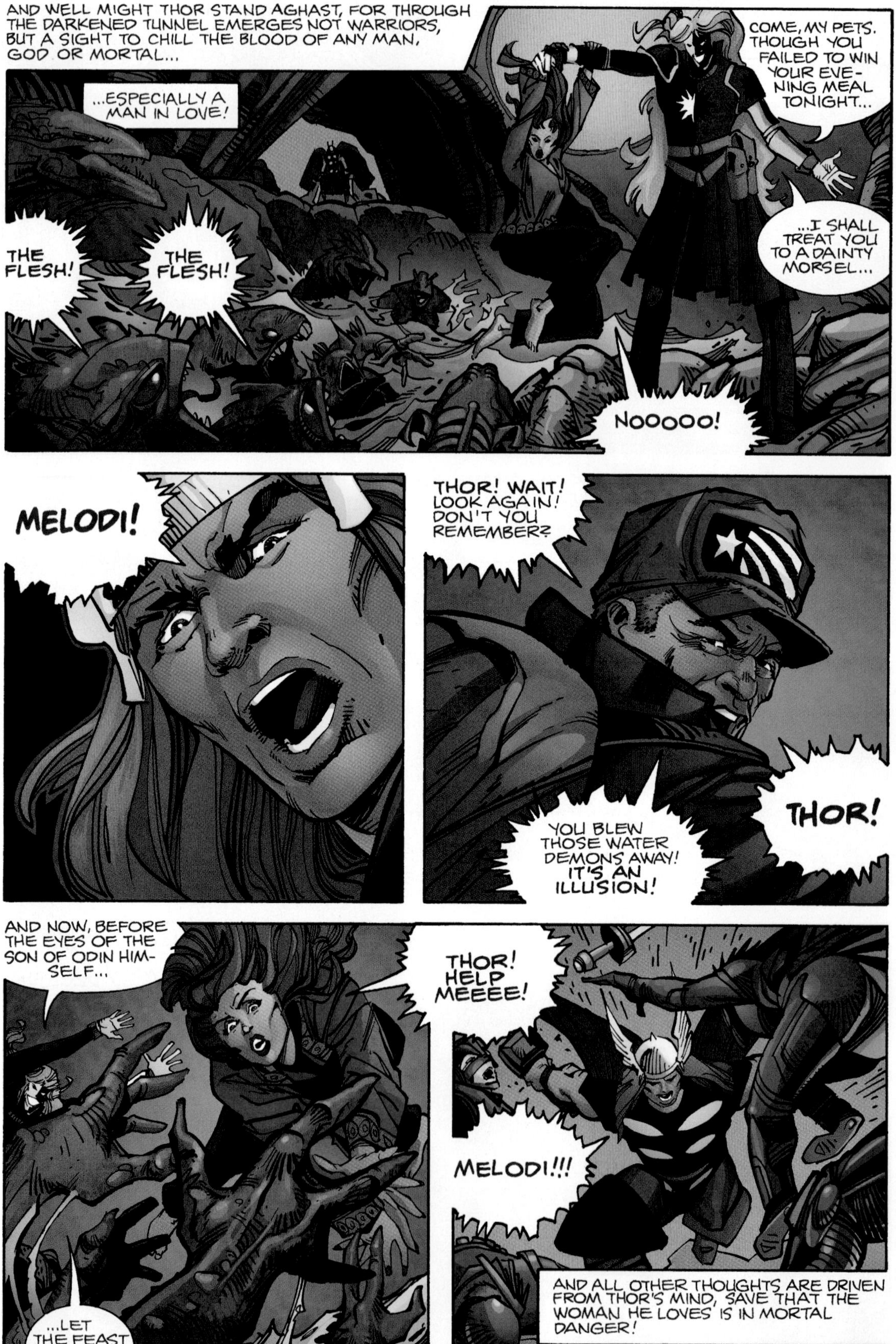

AND WELL MIGHT THOR STAND AGHAST, FOR THROUGH THE DARKENED TUNNEL EMERGES NOT WARRIORS, BUT A SIGHT TO CHILL THE BLOOD OF ANY MAN, GOD OR MORTAL...
...ESPECIALLY A MAN IN LOVE!
COME, MY PETS. THOUGH YOU FAILED TO WIN YOUR EVENING MEAL TONIGHT...
...I SHALL TREAT YOU TO A DAINTY MORSEL...
THE FLESH!
THE FLESH!
NOOOOO!
MELODI!
THOR! WAIT! LOOK AGAIN! DON'T YOU REMEMBER?
THOR!
YOU BLEW THOSE WATER DEMONS AWAY! IT'S AN ILLUSION!
AND NOW, BEFORE THE EYES OF THE SON OF ODIN HIMSELF...
...LET THE FEAST BEGIN!
THOR! HELP MEEEE!
MELODI!!!
AND ALL OTHER THOUGHTS ARE DRIVEN FROM THOR'S MIND, SAVE THAT THE WOMAN HE LOVES IS IN MORTAL DANGER!

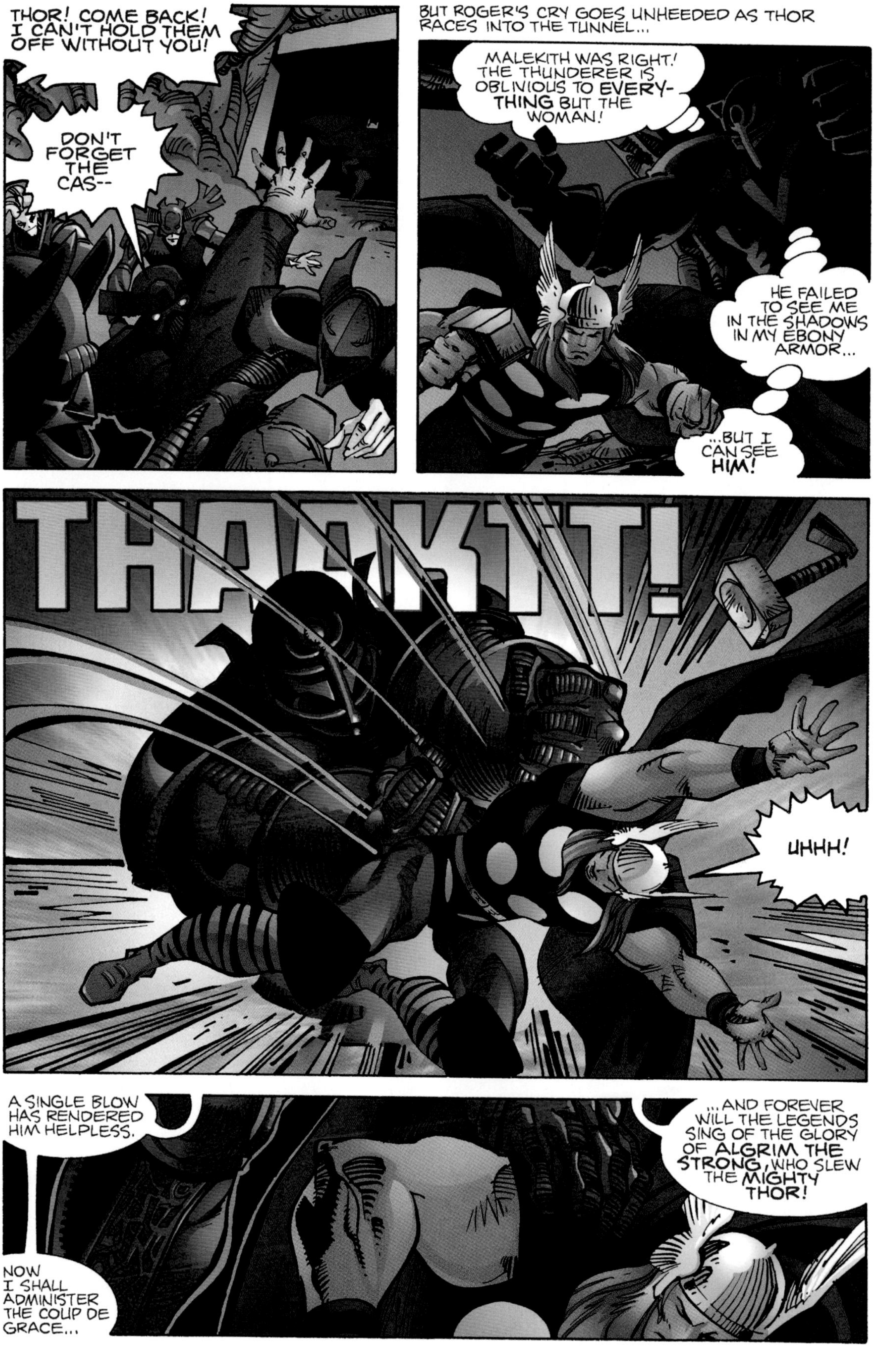
THOR! COME BACK! I CAN'T HOLD THEM OFF WITHOUT YOU!
DON'T FORGET THE CAS--
BUT ROGER'S CRY GOES UNHEEDED AS THOR RACES INTO THE TUNNEL...
MALEKITH WAS RIGHT! THE THUNDERER IS OBLIVIOUS TO EVERY-THING BUT THE WOMAN!
HE FAILED TO SEE ME IN THE SHADOWS IN MY EBONY ARMOR...
...BUT I CAN SEE HIM!
THAKTT!
UHHH!
A SINGLE BLOW HAS RENDERED HIM HELPLESS.
...AND FOREVER WILL THE LEGENDS SING OF THE GLORY OF ALGRIM THE STRONG, WHO SLEW THE MIGHTY THOR!
NOW I SHALL ADMINISTER THE COUP DE GRACE...

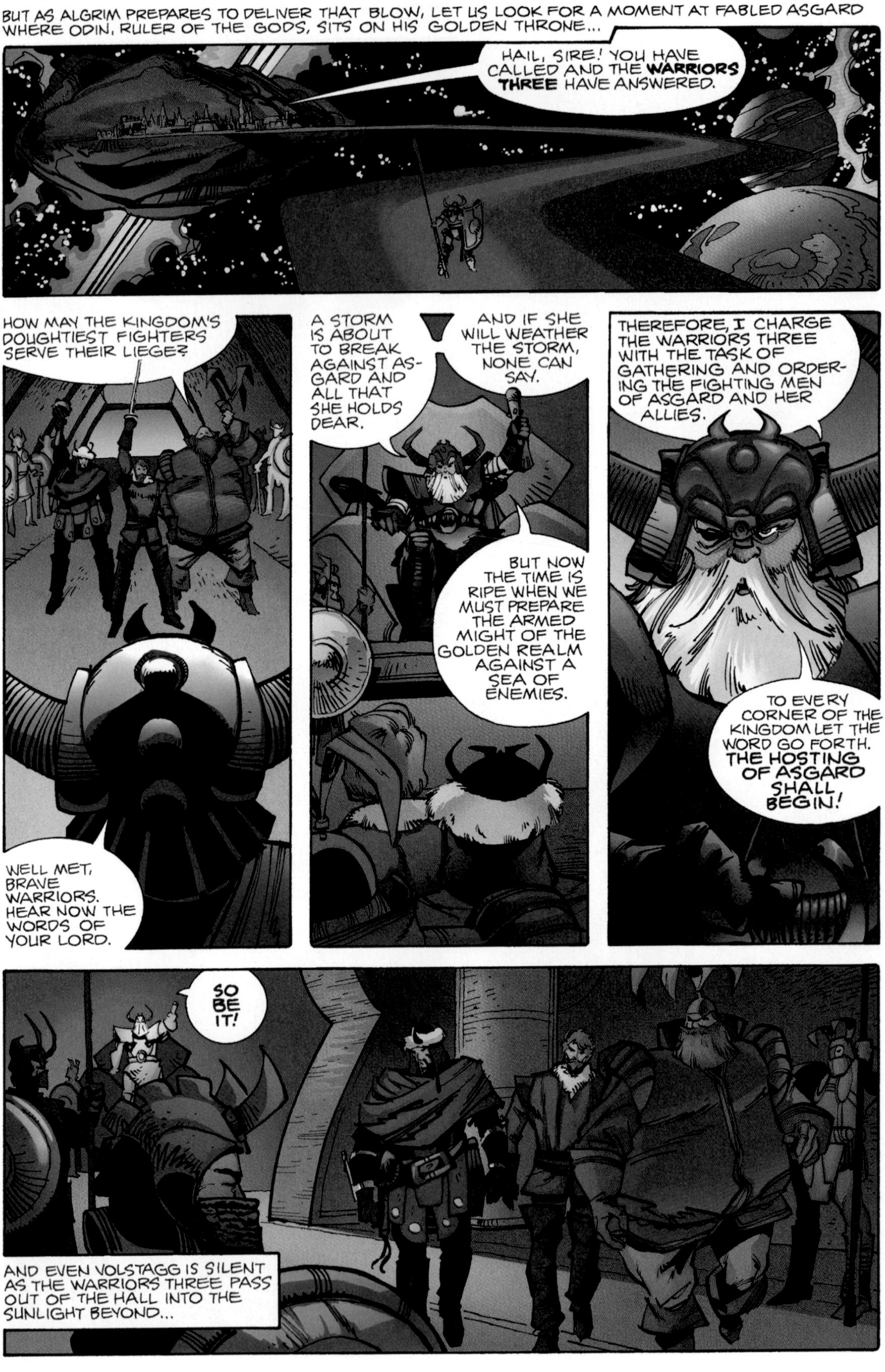

BUT AS ALGRIM PREPARES TO DELIVER THAT BLOW, LET US LOOK FOR A MOMENT AT FABLED ASGARD WHERE ODIN, RULER OF THE GODS, SITS ON HIS GOLDEN THRONE...
HAIL, SIRE! YOU HAVE CALLED AND THE WARRIORS THREE HAVE ANSWERED.
HOW MAY THE KINGDOM'S DOUGHTIEST FIGHTERS SERVE THEIR LIEGE?
WELL MET, BRAVE WARRIORS. HEAR NOW THE WORDS OF YOUR LORD.
A STORM IS ABOUT TO BREAK AGAINST ASGARD AND ALL THAT SHE HOLDS DEAR.
AND IF SHE WILL WEATHER THE STORM, NONE CAN SAY.
BUT NOW THE TIME IS RIPE WHEN WE MUST PREPARE THE ARMED MIGHT OF THE GOLDEN REALM AGAINST A SEA OF ENEMIES.
THEREFORE, I CHARGE THE WARRIORS THREE WITH THE TASK OF GATHERING AND ORDERING THE FIGHTING MEN OF ASGARD AND HER ALLIES.
TO EVERY CORNER OF THE KINGDOM LET THE WORD GO FORTH. THE HOSTING OF ASGARD SHALL BEGIN!
SO BE IT!
AND EVEN VOLSTAGG IS SILENT AS THE WARRIORS THREE PASS OUT OF THE HALL INTO THE SUNLIGHT BEYOND...

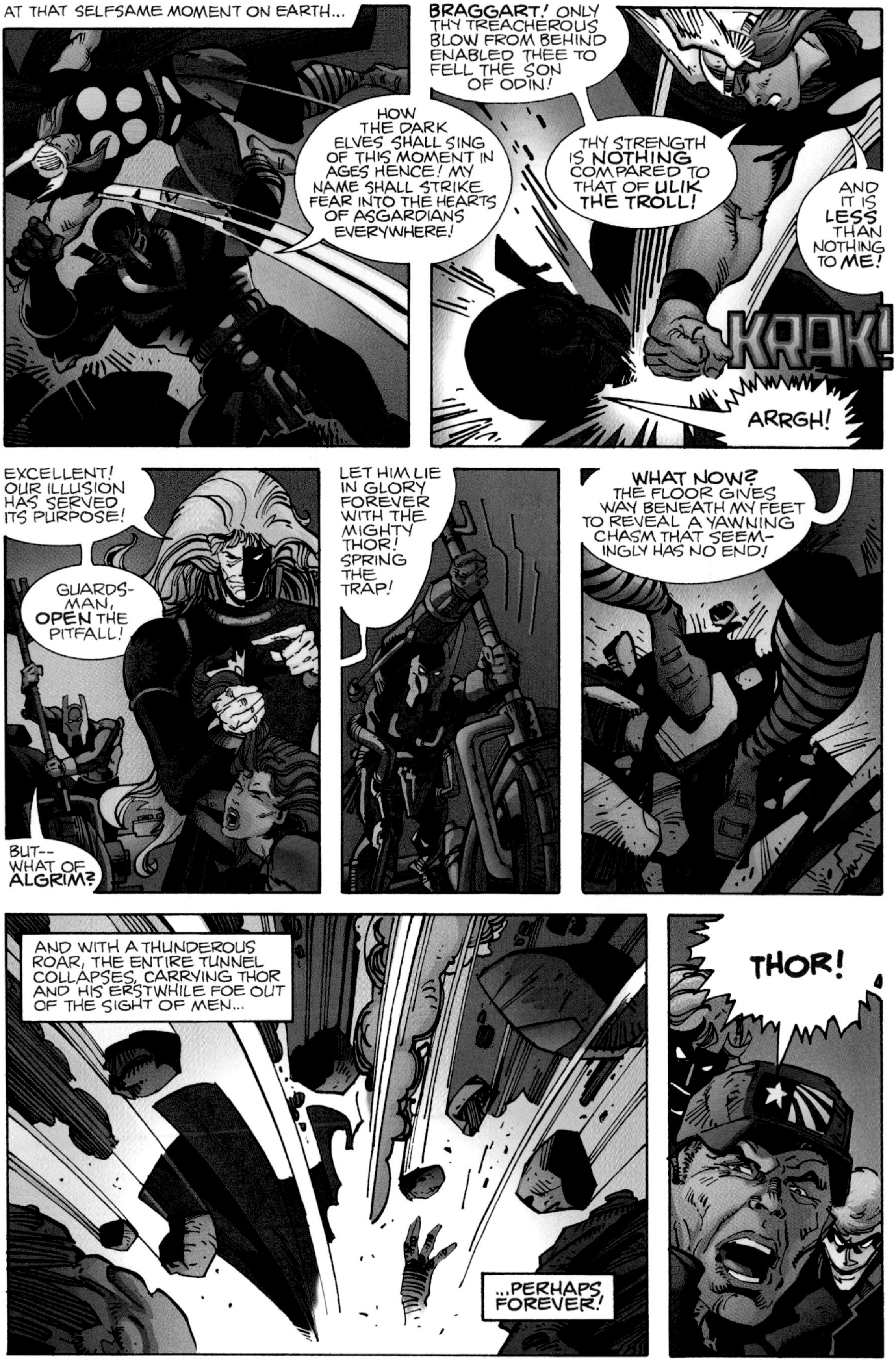
AT THAT SELFSAME MOMENT ON EARTH...
HOW THE DARK ELVES SHALL SING OF THIS MOMENT IN AGES HENCE! MY NAME SHALL STRIKE FEAR INTO THE HEARTS OF ASGARDIANS EVERYWHERE!
BRAGGART! ONLY THY TREACHEROUS BLOW FROM BEHIND ENABLED THEE TO FELL THE SON OF ODIN!
THY STRENGTH IS NOTHING COMPARED TO THAT OF ULIK THE TROLL!
AND IT IS LESS THAN NOTHING TO ME!
KRAK!
ARRGH!
EXCELLENT! OUR ILLUSION HAS SERVED ITS PURPOSE!
GUARDSMAN, OPEN THE PITFALL!
BUT-- WHAT OF ALGRIM?
LET HIM LIE IN GLORY FOREVER WITH THE MIGHTY THOR! SPRING THE TRAP!
WHAT NOW? THE FLOOR GIVES WAY BENEATH MY FEET TO REVEAL A YAWNING CHASM THAT SEEMINGLY HAS NO END!
AND WITH A THUNDEROUS ROAR, THE ENTIRE TUNNEL COLLAPSES, CARRYING THOR AND HIS ERSTWHILE FOE OUT OF THE SIGHT OF MEN...
...PERHAPS FOREVER!
THOR!

ROGER'S CALL IS ALL BUT DROWNED OUT BY THE ROARING AVALANCHE THAT FOLLOWS THOR AND ALGRIM INTO THE BOTTOMLESS CHASM...

...UNTIL THE LAST ECHOES HAVE DIED AWAY AND ONLY SILENCE REMAINS.

AT LAST I AM REVENGED UPON ODIN FOR MY BANISHMENT. FAREWELL, THOR.

YOU WERE NO MATCH FOR MALEKITH THE ACCURSED!

...AN AVALANCHE THAT SHAKES THE VERY ROOTS OF THE FAERIE KINGDOM...

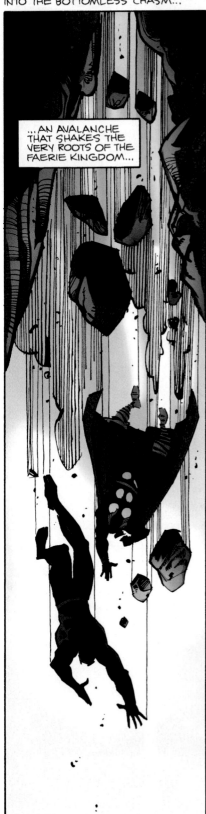

WHAT ABOUT THE WOMAN, LORD?

SHE'S YOURS, WORMWOOD. DO WITH HER WHAT YOU WILL.

BUT TREAT HER AS SHE DESERVES. AFTER ALL, HER GOLDEN MEAD ENABLED US TO DEFEAT THE GOD OF THUNDER.

I WISH TO SEE OUR OTHER MORTAL GUEST.

SO YOU ARE ERIC'S WHELP, EH?

HOW APPROPRIATE THAT THE SON SHOULD RECOVER THE TREASURE WHICH HIS FATHER STOLE FROM ME SO MANY EONS AGO.

OPEN HIS KNAPSACK!

AT LAST! THE CASKET OF ANCIENT WINTERS IS MINE ONCE MORE!

AND WOE TO THE WORLD THAT IT SHOULD BE SO!

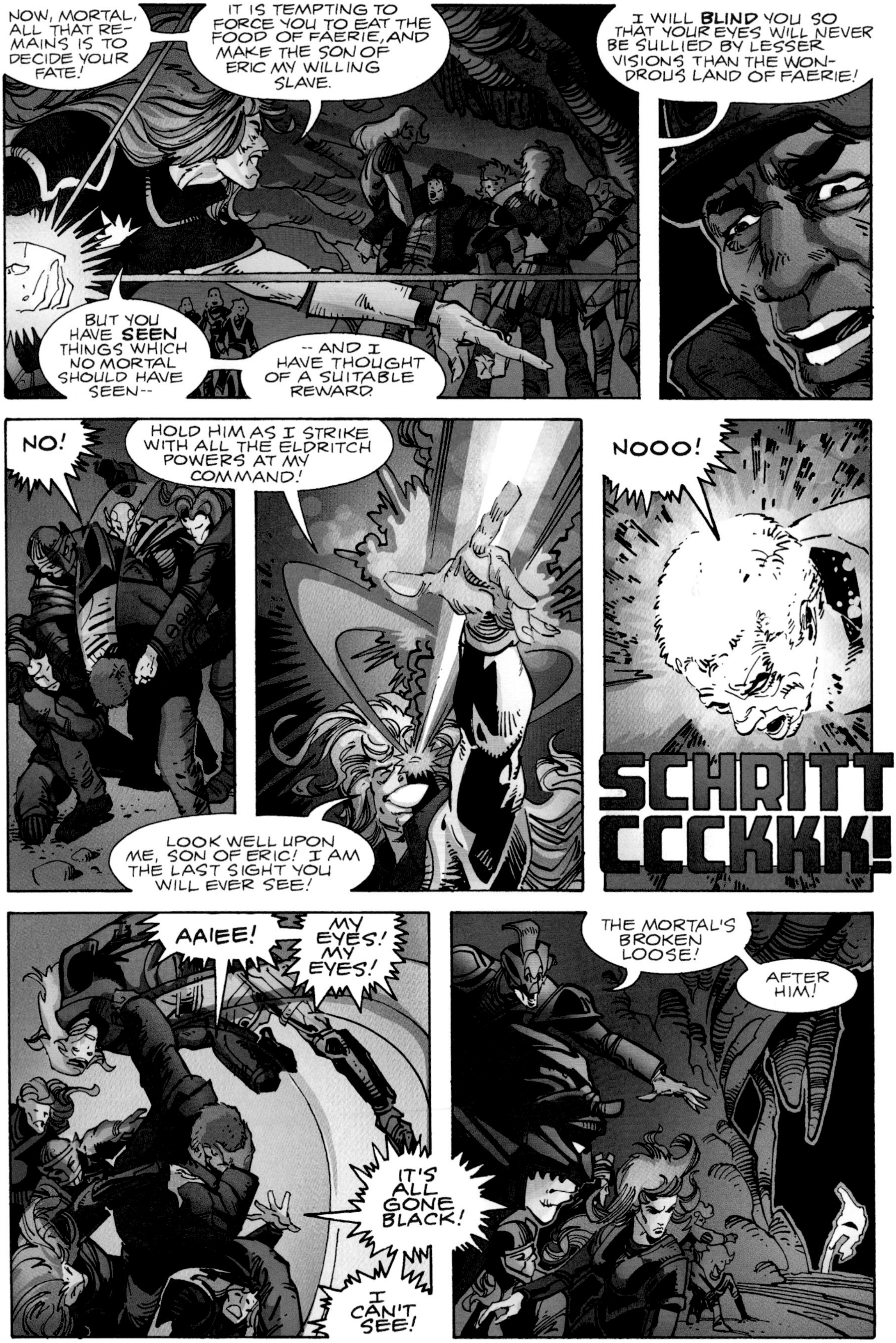
NOW, MORTAL, ALL THAT RE-MAINS IS TO DECIDE YOUR FATE!
IT IS TEMPTING TO FORCE YOU TO EAT THE FOOD OF FAERIE, AND MAKE THE SON OF ERIC MY WILLING SLAVE.
BUT YOU HAVE SEEN THINGS WHICH NO MORTAL SHOULD HAVE SEEN--
-- AND I HAVE THOUGHT OF A SUITABLE REWARD.
I WILL BLIND YOU SO THAT YOUR EYES WILL NEVER BE SULLIED BY LESSER VISIONS THAN THE WON-DROUS LAND OF FAERIE!
NO!
HOLD HIM AS I STRIKE WITH ALL THE ELDRITCH POWERS AT MY COMMAND!
LOOK WELL UPON ME, SON OF ERIC! I AM THE LAST SIGHT YOU WILL EVER SEE!
NOOO!
SCHRITT CCCKKK!
AAIEE!
MY EYES! MY EYES!
IT'S ALL GONE BLACK!
I CAN'T SEE!
THE MORTAL'S BROKEN LOOSE!
AFTER HIM!

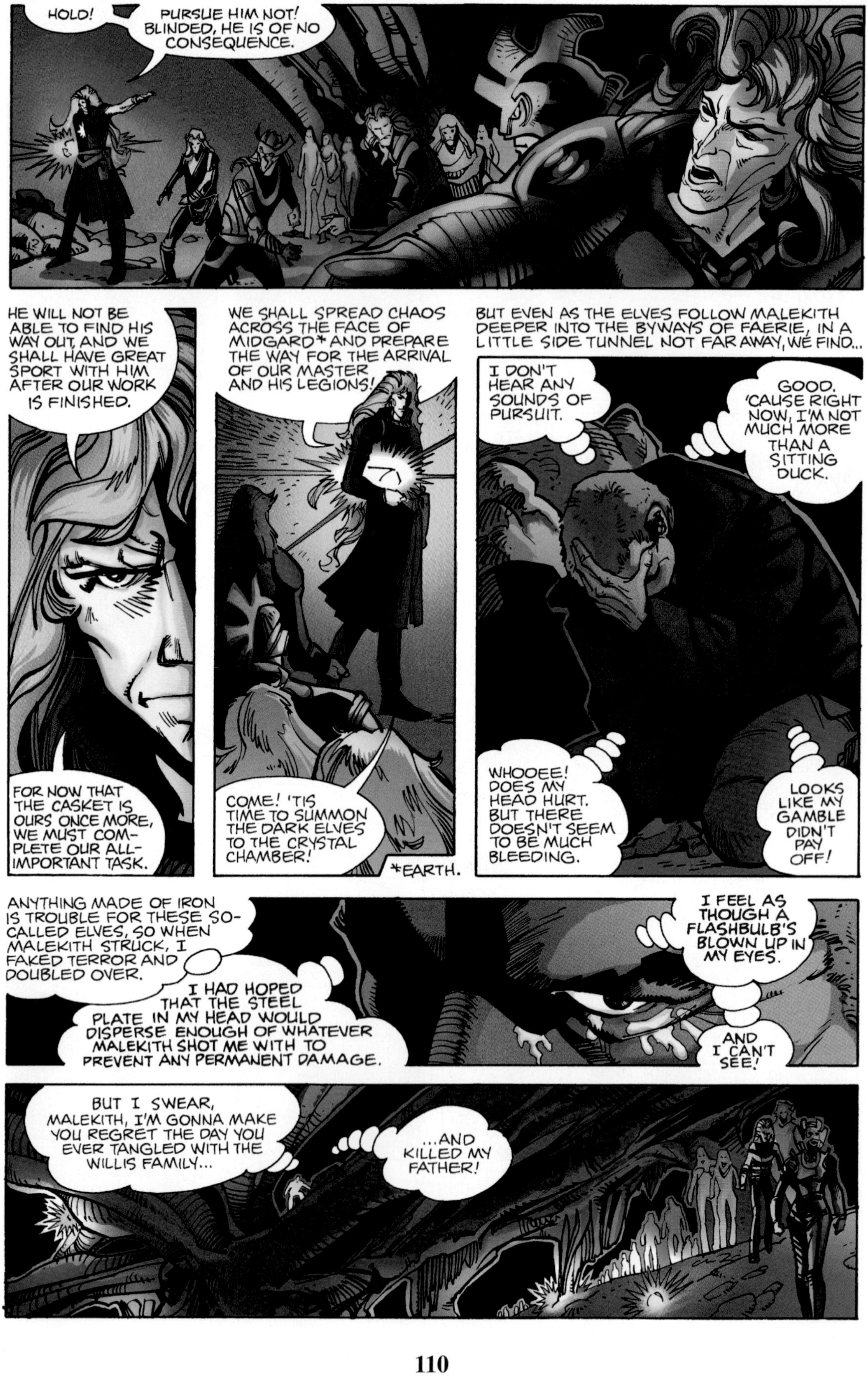
HOLD!
PURSUE HIM NOT! BLINDED, HE IS OF NO CONSEQUENCE.
HE WILL NOT BE ABLE TO FIND HIS WAY OUT, AND WE SHALL HAVE GREAT SPORT WITH HIM AFTER OUR WORK IS FINISHED.
FOR NOW THAT THE CASKET IS OURS ONCE MORE, WE MUST COMPLETE OUR ALL-IMPORTANT TASK.
WE SHALL SPREAD CHAOS ACROSS THE FACE OF MIDGARD* AND PREPARE THE WAY FOR THE ARRIVAL OF OUR MASTER AND HIS LEGIONS!
COME! 'TIS TIME TO SUMMON THE DARK ELVES TO THE CRYSTAL CHAMBER!
*EARTH.
BUT EVEN AS THE ELVES FOLLOW MALEKITH DEEPER INTO THE BYWAYS OF FAERIE, IN A LITTLE SIDE TUNNEL NOT FAR AWAY, WE FIND...
I DON'T HEAR ANY SOUNDS OF PURSUIT.
GOOD. 'CAUSE RIGHT NOW, I'M NOT MUCH MORE THAN A SITTING DUCK.
WHOOEE! DOES MY HEAD HURT. BUT THERE DOESN'T SEEM TO BE MUCH BLEEDING.
LOOKS LIKE MY GAMBLE DIDN'T PAY OFF!
ANYTHING MADE OF IRON IS TROUBLE FOR THESE SO-CALLED ELVES, SO WHEN MALEKITH STRUCK, I FAKED TERROR AND DOUBLED OVER.
I HAD HOPED THAT THE STEEL PLATE IN MY HEAD WOULD DISPERSE ENOUGH OF WHATEVER MALEKITH SHOT ME WITH TO PREVENT ANY PERMANENT DAMAGE.
I FEEL AS THOUGH A FLASHBULB'S BLOWN UP IN MY EYES.
AND I CAN'T SEE!
BUT I SWEAR, MALEKITH, I'M GONNA MAKE YOU REGRET THE DAY YOU EVER TANGLED WITH THE WILLIS FAMILY...
...AND KILLED MY FATHER!

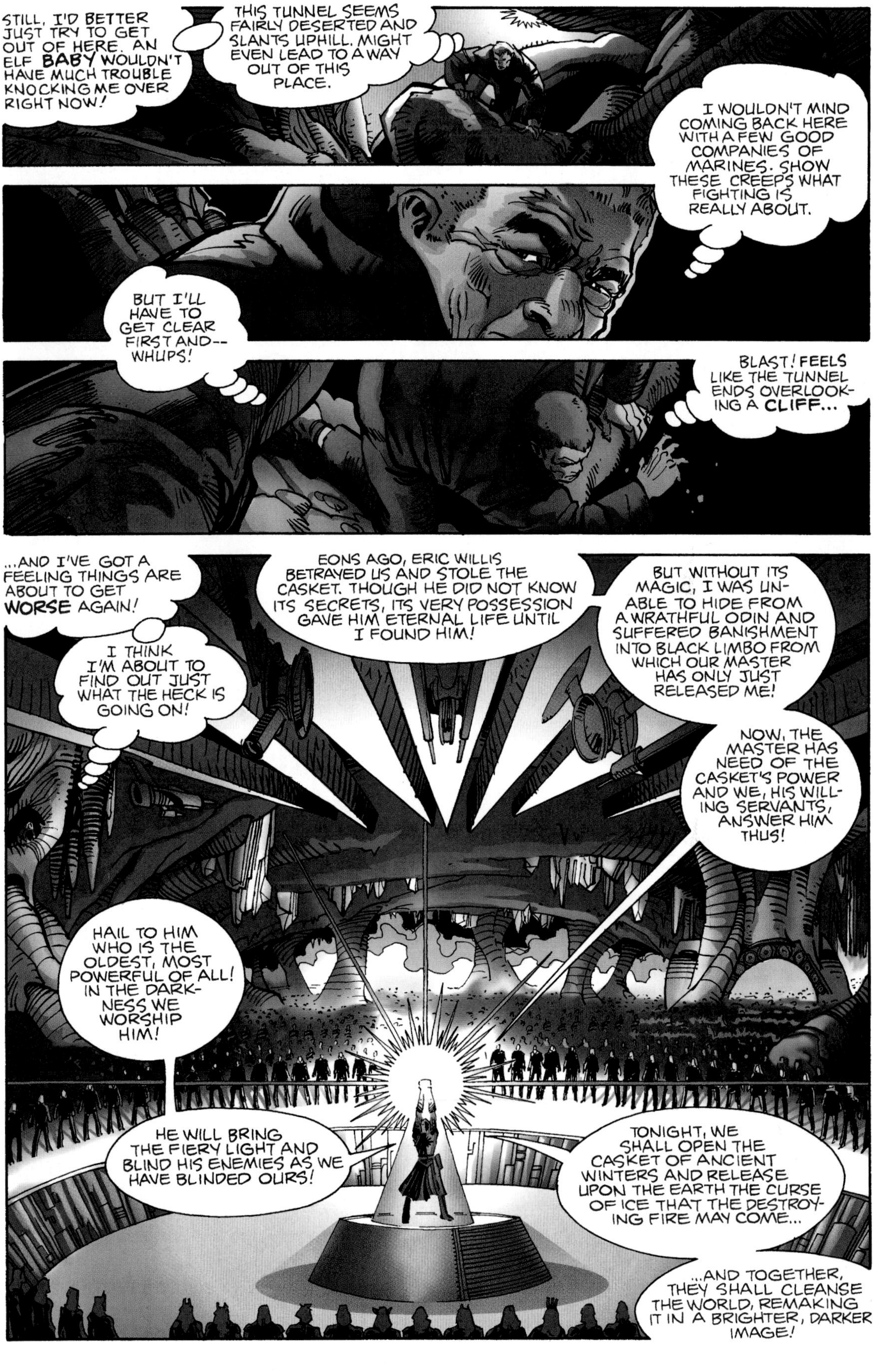
STILL, I'D BETTER JUST TRY TO GET OUT OF HERE. AN ELF BABY WOULDN'T HAVE MUCH TROUBLE KNOCKING ME OVER RIGHT NOW!
THIS TUNNEL SEEMS FAIRLY DESERTED AND SLANTS UPHILL. MIGHT EVEN LEAD TO A WAY OUT OF THIS PLACE.
I WOULDN'T MIND COMING BACK HERE WITH A FEW GOOD COMPANIES OF MARINES. SHOW THESE CREEPS WHAT FIGHTING IS REALLY ABOUT.
BUT I'LL HAVE TO GET CLEAR FIRST AND-- WHUPS!
BLAST! FEELS LIKE THE TUNNEL ENDS OVERLOOKING A CLIFF...
...AND I'VE GOT A FEELING THINGS ARE ABOUT TO GET WORSE AGAIN!
I THINK I'M ABOUT TO FIND OUT JUST WHAT THE HECK IS GOING ON!
EONS AGO, ERIC WILLIS BETRAYED US AND STOLE THE CASKET. THOUGH HE DID NOT KNOW ITS SECRETS, ITS VERY POSSESSION GAVE HIM ETERNAL LIFE UNTIL I FOUND HIM!
BUT WITHOUT ITS MAGIC, I WAS UNABLE TO HIDE FROM A WRATHFUL ODIN AND SUFFERED BANISHMENT INTO BLACK LIMBO FROM WHICH OUR MASTER HAS ONLY JUST RELEASED ME!
NOW, THE MASTER HAS NEED OF THE CASKET'S POWER AND WE, HIS WILLING SERVANTS, ANSWER HIM THUS!
HAIL TO HIM WHO IS THE OLDEST, MOST POWERFUL OF ALL! IN THE DARKNESS WE WORSHIP HIM!
HE WILL BRING THE FIERY LIGHT AND BLIND HIS ENEMIES AS WE HAVE BLINDED OURS!
TONIGHT, WE SHALL OPEN THE CASKET OF ANCIENT WINTERS AND RELEASE UPON THE EARTH THE CURSE OF ICE THAT THE DESTROYING FIRE MAY COME...
...AND TOGETHER, THEY SHALL CLEANSE THE WORLD, REMAKING IT IN A BRIGHTER, DARKER IMAGE!

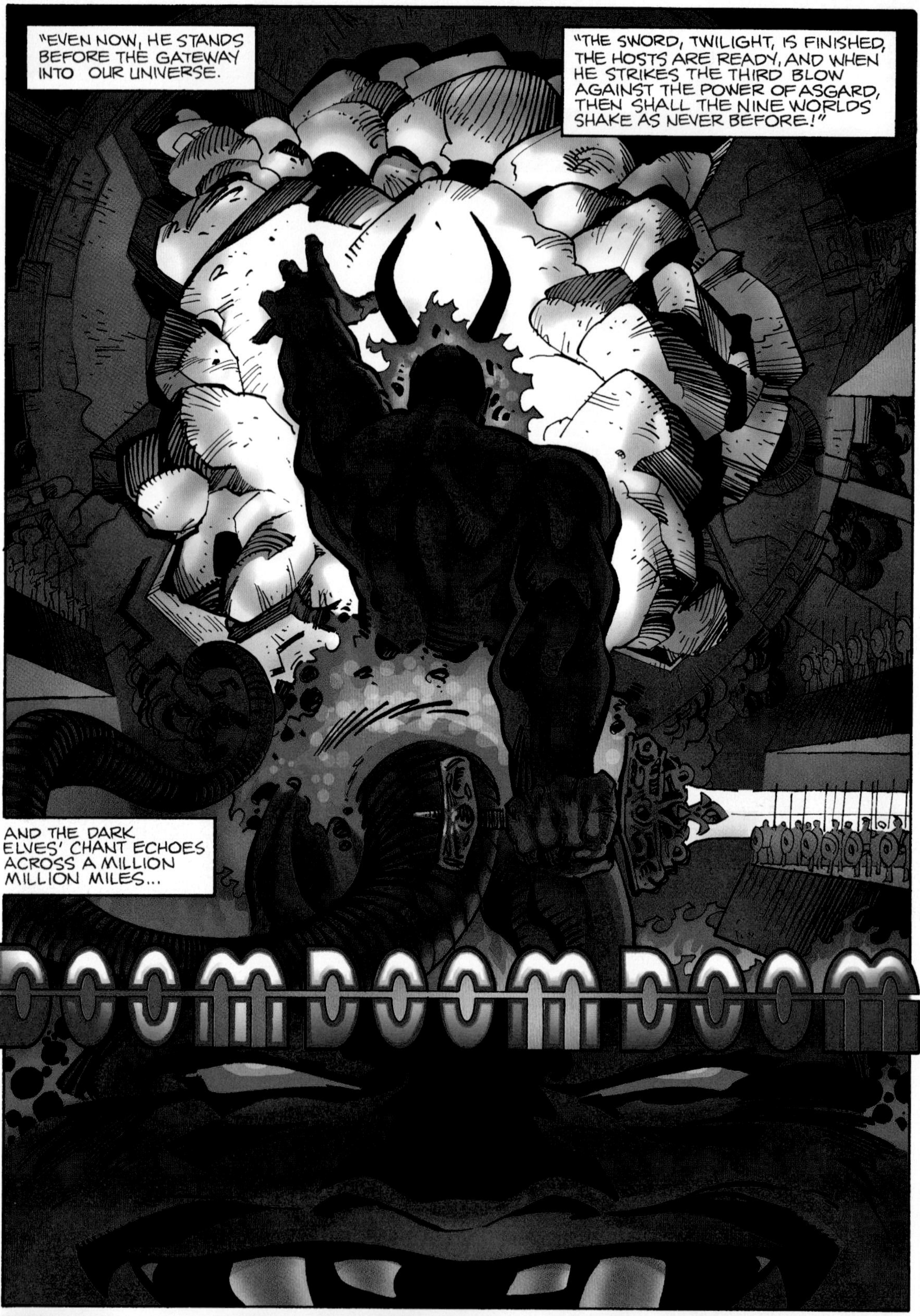
"EVEN NOW, HE STANDS BEFORE THE GATEWAY INTO OUR UNIVERSE.
"THE SWORD, TWILIGHT, IS FINISHED, THE HOSTS ARE READY, AND WHEN HE STRIKES THE THIRD BLOW AGAINST THE POWER OF ASGARD, THEN SHALL THE NINE WORLDS SHAKE AS NEVER BEFORE!"
AND THE DARK ELVES' CHANT ECHOES ACROSS A MILLION MILLION MILES...
DOOM DOOM DOOM
NEXT: THE DARK AND THE LIGHT!

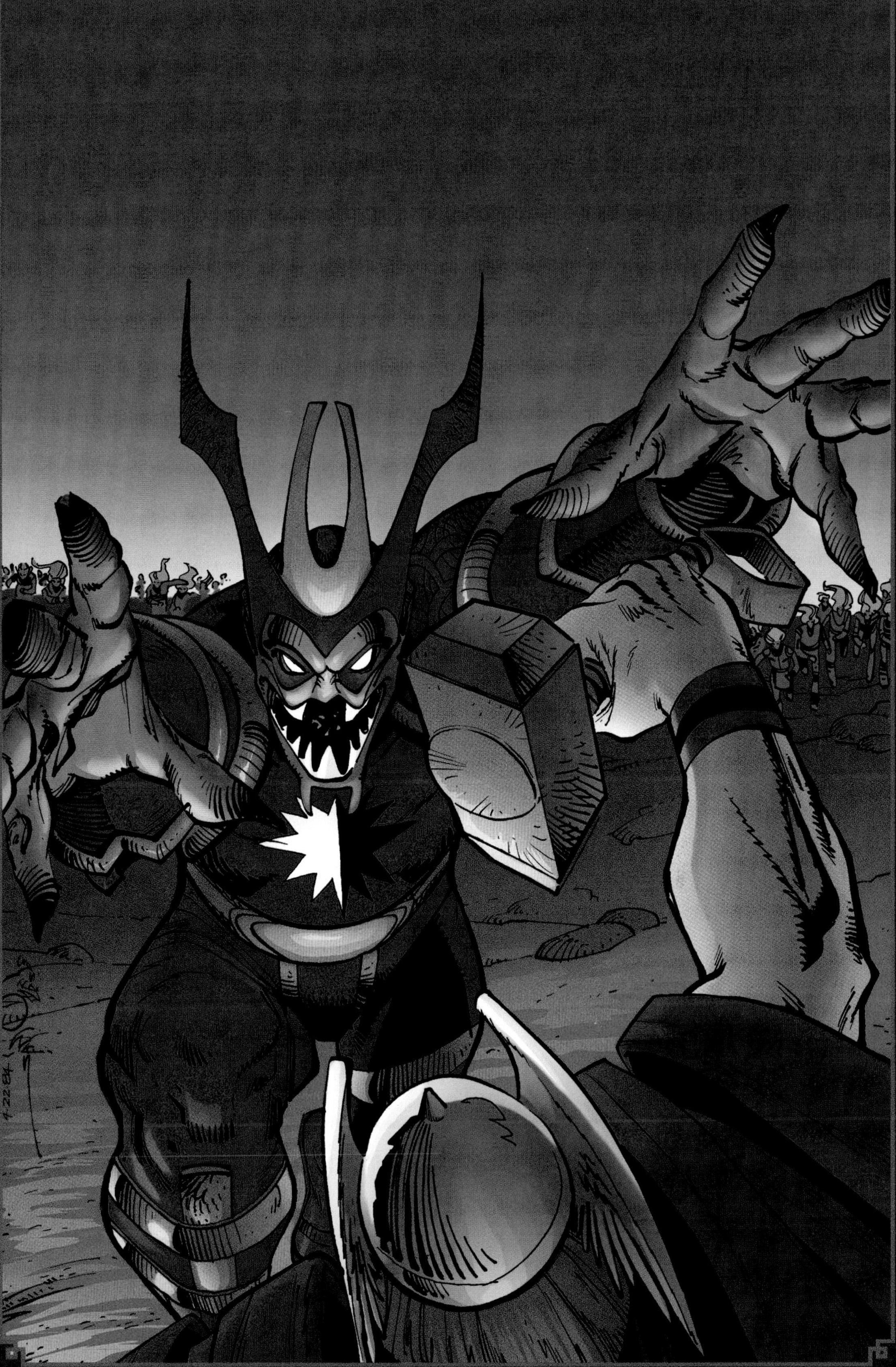

THOR (1966) #348

STAN LEE PRESENTS: the MIGHTY THOR®

# THE DARK AND THE LIGHT

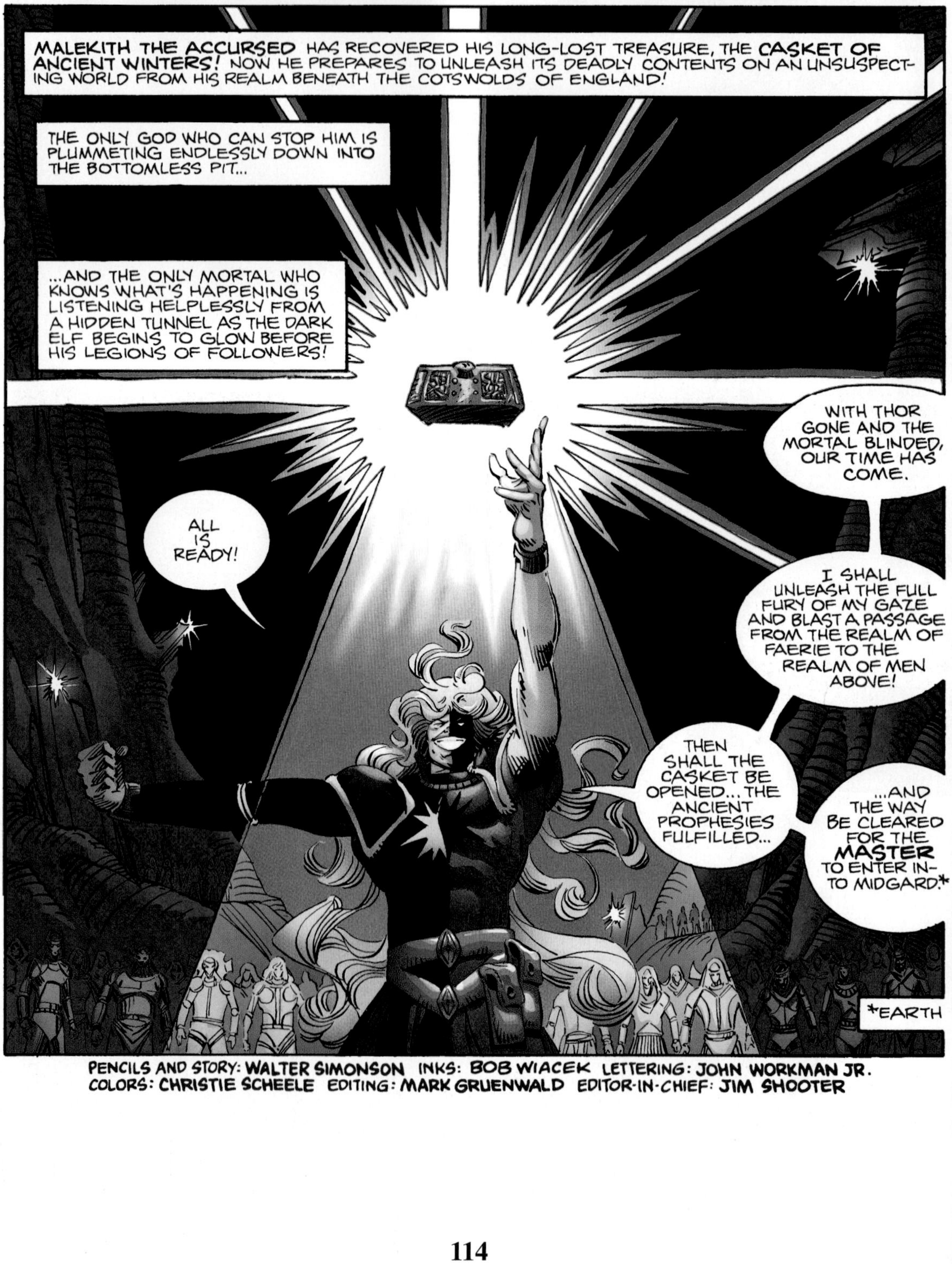

MALEKITH THE ACCURSED HAS RECOVERED HIS LONG-LOST TREASURE, THE CASKET OF ANCIENT WINTERS! NOW HE PREPARES TO UNLEASH ITS DEADLY CONTENTS ON AN UNSUSPECTING WORLD FROM HIS REALM BENEATH THE COTSWOLDS OF ENGLAND!
THE ONLY GOD WHO CAN STOP HIM IS PLUMMETING ENDLESSLY DOWN INTO THE BOTTOMLESS PIT...
...AND THE ONLY MORTAL WHO KNOWS WHAT'S HAPPENING IS LISTENING HELPLESSLY FROM A HIDDEN TUNNEL AS THE DARK ELF BEGINS TO GLOW BEFORE HIS LEGIONS OF FOLLOWERS!
ALL IS READY!
WITH THOR GONE AND THE MORTAL BLINDED, OUR TIME HAS COME.
I SHALL UNLEASH THE FULL FURY OF MY GAZE AND BLAST A PASSAGE FROM THE REALM OF FAERIE TO THE REALM OF MEN ABOVE!
THEN SHALL THE CASKET BE OPENED... THE ANCIENT PROPHESIES FULFILLED...
...AND THE WAY BE CLEARED FOR THE MASTER TO ENTER INTO MIDGARD.*
*EARTH


PENCILS AND STORY: WALTER SIMONSON INKS: BOB WIACEK LETTERING: JOHN WORKMAN JR.
COLORS: CHRISTIE SCHEELE EDITING: MARK GRUENWALD EDITOR-IN-CHIEF: JIM SHOOTER

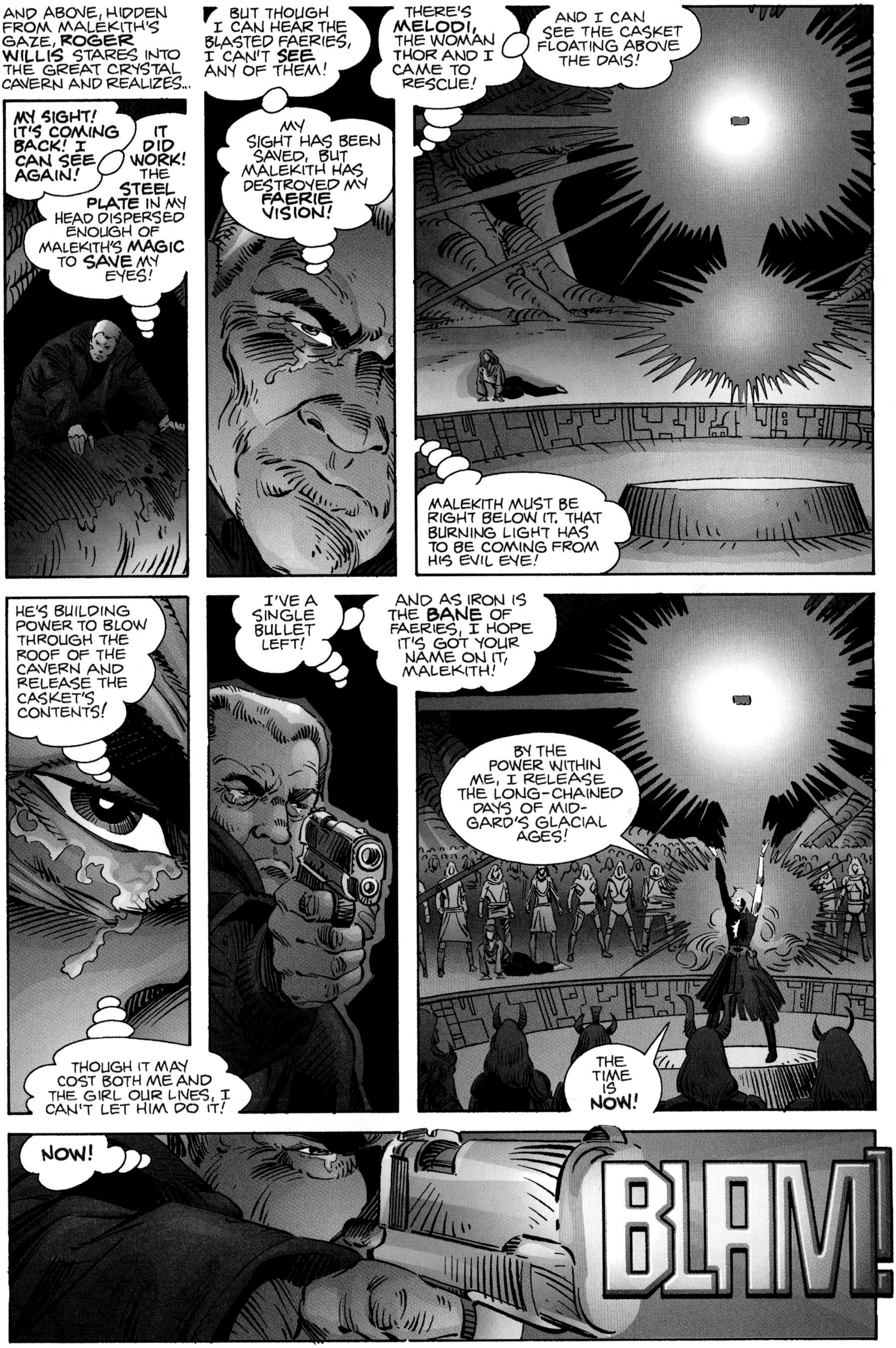
AND ABOVE, HIDDEN FROM MALEKITH'S GAZE, ROGER WILLIS STARES INTO THE GREAT CRYSTAL CAVERN AND REALIZES...
MY SIGHT! IT'S COMING BACK! I CAN SEE AGAIN!
IT DID WORK! THE STEEL PLATE IN MY HEAD DISPERSED ENOUGH OF MALEKITH'S MAGIC TO SAVE MY EYES!
BUT THOUGH I CAN HEAR THE BLASTED FAERIES, I CAN'T SEE ANY OF THEM!
MY SIGHT HAS BEEN SAVED, BUT MALEKITH HAS DESTROYED MY FAERIE VISION!
THERE'S MELODI, THE WOMAN THOR AND I CAME TO RESCUE!
AND I CAN SEE THE CASKET FLOATING ABOVE THE DAIS!
MALEKITH MUST BE RIGHT BELOW IT. THAT BURNING LIGHT HAS TO BE COMING FROM HIS EVIL EYE!
HE'S BUILDING POWER TO BLOW THROUGH THE ROOF OF THE CAVERN AND RELEASE THE CASKET'S CONTENTS!
THOUGH IT MAY COST BOTH ME AND THE GIRL OUR LIVES, I CAN'T LET HIM DO IT!
I'VE A SINGLE BULLET LEFT!
AND AS IRON IS THE BANE OF FAERIES, I HOPE IT'S GOT YOUR NAME ON IT, MALEKITH!
BY THE POWER WITHIN ME, I RELEASE THE LONG-CHAINED DAYS OF MID-GARD'S GLACIAL AGES!
THE TIME IS NOW!
NOW!
BLAM!

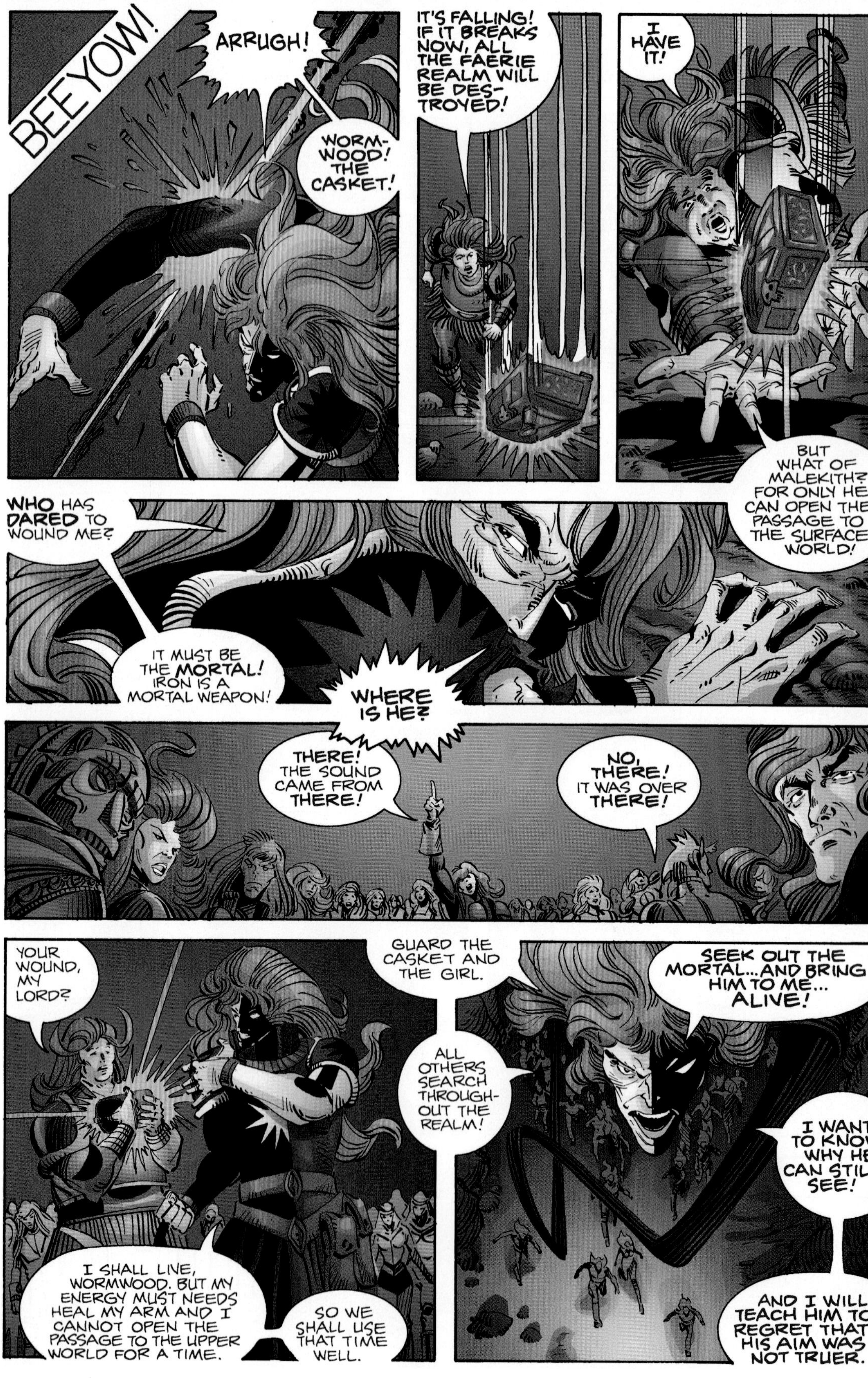
BEEYOW!
ARRUGH!
WORM-WOOD! THE CASKET!
IT'S FALLING! IF IT BREAKS NOW, ALL THE FAERIE REALM WILL BE DES-TROYED!
I HAVE IT!
BUT WHAT OF MALEKITH? FOR ONLY HE CAN OPEN THE PASSAGE TO THE SURFACE WORLD!
WHO HAS DARED TO WOUND ME?
IT MUST BE THE MORTAL! IRON IS A MORTAL WEAPON!
WHERE IS HE?
THERE! THE SOUND CAME FROM THERE!
NO, THERE! IT WAS OVER THERE!
YOUR WOUND, MY LORD?
I SHALL LIVE, WORMWOOD. BUT MY ENERGY MUST NEEDS HEAL MY ARM AND I CANNOT OPEN THE PASSAGE TO THE UPPER WORLD FOR A TIME.
SO WE SHALL USE THAT TIME WELL.
GUARD THE CASKET AND THE GIRL.
ALL OTHERS SEARCH THROUGH-OUT THE REALM!
SEEK OUT THE MORTAL...AND BRING HIM TO ME... ALIVE!
I WANT TO KNOW WHY HE CAN STILL SEE!
AND I WILL TEACH HIM TO REGRET THAT HIS AIM WAS NOT TRUER.

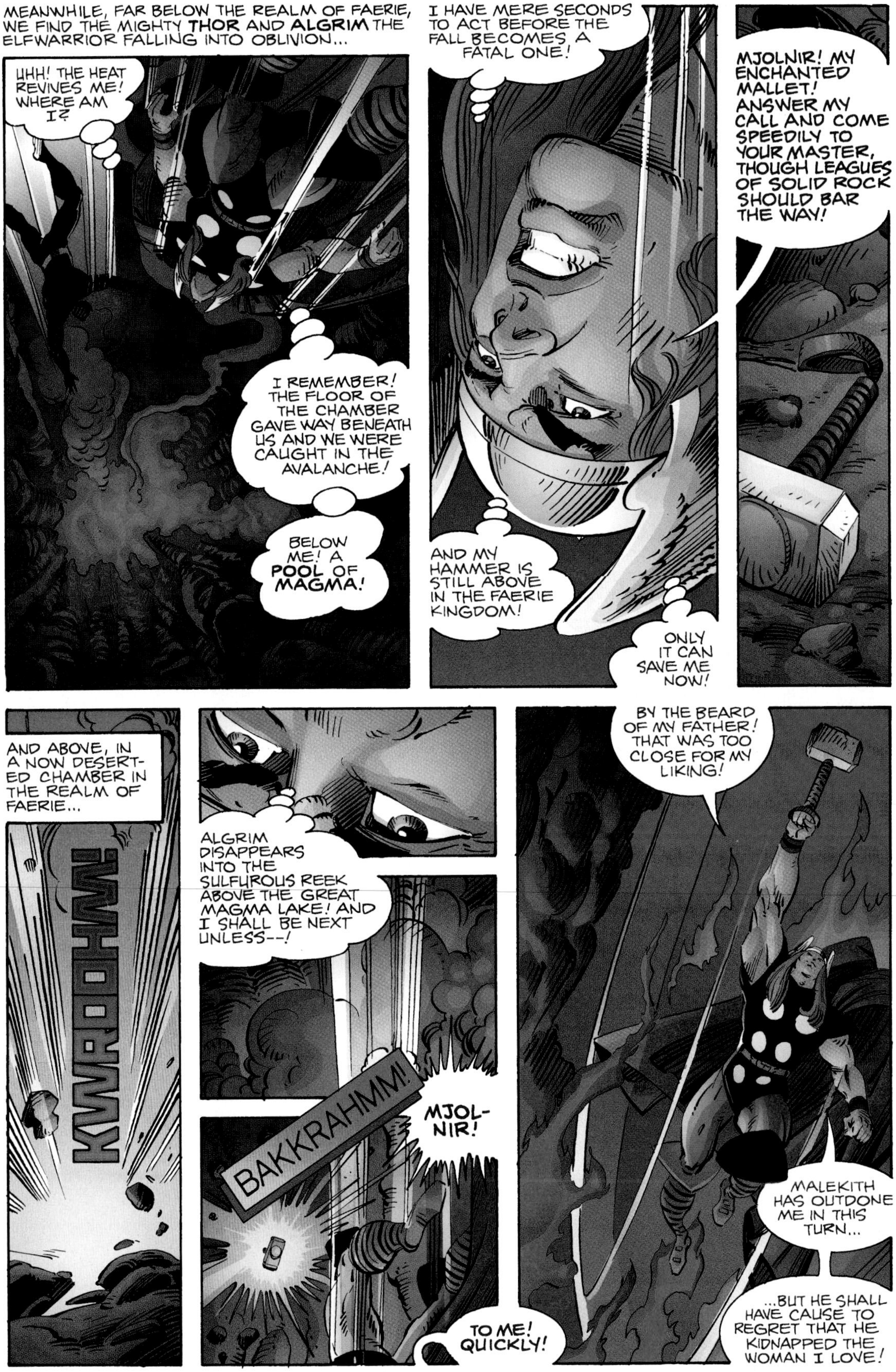
MEANWHILE, FAR BELOW THE REALM OF FAERIE, WE FIND THE MIGHTY THOR AND ALGRIM THE ELFWARRIOR FALLING INTO OBLIVION...
UHH! THE HEAT REVIVES ME! WHERE AM I?
I REMEMBER! THE FLOOR OF THE CHAMBER GAVE WAY BENEATH US AND WE WERE CAUGHT IN THE AVALANCHE!
BELOW ME! A POOL OF MAGMA!
I HAVE MERE SECONDS TO ACT BEFORE THE FALL BECOMES A FATAL ONE!
AND MY HAMMER IS STILL ABOVE IN THE FAERIE KINGDOM!
ONLY IT CAN SAVE ME NOW!
MJOLNIR! MY ENCHANTED MALLET! ANSWER MY CALL AND COME SPEEDILY TO YOUR MASTER, THOUGH LEAGUES OF SOLID ROCK SHOULD BAR THE WAY!
AND ABOVE, IN A NOW DESERTED CHAMBER IN THE REALM OF FAERIE...
KWWROOHMM!
ALGRIM DISAPPEARS INTO THE SULFUROUS REEK ABOVE THE GREAT MAGMA LAKE! AND I SHALL BE NEXT UNLESS--!
BAKKRAHMM!
MJOLNIR!
TO ME! QUICKLY!
BY THE BEARD OF MY FATHER! THAT WAS TOO CLOSE FOR MY LIKING!
MALEKITH HAS OUTDONE ME IN THIS TURN...
...BUT HE SHALL HAVE CAUSE TO REGRET THAT HE KIDNAPPED THE WOMAN I LOVE!

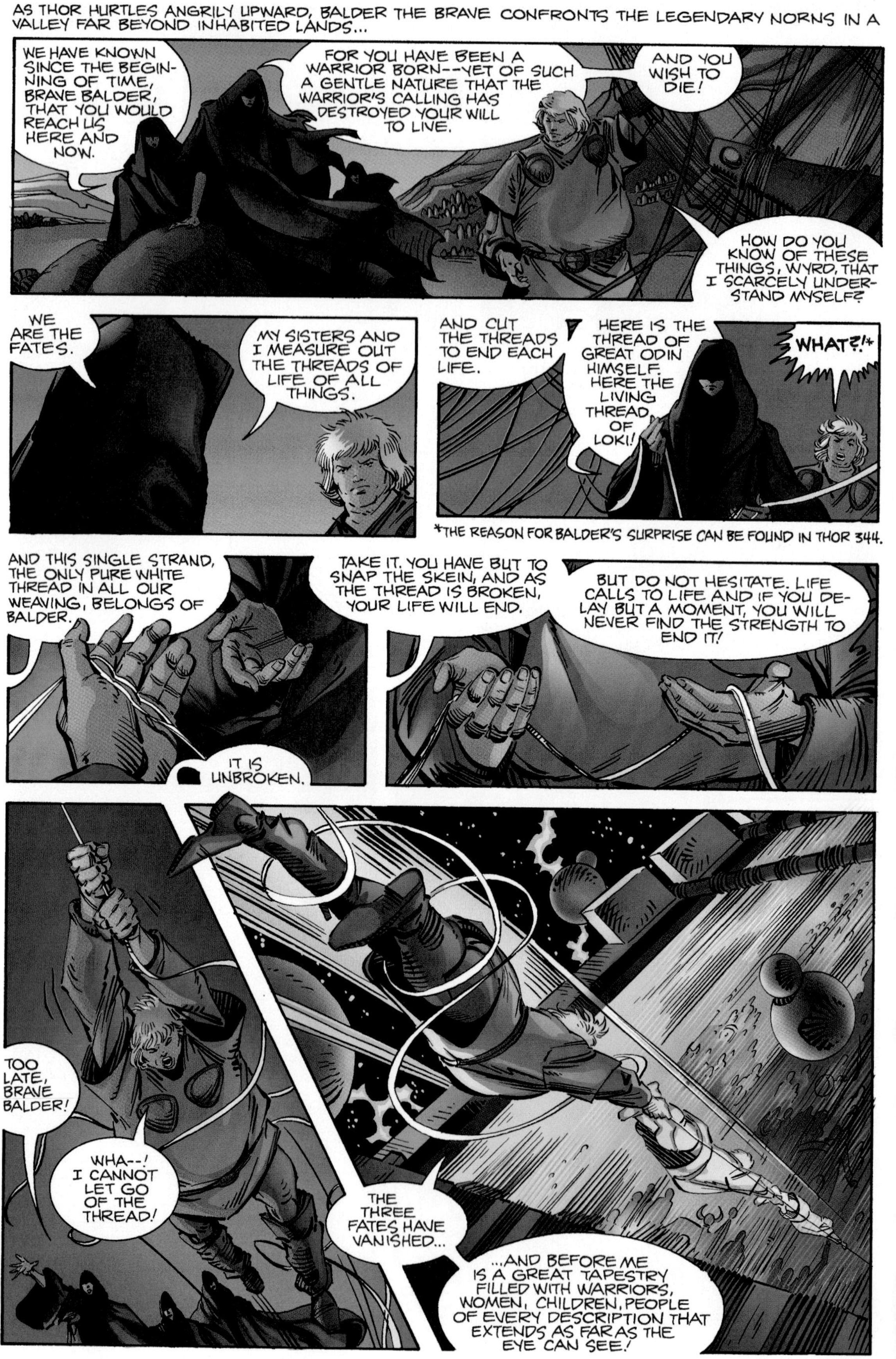
AS THOR HURTLES ANGRILY UPWARD, BALDER THE BRAVE CONFRONTS THE LEGENDARY NORNS IN A VALLEY FAR BEYOND INHABITED LANDS...
WE HAVE KNOWN SINCE THE BEGINNING OF TIME, BRAVE BALDER, THAT YOU WOULD REACH US HERE AND NOW.
FOR YOU HAVE BEEN A WARRIOR BORN--YET OF SUCH A GENTLE NATURE THAT THE WARRIOR'S CALLING HAS DESTROYED YOUR WILL TO LIVE.
AND YOU WISH TO DIE!
HOW DO YOU KNOW OF THESE THINGS, WYRD, THAT I SCARCELY UNDERSTAND MYSELF?
WE ARE THE FATES.
MY SISTERS AND I MEASURE OUT THE THREADS OF LIFE OF ALL THINGS.
AND CUT THE THREADS TO END EACH LIFE.
HERE IS THE THREAD OF GREAT ODIN HIMSELF. HERE THE LIVING THREAD OF LOKI!
WHAT?!*
*THE REASON FOR BALDER'S SURPRISE CAN BE FOUND IN THOR 344.
AND THIS SINGLE STRAND, THE ONLY PURE WHITE THREAD IN ALL OUR WEAVING, BELONGS OF BALDER.
IT IS UNBROKEN.
TAKE IT. YOU HAVE BUT TO SNAP THE SKEIN, AND AS THE THREAD IS BROKEN, YOUR LIFE WILL END.
BUT DO NOT HESITATE. LIFE CALLS TO LIFE AND IF YOU DELAY BUT A MOMENT, YOU WILL NEVER FIND THE STRENGTH TO END IT!
TOO LATE, BRAVE BALDER!
WHA--! I CANNOT LET GO OF THE THREAD!
THE THREE FATES HAVE VANISHED...
...AND BEFORE ME IS A GREAT TAPESTRY FILLED WITH WARRIORS, WOMEN, CHILDREN, PEOPLE OF EVERY DESCRIPTION THAT EXTENDS AS FAR AS THE EYE CAN SEE!

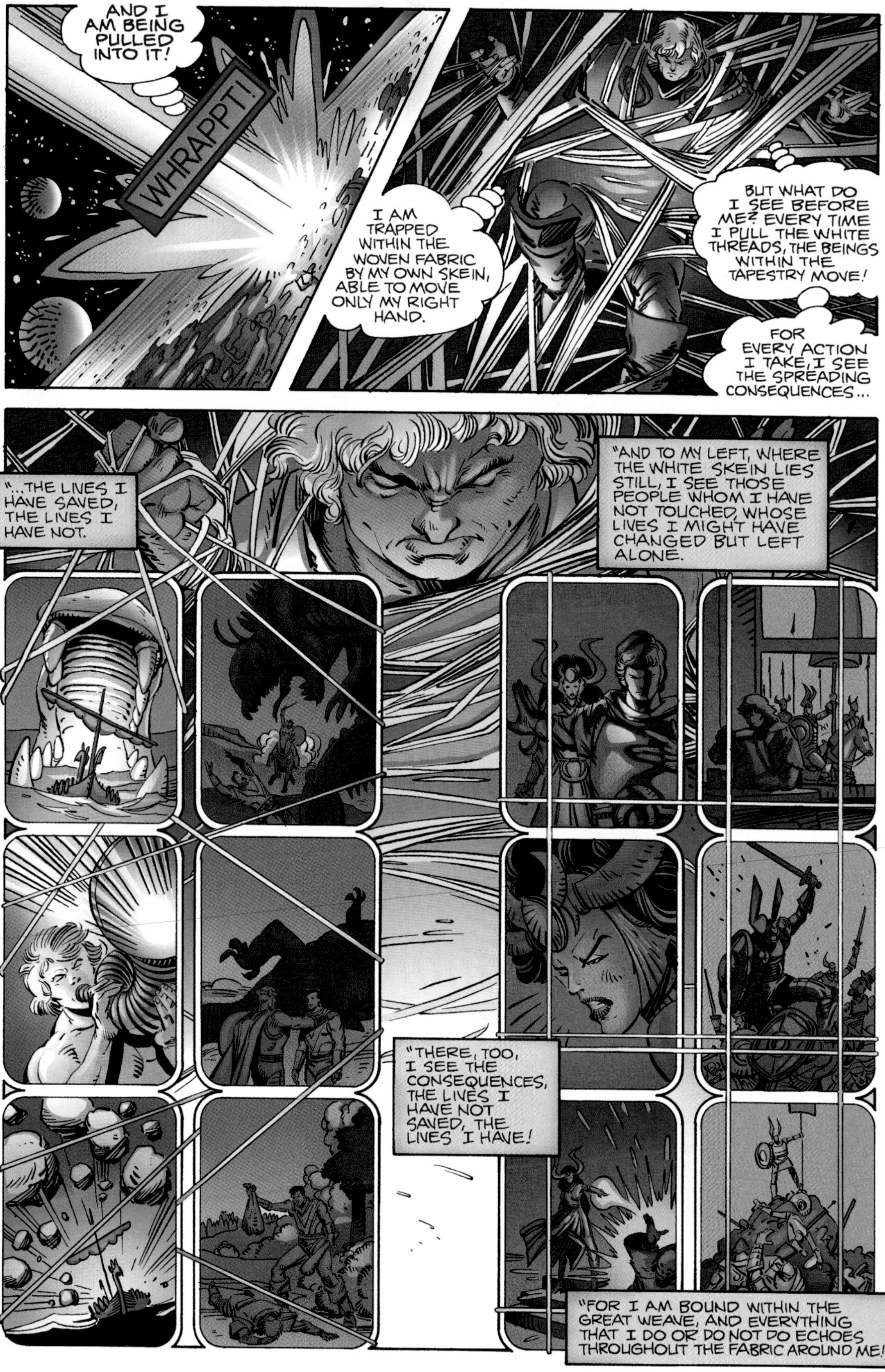
AND I AM BEING PULLED INTO IT!
WHRAPPT!
I AM TRAPPED WITHIN THE WOVEN FABRIC BY MY OWN SKEIN, ABLE TO MOVE ONLY MY RIGHT HAND.
BUT WHAT DO I SEE BEFORE ME? EVERY TIME I PULL THE WHITE THREADS, THE BEINGS WITHIN THE TAPESTRY MOVE!
FOR EVERY ACTION I TAKE, I SEE THE SPREADING CONSEQUENCES...
"...THE LIVES I HAVE SAVED, THE LIVES I HAVE NOT.
"AND TO MY LEFT, WHERE THE WHITE SKEIN LIES STILL, I SEE THOSE PEOPLE WHOM I HAVE NOT TOUCHED, WHOSE LIVES I MIGHT HAVE CHANGED BUT LEFT ALONE.
"THERE, TOO, I SEE THE CONSEQUENCES, THE LIVES I HAVE NOT SAVED, THE LIVES I HAVE!
"FOR I AM BOUND WITHIN THE GREAT WEAVE, AND EVERYTHING THAT I DO OR DO NOT DO ECHOES THROUGHOUT THE FABRIC AROUND ME!"

I CAN BEAR NO MORE! I WILL TEAR MYSELF AWAY FROM THIS DANCING PLAY AND QUIT THE MADNESS OF LIVING!
RRIPPPP!
AND ALL WHO ARE BOUND WITHIN ITS WEAVE FALL WITH ME!
BUT EVEN AS I FALL INTO THE DARK, THE TAPESTRY BEGINS TO UNRAVEL!
THIS MUST NOT BE!
NO MAN OR GOD CAN SET ASIDE THE FATE OF SO MANY AS I HAVE TRIED TO DO!
THERE AHEAD OF ME-- THE TORN ENDS OF THE WHITE THREAD.
AND BEYOND THAT, SOME GREAT SHADOW FLICKERING AS IF WRAPPED IN A DARK FLAME, WAITING TO CATCH THE FALLING TAP-ESTRY AND DESTROY IT!
AS THOUGH MY DEATH HERALDS THE END OF A UNIVERSE!
I HAVE BUT ONE CHANCE TO GRAB THE ENDS!
NOW!
THE SKEINS ARE MINE! BUT HOW CAN I JOIN THEM TOGETHER AGAIN AND REPAIR THE GREAT FABRIC BEFORE IT IS TOO LATE?

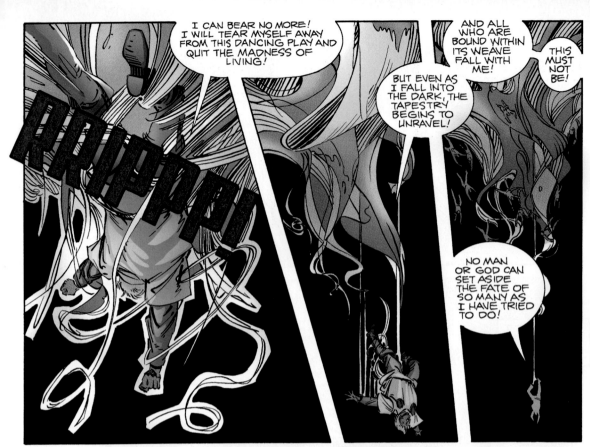

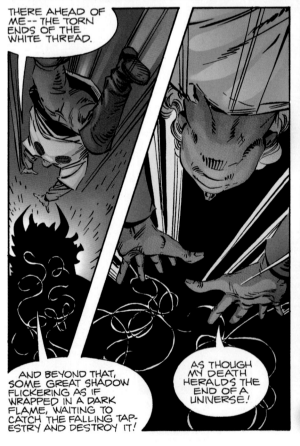

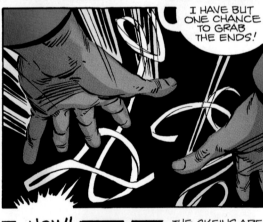

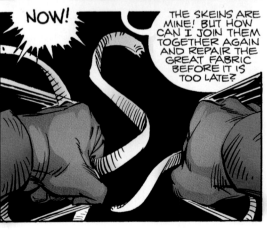

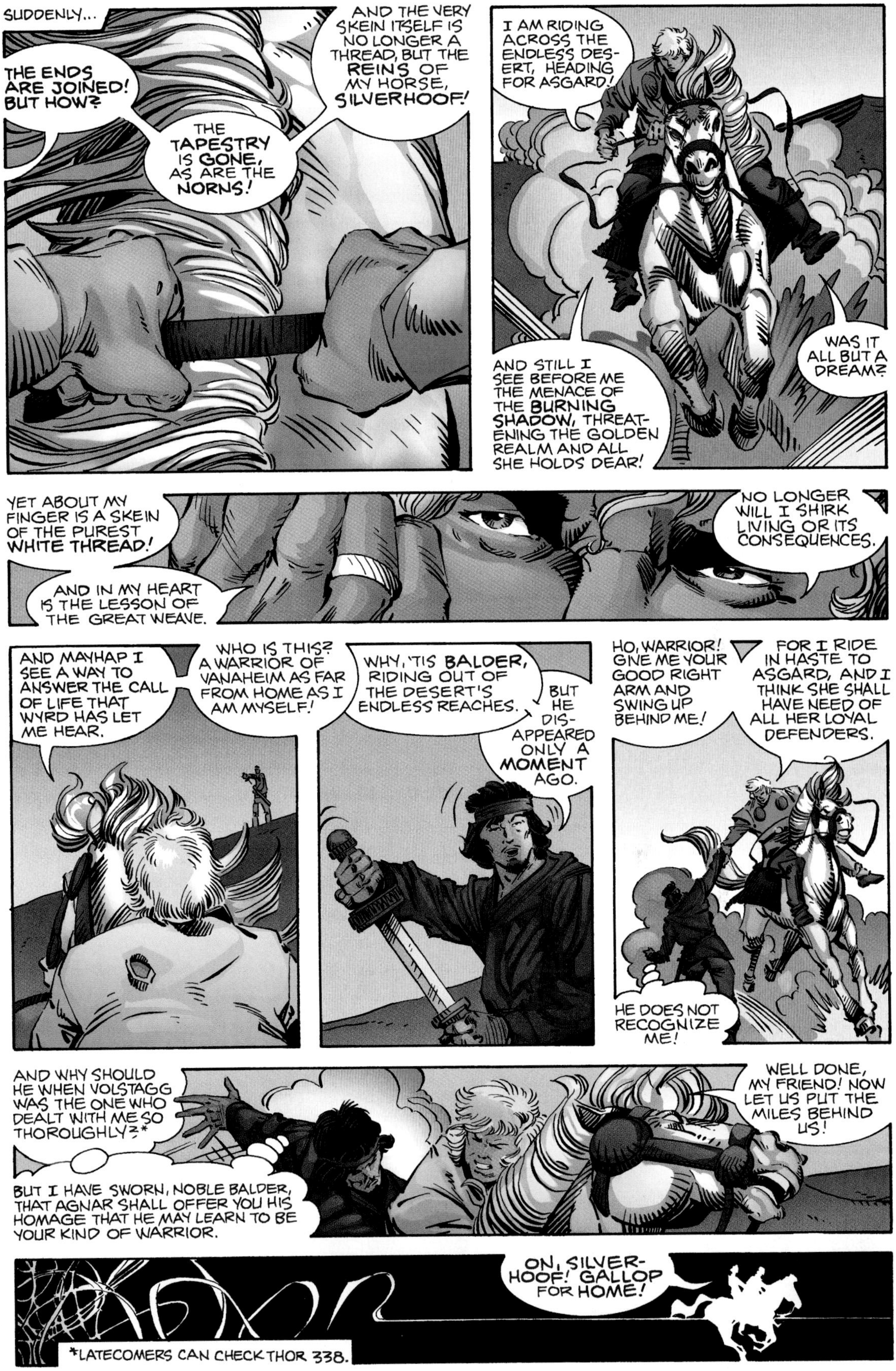
SUDDENLY...
THE ENDS ARE JOINED! BUT HOW?
THE TAPESTRY IS GONE, AS ARE THE NORNS!
AND THE VERY SKEIN ITSELF IS NO LONGER A THREAD, BUT THE REINS OF MY HORSE, SILVERHOOF!
I AM RIDING ACROSS THE ENDLESS DESERT, HEADING FOR ASGARD!
AND STILL I SEE BEFORE ME THE MENACE OF THE BURNING SHADOW, THREATENING THE GOLDEN REALM AND ALL SHE HOLDS DEAR!
WAS IT ALL BUT A DREAM?
YET ABOUT MY FINGER IS A SKEIN OF THE PUREST WHITE THREAD!
AND IN MY HEART IS THE LESSON OF THE GREAT WEAVE.
NO LONGER WILL I SHIRK LIVING OR ITS CONSEQUENCES.
AND MAYHAP I SEE A WAY TO ANSWER THE CALL OF LIFE THAT WYRD HAS LET ME HEAR.
WHO IS THIS? A WARRIOR OF VANAHEIM AS FAR FROM HOME AS I AM MYSELF!
WHY, 'TIS BALDER, RIDING OUT OF THE DESERT'S ENDLESS REACHES.
BUT HE DISAPPEARED ONLY A MOMENT AGO.
HO, WARRIOR! GIVE ME YOUR GOOD RIGHT ARM AND SWING UP BEHIND ME!
FOR I RIDE IN HASTE TO ASGARD, AND I THINK SHE SHALL HAVE NEED OF ALL HER LOYAL DEFENDERS.
HE DOES NOT RECOGNIZE ME!
AND WHY SHOULD HE WHEN VOLSTAGG WAS THE ONE WHO DEALT WITH ME SO THOROUGHLY?*
BUT I HAVE SWORN, NOBLE BALDER, THAT AGNAR SHALL OFFER YOU HIS HOMAGE THAT HE MAY LEARN TO BE YOUR KIND OF WARRIOR.
WELL DONE, MY FRIEND! NOW LET US PUT THE MILES BEHIND US!
ON, SILVERHOOF! GALLOP FOR HOME!
*LATECOMERS CAN CHECK THOR 338.

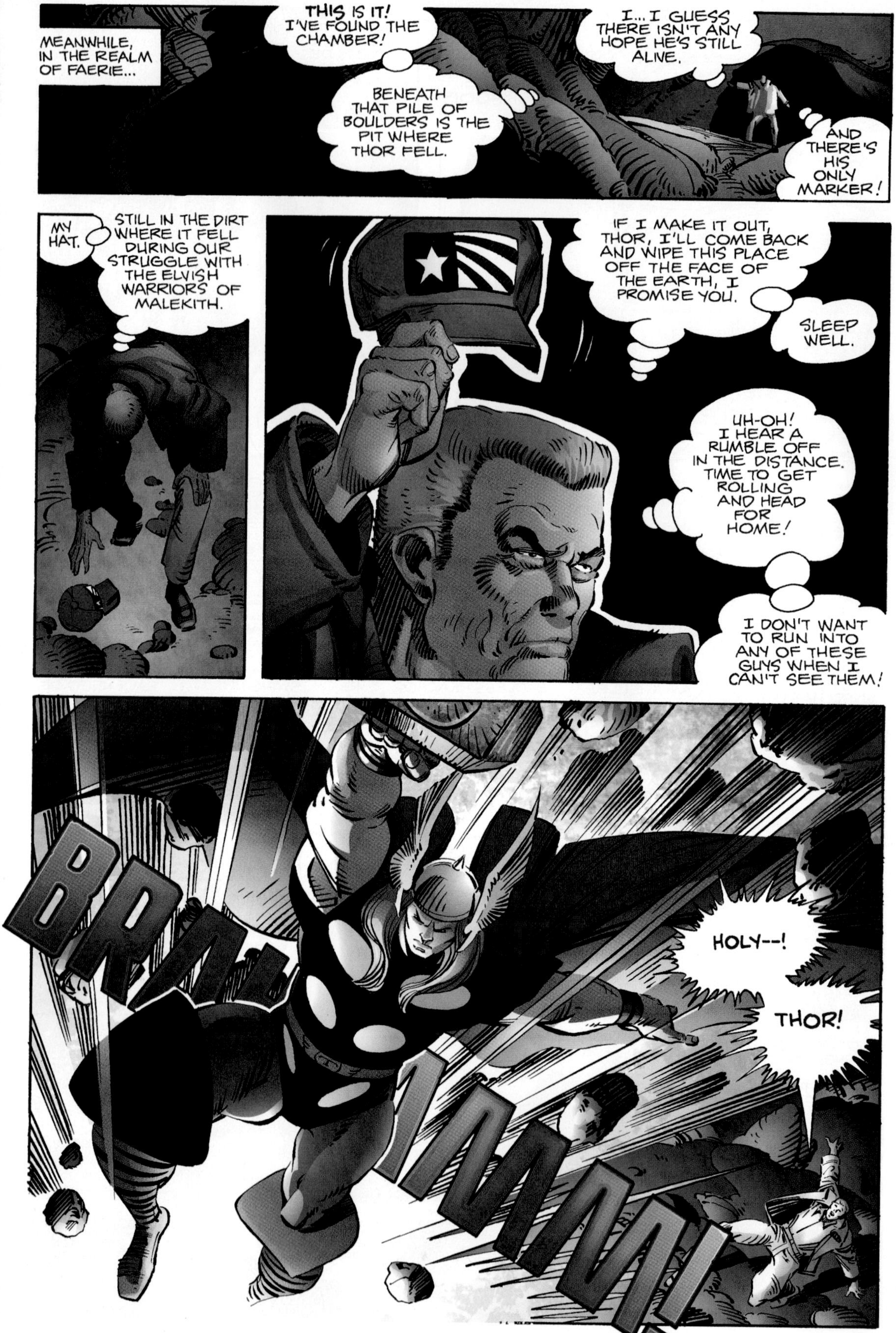
MEANWHILE, IN THE REALM OF FAERIE...
THIS IS IT! I'VE FOUND THE CHAMBER!
BENEATH THAT PILE OF BOULDERS IS THE PIT WHERE THOR FELL.
I... I GUESS THERE ISN'T ANY HOPE HE'S STILL ALIVE.
AND THERE'S HIS ONLY MARKER!
MY HAT.
STILL IN THE DIRT WHERE IT FELL DURING OUR STRUGGLE WITH THE ELVISH WARRIORS OF MALEKITH.
IF I MAKE IT OUT, THOR, I'LL COME BACK AND WIPE THIS PLACE OFF THE FACE OF THE EARTH, I PROMISE YOU.
SLEEP WELL.
UH-OH! I HEAR A RUMBLE OFF IN THE DISTANCE. TIME TO GET ROLLING AND HEAD FOR HOME!
I DON'T WANT TO RUN INTO ANY OF THESE GUYS WHEN I CAN'T SEE THEM!
BRAAAMMM!
HOLY--!
THOR!

AYE, ROGER! **THOR!**

YOU SURE KNOW HOW TO MAKE A DRAMATIC ENTRANCE.

YOU OKAY?

I AM SORRY TO HAVE FAILED YOU BEFORE, ROGER.

THE SON OF ODIN IS NOT USED TO FAILURE, AND YET WHEN I SAW MELODI IN DANGER, ALL OTHER THOUGHTS SEEMED TO FLEE FROM MY MIND.

WHAT HAS HAPPENED DURING MY FALL?

IN 25 WORDS OR LESS, MALEKITH'S GOT THE CASKET, I WINGED HIM, AND HE AND HIS BRAVOS ARE SEARCHING THE CAVES FOR ME.

I **DIDN'T** KILL HIM, WORSE LUCK.

AND MELODI?

"IN THE CAVE WITH THE CASKET UNDER GUARD, LAST TIME I LOOKED. I BEAT A STRATEGIC RETREAT AFTER I TOOK MY SHOT."

"MALEKITH MAY ALREADY HAVE SENSED MY PRESENCE, AND IF HE LEARNS THAT THOR IS STILL ALIVE, HE WILL NOT COME CLOSE ENOUGH FOR US TO GRAPPLE WITH HIM.

"GIVEN HIS ABILITY TO MERGE INTO THE SHADOWS, HE COULD BE MOST DIFFICULT TO CAPTURE."

AND, INDEED...

STRANGE! I FEEL A **PRESENCE** BEFORE ME IN THE CAVE OF THE BOTTOMLESS PIT!

IT HAS A MORTAL SMELL AND MORE BESIDES.

A MOMENT LATER...

WE MEET AGAIN, ROGER WILLIS!

AND THIS TIME, NEITHER **COLD IRON** NOR **THUNDER GOD** SHALL SAVE YOU.

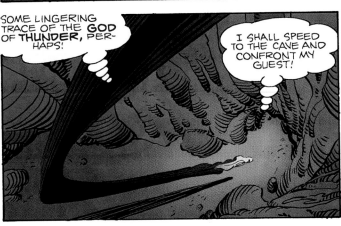

SOME LINGERING TRACE OF THE **GOD** OF **THUNDER,** PERHAPS!

I SHALL SPEED TO THE CAVE AND CONFRONT MY GUEST!

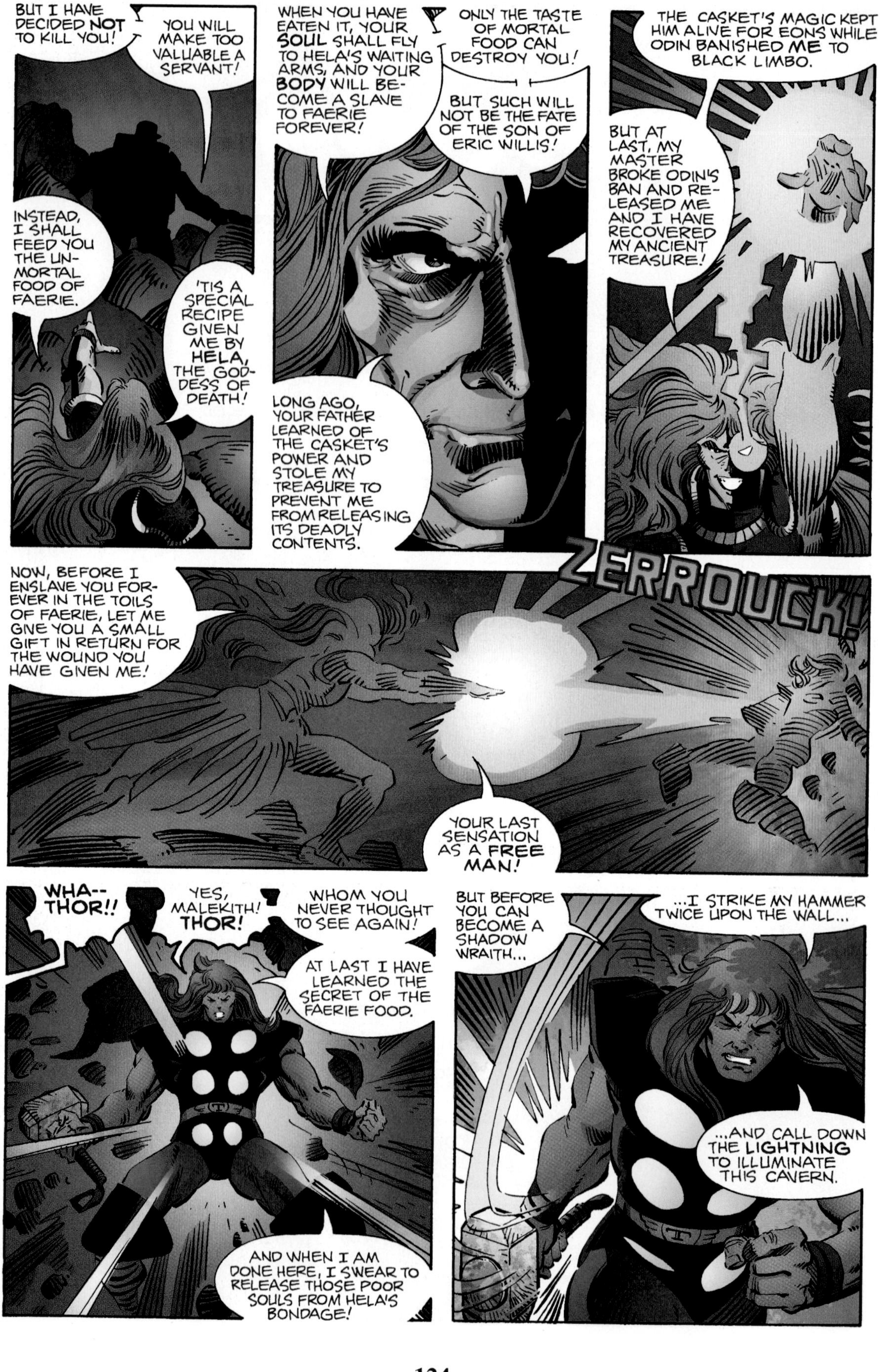

BUT I HAVE DECIDED NOT TO KILL YOU!
YOU WILL MAKE TOO VALUABLE A SERVANT!
INSTEAD, I SHALL FEED YOU THE UN-MORTAL FOOD OF FAERIE.
'TIS A SPECIAL RECIPE GIVEN ME BY HELA, THE GOD-DESS OF DEATH!
WHEN YOU HAVE EATEN IT, YOUR SOUL SHALL FLY TO HELA'S WAITING ARMS, AND YOUR BODY WILL BE-COME A SLAVE TO FAERIE FOREVER!
ONLY THE TASTE OF MORTAL FOOD CAN DESTROY YOU!
BUT SUCH WILL NOT BE THE FATE OF THE SON OF ERIC WILLIS!
LONG AGO, YOUR FATHER LEARNED OF THE CASKET'S POWER AND STOLE MY TREASURE TO PREVENT ME FROM RELEASING ITS DEADLY CONTENTS.
THE CASKET'S MAGIC KEPT HIM ALIVE FOR EONS WHILE ODIN BANISHED ME TO BLACK LIMBO.
BUT AT LAST, MY MASTER BROKE ODIN'S BAN AND RE-LEASED ME AND I HAVE RECOVERED MY ANCIENT TREASURE!
NOW, BEFORE I ENSLAVE YOU FOR-EVER IN THE TOILS OF FAERIE, LET ME GIVE YOU A SMALL GIFT IN RETURN FOR THE WOUND YOU HAVE GIVEN ME!
ZERROUCK!
YOUR LAST SENSATION AS A FREE MAN!
WHA-- THOR!!
YES, MALEKITH! THOR!
WHOM YOU NEVER THOUGHT TO SEE AGAIN!
AT LAST I HAVE LEARNED THE SECRET OF THE FAERIE FOOD.
AND WHEN I AM DONE HERE, I SWEAR TO RELEASE THOSE POOR SOULS FROM HELA'S BONDAGE!
BUT BEFORE YOU CAN BECOME A SHADOW WRAITH...
...I STRIKE MY HAMMER TWICE UPON THE WALL...
...AND CALL DOWN THE LIGHTNING TO ILLUMINATE THIS CAVERN.

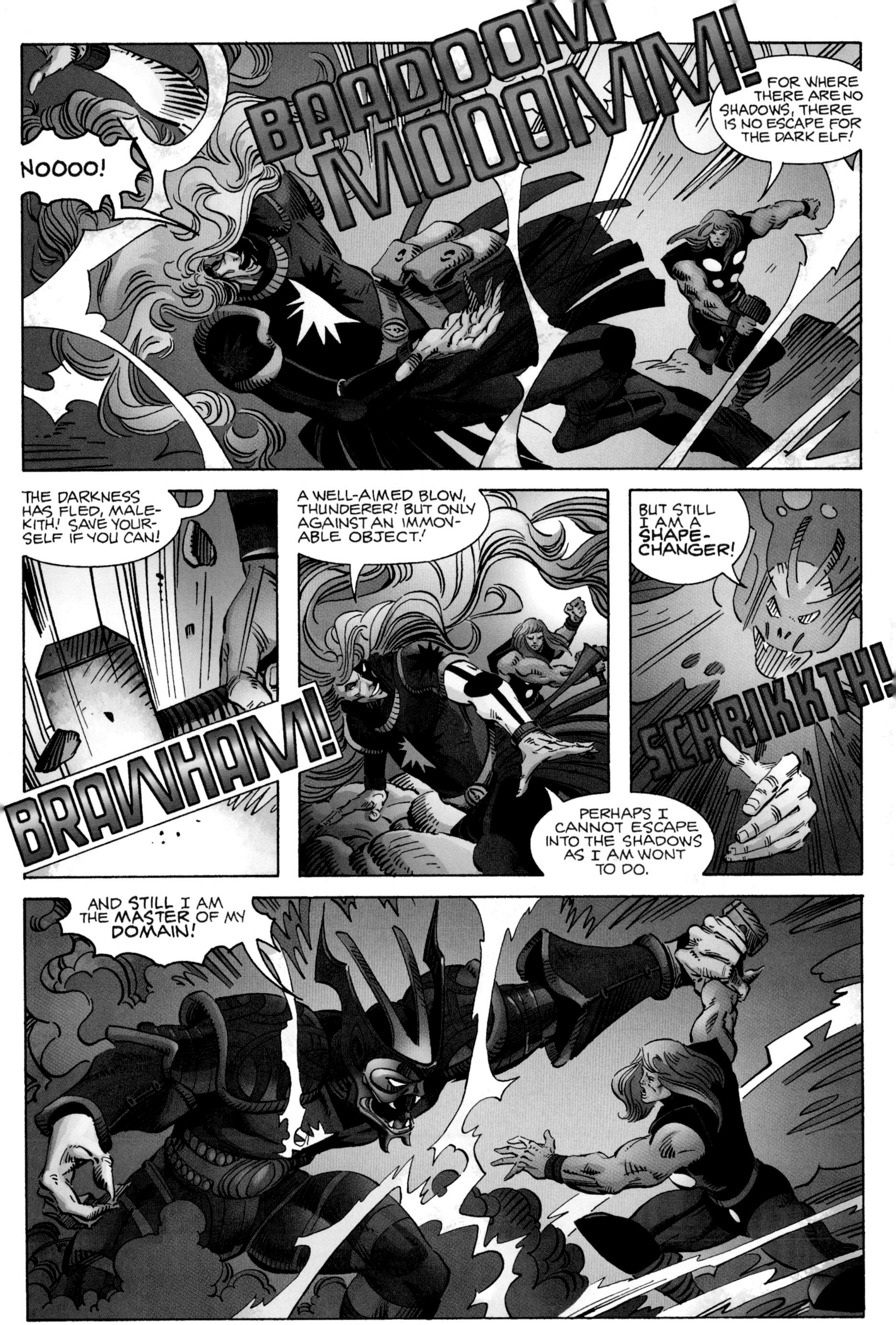
BAADOOM MOOOMMM!
NOOOO!
FOR WHERE THERE ARE NO SHADOWS, THERE IS NO ESCAPE FOR THE DARK ELF!
THE DARKNESS HAS FLED, MALEKITH! SAVE YOURSELF IF YOU CAN!
BRAWHAM!
A WELL-AIMED BLOW, THUNDERER! BUT ONLY AGAINST AN IMMOVABLE OBJECT!
PERHAPS I CANNOT ESCAPE INTO THE SHADOWS AS I AM WONT TO DO.
BUT STILL I AM A SHAPE-CHANGER!
SCHRIKKTH!
AND STILL I AM THE MASTER OF MY DOMAIN!

ONLY A MASTER OF **EVIL**, MALEKITH!

FOR THOUGH YOU HAVE TAKEN THE SHAPE OF A TRULY FEARSOME WARRIOR, 'TIS **THOR** WHO HAS THE POWER HERE!

THOR WHOM YOU HAVE **WRONGED!**

**KEERASH!**

THOR WHOM YOU HAVE TRIED TO **DESTROY!**

**THRAUUAHNN!**

THOR WHOSE LADY YOU HAVE STOLEN FOR THE SAKE OF **RANSOM** AND BETRAYAL!

**BLOUAKKATH!**

AND THOR WHO WILL HAVE HIS **VENGEANCE...**

**THRASH!**

...UPON THE **DARK ELF** AND **ALL** WHO FOLLOW HIM!

UH, THOR, I DON'T THINK HE CAN HEAR YOU ANYMORE.

WHAT?

OH.

VERY WELL. LET THE LIGHTNING CEASE!

WE SHALL TAKE HIM WITH US. MY FATHER WILL NO DOUBT WISH TO SEE HIM!

AND I WISH TO SEE MELODI. LET ME SHOULDER THE UNCONSCIOUS MALEKITH AND THEN, ROGER, YOU SHALL LEAD ME TO BOTH MELODI AND THE CASKET.

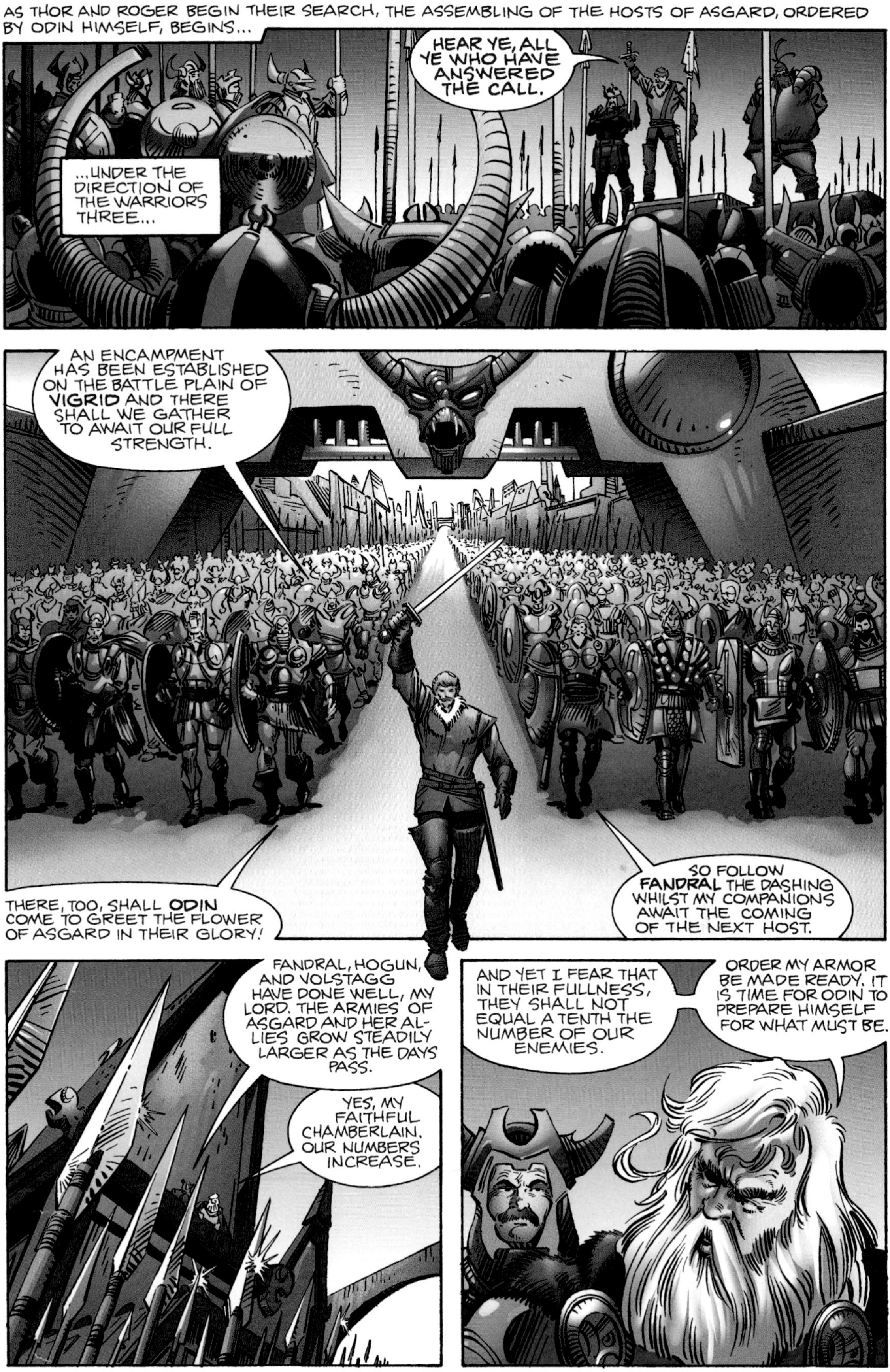
AS THOR AND ROGER BEGIN THEIR SEARCH, THE ASSEMBLING OF THE HOSTS OF ASGARD, ORDERED BY ODIN HIMSELF, BEGINS...
HEAR YE, ALL YE WHO HAVE ANSWERED THE CALL.
...UNDER THE DIRECTION OF THE WARRIORS THREE...
AN ENCAMPMENT HAS BEEN ESTABLISHED ON THE BATTLE PLAIN OF VIGRID AND THERE SHALL WE GATHER TO AWAIT OUR FULL STRENGTH.
THERE, TOO, SHALL ODIN COME TO GREET THE FLOWER OF ASGARD IN THEIR GLORY!
SO FOLLOW FANDRAL THE DASHING WHILST MY COMPANIONS AWAIT THE COMING OF THE NEXT HOST.
FANDRAL, HOGUN, AND VOLSTAGG HAVE DONE WELL, MY LORD. THE ARMIES OF ASGARD AND HER ALLIES GROW STEADILY LARGER AS THE DAYS PASS.
YES, MY FAITHFUL CHAMBERLAIN. OUR NUMBERS INCREASE.
AND YET I FEAR THAT IN THEIR FULLNESS, THEY SHALL NOT EQUAL A TENTH THE NUMBER OF OUR ENEMIES.
ORDER MY ARMOR BE MADE READY. IT IS TIME FOR ODIN TO PREPARE HIMSELF FOR WHAT MUST BE.

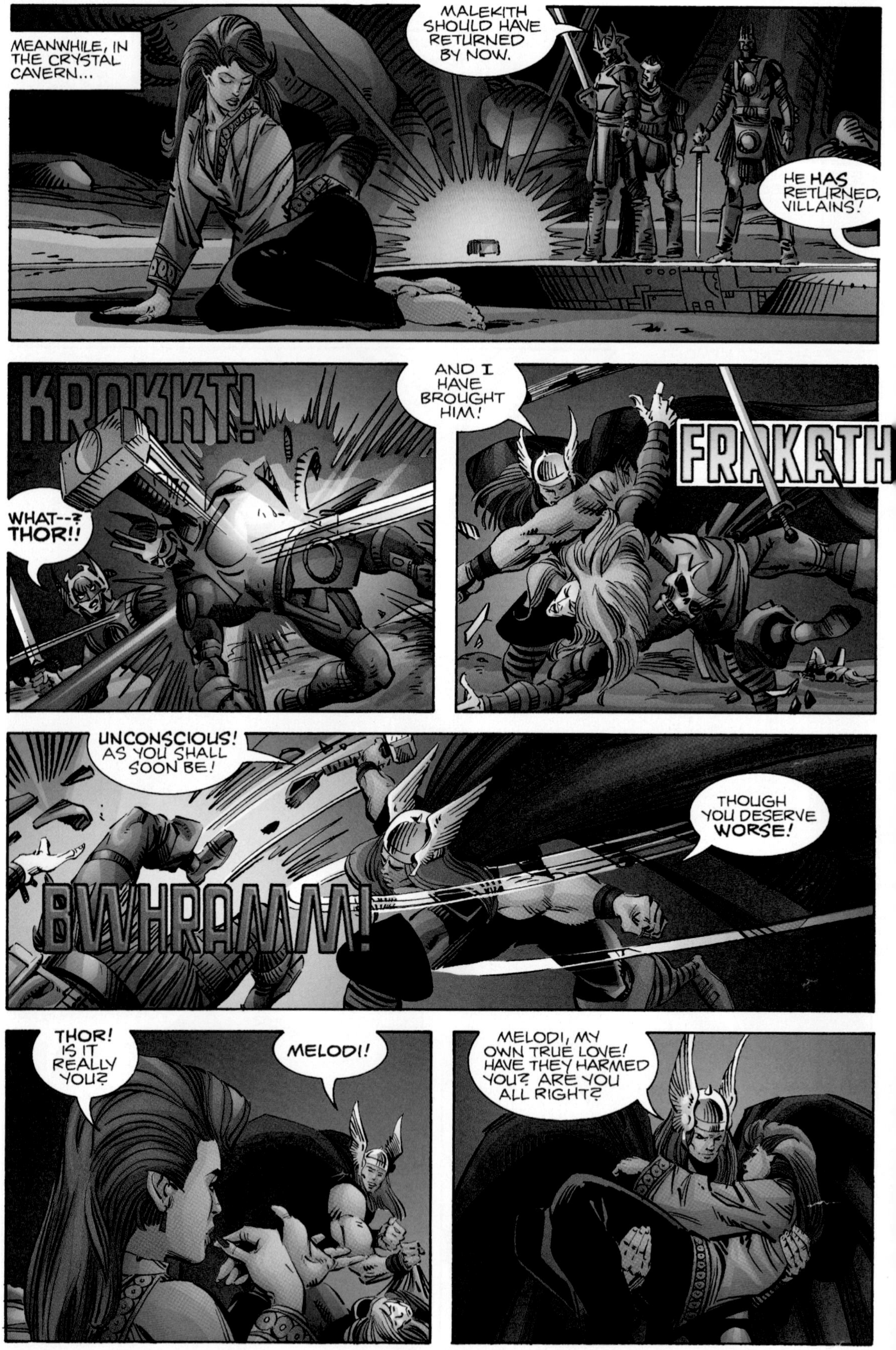
MEANWHILE, IN THE CRYSTAL CAVERN...
MALEKITH SHOULD HAVE RETURNED BY NOW.
HE HAS RETURNED, VILLAINS!
KROKKT!
AND I HAVE BROUGHT HIM!
WHAT--? THOR!!
FRAKATH
UNCONSCIOUS! AS YOU SHALL SOON BE!
THOUGH YOU DESERVE WORSE!
BWHRAMM!
THOR! IS IT REALLY YOU?
MELODI!
MELODI, MY OWN TRUE LOVE! HAVE THEY HARMED YOU? ARE YOU ALL RIGHT?

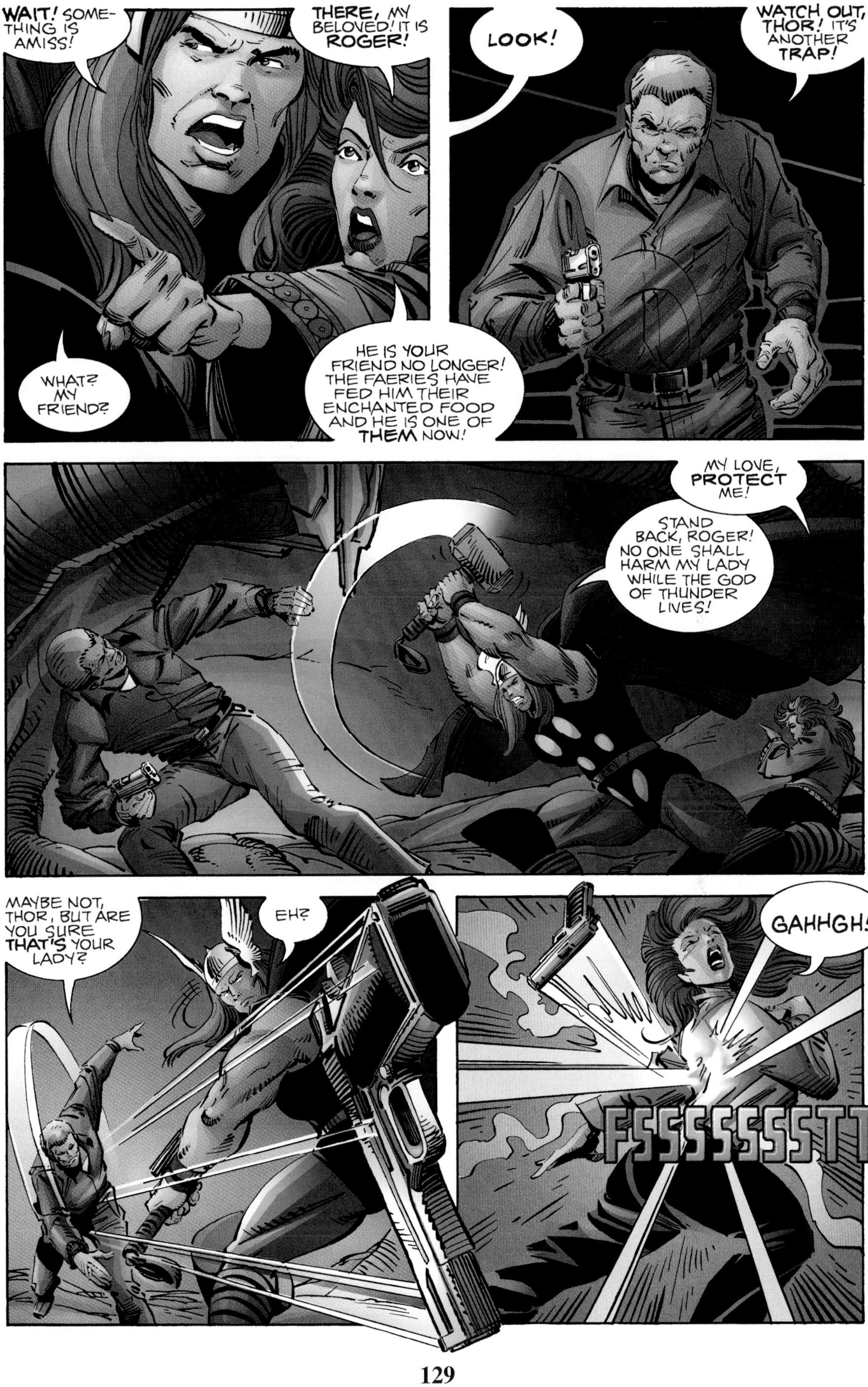
WAIT! SOMETHING IS AMISS!
THERE, MY BELOVED! IT IS ROGER!
WHAT? MY FRIEND?
HE IS YOUR FRIEND NO LONGER! THE FAERIES HAVE FED HIM THEIR ENCHANTED FOOD AND HE IS ONE OF THEM NOW!
LOOK!
WATCH OUT, THOR! IT'S ANOTHER TRAP!
MY LOVE, PROTECT ME!
STAND BACK, ROGER! NO ONE SHALL HARM MY LADY WHILE THE GOD OF THUNDER LIVES!
MAYBE NOT, THOR, BUT ARE YOU SURE THAT'S YOUR LADY?
EH?
GAHHGH!
FSSSSSSSTT!

MELODI'S FORM! IT SHIFTS LIKE A MIRAGE IN THE DESERT!

OH, NO! THE CURSED IRON HAS DISRUPTED MY DISGUISE!

SO!

WITHOUT THE FAERIE VISION THAT MALEKITH DESTROYED, I COULDN'T SEE ANYONE. BUT I COULD STILL HEAR 'IM.

SO I THREW MY GUN AT THE SOUND.

AND I'VE HEARD THIS ONE BEFORE. MALEKITH CALLED HIM WORMWOOD!

HE WAS GUARDING MELODI!

WHAKKKK!

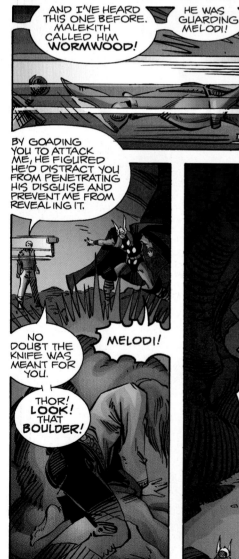

BY GOADING YOU TO ATTACK ME, HE FIGURED HE'D DISTRACT YOU FROM PENETRATING HIS DISGUISE AND PREVENT ME FROM REVEALING IT.

NO DOUBT THE KNIFE WAS MEANT FOR YOU.

MELODI!

THOR! LOOK! THAT BOULDER!

YOU HAVE DISCOVERED HER TOO LATE, THUNDER GOD!

FOR THE WARRIORS OF FAERIE HAVE FOUND YOU NOW, AND NEITHER YOU NOR YOUR COMPANIONS SHALL EVER SEE THE LIGHT OF DAY AGAIN!

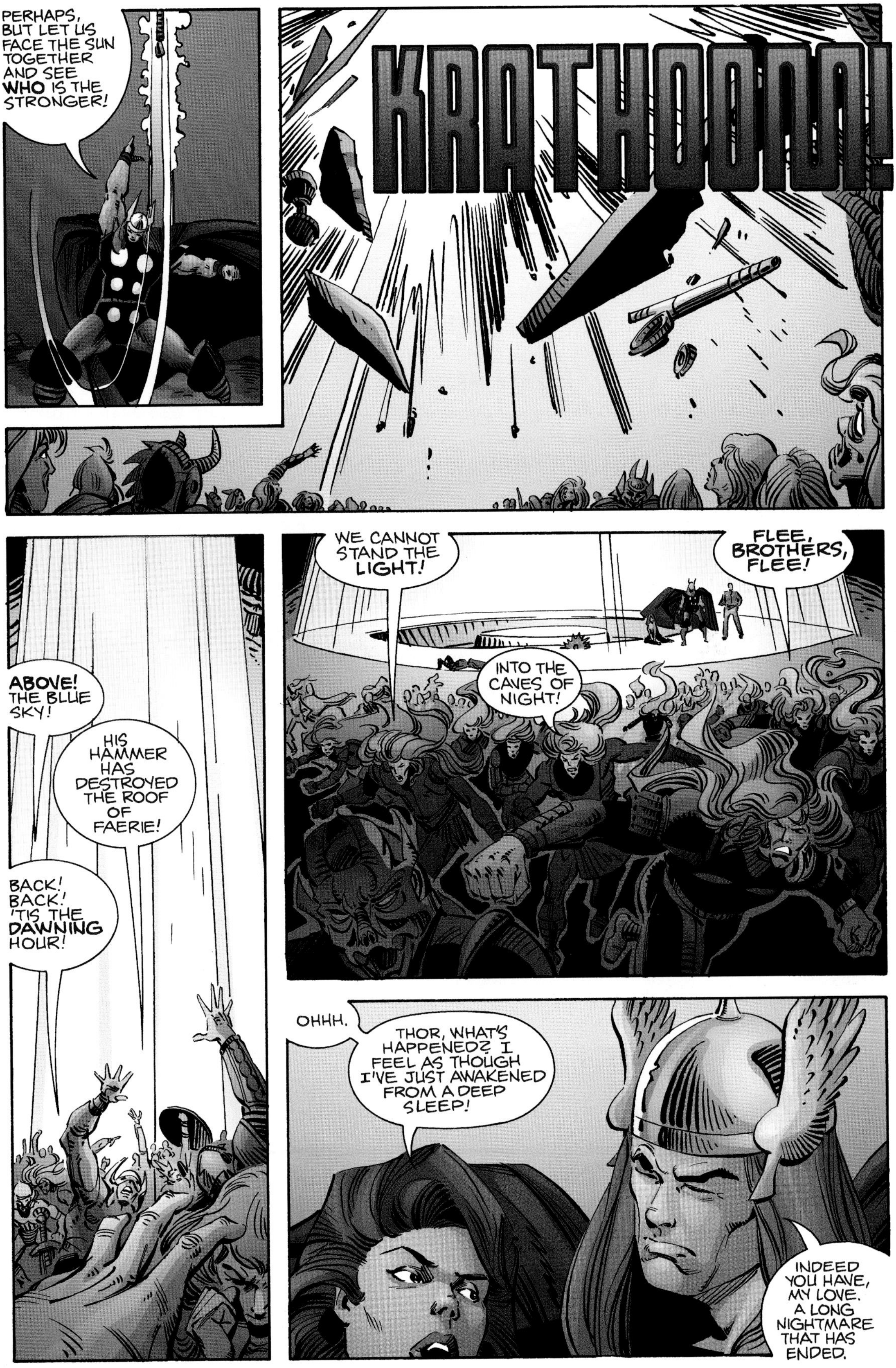
PERHAPS, BUT LET US FACE THE SUN TOGETHER AND SEE WHO IS THE STRONGER!
KRATHOOM!
ABOVE! THE BLUE SKY!
HIS HAMMER HAS DESTROYED THE ROOF OF FAERIE!
BACK! BACK! 'TIS THE DAWNING HOUR!
WE CANNOT STAND THE LIGHT!
FLEE, BROTHERS, FLEE!
INTO THE CAVES OF NIGHT!
OHHH.
THOR, WHAT'S HAPPENED? I FEEL AS THOUGH I'VE JUST AWAKENED FROM A DEEP SLEEP!
INDEED YOU HAVE, MY LOVE. A LONG NIGHTMARE THAT HAS ENDED.

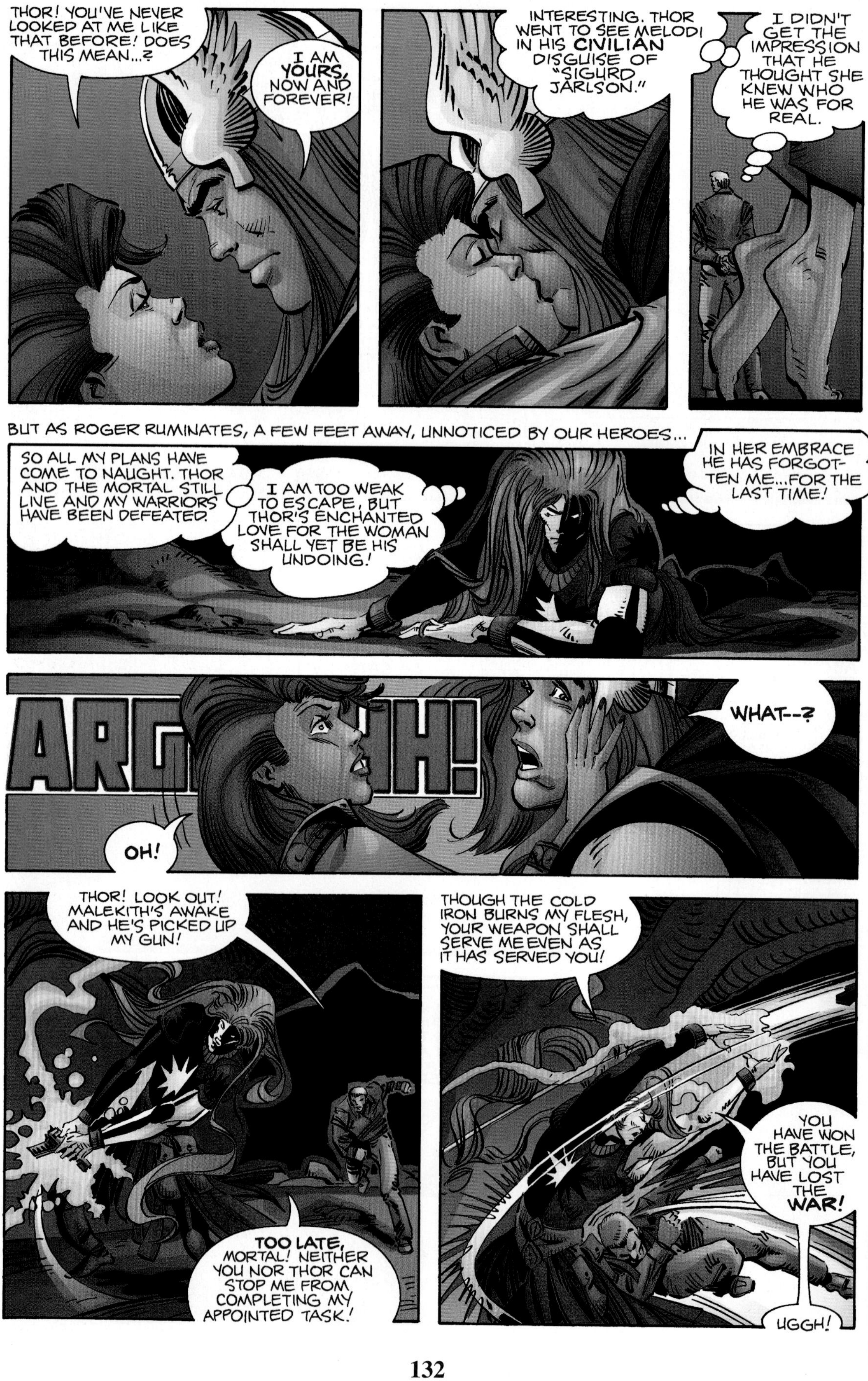

THOR! YOU'VE NEVER LOOKED AT ME LIKE THAT BEFORE! DOES THIS MEAN...?
I AM YOURS, NOW AND FOREVER!
INTERESTING. THOR WENT TO SEE MELODI IN HIS CIVILIAN DISGUISE OF "SIGURD JARLSON."
I DIDN'T GET THE IMPRESSION THAT HE THOUGHT SHE KNEW WHO HE WAS FOR REAL.
BUT AS ROGER RUMINATES, A FEW FEET AWAY, UNNOTICED BY OUR HEROES...
SO ALL MY PLANS HAVE COME TO NAUGHT. THOR AND THE MORTAL STILL LIVE AND MY WARRIORS HAVE BEEN DEFEATED.
I AM TOO WEAK TO ESCAPE, BUT THOR'S ENCHANTED LOVE FOR THE WOMAN SHALL YET BE HIS UNDOING!
IN HER EMBRACE HE HAS FORGOTTEN ME...FOR THE LAST TIME!
WHAT--?
OH!
THOR! LOOK OUT! MALEKITH'S AWAKE AND HE'S PICKED UP MY GUN!
TOO LATE, MORTAL! NEITHER YOU NOR THOR CAN STOP ME FROM COMPLETING MY APPOINTED TASK!
THOUGH THE COLD IRON BURNS MY FLESH, YOUR WEAPON SHALL SERVE ME EVEN AS IT HAS SERVED YOU!
YOU HAVE WON THE BATTLE, BUT YOU HAVE LOST THE WAR!
UGGH!

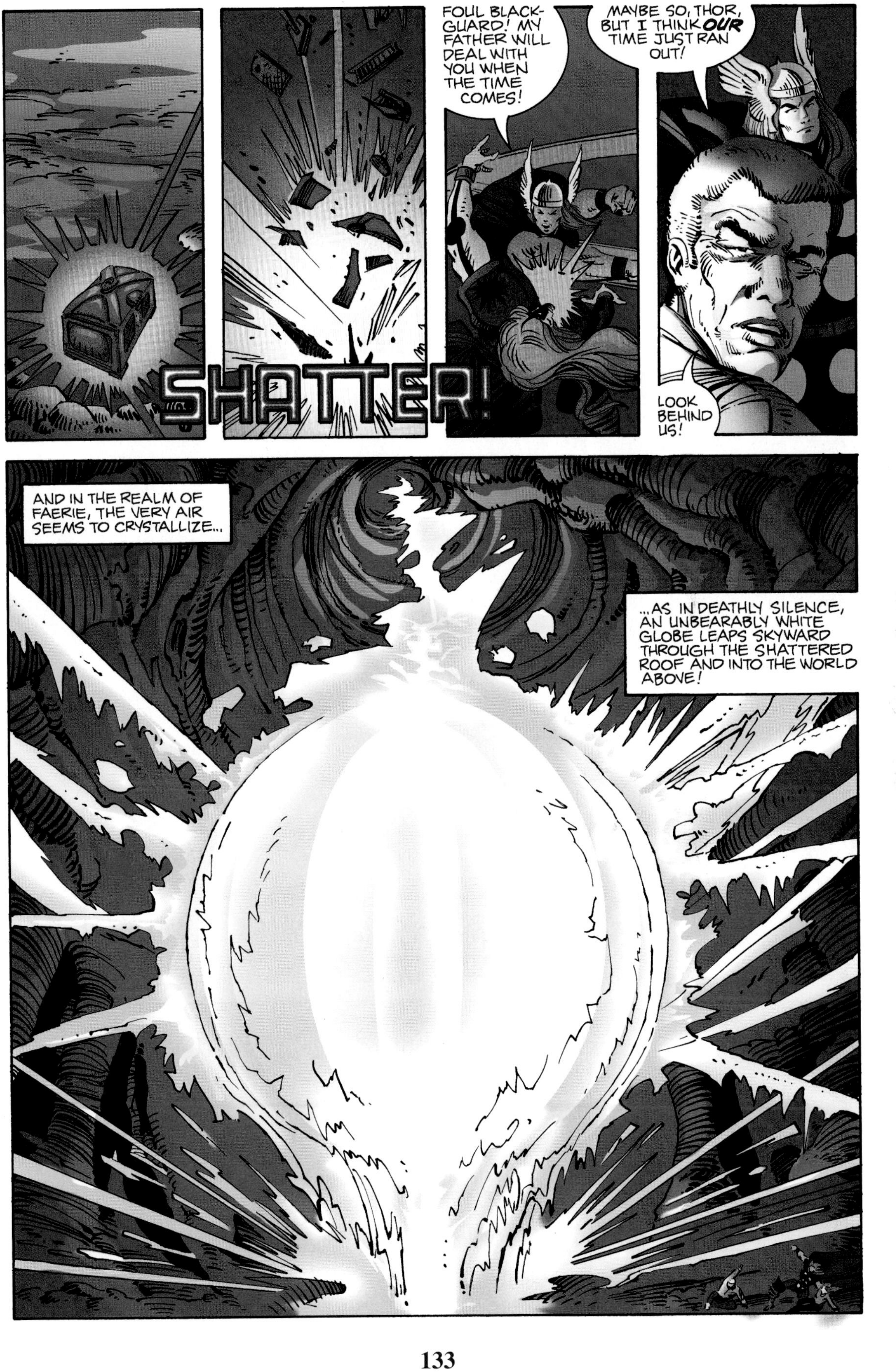
SHATTER!
FOUL BLACK-GUARD! MY FATHER WILL DEAL WITH YOU WHEN THE TIME COMES!
MAYBE SO, THOR, BUT I THINK OUR TIME JUST RAN OUT!
LOOK BEHIND US!
AND IN THE REALM OF FAERIE, THE VERY AIR SEEMS TO CRYSTALLIZE...
...AS IN DEATHLY SILENCE, AN UNBEARABLY WHITE GLOBE LEAPS SKYWARD THROUGH THE SHATTERED ROOF AND INTO THE WORLD ABOVE!

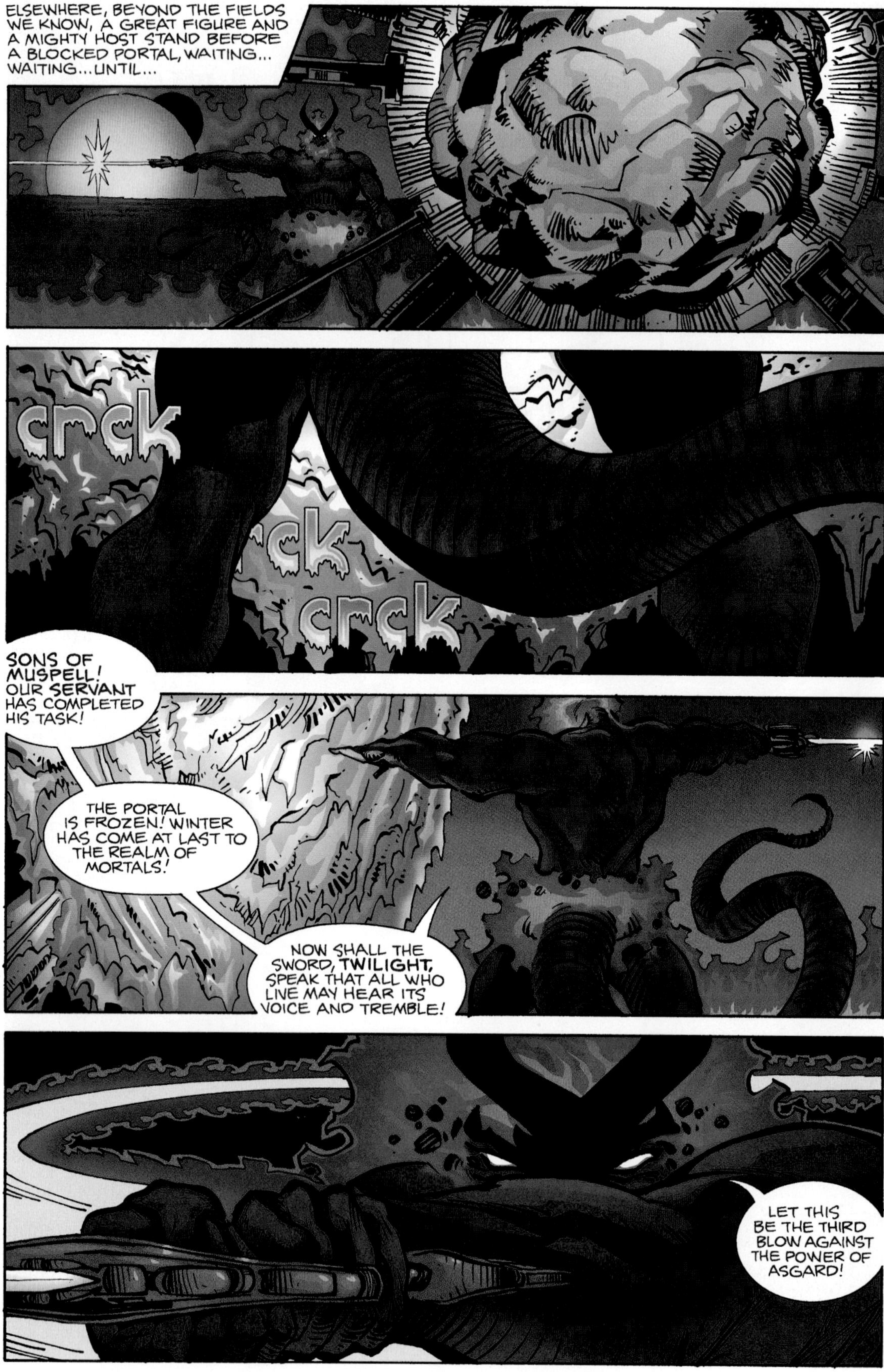
ELSEWHERE, BEYOND THE FIELDS WE KNOW, A GREAT FIGURE AND A MIGHTY HOST STAND BEFORE A BLOCKED PORTAL, WAITING... WAITING... UNTIL...
crck
crck
crck
SONS OF MUSPELL! OUR SERVANT HAS COMPLETED HIS TASK!
THE PORTAL IS FROZEN! WINTER HAS COME AT LAST TO THE REALM OF MORTALS!
NOW SHALL THE SWORD, TWILIGHT, SPEAK THAT ALL WHO LIVE MAY HEAR ITS VOICE AND TREMBLE!
LET THIS BE THE THIRD BLOW AGAINST THE POWER OF ASGARD!

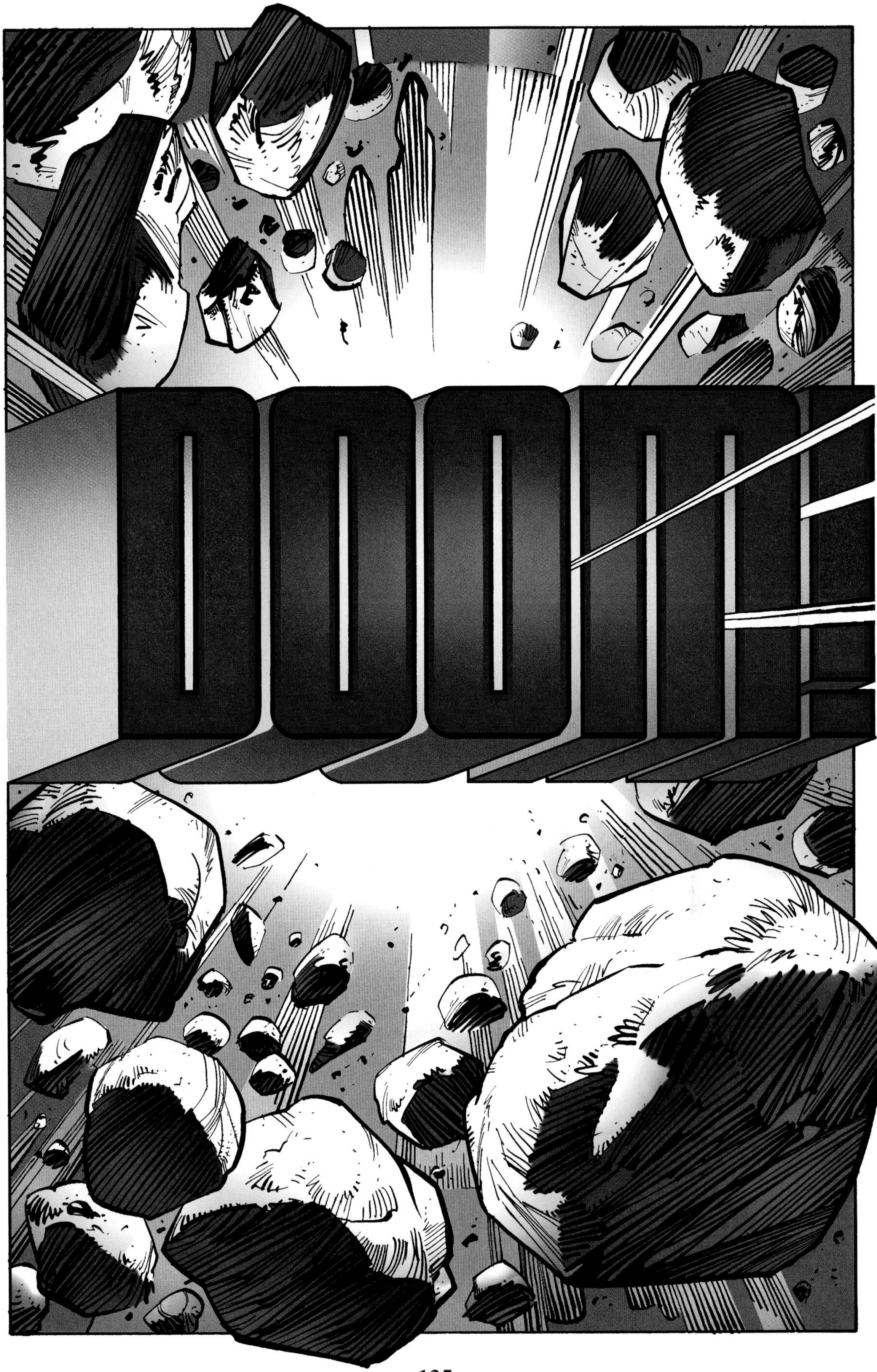
DOOM!

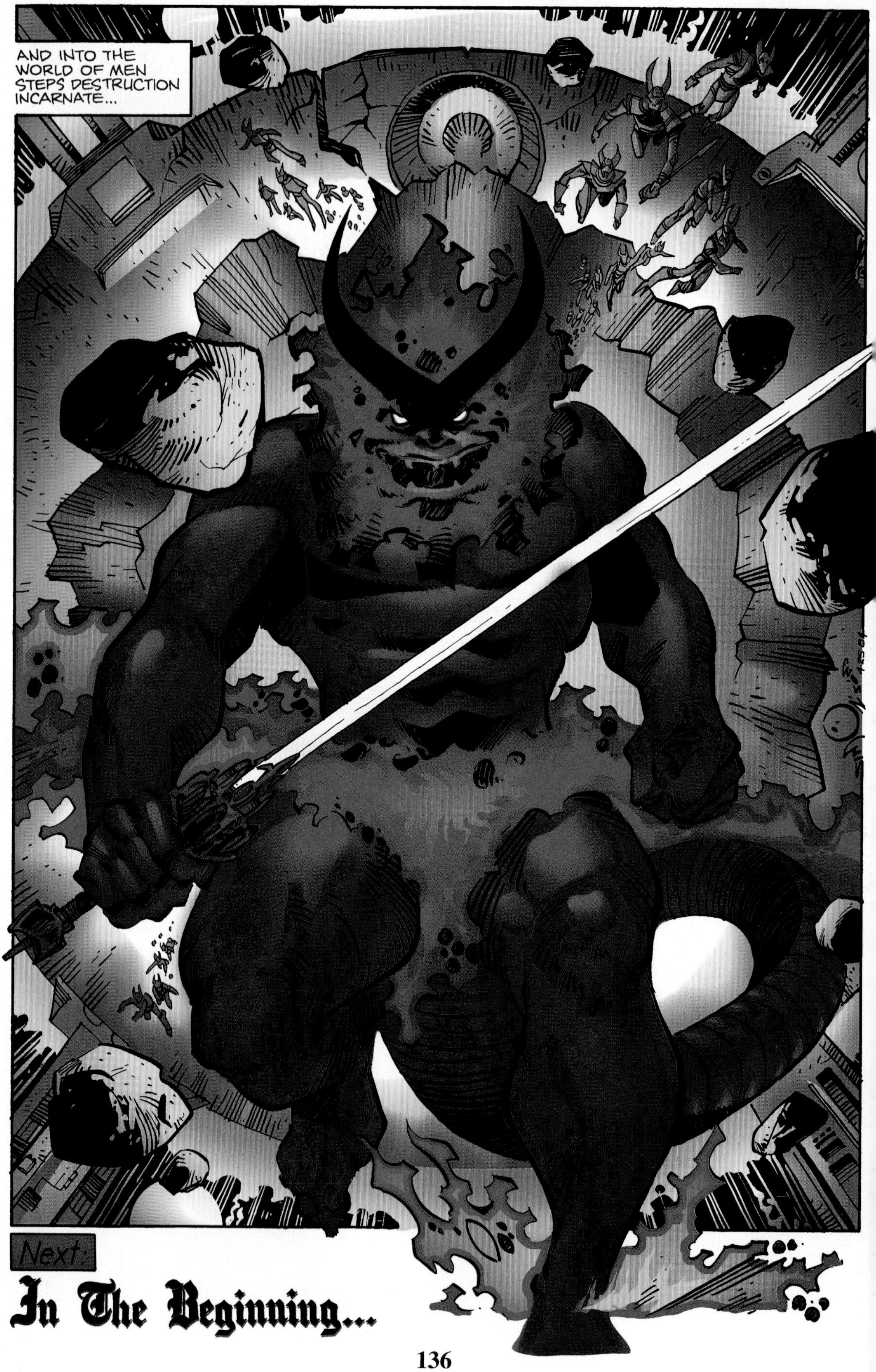
AND INTO THE WORLD OF MEN STEPS DESTRUCTION INCARNATE...

Next:

# In The Beginning...

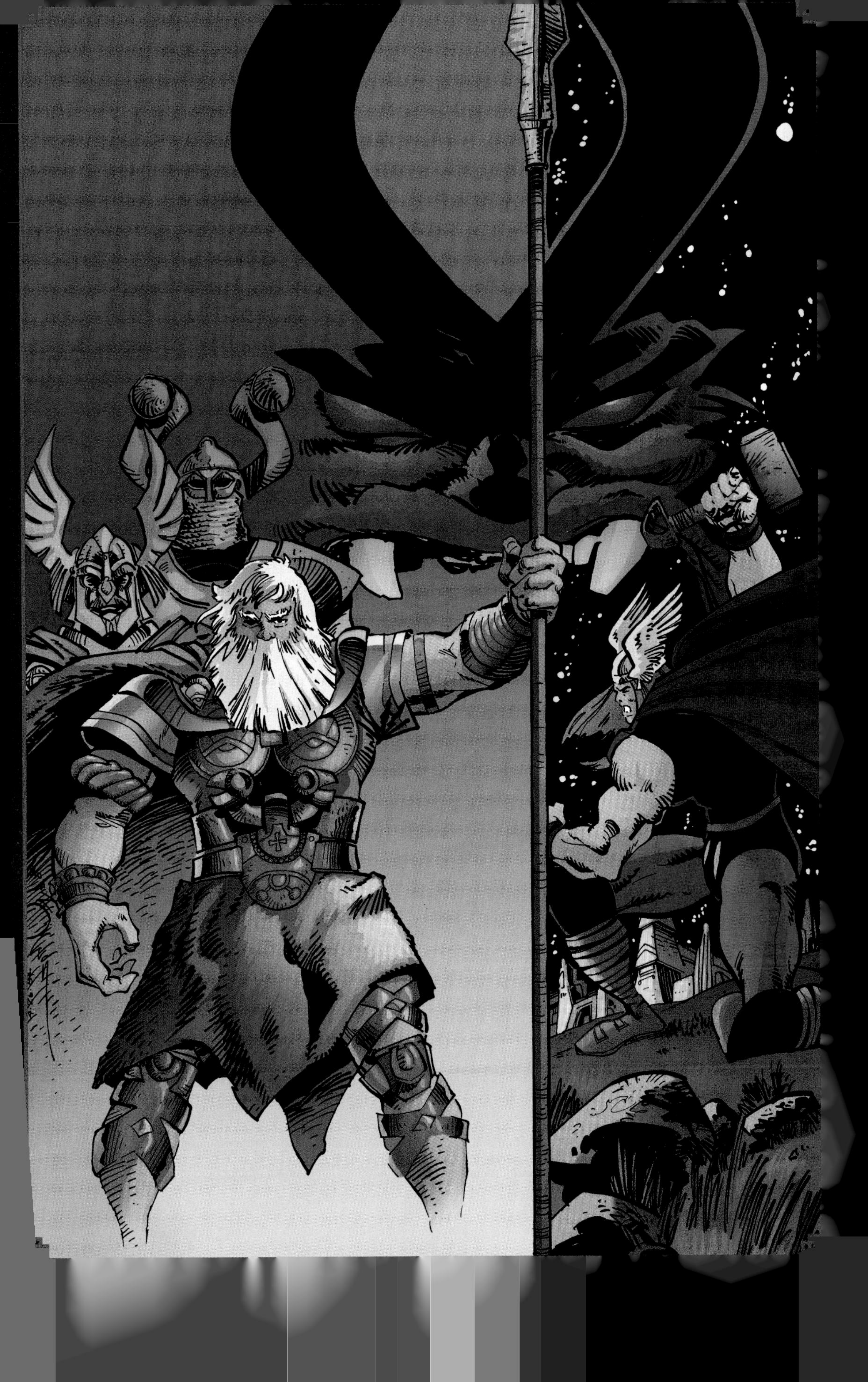

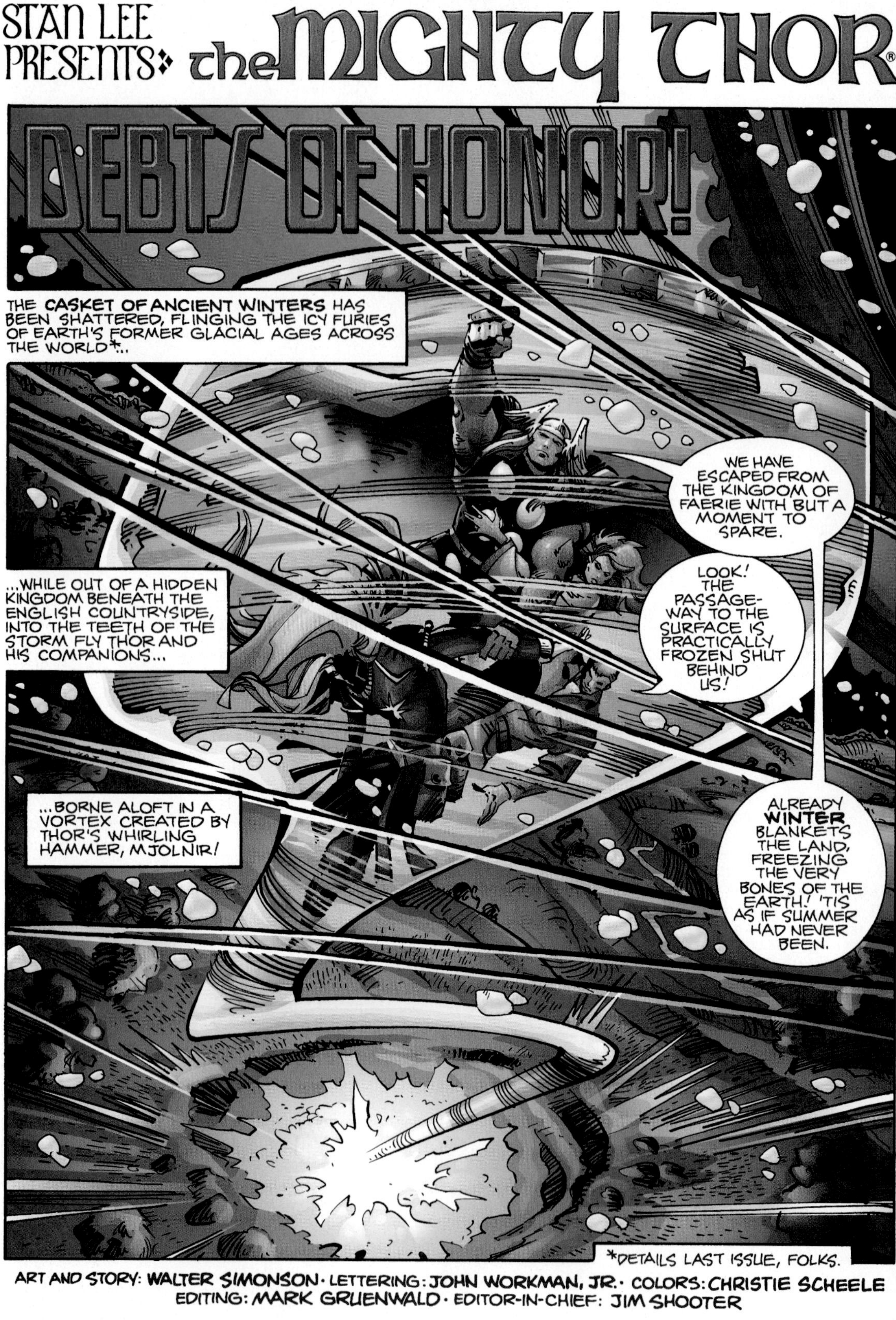
STAN LEE PRESENTS: the MIGHTY THOR®
DEBTS OF HONOR!
THE CASKET OF ANCIENT WINTERS HAS BEEN SHATTERED, FLINGING THE ICY FURIES OF EARTH'S FORMER GLACIAL AGES ACROSS THE WORLD*...
...WHILE OUT OF A HIDDEN KINGDOM BENEATH THE ENGLISH COUNTRYSIDE, INTO THE TEETH OF THE STORM FLY THOR AND HIS COMPANIONS...
...BORNE ALOFT IN A VORTEX CREATED BY THOR'S WHIRLING HAMMER, MJOLNIR!
WE HAVE ESCAPED FROM THE KINGDOM OF FAERIE WITH BUT A MOMENT TO SPARE.
LOOK! THE PASSAGEWAY TO THE SURFACE IS PRACTICALLY FROZEN SHUT BEHIND US!
ALREADY WINTER BLANKETS THE LAND, FREEZING THE VERY BONES OF THE EARTH! 'TIS AS IF SUMMER HAD NEVER BEEN.
*DETAILS LAST ISSUE, FOLKS.
ART AND STORY: WALTER SIMONSON · LETTERING: JOHN WORKMAN, JR. · COLORS: CHRISTIE SCHEELE
EDITING: MARK GRUENWALD · EDITOR-IN-CHIEF: JIM SHOOTER

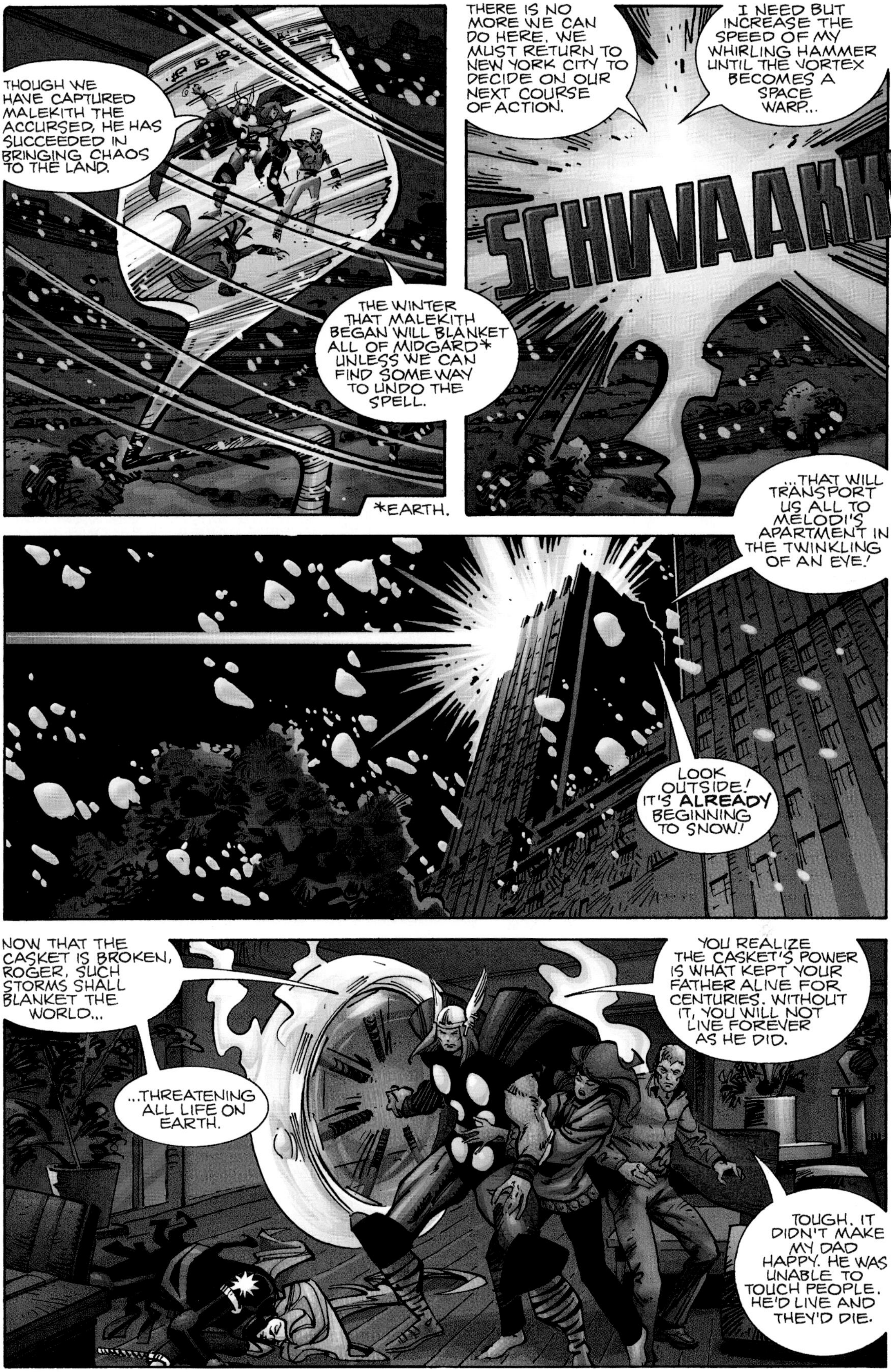
THOUGH WE HAVE CAPTURED MALEKITH THE ACCURSED, HE HAS SUCCEEDED IN BRINGING CHAOS TO THE LAND.
THE WINTER THAT MALEKITH BEGAN WILL BLANKET ALL OF MIDGARD* UNLESS WE CAN FIND SOME WAY TO UNDO THE SPELL.
*EARTH.
THERE IS NO MORE WE CAN DO HERE. WE MUST RETURN TO NEW YORK CITY TO DECIDE ON OUR NEXT COURSE OF ACTION.
I NEED BUT INCREASE THE SPEED OF MY WHIRLING HAMMER UNTIL THE VORTEX BECOMES A SPACE WARP...
SCHVVAAKK!
...THAT WILL TRANSPORT US ALL TO MELODI'S APARTMENT IN THE TWINKLING OF AN EYE!
LOOK OUTSIDE! IT'S ALREADY BEGINNING TO SNOW!
NOW THAT THE CASKET IS BROKEN, ROGER, SUCH STORMS SHALL BLANKET THE WORLD...
...THREATENING ALL LIFE ON EARTH.
YOU REALIZE THE CASKET'S POWER IS WHAT KEPT YOUR FATHER ALIVE FOR CENTURIES. WITHOUT IT, YOU WILL NOT LIVE FOREVER AS HE DID.
TOUGH. IT DIDN'T MAKE MY DAD HAPPY. HE WAS UNABLE TO TOUCH PEOPLE. HE'D LIVE AND THEY'D DIE.

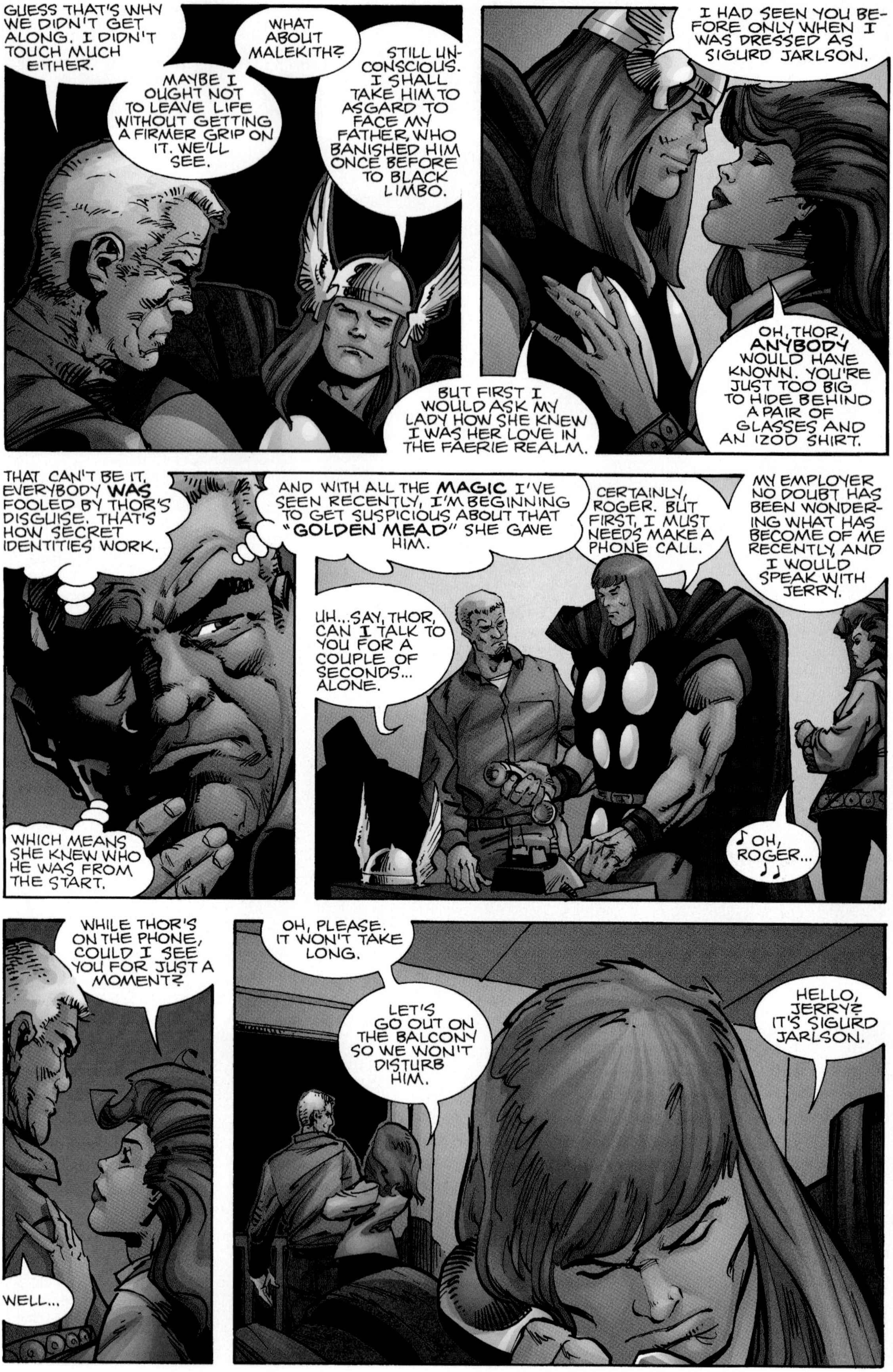
GUESS THAT'S WHY WE DIDN'T GET ALONG. I DIDN'T TOUCH MUCH EITHER.
WHAT ABOUT MALEKITH?
MAYBE I OUGHT NOT TO LEAVE LIFE WITHOUT GETTING A FIRMER GRIP ON IT. WE'LL SEE.
STILL UNCONSCIOUS. I SHALL TAKE HIM TO ASGARD TO FACE MY FATHER, WHO BANISHED HIM ONCE BEFORE TO BLACK LIMBO.
BUT FIRST I WOULD ASK MY LADY HOW SHE KNEW I WAS HER LOVE IN THE FAERIE REALM.
I HAD SEEN YOU BEFORE ONLY WHEN I WAS DRESSED AS SIGURD JARLSON.
OH, THOR, ANYBODY WOULD HAVE KNOWN. YOU'RE JUST TOO BIG TO HIDE BEHIND A PAIR OF GLASSES AND AN IZOD SHIRT.
THAT CAN'T BE IT. EVERYBODY WAS FOOLED BY THOR'S DISGUISE. THAT'S HOW SECRET IDENTITIES WORK.
AND WITH ALL THE MAGIC I'VE SEEN RECENTLY, I'M BEGINNING TO GET SUSPICIOUS ABOUT THAT "GOLDEN MEAD" SHE GAVE HIM.
WHICH MEANS SHE KNEW WHO HE WAS FROM THE START.
CERTAINLY, ROGER. BUT FIRST, I MUST NEEDS MAKE A PHONE CALL.
MY EMPLOYER NO DOUBT HAS BEEN WONDERING WHAT HAS BECOME OF ME RECENTLY, AND I WOULD SPEAK WITH JERRY.
UH...SAY, THOR, CAN I TALK TO YOU FOR A COUPLE OF SECONDS... ALONE.
♪ OH, ROGER... ♪♪
WHILE THOR'S ON THE PHONE, COULD I SEE YOU FOR JUST A MOMENT?
WELL...
OH, PLEASE. IT WON'T TAKE LONG.
LET'S GO OUT ON THE BALCONY SO WE WON'T DISTURB HIM.
HELLO, JERRY? IT'S SIGURD JARLSON.

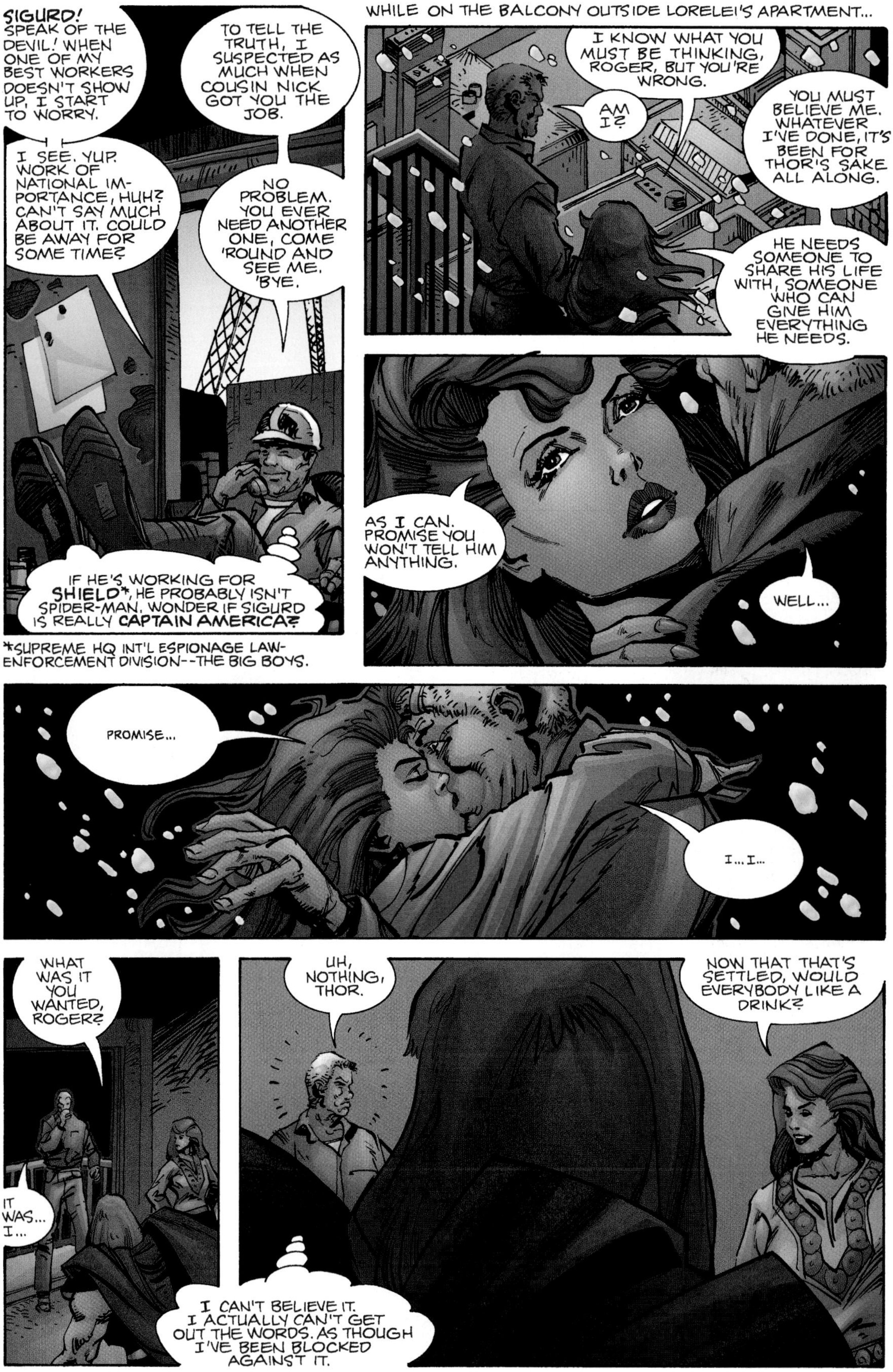
SIGURD! SPEAK OF THE DEVIL! WHEN ONE OF MY BEST WORKERS DOESN'T SHOW UP, I START TO WORRY.
TO TELL THE TRUTH, I SUSPECTED AS MUCH WHEN COUSIN NICK GOT YOU THE JOB.
I SEE. YUP. WORK OF NATIONAL IMPORTANCE, HUH? CAN'T SAY MUCH ABOUT IT. COULD BE AWAY FOR SOME TIME?
NO PROBLEM. YOU EVER NEED ANOTHER ONE, COME 'ROUND AND SEE ME. 'BYE.
IF HE'S WORKING FOR SHIELD*, HE PROBABLY ISN'T SPIDER-MAN. WONDER IF SIGURD IS REALLY CAPTAIN AMERICA?
WHILE ON THE BALCONY OUTSIDE LORELEI'S APARTMENT...
I KNOW WHAT YOU MUST BE THINKING, ROGER, BUT YOU'RE WRONG.
AM I?
YOU MUST BELIEVE ME. WHATEVER I'VE DONE, IT'S BEEN FOR THOR'S SAKE ALL ALONG.
HE NEEDS SOMEONE TO SHARE HIS LIFE WITH, SOMEONE WHO CAN GIVE HIM EVERYTHING HE NEEDS.
AS I CAN. PROMISE YOU WON'T TELL HIM ANYTHING.
WELL...
PROMISE...
I... I...
WHAT WAS IT YOU WANTED, ROGER?
IT WAS... I...
UH, NOTHING, THOR.
NOW THAT THAT'S SETTLED, WOULD EVERYBODY LIKE A DRINK?
I CAN'T BELIEVE IT. I ACTUALLY CAN'T GET OUT THE WORDS. AS THOUGH I'VE BEEN BLOCKED AGAINST IT.

*SUPREME HQ INT'L ESPIONAGE LAW-ENFORCEMENT DIVISION--THE BIG BOYS.

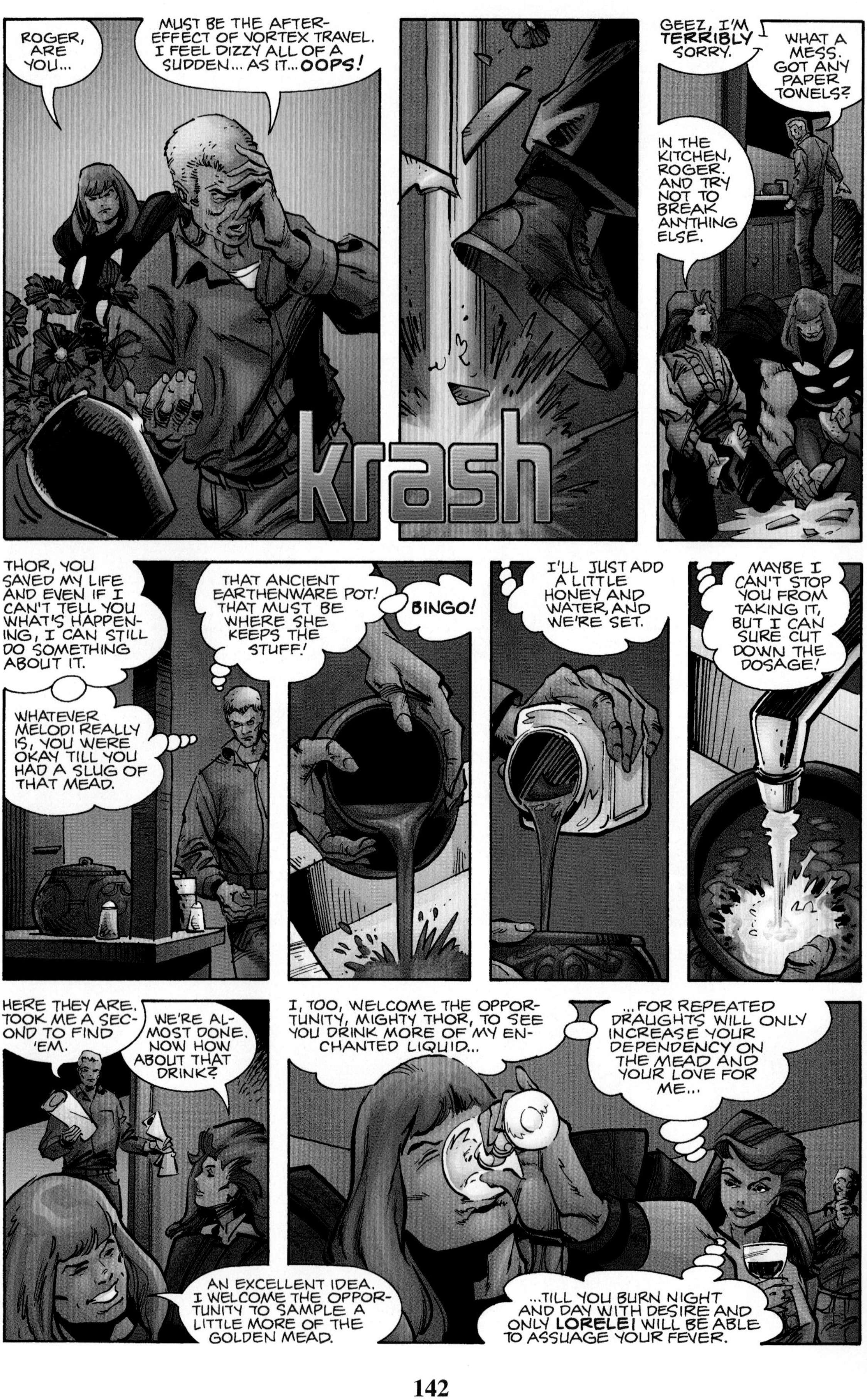
ROGER, ARE YOU...
MUST BE THE AFTER-EFFECT OF VORTEX TRAVEL. I FEEL DIZZY ALL OF A SUDDEN... AS IT... OOPS!
krash
GEEZ, I'M TERRIBLY SORRY.
WHAT A MESS. GOT ANY PAPER TOWELS?
IN THE KITCHEN, ROGER. AND TRY NOT TO BREAK ANYTHING ELSE.
THOR, YOU SAVED MY LIFE AND EVEN IF I CAN'T TELL YOU WHAT'S HAPPENING, I CAN STILL DO SOMETHING ABOUT IT.
WHATEVER MELODI REALLY IS, YOU WERE OKAY TILL YOU HAD A SLUG OF THAT MEAD.
THAT ANCIENT EARTHENWARE POT! THAT MUST BE WHERE SHE KEEPS THE STUFF!
BINGO!
I'LL JUST ADD A LITTLE HONEY AND WATER, AND WE'RE SET.
MAYBE I CAN'T STOP YOU FROM TAKING IT, BUT I CAN SURE CUT DOWN THE DOSAGE!
HERE THEY ARE. TOOK ME A SECOND TO FIND 'EM.
WE'RE ALMOST DONE. NOW HOW ABOUT THAT DRINK?
AN EXCELLENT IDEA. I WELCOME THE OPPORTUNITY TO SAMPLE A LITTLE MORE OF THE GOLDEN MEAD.
I, TOO, WELCOME THE OPPORTUNITY, MIGHTY THOR, TO SEE YOU DRINK MORE OF MY ENCHANTED LIQUID...
...FOR REPEATED DRAUGHTS WILL ONLY INCREASE YOUR DEPENDENCY ON THE MEAD AND YOUR LOVE FOR ME...
...TILL YOU BURN NIGHT AND DAY WITH DESIRE AND ONLY LORELEI WILL BE ABLE TO ASSUAGE YOUR FEVER.

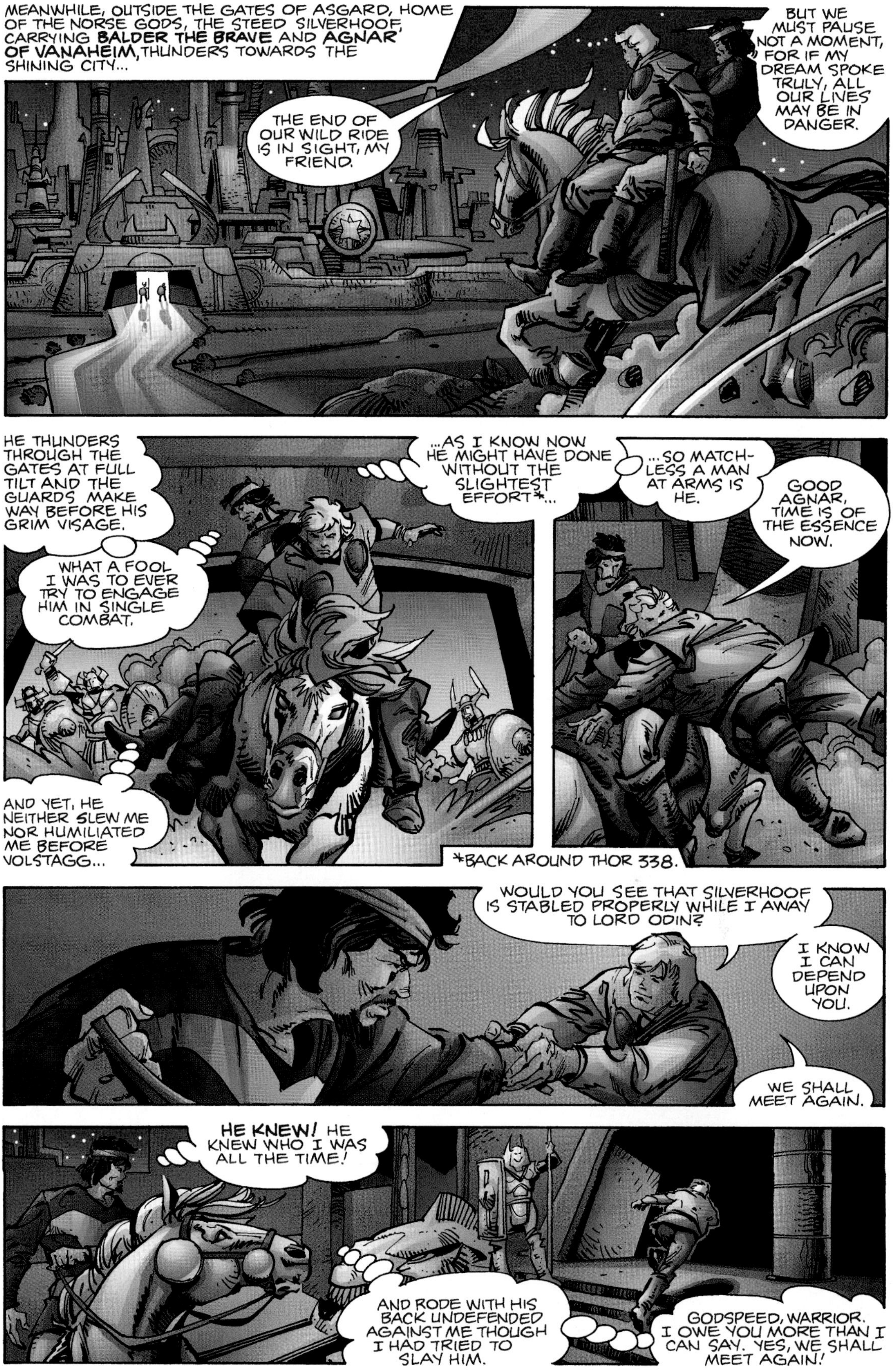
MEANWHILE, OUTSIDE THE GATES OF ASGARD, HOME OF THE NORSE GODS, THE STEED SILVERHOOF, CARRYING **BALDER THE BRAVE** AND **AGNAR OF VANAHEIM**, THUNDERS TOWARDS THE SHINING CITY...
THE END OF OUR WILD RIDE IS IN SIGHT, MY FRIEND.
BUT WE MUST PAUSE NOT A MOMENT, FOR IF MY DREAM SPOKE TRULY, ALL OUR LIVES MAY BE IN DANGER.
HE THUNDERS THROUGH THE GATES AT FULL TILT AND THE GUARDS MAKE WAY BEFORE HIS GRIM VISAGE.
WHAT A FOOL I WAS TO EVER TRY TO ENGAGE HIM IN SINGLE COMBAT.
AND YET, HE NEITHER SLEW ME NOR HUMILIATED ME BEFORE VOLSTAGG...
...AS I KNOW NOW HE MIGHT HAVE DONE WITHOUT THE SLIGHTEST EFFORT*...
...SO MATCHLESS A MAN AT ARMS IS HE.
GOOD AGNAR, TIME IS OF THE ESSENCE NOW.
*BACK AROUND THOR 338.
WOULD YOU SEE THAT SILVERHOOF IS STABLED PROPERLY WHILE I AWAY TO LORD ODIN?
I KNOW I CAN DEPEND UPON YOU.
WE SHALL MEET AGAIN.
**HE KNEW!** HE KNEW WHO I WAS ALL THE TIME!
AND RODE WITH HIS BACK UNDEFENDED AGAINST ME THOUGH I HAD TRIED TO SLAY HIM.
GODSPEED, WARRIOR. I OWE YOU MORE THAN I CAN SAY. YES, WE SHALL MEET AGAIN!

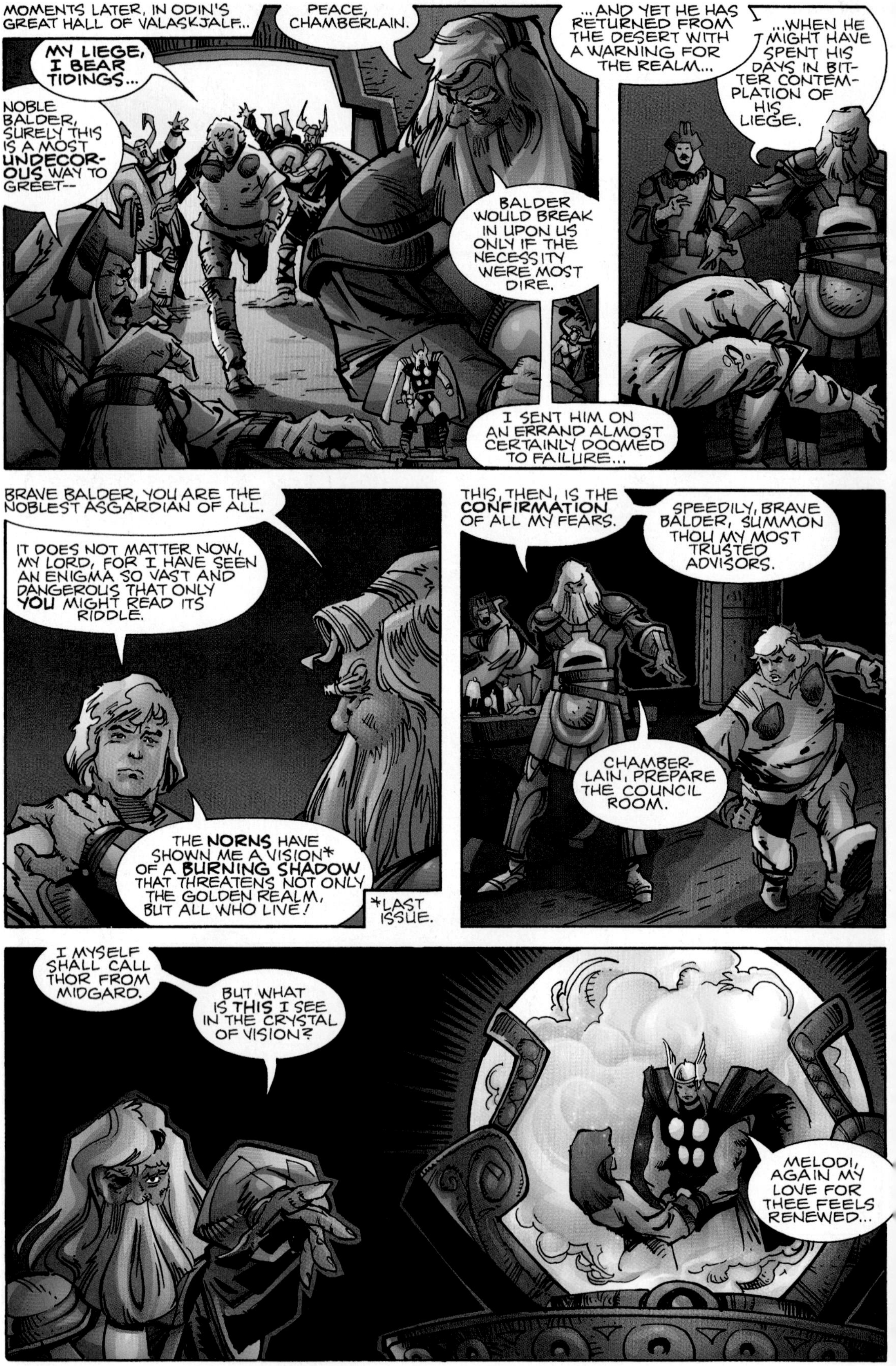

MOMENTS LATER, IN ODIN'S GREAT HALL OF VALASKJALF...
MY LIEGE, I BEAR TIDINGS...
NOBLE BALDER, SURELY THIS IS A MOST UNDECOROUS WAY TO GREET--
PEACE, CHAMBERLAIN.
BALDER WOULD BREAK IN UPON US ONLY IF THE NECESSITY WERE MOST DIRE.
I SENT HIM ON AN ERRAND ALMOST CERTAINLY DOOMED TO FAILURE...
...AND YET HE HAS RETURNED FROM THE DESERT WITH A WARNING FOR THE REALM...
...WHEN HE MIGHT HAVE SPENT HIS DAYS IN BITTER CONTEMPLATION OF HIS LIEGE.
BRAVE BALDER, YOU ARE THE NOBLEST ASGARDIAN OF ALL.
IT DOES NOT MATTER NOW, MY LORD, FOR I HAVE SEEN AN ENIGMA SO VAST AND DANGEROUS THAT ONLY YOU MIGHT READ ITS RIDDLE.
THE NORNS HAVE SHOWN ME A VISION* OF A BURNING SHADOW THAT THREATENS NOT ONLY THE GOLDEN REALM, BUT ALL WHO LIVE!
*LAST ISSUE.
THIS, THEN, IS THE CONFIRMATION OF ALL MY FEARS.
SPEEDILY, BRAVE BALDER, SUMMON THOU MY MOST TRUSTED ADVISORS.
CHAMBERLAIN, PREPARE THE COUNCIL ROOM.
I MYSELF SHALL CALL THOR FROM MIDGARD.
BUT WHAT IS THIS I SEE IN THE CRYSTAL OF VISION?
MELODI, AGAIN MY LOVE FOR THEE FEELS RENEWED...

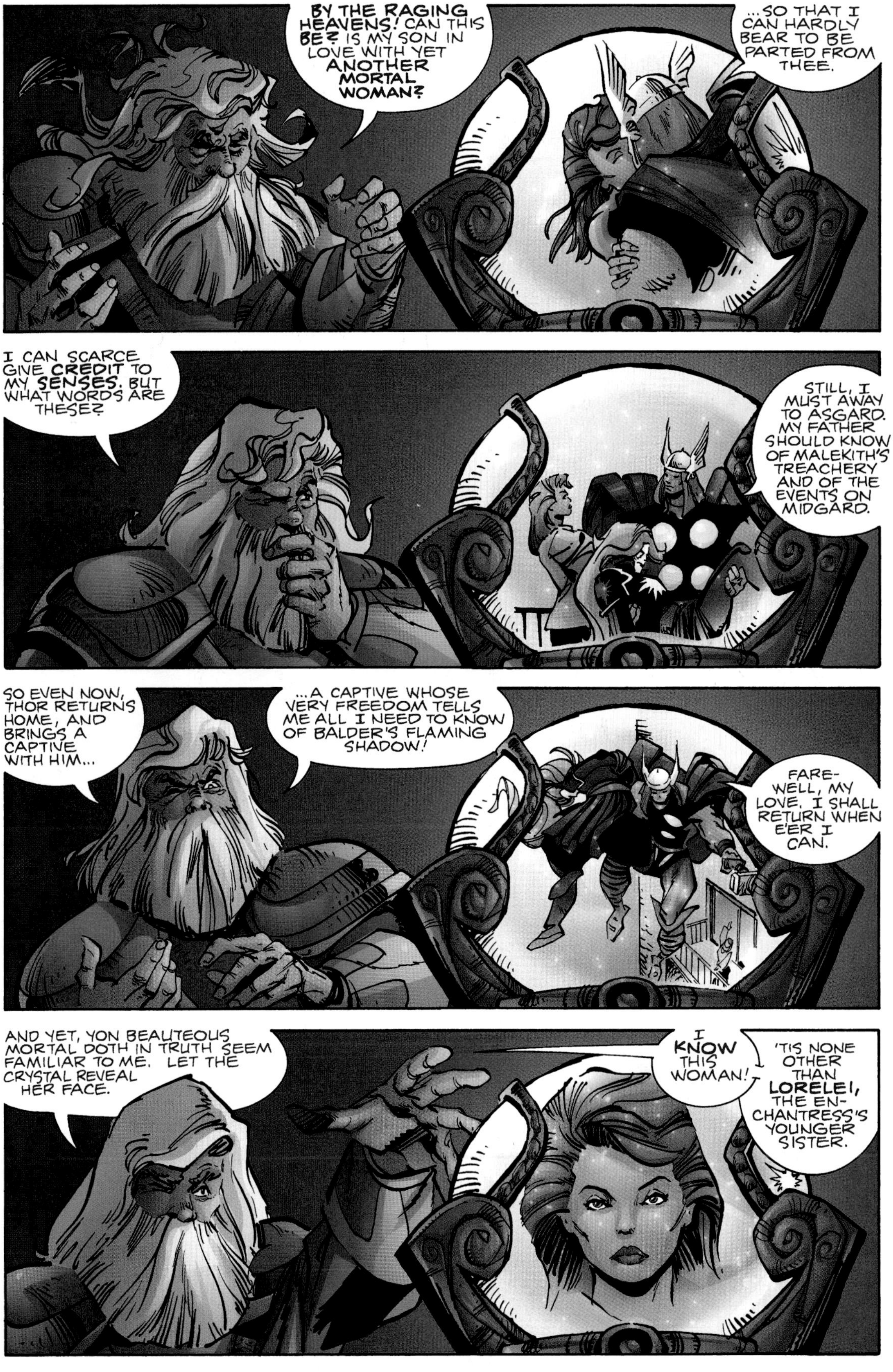
BY THE RAGING HEAVENS! CAN THIS BE? IS MY SON IN LOVE WITH YET ANOTHER MORTAL WOMAN?
...SO THAT I CAN HARDLY BEAR TO BE PARTED FROM THEE.
I CAN SCARCE GIVE CREDIT TO MY SENSES. BUT WHAT WORDS ARE THESE?
STILL, I MUST AWAY TO ASGARD. MY FATHER SHOULD KNOW OF MALEKITH'S TREACHERY AND OF THE EVENTS ON MIDGARD.
SO EVEN NOW, THOR RETURNS HOME, AND BRINGS A CAPTIVE WITH HIM...
...A CAPTIVE WHOSE VERY FREEDOM TELLS ME ALL I NEED TO KNOW OF BALDER'S FLAMING SHADOW!
FARE-WELL, MY LOVE. I SHALL RETURN WHEN E'ER I CAN.
AND YET, YON BEAUTEOUS MORTAL DOTH IN TRUTH SEEM FAMILIAR TO ME. LET THE CRYSTAL REVEAL HER FACE.
I KNOW THIS WOMAN!
'TIS NONE OTHER THAN LORELEI, THE EN-CHANTRESS'S YOUNGER SISTER.

YET APPARENTLY THOR KNOWS IT NOT. DID HE NOT CALL HER "MELODI"?

A WONDERFUL JEST.

I WILL NOT INTERFERE IN THIS RELATIONSHIP.

SO LONG AS HE HAS NOT FORMED AN ATTACHMENT WITH A MORTAL WOMAN, I AM CONTENT.

AND A SON **SHOULD** HAVE SOME SECRETS FROM HIS FATHER.

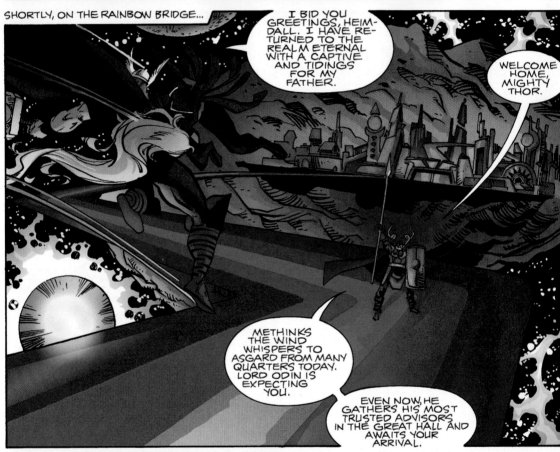

SHORTLY, ON THE RAINBOW BRIDGE...

I BID YOU GREETINGS, HEIMDALL. I HAVE RETURNED TO THE REALM ETERNAL WITH A CAPTIVE AND TIDINGS FOR MY FATHER.

WELCOME HOME, MIGHTY THOR.

METHINKS THE WIND WHISPERS TO ASGARD FROM MANY QUARTERS TODAY. LORD ODIN IS EXPECTING YOU.

EVEN NOW, HE GATHERS HIS MOST TRUSTED ADVISORS IN THE GREAT HALL AND AWAITS YOUR ARRIVAL.

...BUT MAYHAP BEFORE THE SUN HAS SET, I SHALL LEARN THE ANSWERS TO THE QUESTIONS I HAVE BEGUN TO ASK ABOUT THE SHADOWS LOOMING OVER MIDGARD THESE PAST FEW WEEKS.

I CAN SEE THAT MY NEWS WILL BE NO NEWS.

STILL, SOMEDAY, I HOPE TO SURPRISE MY FATHER AT SOMETHING...

146

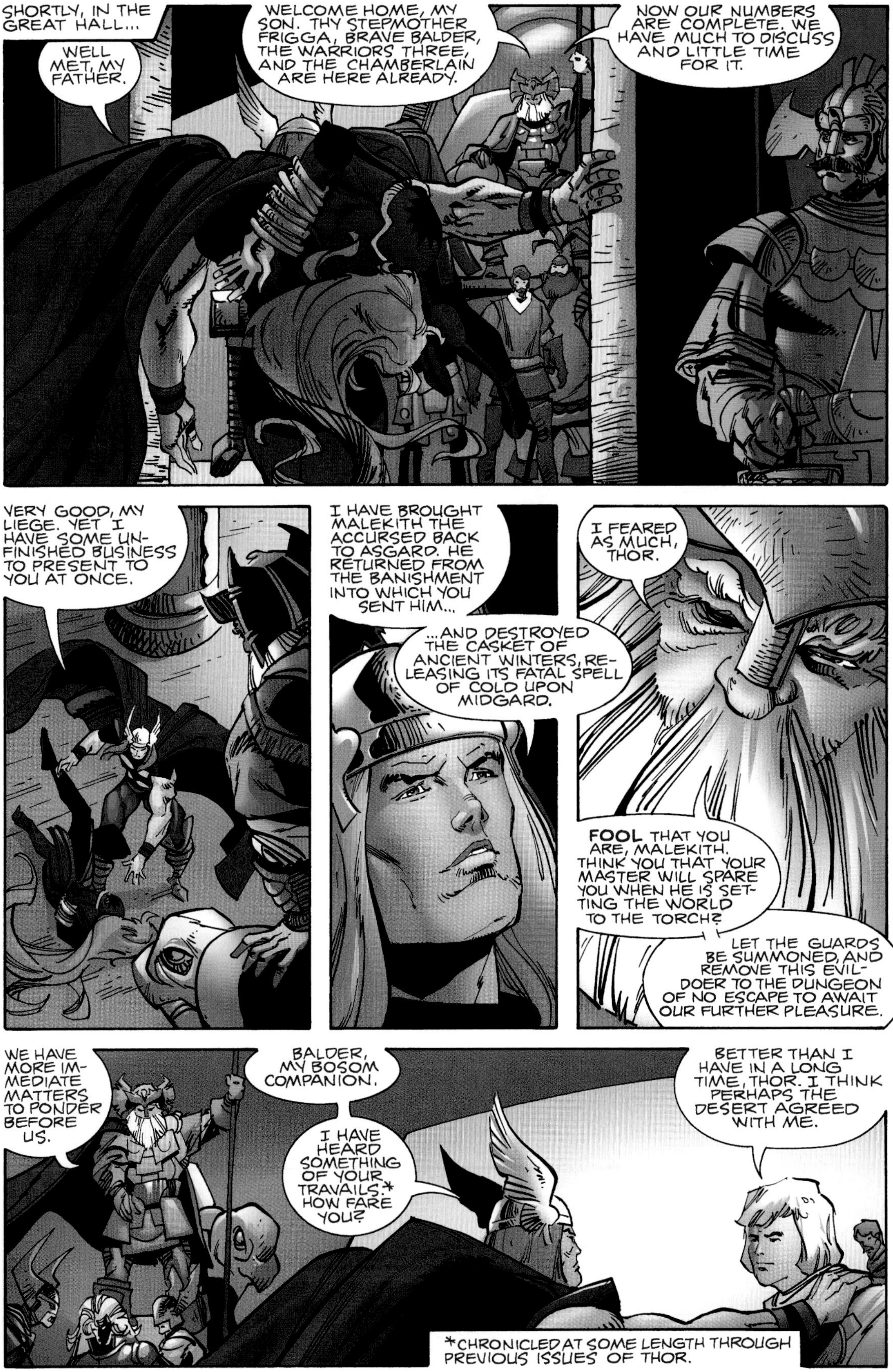
SHORTLY, IN THE GREAT HALL...
WELL MET, MY FATHER.
WELCOME HOME, MY SON. THY STEPMOTHER FRIGGA, BRAVE BALDER, THE WARRIORS THREE, AND THE CHAMBERLAIN ARE HERE ALREADY.
NOW OUR NUMBERS ARE COMPLETE. WE HAVE MUCH TO DISCUSS AND LITTLE TIME FOR IT.
VERY GOOD, MY LIEGE. YET I HAVE SOME UN-FINISHED BUSINESS TO PRESENT TO YOU AT ONCE.
I HAVE BROUGHT MALEKITH THE ACCURSED BACK TO ASGARD. HE RETURNED FROM THE BANISHMENT INTO WHICH YOU SENT HIM...
...AND DESTROYED THE CASKET OF ANCIENT WINTERS, RE-LEASING ITS FATAL SPELL OF COLD UPON MIDGARD.
I FEARED AS MUCH, THOR.
FOOL THAT YOU ARE, MALEKITH. THINK YOU THAT YOUR MASTER WILL SPARE YOU WHEN HE IS SET-TING THE WORLD TO THE TORCH?
LET THE GUARDS BE SUMMONED, AND REMOVE THIS EVIL-DOER TO THE DUNGEON OF NO ESCAPE TO AWAIT OUR FURTHER PLEASURE.
WE HAVE MORE IM-MEDIATE MATTERS TO PONDER BEFORE US.
BALDER, MY BOSOM COMPANION.
I HAVE HEARD SOMETHING OF YOUR TRAVAILS.* HOW FARE YOU?
BETTER THAN I HAVE IN A LONG TIME, THOR. I THINK PERHAPS THE DESERT AGREED WITH ME.
*CHRONICLED AT SOME LENGTH THROUGH PREVIOUS ISSUES OF THOR.

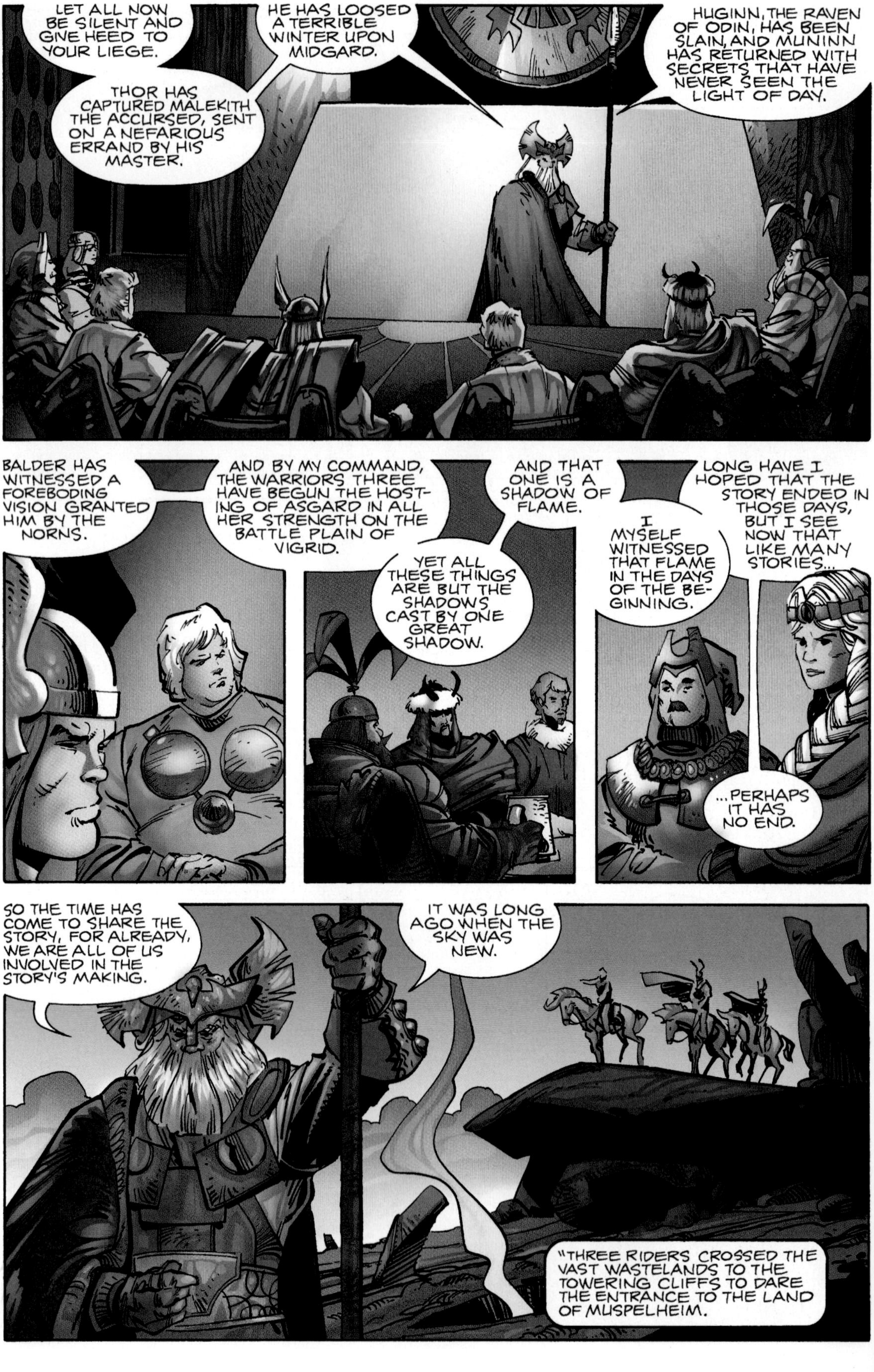
LET ALL NOW BE SILENT AND GIVE HEED TO YOUR LIEGE.
THOR HAS CAPTURED MALEKITH THE ACCURSED, SENT ON A NEFARIOUS ERRAND BY HIS MASTER.
HE HAS LOOSED A TERRIBLE WINTER UPON MIDGARD.
HUGINN, THE RAVEN OF ODIN, HAS BEEN SLAIN, AND MUNINN HAS RETURNED WITH SECRETS THAT HAVE NEVER SEEN THE LIGHT OF DAY.
BALDER HAS WITNESSED A FOREBODING VISION GRANTED HIM BY THE NORNS.
AND BY MY COMMAND, THE WARRIORS THREE HAVE BEGUN THE HOSTING OF ASGARD IN ALL HER STRENGTH ON THE BATTLE PLAIN OF VIGRID.
YET ALL THESE THINGS ARE BUT THE SHADOWS CAST BY ONE GREAT SHADOW.
AND THAT ONE IS A SHADOW OF FLAME.
I MYSELF WITNESSED THAT FLAME IN THE DAYS OF THE BEGINNING.
LONG HAVE I HOPED THAT THE STORY ENDED IN THOSE DAYS, BUT I SEE NOW THAT LIKE MANY STORIES...
...PERHAPS IT HAS NO END.
SO THE TIME HAS COME TO SHARE THE STORY, FOR ALREADY, WE ARE ALL OF US INVOLVED IN THE STORY'S MAKING.
IT WAS LONG AGO WHEN THE SKY WAS NEW.
"THREE RIDERS CROSSED THE VAST WASTELANDS TO THE TOWERING CLIFFS TO DARE THE ENTRANCE TO THE LAND OF MUSPELHEIM.

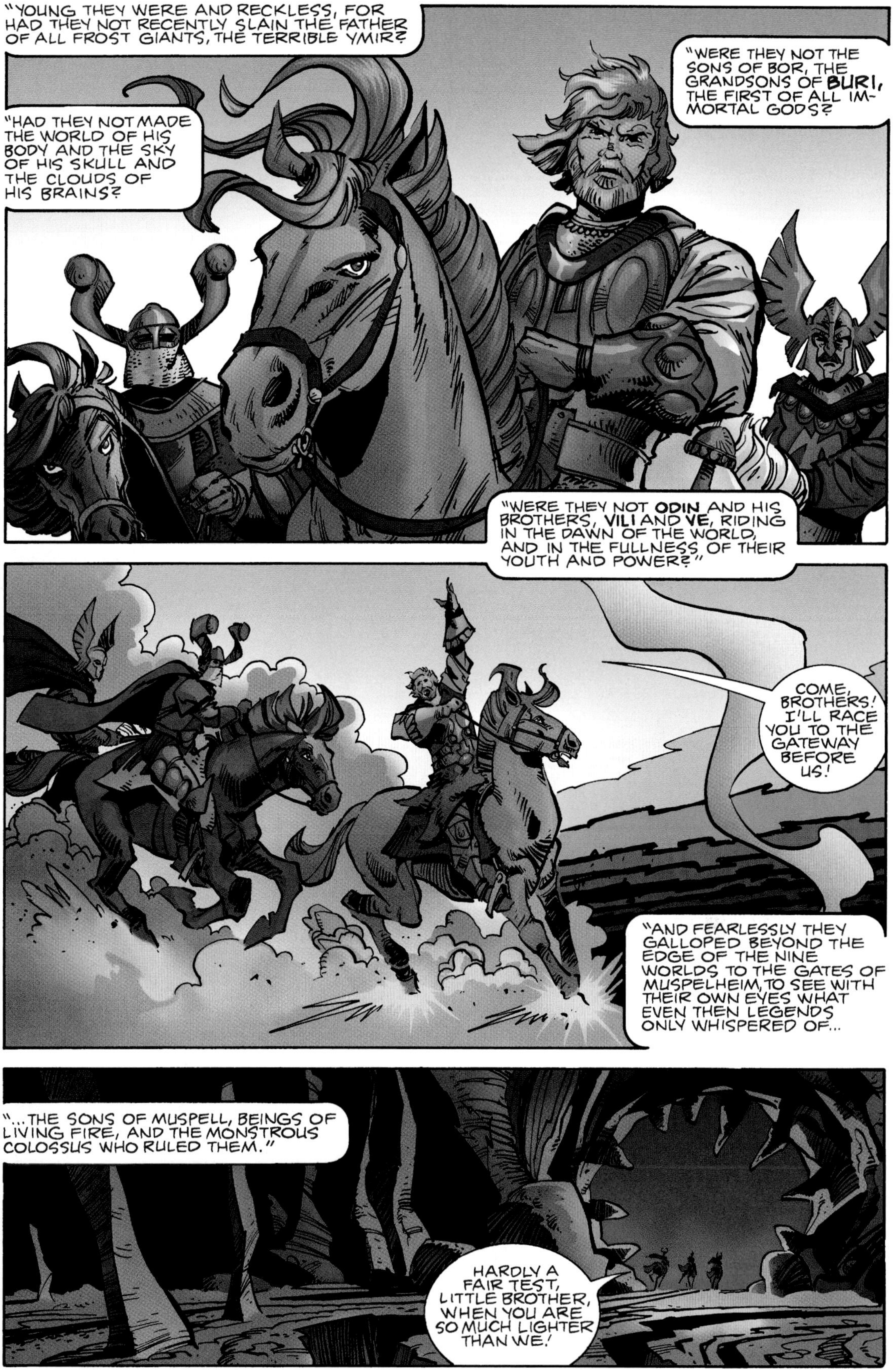
"YOUNG THEY WERE AND RECKLESS, FOR HAD THEY NOT RECENTLY SLAIN THE FATHER OF ALL FROST GIANTS, THE TERRIBLE YMIR?
"WERE THEY NOT THE SONS OF BOR, THE GRANDSONS OF BURI, THE FIRST OF ALL IMMORTAL GODS?
"HAD THEY NOT MADE THE WORLD OF HIS BODY AND THE SKY OF HIS SKULL AND THE CLOUDS OF HIS BRAINS?
"WERE THEY NOT ODIN AND HIS BROTHERS, VILI AND VE, RIDING IN THE DAWN OF THE WORLD, AND IN THE FULLNESS OF THEIR YOUTH AND POWER?"
COME, BROTHERS! I'LL RACE YOU TO THE GATEWAY BEFORE US!
"AND FEARLESSLY THEY GALLOPED BEYOND THE EDGE OF THE NINE WORLDS TO THE GATES OF MUSPELHEIM, TO SEE WITH THEIR OWN EYES WHAT EVEN THEN LEGENDS ONLY WHISPERED OF...
"...THE SONS OF MUSPELL, BEINGS OF LIVING FIRE, AND THE MONSTROUS COLOSSUS WHO RULED THEM."
HARDLY A FAIR TEST, LITTLE BROTHER, WHEN YOU ARE SO MUCH LIGHTER THAN WE!

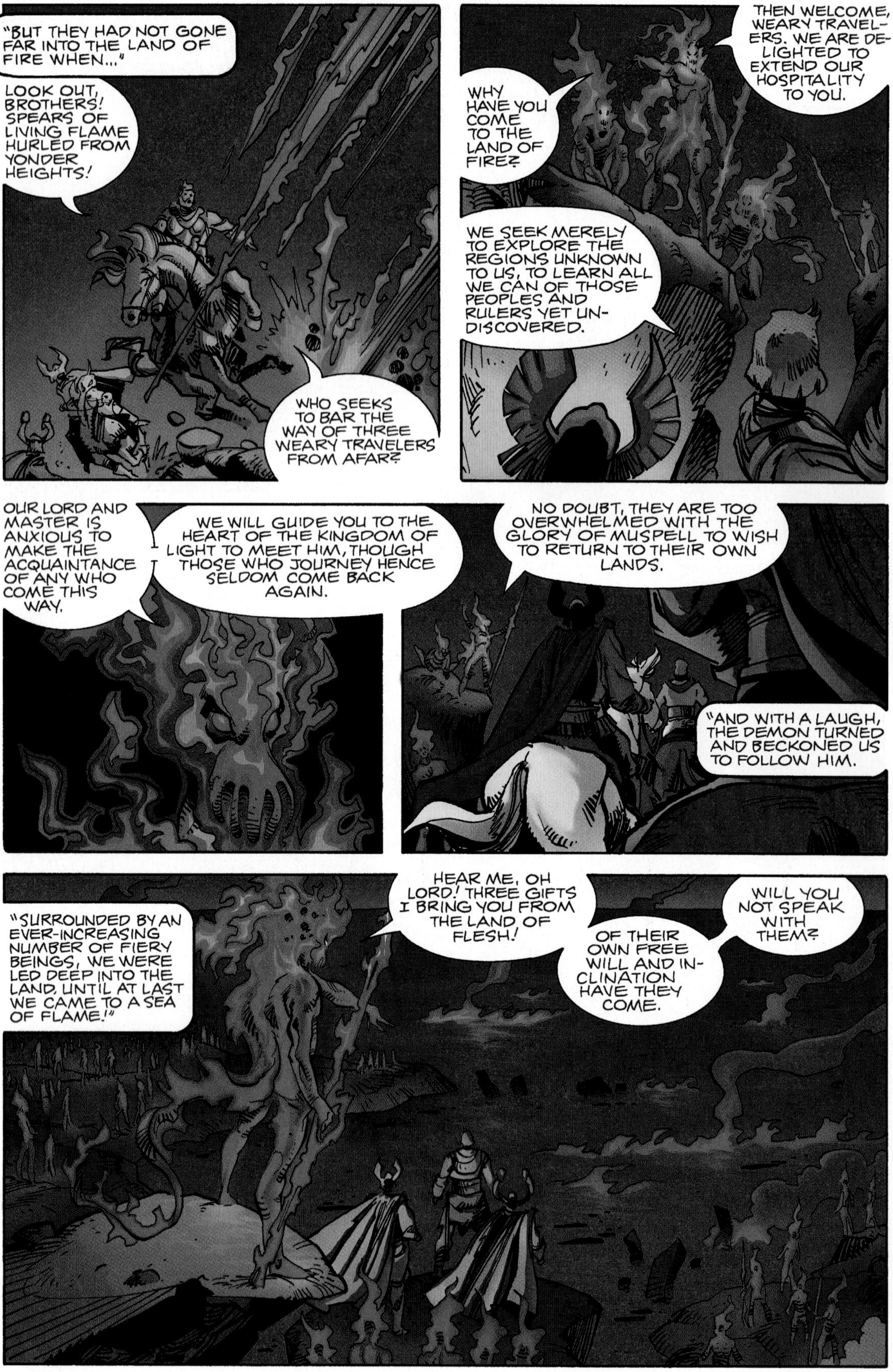
"BUT THEY HAD NOT GONE FAR INTO THE LAND OF FIRE WHEN..."
LOOK OUT, BROTHERS! SPEARS OF LIVING FLAME HURLED FROM YONDER HEIGHTS!
WHO SEEKS TO BAR THE WAY OF THREE WEARY TRAVELERS FROM AFAR?
WHY HAVE YOU COME TO THE LAND OF FIRE?
WE SEEK MERELY TO EXPLORE THE REGIONS UNKNOWN TO US, TO LEARN ALL WE CAN OF THOSE PEOPLES AND RULERS YET UNDISCOVERED.
THEN WELCOME, WEARY TRAVELERS. WE ARE DELIGHTED TO EXTEND OUR HOSPITALITY TO YOU.
OUR LORD AND MASTER IS ANXIOUS TO MAKE THE ACQUAINTANCE OF ANY WHO COME THIS WAY.
WE WILL GUIDE YOU TO THE HEART OF THE KINGDOM OF LIGHT TO MEET HIM, THOUGH THOSE WHO JOURNEY HENCE SELDOM COME BACK AGAIN.
NO DOUBT, THEY ARE TOO OVERWHELMED WITH THE GLORY OF MUSPELL TO WISH TO RETURN TO THEIR OWN LANDS.
"AND WITH A LAUGH, THE DEMON TURNED AND BECKONED US TO FOLLOW HIM.
"SURROUNDED BY AN EVER-INCREASING NUMBER OF FIERY BEINGS, WE WERE LED DEEP INTO THE LAND, UNTIL AT LAST WE CAME TO A SEA OF FLAME!"
HEAR ME, OH LORD! THREE GIFTS I BRING YOU FROM THE LAND OF FLESH!
OF THEIR OWN FREE WILL AND INCLINATION HAVE THEY COME.
WILL YOU NOT SPEAK WITH THEM?

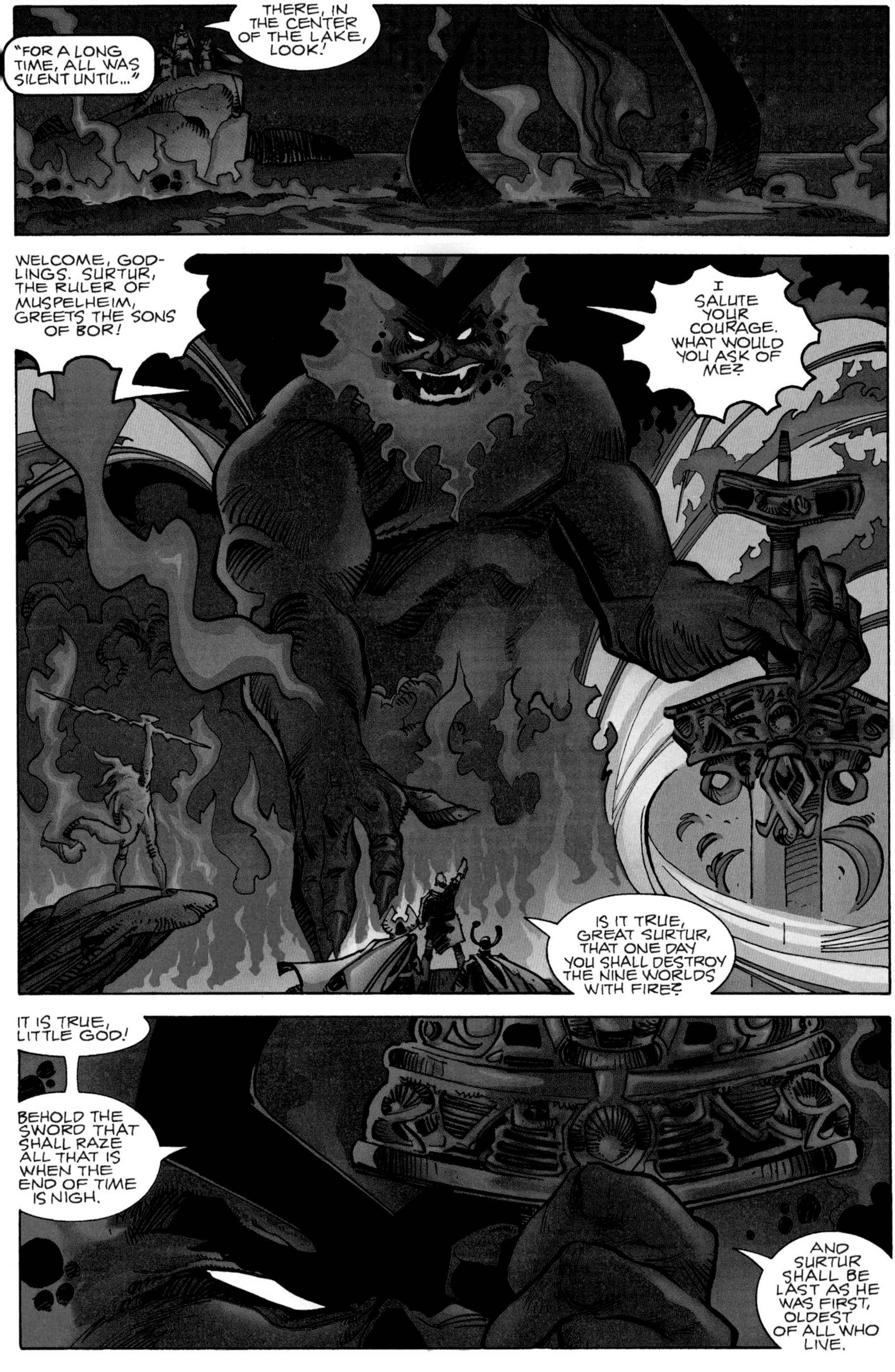
"FOR A LONG TIME, ALL WAS SILENT UNTIL..."
THERE, IN THE CENTER OF THE LAKE, LOOK!
WELCOME, GOD-LINGS. SURTUR, THE RULER OF MUSPELHEIM, GREETS THE SONS OF BOR!
I SALUTE YOUR COURAGE. WHAT WOULD YOU ASK OF ME?
IS IT TRUE, GREAT SURTUR, THAT ONE DAY YOU SHALL DESTROY THE NINE WORLDS WITH FIRE?
IT IS TRUE, LITTLE GOD!
BEHOLD THE SWORD THAT SHALL RAZE ALL THAT IS WHEN THE END OF TIME IS NIGH.
AND SURTUR SHALL BE LAST AS HE WAS FIRST, OLDEST OF ALL WHO LIVE.

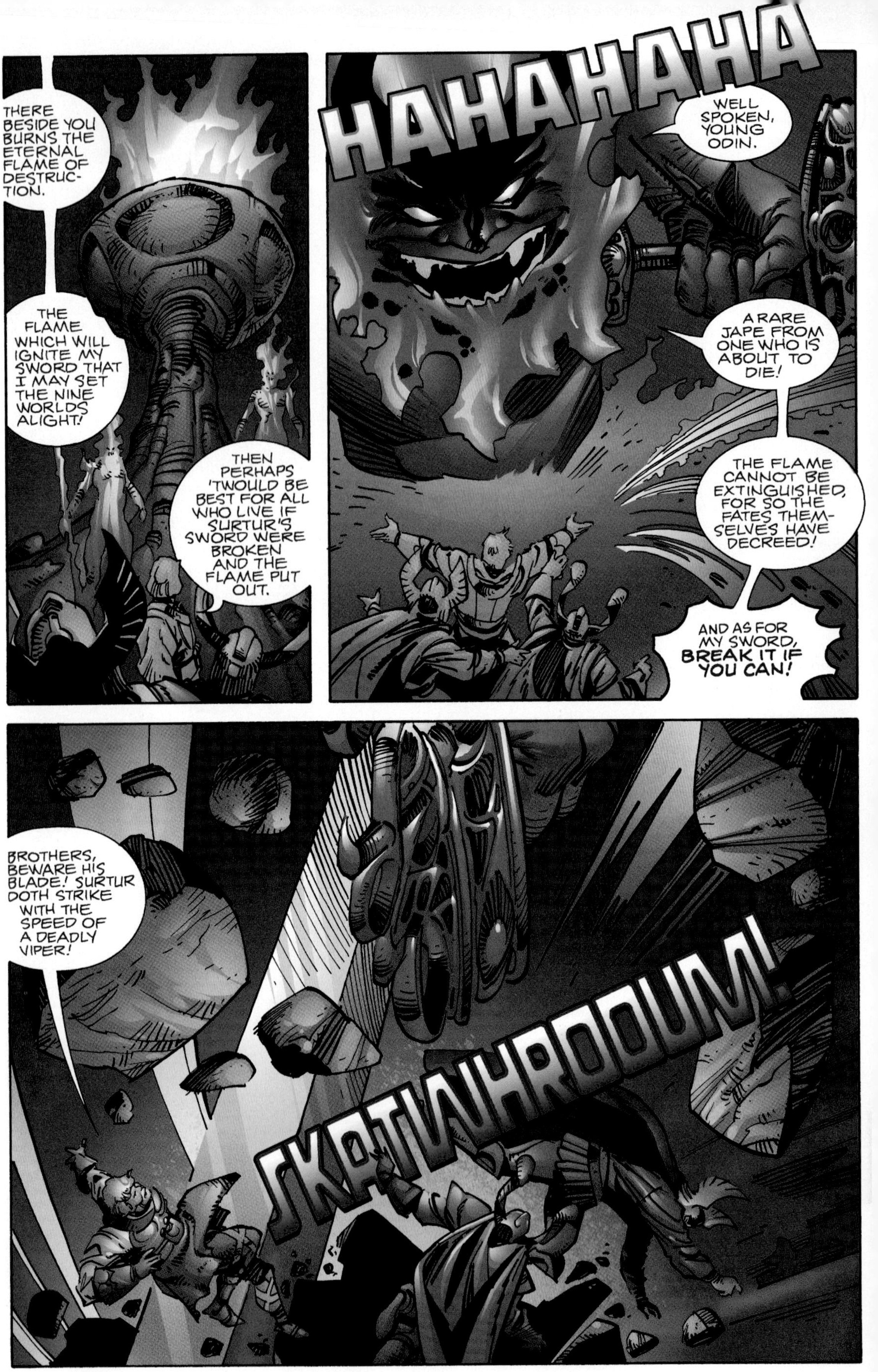
THERE BESIDE YOU BURNS THE ETERNAL FLAME OF DESTRUCTION.
THE FLAME WHICH WILL IGNITE MY SWORD THAT I MAY SET THE NINE WORLDS ALIGHT!
THEN PERHAPS 'TWOULD BE BEST FOR ALL WHO LIVE IF SURTUR'S SWORD WERE BROKEN AND THE FLAME PUT OUT.
HAHAHAHAHA
WELL SPOKEN, YOUNG ODIN.
A RARE JAPE FROM ONE WHO IS ABOUT TO DIE!
THE FLAME CANNOT BE EXTINGUISHED, FOR SO THE FATES THEMSELVES HAVE DECREED!
AND AS FOR MY SWORD, BREAK IT IF YOU CAN!
BROTHERS, BEWARE HIS BLADE! SURTUR DOTH STRIKE WITH THE SPEED OF A DEADLY VIPER!
SKATWHROOUM!

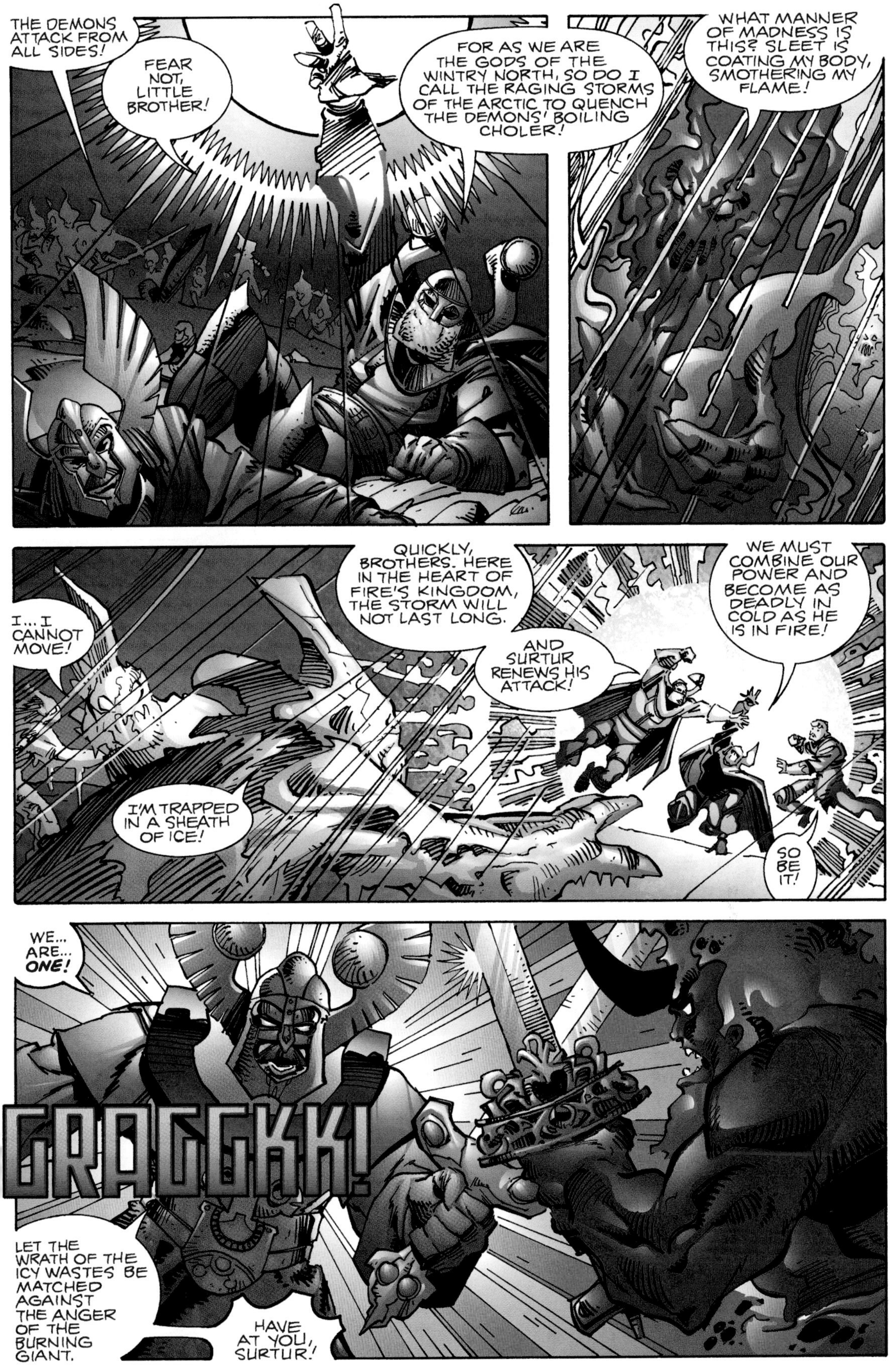
THE DEMONS ATTACK FROM ALL SIDES!
FEAR NOT, LITTLE BROTHER!
FOR AS WE ARE THE GODS OF THE WINTRY NORTH, SO DO I CALL THE RAGING STORMS OF THE ARCTIC TO QUENCH THE DEMONS' BOILING CHOLER!
WHAT MANNER OF MADNESS IS THIS? SLEET IS COATING MY BODY, SMOTHERING MY FLAME!
I... I CANNOT MOVE!
QUICKLY, BROTHERS. HERE IN THE HEART OF FIRE'S KINGDOM, THE STORM WILL NOT LAST LONG.
AND SURTUR RENEWS HIS ATTACK!
WE MUST COMBINE OUR POWER AND BECOME AS DEADLY IN COLD AS HE IS IN FIRE!
I'M TRAPPED IN A SHEATH OF ICE!
SO BE IT!
WE... ARE... **ONE!**
GRAGGKK!
LET THE WRATH OF THE ICY WASTES BE MATCHED AGAINST THE ANGER OF THE BURNING GIANT.
HAVE AT YOU, SURTUR!

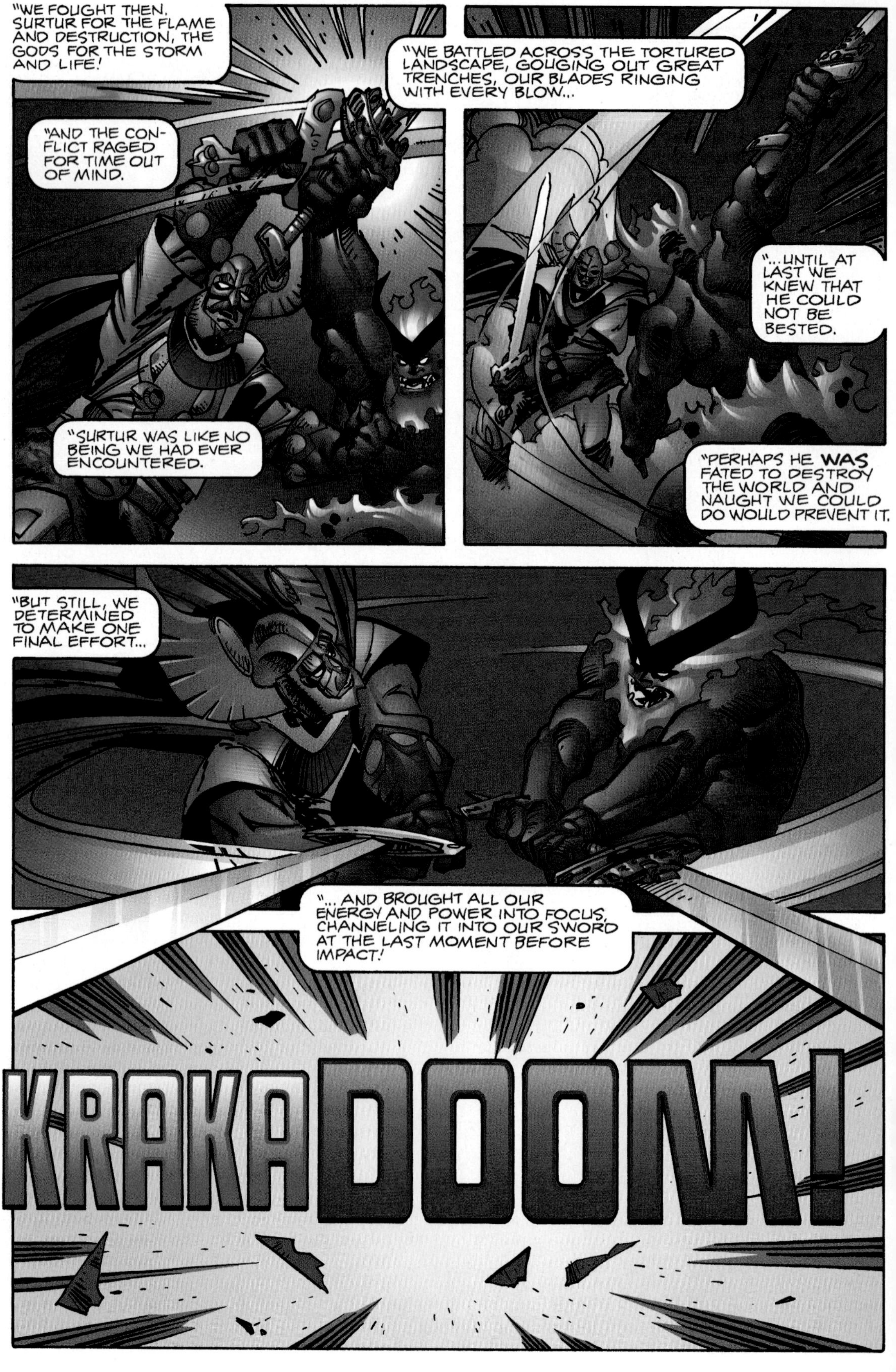
"WE FOUGHT THEN. SURTUR FOR THE FLAME AND DESTRUCTION, THE GODS FOR THE STORM AND LIFE!
"AND THE CONFLICT RAGED FOR TIME OUT OF MIND.
"SURTUR WAS LIKE NO BEING WE HAD EVER ENCOUNTERED.
"WE BATTLED ACROSS THE TORTURED LANDSCAPE, GOUGING OUT GREAT TRENCHES, OUR BLADES RINGING WITH EVERY BLOW...
"...UNTIL AT LAST WE KNEW THAT HE COULD NOT BE BESTED.
"PERHAPS HE **WAS** FATED TO DESTROY THE WORLD AND NAUGHT WE COULD DO WOULD PREVENT IT.
"BUT STILL, WE DETERMINED TO MAKE ONE FINAL EFFORT...
"... AND BROUGHT ALL OUR ENERGY AND POWER INTO FOCUS, CHANNELING IT INTO OUR SWORD AT THE LAST MOMENT BEFORE IMPACT!
KRAKADOOM!

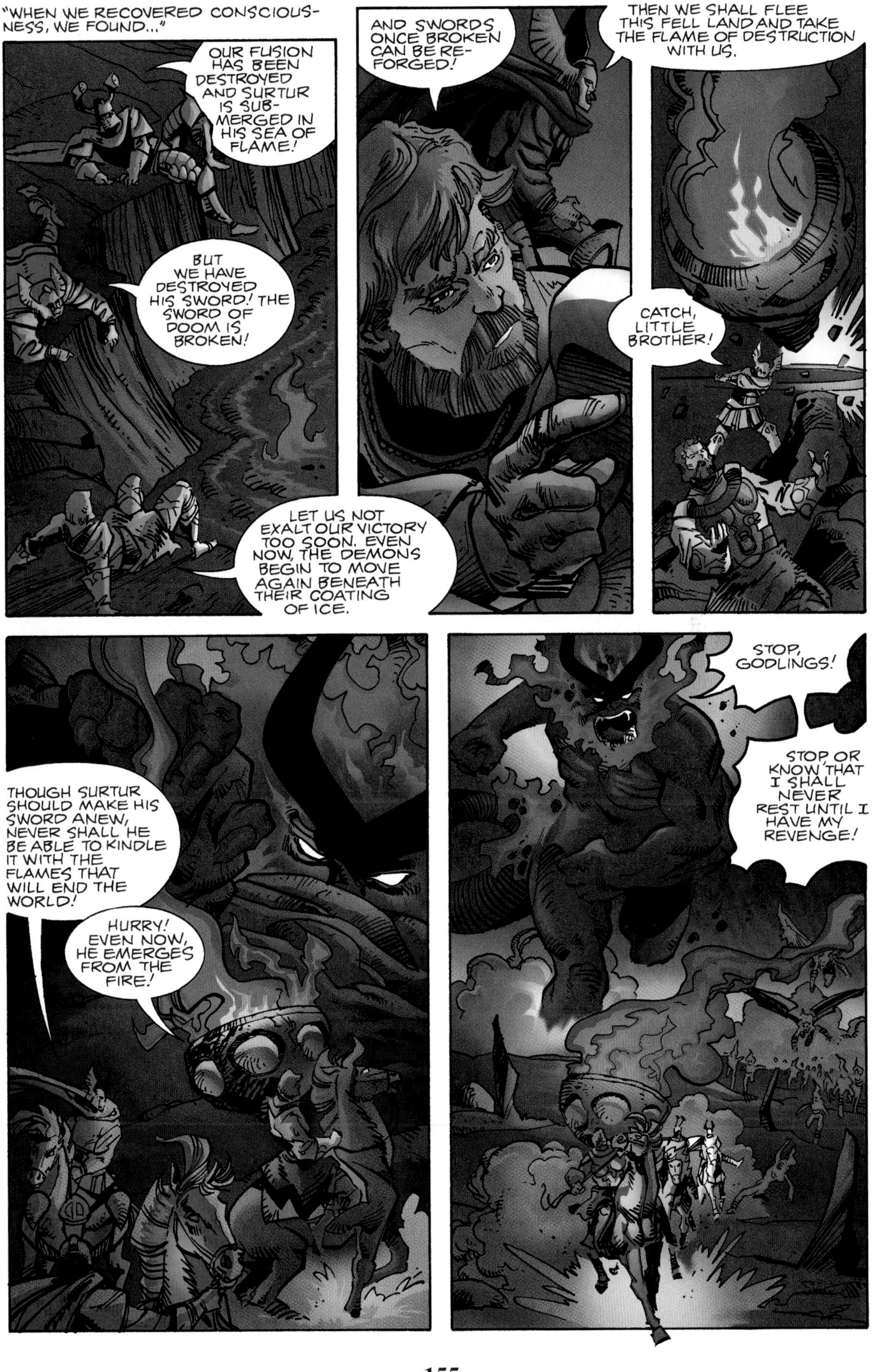
"WHEN WE RECOVERED CONSCIOUSNESS, WE FOUND..."
OUR FUSION HAS BEEN DESTROYED AND SURTUR IS SUBMERGED IN HIS SEA OF FLAME!
BUT WE HAVE DESTROYED HIS SWORD! THE SWORD OF DOOM IS BROKEN!
AND SWORDS ONCE BROKEN CAN BE REFORGED!
LET US NOT EXALT OUR VICTORY TOO SOON. EVEN NOW, THE DEMONS BEGIN TO MOVE AGAIN BENEATH THEIR COATING OF ICE.
THEN WE SHALL FLEE THIS FELL LAND AND TAKE THE FLAME OF DESTRUCTION WITH US.
CATCH, LITTLE BROTHER!
THOUGH SURTUR SHOULD MAKE HIS SWORD ANEW, NEVER SHALL HE BE ABLE TO KINDLE IT WITH THE FLAMES THAT WILL END THE WORLD!
HURRY! EVEN NOW, HE EMERGES FROM THE FIRE!
STOP, GODLINGS!
STOP OR KNOW THAT I SHALL NEVER REST UNTIL I HAVE MY REVENGE!

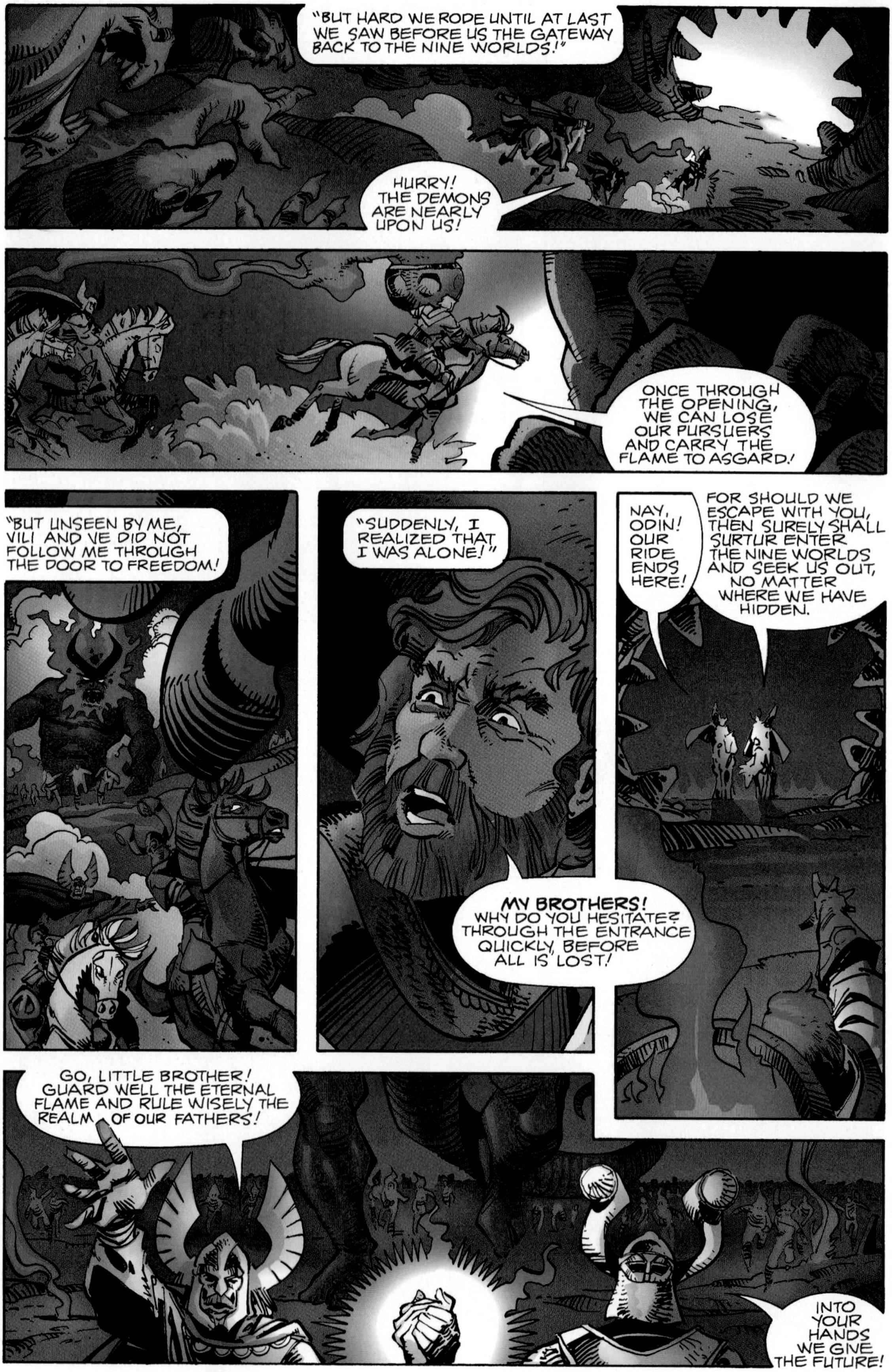
"BUT HARD WE RODE UNTIL AT LAST WE SAW BEFORE US THE GATEWAY BACK TO THE NINE WORLDS!"
HURRY! THE DEMONS ARE NEARLY UPON US!
ONCE THROUGH THE OPENING, WE CAN LOSE OUR PURSUERS AND CARRY THE FLAME TO ASGARD!
"BUT UNSEEN BY ME, VILI AND VE DID NOT FOLLOW ME THROUGH THE DOOR TO FREEDOM!
"SUDDENLY, I REALIZED THAT I WAS ALONE!"
MY BROTHERS! WHY DO YOU HESITATE? THROUGH THE ENTRANCE QUICKLY, BEFORE ALL IS LOST!
NAY, ODIN! OUR RIDE ENDS HERE!
FOR SHOULD WE ESCAPE WITH YOU, THEN SURELY SHALL SURTUR ENTER THE NINE WORLDS AND SEEK US OUT, NO MATTER WHERE WE HAVE HIDDEN.
GO, LITTLE BROTHER! GUARD WELL THE ETERNAL FLAME AND RULE WISELY THE REALM OF OUR FATHERS!
INTO YOUR HANDS WE GIVE THE FUTURE!

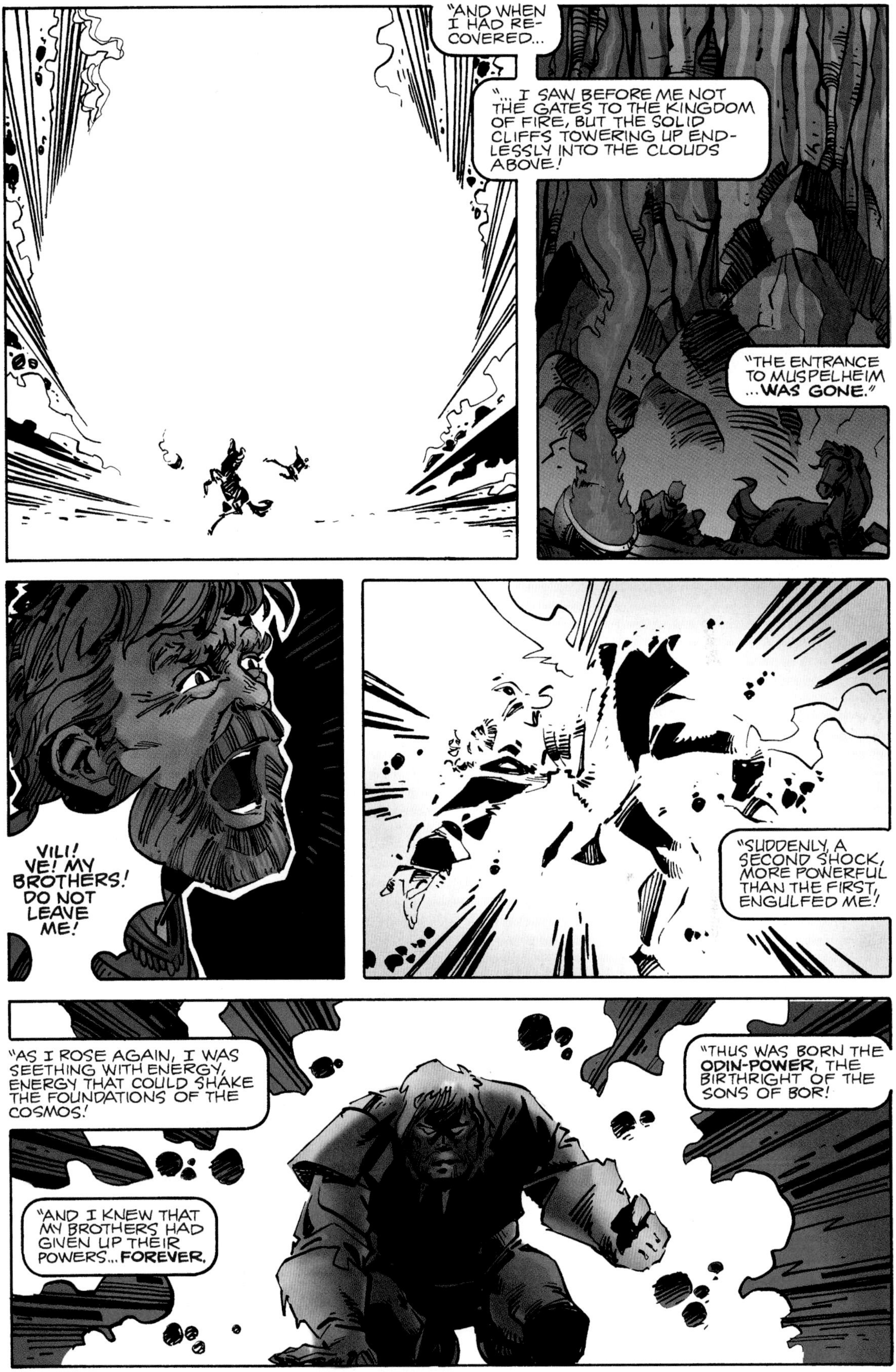
"AND WHEN I HAD RE-COVERED...
"... I SAW BEFORE ME NOT THE GATES TO THE KINGDOM OF FIRE, BUT THE SOLID CLIFFS TOWERING UP END-LESSLY INTO THE CLOUDS ABOVE!
"THE ENTRANCE TO MUSPELHEIM ...**WAS GONE.**"
VILI! VE! MY BROTHERS! DO NOT LEAVE ME!
"SUDDENLY, A SECOND SHOCK, MORE POWERFUL THAN THE FIRST, ENGULFED ME!
"AS I ROSE AGAIN, I WAS SEETHING WITH ENERGY, ENERGY THAT COULD SHAKE THE FOUNDATIONS OF THE COSMOS!
"THUS WAS BORN THE **ODIN-POWER**, THE BIRTHRIGHT OF THE SONS OF BOR!
"AND I KNEW THAT MY BROTHERS HAD GIVEN UP THEIR POWERS...**FOREVER.**

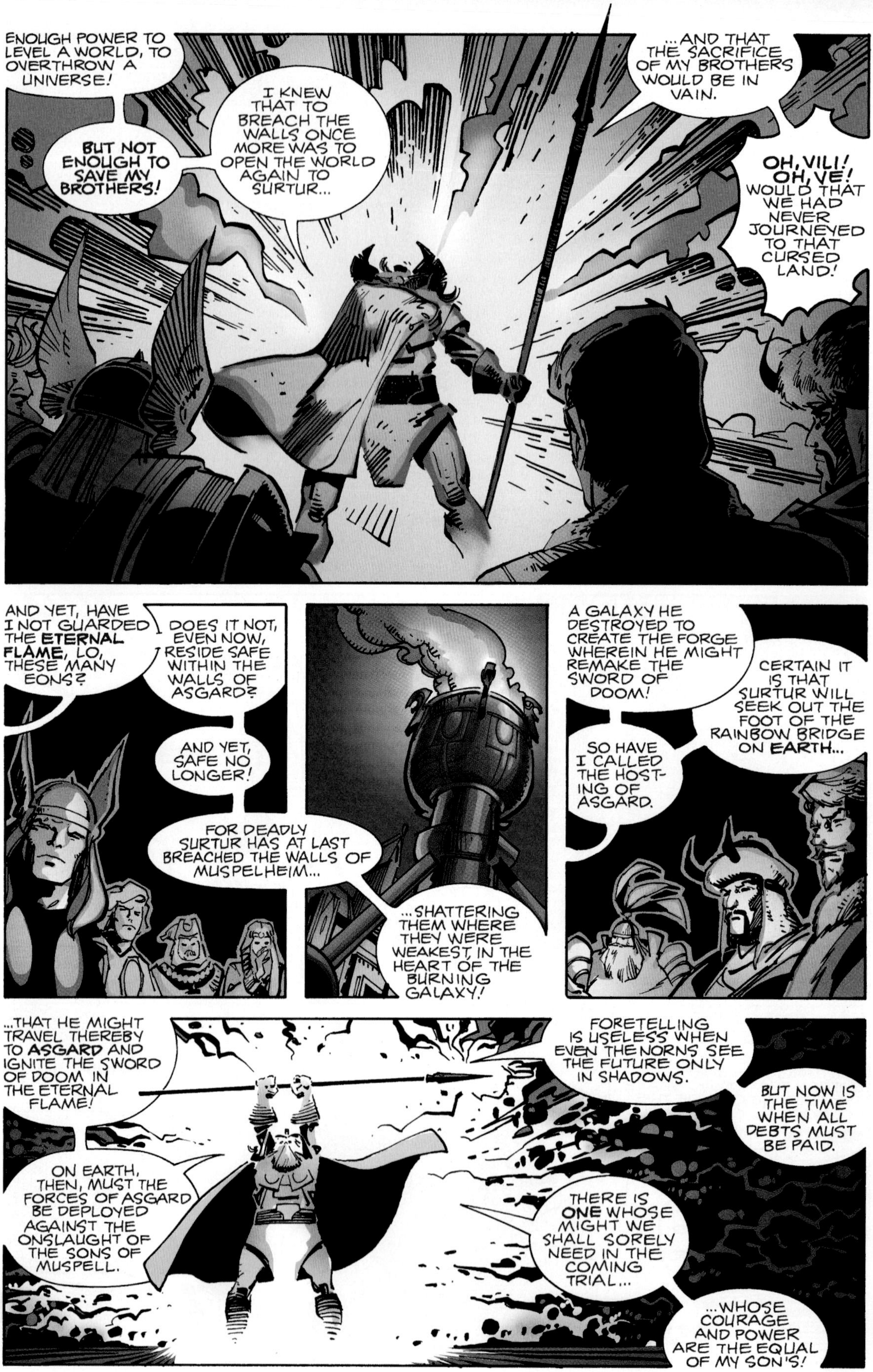

ENOUGH POWER TO LEVEL A WORLD, TO OVERTHROW A UNIVERSE!
BUT NOT ENOUGH TO SAVE MY BROTHERS!
I KNEW THAT TO BREACH THE WALLS ONCE MORE WAS TO OPEN THE WORLD AGAIN TO SURTUR...
...AND THAT THE SACRIFICE OF MY BROTHERS WOULD BE IN VAIN.
OH, VILI! OH, VE! WOULD THAT WE HAD NEVER JOURNEYED TO THAT CURSED LAND!
AND YET, HAVE I NOT GUARDED THE ETERNAL FLAME, LO, THESE MANY EONS?
DOES IT NOT, EVEN NOW, RESIDE SAFE WITHIN THE WALLS OF ASGARD?
AND YET, SAFE NO LONGER!
FOR DEADLY SURTUR HAS AT LAST BREACHED THE WALLS OF MUSPELHEIM...
...SHATTERING THEM WHERE THEY WERE WEAKEST, IN THE HEART OF THE BURNING GALAXY!
A GALAXY HE DESTROYED TO CREATE THE FORGE WHEREIN HE MIGHT REMAKE THE SWORD OF DOOM!
CERTAIN IT IS THAT SURTUR WILL SEEK OUT THE FOOT OF THE RAINBOW BRIDGE ON EARTH...
SO HAVE I CALLED THE HOST-ING OF ASGARD.
...THAT HE MIGHT TRAVEL THEREBY TO ASGARD AND IGNITE THE SWORD OF DOOM IN THE ETERNAL FLAME!
ON EARTH, THEN, MUST THE FORCES OF ASGARD BE DEPLOYED AGAINST THE ONSLAUGHT OF THE SONS OF MUSPELL.
FORETELLING IS USELESS WHEN EVEN THE NORNS SEE THE FUTURE ONLY IN SHADOWS.
BUT NOW IS THE TIME WHEN ALL DEBTS MUST BE PAID.
THERE IS ONE WHOSE MIGHT WE SHALL SORELY NEED IN THE COMING TRIAL...
...WHOSE COURAGE AND POWER ARE THE EQUAL OF MY SON'S!

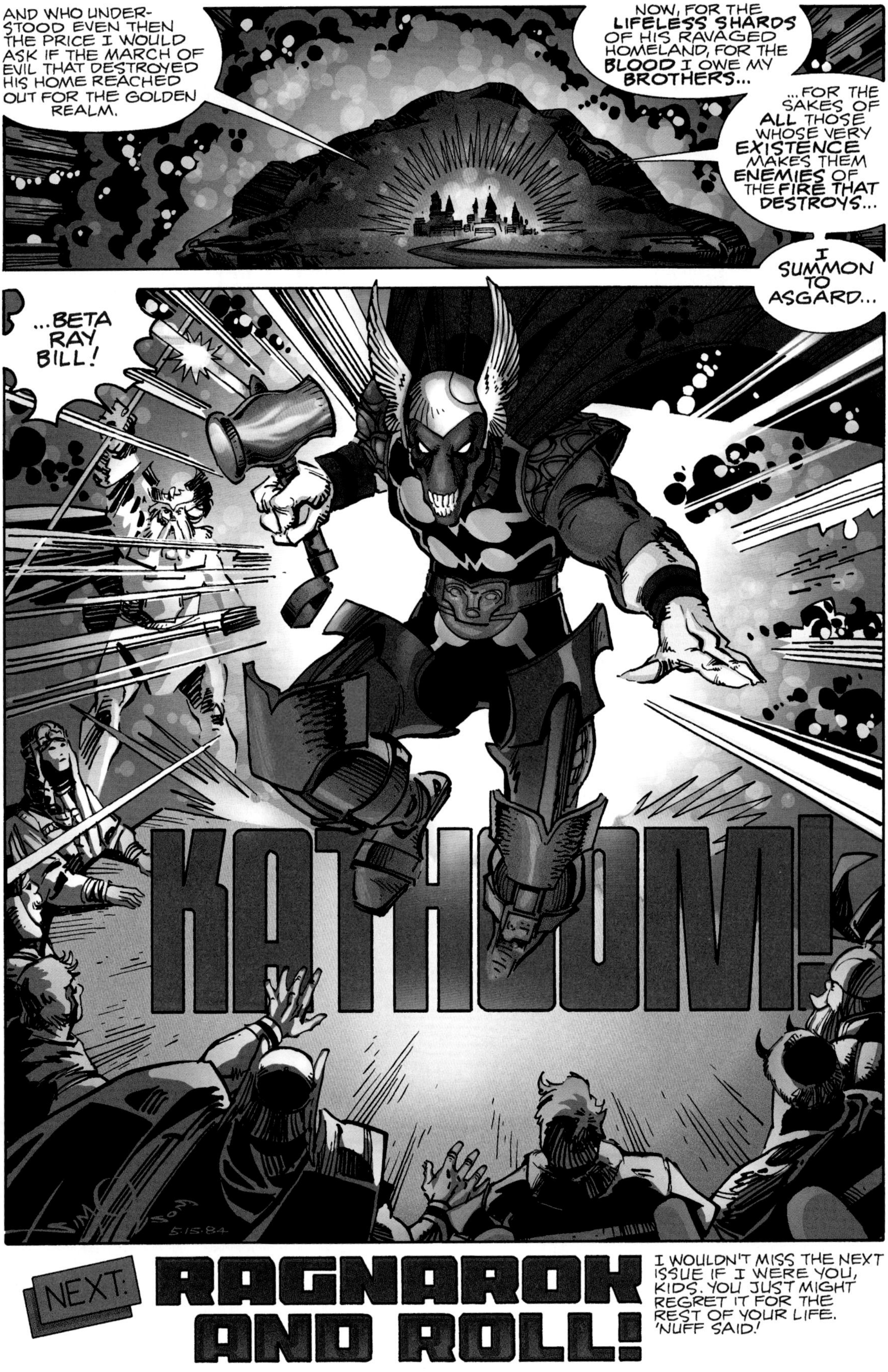
AND WHO UNDER-STOOD EVEN THEN THE PRICE I WOULD ASK IF THE MARCH OF EVIL THAT DESTROYED HIS HOME REACHED OUT FOR THE GOLDEN REALM.
NOW, FOR THE LIFELESS SHARDS OF HIS RAVAGED HOMELAND, FOR THE BLOOD I OWE MY BROTHERS...
...FOR THE SAKES OF ALL THOSE WHOSE VERY EXISTENCE MAKES THEM ENEMIES OF THE FIRE THAT DESTROYS...
I SUMMON TO ASGARD...
...BETA RAY BILL!
KATHOOM!
NEXT: RAGNAROK AND ROLL!
I WOULDN'T MISS THE NEXT ISSUE IF I WERE YOU, KIDS. YOU JUST MIGHT REGRET IT FOR THE REST OF YOUR LIFE. 'NUFF SAID!

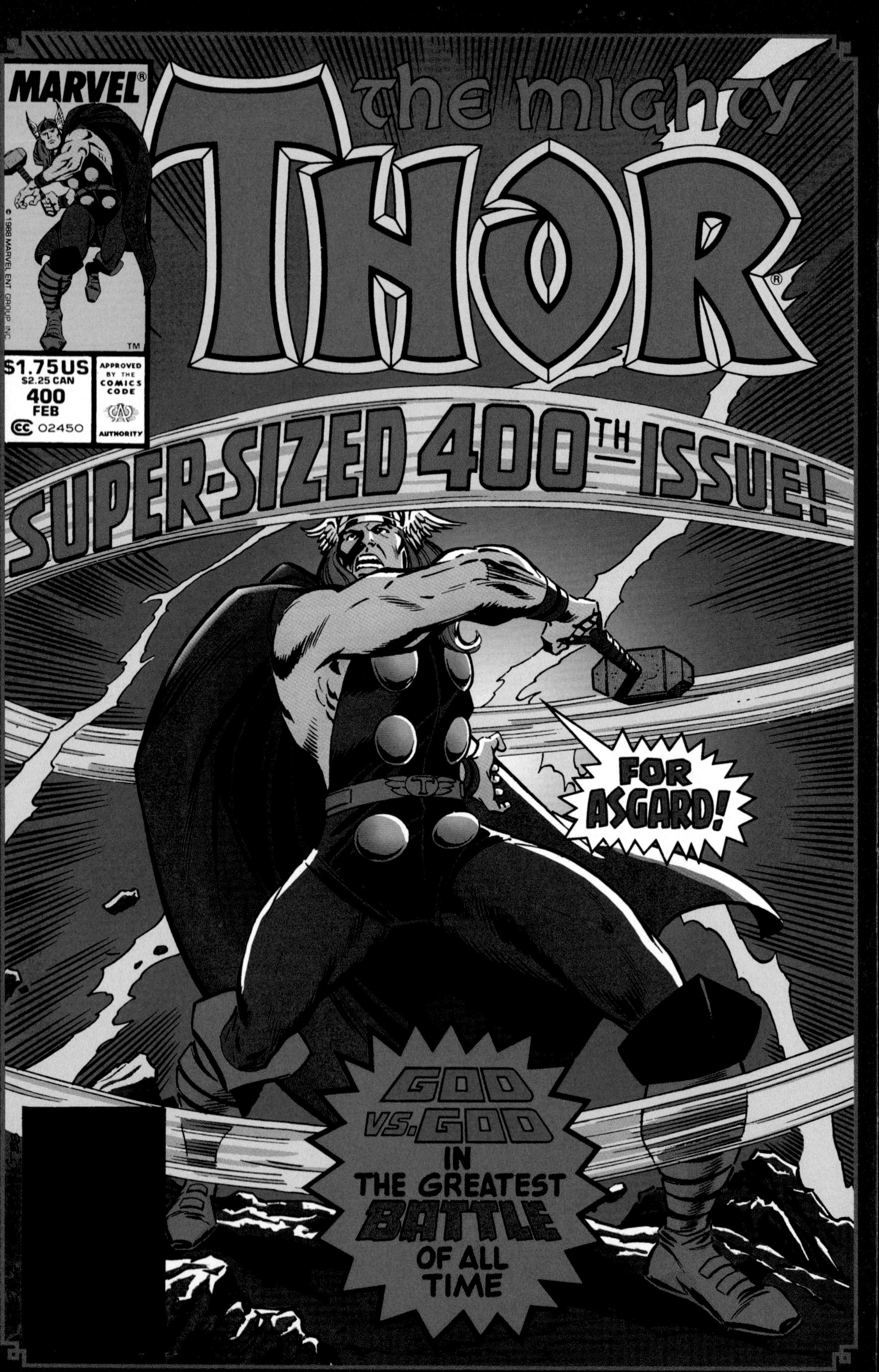
MARVEL®
© 1988 MARVEL ENT. GROUP, INC.
TM
$1.75US
$2.25 CAN
400
FEB
CC 02450
APPROVED BY THE COMICS CODE AUTHORITY
the mighty
THOR®
SUPER-SIZED 400TH ISSUE!
FOR ASGARD!
GOD VS. GOD IN THE GREATEST BATTLE OF ALL TIME

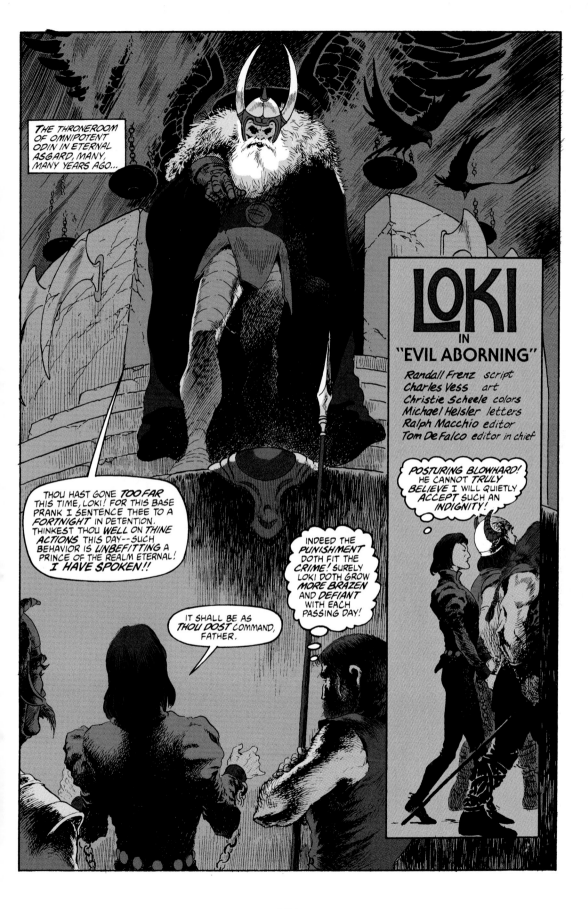

THE THRONEROOM OF OMNIPOTENT ODIN IN ETERNAL ASGARD, MANY, MANY YEARS AGO...

# LOKI
## IN
## "EVIL ABORNING"

Randall Frenz script
Charles Vess art
Christie Scheele colors
Michael Heisler letters
Ralph Macchio editor
Tom DeFalco editor in chief

THOU HAST GONE *TOO FAR* THIS TIME, LOKI! FOR THIS BASE PRANK I SENTENCE THEE TO A *FORTNIGHT* IN DETENTION. THINKEST THOU *WELL* ON *THINE ACTIONS* THIS DAY--SUCH BEHAVIOR IS *UNBEFITTING* A PRINCE OF THE REALM ETERNAL! *I HAVE SPOKEN!!*

IT SHALL BE AS *THOU DOST* COMMAND, FATHER.

INDEED THE *PUNISHMENT* DOTH FIT THE *CRIME!* SURELY LOKI DOTH GROW *MORE BRAZEN* AND *DEFIANT* WITH EACH PASSING DAY!

POSTURING BLOWHARD! HE CANNOT *TRULY BELIEVE* I WILL QUIETLY *ACCEPT* SUCH AN *INDIGNITY!*

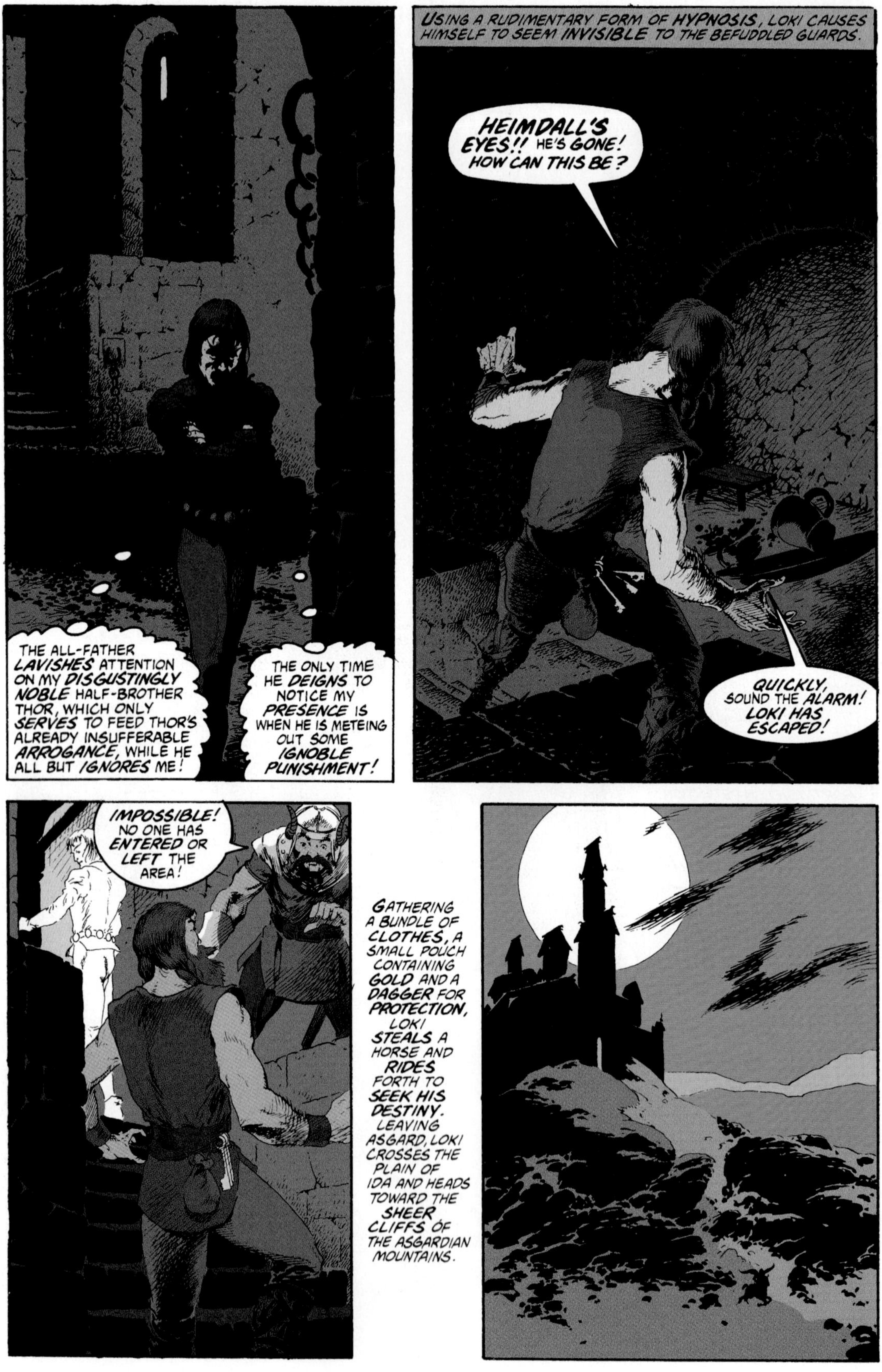
THE ALL-FATHER LAVISHES ATTENTION ON MY DISGUSTINGLY NOBLE HALF-BROTHER THOR, WHICH ONLY SERVES TO FEED THOR'S ALREADY INSUFFERABLE ARROGANCE, WHILE HE ALL BUT IGNORES ME!
THE ONLY TIME HE DEIGNS TO NOTICE MY PRESENCE IS WHEN HE IS METEING OUT SOME IGNOBLE PUNISHMENT!
USING A RUDIMENTARY FORM OF HYPNOSIS, LOKI CAUSES HIMSELF TO SEEM INVISIBLE TO THE BEFUDDLED GUARDS.
HEIMDALL'S EYES!! HE'S GONE! HOW CAN THIS BE?
QUICKLY, SOUND THE ALARM! LOKI HAS ESCAPED!
IMPOSSIBLE! NO ONE HAS ENTERED OR LEFT THE AREA!
GATHERING A BUNDLE OF CLOTHES, A SMALL POUCH CONTAINING GOLD AND A DAGGER FOR PROTECTION, LOKI STEALS A HORSE AND RIDES FORTH TO SEEK HIS DESTINY. LEAVING ASGARD, LOKI CROSSES THE PLAIN OF IDA AND HEADS TOWARD THE SHEER CLIFFS OF THE ASGARDIAN MOUNTAINS.

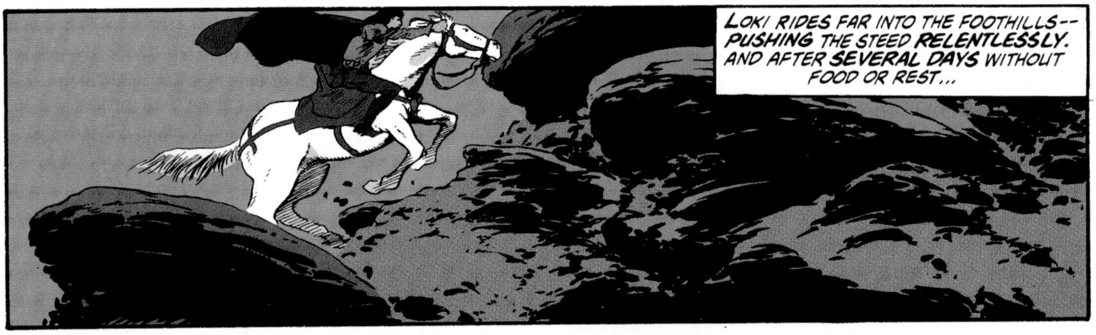
LOKI RIDES FAR INTO THE FOOTHILLS--
PUSHING THE STEED RELENTLESSLY.
AND AFTER SEVERAL DAYS WITHOUT
FOOD OR REST...

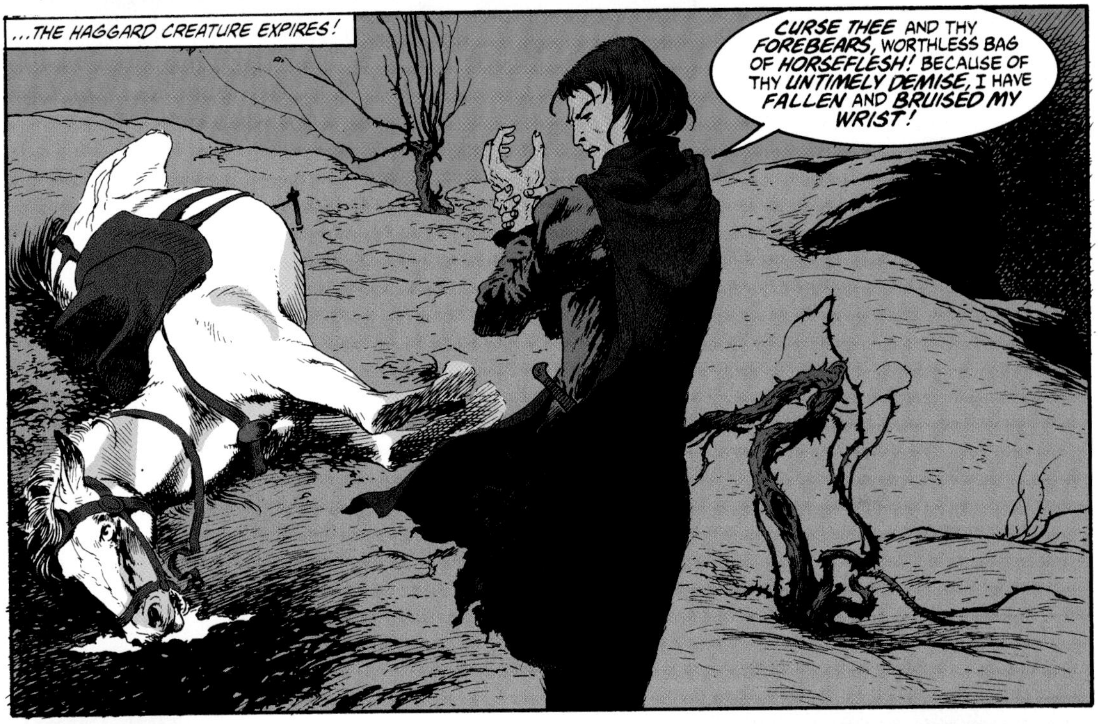
...THE HAGGARD CREATURE EXPIRES!
CURSE THEE AND THY FOREBEARS, WORTHLESS BAG OF HORSEFLESH! BECAUSE OF THY UNTIMELY DEMISE, I HAVE FALLEN AND BRUISED MY WRIST!

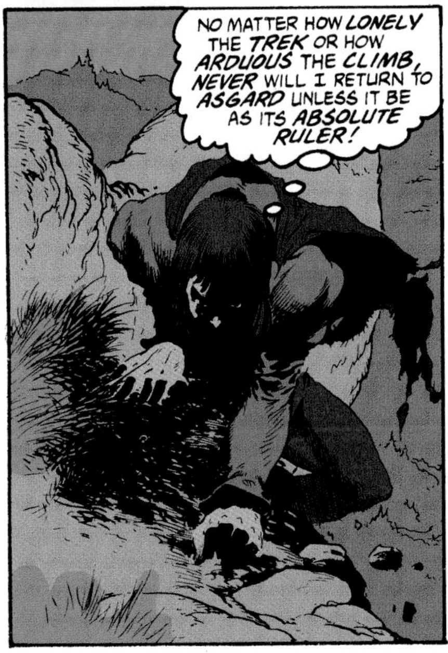
NO MATTER HOW LONELY THE TREK OR HOW ARDUOUS THE CLIMB, NEVER WILL I RETURN TO ASGARD UNLESS IT BE AS ITS ABSOLUTE RULER!

AFTER A LONG AND DANGEROUS ASCENT, HE FINALLY CROSSES INTO ALFHEIM, THE ABODE OF THE LIGHT ELVES. DAYS HAVE PASSED SINCE HE HAS EATEN, BUT HE IS NOURISHED BY THE BITTER TASTE OF HATRED. HE IS DRIVEN BY THE KNOWLEDGE THAT ONE DAY HE WILL KNOW THE SWEET TASTE OF HIS REVENGE!

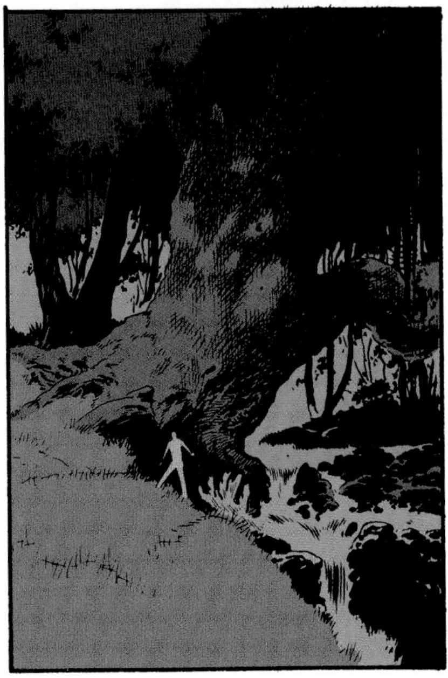

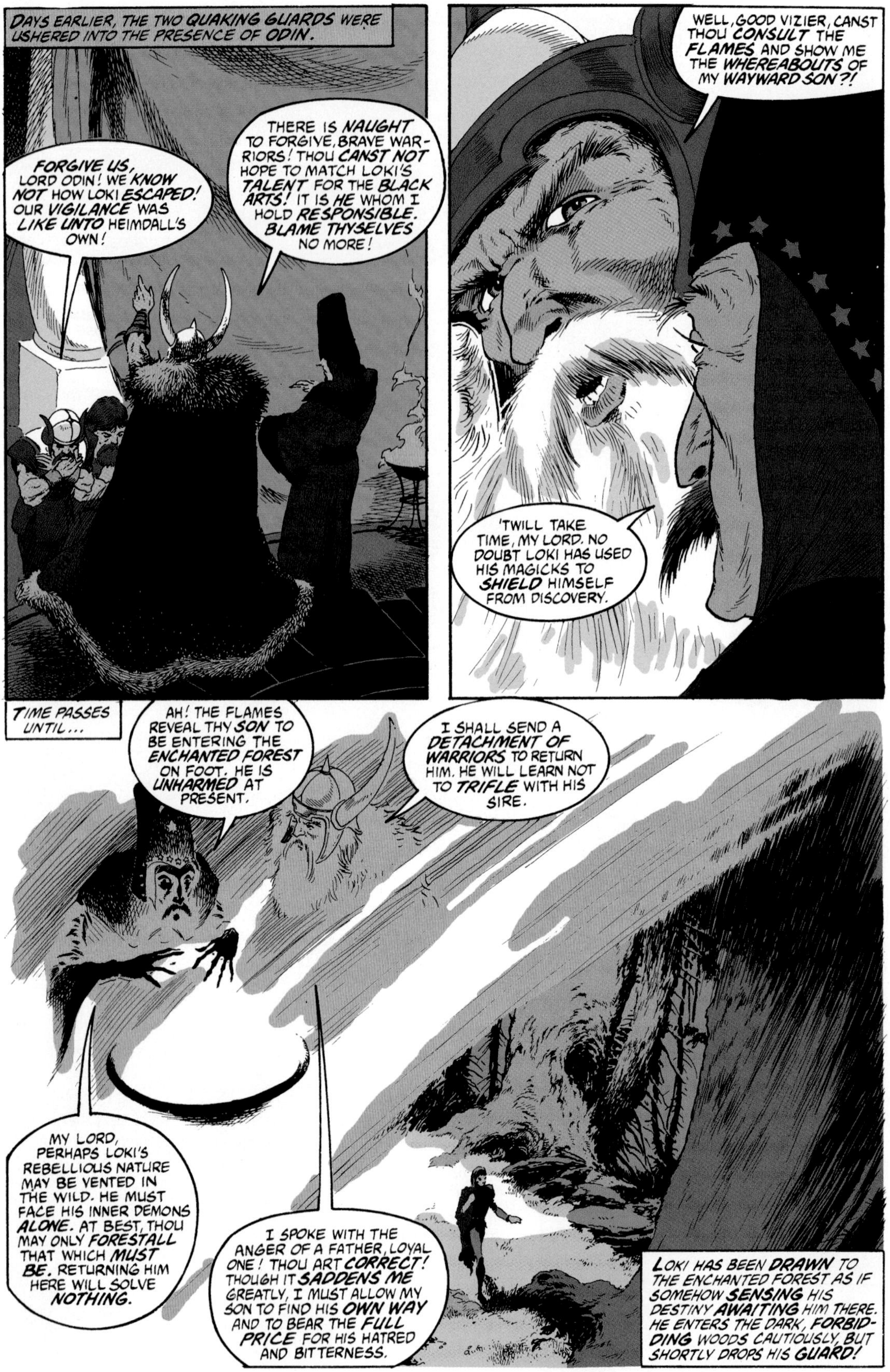
DAYS EARLIER, THE TWO QUAKING GUARDS WERE USHERED INTO THE PRESENCE OF ODIN.
FORGIVE US, LORD ODIN! WE KNOW NOT HOW LOKI ESCAPED! OUR VIGILANCE WAS LIKE UNTO HEIMDALL'S OWN!
THERE IS NAUGHT TO FORGIVE, BRAVE WARRIORS! THOU CANST NOT HOPE TO MATCH LOKI'S TALENT FOR THE BLACK ARTS! IT IS HE WHOM I HOLD RESPONSIBLE. BLAME THYSELVES NO MORE!
WELL, GOOD VIZIER, CANST THOU CONSULT THE FLAMES AND SHOW ME THE WHEREABOUTS OF MY WAYWARD SON?!
'TWILL TAKE TIME, MY LORD. NO DOUBT LOKI HAS USED HIS MAGICKS TO SHIELD HIMSELF FROM DISCOVERY.
TIME PASSES UNTIL...
AH! THE FLAMES REVEAL THY SON TO BE ENTERING THE ENCHANTED FOREST ON FOOT. HE IS UNHARMED AT PRESENT.
I SHALL SEND A DETACHMENT OF WARRIORS TO RETURN HIM. HE WILL LEARN NOT TO TRIFLE WITH HIS SIRE.
MY LORD, PERHAPS LOKI'S REBELLIOUS NATURE MAY BE VENTED IN THE WILD. HE MUST FACE HIS INNER DEMONS ALONE. AT BEST, THOU MAY ONLY FORESTALL THAT WHICH MUST BE. RETURNING HIM HERE WILL SOLVE NOTHING.
I SPOKE WITH THE ANGER OF A FATHER, LOYAL ONE! THOU ART CORRECT! THOUGH IT SADDENS ME GREATLY, I MUST ALLOW MY SON TO FIND HIS OWN WAY AND TO BEAR THE FULL PRICE FOR HIS HATRED AND BITTERNESS.
LOKI HAS BEEN DRAWN TO THE ENCHANTED FOREST AS IF SOMEHOW SENSING HIS DESTINY AWAITING HIM THERE. HE ENTERS THE DARK, FORBIDDING WOODS CAUTIOUSLY, BUT SHORTLY DROPS HIS GUARD!

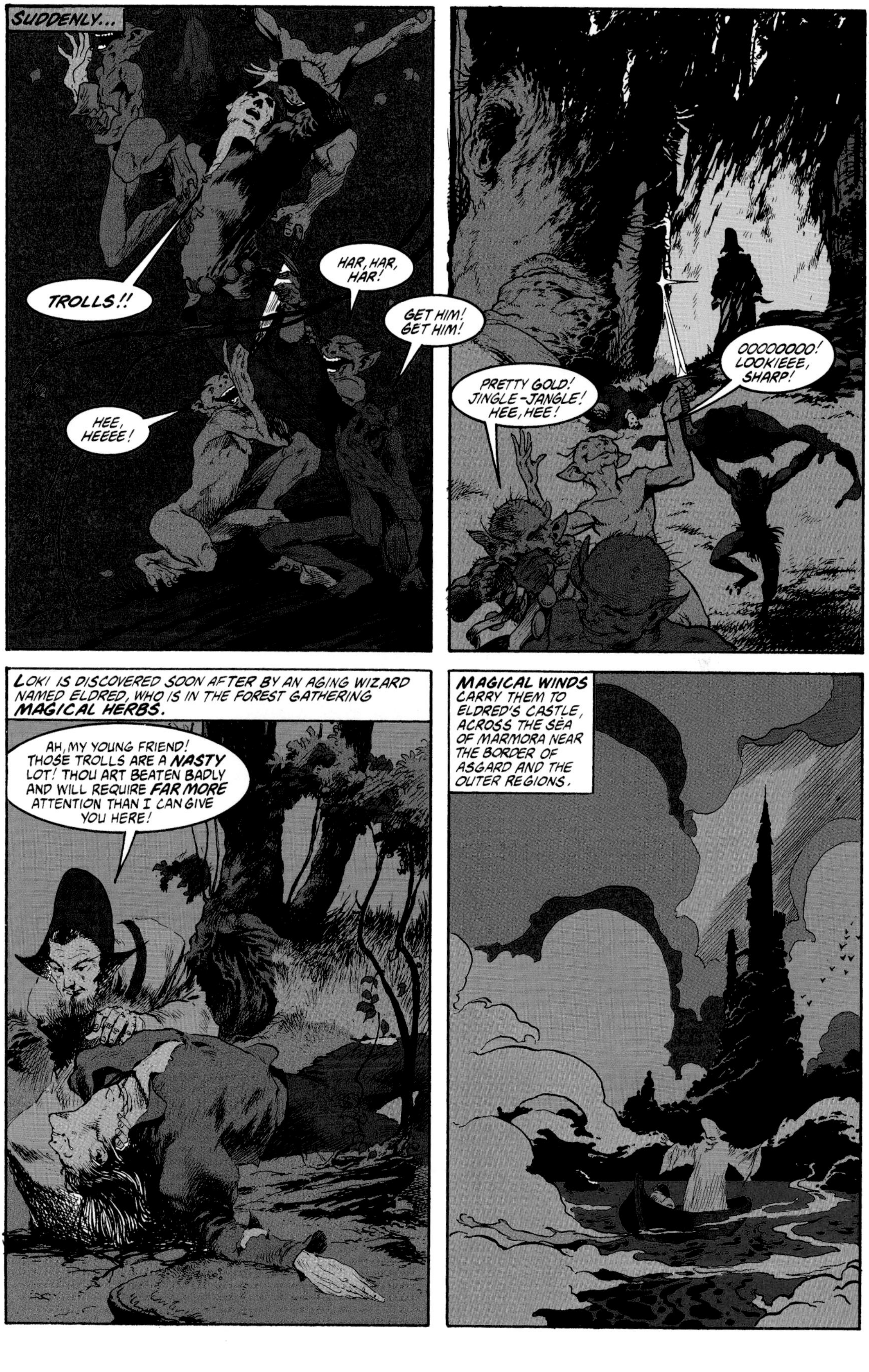
SUDDENLY...
TROLLS!!
HAR, HAR, HAR!
GET HIM! GET HIM!
HEE, HEEEE!
PRETTY GOLD! JINGLE-JANGLE! HEE, HEE!
OOOOOOOO! LOOKIEEE, SHARP!
LOKI IS DISCOVERED SOON AFTER BY AN AGING WIZARD NAMED ELDRED, WHO IS IN THE FOREST GATHERING MAGICAL HERBS.
AH, MY YOUNG FRIEND! THOSE TROLLS ARE A NASTY LOT! THOU ART BEATEN BADLY AND WILL REQUIRE FAR MORE ATTENTION THAN I CAN GIVE YOU HERE!
MAGICAL WINDS CARRY THEM TO ELDRED'S CASTLE, ACROSS THE SEA OF MARMORA NEAR THE BORDER OF ASGARD AND THE OUTER REGIONS.

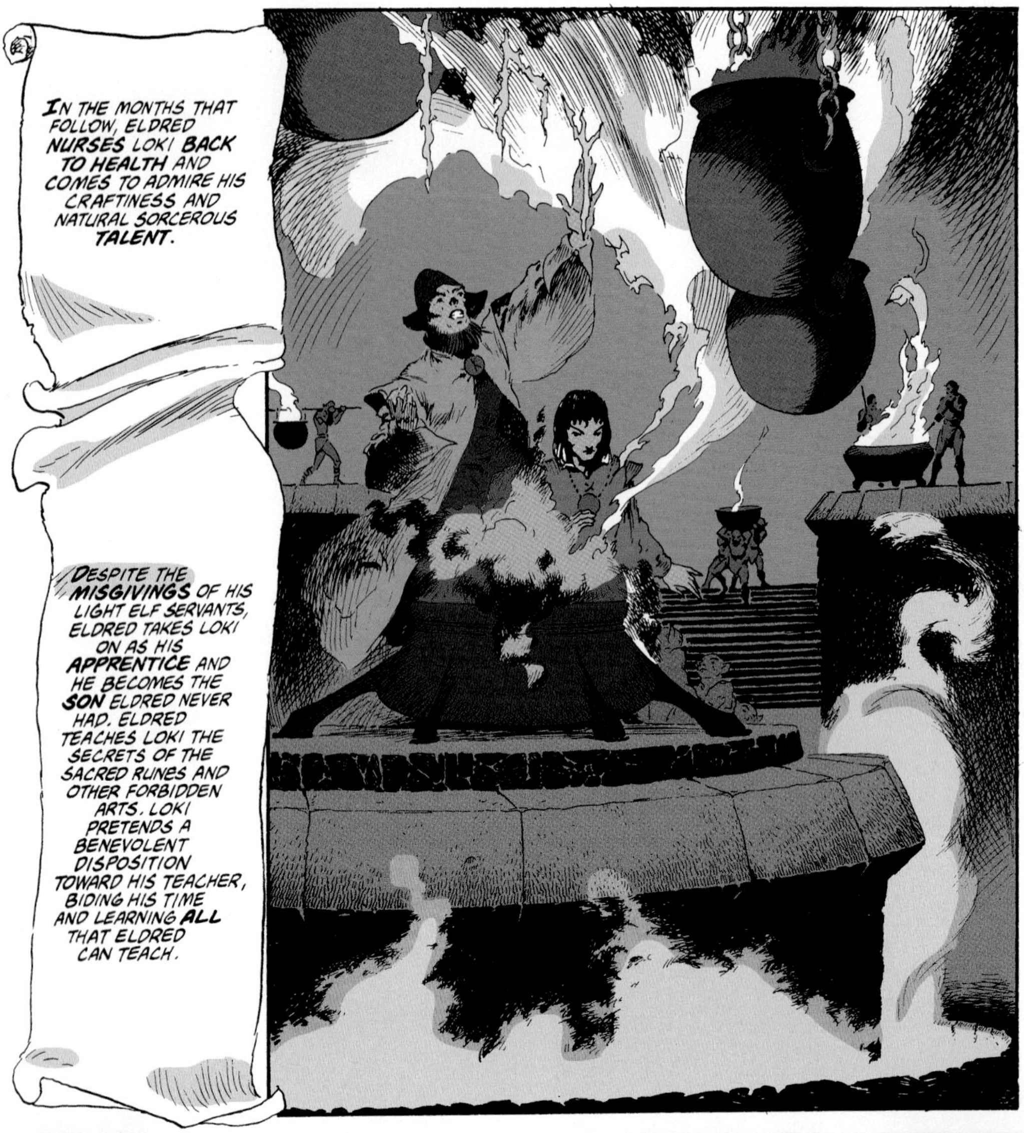
IN THE MONTHS THAT FOLLOW, ELDRED NURSES LOKI BACK TO HEALTH AND COMES TO ADMIRE HIS CRAFTINESS AND NATURAL SORCEROUS TALENT.
DESPITE THE MISGIVINGS OF HIS LIGHT ELF SERVANTS, ELDRED TAKES LOKI ON AS HIS APPRENTICE AND HE BECOMES THE SON ELDRED NEVER HAD. ELDRED TEACHES LOKI THE SECRETS OF THE SACRED RUNES AND OTHER FORBIDDEN ARTS. LOKI PRETENDS A BENEVOLENT DISPOSITION TOWARD HIS TEACHER, BIDING HIS TIME AND LEARNING ALL THAT ELDRED CAN TEACH.

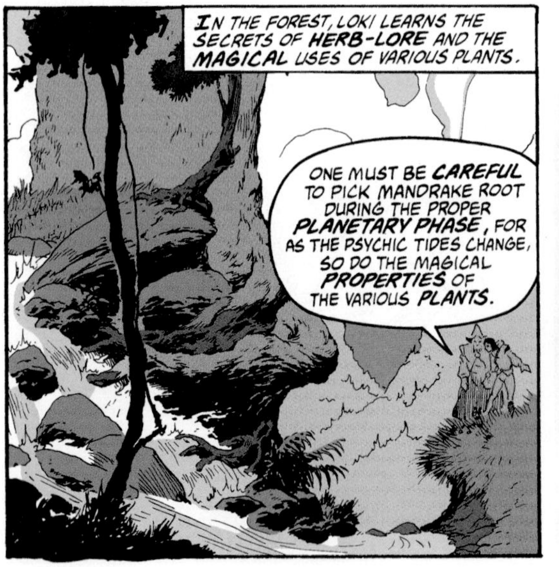
IN THE FOREST, LOKI LEARNS THE SECRETS OF HERB-LORE AND THE MAGICAL USES OF VARIOUS PLANTS.
ONE MUST BE CAREFUL TO PICK MANDRAKE ROOT DURING THE PROPER PLANETARY PHASE, FOR AS THE PSYCHIC TIDES CHANGE, SO DO THE MAGICAL PROPERTIES OF THE VARIOUS PLANTS.

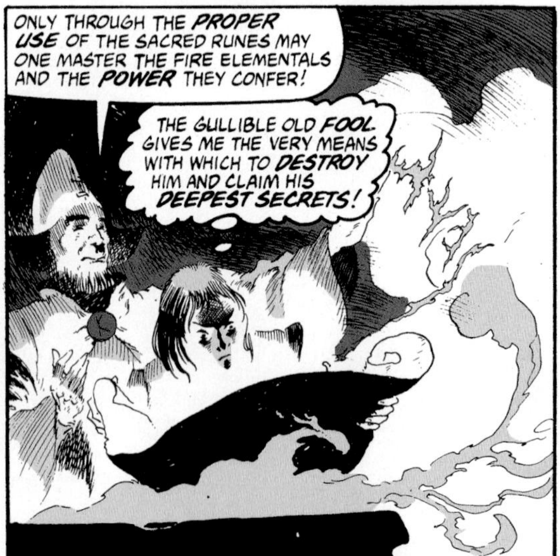
ONLY THROUGH THE PROPER USE OF THE SACRED RUNES MAY ONE MASTER THE FIRE ELEMENTALS AND THE POWER THEY CONFER!
THE GULLIBLE OLD FOOL GIVES ME THE VERY MEANS WITH WHICH TO DESTROY HIM AND CLAIM HIS DEEPEST SECRETS!

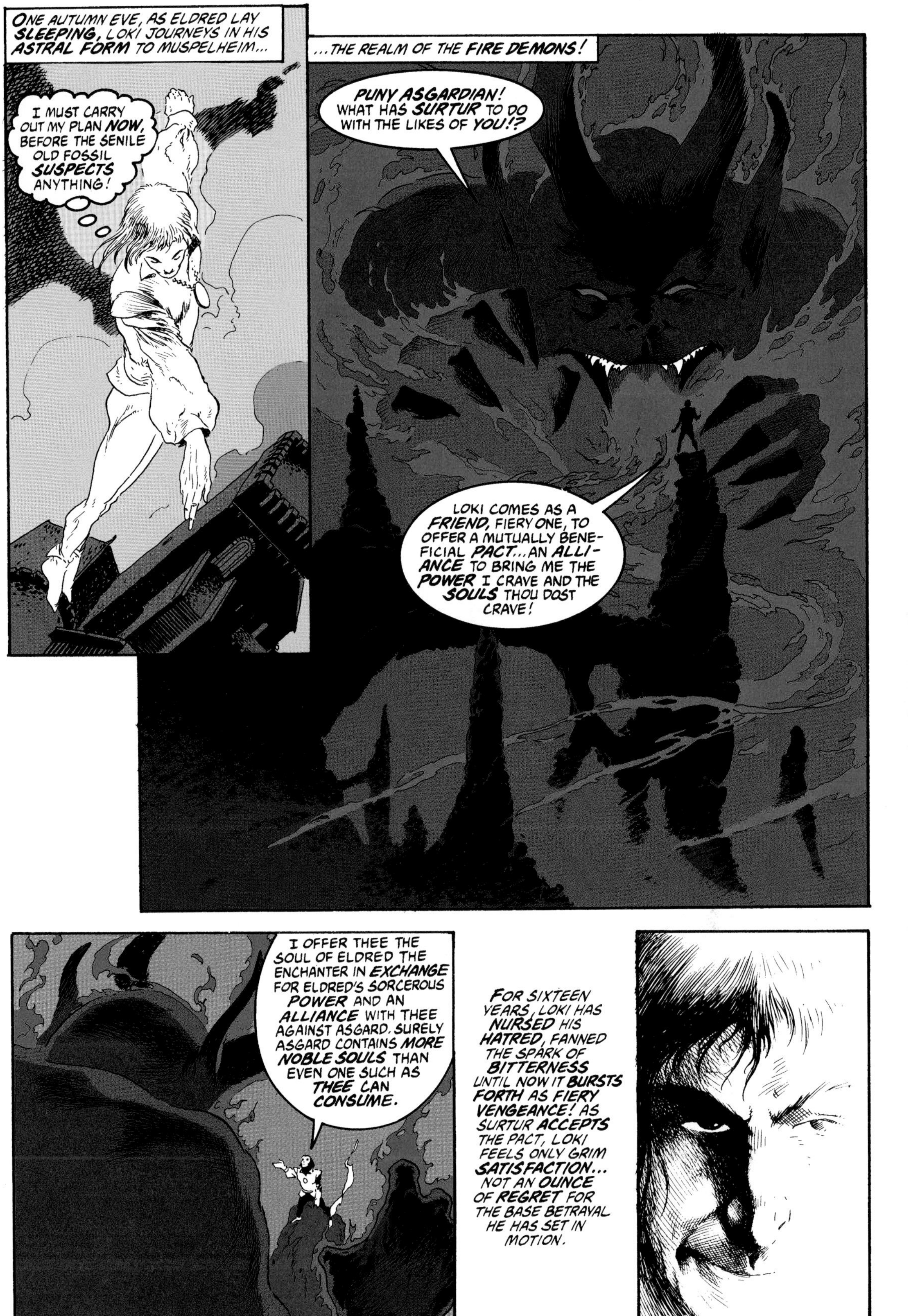
ONE AUTUMN EVE, AS ELDRED LAY SLEEPING, LOKI JOURNEYS IN HIS ASTRAL FORM TO MUSPELHEIM...
I MUST CARRY OUT MY PLAN NOW, BEFORE THE SENILE OLD FOSSIL SUSPECTS ANYTHING!
...THE REALM OF THE FIRE DEMONS!
PUNY ASGARDIAN! WHAT HAS SURTUR TO DO WITH THE LIKES OF YOU!?
LOKI COMES AS A FRIEND, FIERY ONE, TO OFFER A MUTUALLY BENEFICIAL PACT...AN ALLIANCE TO BRING ME THE POWER I CRAVE AND THE SOULS THOU DOST CRAVE!
I OFFER THEE THE SOUL OF ELDRED THE ENCHANTER IN EXCHANGE FOR ELDRED'S SORCEROUS POWER AND AN ALLIANCE WITH THEE AGAINST ASGARD. SURELY ASGARD CONTAINS MORE NOBLE SOULS THAN EVEN ONE SUCH AS THEE CAN CONSUME.
FOR SIXTEEN YEARS, LOKI HAS NURSED HIS HATRED, FANNED THE SPARK OF BITTERNESS UNTIL NOW IT BURSTS FORTH AS FIERY VENGEANCE! AS SURTUR ACCEPTS THE PACT, LOKI FEELS ONLY GRIM SATISFACTION... NOT AN OUNCE OF REGRET FOR THE BASE BETRAYAL HE HAS SET IN MOTION.

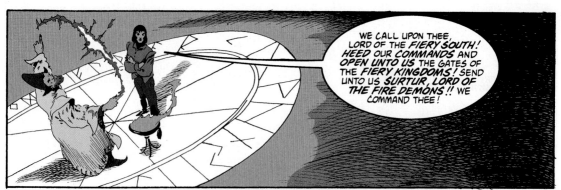

WE CALL UPON THEE, LORD OF THE *FIERY SOUTH!* *HEED* OUR *COMMANDS* AND *OPEN UNTO US* THE GATES OF THE *FIERY KINGDOMS!* SEND UNTO US *SURTUR, LORD OF THE FIRE DEMONS!!* WE COMMAND THEE!

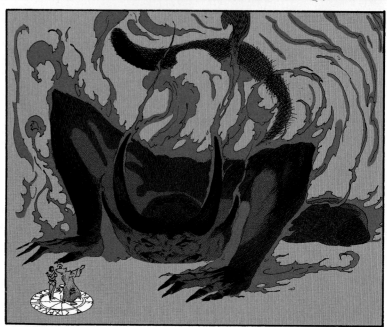

IT HAS TAKEN *SEVERAL DAYS* FOR LOKI TO CONVINCE ELDRED THAT HE IS READY TO INVOKE SUCH A DEMON TO *VISIBLE APPEARANCE.* ELDRED SUSPECTED NO MORE THAN *YOUTHFUL EXUBERANCE.* NOW HE IS IN THE GRIP OF *ICY FEAR!* HE KNOWS THAT LOKI HAS BEEN HIDING THE *TRUE EXTENT* OF HIS *POWER!* HE KNOWS THAT LOKI *TRICKED* HIM INTO MAKING HIMSELF *VULNERABLE!* HE KNOWS... *TOO LATE!*

YOU KNOW *MUCH* OF THE BLACK ARTS, *OLD FOOL!* BUT YOUR KNOWLEDGE OF THE *DARKNESS* THAT MAY LURK IN A GOD'S *SOUL* IS SORELY LACKING!

*BY THE GODS! NO!* DON'T PUSH ME FROM THE PROTECTION OF THE CIRCLE!

*NOOOOO!*

*AHH!* I CAN FEEL ELDRED'S *POWER* AS IT *COURSES THROUGH* MY VERY *BEING!* I AM *TRIUMPHANT!*

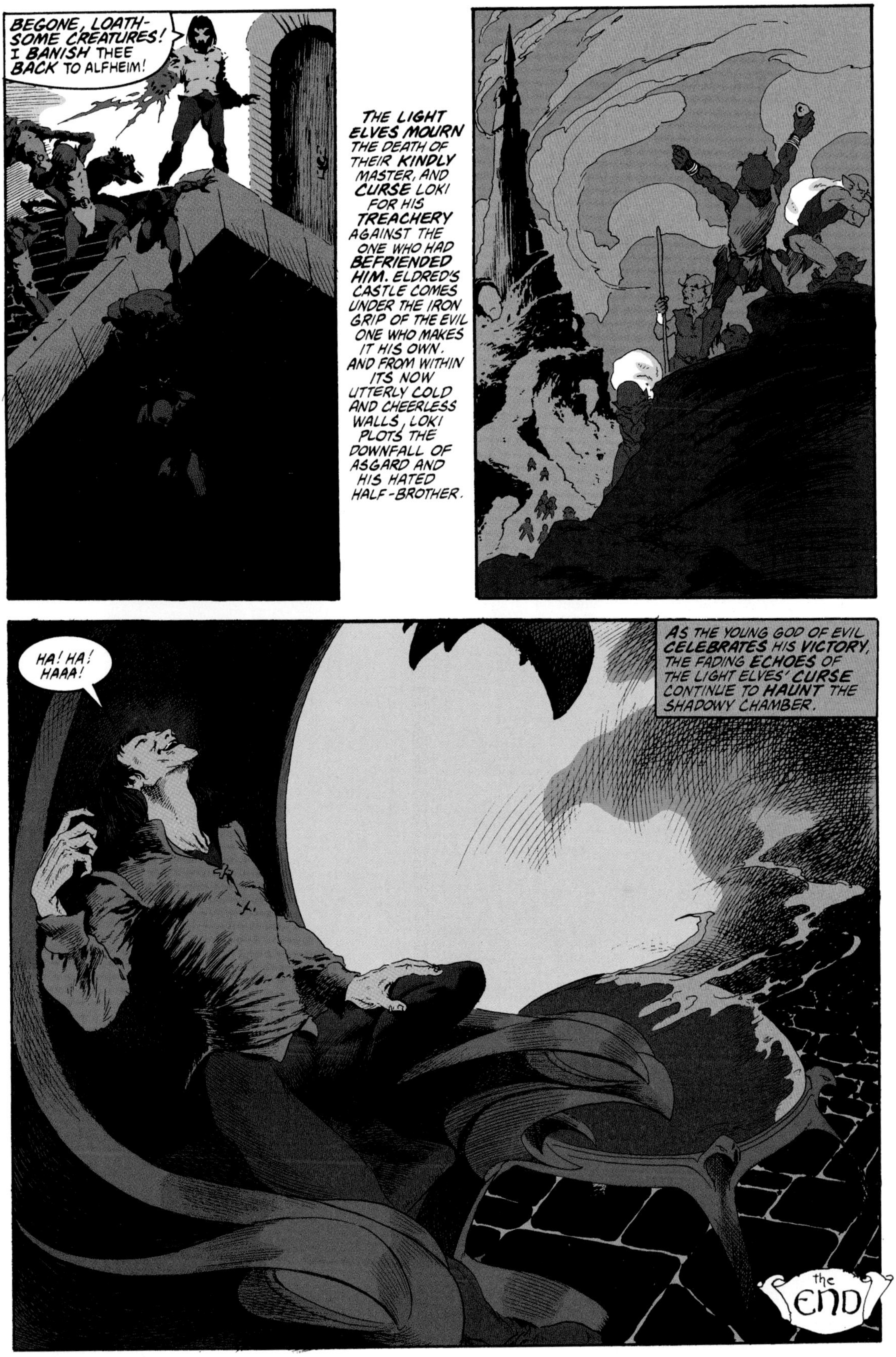
BEGONE, LOATHSOME CREATURES! I BANISH THEE BACK TO ALFHEIM!
THE LIGHT ELVES MOURN THE DEATH OF THEIR KINDLY MASTER, AND CURSE LOKI FOR HIS TREACHERY AGAINST THE ONE WHO HAD BEFRIENDED HIM. ELDRED'S CASTLE COMES UNDER THE IRON GRIP OF THE EVIL ONE WHO MAKES IT HIS OWN. AND FROM WITHIN ITS NOW UTTERLY COLD AND CHEERLESS WALLS, LOKI PLOTS THE DOWNFALL OF ASGARD AND HIS HATED HALF-BROTHER.
HA! HA! HAAA!
AS THE YOUNG GOD OF EVIL CELEBRATES HIS VICTORY, THE FADING ECHOES OF THE LIGHT ELVES' CURSE CONTINUE TO HAUNT THE SHADOWY CHAMBER.
the END

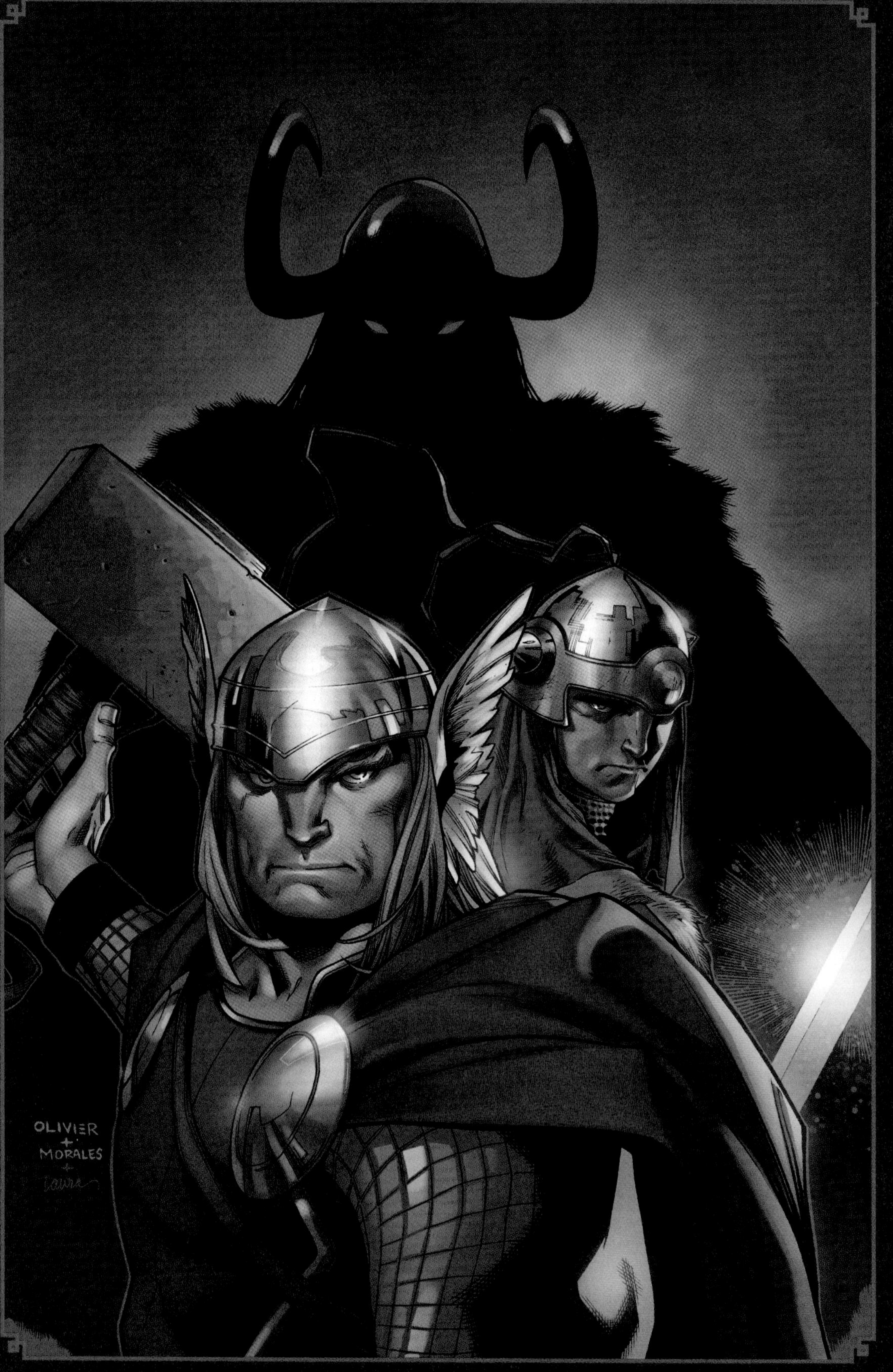
OLIVIER
+
MORALES
+
Laura

THOR (2007) #12

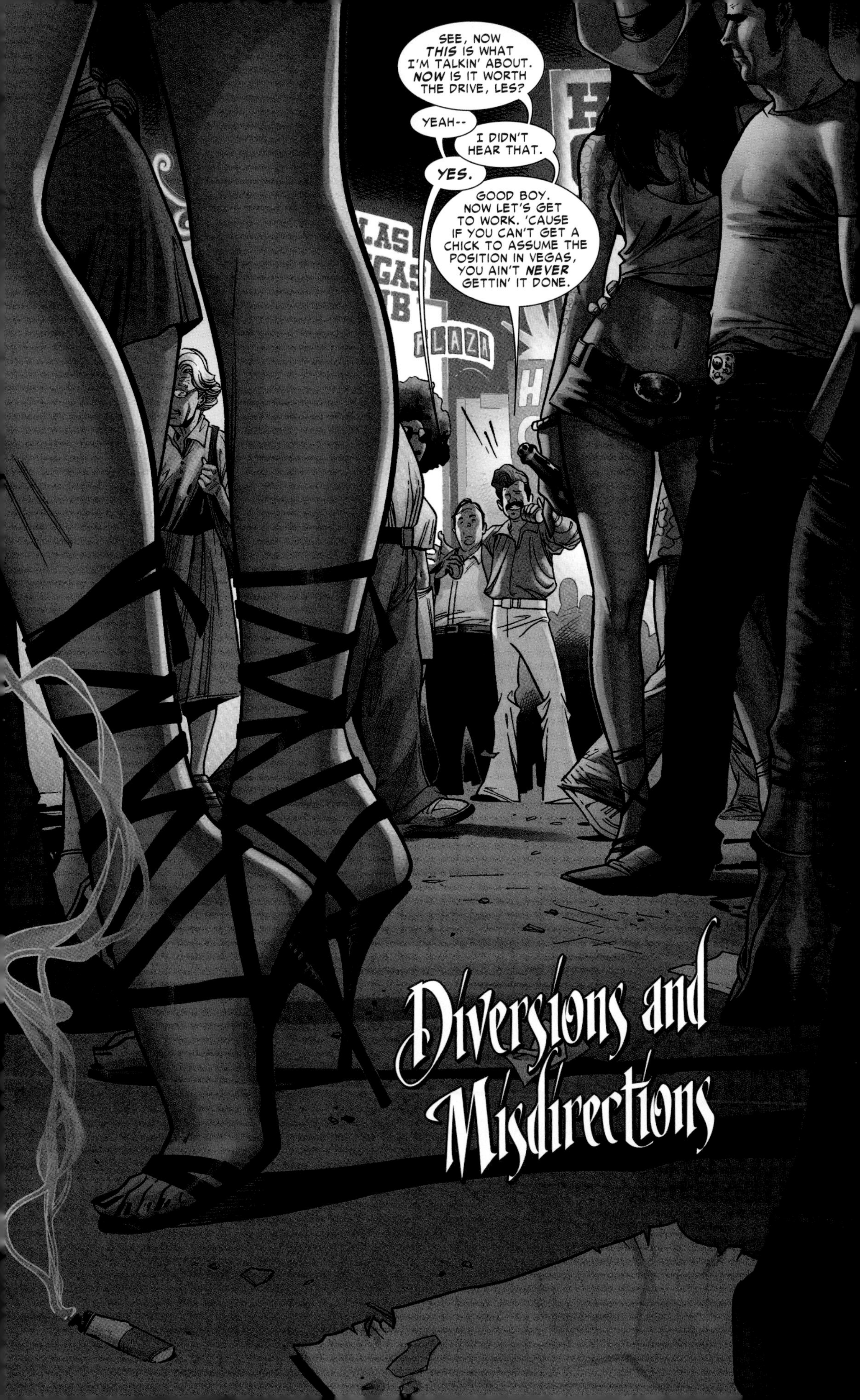
SEE, NOW *THIS* IS WHAT I'M TALKIN' ABOUT. *NOW* IS IT WORTH THE DRIVE, LES?
YEAH--
I DIDN'T HEAR THAT.
*YES.*
GOOD BOY. NOW LET'S GET TO WORK. 'CAUSE IF YOU CAN'T GET A CHICK TO ASSUME THE POSITION IN VEGAS, YOU AIN'T *NEVER* GETTIN' IT DONE.
LAS VEGAS CLUB
PLAZA
Diversions and Misdirections

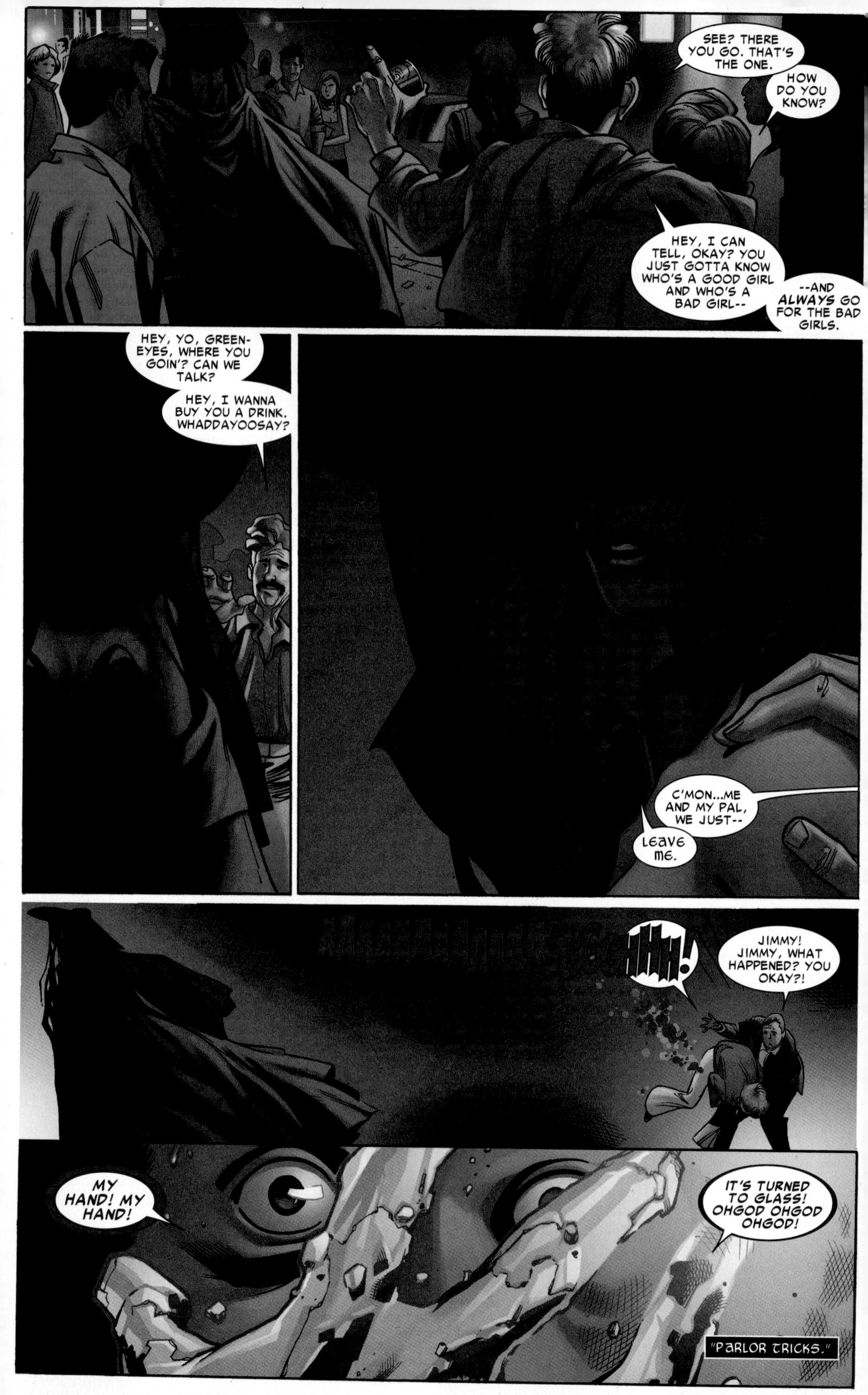
SEE? THERE YOU GO. THAT'S THE ONE.
HOW DO YOU KNOW?
HEY, I CAN TELL, OKAY? YOU JUST GOTTA KNOW WHO'S A GOOD GIRL AND WHO'S A BAD GIRL--
--AND ALWAYS GO FOR THE BAD GIRLS.
HEY, YO, GREEN-EYES, WHERE YOU GOIN'? CAN WE TALK?
HEY, I WANNA BUY YOU A DRINK. WHADDAYOOSAY?
C'MON...ME AND MY PAL, WE JUST--
LEAVE ME.
JIMMY! JIMMY, WHAT HAPPENED? YOU OKAY?!
MY HAND! MY HAND!
IT'S TURNED TO GLASS! OHGOD OHGOD OHGOD!
"PARLOR TRICKS."

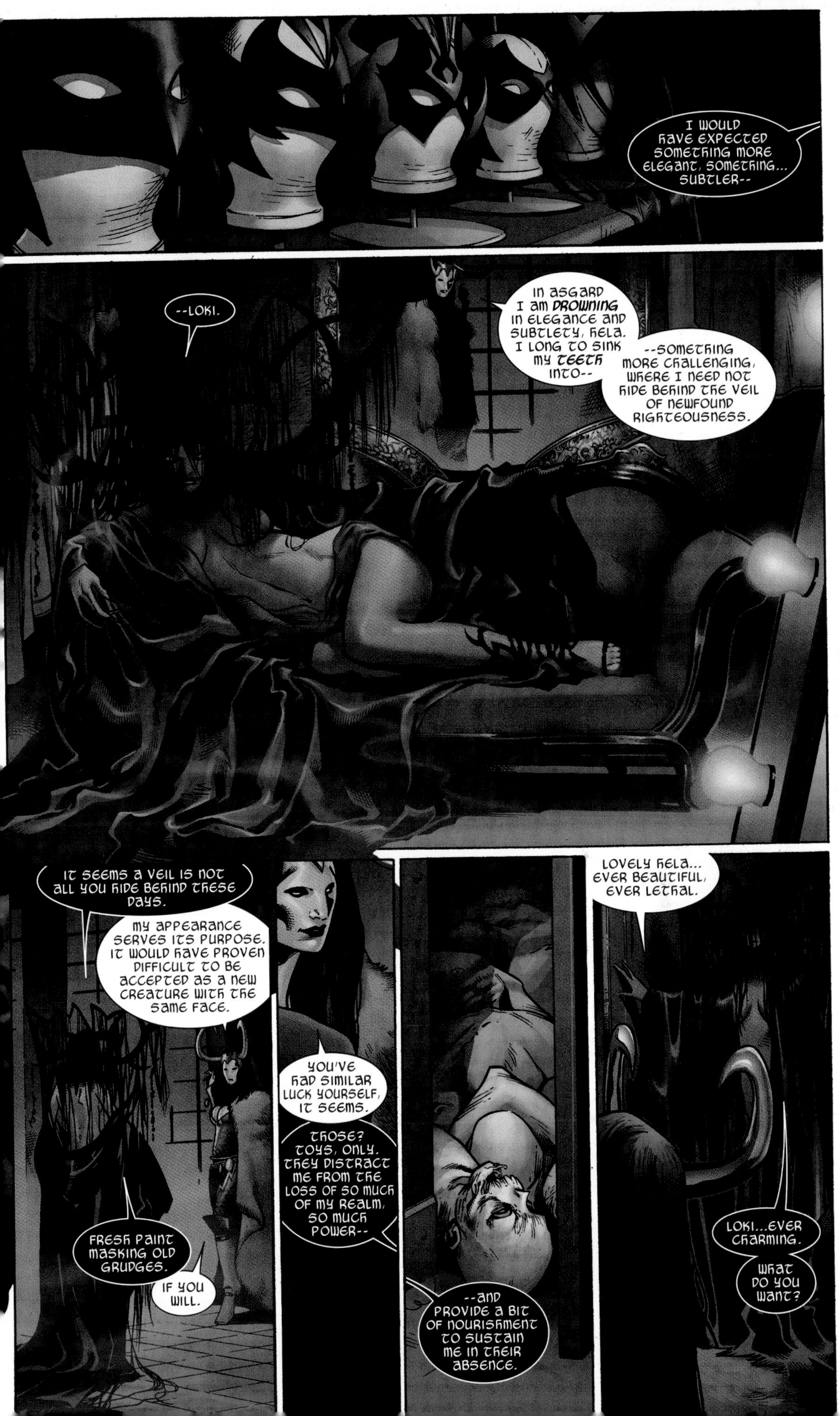
I WOULD HAVE EXPECTED SOMETHING MORE ELEGANT, SOMETHING... SUBTLER--
--LOKI.
IN ASGARD I AM DROWNING IN ELEGANCE AND SUBTLETY, HELA. I LONG TO SINK MY TEETH INTO--
--SOMETHING MORE CHALLENGING, WHERE I NEED NOT HIDE BEHIND THE VEIL OF NEWFOUND RIGHTEOUSNESS.
IT SEEMS A VEIL IS NOT ALL YOU HIDE BEHIND THESE DAYS.
MY APPEARANCE SERVES ITS PURPOSE. IT WOULD HAVE PROVEN DIFFICULT TO BE ACCEPTED AS A NEW CREATURE WITH THE SAME FACE.
FRESH PAINT MASKING OLD GRUDGES.
IF YOU WILL.
YOU'VE HAD SIMILAR LUCK YOURSELF, IT SEEMS.
THOSE? TOYS, ONLY. THEY DISTRACT ME FROM THE LOSS OF SO MUCH OF MY REALM, SO MUCH POWER--
--AND PROVIDE A BIT OF NOURISHMENT TO SUSTAIN ME IN THEIR ABSENCE.
LOVELY HELA... EVER BEAUTIFUL, EVER LETHAL.
LOKI...EVER CHARMING.
WHAT DO YOU WANT?

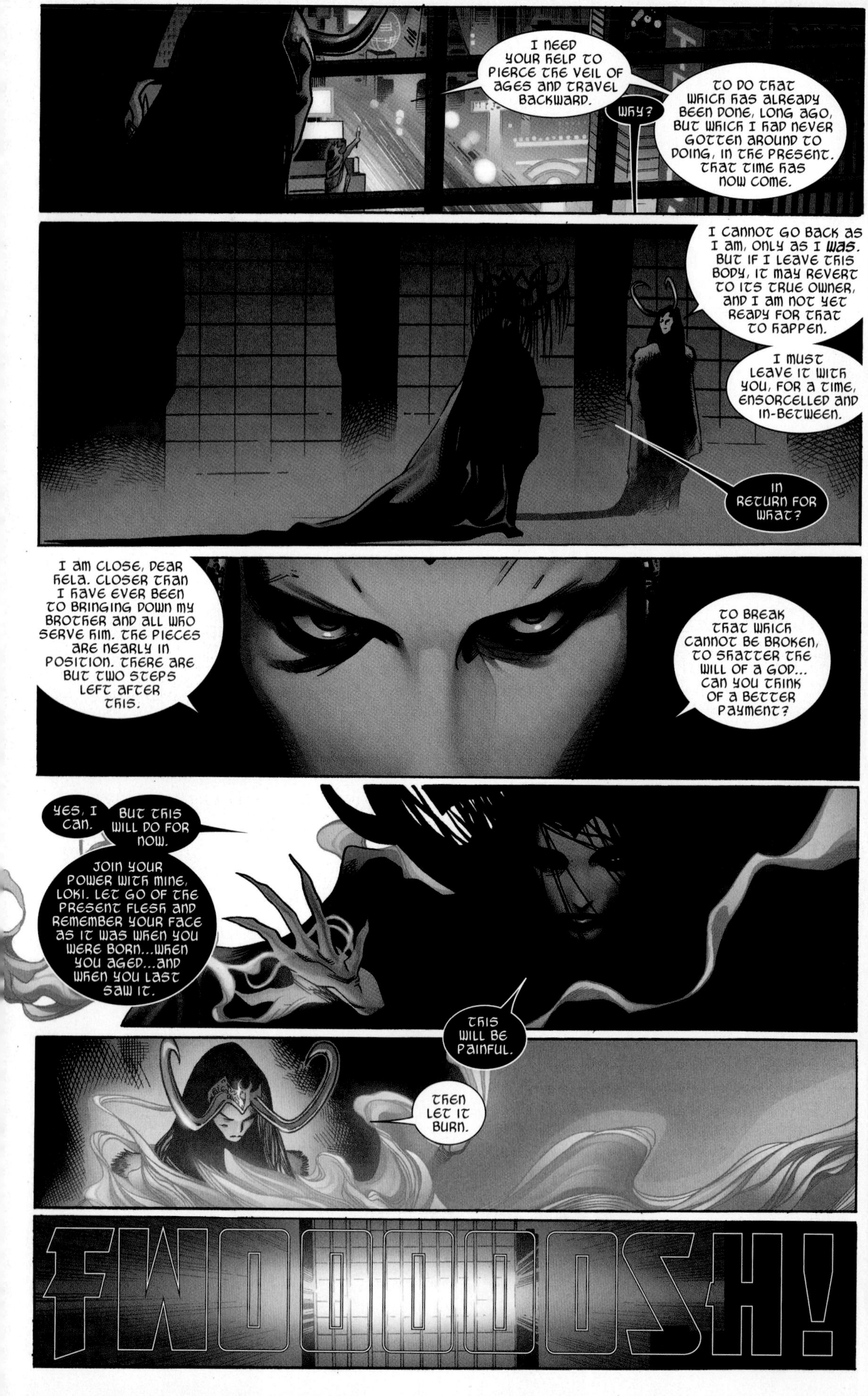
I NEED YOUR HELP TO PIERCE THE VEIL OF AGES AND TRAVEL BACKWARD.
WHY?
TO DO THAT WHICH HAS ALREADY BEEN DONE, LONG AGO, BUT WHICH I HAD NEVER GOTTEN AROUND TO DOING, IN THE PRESENT. THAT TIME HAS NOW COME.
I CANNOT GO BACK AS I AM, ONLY AS I *WAS*. BUT IF I LEAVE THIS BODY, IT MAY REVERT TO ITS TRUE OWNER, AND I AM NOT YET READY FOR THAT TO HAPPEN.
I MUST LEAVE IT WITH YOU, FOR A TIME, ENSORCELLED AND IN-BETWEEN.
IN RETURN FOR WHAT?
I AM CLOSE, DEAR HELA. CLOSER THAN I HAVE EVER BEEN TO BRINGING DOWN MY BROTHER AND ALL WHO SERVE HIM. THE PIECES ARE NEARLY IN POSITION. THERE ARE BUT TWO STEPS LEFT AFTER THIS.
TO BREAK THAT WHICH CANNOT BE BROKEN, TO SHATTER THE WILL OF A GOD... CAN YOU THINK OF A BETTER PAYMENT?
YES, I CAN.
BUT THIS WILL DO FOR NOW.
JOIN YOUR POWER WITH MINE, LOKI. LET GO OF THE PRESENT FLESH AND REMEMBER YOUR FACE AS IT WAS WHEN YOU WERE BORN...WHEN YOU AGED...AND WHEN YOU LAST SAW IT.
THIS WILL BE PAINFUL.
THEN LET IT BURN.
FWOOOOSH!

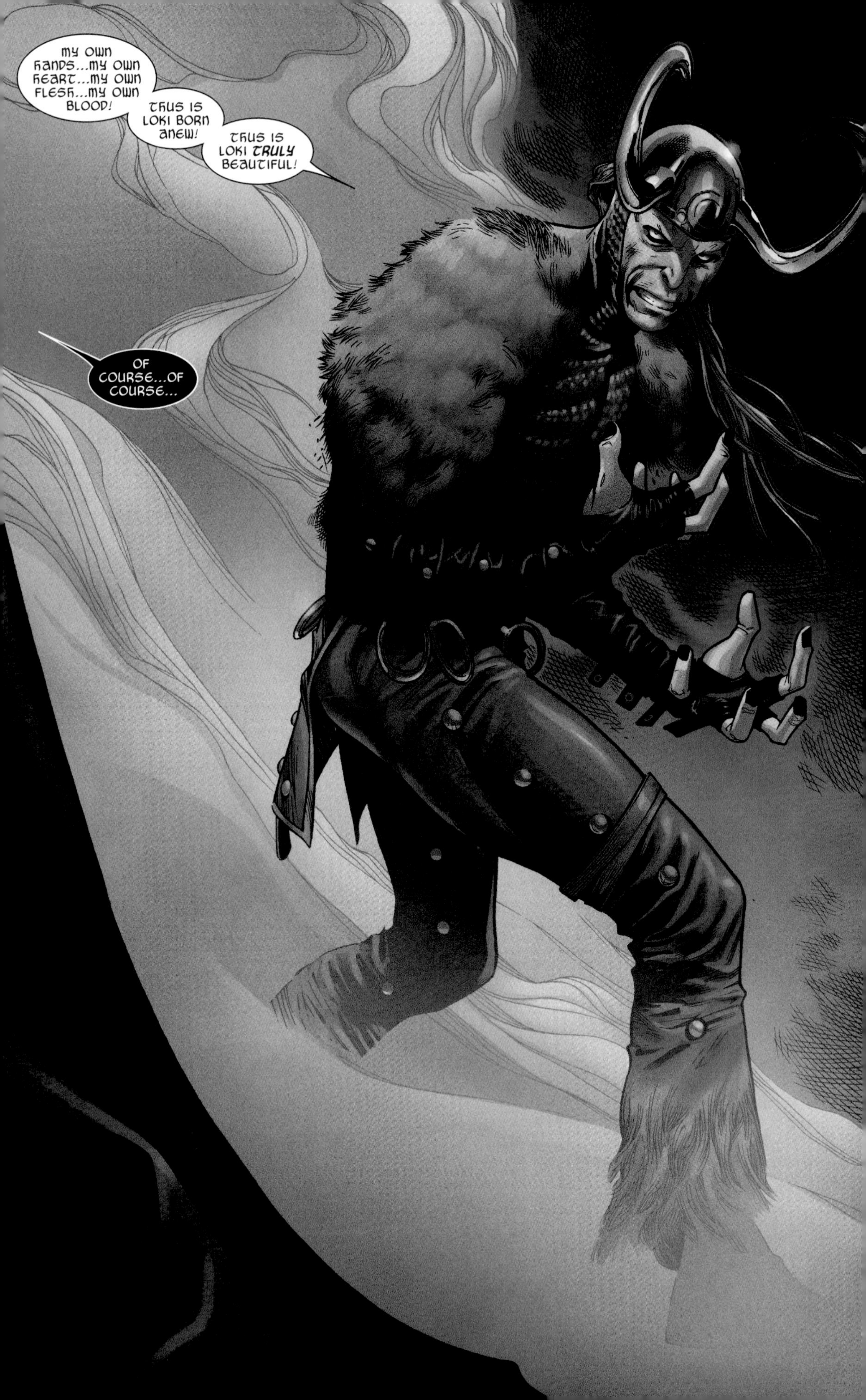
MY OWN HANDS...MY OWN HEART...MY OWN FLESH...MY OWN BLOOD!
THUS IS LOKI BORN ANEW!
THUS IS LOKI *TRULY* BEAUTIFUL!
OF COURSE...OF COURSE...

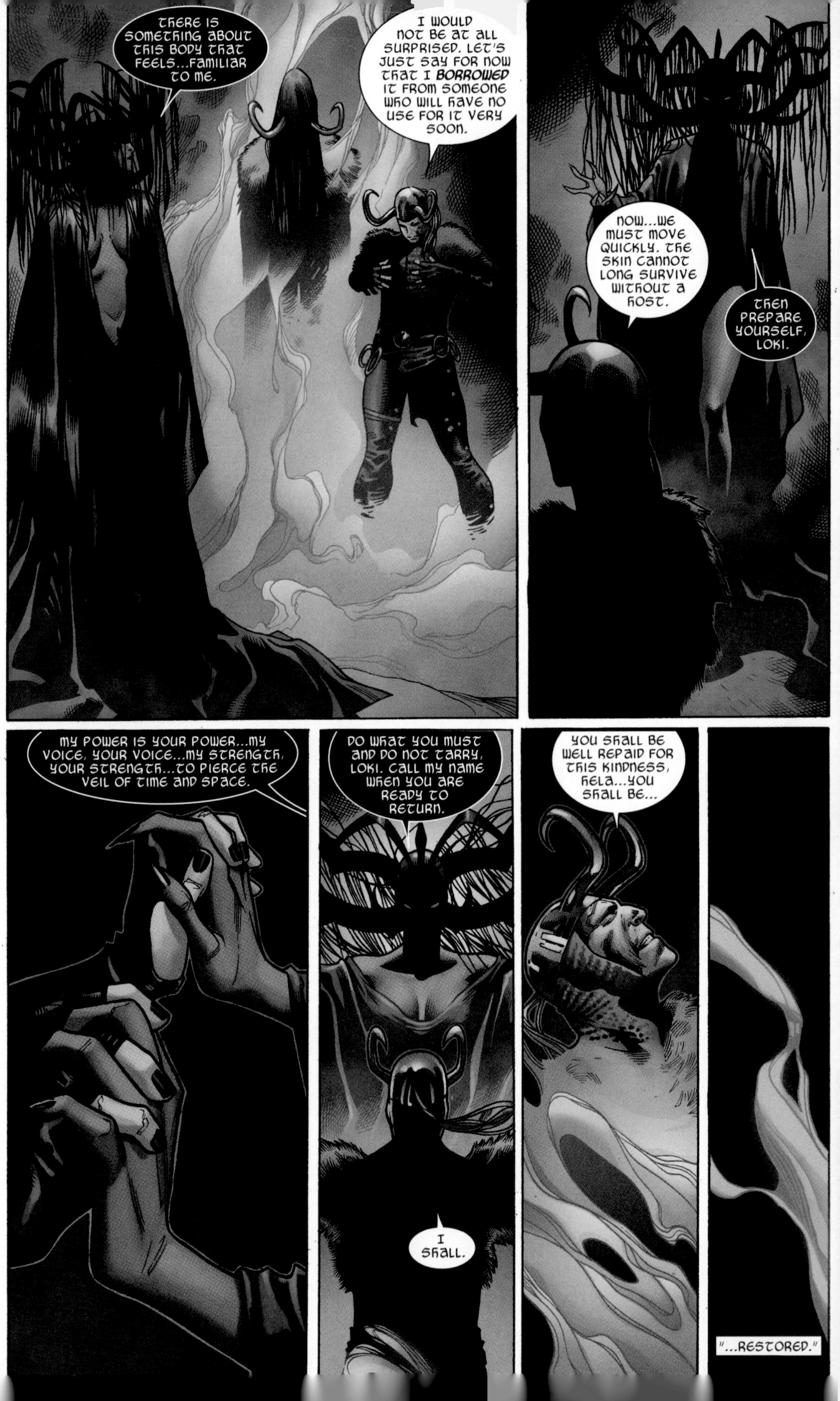
THERE IS SOMETHING ABOUT THIS BODY THAT FEELS...FAMILIAR TO ME.
I WOULD NOT BE AT ALL SURPRISED. LET'S JUST SAY FOR NOW THAT I **BORROWED** IT FROM SOMEONE WHO WILL HAVE NO USE FOR IT VERY SOON.
NOW...WE MUST MOVE QUICKLY. THE SKIN CANNOT LONG SURVIVE WITHOUT A HOST.
THEN PREPARE YOURSELF, LOKI.
MY POWER IS YOUR POWER...MY VOICE, YOUR VOICE...MY STRENGTH, YOUR STRENGTH...TO PIERCE THE VEIL OF TIME AND SPACE.
DO WHAT YOU MUST AND DO NOT TARRY, LOKI. CALL MY NAME WHEN YOU ARE READY TO RETURN.
I SHALL.
YOU SHALL BE WELL REPAID FOR THIS KINDNESS, HELA...YOU SHALL BE...
"...RESTORED."

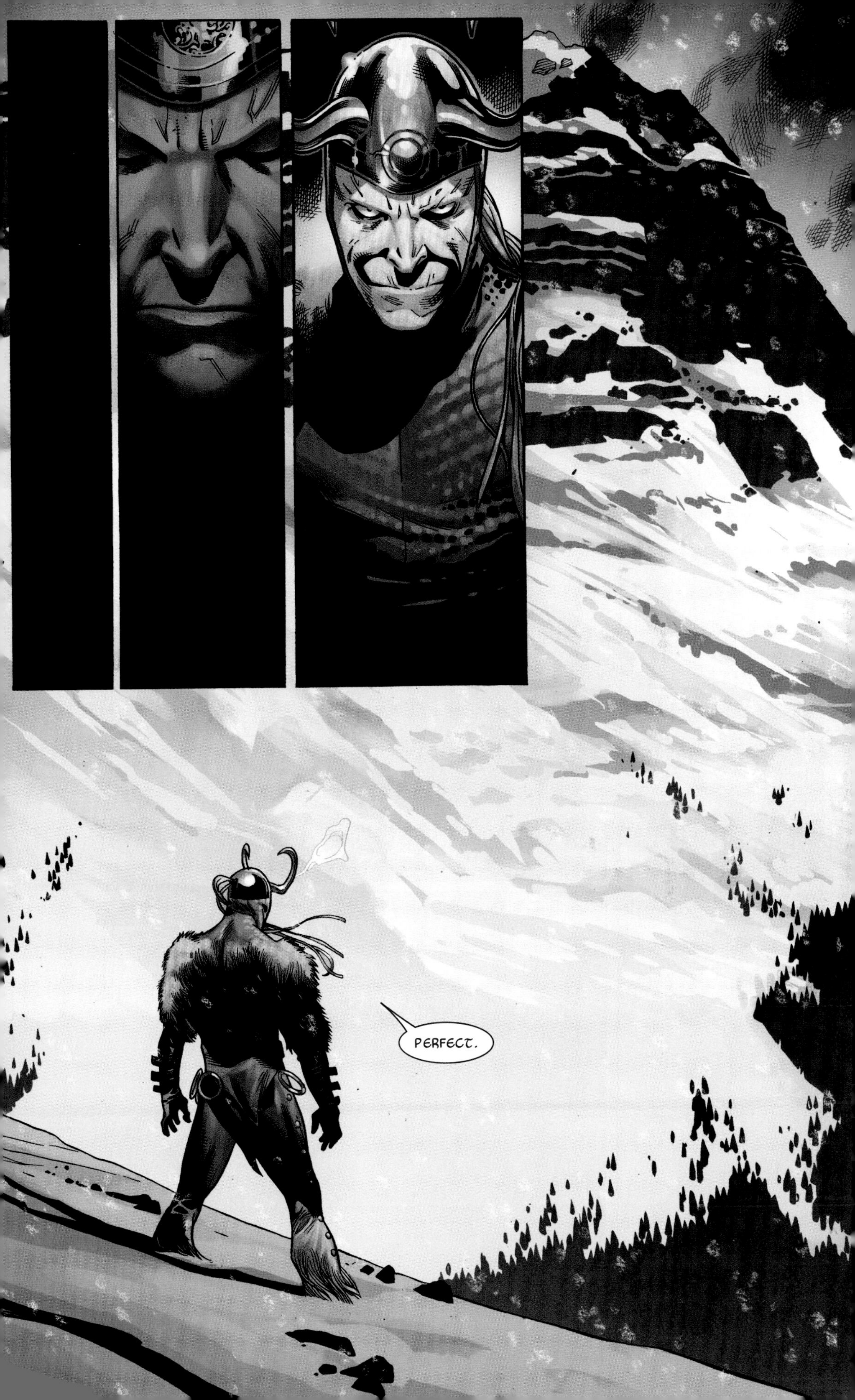
PERFECT.

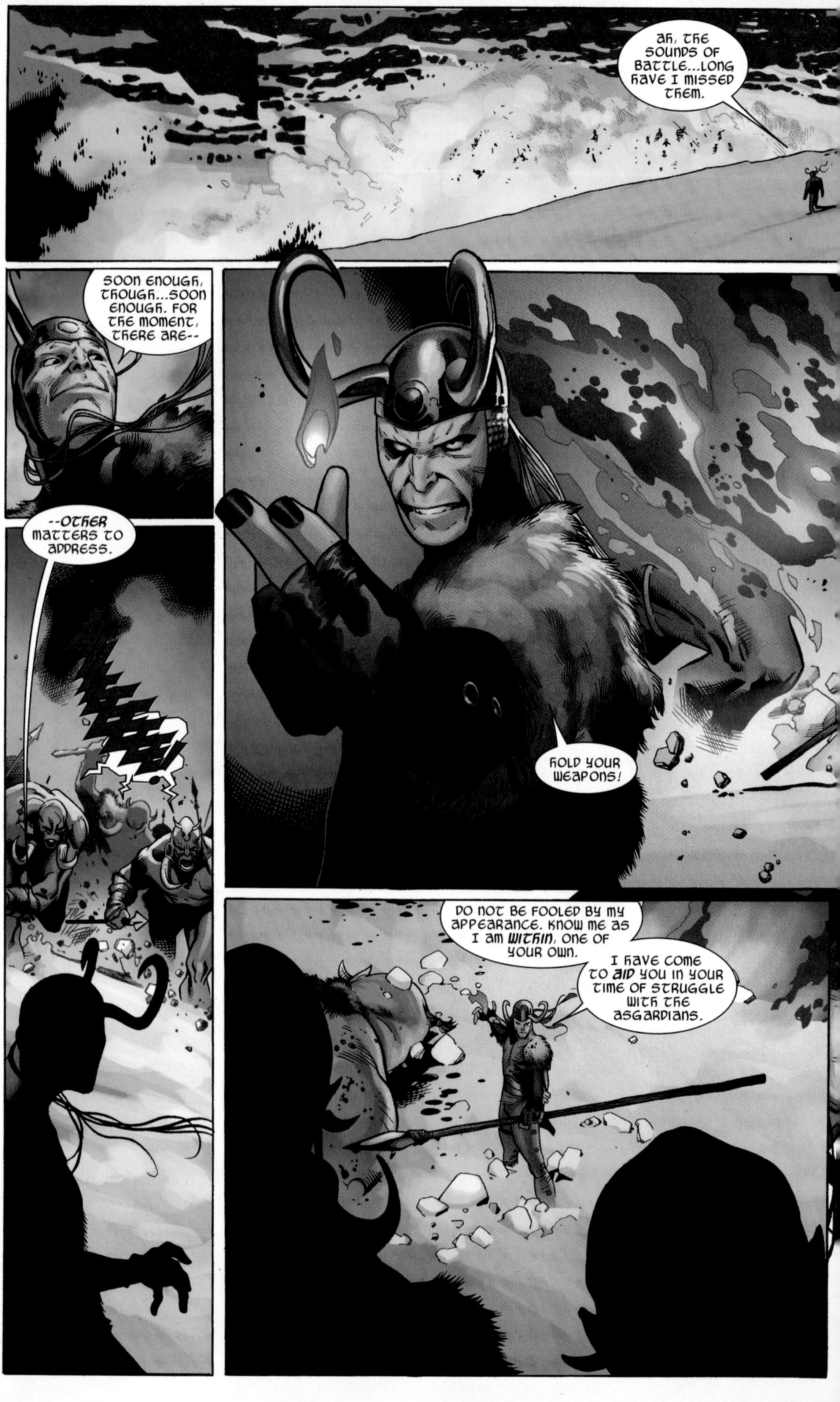
AH, THE SOUNDS OF BATTLE...LONG HAVE I MISSED THEM.
SOON ENOUGH, THOUGH...SOON ENOUGH. FOR THE MOMENT, THERE ARE--
--OTHER MATTERS TO ADDRESS.
HOLD YOUR WEAPONS!
DO NOT BE FOOLED BY MY APPEARANCE. KNOW ME AS I AM WITHIN, ONE OF YOUR OWN.
I HAVE COME TO AID YOU IN YOUR TIME OF STRUGGLE WITH THE ASGARDIANS.

I said--

...OLD!

I SMELL IN YOU THE BLOOD THAT RUNS THROUGH MY VEINS.

WHAT DO YOU WANT FROM US?

A MOMENT ONLY. A FLICKER OF TIME.

A CLOAK, THAT I MAY CONCEAL MY APPEARANCE.

AND YOUR FASTEST RUNNER.

"ONE WHOSE SPEED AND SKILL WILL DRAW THE ATTENTION OF THE LORD OF ASGARD--

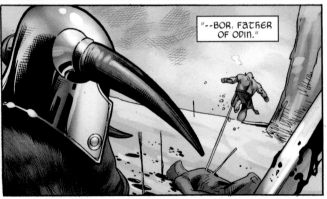

"--BOR, FATHER OF ODIN."

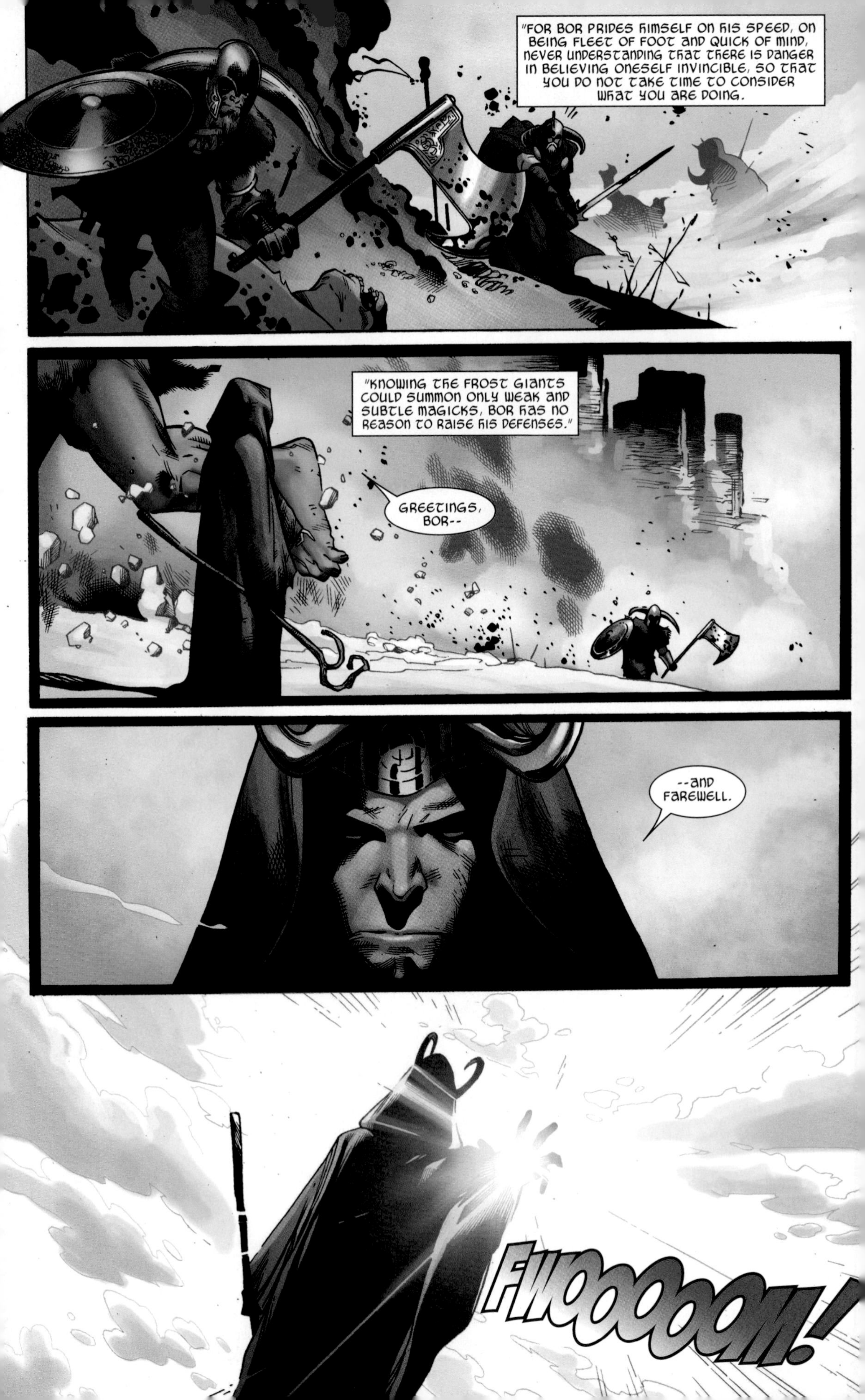
"FOR BOR PRIDES HIMSELF ON HIS SPEED, ON BEING FLEET OF FOOT AND QUICK OF MIND, NEVER UNDERSTANDING THAT THERE IS DANGER IN BELIEVING ONESELF INVINCIBLE, SO THAT YOU DO NOT TAKE TIME TO CONSIDER WHAT YOU ARE DOING.
"KNOWING THE FROST GIANTS COULD SUMMON ONLY WEAK AND SUBTLE MAGICKS, BOR HAS NO REASON TO RAISE HIS DEFENSES."
GREETINGS, BOR--
--AND FAREWELL.
FWOOOOOOM!

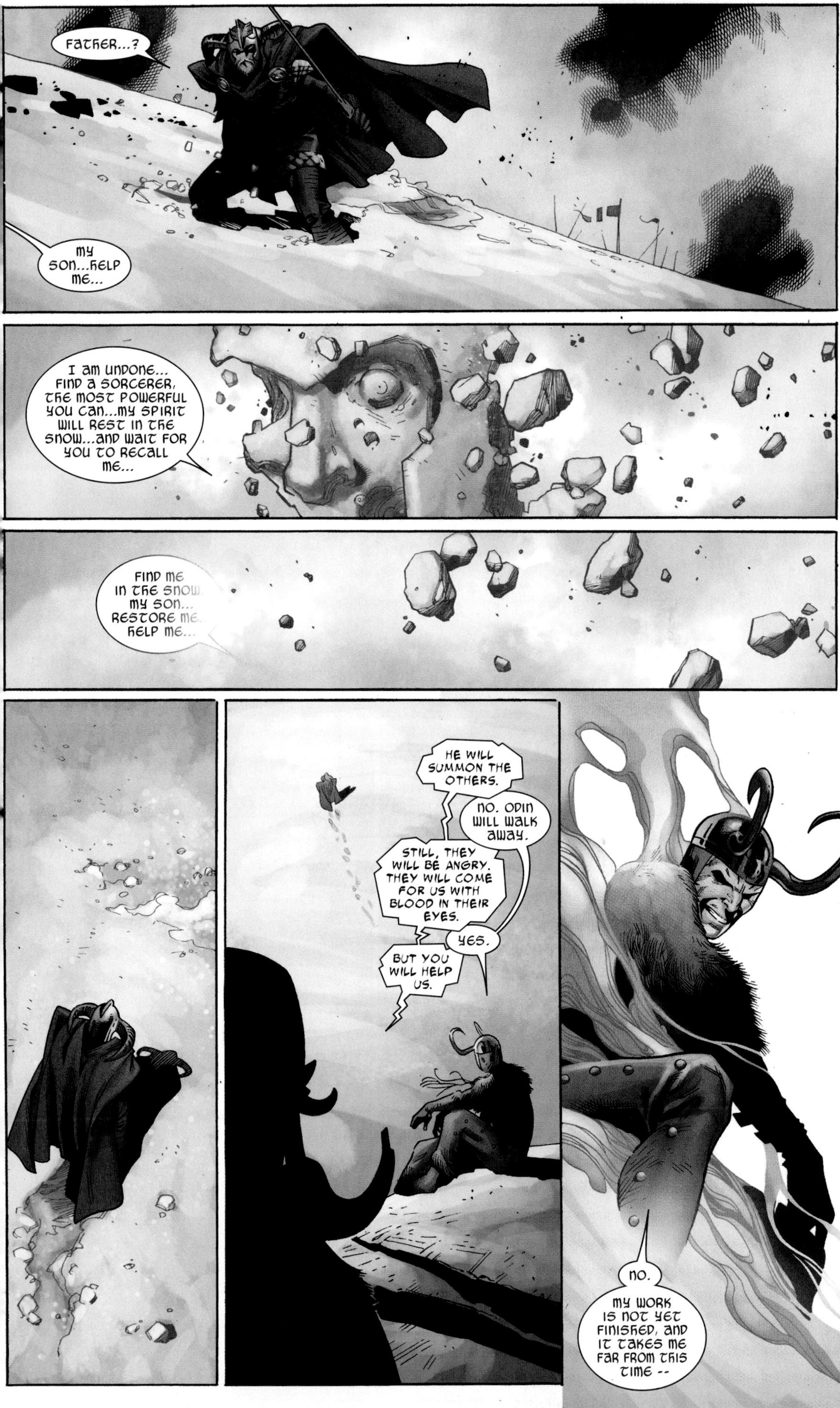
FATHER...?
MY SON...HELP ME...
I AM UNDONE... FIND A SORCERER, THE MOST POWERFUL YOU CAN...MY SPIRIT WILL REST IN THE SNOW...AND WAIT FOR YOU TO RECALL ME...
FIND ME IN THE SNOW... MY SON... RESTORE ME... HELP ME...
HE WILL SUMMON THE OTHERS.
NO. ODIN WILL WALK AWAY.
STILL, THEY WILL BE ANGRY. THEY WILL COME FOR US WITH BLOOD IN THEIR EYES.
YES.
BUT YOU WILL HELP US.
NO.
MY WORK IS NOT YET FINISHED, AND IT TAKES ME FAR FROM THIS TIME --

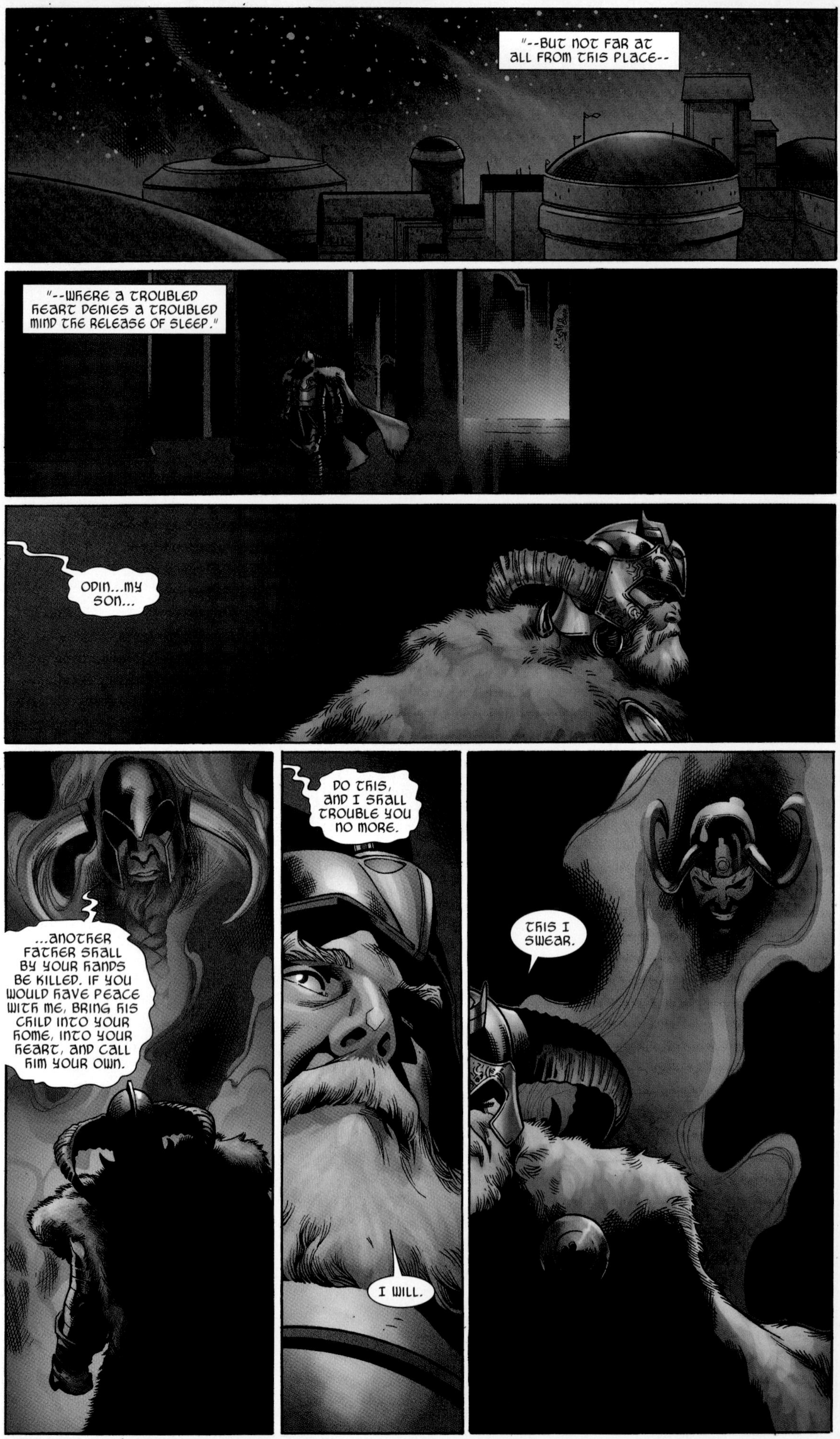
"--BUT NOT FAR AT ALL FROM THIS PLACE--
"--WHERE A TROUBLED HEART DENIES A TROUBLED MIND THE RELEASE OF SLEEP."
ODIN...MY SON...
...ANOTHER FATHER SHALL BY YOUR HANDS BE KILLED. IF YOU WOULD HAVE PEACE WITH ME, BRING HIS CHILD INTO YOUR HOME, INTO YOUR HEART, AND CALL HIM YOUR OWN.
DO THIS, AND I SHALL TROUBLE YOU NO MORE.
I WILL.
THIS I SWEAR.

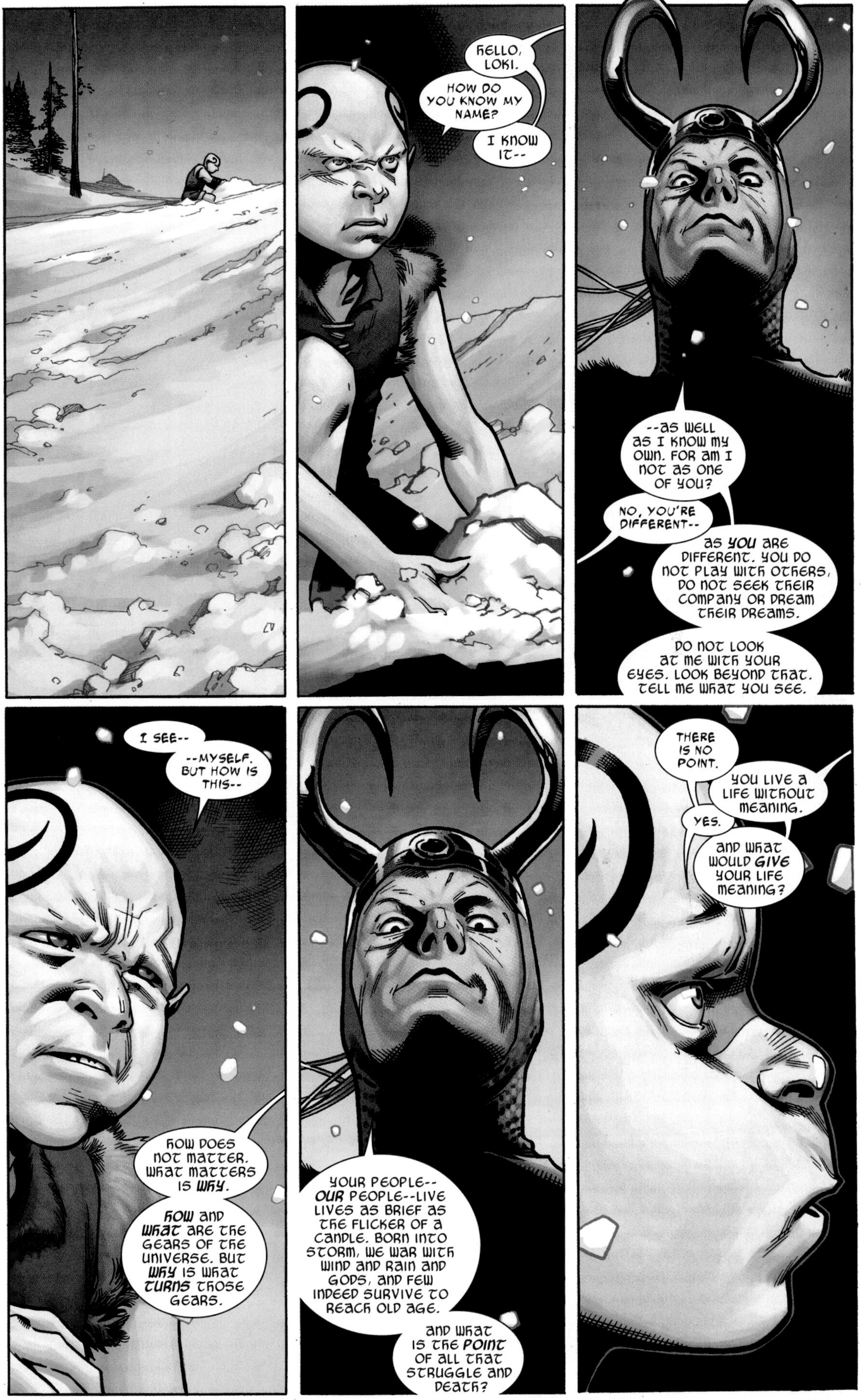
HELLO, LOKI.
HOW DO YOU KNOW MY NAME?
I KNOW IT--
--AS WELL AS I KNOW MY OWN. FOR AM I NOT AS ONE OF YOU?
NO, YOU'RE DIFFERENT--
AS YOU ARE DIFFERENT. YOU DO NOT PLAY WITH OTHERS, DO NOT SEEK THEIR COMPANY OR DREAM THEIR DREAMS.
DO NOT LOOK AT ME WITH YOUR EYES. LOOK BEYOND THAT. TELL ME WHAT YOU SEE.
I SEE--
--MYSELF. BUT HOW IS THIS--
HOW DOES NOT MATTER. WHAT MATTERS IS WHY.
HOW AND WHAT ARE THE GEARS OF THE UNIVERSE. BUT WHY IS WHAT TURNS THOSE GEARS.
YOUR PEOPLE-- OUR PEOPLE--LIVE LIVES AS BRIEF AS THE FLICKER OF A CANDLE. BORN INTO STORM, WE WAR WITH WIND AND RAIN AND GODS, AND FEW INDEED SURVIVE TO REACH OLD AGE.
AND WHAT IS THE POINT OF ALL THAT STRUGGLE AND DEATH?
THERE IS NO POINT.
YOU LIVE A LIFE WITHOUT MEANING.
YES.
AND WHAT WOULD GIVE YOUR LIFE MEANING?

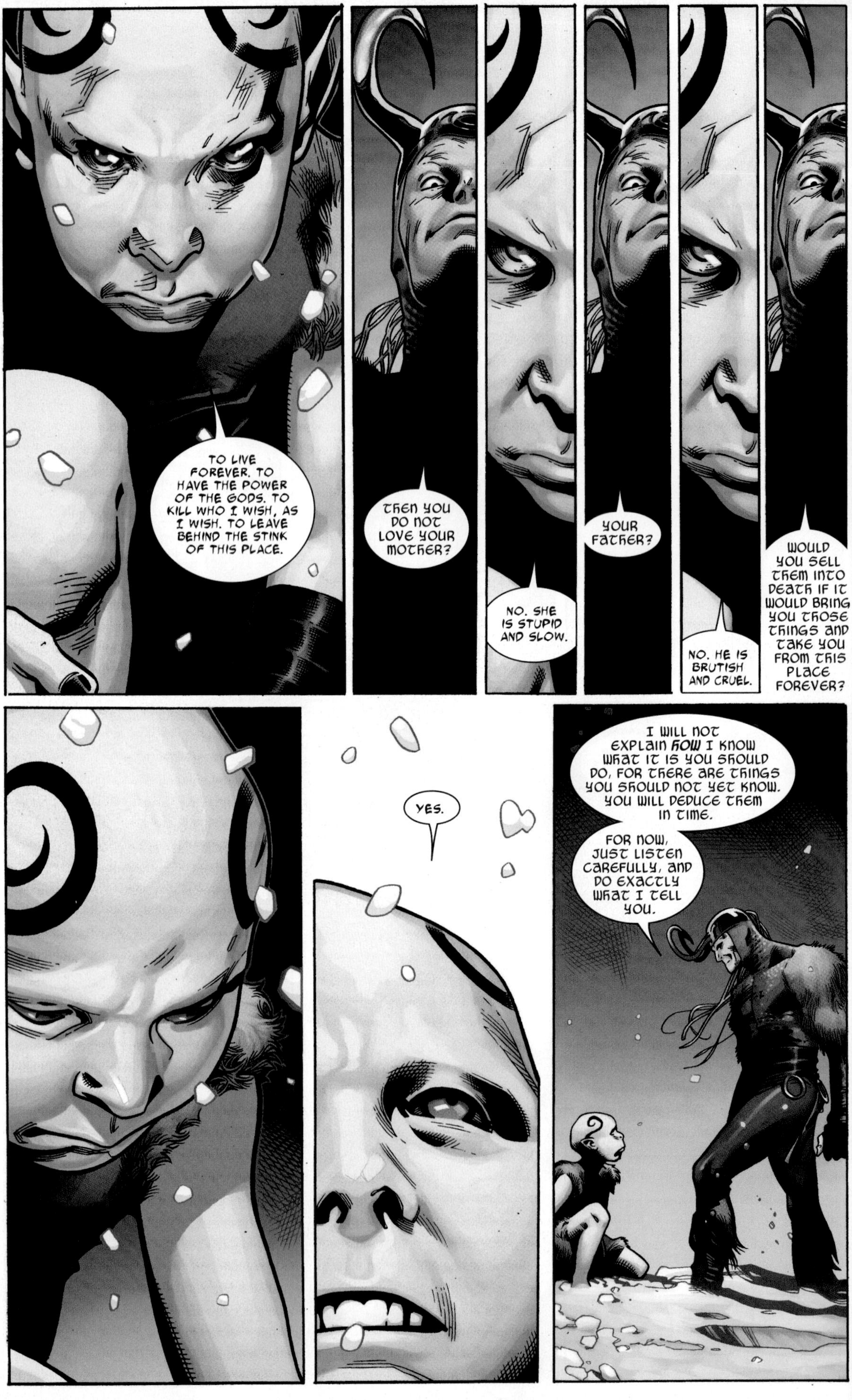
TO LIVE FOREVER. TO HAVE THE POWER OF THE GODS. TO KILL WHO I WISH, AS I WISH. TO LEAVE BEHIND THE STINK OF THIS PLACE.
THEN YOU DO NOT LOVE YOUR MOTHER?
NO. SHE IS STUPID AND SLOW.
YOUR FATHER?
NO. HE IS BRUTISH AND CRUEL.
WOULD YOU SELL THEM INTO DEATH IF IT WOULD BRING YOU THOSE THINGS AND TAKE YOU FROM THIS PLACE FOREVER?
YES.
I WILL NOT EXPLAIN HOW I KNOW WHAT IT IS YOU SHOULD DO, FOR THERE ARE THINGS YOU SHOULD NOT YET KNOW. YOU WILL DEDUCE THEM IN TIME.
FOR NOW, JUST LISTEN CAREFULLY, AND DO EXACTLY WHAT I TELL YOU.

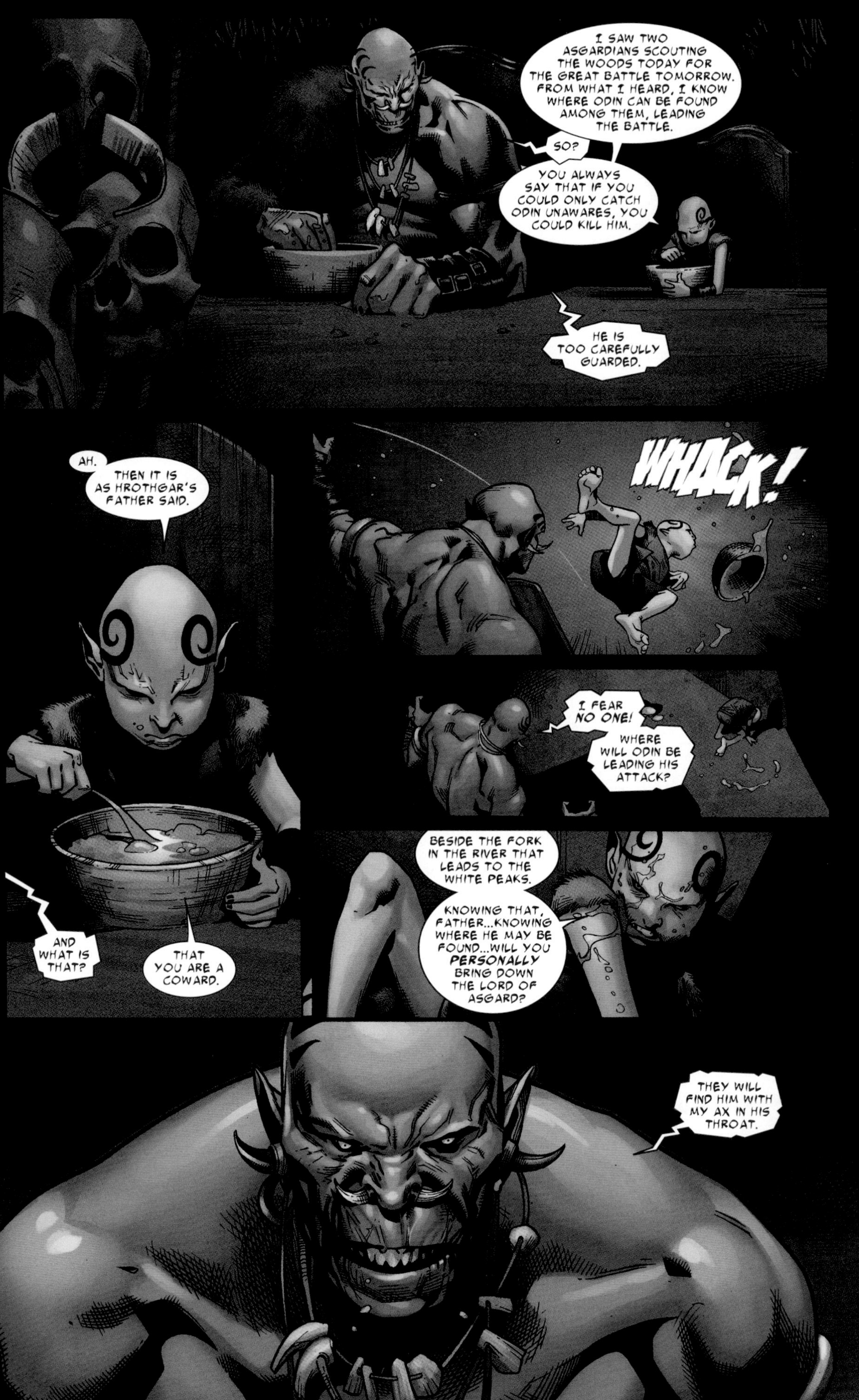
I SAW TWO ASGARDIANS SCOUTING THE WOODS TODAY FOR THE GREAT BATTLE TOMORROW. FROM WHAT I HEARD, I KNOW WHERE ODIN CAN BE FOUND AMONG THEM, LEADING THE BATTLE.
SO?
YOU ALWAYS SAY THAT IF YOU COULD ONLY CATCH ODIN UNAWARES, YOU COULD KILL HIM.
HE IS TOO CAREFULLY GUARDED.
AH.
THEN IT IS AS HROTHGAR'S FATHER SAID.
AND WHAT IS THAT?
THAT YOU ARE A COWARD.
WHACK!
I FEAR NO ONE!
WHERE WILL ODIN BE LEADING HIS ATTACK?
BESIDE THE FORK IN THE RIVER THAT LEADS TO THE WHITE PEAKS.
KNOWING THAT, FATHER...KNOWING WHERE HE MAY BE FOUND...WILL YOU PERSONALLY BRING DOWN THE LORD OF ASGARD?
THEY WILL FIND HIM WITH MY AX IN HIS THROAT.

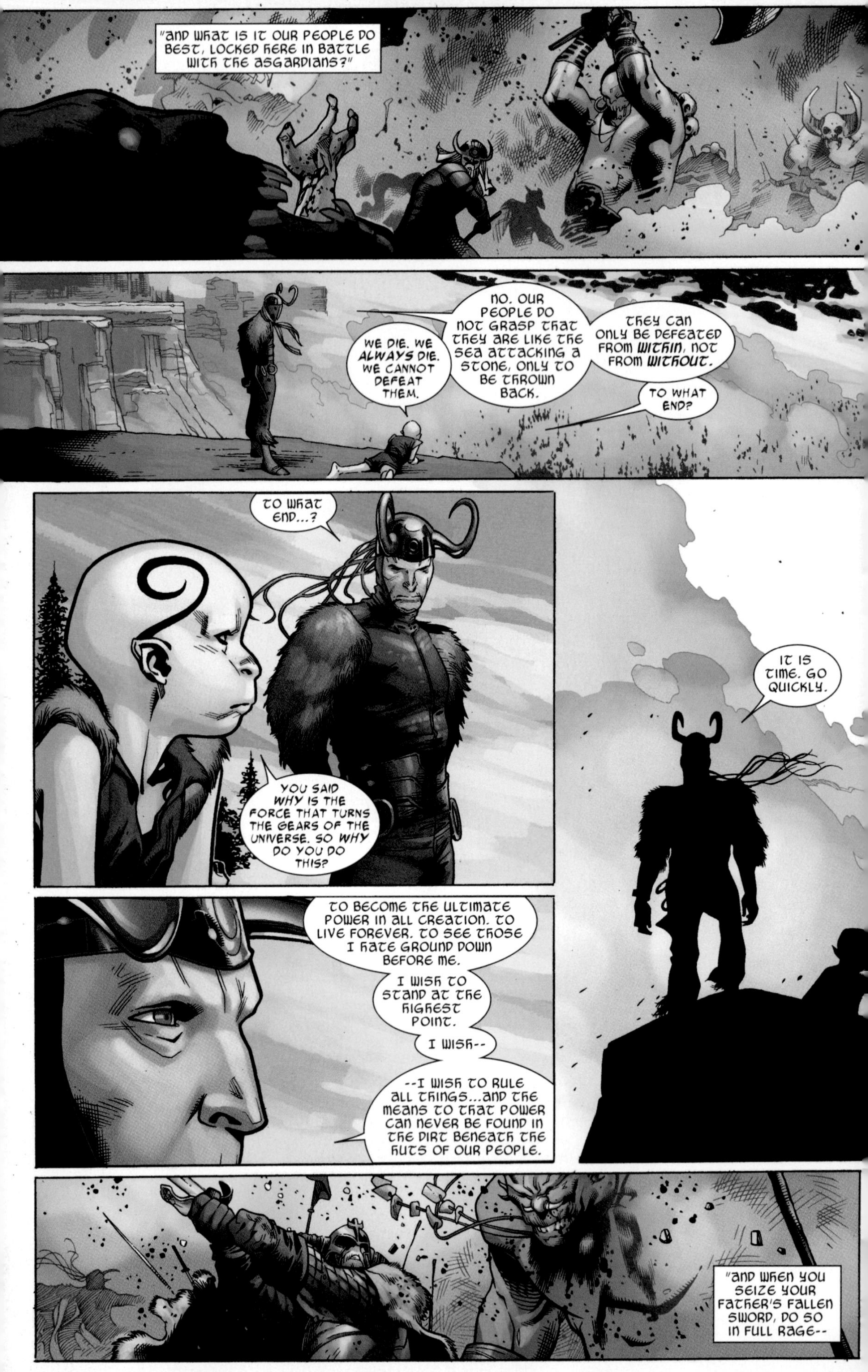
"AND WHAT IS IT OUR PEOPLE DO BEST, LOCKED HERE IN BATTLE WITH THE ASGARDIANS?"
WE DIE. WE ALWAYS DIE. WE CANNOT DEFEAT THEM.
NO. OUR PEOPLE DO NOT GRASP THAT THEY ARE LIKE THE SEA ATTACKING A STONE, ONLY TO BE THROWN BACK.
THEY CAN ONLY BE DEFEATED FROM WITHIN, NOT FROM WITHOUT.
TO WHAT END?
TO WHAT END...?
YOU SAID WHY IS THE FORCE THAT TURNS THE GEARS OF THE UNIVERSE. SO WHY DO YOU DO THIS?
TO BECOME THE ULTIMATE POWER IN ALL CREATION. TO LIVE FOREVER. TO SEE THOSE I HATE GROUND DOWN BEFORE ME.
I WISH TO STAND AT THE HIGHEST POINT.
I WISH--
--I WISH TO RULE ALL THINGS...AND THE MEANS TO THAT POWER CAN NEVER BE FOUND IN THE DIRT BENEATH THE HUTS OF OUR PEOPLE.
IT IS TIME. GO QUICKLY.
"AND WHEN YOU SEIZE YOUR FATHER'S FALLEN SWORD, DO SO IN FULL RAGE--

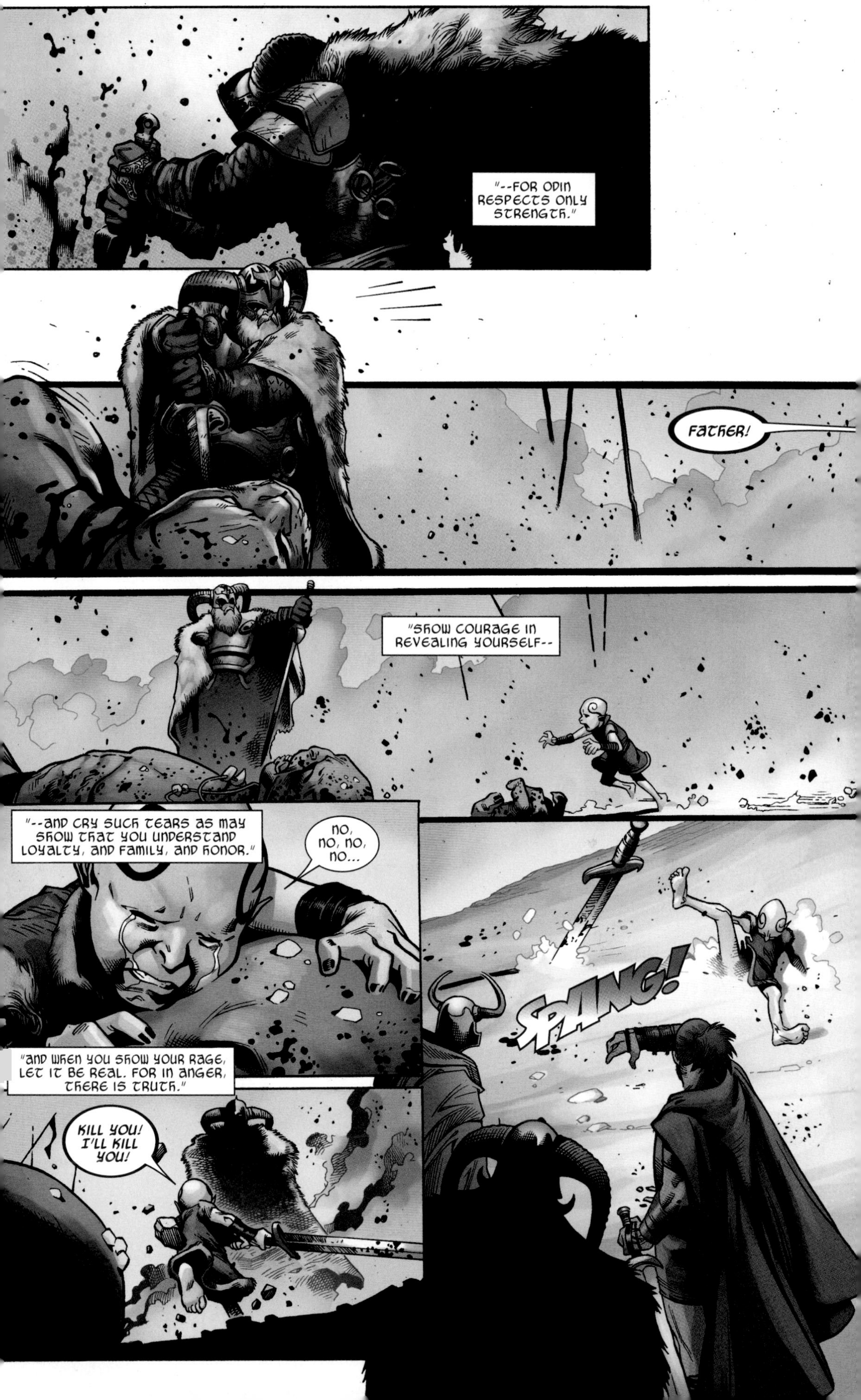
"--FOR ODIN RESPECTS ONLY STRENGTH."
FATHER!
"SHOW COURAGE IN REVEALING YOURSELF--
"--AND CRY SUCH TEARS AS MAY SHOW THAT YOU UNDERSTAND LOYALTY, AND FAMILY, AND HONOR."
NO, NO, NO, NO...
"AND WHEN YOU SHOW YOUR RAGE, LET IT BE REAL. FOR IN ANGER, THERE IS TRUTH."
KILL YOU! I'LL KILL YOU!
SPANG!

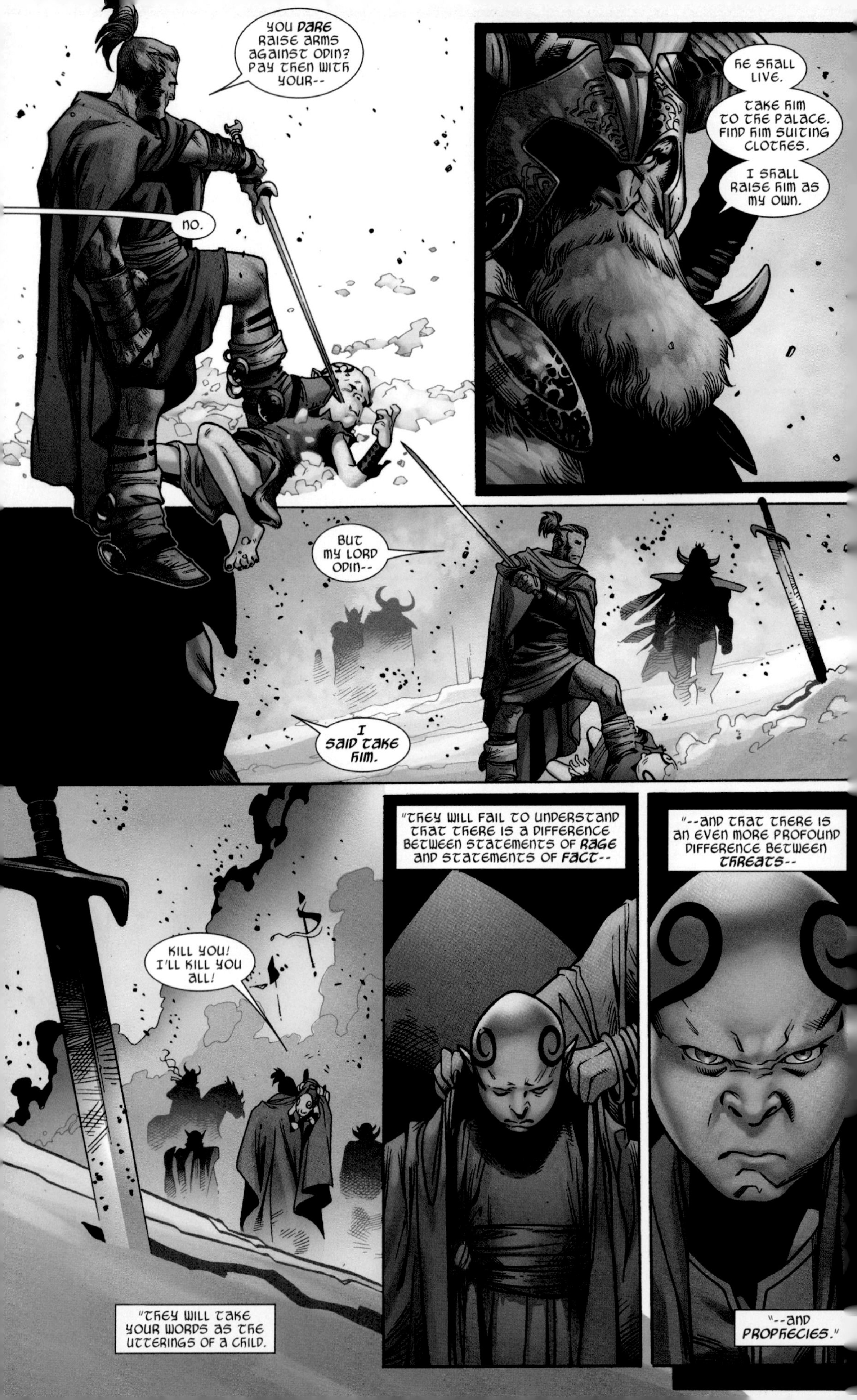
YOU DARE RAISE ARMS AGAINST ODIN? PAY THEN WITH YOUR--
NO.
HE SHALL LIVE.
TAKE HIM TO THE PALACE. FIND HIM SUITING CLOTHES.
I SHALL RAISE HIM AS MY OWN.
BUT MY LORD ODIN--
I SAID TAKE HIM.
KILL YOU! I'LL KILL YOU ALL!
"THEY WILL TAKE YOUR WORDS AS THE UTTERINGS OF A CHILD.
"THEY WILL FAIL TO UNDERSTAND THAT THERE IS A DIFFERENCE BETWEEN STATEMENTS OF RAGE AND STATEMENTS OF FACT--
"--AND THAT THERE IS AN EVEN MORE PROFOUND DIFFERENCE BETWEEN THREATS--
"--AND PROPHECIES."

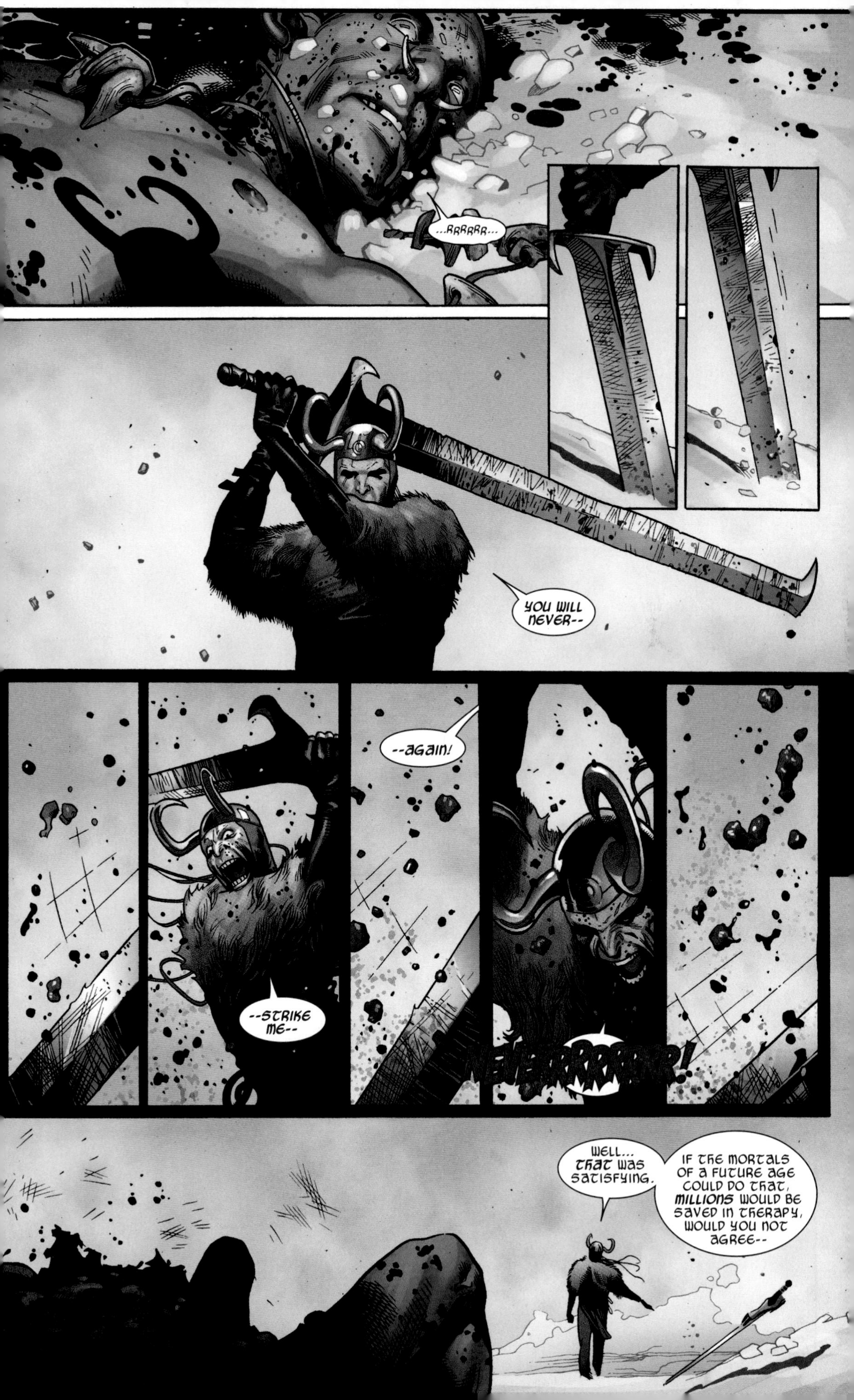
...RRRRRR...
YOU WILL NEVER--
--STRIKE ME--
--AGAIN!
NEVERRRRRRR!
WELL... THAT WAS SATISFYING.
IF THE MORTALS OF A FUTURE AGE COULD DO THAT, MILLIONS WOULD BE SAVED IN THERAPY, WOULD YOU NOT AGREE--

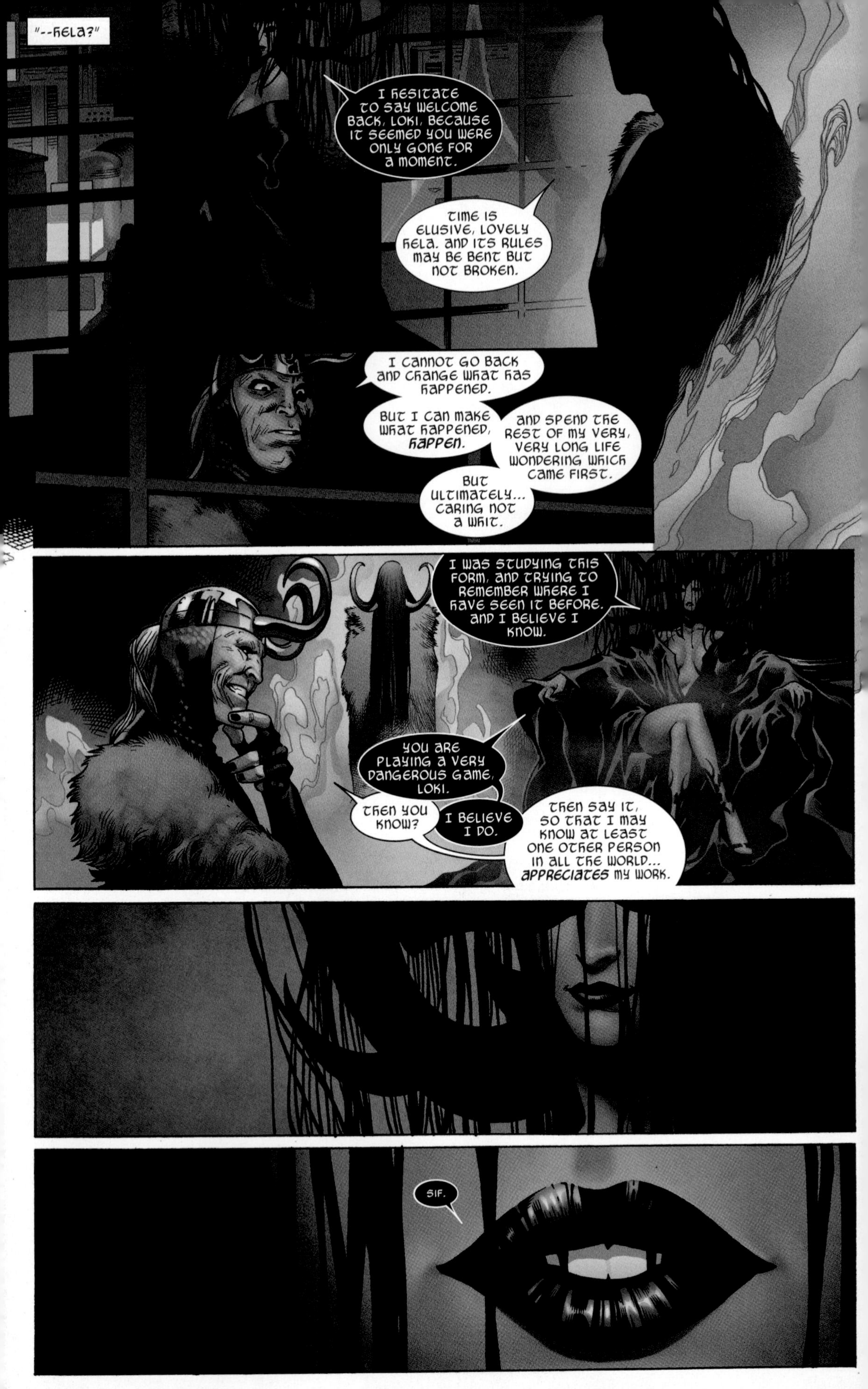
"--HELA?"
I HESITATE TO SAY WELCOME BACK, LOKI, BECAUSE IT SEEMED YOU WERE ONLY GONE FOR A MOMENT.
TIME IS ELUSIVE, LOVELY HELA. AND ITS RULES MAY BE BENT BUT NOT BROKEN.
I CANNOT GO BACK AND CHANGE WHAT HAS HAPPENED.
BUT I CAN MAKE WHAT HAPPENED, HAPPEN.
AND SPEND THE REST OF MY VERY, VERY LONG LIFE WONDERING WHICH CAME FIRST.
BUT ULTIMATELY... CARING NOT A WHIT.
I WAS STUDYING THIS FORM, AND TRYING TO REMEMBER WHERE I HAVE SEEN IT BEFORE. AND I BELIEVE I KNOW.
YOU ARE PLAYING A VERY DANGEROUS GAME, LOKI.
THEN YOU KNOW?
I BELIEVE I DO.
THEN SAY IT, SO THAT I MAY KNOW AT LEAST ONE OTHER PERSON IN ALL THE WORLD... APPRECIATES MY WORK.
SIF.

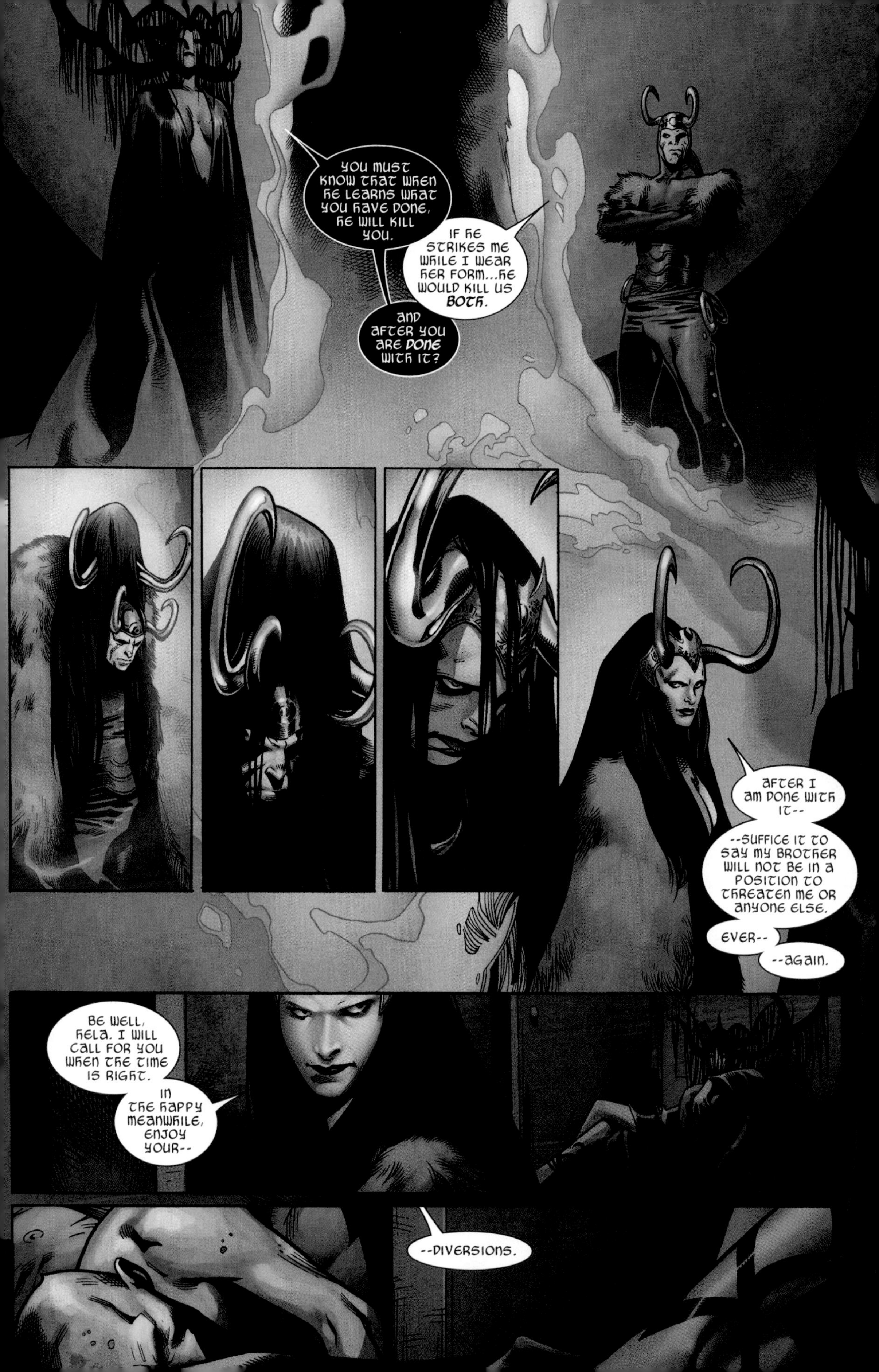

YOU MUST KNOW THAT WHEN HE LEARNS WHAT YOU HAVE DONE, HE WILL KILL YOU.
IF HE STRIKES ME WHILE I WEAR HER FORM...HE WOULD KILL US BOTH.
AND AFTER YOU ARE DONE WITH IT?
AFTER I AM DONE WITH IT--
--SUFFICE IT TO SAY MY BROTHER WILL NOT BE IN A POSITION TO THREATEN ME OR ANYONE ELSE.
EVER--
--AGAIN.
BE WELL, HELA. I WILL CALL FOR YOU WHEN THE TIME IS RIGHT.
IN THE HAPPY MEANWHILE, ENJOY YOUR--
--DIVERSIONS.

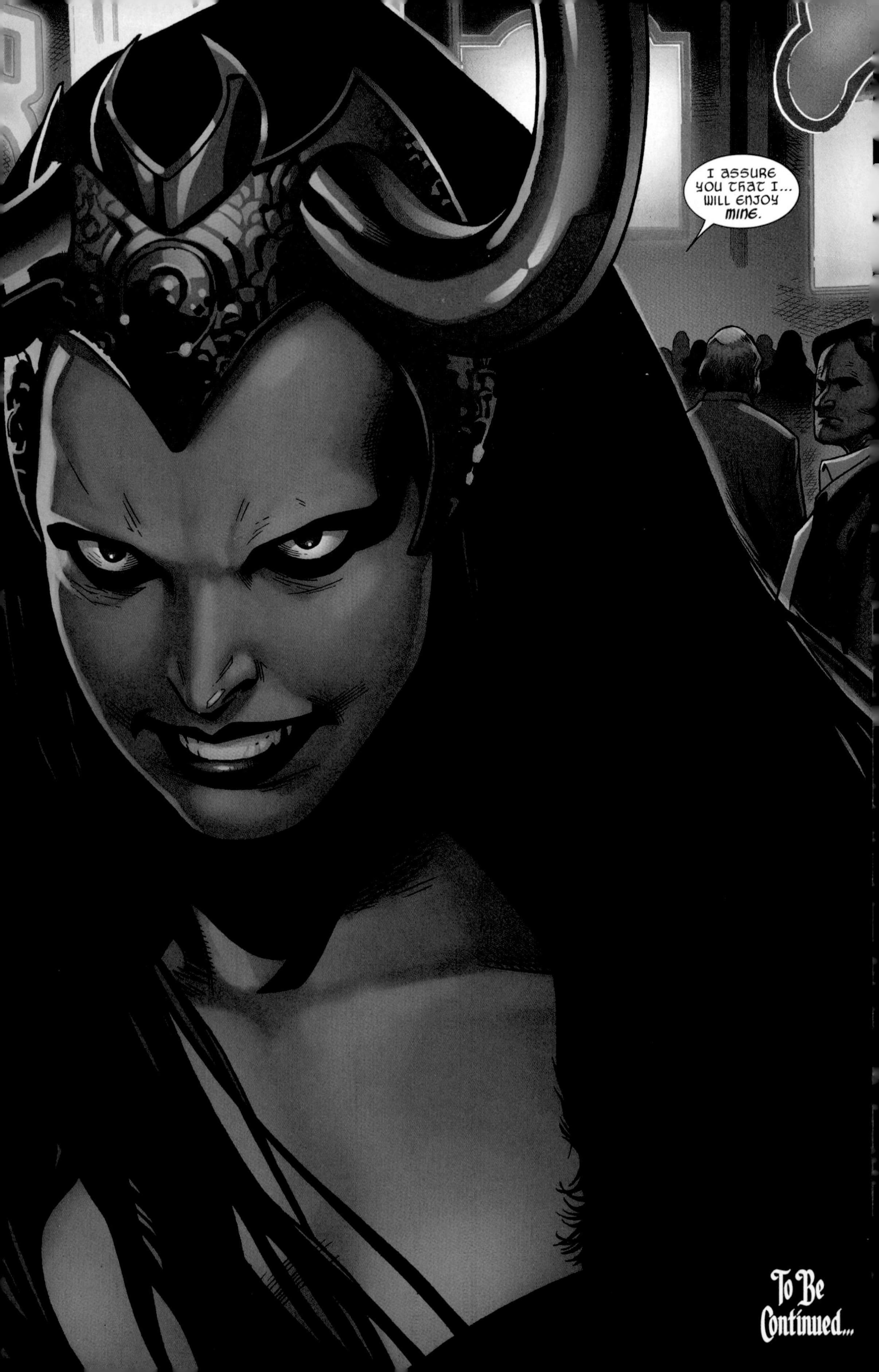
I ASSURE YOU THAT I... WILL ENJOY MINE.
To Be Continued...

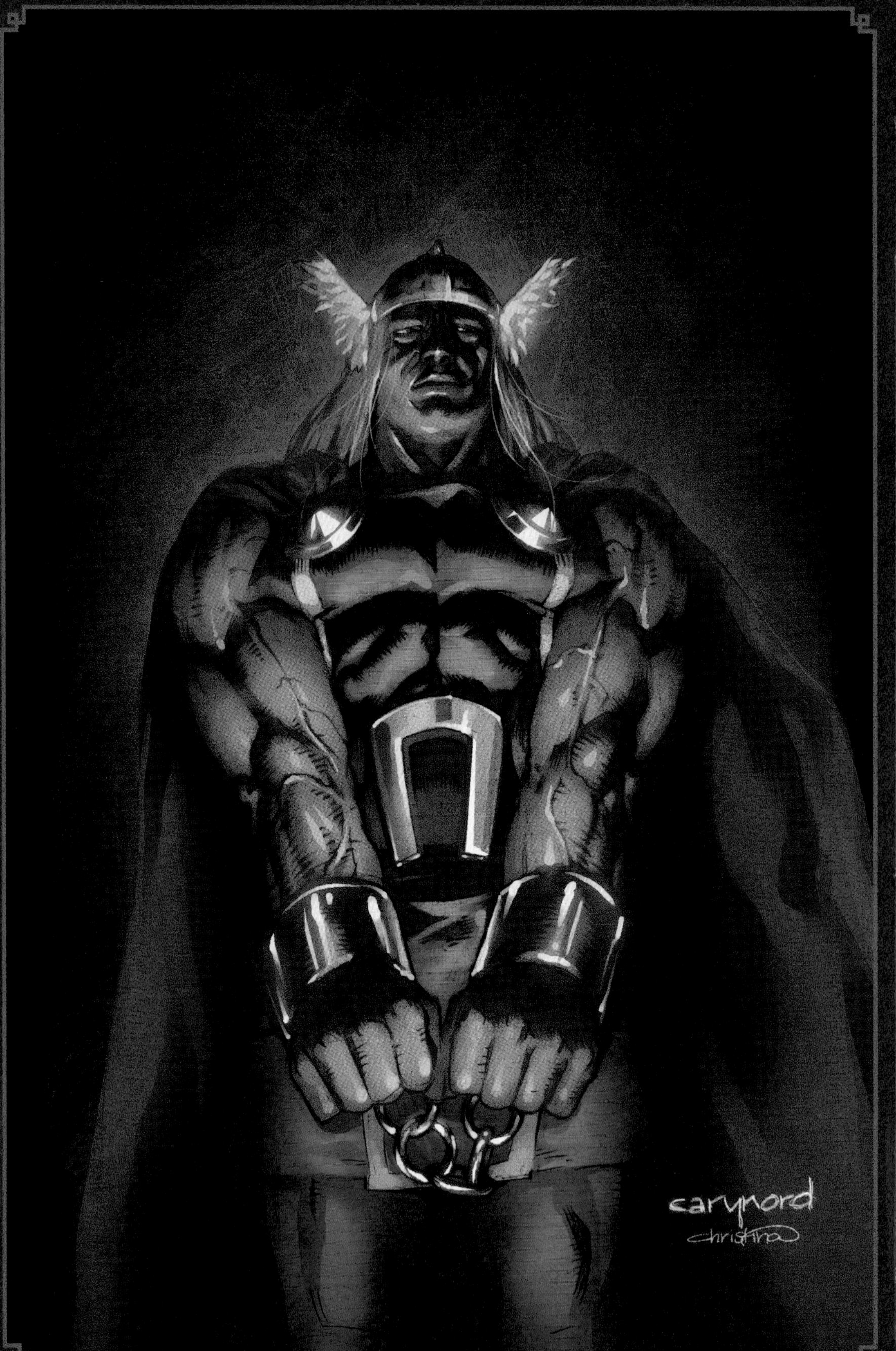
carynord

# THOR: THE TRIAL OF THOR

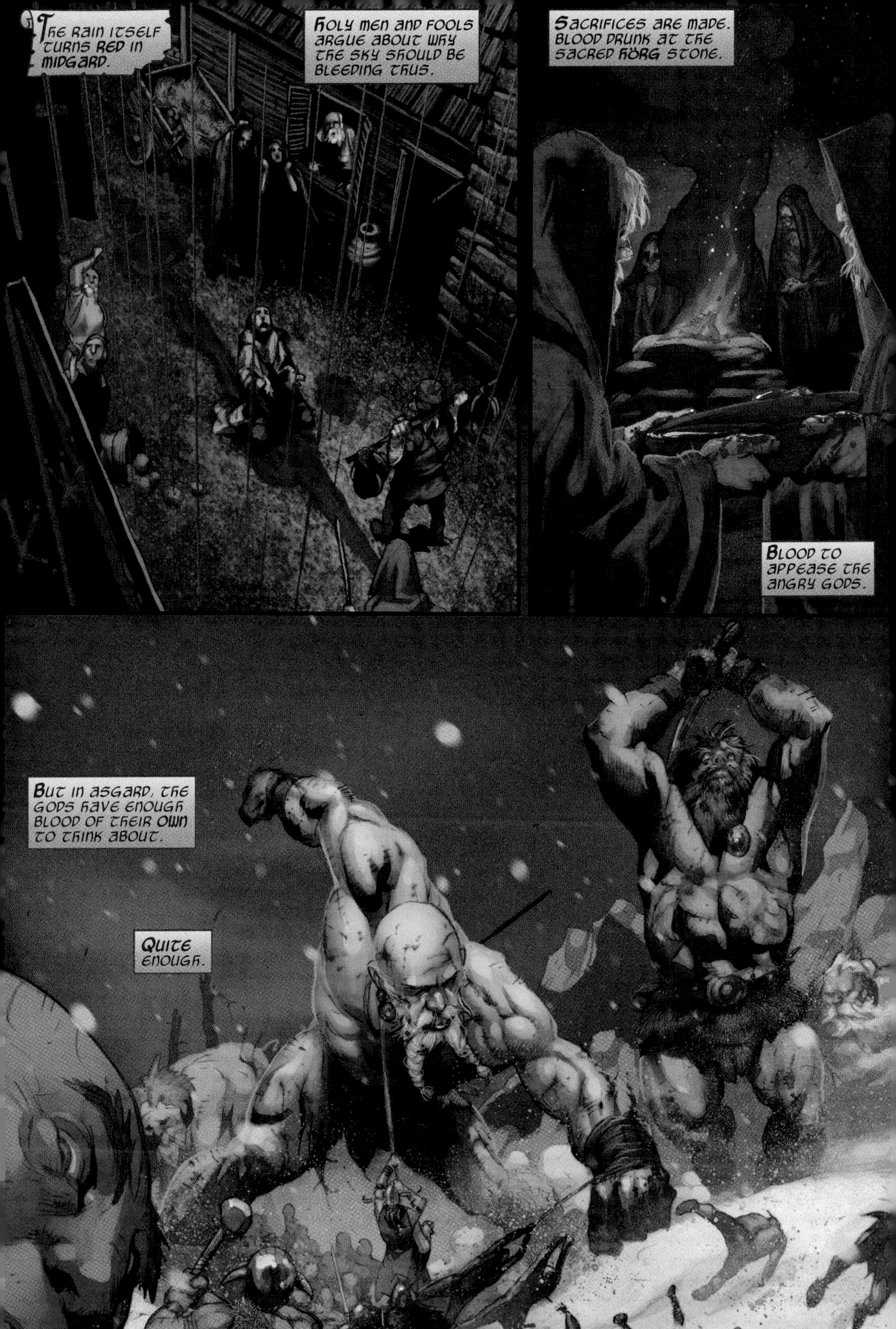
THE RAIN ITSELF TURNS RED IN MIDGARD.
HOLY MEN AND FOOLS ARGUE ABOUT WHY THE SKY SHOULD BE BLEEDING THUS.
SACRIFICES ARE MADE. BLOOD DRUNK AT THE SACRED HÖRG STONE.
BLOOD TO APPEASE THE ANGRY GODS.
BUT IN ASGARD, THE GODS HAVE ENOUGH BLOOD OF THEIR OWN TO THINK ABOUT.
QUITE ENOUGH.

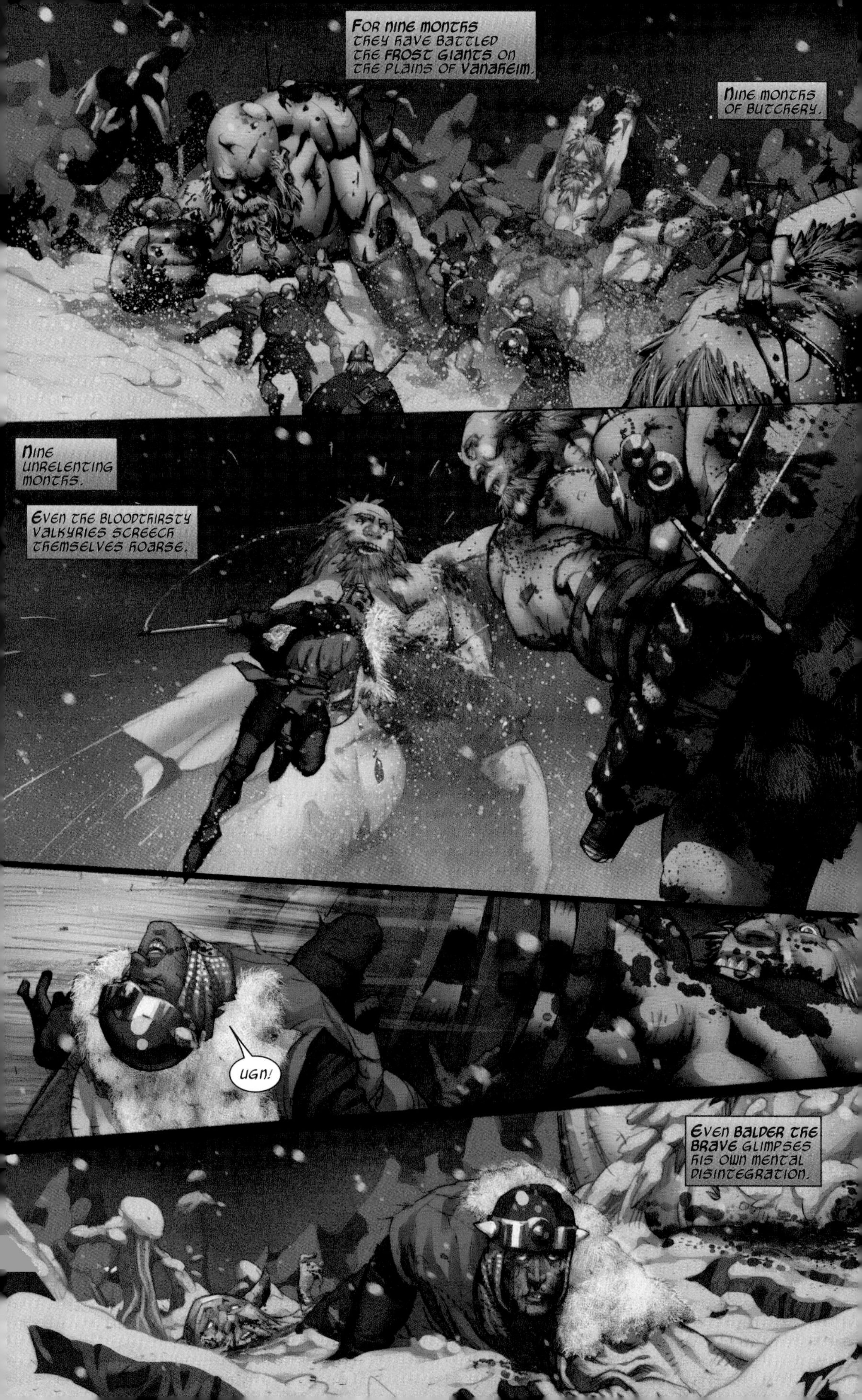
For nine months they have battled the FROST GIANTS on the plains of Vanaheim.
Nine months of butchery.
Nine unrelenting months.
Even the bloodthirsty Valkyries screech themselves hoarse.
UGN!
Even BALDER THE BRAVE glimpses his own mental disintegration.

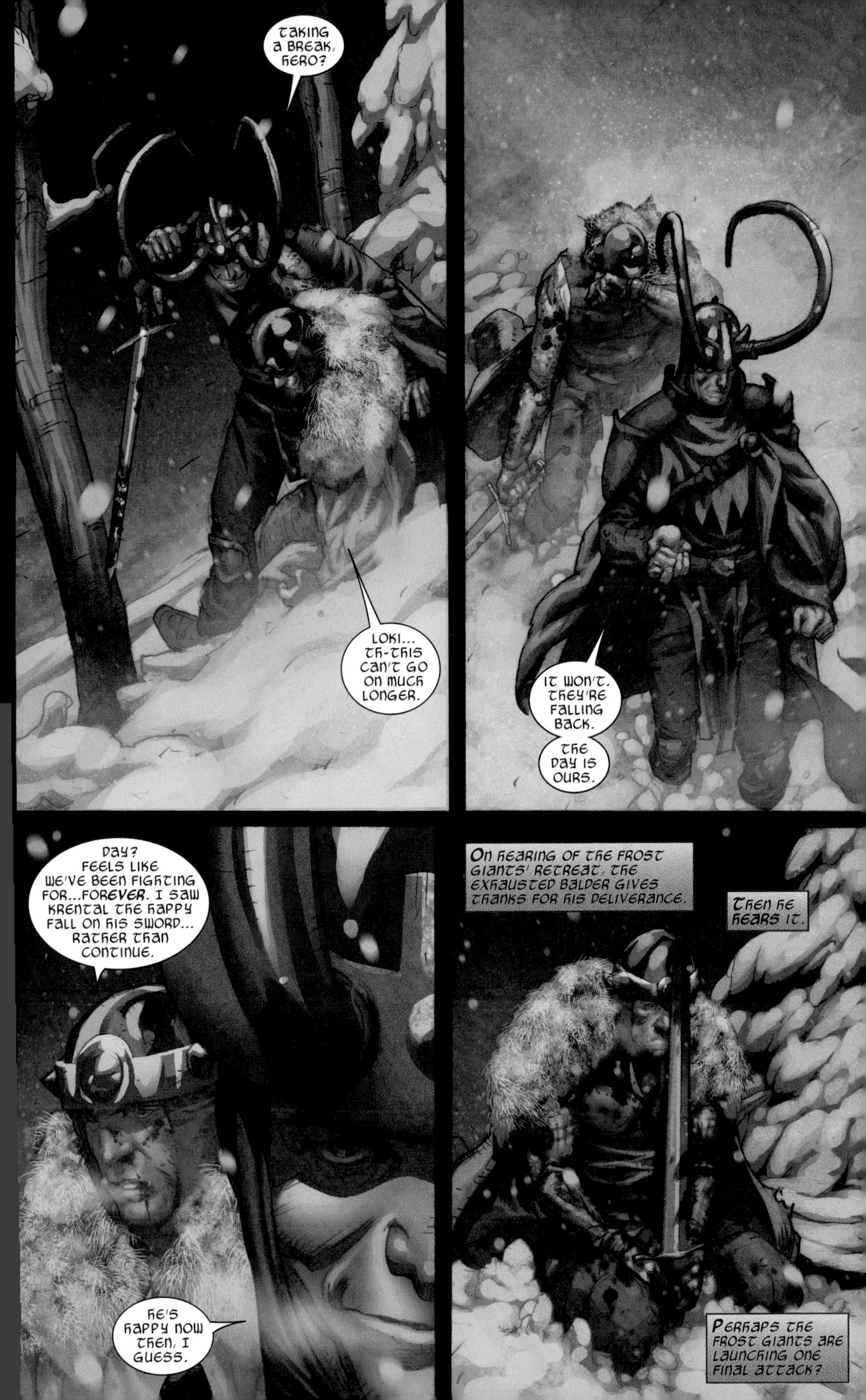
TAKING A BREAK, HERO?
LOKI... TH-THIS CAN'T GO ON MUCH LONGER.
IT WON'T. THEY'RE FALLING BACK.
THE DAY IS OURS.
DAY? FEELS LIKE WE'VE BEEN FIGHTING FOR...FOREVER. I SAW KRENTAL THE HAPPY FALL ON HIS SWORD... RATHER THAN CONTINUE.
HE'S HAPPY NOW THEN, I GUESS.
ON HEARING OF THE FROST GIANTS' RETREAT, THE EXHAUSTED BALDER GIVES THANKS FOR HIS DELIVERANCE.
THEN HE HEARS IT.
PERHAPS THE FROST GIANTS ARE LAUNCHING ONE FINAL ATTACK?

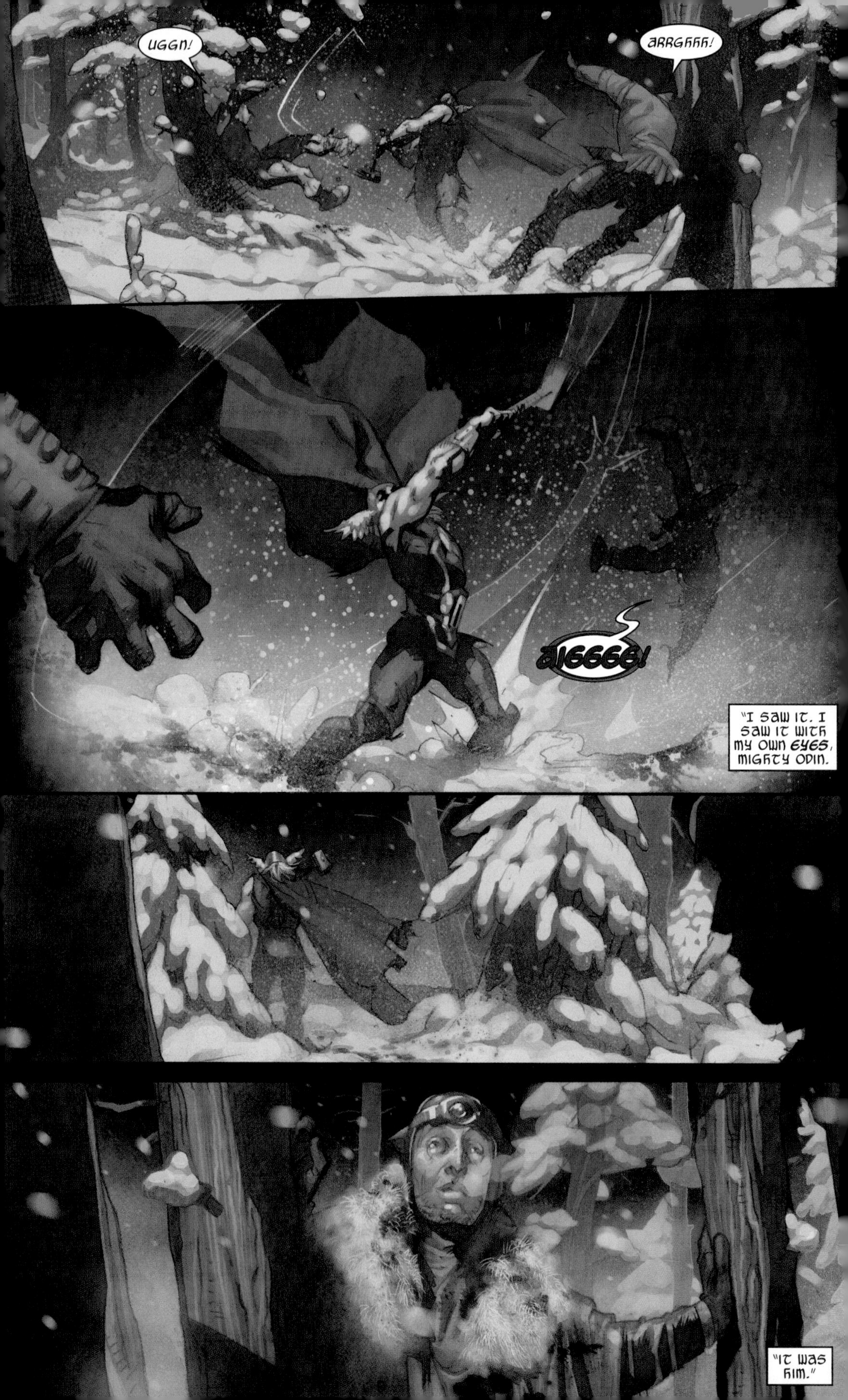
UGGN!
ARRGHHH!
AIGGGG!
"I SAW IT. I SAW IT WITH MY OWN *EYES*, MIGHTY ODIN.
"IT WAS HIM."

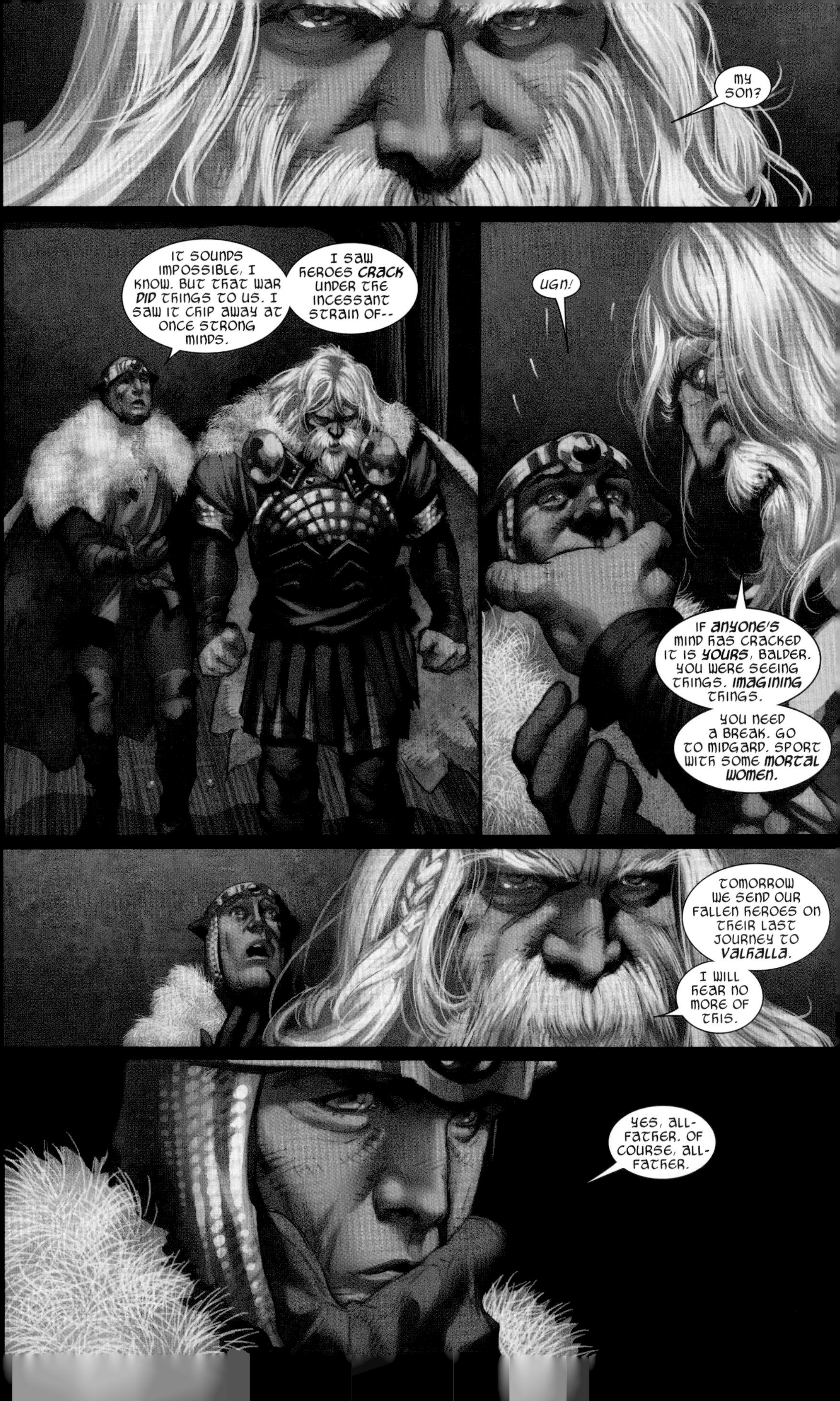
MY SON?
IT SOUNDS IMPOSSIBLE, I KNOW. BUT THAT WAR DID THINGS TO US. I SAW IT CHIP AWAY AT ONCE STRONG MINDS.
I SAW HEROES CRACK UNDER THE INCESSANT STRAIN OF--
UGN!
IF ANYONE'S MIND HAS CRACKED IT IS YOURS, BALDER. YOU WERE SEEING THINGS. IMAGINING THINGS.
YOU NEED A BREAK. GO TO MIDGARD. SPORT WITH SOME MORTAL WOMEN.
TOMORROW WE SEND OUR FALLEN HEROES ON THEIR LAST JOURNEY TO VALHALLA.
I WILL HEAR NO MORE OF THIS.
YES, ALL-FATHER. OF COURSE, ALL-FATHER.

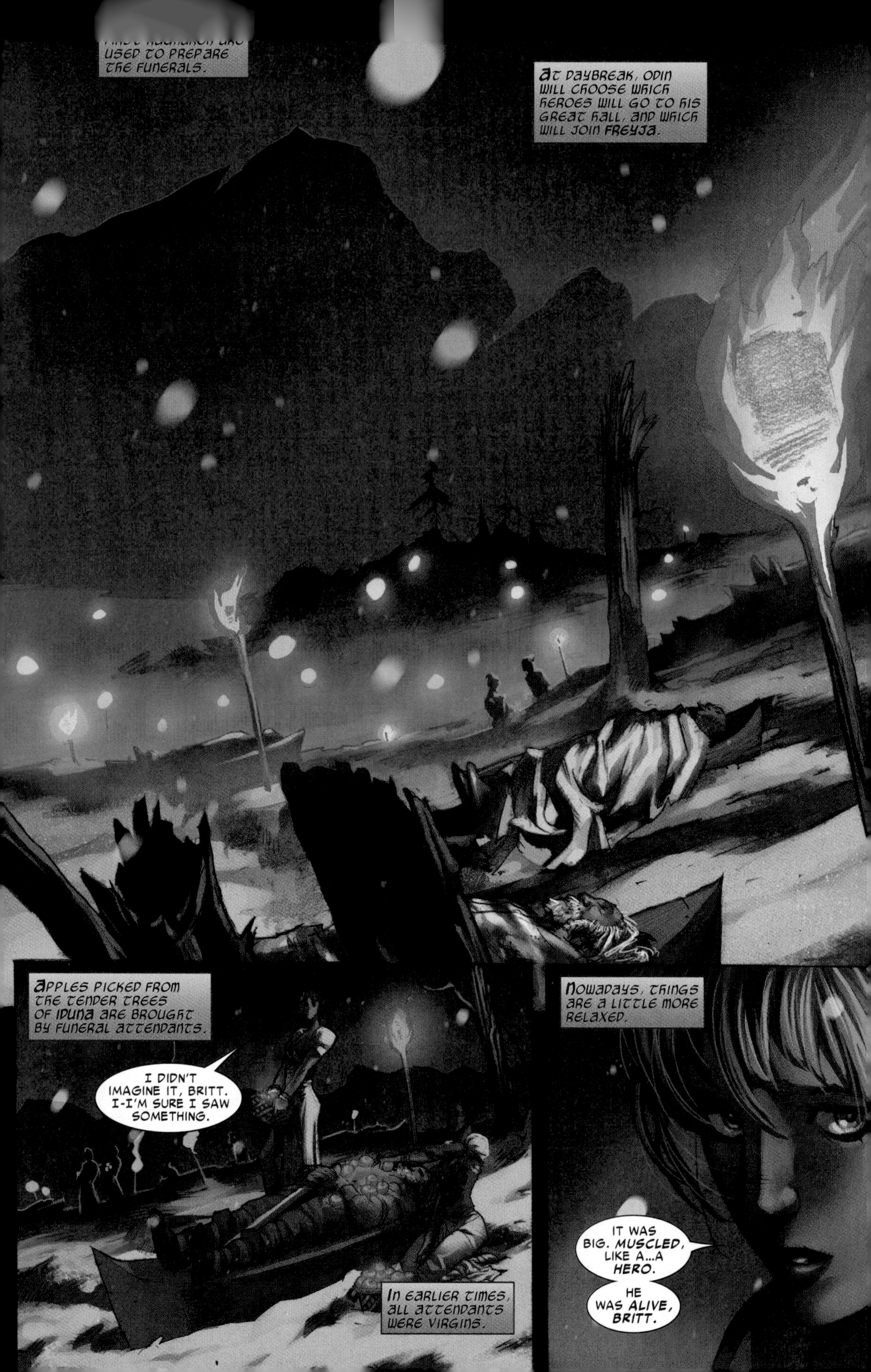
USED TO PREPARE THE FUNERALS.
AT DAYBREAK, ODIN WILL CHOOSE WHICH HEROES WILL GO TO HIS GREAT HALL, AND WHICH WILL JOIN FREYJA.
APPLES PICKED FROM THE TENDER TREES OF IDUNA ARE BROUGHT BY FUNERAL ATTENDANTS.
I DIDN'T IMAGINE IT, BRITT. I-I'M SURE I SAW SOMETHING.
IN EARLIER TIMES, ALL ATTENDANTS WERE VIRGINS.
NOWADAYS, THINGS ARE A LITTLE MORE RELAXED.
IT WAS BIG. MUSCLED, LIKE A...A HERO.
HE WAS ALIVE, BRITT.

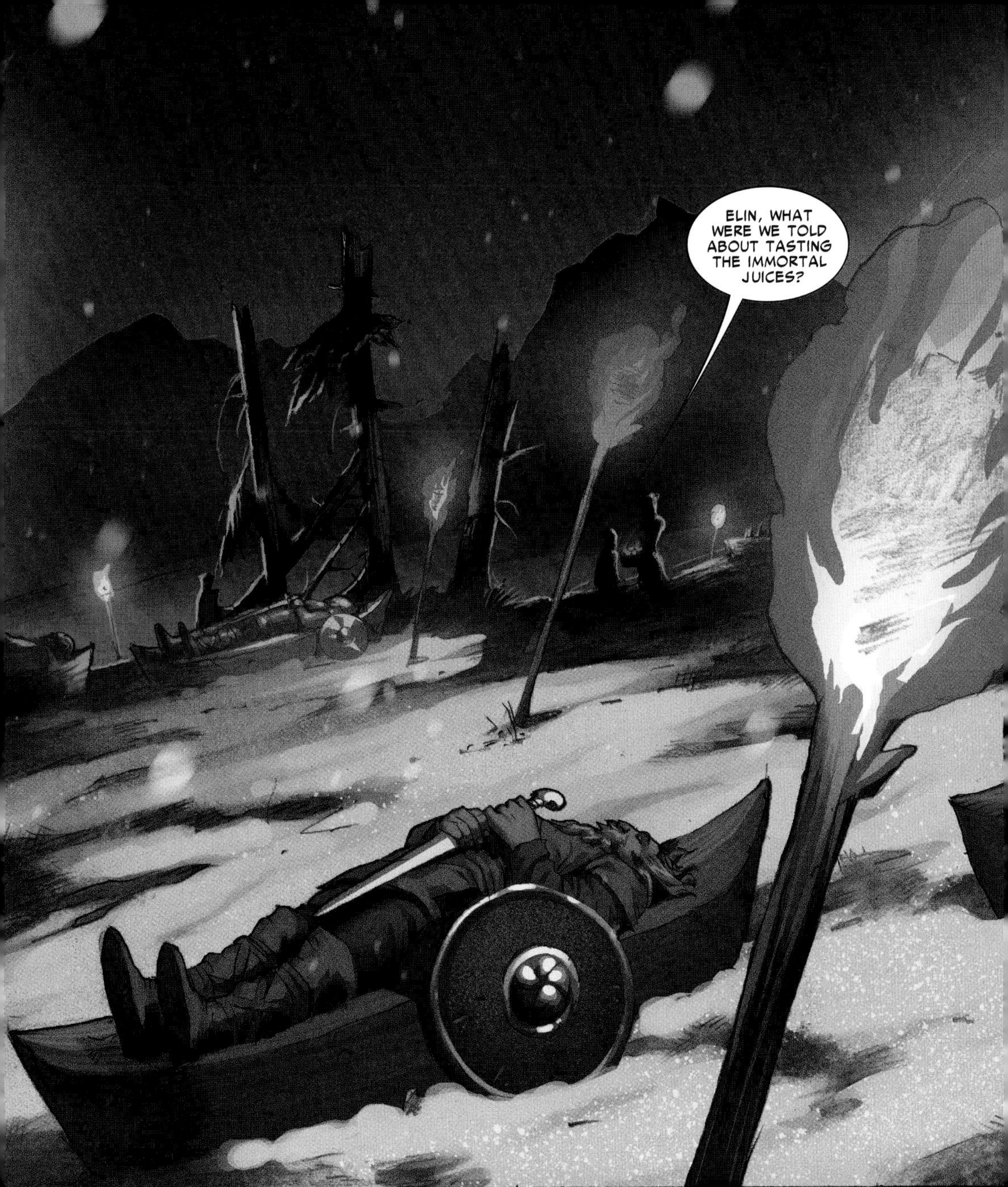
ELIN, WHAT WERE WE TOLD ABOUT TASTING THE IMMORTAL JUICES?
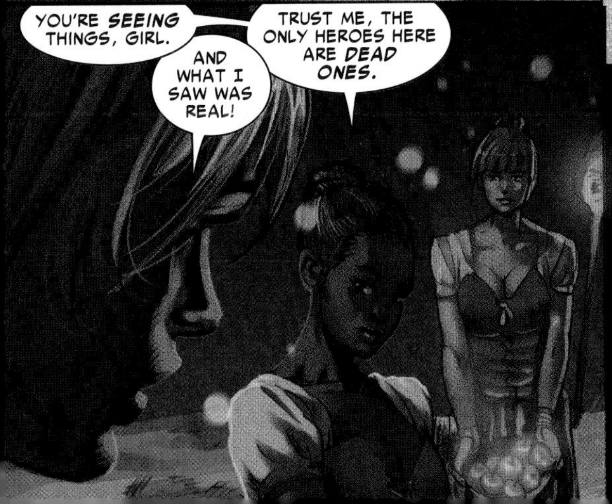
YOU'RE *SEEING* THINGS, GIRL.
AND WHAT I SAW WAS REAL!
TRUST ME, THE ONLY HEROES HERE ARE *DEAD ONES.*
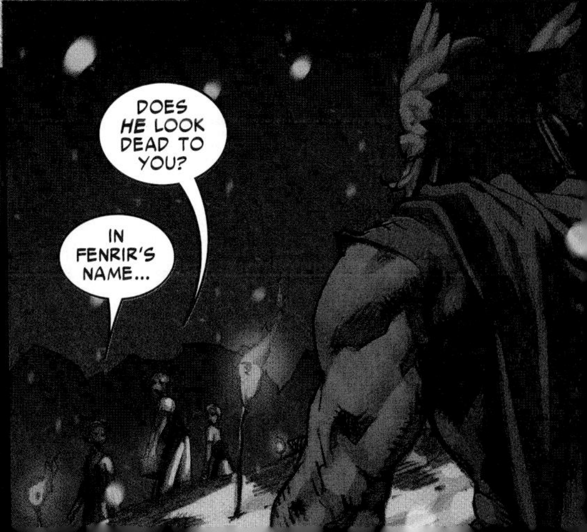
DOES *HE* LOOK DEAD TO YOU?
IN FENRIR'S NAME...

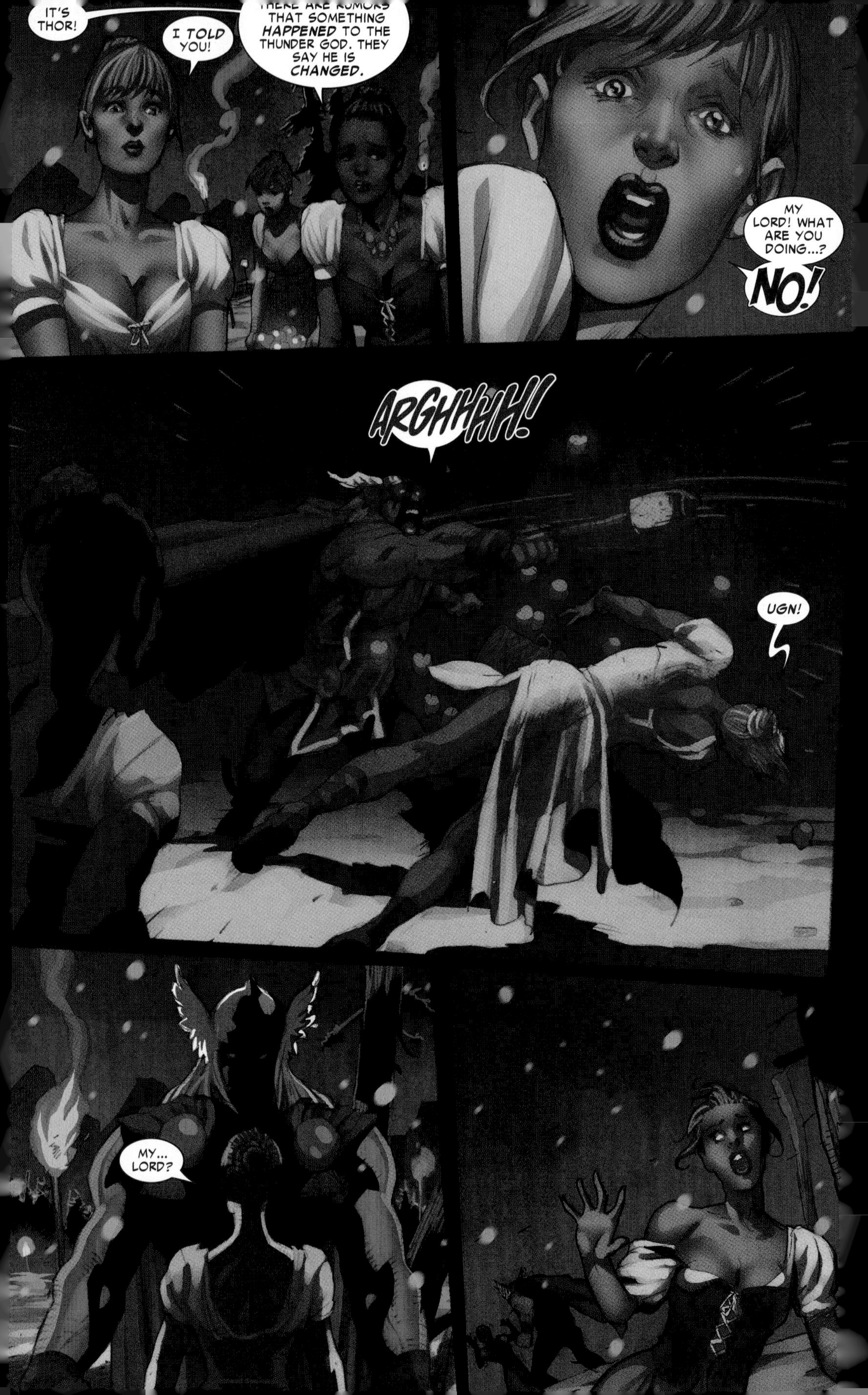

IT'S THOR!
I TOLD YOU!
THERE ARE RUMORS THAT SOMETHING HAPPENED TO THE THUNDER GOD. THEY SAY HE IS CHANGED.
MY LORD! WHAT ARE YOU DOING...?
NO!
ARGHHHH!
UGN!
MY... LORD?

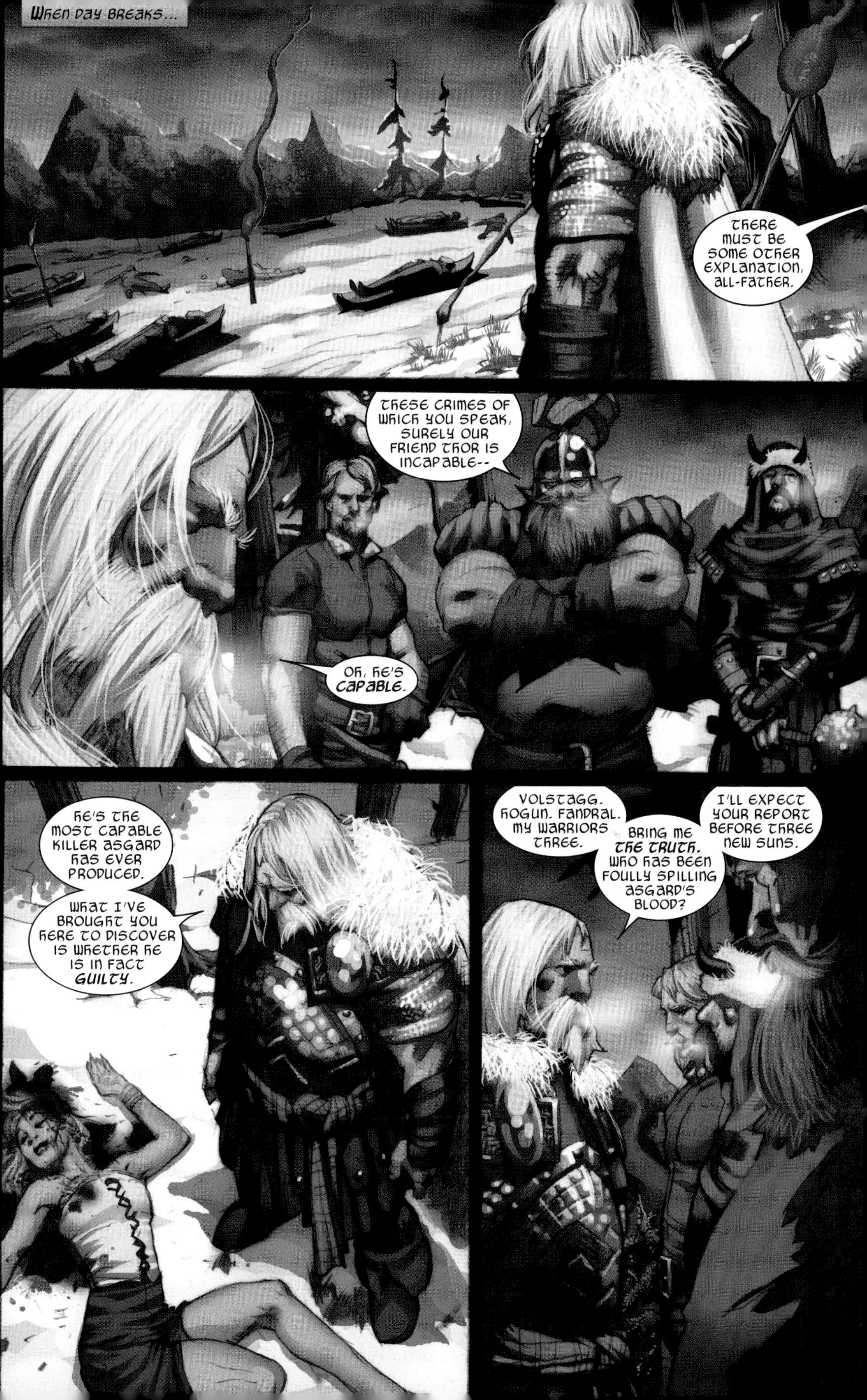
WHEN DAY BREAKS...
THERE MUST BE SOME OTHER EXPLANATION, ALL-FATHER.
THESE CRIMES OF WHICH YOU SPEAK, SURELY OUR FRIEND THOR IS INCAPABLE--
OH, HE'S CAPABLE.
HE'S THE MOST CAPABLE KILLER ASGARD HAS EVER PRODUCED.
WHAT I'VE BROUGHT YOU HERE TO DISCOVER IS WHETHER HE IS IN FACT GUILTY.
VOLSTAGG. HOGUN. FANDRAL. MY WARRIORS THREE.
BRING ME THE TRUTH. WHO HAS BEEN FOULLY SPILLING ASGARD'S BLOOD?
I'LL EXPECT YOUR REPORT BEFORE THREE NEW SUNS.

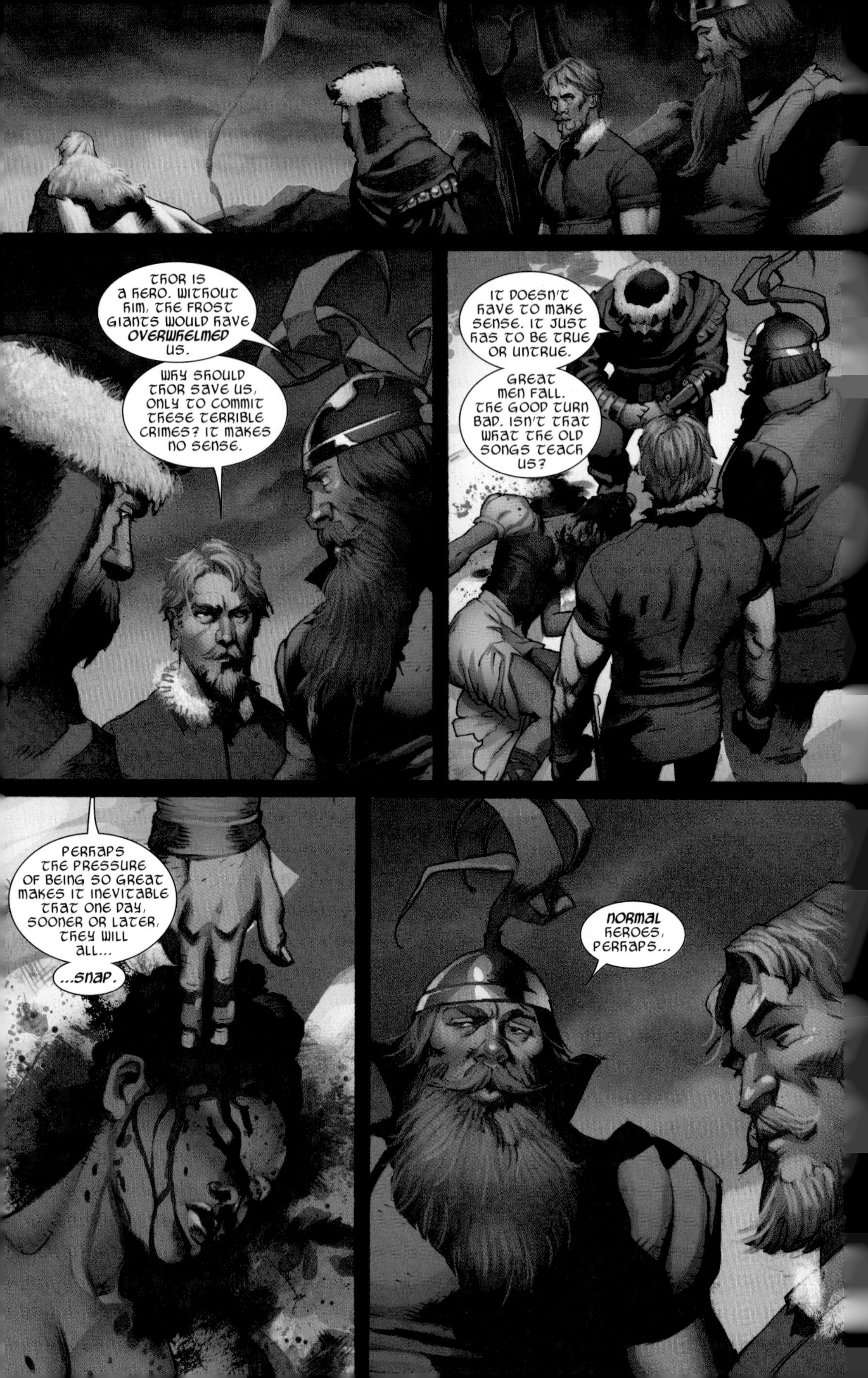
THOR IS A HERO. WITHOUT HIM, THE FROST GIANTS WOULD HAVE **OVERWHELMED** US.
WHY SHOULD THOR SAVE US, ONLY TO COMMIT THESE TERRIBLE CRIMES? IT MAKES NO SENSE.
IT DOESN'T HAVE TO MAKE SENSE. IT JUST HAS TO BE TRUE OR UNTRUE.
GREAT MEN FALL. THE GOOD TURN BAD. ISN'T THAT WHAT THE OLD SONGS TEACH US?
PERHAPS THE PRESSURE OF BEING SO GREAT MAKES IT INEVITABLE THAT ONE DAY, SOONER OR LATER, THEY WILL ALL...
...**SNAP**.
**NORMAL** HEROES, PERHAPS...

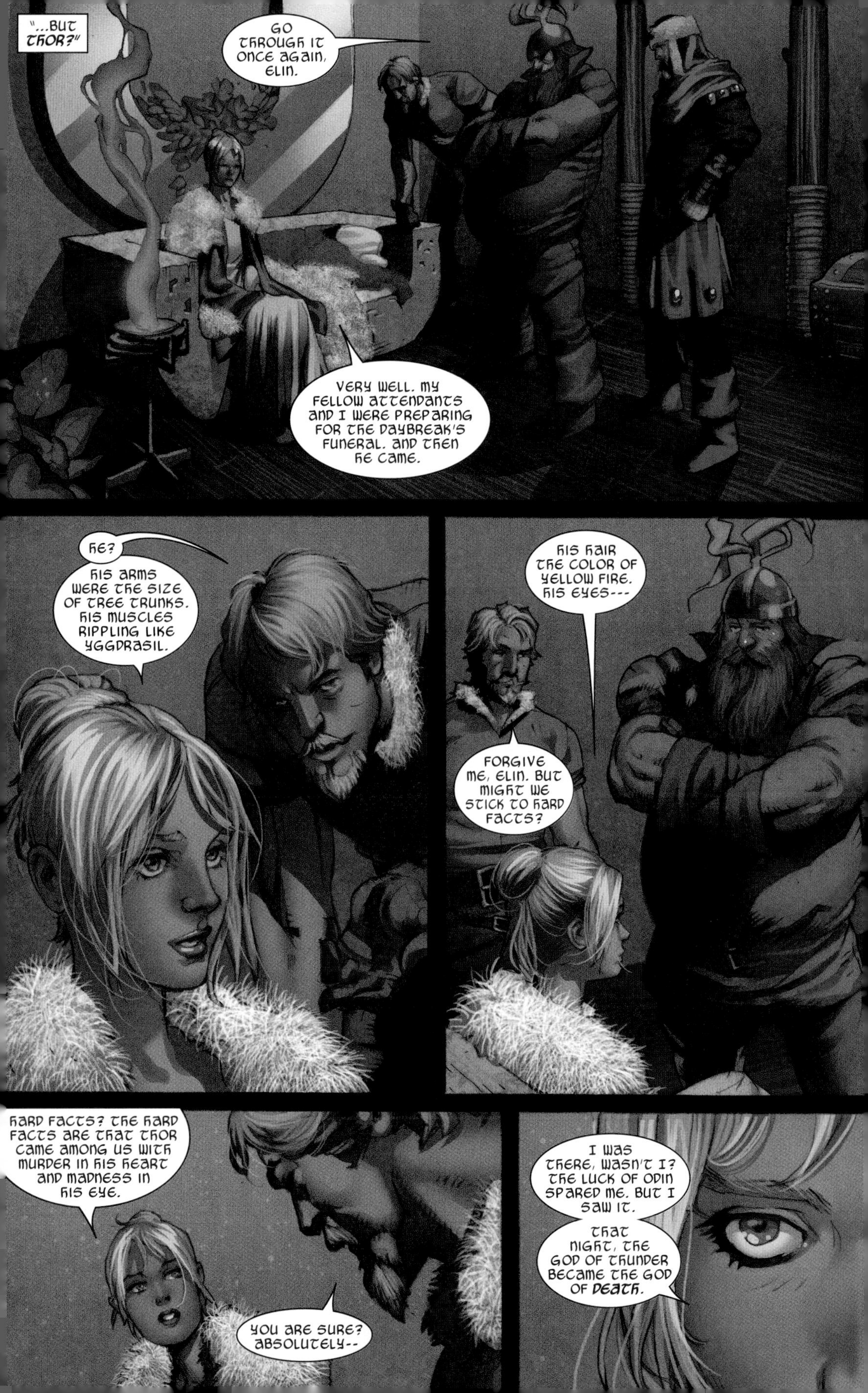
"...BUT THOR?"
GO THROUGH IT ONCE AGAIN, ELIN.
VERY WELL. MY FELLOW ATTENDANTS AND I WERE PREPARING FOR THE DAYBREAK'S FUNERAL. AND THEN HE CAME.
HE?
HIS ARMS WERE THE SIZE OF TREE TRUNKS. HIS MUSCLES RIPPLING LIKE YGGDRASIL.
HIS HAIR THE COLOR OF YELLOW FIRE. HIS EYES---
FORGIVE ME, ELIN. BUT MIGHT WE STICK TO HARD FACTS?
HARD FACTS? THE HARD FACTS ARE THAT THOR CAME AMONG US WITH MURDER IN HIS HEART AND MADNESS IN HIS EYE.
YOU ARE SURE? ABSOLUTELY--
I WAS THERE, WASN'T I? THE LUCK OF ODIN SPARED ME. BUT I SAW IT.
THAT NIGHT, THE GOD OF THUNDER BECAME THE GOD OF *DEATH*.

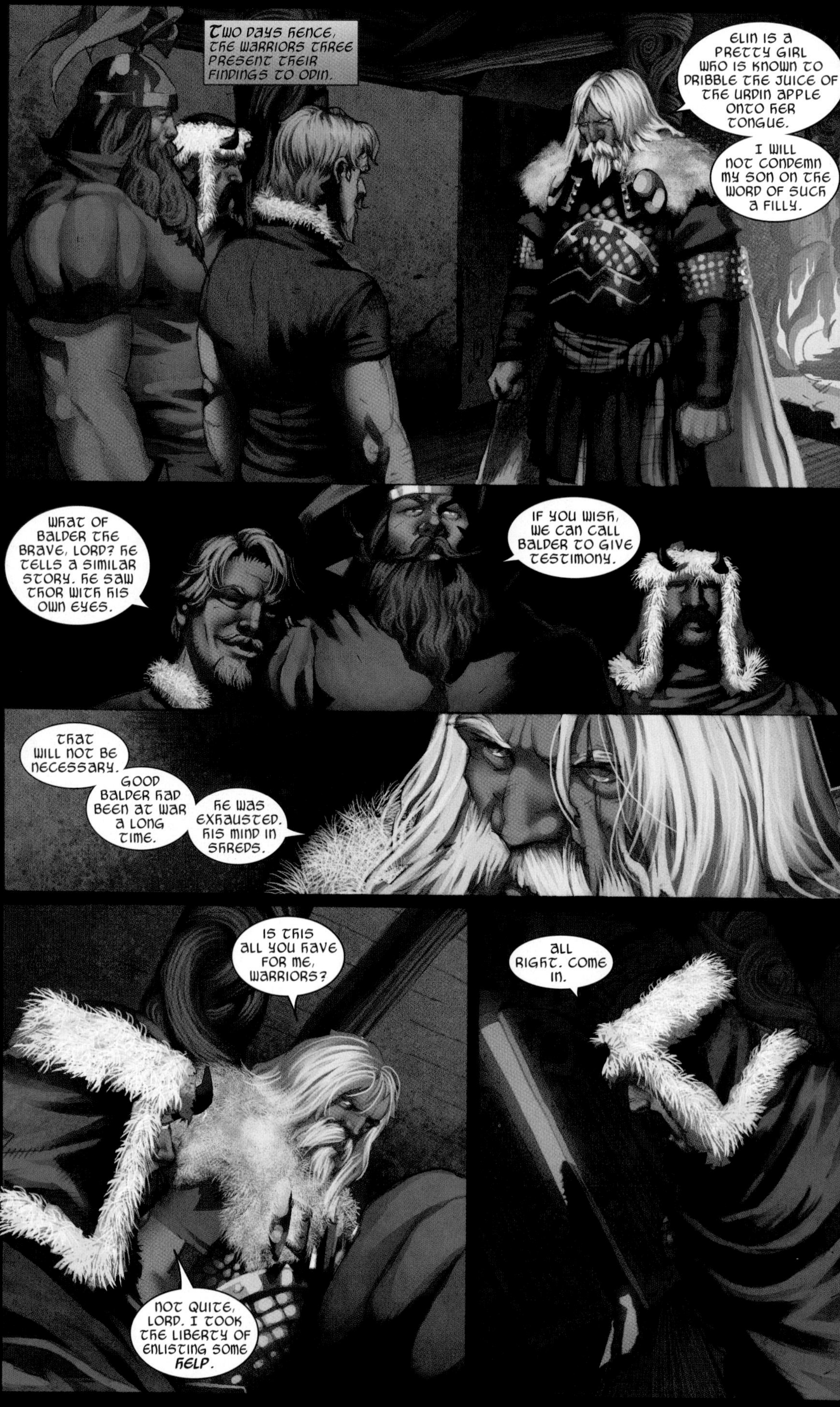
TWO DAYS HENCE, THE WARRIORS THREE PRESENT THEIR FINDINGS TO ODIN.
ELIN IS A PRETTY GIRL WHO IS KNOWN TO DRIBBLE THE JUICE OF THE URDIN APPLE ONTO HER TONGUE.
I WILL NOT CONDEMN MY SON ON THE WORD OF SUCH A FILLY.
WHAT OF BALDER THE BRAVE, LORD? HE TELLS A SIMILAR STORY. HE SAW THOR WITH HIS OWN EYES.
IF YOU WISH, WE CAN CALL BALDER TO GIVE TESTIMONY.
THAT WILL NOT BE NECESSARY.
GOOD BALDER HAD BEEN AT WAR A LONG TIME.
HE WAS EXHAUSTED. HIS MIND IN SHREDS.
IS THIS ALL YOU HAVE FOR ME, WARRIORS?
NOT QUITE, LORD. I TOOK THE LIBERTY OF ENLISTING SOME HELP.
ALL RIGHT. COME IN.

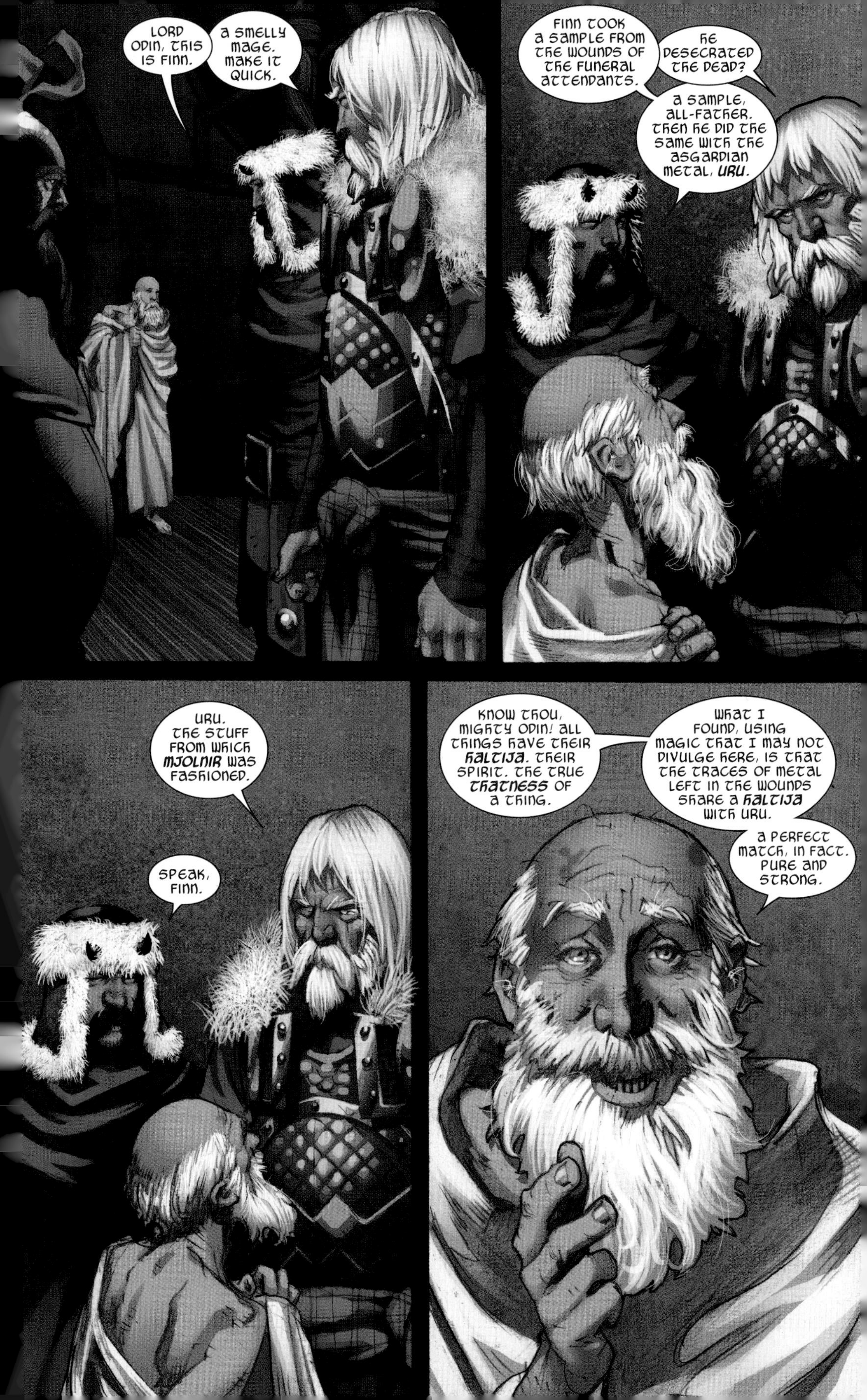
LORD ODIN, THIS IS FINN.
A SMELLY MAGE. MAKE IT QUICK.
FINN TOOK A SAMPLE FROM THE WOUNDS OF THE FUNERAL ATTENDANTS.
HE DESECRATED THE DEAD?
A SAMPLE, ALL-FATHER. THEN HE DID THE SAME WITH THE ASGARDIAN METAL, URU.
URU. THE STUFF FROM WHICH MJOLNIR WAS FASHIONED.
SPEAK, FINN.
KNOW THOU, MIGHTY ODIN! ALL THINGS HAVE THEIR HALTIJA. THEIR SPIRIT. THE TRUE THATNESS OF A THING.
WHAT I FOUND, USING MAGIC THAT I MAY NOT DIVULGE HERE, IS THAT THE TRACES OF METAL LEFT IN THE WOUNDS SHARE A HALTIJA WITH URU.
A PERFECT MATCH, IN FACT. PURE AND STRONG.

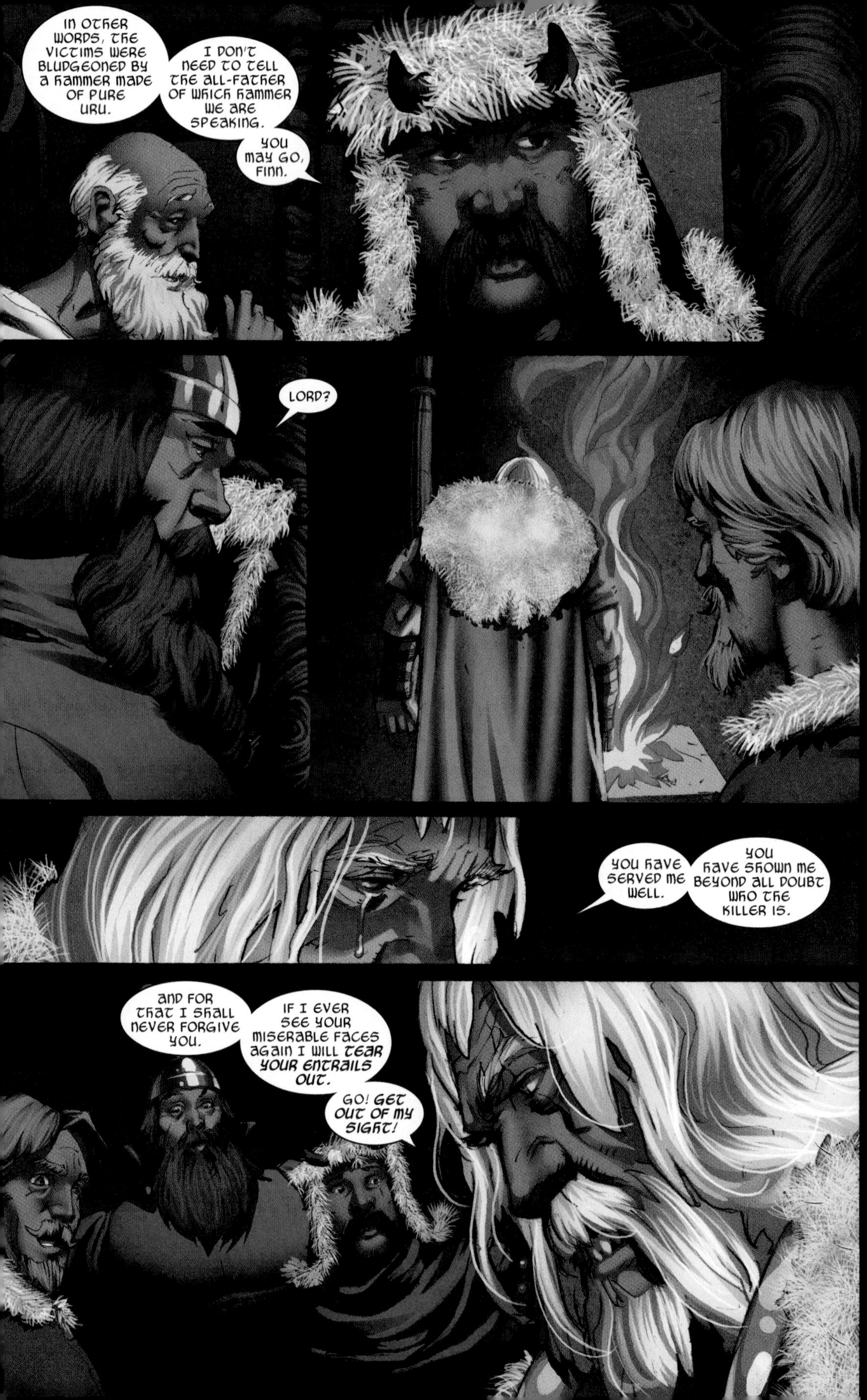
IN OTHER WORDS, THE VICTIMS WERE BLUDGEONED BY A HAMMER MADE OF PURE URU.
I DON'T NEED TO TELL THE ALL-FATHER OF WHICH HAMMER WE ARE SPEAKING.
YOU MAY GO, FINN.
LORD?
YOU HAVE SERVED ME WELL.
YOU HAVE SHOWN ME BEYOND ALL DOUBT WHO THE KILLER IS.
AND FOR THAT I SHALL NEVER FORGIVE YOU.
IF I EVER SEE YOUR MISERABLE FACES AGAIN I WILL TEAR YOUR ENTRAILS OUT.
GO! GET OUT OF MY SIGHT!

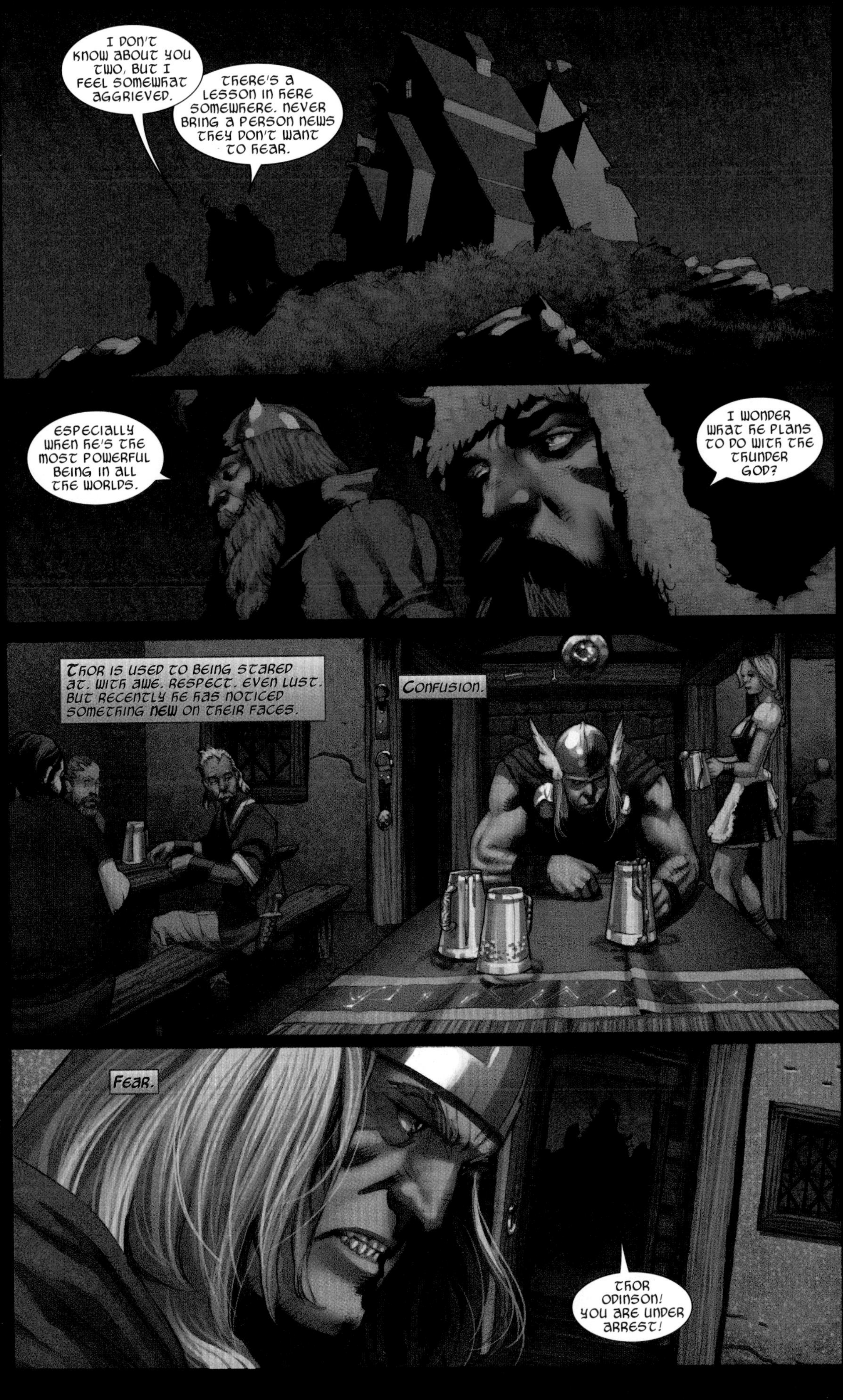
I DON'T KNOW ABOUT YOU TWO, BUT I FEEL SOMEWHAT AGGRIEVED.
THERE'S A LESSON IN HERE SOMEWHERE. NEVER BRING A PERSON NEWS THEY DON'T WANT TO HEAR.
ESPECIALLY WHEN HE'S THE MOST POWERFUL BEING IN ALL THE WORLDS.
I WONDER WHAT HE PLANS TO DO WITH THE THUNDER GOD?
THOR IS USED TO BEING STARED AT. WITH AWE. RESPECT. EVEN LUST. BUT RECENTLY HE HAS NOTICED SOMETHING NEW ON THEIR FACES.
CONFUSION.
FEAR.
THOR ODINSON! YOU ARE UNDER ARREST!

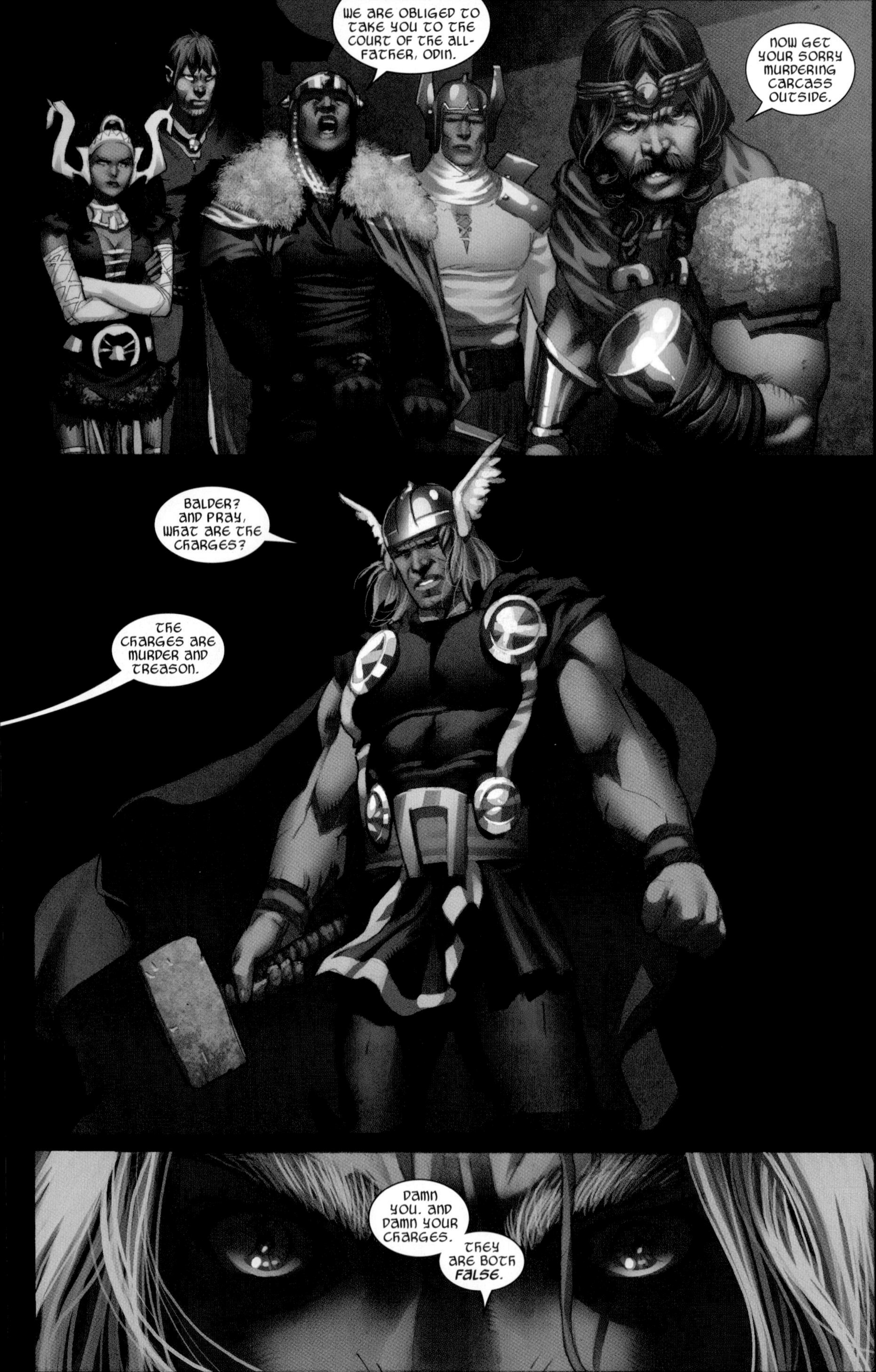
WE ARE OBLIGED TO TAKE YOU TO THE COURT OF THE ALL-FATHER, ODIN.
NOW GET YOUR SORRY MURDERING CARCASS OUTSIDE.
BALDER? AND PRAY, WHAT ARE THE CHARGES?
THE CHARGES ARE MURDER AND TREASON.
DAMN YOU. AND DAMN YOUR CHARGES.
THEY ARE BOTH *FALSE*.

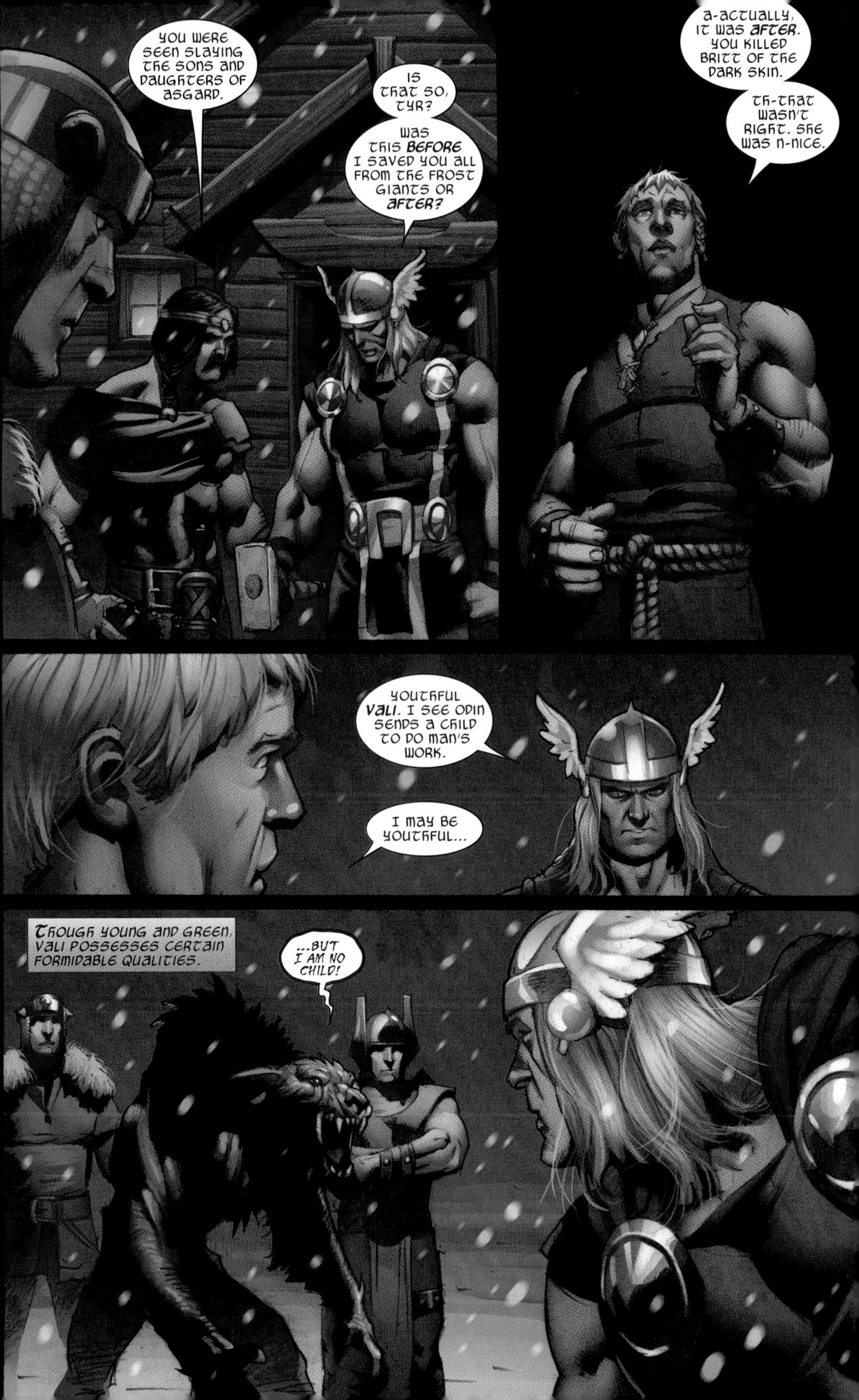
YOU WERE SEEN SLAYING THE SONS AND DAUGHTERS OF ASGARD.
IS THAT SO, TYR?
WAS THIS BEFORE I SAVED YOU ALL FROM THE FROST GIANTS OR AFTER?
A-ACTUALLY, IT WAS AFTER. YOU KILLED BRITT OF THE DARK SKIN.
TH-THAT WASN'T RIGHT. SHE WAS N-NICE.
YOUTHFUL VALI. I SEE ODIN SENDS A CHILD TO DO MAN'S WORK.
I MAY BE YOUTHFUL...
THOUGH YOUNG AND GREEN, VALI POSSESSES CERTAIN FORMIDABLE QUALITIES.
...BUT I AM NO CHILD!

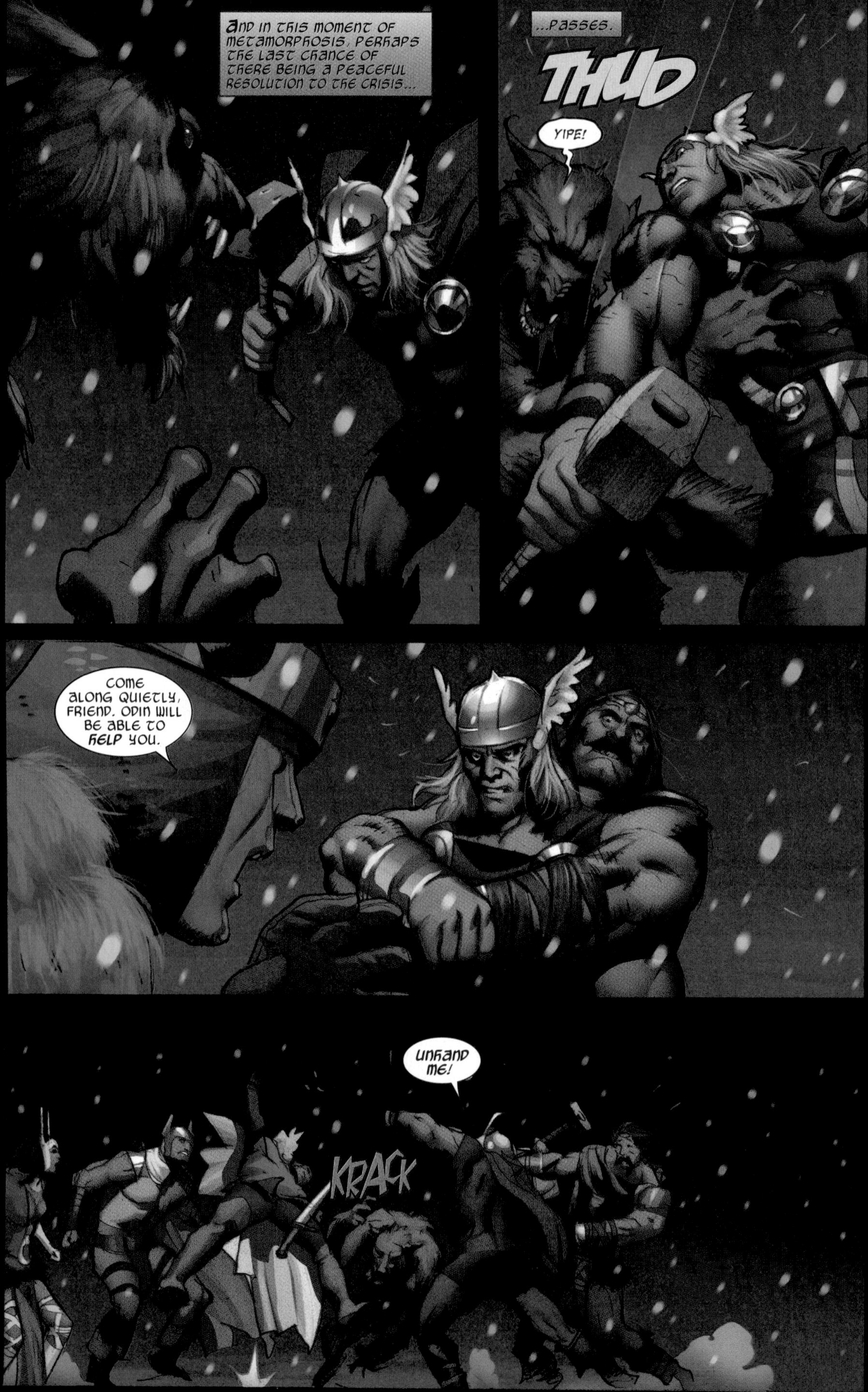
And in this moment of metamorphosis, perhaps the last chance of there being a peaceful resolution to the crisis...
...passes.
THUD
YIPE!
Come along quietly, friend. Odin will be able to help you.
Unhand me!
KRACK

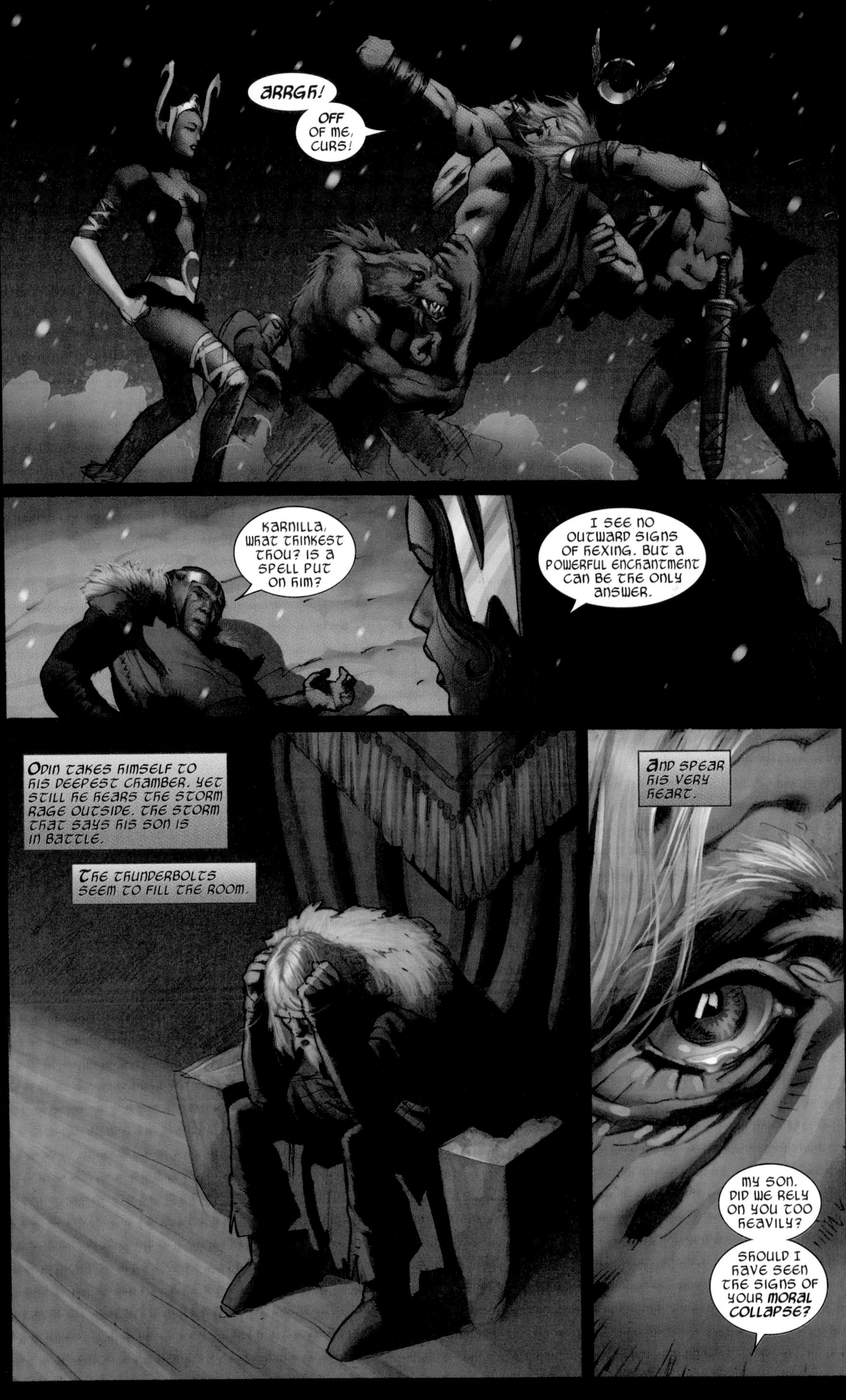
ARRGH!
OFF OF ME, CURS!
KARNILLA, WHAT THINKEST THOU? IS A SPELL PUT ON HIM?
I SEE NO OUTWARD SIGNS OF HEXING. BUT A POWERFUL ENCHANTMENT CAN BE THE ONLY ANSWER.
ODIN TAKES HIMSELF TO HIS DEEPEST CHAMBER. YET STILL HE HEARS THE STORM RAGE OUTSIDE. THE STORM THAT SAYS HIS SON IS IN BATTLE.
THE THUNDERBOLTS SEEM TO FILL THE ROOM.
AND SPEAR HIS VERY HEART.
MY SON. DID WE RELY ON YOU TOO HEAVILY?
SHOULD I HAVE SEEN THE SIGNS OF YOUR MORAL COLLAPSE?

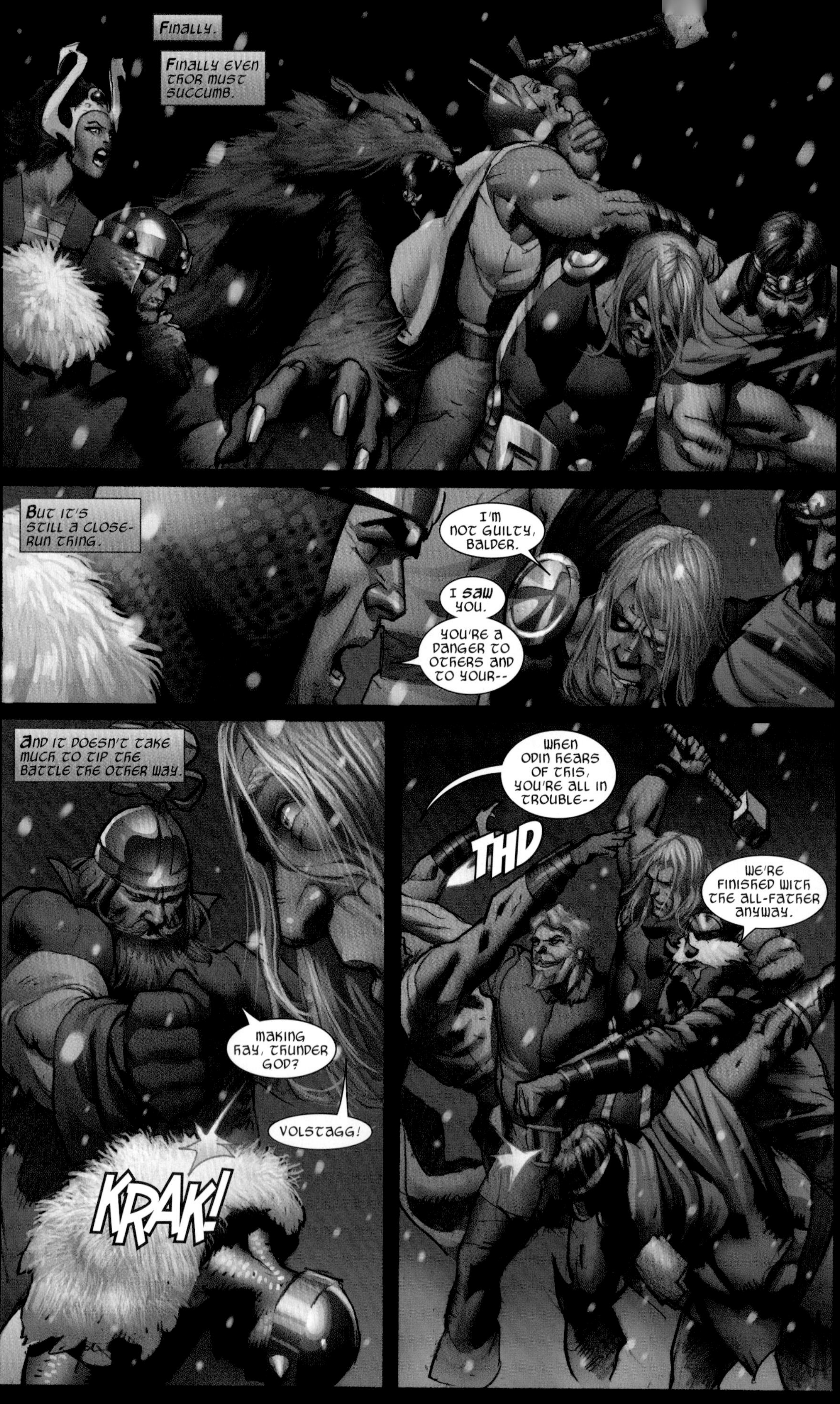
Finally.
Finally even Thor must succumb.
But it's still a close-run thing.
I'm not guilty, Balder.
I saw you.
You're a danger to others and to your--
And it doesn't take much to tip the battle the other way.
Making hay, Thunder God?
Volstagg!
KRAK!
When Odin hears of this, you're all in trouble--
THD
We're finished with the All-Father anyway.

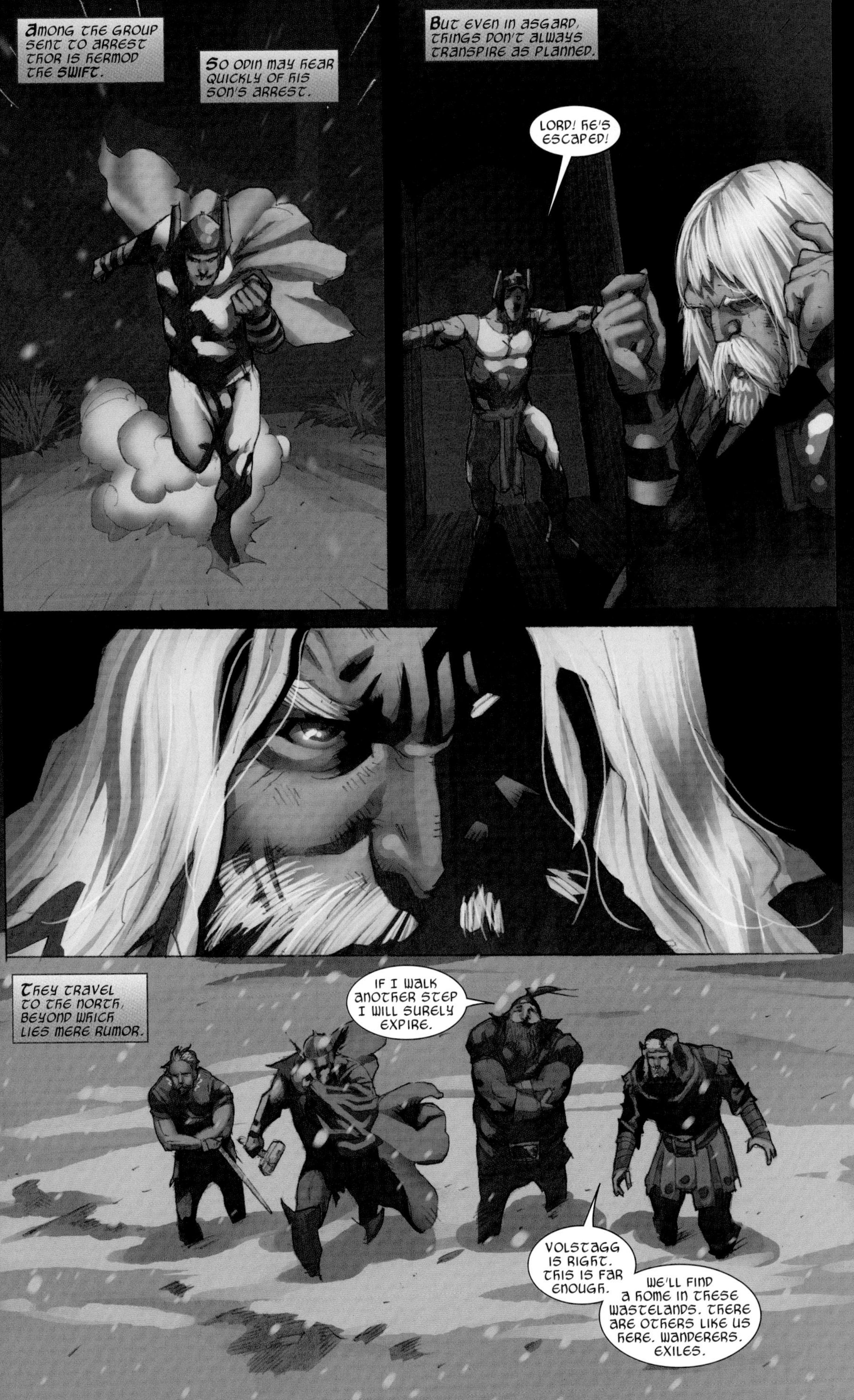
Among the group sent to arrest Thor is Hermod the Swift.
So Odin may hear quickly of his son's arrest.
But even in Asgard, things don't always transpire as planned.
LORD! HE'S ESCAPED!
They travel to the north, beyond which lies mere rumor.
IF I WALK ANOTHER STEP I WILL SURELY EXPIRE.
VOLSTAGG IS RIGHT. THIS IS FAR ENOUGH.
WE'LL FIND A HOME IN THESE WASTELANDS. THERE ARE OTHERS LIKE US HERE. WANDERERS. EXILES.

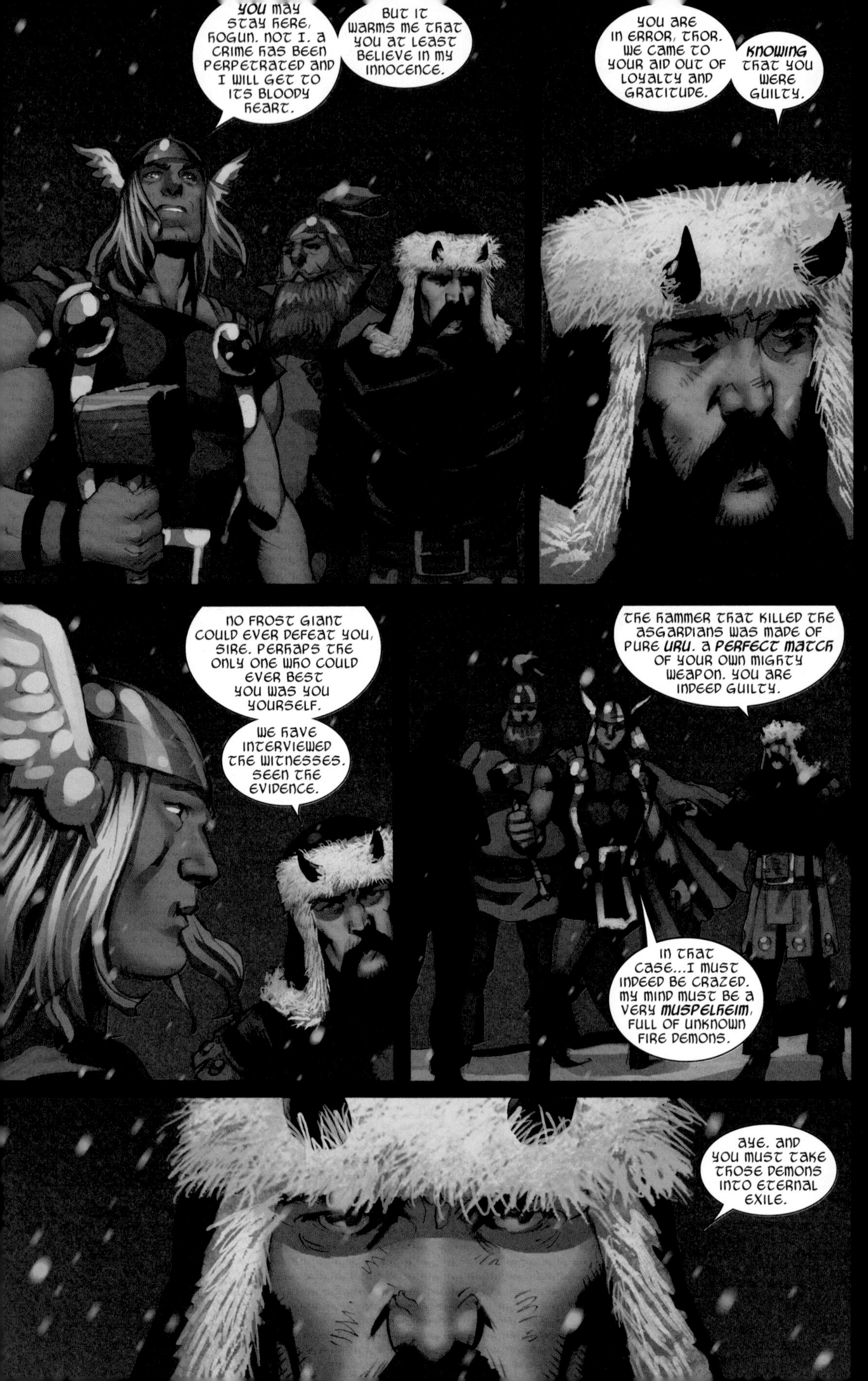
YOU MAY STAY HERE, HOGUN. NOT I. A CRIME HAS BEEN PERPETRATED AND I WILL GET TO ITS BLOODY HEART.
BUT IT WARMS ME THAT YOU AT LEAST BELIEVE IN MY INNOCENCE.
YOU ARE IN ERROR, THOR. WE CAME TO YOUR AID OUT OF LOYALTY AND GRATITUDE.
KNOWING THAT YOU WERE GUILTY.
NO FROST GIANT COULD EVER DEFEAT YOU, SIRE. PERHAPS THE ONLY ONE WHO COULD EVER BEST YOU WAS YOU YOURSELF.
WE HAVE INTERVIEWED THE WITNESSES. SEEN THE EVIDENCE.
THE HAMMER THAT KILLED THE ASGARDIANS WAS MADE OF PURE URU. A PERFECT MATCH OF YOUR OWN MIGHTY WEAPON. YOU ARE INDEED GUILTY.
IN THAT CASE...I MUST INDEED BE CRAZED. MY MIND MUST BE A VERY MUSPELHEIM, FULL OF UNKNOWN FIRE DEMONS.
AYE. AND YOU MUST TAKE THOSE DEMONS INTO ETERNAL EXILE.

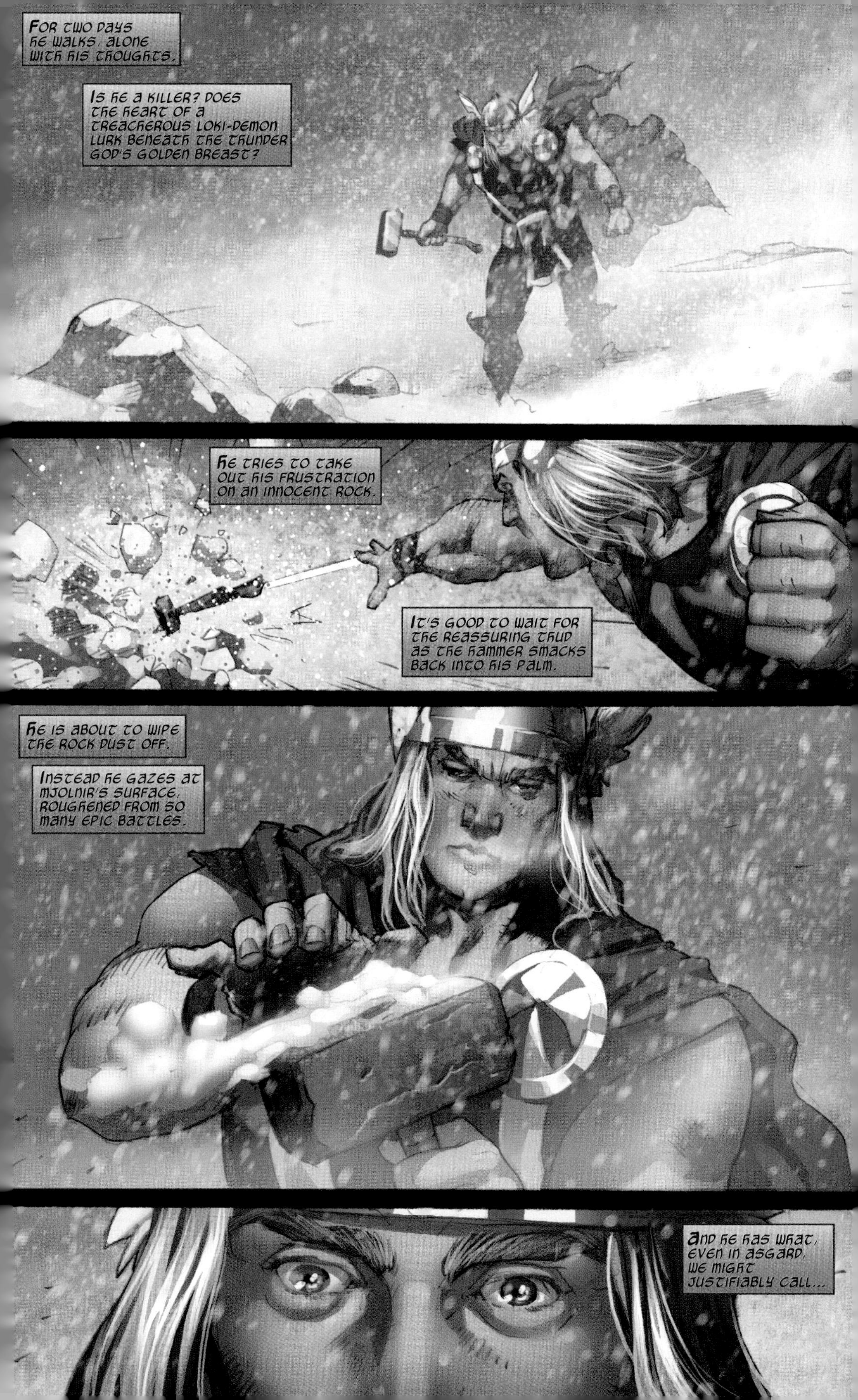
For two days he walks, alone with his thoughts.
Is he a killer? Does the heart of a treacherous Loki-demon lurk beneath the thunder god's golden breast?
He tries to take out his frustration on an innocent rock.
It's good to wait for the reassuring thud as the hammer smacks back into his palm.
He is about to wipe the rock dust off.
Instead he gazes at Mjolnir's surface, roughened from so many epic battles.
And he has what, even in Asgard, we might justifiably call...

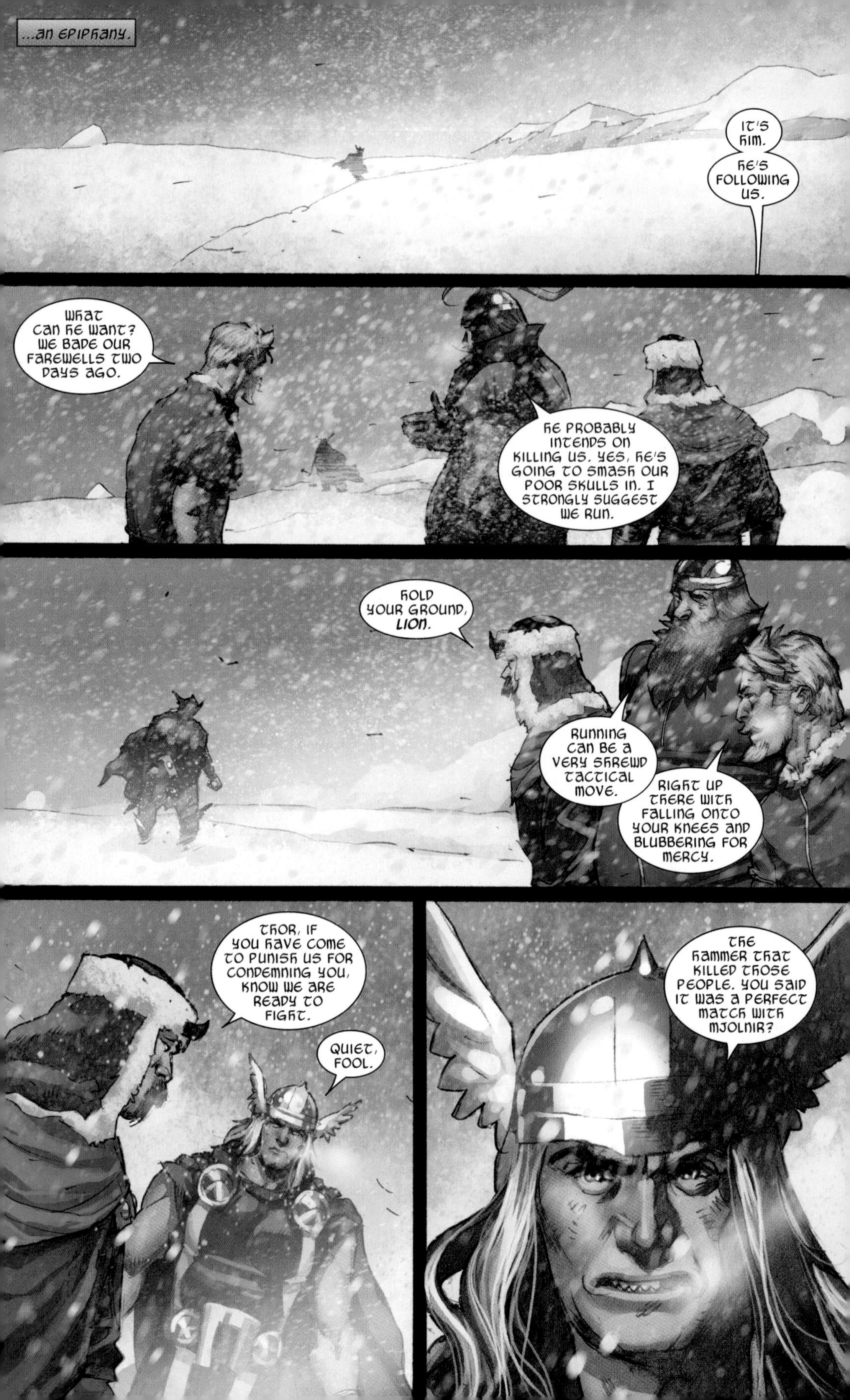
...an epiphany.
It's him.
He's following us.
What can he want? We bade our farewells two days ago.
He probably intends on killing us. Yes, he's going to smash our poor skulls in. I strongly suggest we run.
Hold your ground, Lion.
Running can be a very shrewd tactical move.
Right up there with falling onto your knees and blubbering for mercy.
Thor, if you have come to punish us for condemning you, know we are ready to fight.
Quiet, fool.
The hammer that killed those people. You said it was a perfect match with Mjolnir?

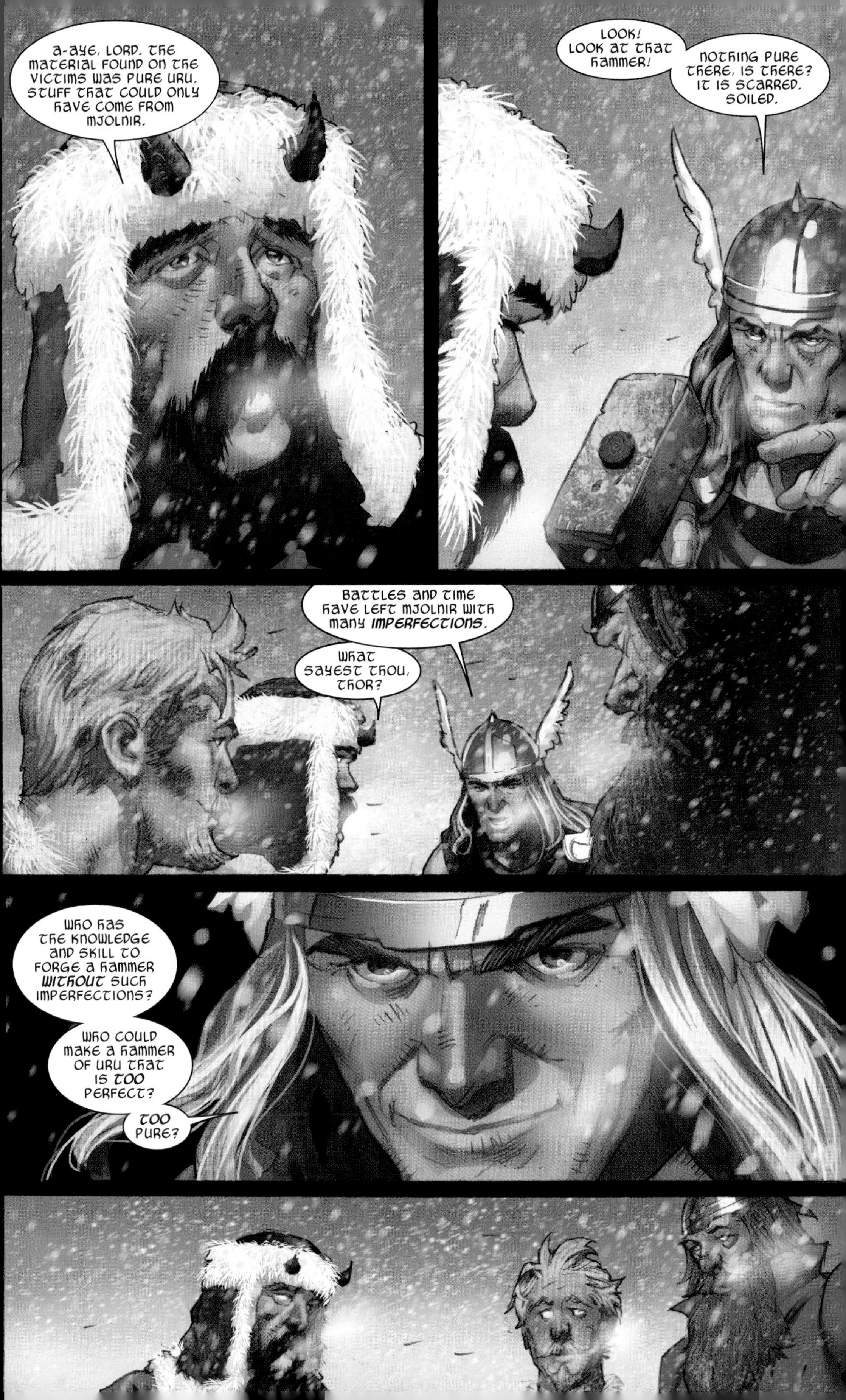
A-AYE, LORD. THE MATERIAL FOUND ON THE VICTIMS WAS PURE URU. STUFF THAT COULD ONLY HAVE COME FROM MJOLNIR.
LOOK! LOOK AT THAT HAMMER!
NOTHING PURE THERE, IS THERE? IT IS SCARRED. SOILED.
BATTLES AND TIME HAVE LEFT MJOLNIR WITH MANY IMPERFECTIONS.
WHAT SAYEST THOU, THOR?
WHO HAS THE KNOWLEDGE AND SKILL TO FORGE A HAMMER WITHOUT SUCH IMPERFECTIONS?
WHO COULD MAKE A HAMMER OF URU THAT IS TOO PERFECT?
TOO PURE?

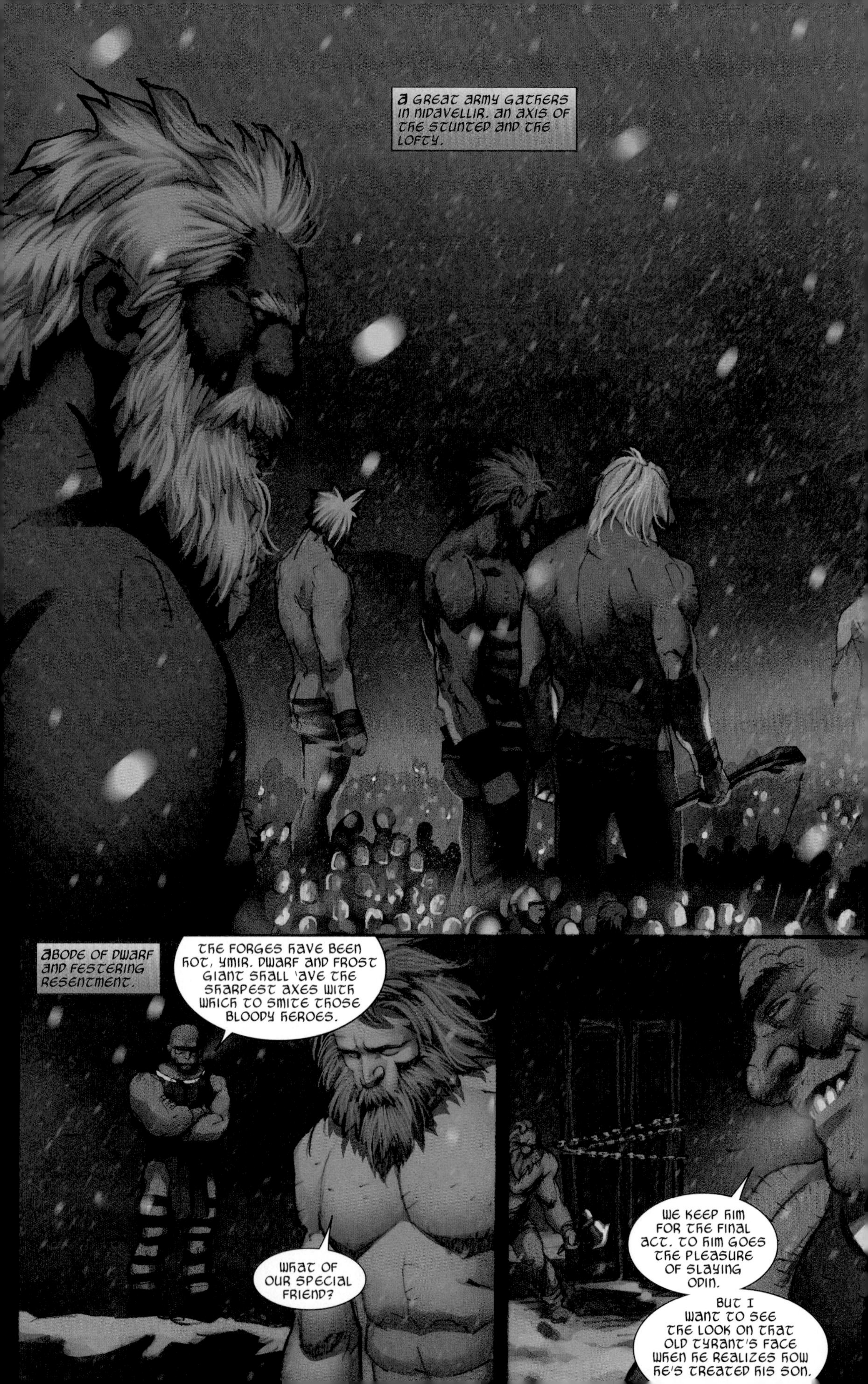

A GREAT ARMY GATHERS IN NIDAVELLIR. AN AXIS OF THE STUNTED AND THE LOFTY.
ABODE OF DWARF AND FESTERING RESENTMENT.
THE FORGES HAVE BEEN HOT, YMIR. DWARF AND FROST GIANT SHALL 'AVE THE SHARPEST AXES WITH WHICH TO SMITE THOSE BLOODY HEROES.
WHAT OF OUR SPECIAL FRIEND?
WE KEEP HIM FOR THE FINAL ACT. TO HIM GOES THE PLEASURE OF SLAYING ODIN.
BUT I WANT TO SEE THE LOOK ON THAT OLD TYRANT'S FACE WHEN HE REALIZES HOW HE'S TREATED HIS SON.

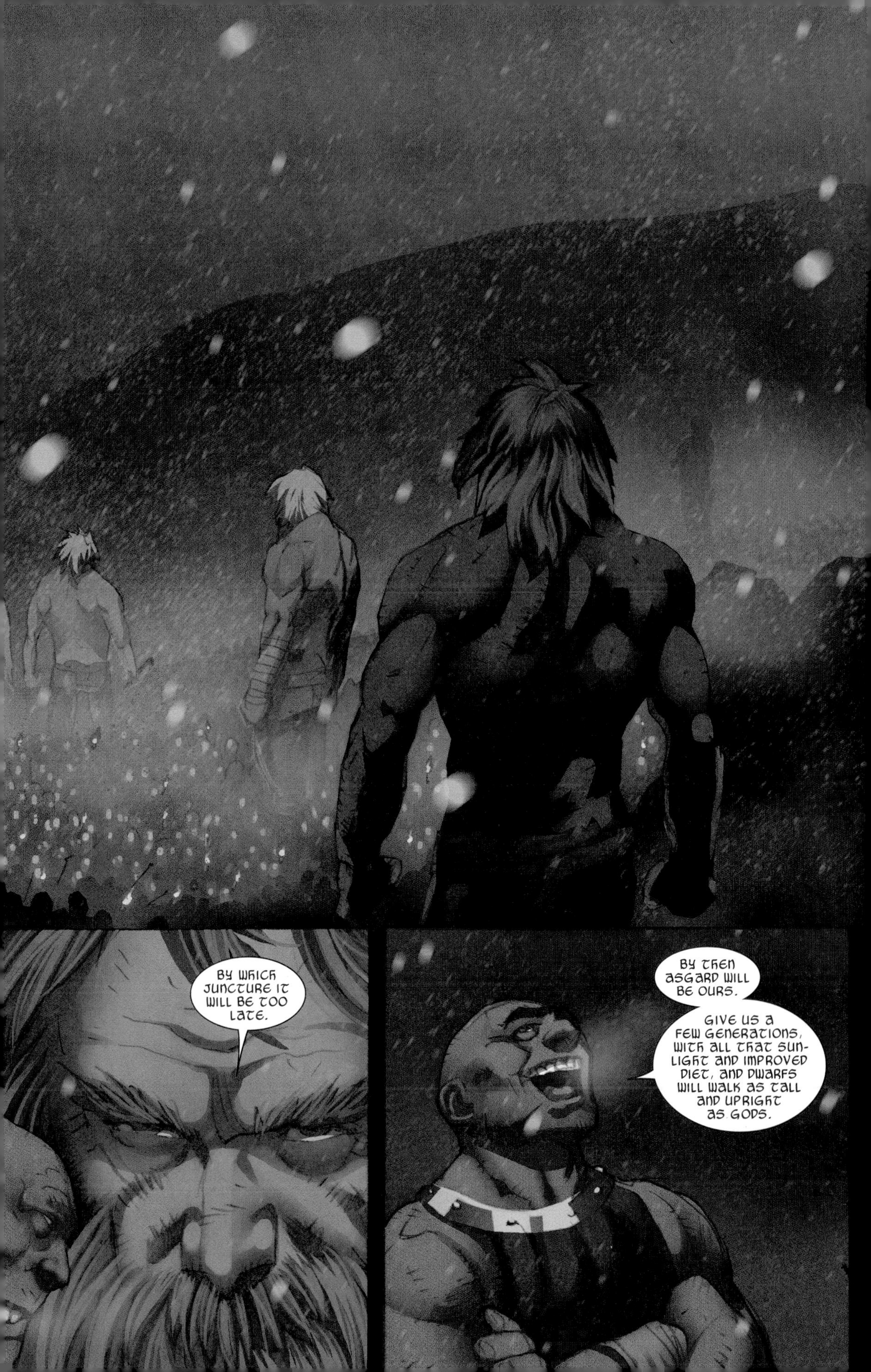

BY WHICH JUNCTURE IT WILL BE TOO LATE.
BY THEN ASGARD WILL BE OURS.
GIVE US A FEW GENERATIONS, WITH ALL THAT SUNLIGHT AND IMPROVED DIET, AND DWARFS WILL WALK AS TALL AND UPRIGHT AS GODS.

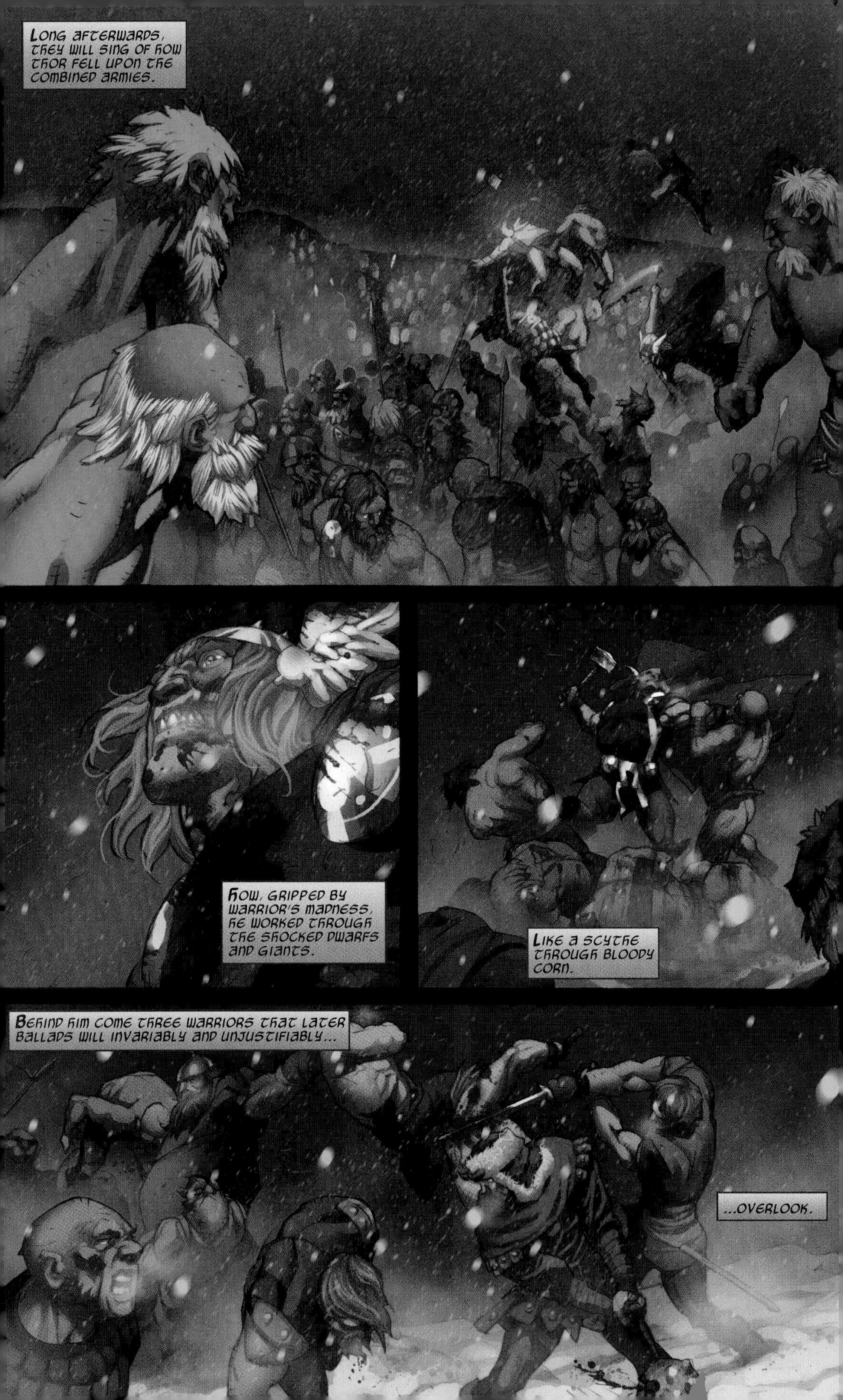
LONG AFTERWARDS, THEY WILL SING OF HOW THOR FELL UPON THE COMBINED ARMIES.
HOW, GRIPPED BY WARRIOR'S MADNESS, HE WORKED THROUGH THE SHOCKED DWARFS AND GIANTS.
LIKE A SCYTHE THROUGH BLOODY CORN.
BEHIND HIM COME THREE WARRIORS THAT LATER BALLADS WILL INVARIABLY AND UNJUSTIFIABLY...
...OVERLOOK.

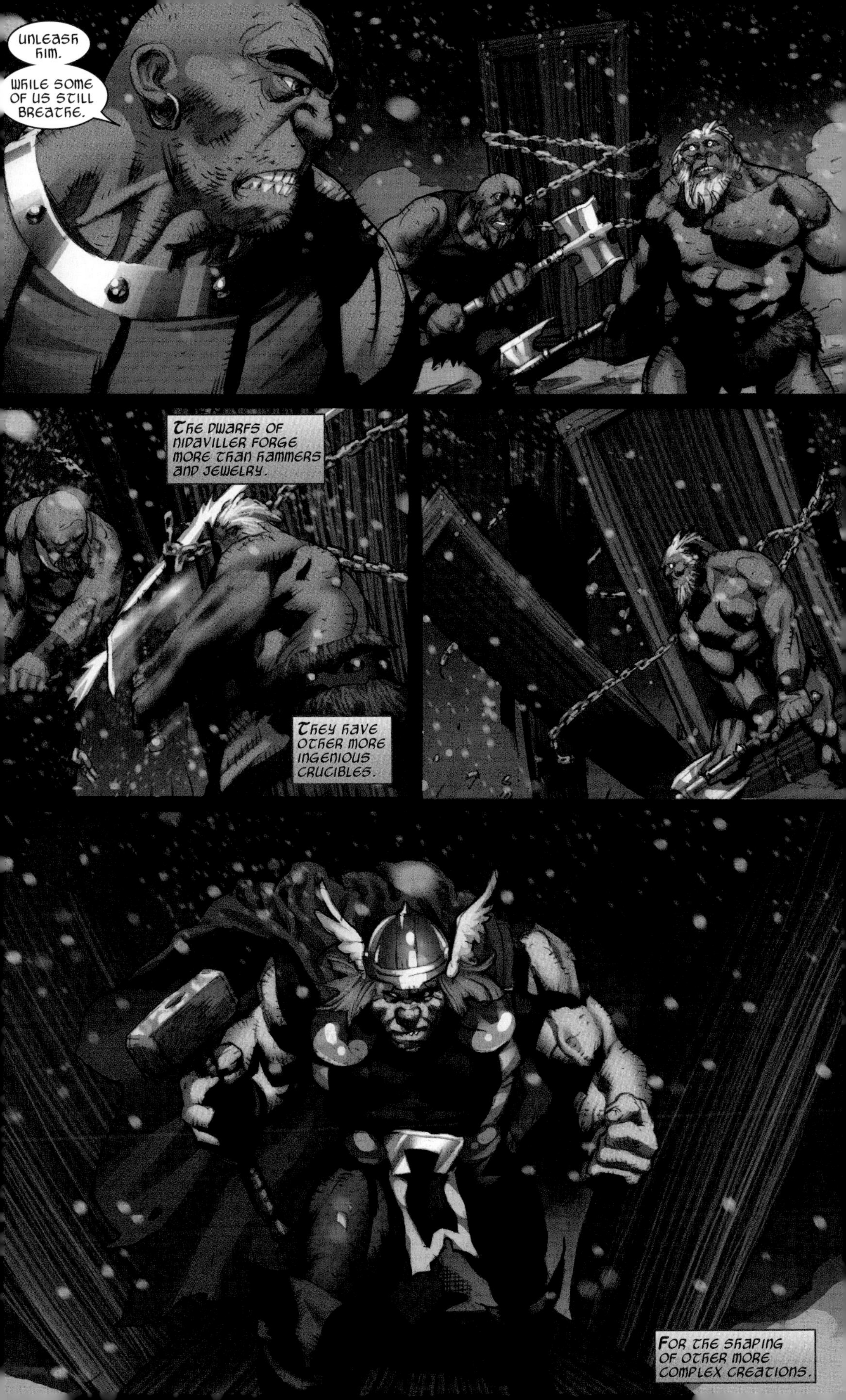
UNLEASH HIM.
WHILE SOME OF US STILL BREATHE.
THE DWARFS OF NIDAVILLER FORGE MORE THAN HAMMERS AND JEWELRY.
THEY HAVE OTHER MORE INGENIOUS CRUCIBLES.
FOR THE SHAPING OF OTHER MORE COMPLEX CREATIONS.

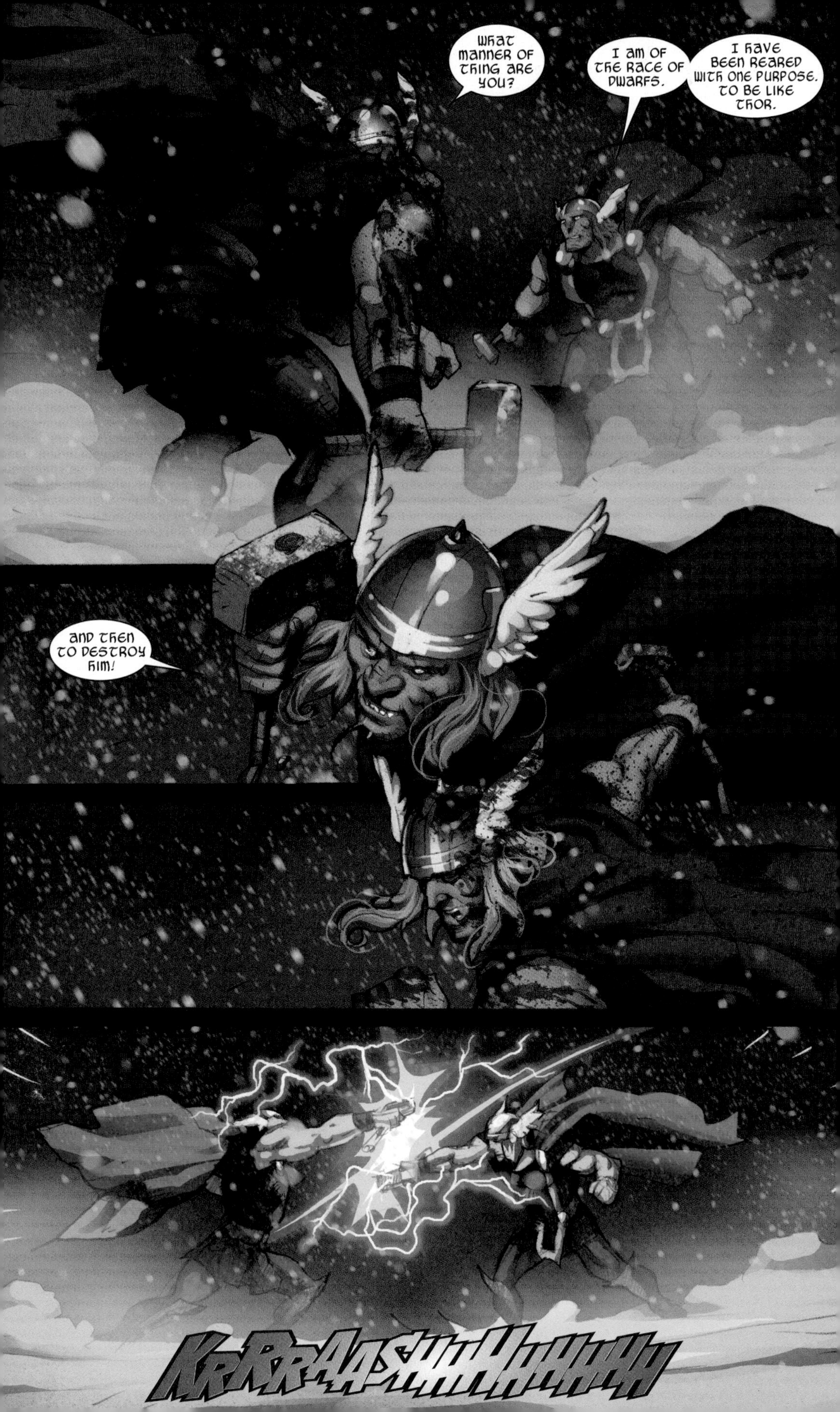

WHAT MANNER OF THING ARE YOU?
I AM OF THE RACE OF DWARFS.
I HAVE BEEN REARED WITH ONE PURPOSE. TO BE LIKE THOR.
AND THEN TO DESTROY HIM!
KRRRAASHHHHHHHH

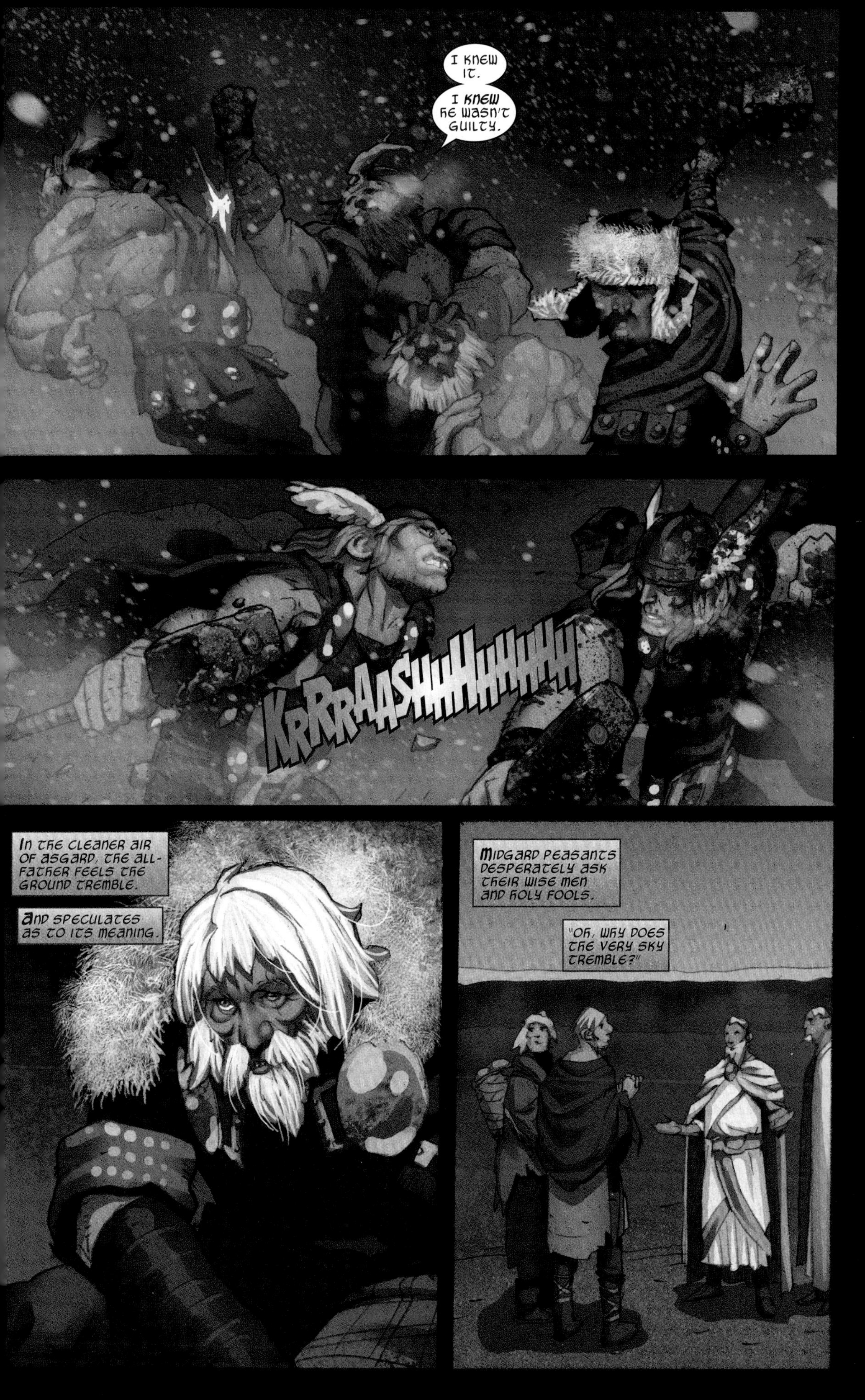
I KNEW IT.
I KNEW HE WASN'T GUILTY.
KRRRAASHHHHHHHHH
IN THE CLEANER AIR OF ASGARD, THE ALL-FATHER FEELS THE GROUND TREMBLE.
AND SPECULATES AS TO ITS MEANING.
MIDGARD PEASANTS DESPERATELY ASK THEIR WISE MEN AND HOLY FOOLS.
"OH, WHY DOES THE VERY SKY TREMBLE?"

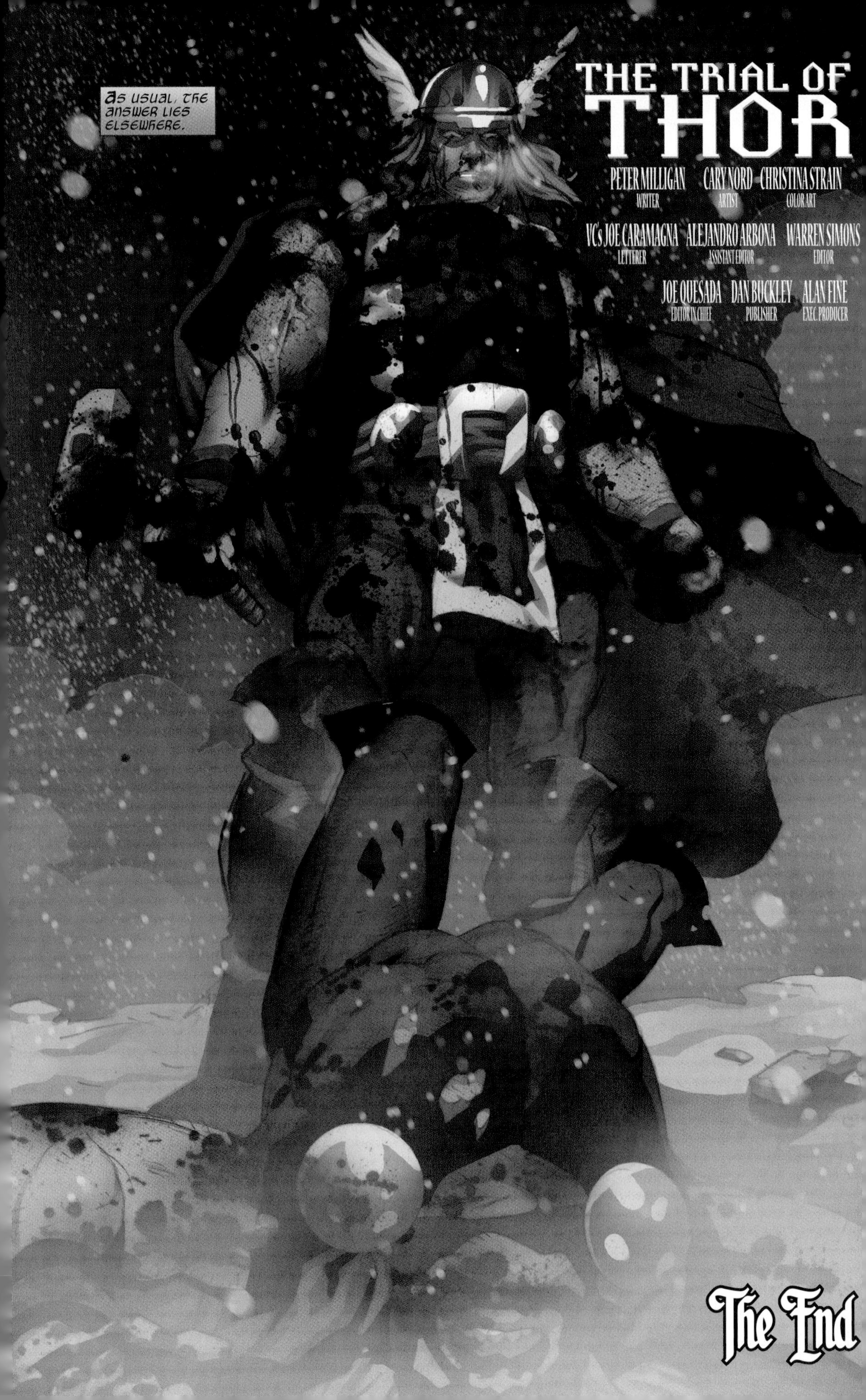
AS USUAL, THE ANSWER LIES ELSEWHERE.
THE TRIAL OF THOR
PETER MILLIGAN WRITER
CARY NORD ARTIST
CHRISTINA STRAIN COLOR ART
VC's JOE CARAMAGNA LETTERER
ALEJANDRO ARBONA ASSISTANT EDITOR
WARREN SIMONS EDITOR
JOE QUESADA EDITOR IN CHIEF
DAN BUCKLEY PUBLISHER
ALAN FINE EXEC. PRODUCER
The End

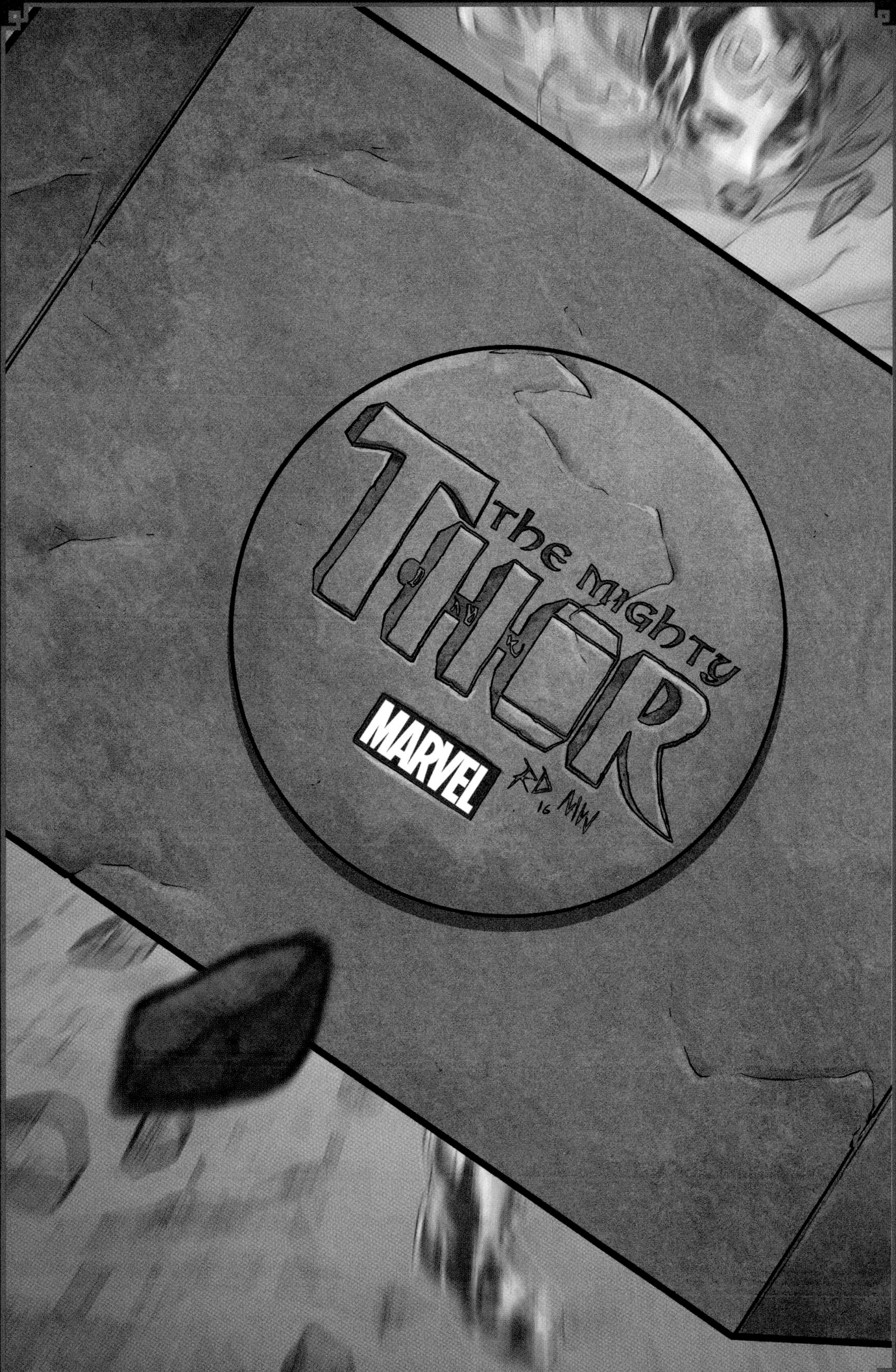

THE MIGHTY THOR
MARVEL
RD 16 MW

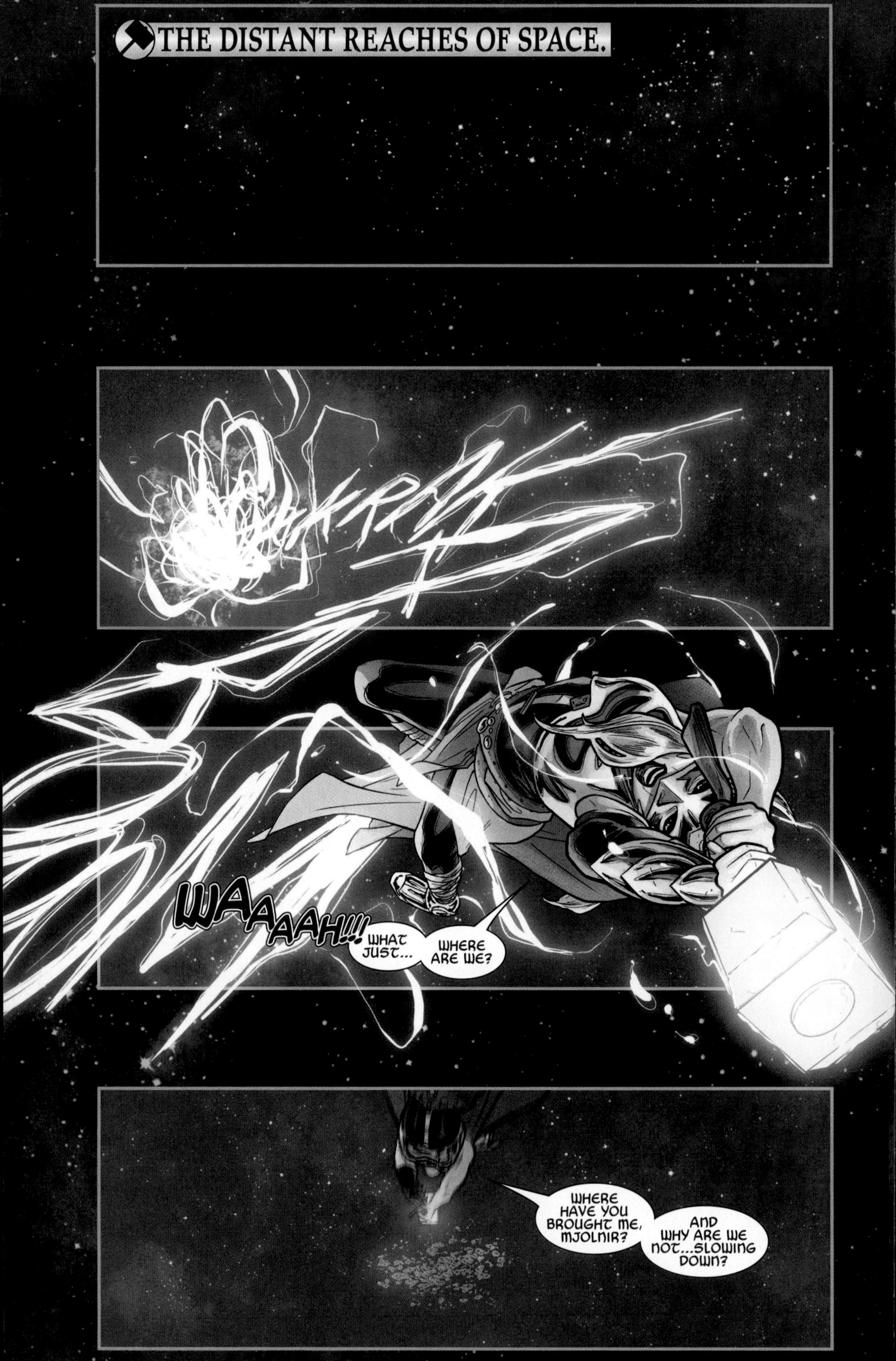
THE DISTANT REACHES OF SPACE.
WAAAAAH!!!
WHAT JUST...
WHERE ARE WE?
WHERE HAVE YOU BROUGHT ME, MJOLNIR?
AND WHY ARE WE NOT...SLOWING DOWN?

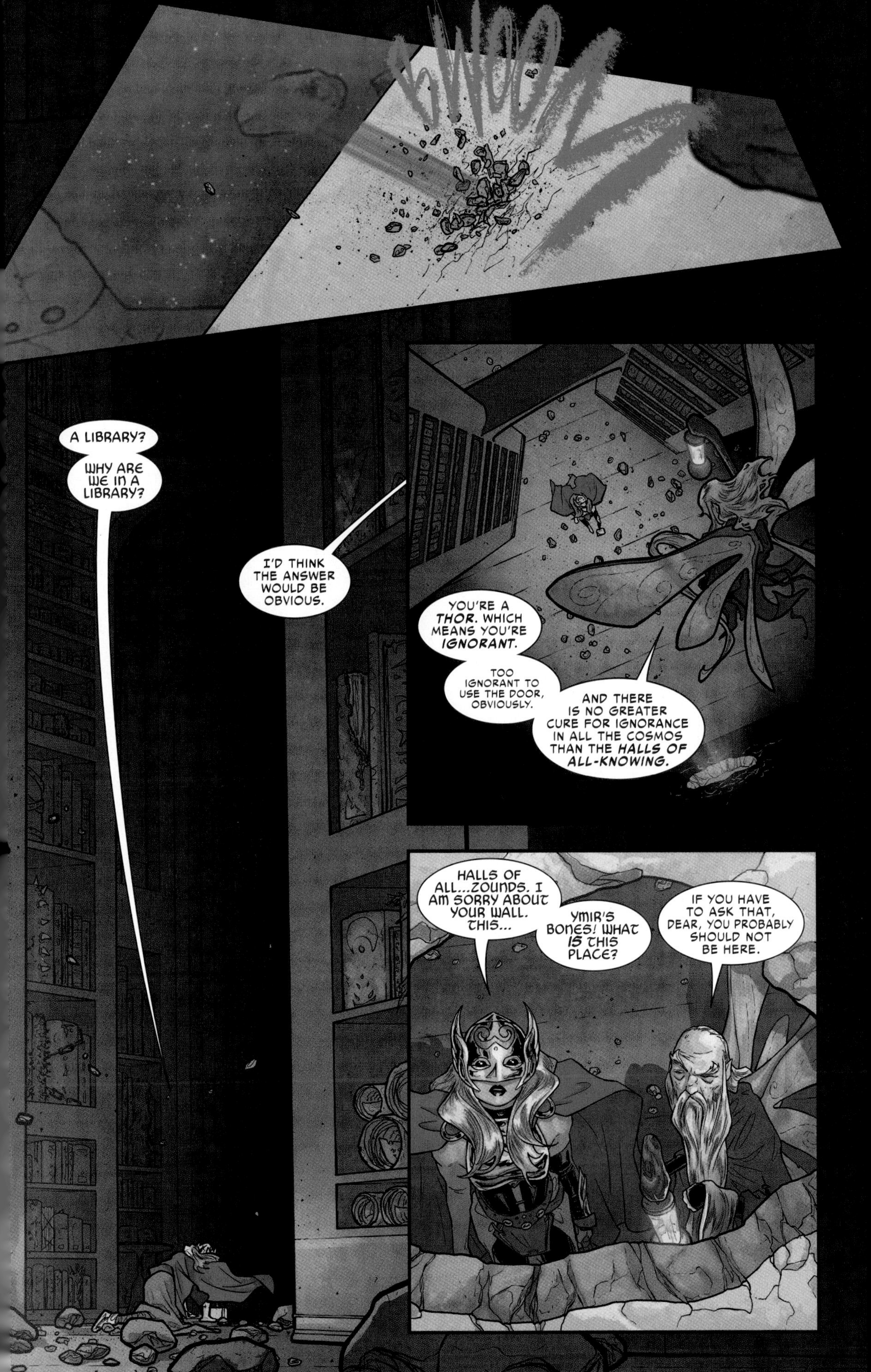

A LIBRARY?
WHY ARE WE IN A LIBRARY?
I'D THINK THE ANSWER WOULD BE OBVIOUS.
YOU'RE A THOR. WHICH MEANS YOU'RE IGNORANT.
TOO IGNORANT TO USE THE DOOR, OBVIOUSLY.
AND THERE IS NO GREATER CURE FOR IGNORANCE IN ALL THE COSMOS THAN THE HALLS OF ALL-KNOWING.
HALLS OF ALL...ZOUNDS. I AM SORRY ABOUT YOUR WALL. THIS...
YMIR'S BONES! WHAT IS THIS PLACE?
IF YOU HAVE TO ASK THAT, DEAR, YOU PROBABLY SHOULD NOT BE HERE.

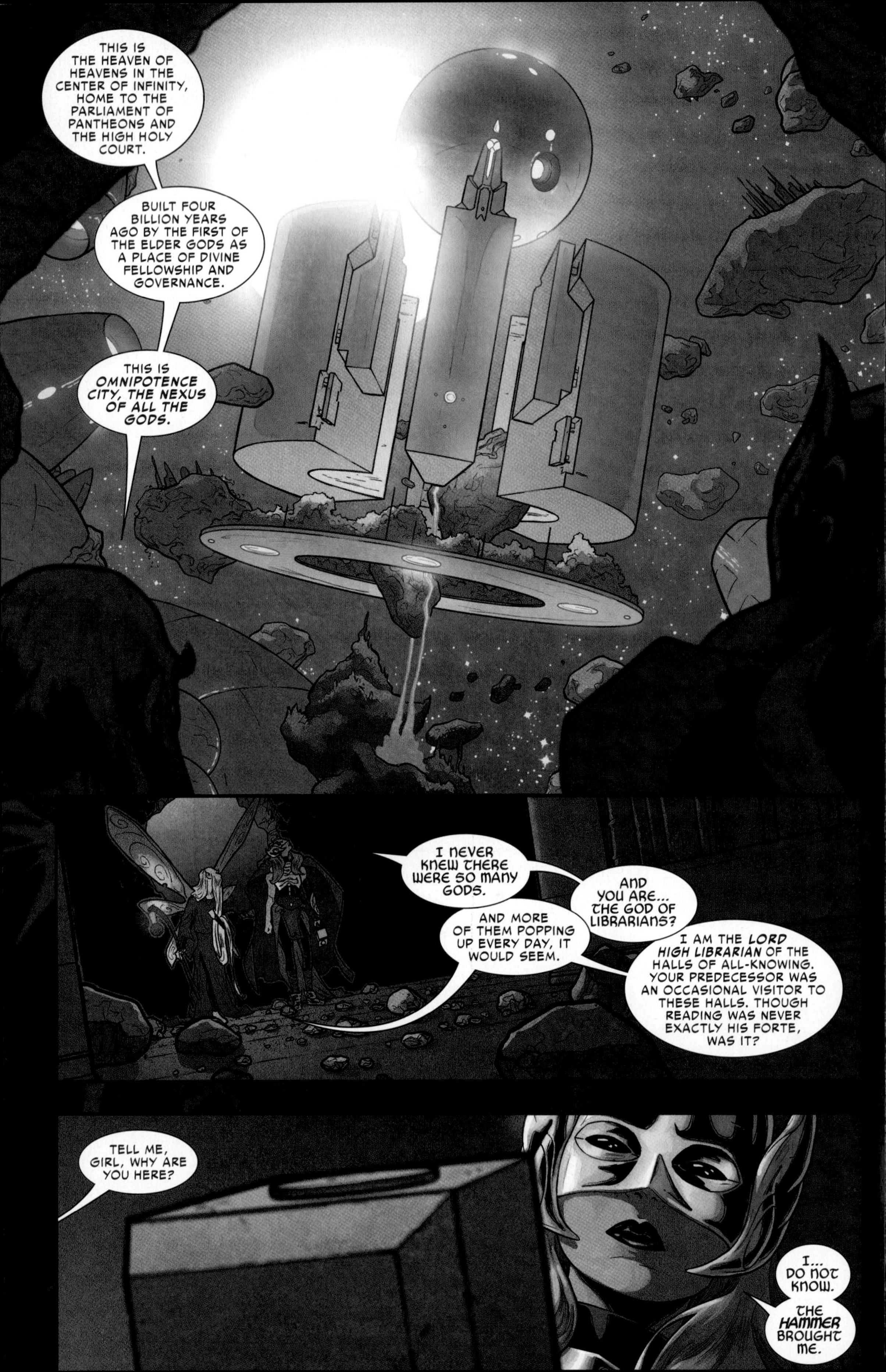
THIS IS THE HEAVEN OF HEAVENS IN THE CENTER OF INFINITY, HOME TO THE PARLIAMENT OF PANTHEONS AND THE HIGH HOLY COURT.
BUILT FOUR BILLION YEARS AGO BY THE FIRST OF THE ELDER GODS AS A PLACE OF DIVINE FELLOWSHIP AND GOVERNANCE.
THIS IS *OMNIPOTENCE CITY, THE NEXUS OF ALL THE GODS.*
I NEVER KNEW THERE WERE SO MANY GODS.
AND MORE OF THEM POPPING UP EVERY DAY, IT WOULD SEEM.
AND YOU ARE... THE GOD OF LIBRARIANS?
I AM THE *LORD HIGH LIBRARIAN* OF THE HALLS OF ALL-KNOWING. YOUR PREDECESSOR WAS AN OCCASIONAL VISITOR TO THESE HALLS. THOUGH READING WAS NEVER EXACTLY HIS FORTE, WAS IT?
TELL ME, GIRL, WHY ARE YOU HERE?
I... DO NOT KNOW.
THE ***HAMMER*** BROUGHT ME.

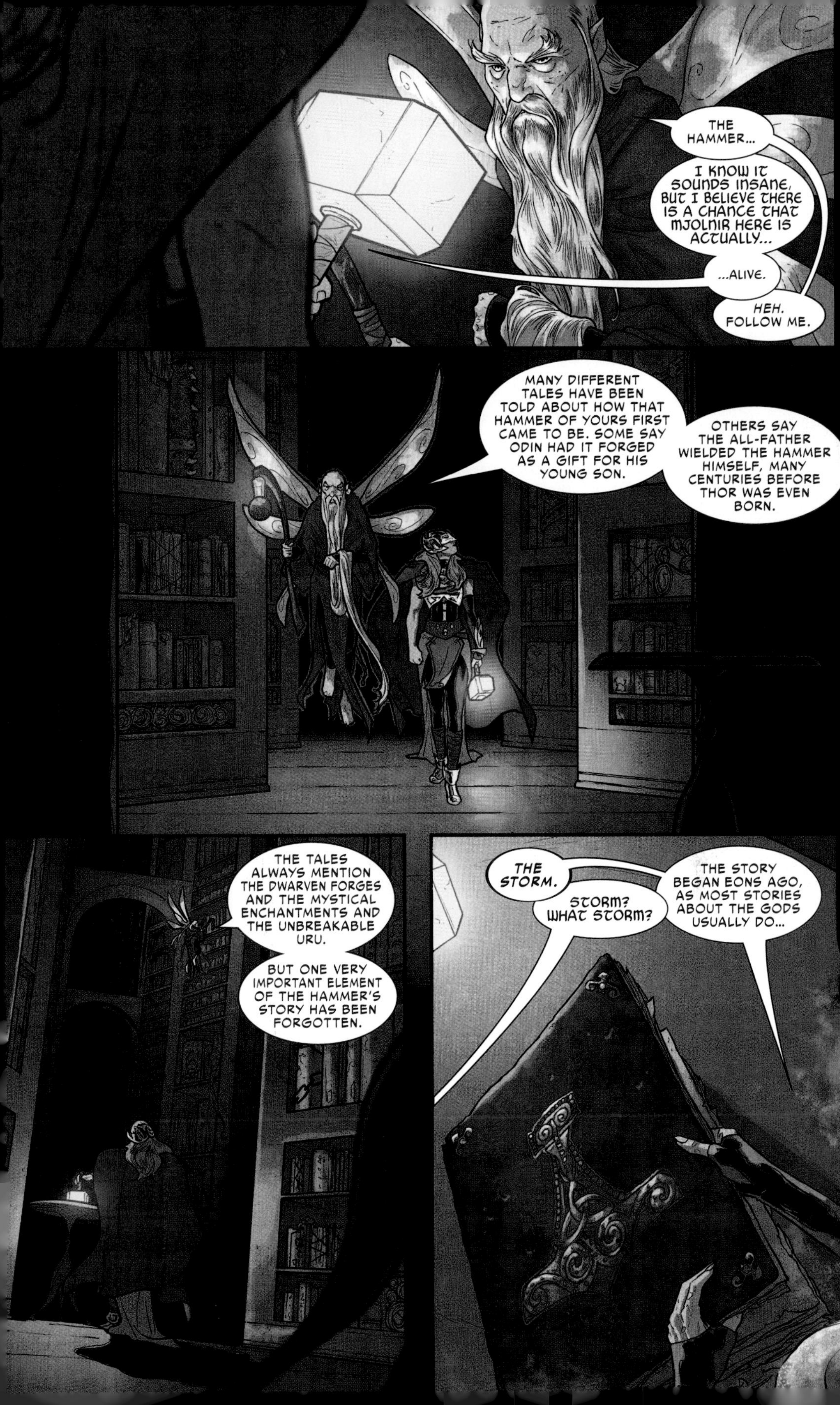
THE HAMMER...
I KNOW IT SOUNDS INSANE, BUT I BELIEVE THERE IS A CHANCE THAT MJOLNIR HERE IS ACTUALLY...
...ALIVE.
HEH. FOLLOW ME.
MANY DIFFERENT TALES HAVE BEEN TOLD ABOUT HOW THAT HAMMER OF YOURS FIRST CAME TO BE. SOME SAY ODIN HAD IT FORGED AS A GIFT FOR HIS YOUNG SON.
OTHERS SAY THE ALL-FATHER WIELDED THE HAMMER HIMSELF, MANY CENTURIES BEFORE THOR WAS EVEN BORN.
THE TALES ALWAYS MENTION THE DWARVEN FORGES AND THE MYSTICAL ENCHANTMENTS AND THE UNBREAKABLE URU.
BUT ONE VERY IMPORTANT ELEMENT OF THE HAMMER'S STORY HAS BEEN FORGOTTEN.
THE STORM.
STORM? WHAT STORM?
THE STORY BEGAN EONS AGO, AS MOST STORIES ABOUT THE GODS USUALLY DO...

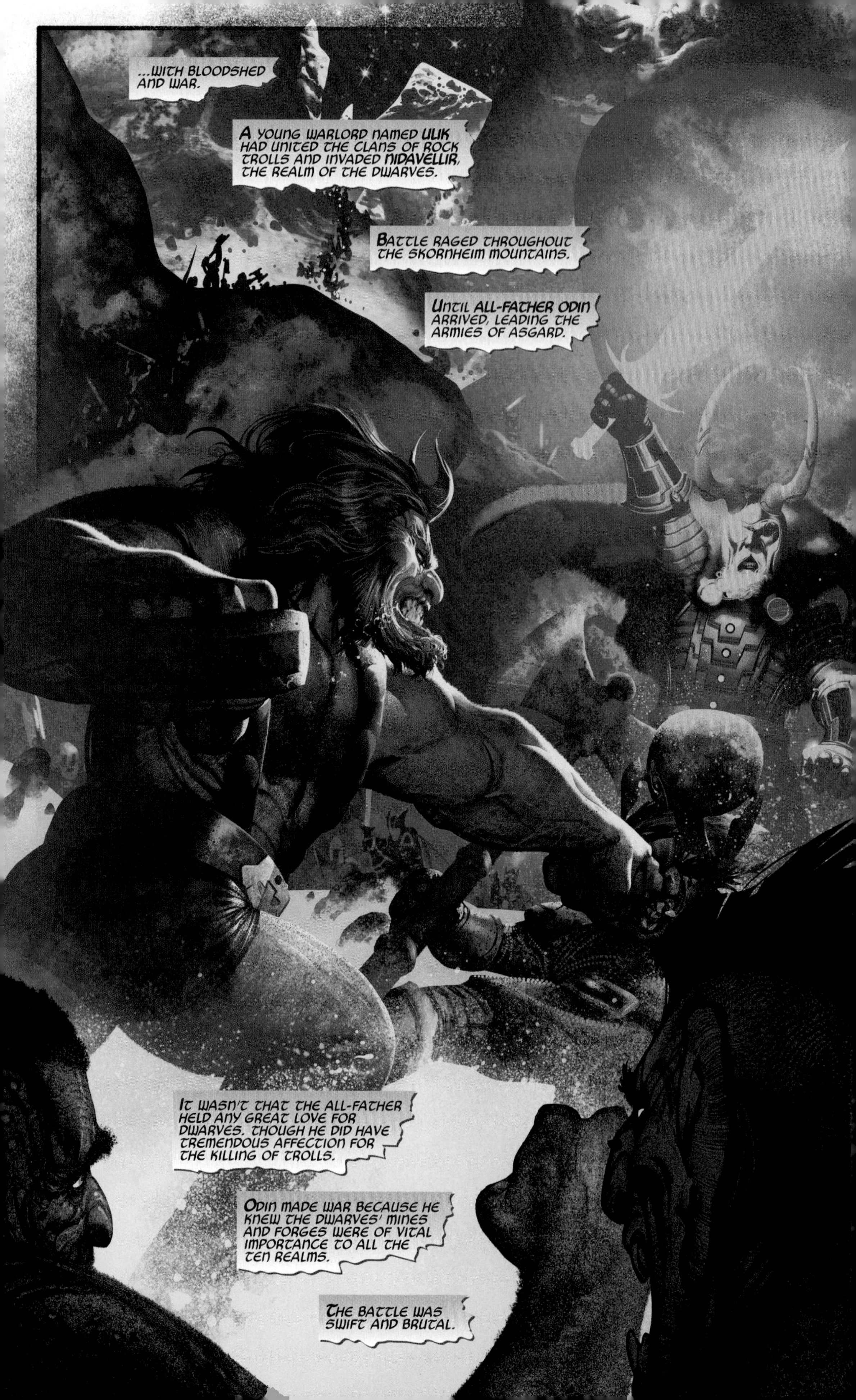
...WITH BLOODSHED AND WAR.
A YOUNG WARLORD NAMED ULIK HAD UNITED THE CLANS OF ROCK TROLLS AND INVADED NIDAVELLIR, THE REALM OF THE DWARVES.
BATTLE RAGED THROUGHOUT THE SKORNHEIM MOUNTAINS.
UNTIL ALL-FATHER ODIN ARRIVED, LEADING THE ARMIES OF ASGARD.
IT WASN'T THAT THE ALL-FATHER HELD ANY GREAT LOVE FOR DWARVES. THOUGH HE DID HAVE TREMENDOUS AFFECTION FOR THE KILLING OF TROLLS.
ODIN MADE WAR BECAUSE HE KNEW THE DWARVES' MINES AND FORGES WERE OF VITAL IMPORTANCE TO ALL THE TEN REALMS.
THE BATTLE WAS SWIFT AND BRUTAL.

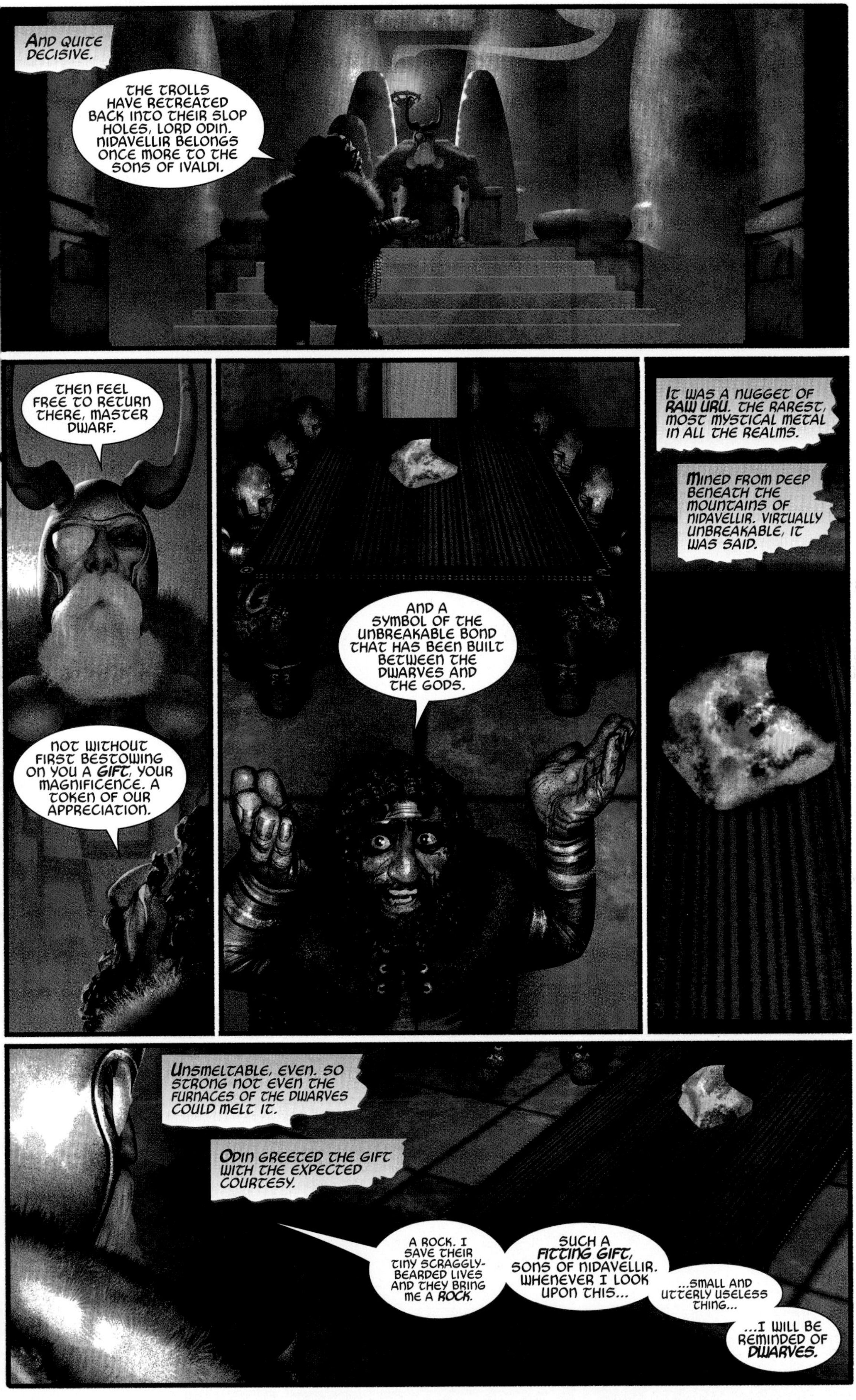
AND QUITE DECISIVE.
THE TROLLS HAVE RETREATED BACK INTO THEIR SLOP HOLES, LORD ODIN. NIDAVELLIR BELONGS ONCE MORE TO THE SONS OF IVALDI.
THEN FEEL FREE TO RETURN THERE, MASTER DWARF.
NOT WITHOUT FIRST BESTOWING ON YOU A GIFT, YOUR MAGNIFICENCE. A TOKEN OF OUR APPRECIATION.
AND A SYMBOL OF THE UNBREAKABLE BOND THAT HAS BEEN BUILT BETWEEN THE DWARVES AND THE GODS.
IT WAS A NUGGET OF RAW URU. THE RAREST, MOST MYSTICAL METAL IN ALL THE REALMS.
MINED FROM DEEP BENEATH THE MOUNTAINS OF NIDAVELLIR. VIRTUALLY UNBREAKABLE, IT WAS SAID.
UNSMELTABLE, EVEN. SO STRONG NOT EVEN THE FURNACES OF THE DWARVES COULD MELT IT.
ODIN GREETED THE GIFT WITH THE EXPECTED COURTESY.
A ROCK. I SAVE THEIR TINY SCRAGGLY-BEARDED LIVES AND THEY BRING ME A ROCK.
SUCH A FITTING GIFT, SONS OF NIDAVELLIR. WHENEVER I LOOK UPON THIS...
...SMALL AND UTTERLY USELESS THING...
...I WILL BE REMINDED OF DWARVES.

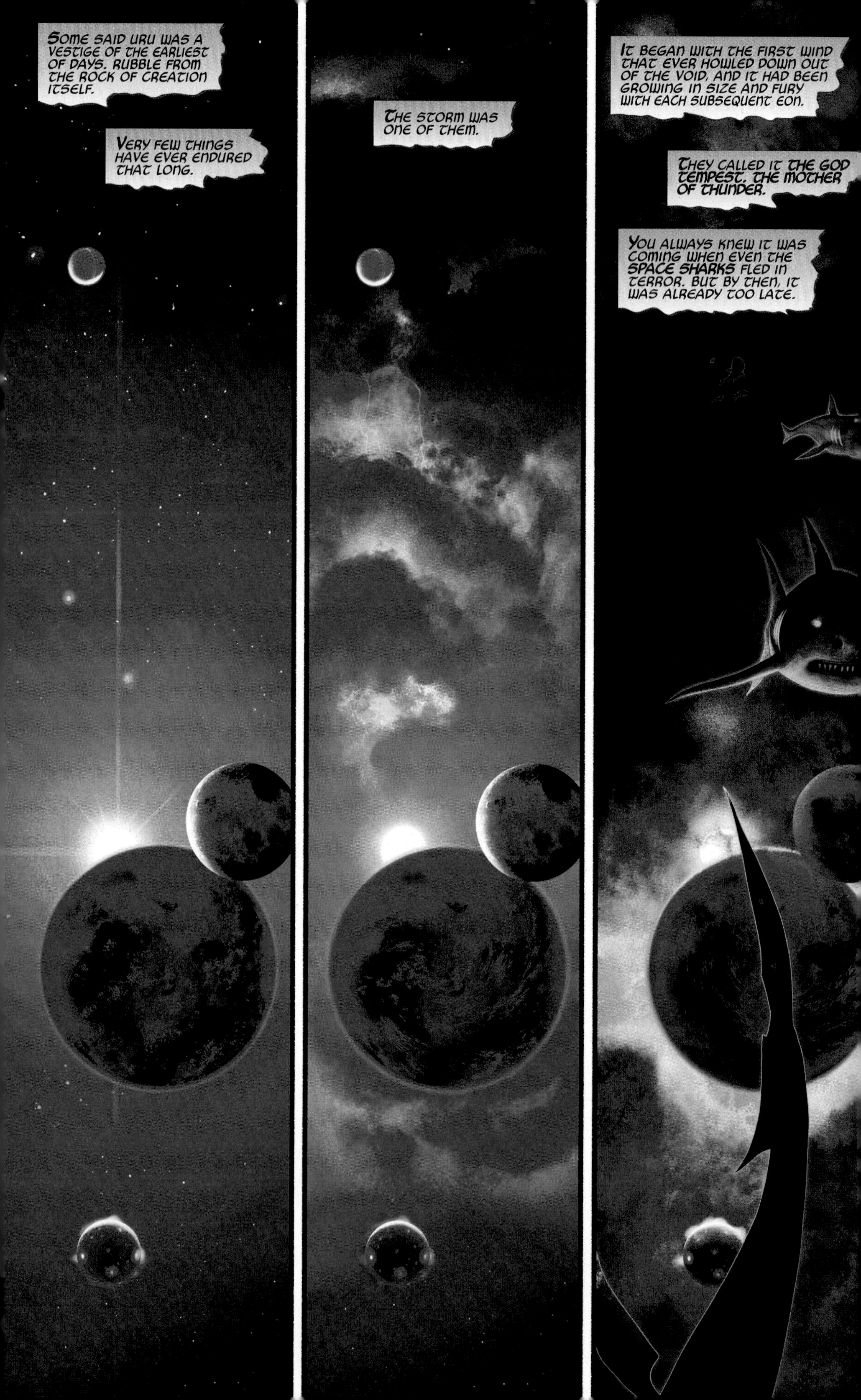

SOME SAID URU WAS A VESTIGE OF THE EARLIEST OF DAYS. RUBBLE FROM THE ROCK OF CREATION ITSELF.
VERY FEW THINGS HAVE EVER ENDURED THAT LONG.
THE STORM WAS ONE OF THEM.
IT BEGAN WITH THE FIRST WIND THAT EVER HOWLED DOWN OUT OF THE VOID, AND IT HAD BEEN GROWING IN SIZE AND FURY WITH EACH SUBSEQUENT EON.
THEY CALLED IT THE GOD TEMPEST. THE MOTHER OF THUNDER.
YOU ALWAYS KNEW IT WAS COMING WHEN EVEN THE SPACE SHARKS FLED IN TERROR. BUT BY THEN, IT WAS ALREADY TOO LATE.

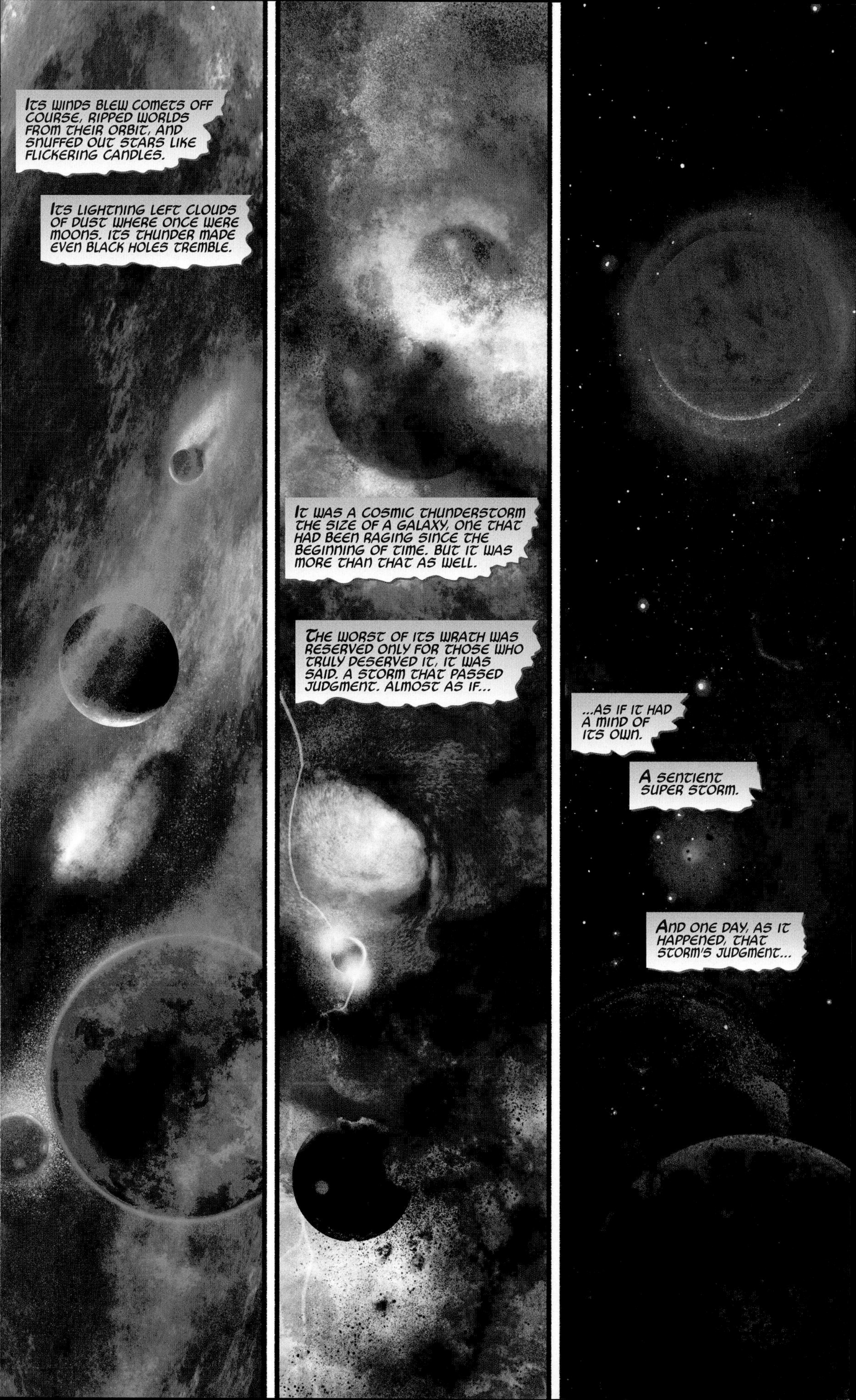
ITS WINDS BLEW COMETS OFF COURSE, RIPPED WORLDS FROM THEIR ORBIT, AND SNUFFED OUT STARS LIKE FLICKERING CANDLES.
ITS LIGHTNING LEFT CLOUDS OF DUST WHERE ONCE WERE MOONS. ITS THUNDER MADE EVEN BLACK HOLES TREMBLE.
IT WAS A COSMIC THUNDERSTORM THE SIZE OF A GALAXY, ONE THAT HAD BEEN RAGING SINCE THE BEGINNING OF TIME. BUT IT WAS MORE THAN THAT AS WELL.
THE WORST OF ITS WRATH WAS RESERVED ONLY FOR THOSE WHO TRULY DESERVED IT, IT WAS SAID. A STORM THAT PASSED JUDGMENT. ALMOST AS IF...
...AS IF IT HAD A MIND OF ITS OWN.
A SENTIENT SUPER STORM.
AND ONE DAY, AS IT HAPPENED, THAT STORM'S JUDGMENT...

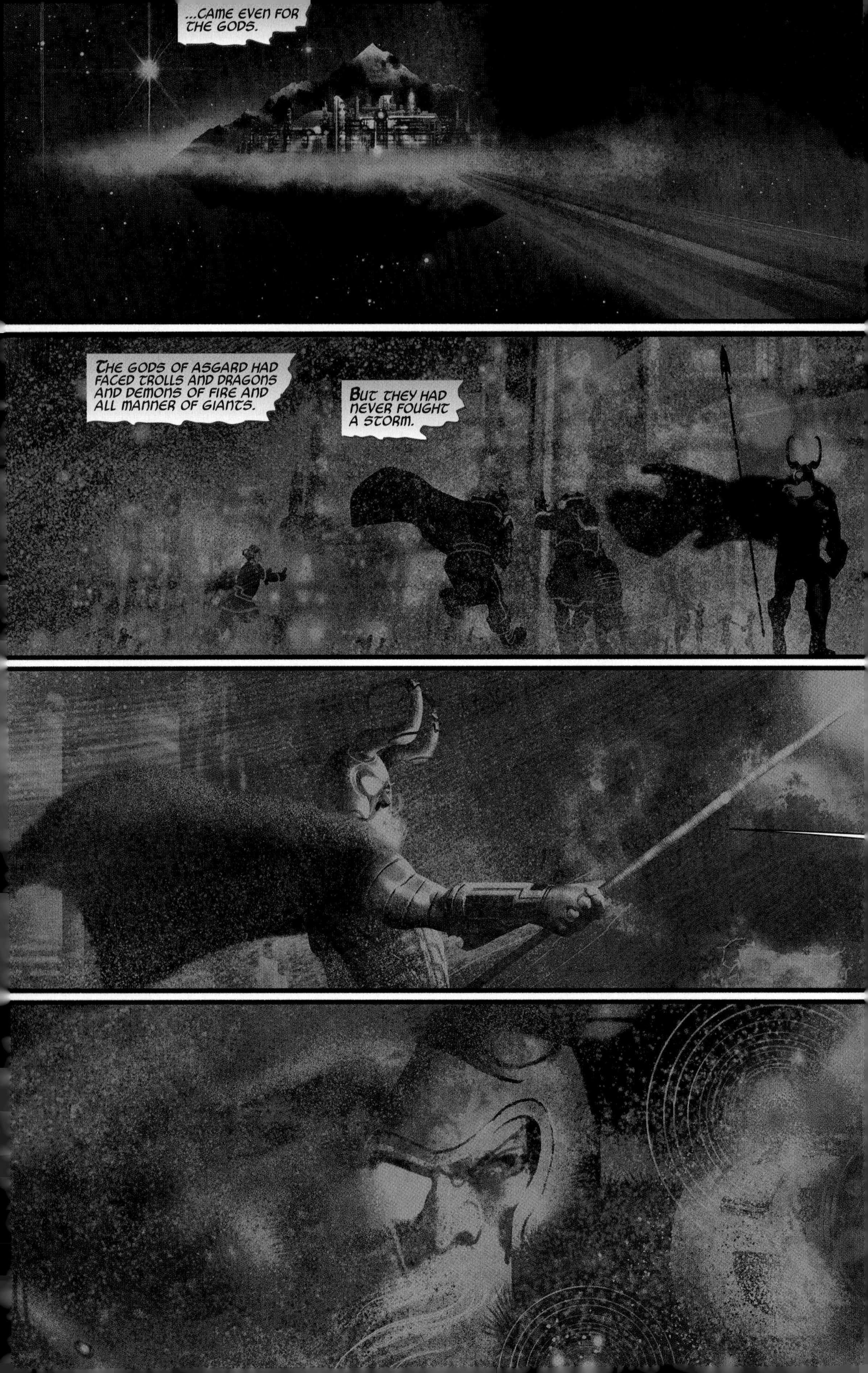
...CAME EVEN FOR THE GODS.
THE GODS OF ASGARD HAD FACED TROLLS AND DRAGONS AND DEMONS OF FIRE AND ALL MANNER OF GIANTS.
BUT THEY HAD NEVER FOUGHT A STORM.

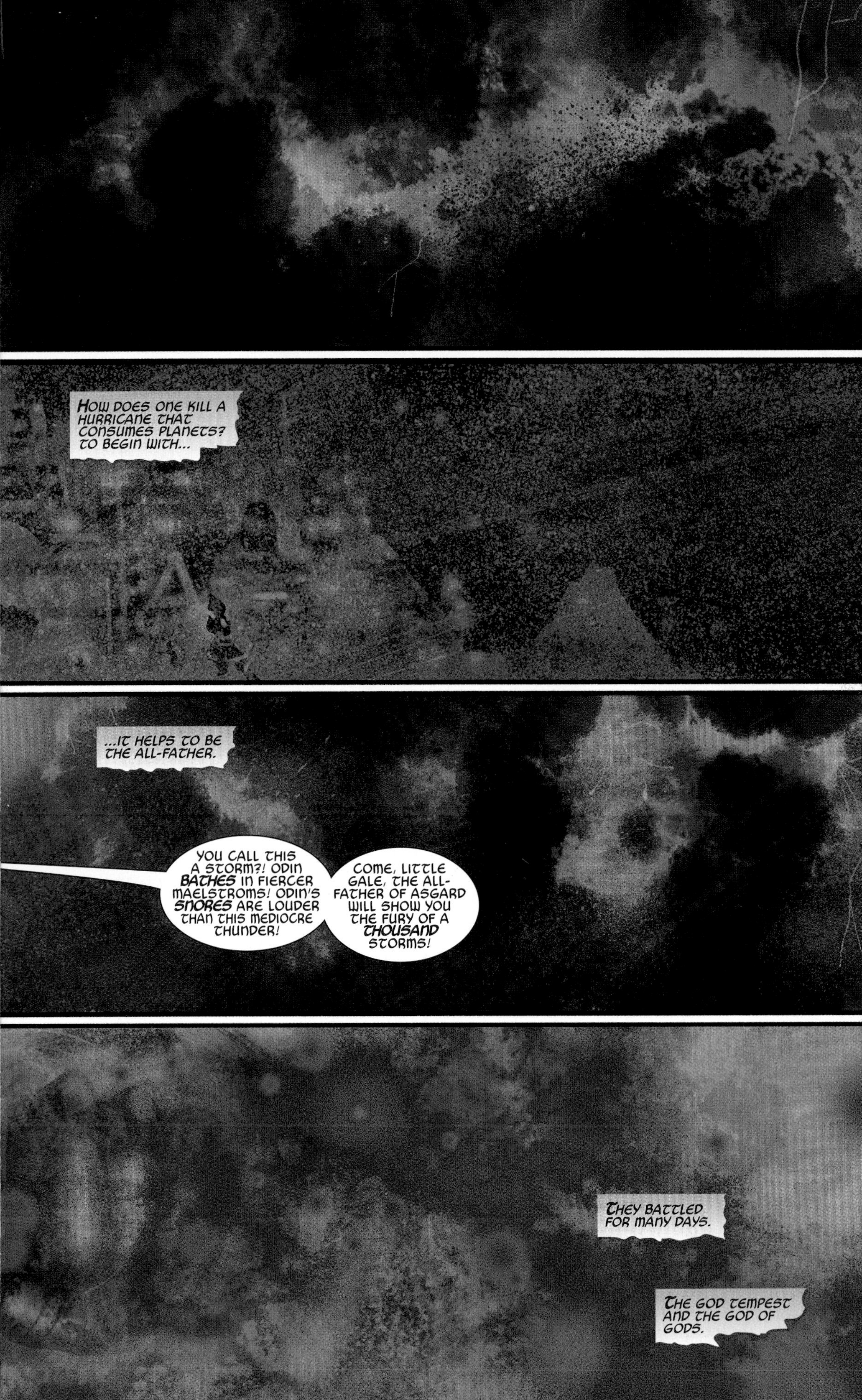
HOW DOES ONE KILL A HURRICANE THAT CONSUMES PLANETS? TO BEGIN WITH...
...IT HELPS TO BE THE ALL-FATHER.
YOU CALL THIS A STORM?! ODIN BATHES IN FIERCER MAELSTROMS! ODIN'S SNORES ARE LOUDER THAN THIS MEDIOCRE THUNDER!
COME, LITTLE GALE, THE ALL-FATHER OF ASGARD WILL SHOW YOU THE FURY OF A THOUSAND STORMS!
THEY BATTLED FOR MANY DAYS.
THE GOD TEMPEST AND THE GOD OF GODS.

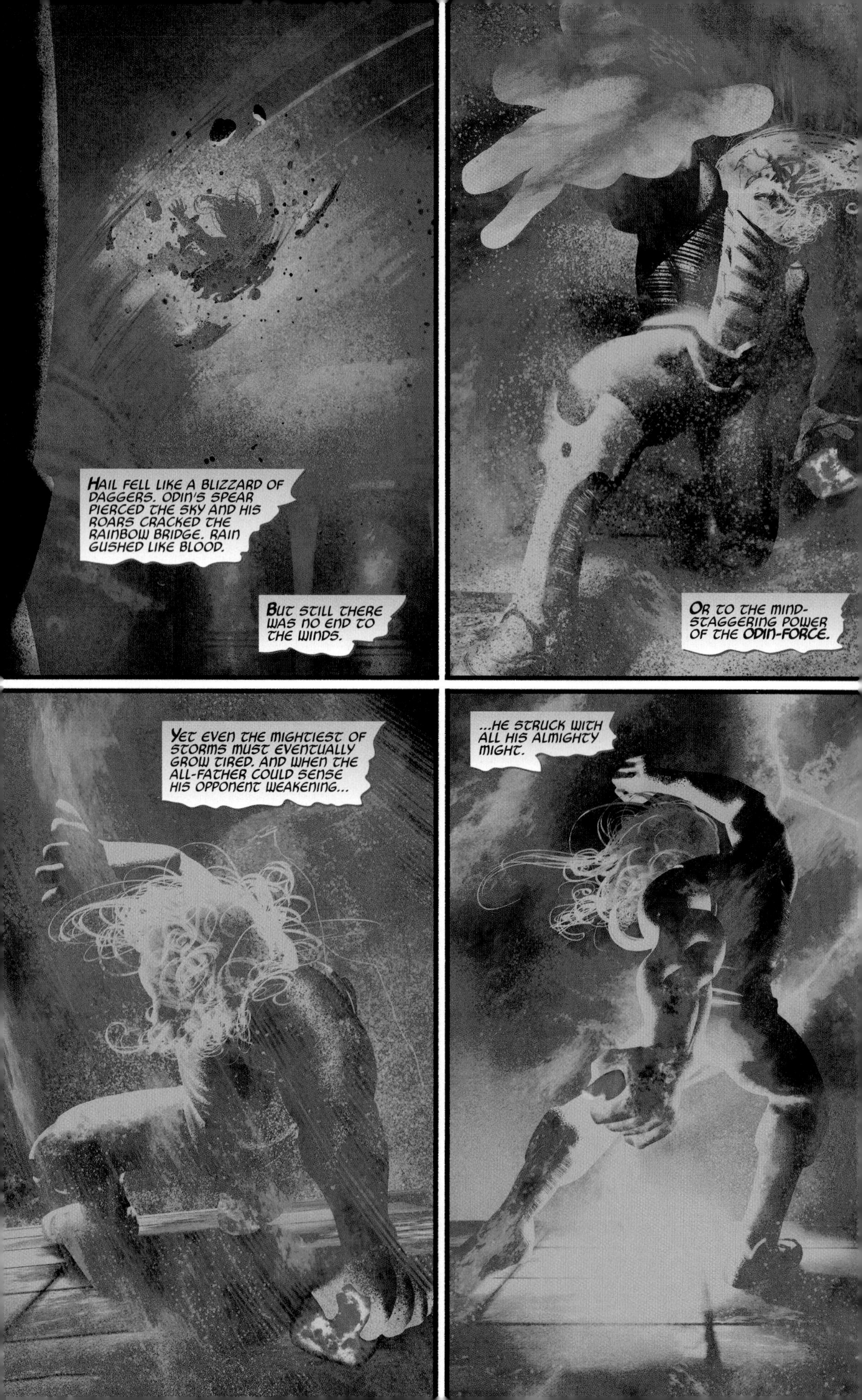
HAIL FELL LIKE A BLIZZARD OF DAGGERS. ODIN'S SPEAR PIERCED THE SKY AND HIS ROARS CRACKED THE RAINBOW BRIDGE. RAIN GUSHED LIKE BLOOD.
BUT STILL THERE WAS NO END TO THE WINDS.
OR TO THE MIND-STAGGERING POWER OF THE ODIN-FORCE.
YET EVEN THE MIGHTIEST OF STORMS MUST EVENTUALLY GROW TIRED. AND WHEN THE ALL-FATHER COULD SENSE HIS OPPONENT WEAKENING...
...HE STRUCK WITH ALL HIS ALMIGHTY MIGHT.

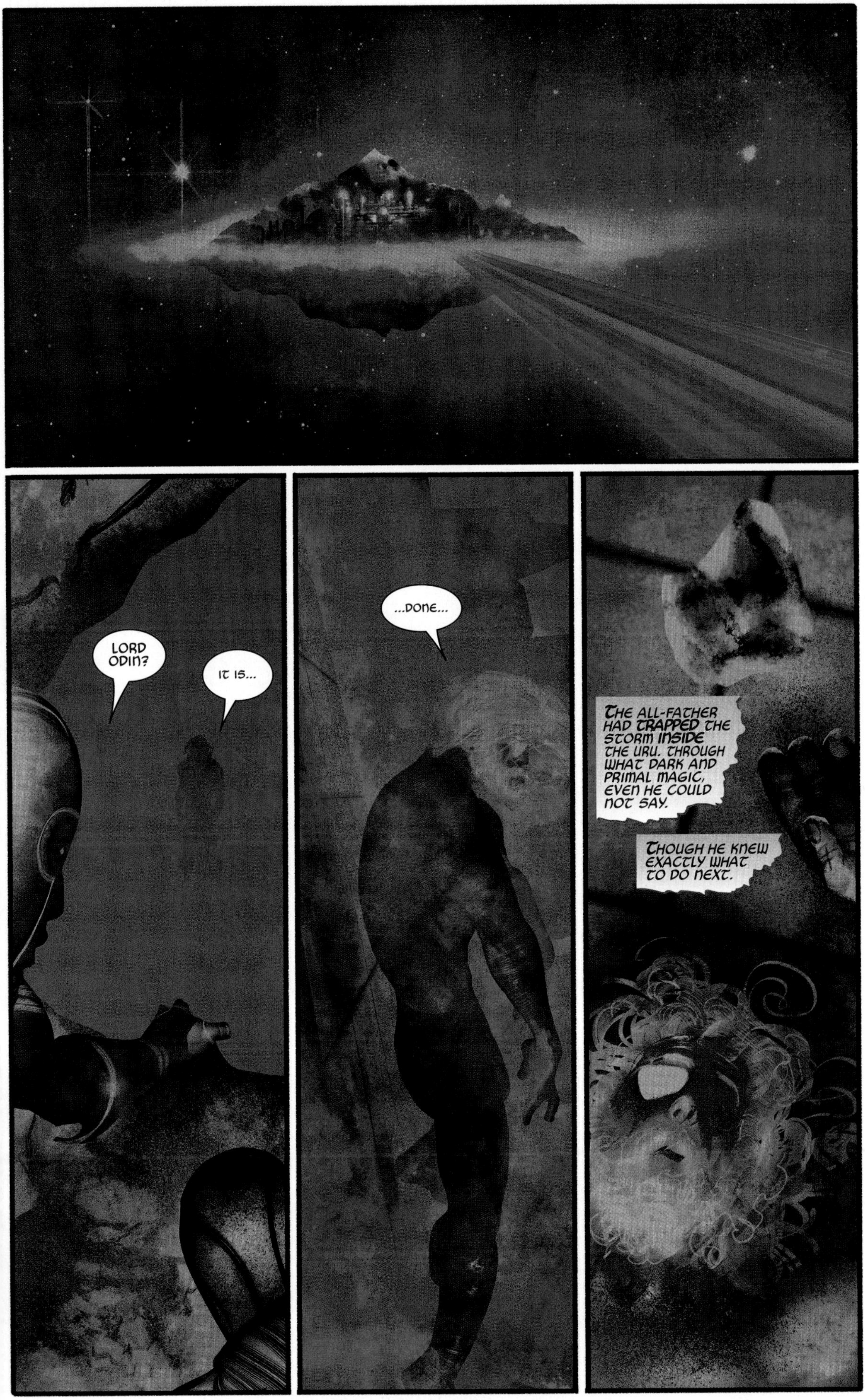
LORD ODIN?
IT IS...
...DONE...
THE ALL-FATHER HAD TRAPPED THE STORM INSIDE THE URU. THROUGH WHAT DARK AND PRIMAL MAGIC, EVEN HE COULD NOT SAY.
THOUGH HE KNEW EXACTLY WHAT TO DO NEXT.

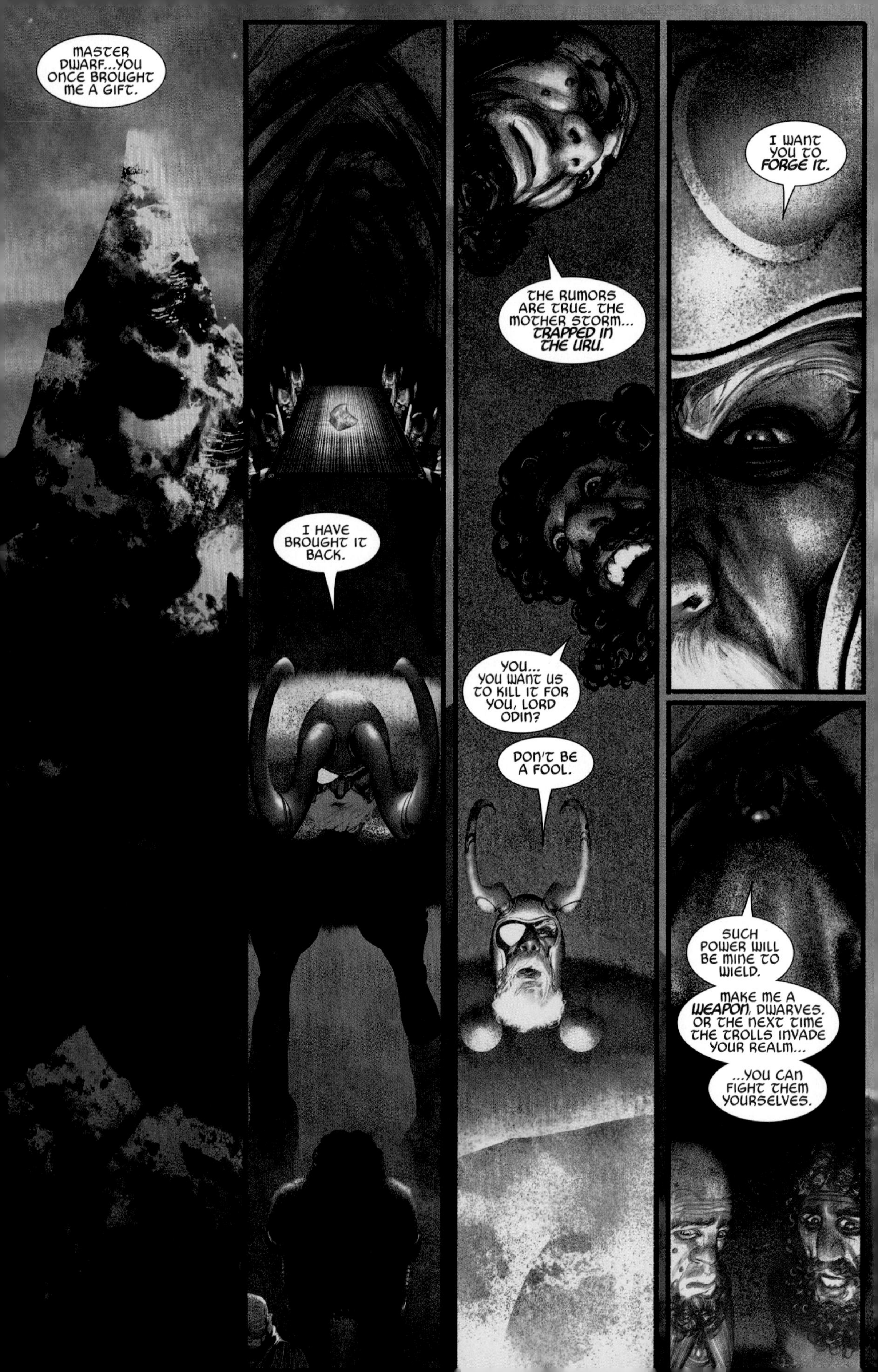
MASTER DWARF...YOU ONCE BROUGHT ME A GIFT.
I HAVE BROUGHT IT BACK.
THE RUMORS ARE TRUE. THE MOTHER STORM... TRAPPED IN THE URU.
YOU... YOU WANT US TO KILL IT FOR YOU, LORD ODIN?
DON'T BE A FOOL.
I WANT YOU TO FORGE IT.
SUCH POWER WILL BE MINE TO WIELD.
MAKE ME A WEAPON, DWARVES. OR THE NEXT TIME THE TROLLS INVADE YOUR REALM...
...YOU CAN FIGHT THEM YOURSELVES.

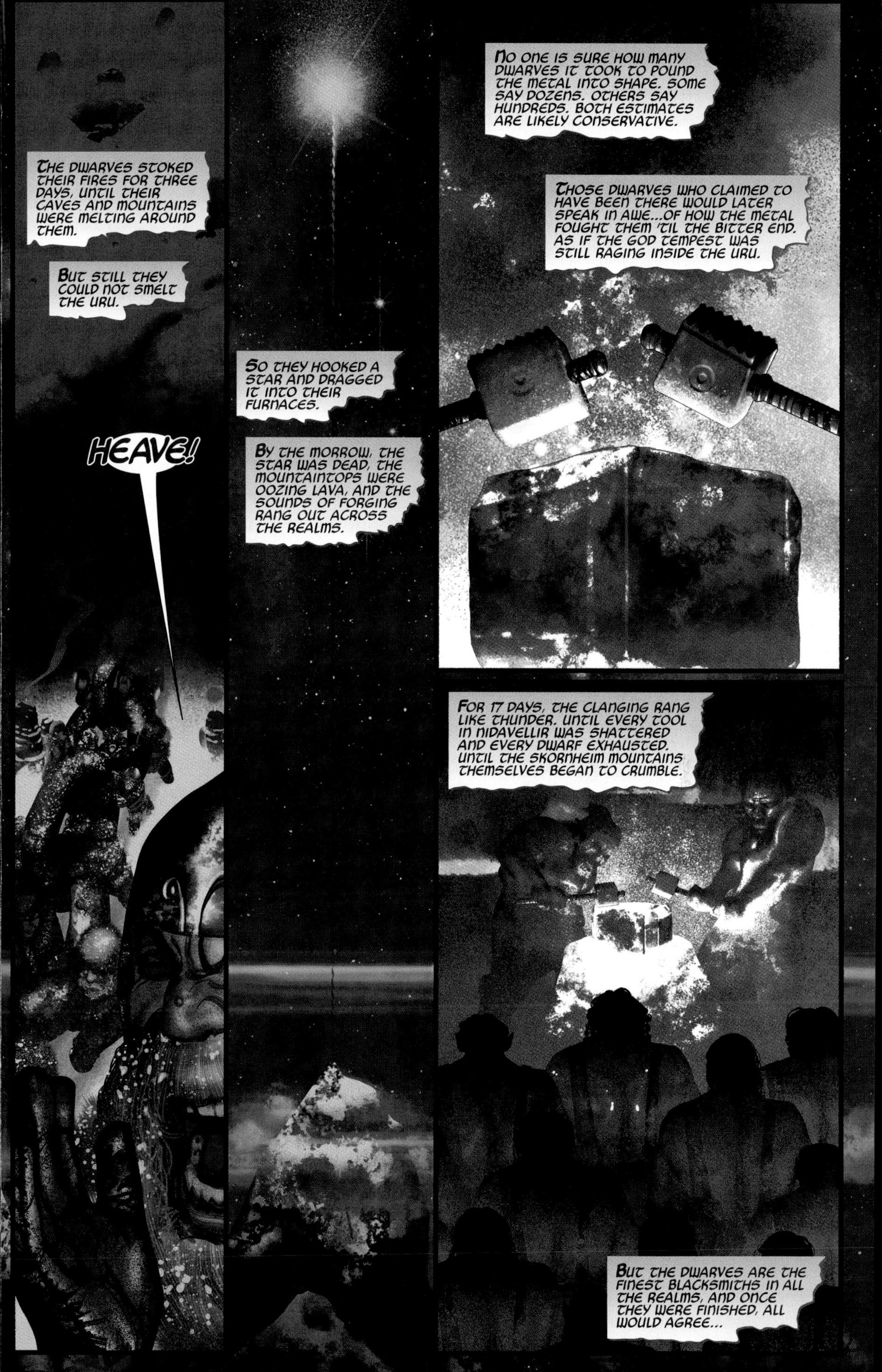
THE DWARVES STOKED THEIR FIRES FOR THREE DAYS, UNTIL THEIR CAVES AND MOUNTAINS WERE MELTING AROUND THEM.
BUT STILL THEY COULD NOT SMELT THE URU.
HEAVE!
SO THEY HOOKED A STAR AND DRAGGED IT INTO THEIR FURNACES.
BY THE MORROW, THE STAR WAS DEAD, THE MOUNTAINTOPS WERE OOZING LAVA, AND THE SOUNDS OF FORGING RANG OUT ACROSS THE REALMS.
NO ONE IS SURE HOW MANY DWARVES IT TOOK TO POUND THE METAL INTO SHAPE. SOME SAY DOZENS. OTHERS SAY HUNDREDS. BOTH ESTIMATES ARE LIKELY CONSERVATIVE.
THOSE DWARVES WHO CLAIMED TO HAVE BEEN THERE WOULD LATER SPEAK IN AWE...OF HOW THE METAL FOUGHT THEM 'TIL THE BITTER END. AS IF THE GOD TEMPEST WAS STILL RAGING INSIDE THE URU.
FOR 17 DAYS, THE CLANGING RANG LIKE THUNDER. UNTIL EVERY TOOL IN NIDAVELLIR WAS SHATTERED AND EVERY DWARF EXHAUSTED. UNTIL THE SKORNHEIM MOUNTAINS THEMSELVES BEGAN TO CRUMBLE.
BUT THE DWARVES ARE THE FINEST BLACKSMITHS IN ALL THE REALMS, AND ONCE THEY WERE FINISHED, ALL WOULD AGREE...

...THEY HAD FORGED THEIR FINEST CREATION.

THEY DELIVERED THE WEAPON TO ODIN, AS PROMISED. THOUGH WITH ONE CAVEAT...

...THAT THEY WOULD NEVER HAVE TO SEE THAT DAMNED HAMMER AGAIN.

I NAME THEE... MJOLNIR, THE THUNDER WEAPON.

FIRST AMONG HAMMERS. THE BREAKER OF ALL THINGS.

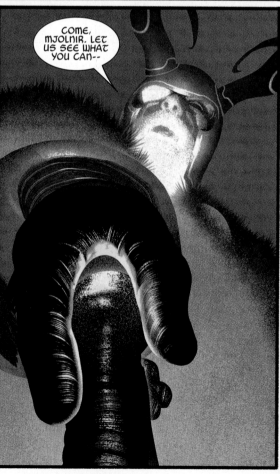

COME, MJOLNIR. LET US SEE WHAT YOU CAN--

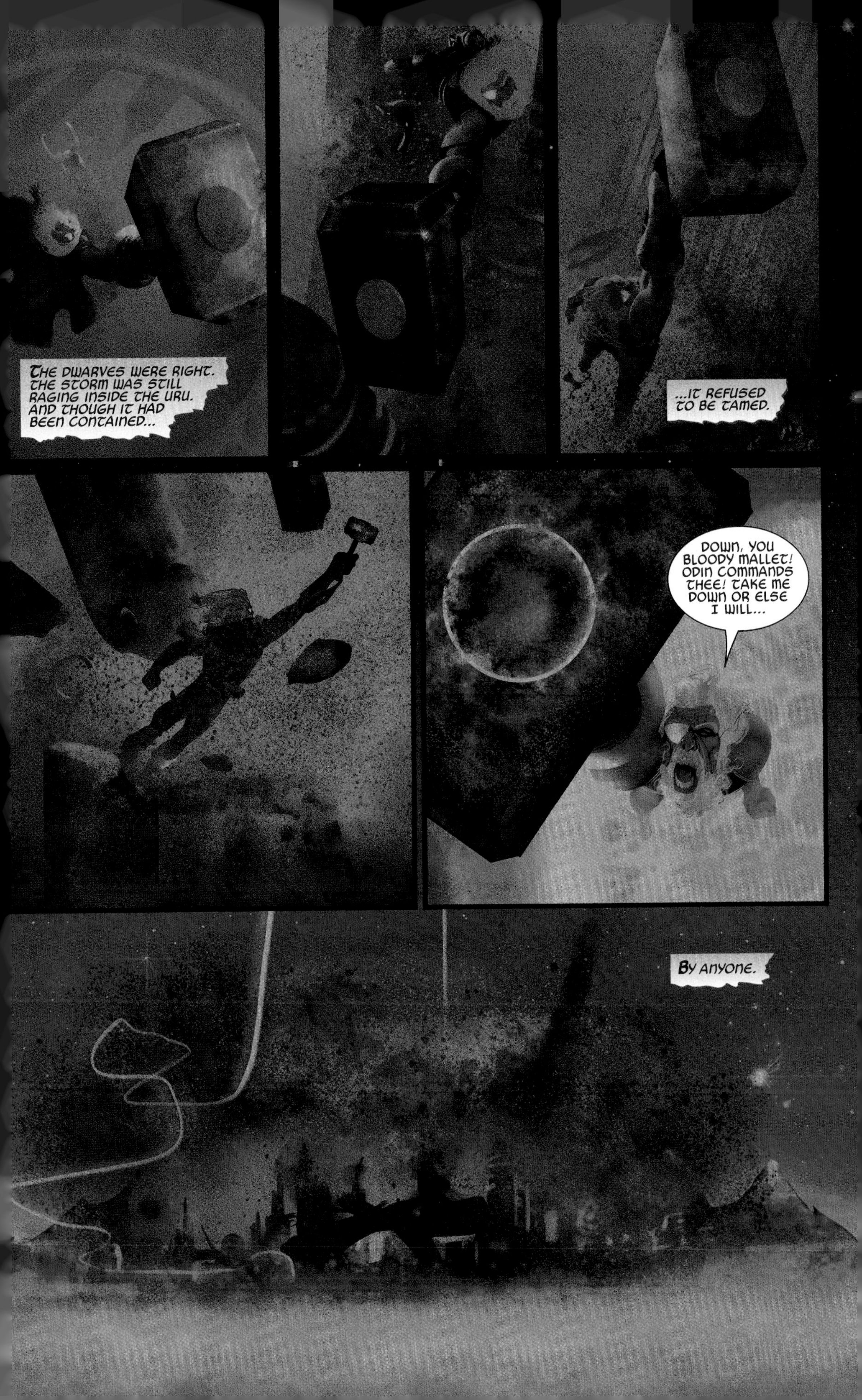
THE DWARVES WERE RIGHT. THE STORM WAS STILL RAGING INSIDE THE URU. AND THOUGH IT HAD BEEN CONTAINED...
...IT REFUSED TO BE TAMED.
DOWN, YOU BLOODY MALLET! ODIN COMMANDS THEE! TAKE ME DOWN OR ELSE I WILL...
By anyone.

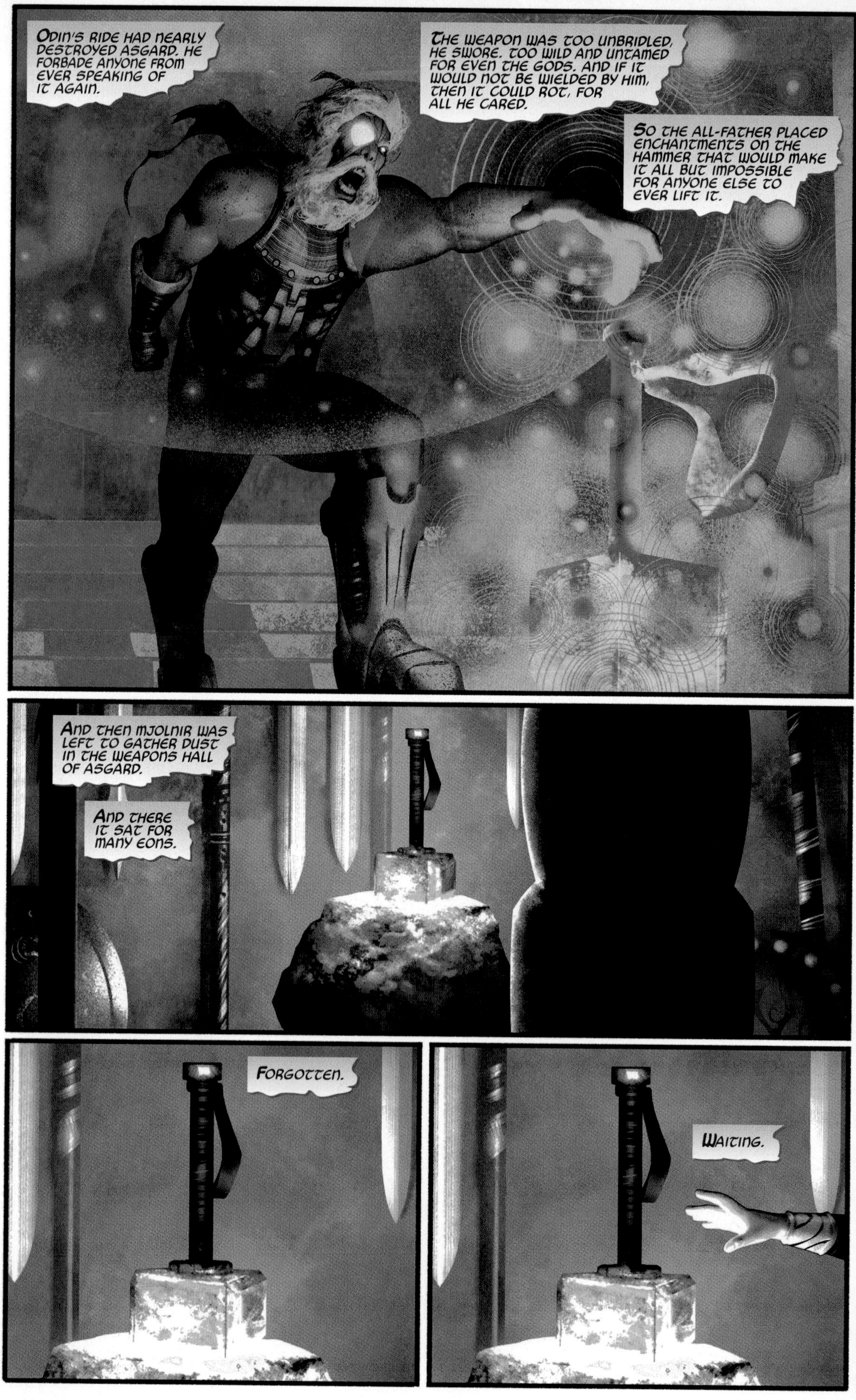
ODIN'S RIDE HAD NEARLY DESTROYED ASGARD. HE FORBADE ANYONE FROM EVER SPEAKING OF IT AGAIN.
THE WEAPON WAS TOO UNBRIDLED, HE SWORE. TOO WILD AND UNTAMED FOR EVEN THE GODS. AND IF IT WOULD NOT BE WIELDED BY HIM, THEN IT COULD ROT, FOR ALL HE CARED.
SO THE ALL-FATHER PLACED ENCHANTMENTS ON THE HAMMER THAT WOULD MAKE IT ALL BUT IMPOSSIBLE FOR ANYONE ELSE TO EVER LIFT IT.
AND THEN MJOLNIR WAS LEFT TO GATHER DUST IN THE WEAPONS HALL OF ASGARD.
AND THERE IT SAT FOR MANY EONS.
FORGOTTEN.
WAITING.

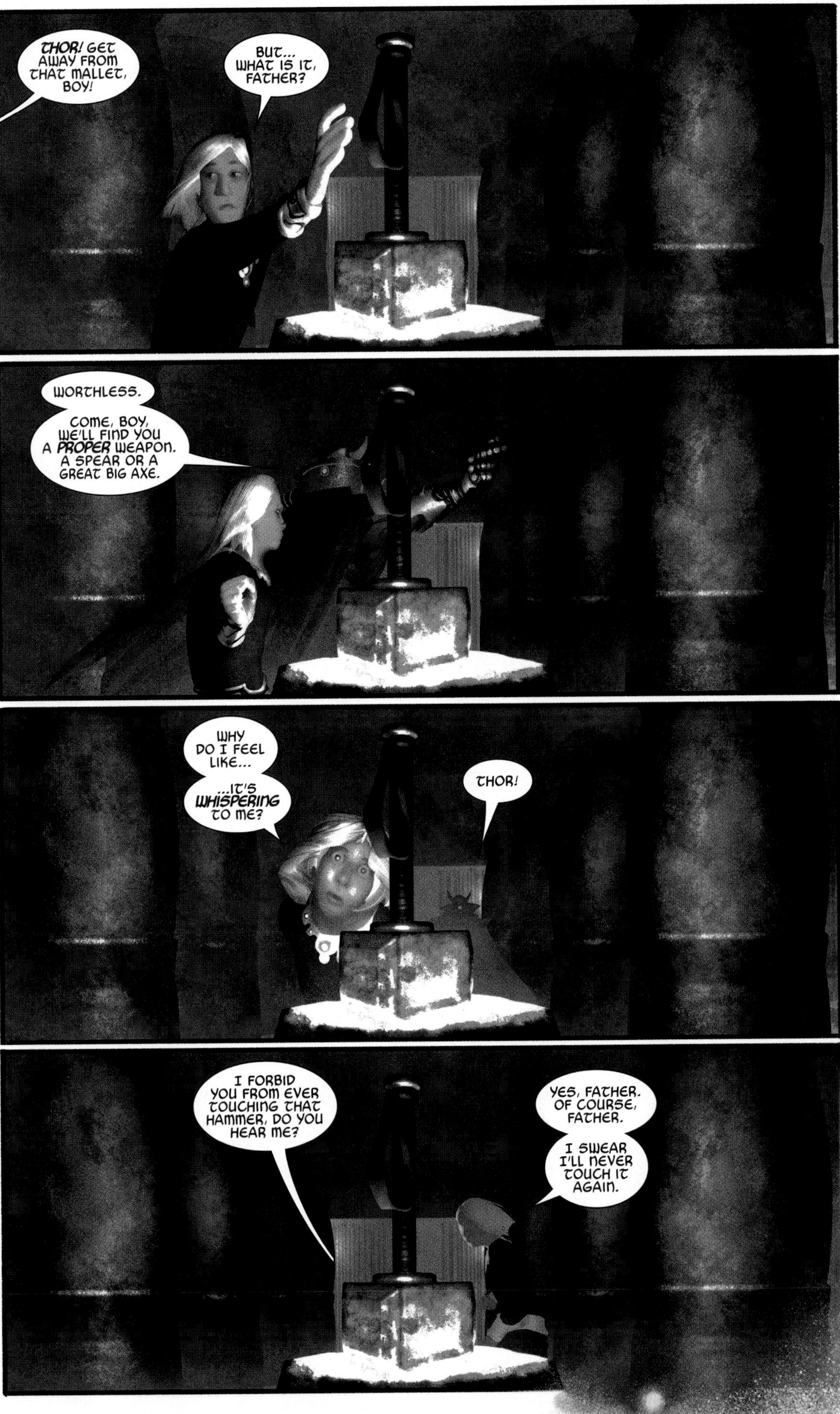
THOR! GET AWAY FROM THAT MALLET, BOY!
BUT... WHAT IS IT, FATHER?
WORTHLESS.
COME, BOY, WE'LL FIND YOU A PROPER WEAPON. A SPEAR OR A GREAT BIG AXE.
WHY DO I FEEL LIKE...
...IT'S WHISPERING TO ME?
THOR!
I FORBID YOU FROM EVER TOUCHING THAT HAMMER, DO YOU HEAR ME?
YES, FATHER. OF COURSE, FATHER.
I SWEAR I'LL NEVER TOUCH IT AGAIN.

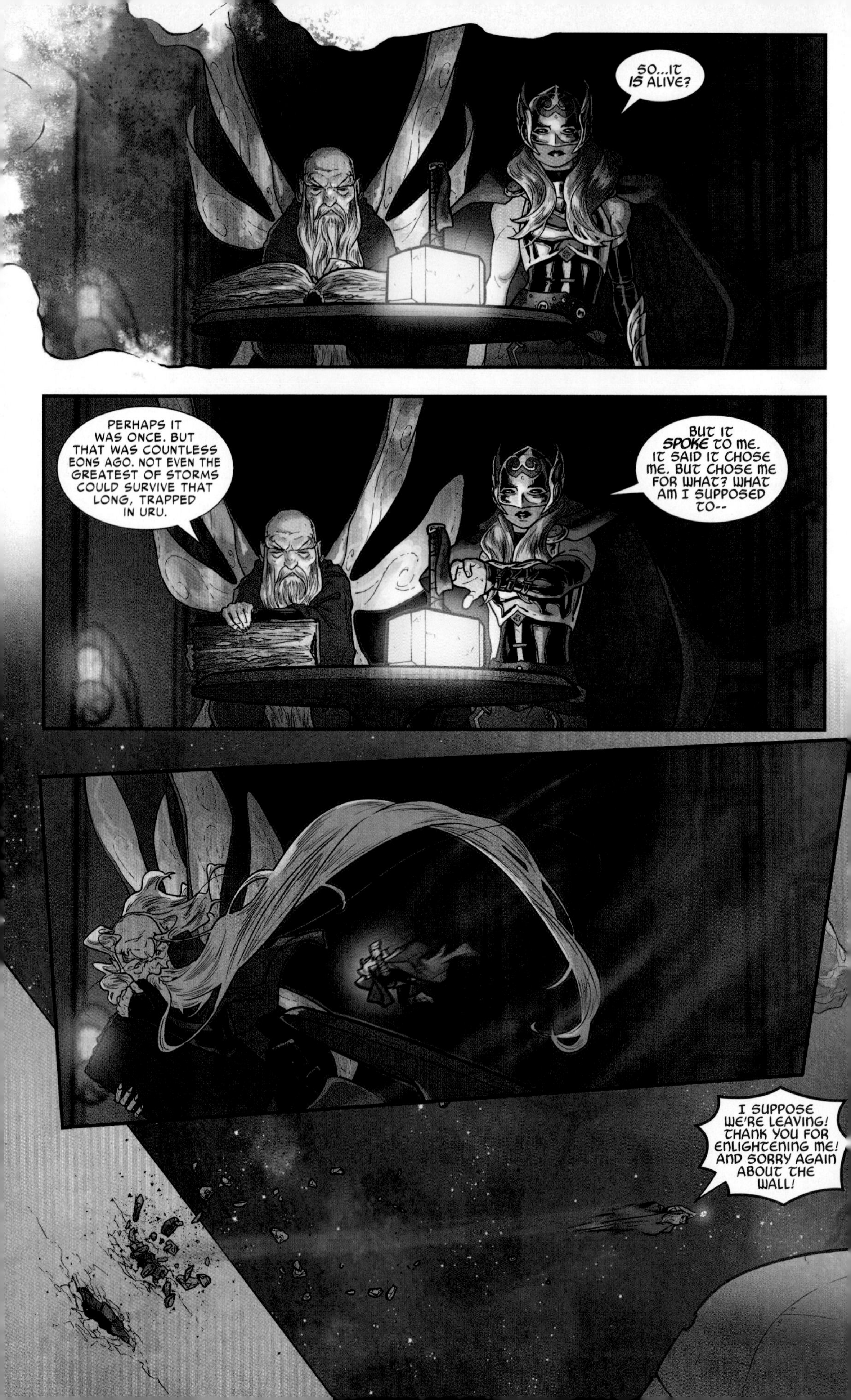
SO...IT *IS* ALIVE?
PERHAPS IT WAS ONCE. BUT THAT WAS COUNTLESS EONS AGO. NOT EVEN THE GREATEST OF STORMS COULD SURVIVE THAT LONG, TRAPPED IN URU.
BUT IT *SPOKE* TO ME. IT SAID IT CHOSE ME. BUT CHOSE ME FOR WHAT? WHAT AM I SUPPOSED TO--
I SUPPOSE WE'RE LEAVING! THANK YOU FOR ENLIGHTENING ME! AND SORRY AGAIN ABOUT THE WALL!

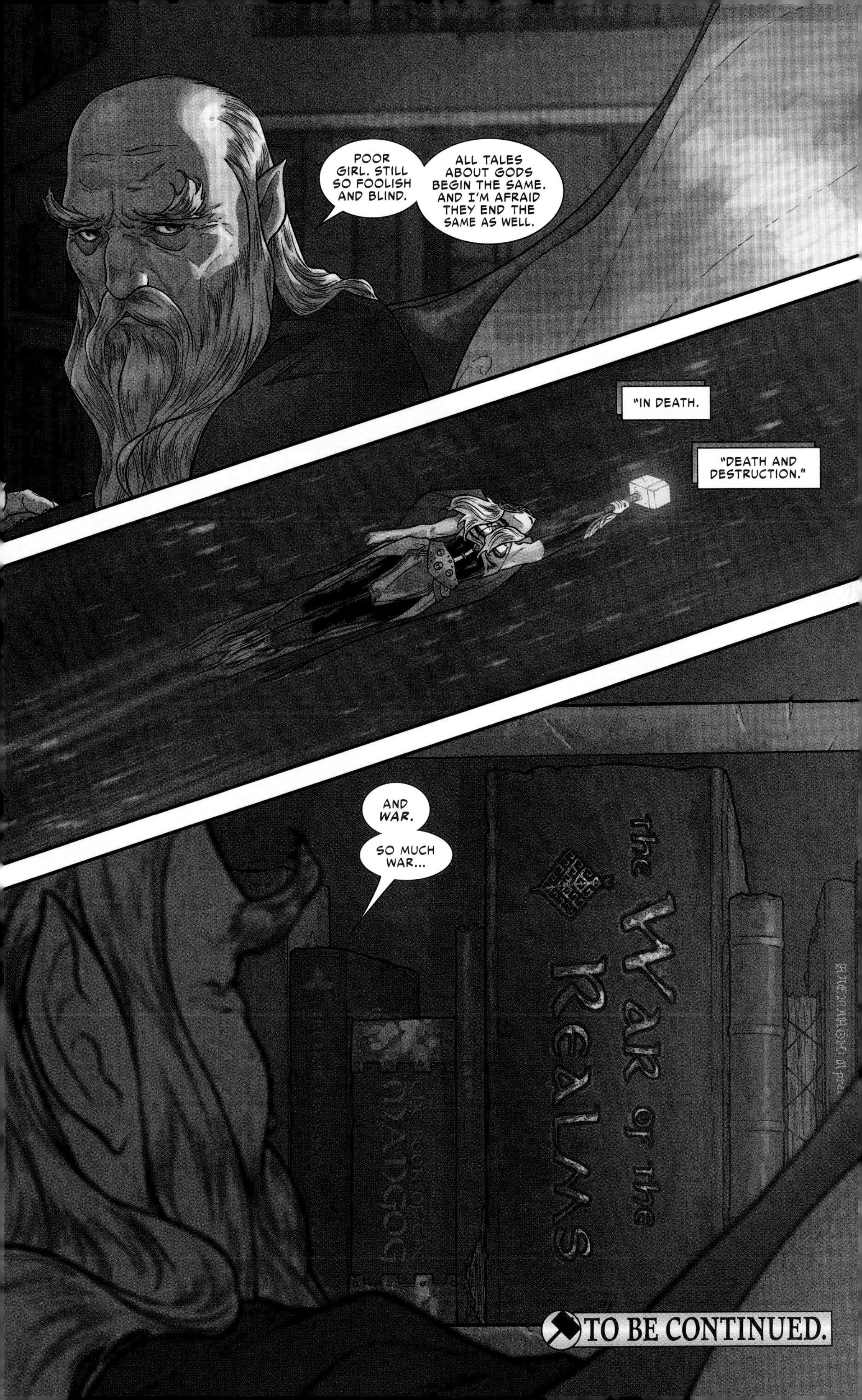
POOR GIRL. STILL SO FOOLISH AND BLIND.
ALL TALES ABOUT GODS BEGIN THE SAME. AND I'M AFRAID THEY END THE SAME AS WELL.
"IN DEATH.
"DEATH AND DESTRUCTION."
AND WAR.
SO MUCH WAR...
the War of the Realms
TO BE CONTINUED.

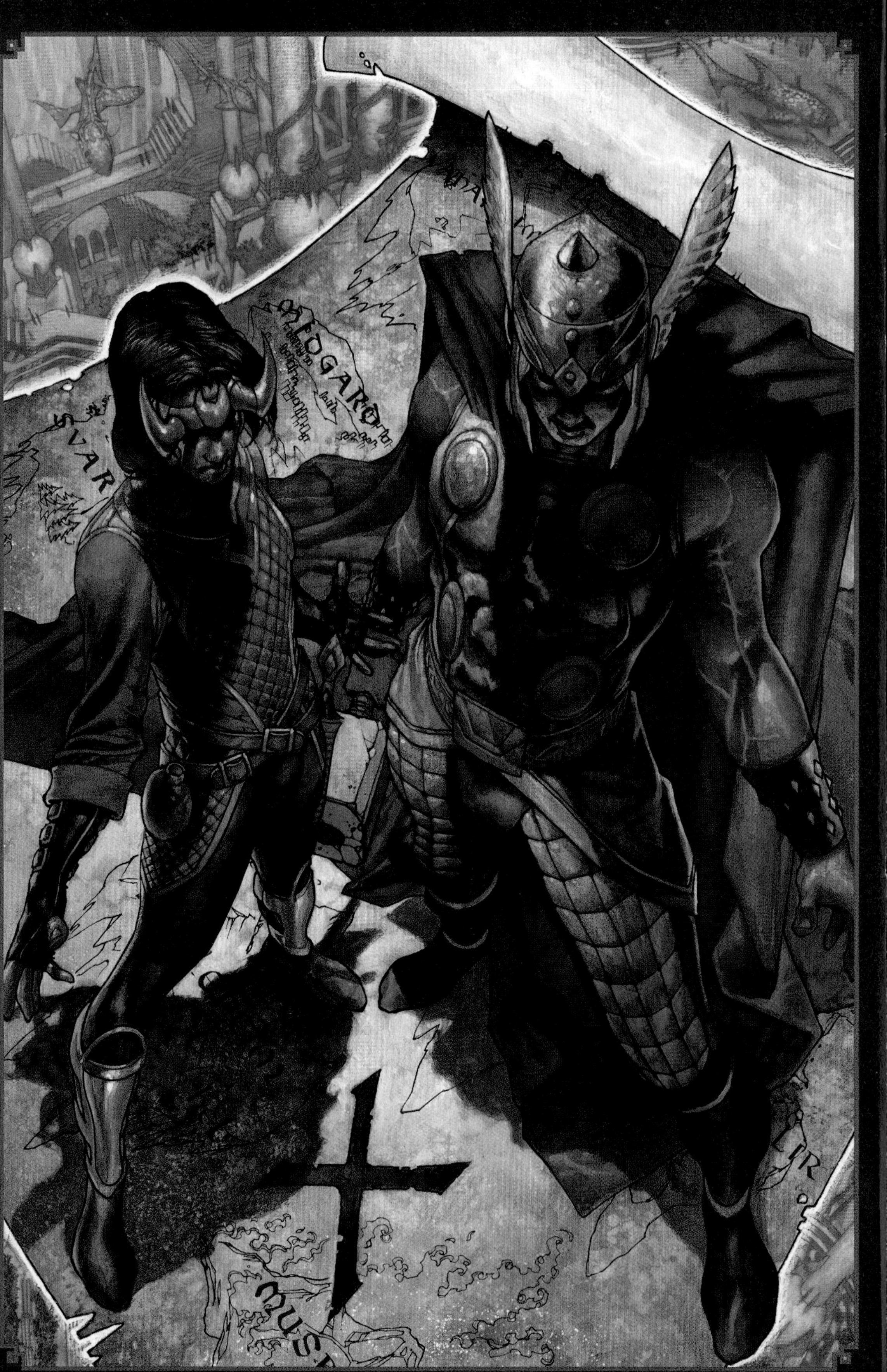
SVAR

ORIGINAL SIN #5.1

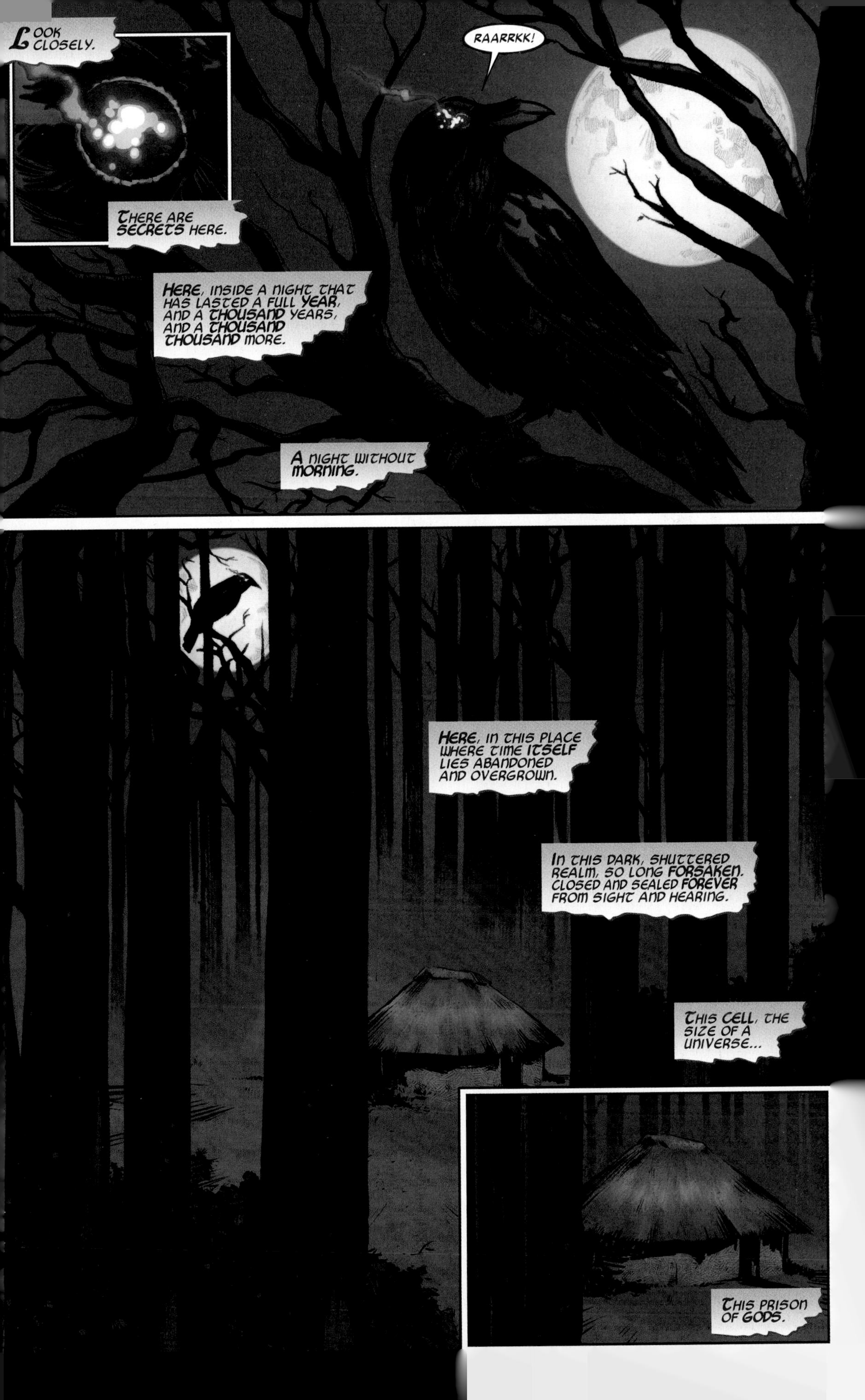
LOOK CLOSELY.
RAARRKK!
THERE ARE SECRETS HERE.
HERE, INSIDE A NIGHT THAT HAS LASTED A FULL YEAR, AND A THOUSAND YEARS, AND A THOUSAND THOUSAND MORE.
A NIGHT WITHOUT MORNING.
HERE, IN THIS PLACE WHERE TIME ITSELF LIES ABANDONED AND OVERGROWN.
IN THIS DARK, SHUTTERED REALM, SO LONG FORSAKEN. CLOSED AND SEALED FOREVER FROM SIGHT AND HEARING.
THIS CELL, THE SIZE OF A UNIVERSE...
THIS PRISON OF GODS.

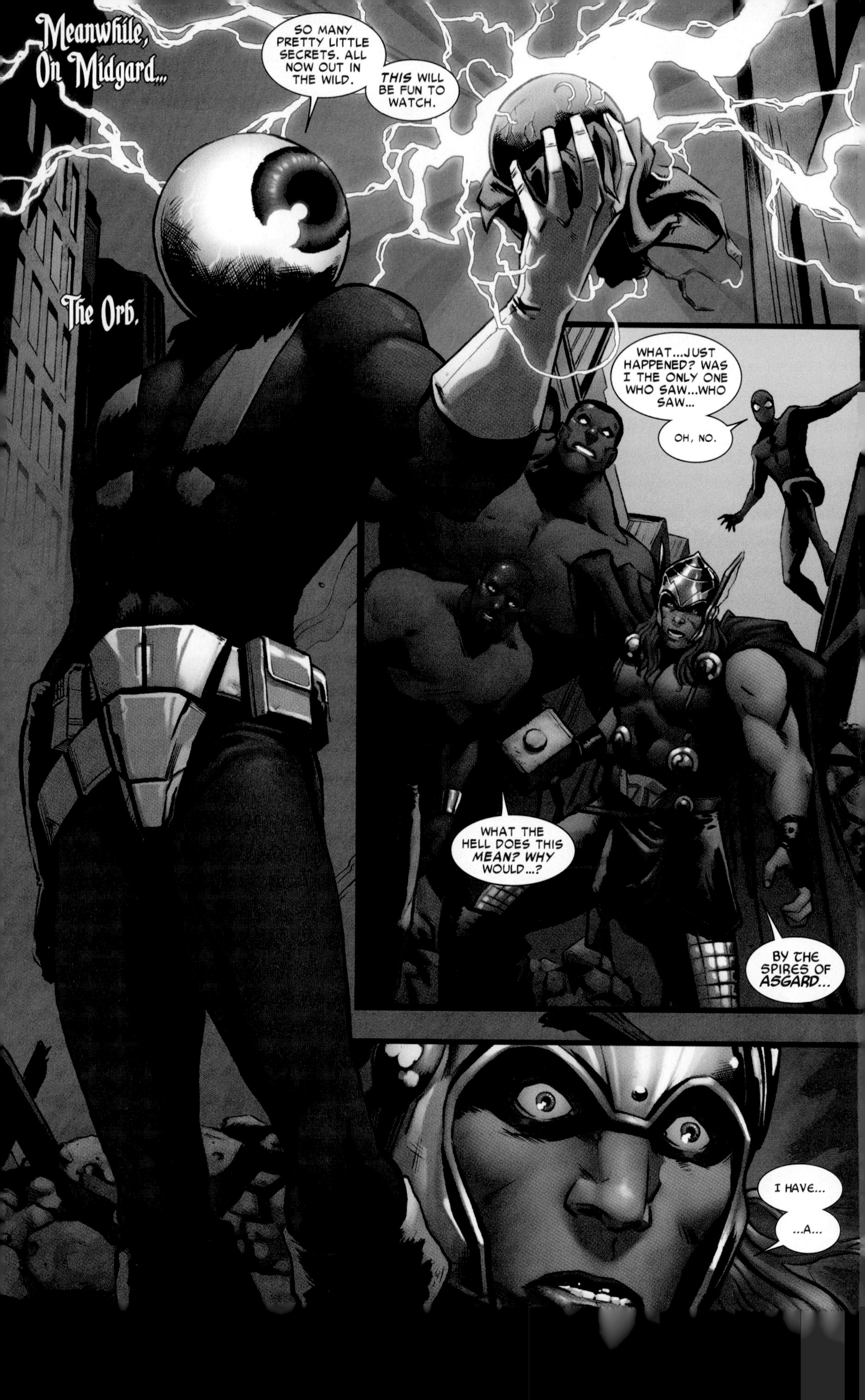
Meanwhile, On Midgard...
SO MANY PRETTY LITTLE SECRETS. ALL NOW OUT IN THE WILD.
THIS WILL BE FUN TO WATCH.
The Orb.
WHAT...JUST HAPPENED? WAS I THE ONLY ONE WHO SAW...WHO SAW...
OH, NO.
WHAT THE HELL DOES THIS MEAN? WHY WOULD...?
BY THE SPIRES OF ASGARD...
I HAVE...
...A...

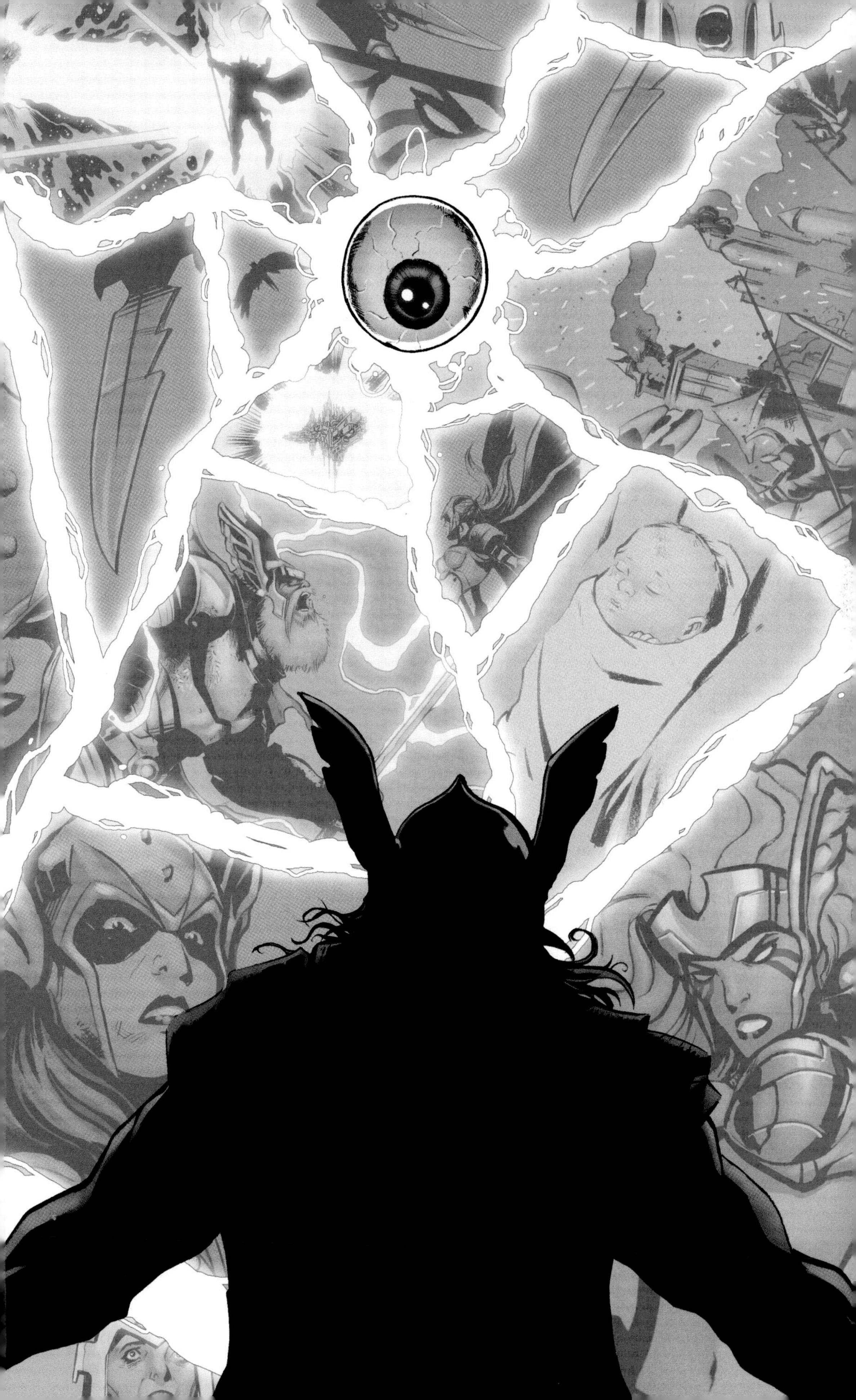

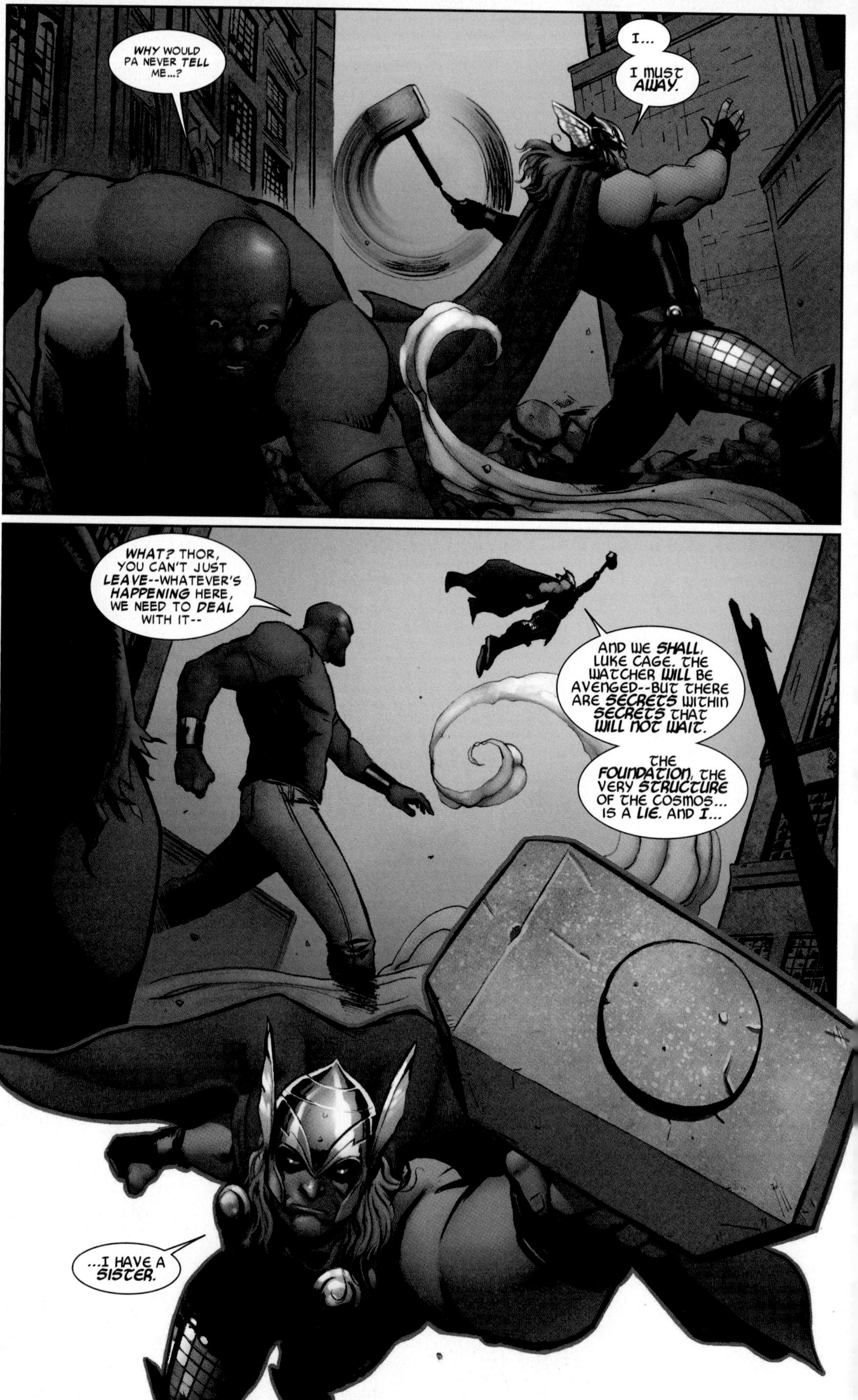

WHY WOULD PA NEVER TELL ME...?
I...
I MUST AWAY.
WHAT? THOR, YOU CAN'T JUST LEAVE--WHATEVER'S HAPPENING HERE, WE NEED TO DEAL WITH IT--
AND WE SHALL, LUKE CAGE. THE WATCHER WILL BE AVENGED--BUT THERE ARE SECRETS WITHIN SECRETS THAT WILL NOT WAIT.
THE FOUNDATION, THE VERY STRUCTURE OF THE COSMOS... IS A LIE. AND I...
...I HAVE A SISTER.

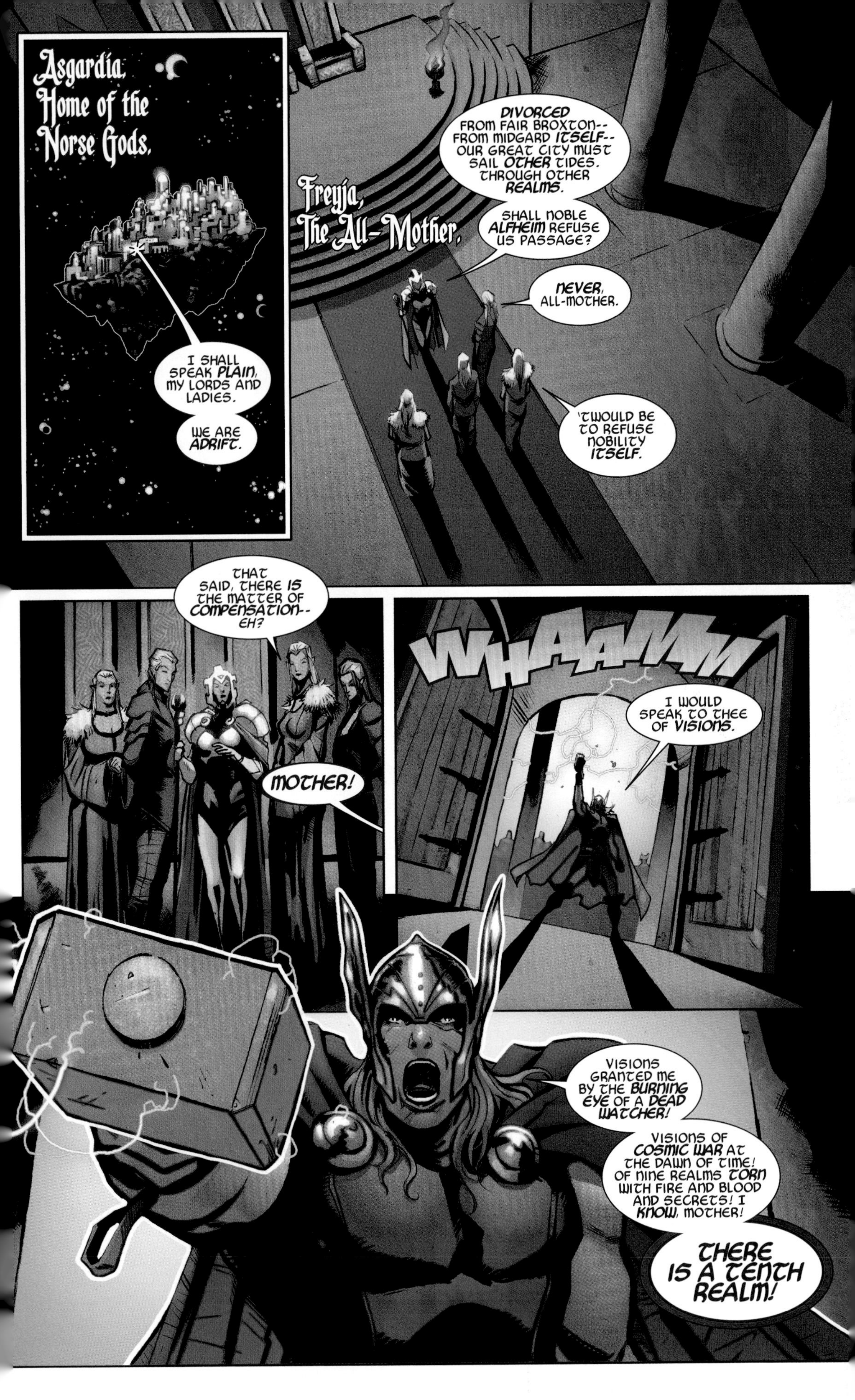
Asgardia. Home of the Norse Gods.
I SHALL SPEAK PLAIN, MY LORDS AND LADIES.
WE ARE ADRIFT.
Freyja, The All-Mother.
DIVORCED FROM FAIR BROXTON-- FROM MIDGARD ITSELF-- OUR GREAT CITY MUST SAIL OTHER TIDES. THROUGH OTHER REALMS.
SHALL NOBLE ALFHEIM REFUSE US PASSAGE?
NEVER, ALL-MOTHER.
'TWOULD BE TO REFUSE NOBILITY ITSELF.
THAT SAID, THERE IS THE MATTER OF COMPENSATION-- EH?
MOTHER!
WHAAMM
I WOULD SPEAK TO THEE OF VISIONS.
VISIONS GRANTED ME BY THE BURNING EYE OF A DEAD WATCHER!
VISIONS OF COSMIC WAR AT THE DAWN OF TIME! OF NINE REALMS TORN WITH FIRE AND BLOOD AND SECRETS! I KNOW, MOTHER!
THERE IS A TENTH REALM!

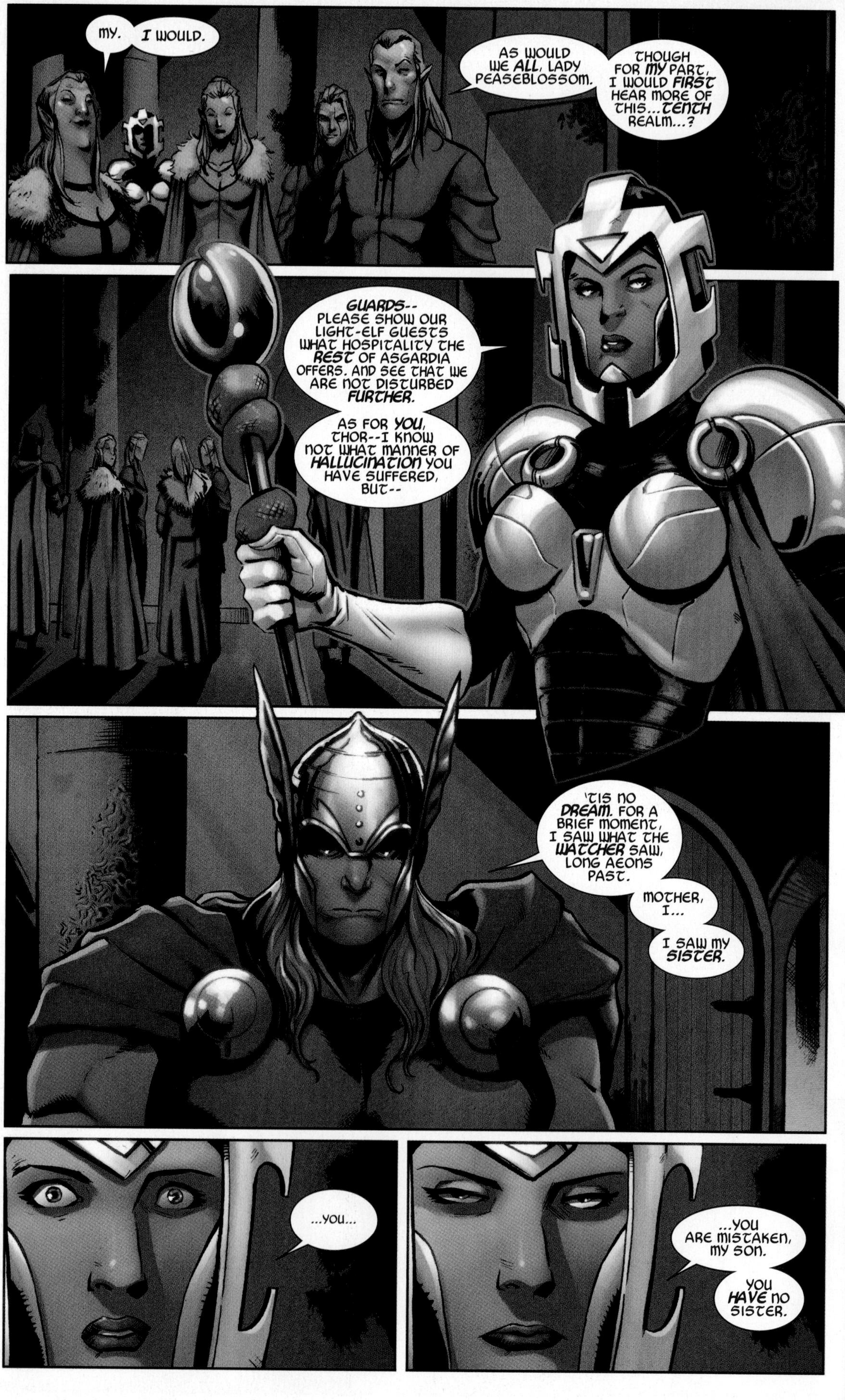
my.
I WOULD.
AS WOULD WE ALL, LADY PEASEBLOSSOM.
THOUGH FOR MY PART, I WOULD FIRST HEAR MORE OF THIS...TENTH REALM...?
GUARDS-- PLEASE SHOW OUR LIGHT-ELF GUESTS WHAT HOSPITALITY THE REST OF ASGARDIA OFFERS. AND SEE THAT WE ARE NOT DISTURBED FURTHER.
AS FOR YOU, THOR--I KNOW NOT WHAT MANNER OF HALLUCINATION YOU HAVE SUFFERED, BUT--
'TIS NO DREAM. FOR A BRIEF MOMENT, I SAW WHAT THE WATCHER SAW, LONG AEONS PAST.
MOTHER, I...
I SAW MY SISTER.
...YOU...
...YOU ARE MISTAKEN, MY SON.
YOU HAVE NO SISTER.

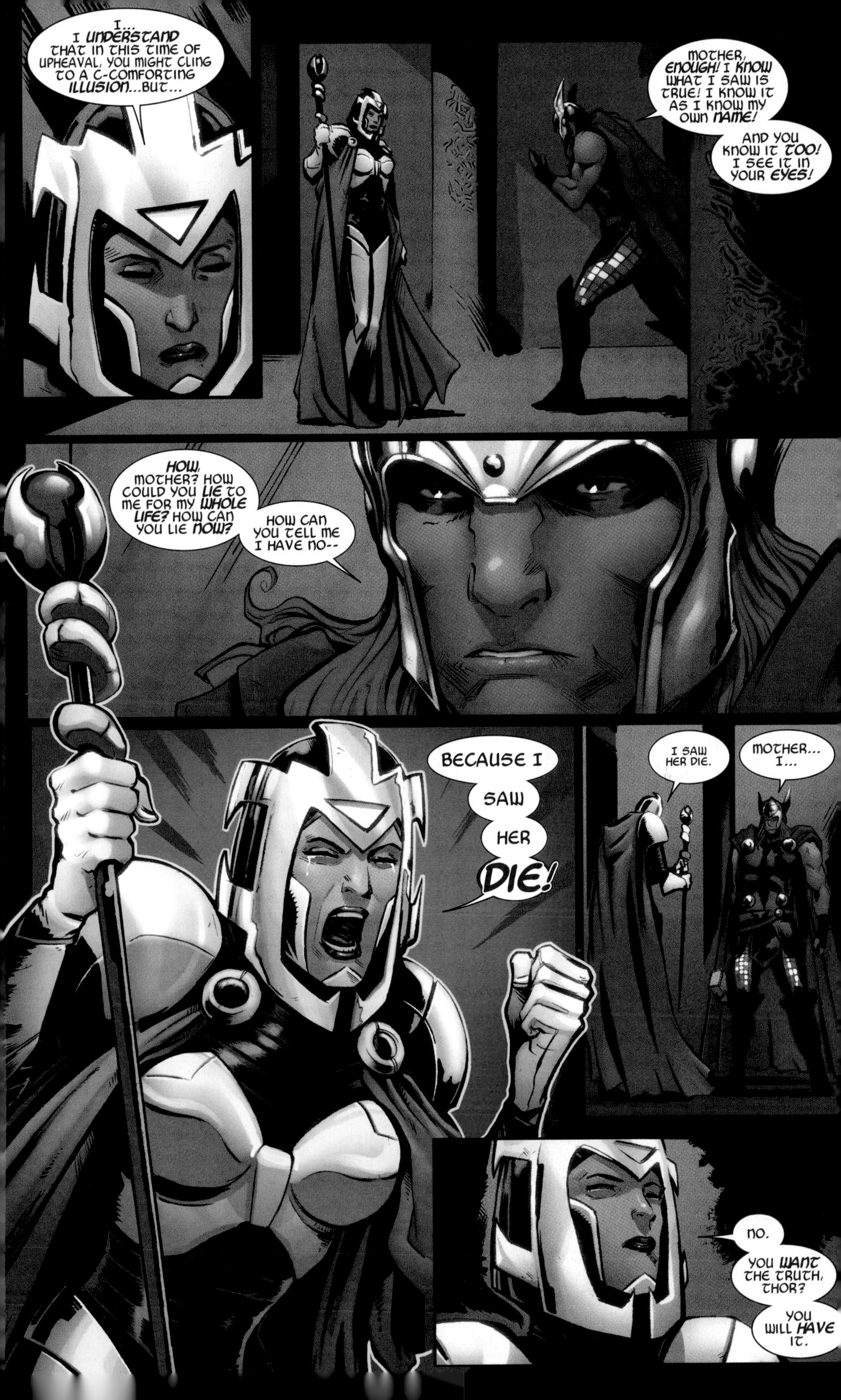
I... I UNDERSTAND THAT IN THIS TIME OF UPHEAVAL, YOU MIGHT CLING TO A C-COMFORTING ILLUSION...BUT...
MOTHER, ENOUGH! I KNOW WHAT I SAW IS TRUE! I KNOW IT AS I KNOW MY OWN NAME!
AND YOU KNOW IT TOO! I SEE IT IN YOUR EYES!
HOW, MOTHER? HOW COULD YOU LIE TO ME FOR MY WHOLE LIFE? HOW CAN YOU LIE NOW?
HOW CAN YOU TELL ME I HAVE NO--
BECAUSE I SAW HER DIE!
I SAW HER DIE.
MOTHER... I...
NO.
YOU WANT THE TRUTH, THOR?
YOU WILL HAVE IT.

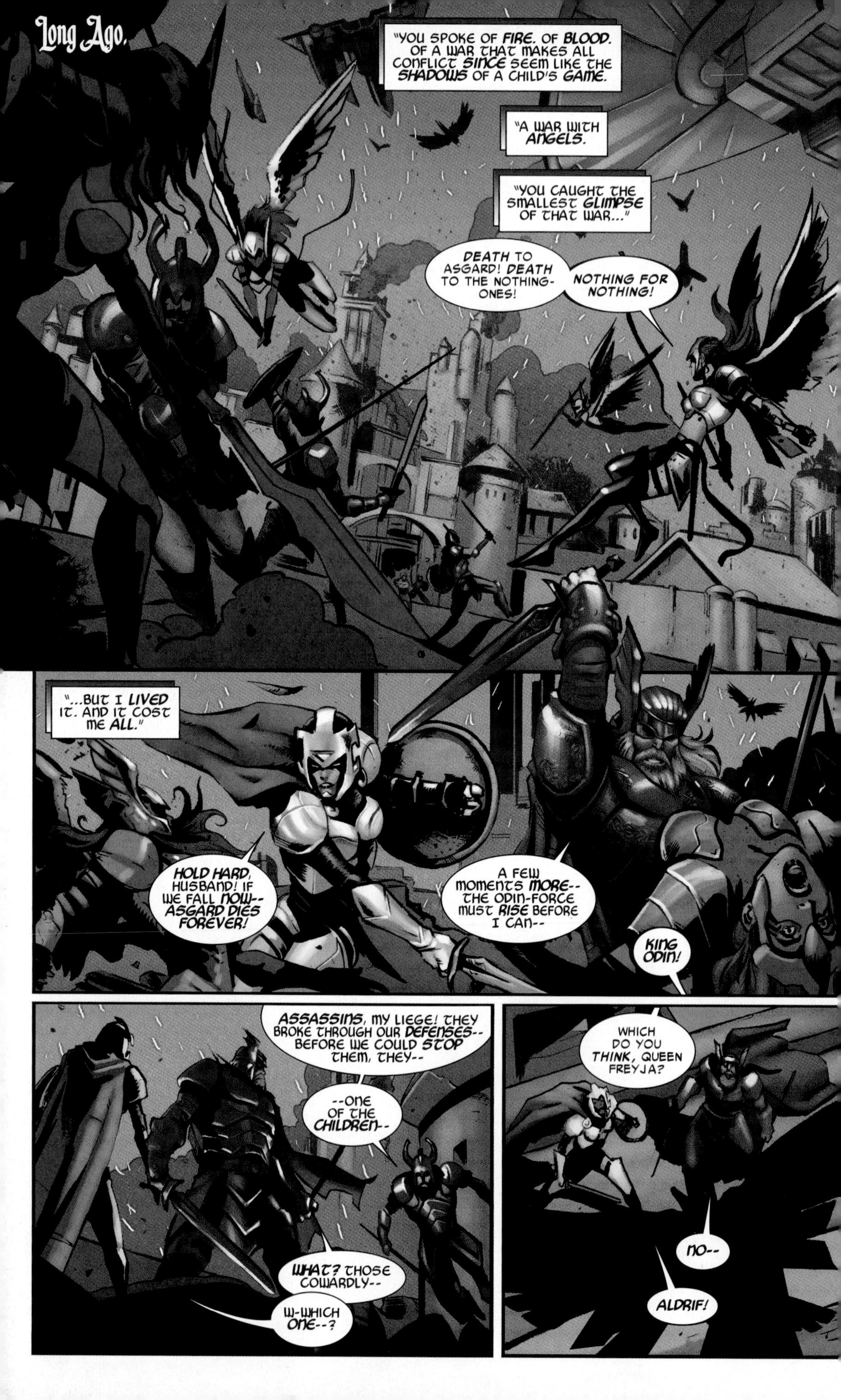

Long Ago.
"YOU SPOKE OF FIRE. OF BLOOD. OF A WAR THAT MAKES ALL CONFLICT SINCE SEEM LIKE THE SHADOWS OF A CHILD'S GAME.
"A WAR WITH ANGELS.
"YOU CAUGHT THE SMALLEST GLIMPSE OF THAT WAR..."
DEATH TO ASGARD! DEATH TO THE NOTHING-ONES!
NOTHING FOR NOTHING!
"...BUT I LIVED IT. AND IT COST ME ALL."
HOLD HARD, HUSBAND! IF WE FALL NOW-- ASGARD DIES FOREVER!
A FEW MOMENTS MORE-- THE ODIN-FORCE MUST RISE BEFORE I CAN--
KING ODIN!
ASSASSINS, MY LIEGE! THEY BROKE THROUGH OUR DEFENSES-- BEFORE WE COULD STOP THEM, THEY--
--ONE OF THE CHILDREN--
WHAT? THOSE COWARDLY--
W-WHICH ONE--?
WHICH DO YOU THINK, QUEEN FREYJA?
NO--
ALDRIF!

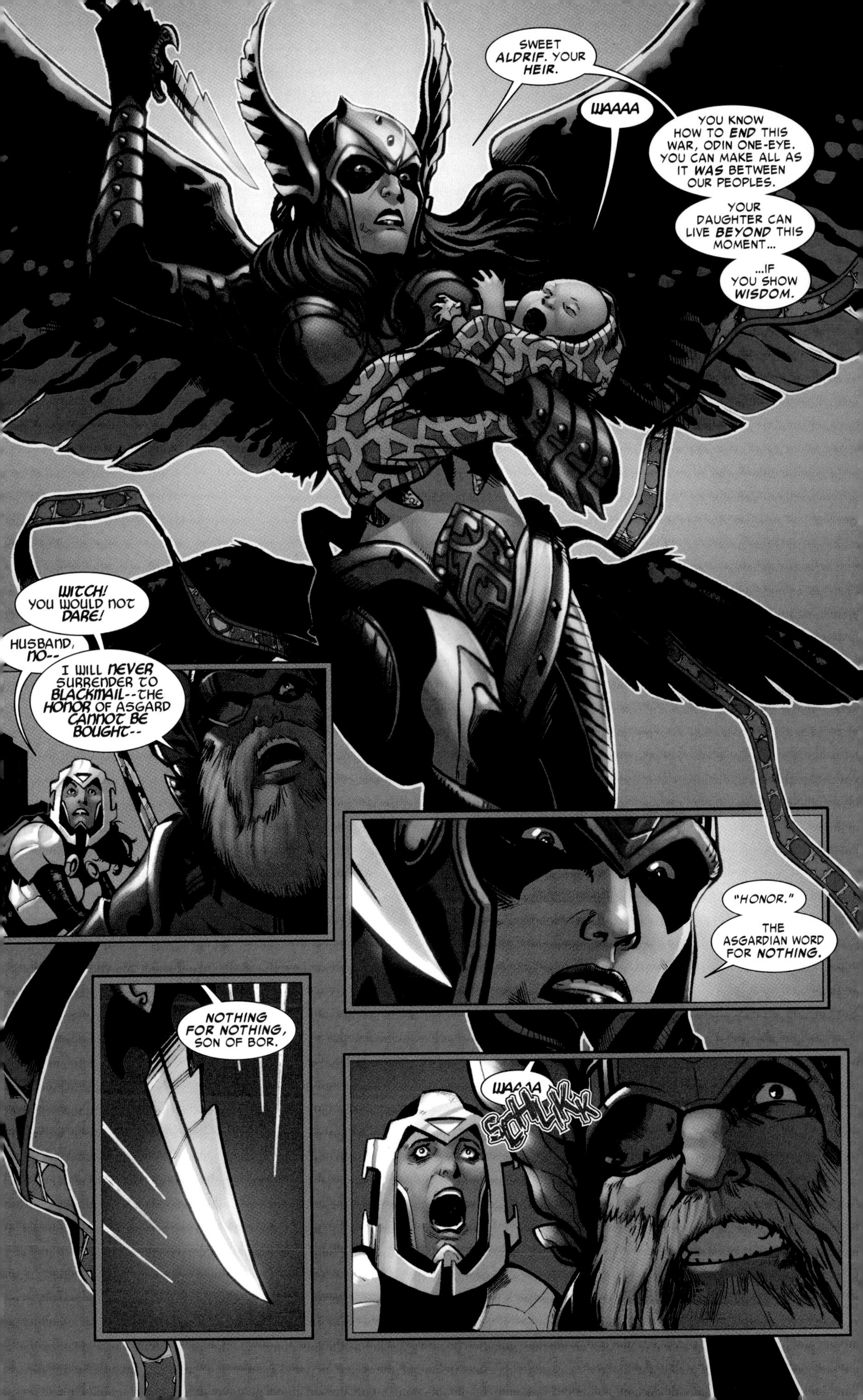
SWEET ALDRIF. YOUR HEIR.
WAAAA
YOU KNOW HOW TO END THIS WAR, ODIN ONE-EYE. YOU CAN MAKE ALL AS IT WAS BETWEEN OUR PEOPLES.
YOUR DAUGHTER CAN LIVE BEYOND THIS MOMENT...
...IF YOU SHOW WISDOM.
WITCH! YOU WOULD NOT DARE!
HUSBAND, NO--
I WILL NEVER SURRENDER TO BLACKMAIL--THE HONOR OF ASGARD CANNOT BE BOUGHT--
"HONOR."
THE ASGARDIAN WORD FOR NOTHING.
NOTHING FOR NOTHING, SON OF BOR.
WAAAA
SCHUKK

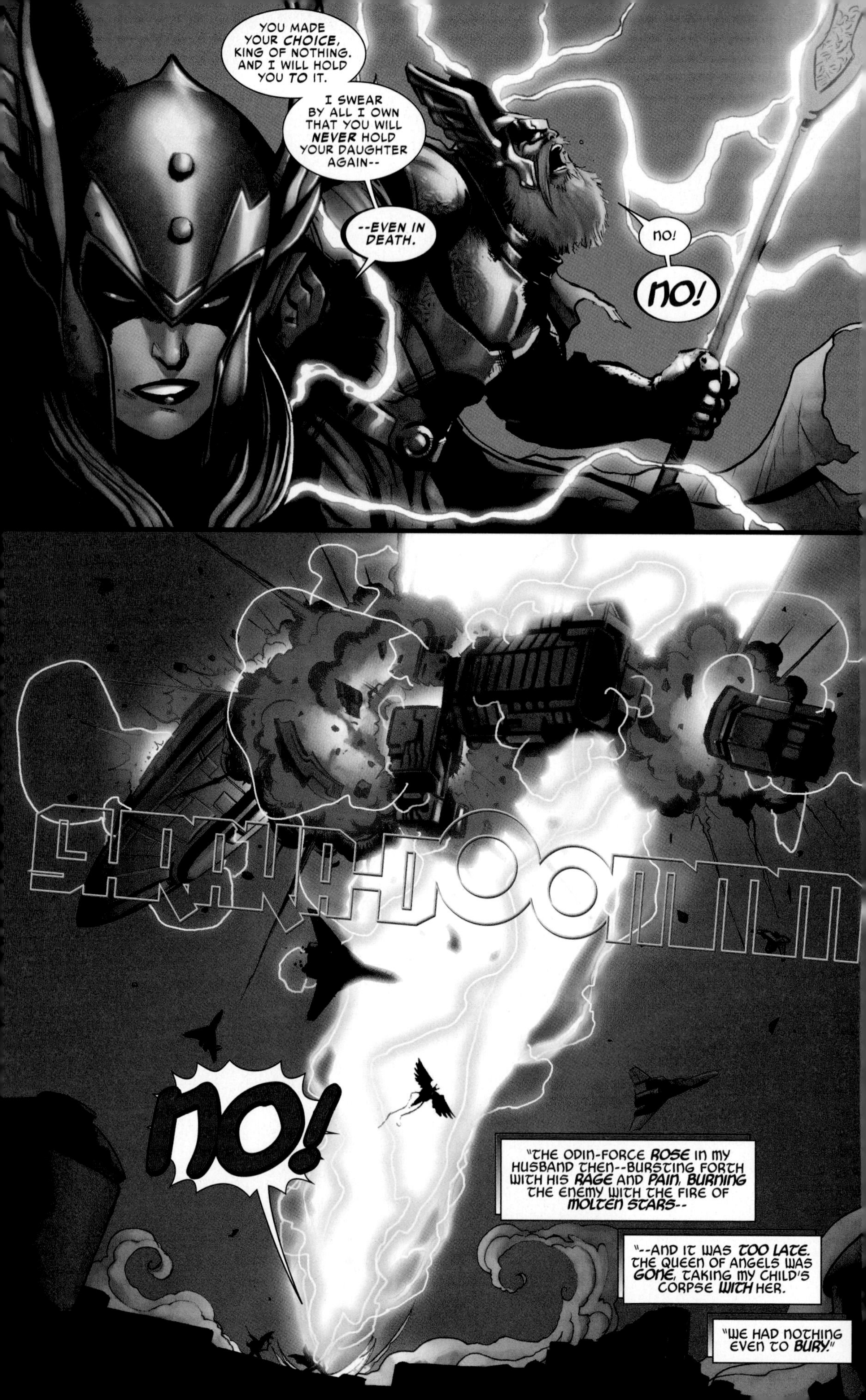
YOU MADE YOUR *CHOICE*, KING OF NOTHING. AND I WILL HOLD YOU *TO* IT.
I SWEAR BY ALL I OWN THAT YOU WILL *NEVER* HOLD YOUR DAUGHTER AGAIN--
--EVEN IN DEATH.
NO!
NO!
NO!
"THE ODIN-FORCE *ROSE* IN MY HUSBAND THEN--BURSTING FORTH WITH HIS *RAGE* AND *PAIN*, *BURNING* THE ENEMY WITH THE FIRE OF *MOLTEN STARS*--
"--AND IT WAS *TOO LATE*. THE QUEEN OF ANGELS WAS *GONE*, TAKING MY CHILD'S CORPSE *WITH* HER.
"WE HAD NOTHING EVEN TO *BURY*."

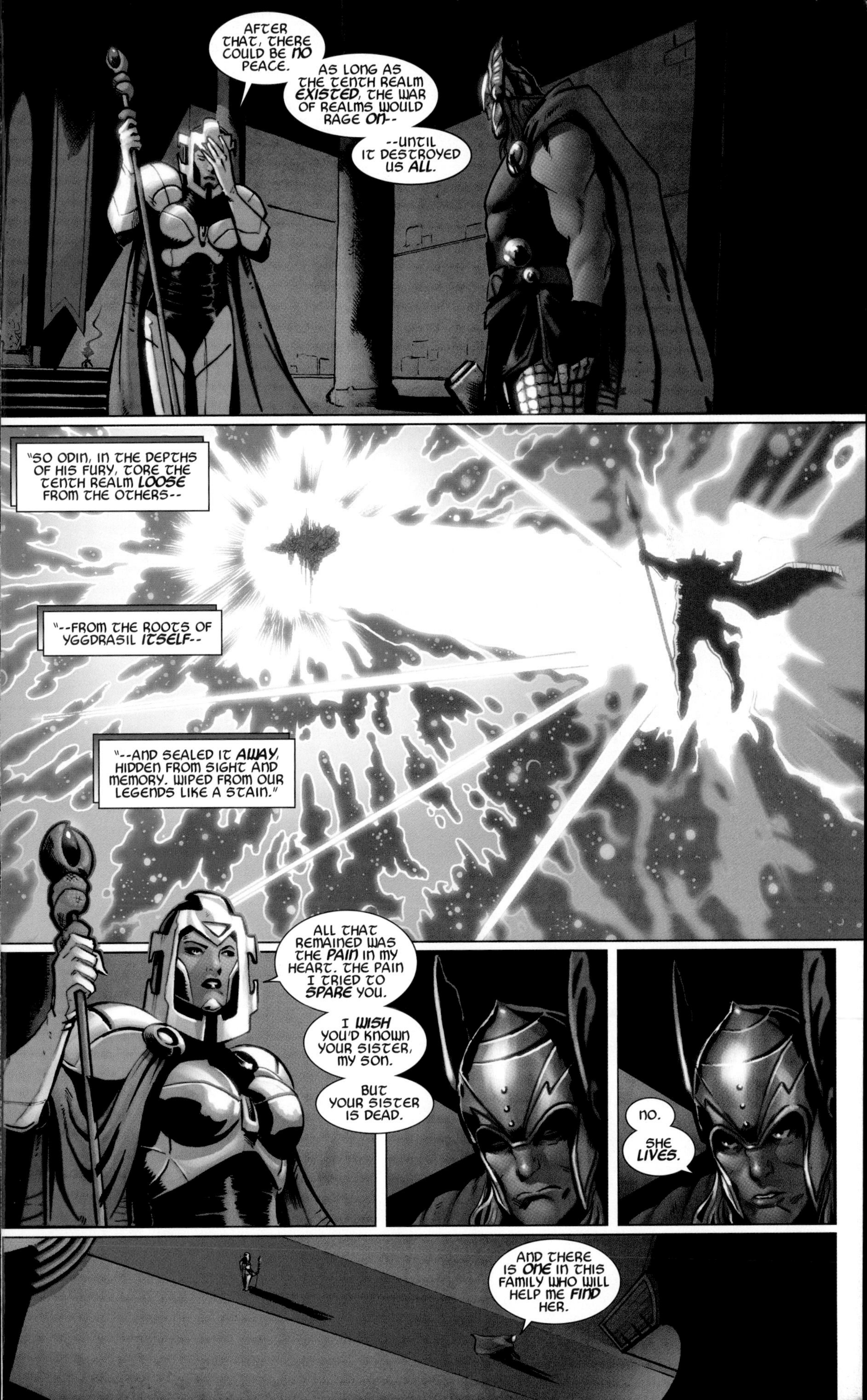
AFTER THAT, THERE COULD BE NO PEACE.
AS LONG AS THE TENTH REALM EXISTED, THE WAR OF REALMS WOULD RAGE ON--
--UNTIL IT DESTROYED US ALL.
"SO ODIN, IN THE DEPTHS OF HIS FURY, TORE THE TENTH REALM LOOSE FROM THE OTHERS--
"--FROM THE ROOTS OF YGGDRASIL ITSELF--
"--AND SEALED IT AWAY, HIDDEN FROM SIGHT AND MEMORY. WIPED FROM OUR LEGENDS LIKE A STAIN."
ALL THAT REMAINED WAS THE PAIN IN MY HEART. THE PAIN I TRIED TO SPARE YOU.
I WISH YOU'D KNOWN YOUR SISTER, MY SON.
BUT YOUR SISTER IS DEAD.
NO.
SHE LIVES.
AND THERE IS ONE IN THIS FAMILY WHO WILL HELP ME FIND HER.

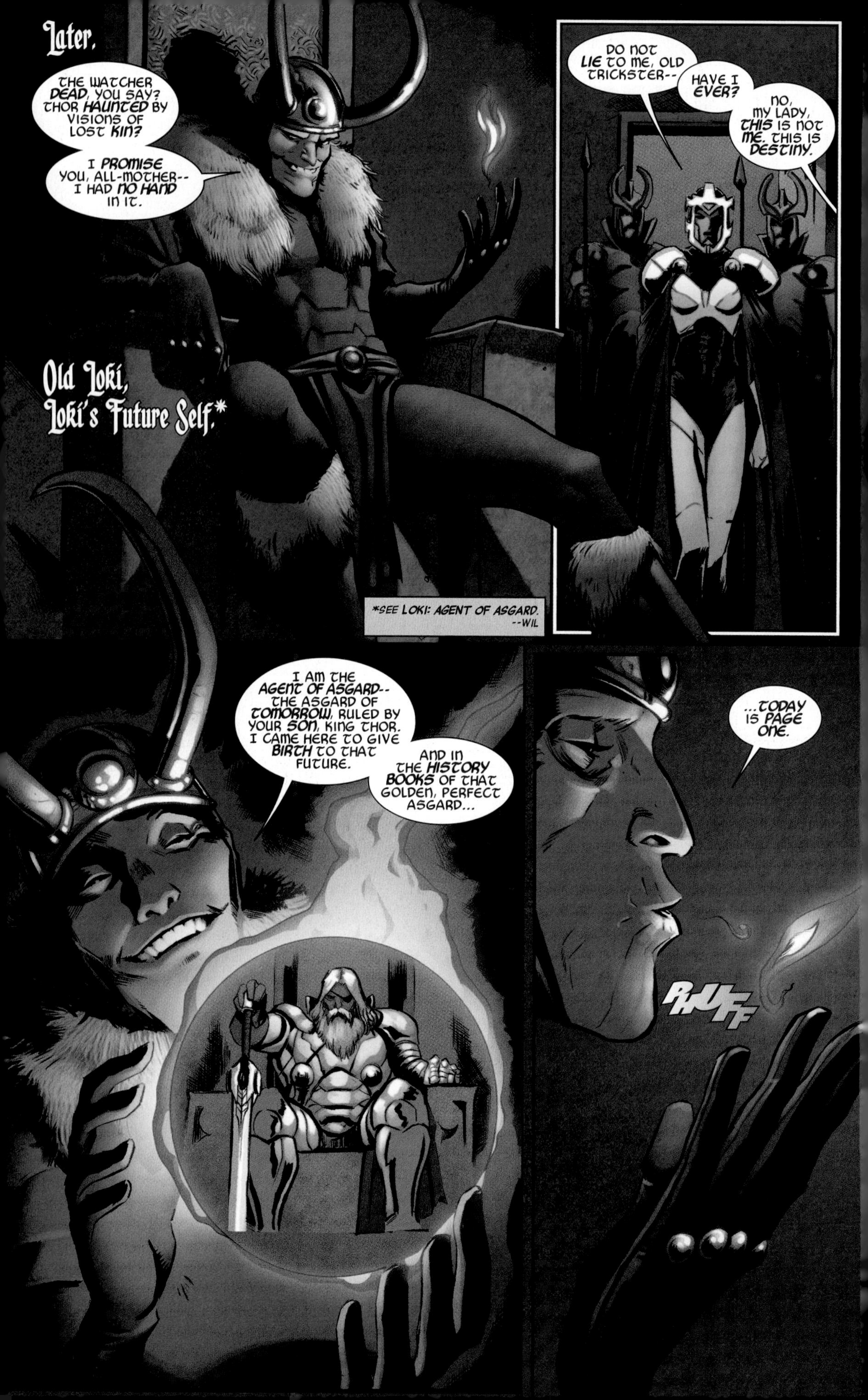
Later.
THE WATCHER DEAD, YOU SAY? THOR HAUNTED BY VISIONS OF LOST KIN?
I PROMISE YOU, ALL-MOTHER-- I HAD NO HAND IN IT.
Old Loki, Loki's Future Self.*
DO NOT LIE TO ME, OLD TRICKSTER--
HAVE I EVER?
NO, MY LADY, THIS IS NOT ME. THIS IS DESTINY.
*SEE LOKI: AGENT OF ASGARD. --WIL
I AM THE AGENT OF ASGARD-- THE ASGARD OF TOMORROW, RULED BY YOUR SON, KING THOR. I CAME HERE TO GIVE BIRTH TO THAT FUTURE.
AND IN THE HISTORY BOOKS OF THAT GOLDEN, PERFECT ASGARD...
...TODAY IS PAGE ONE.
PHUFF

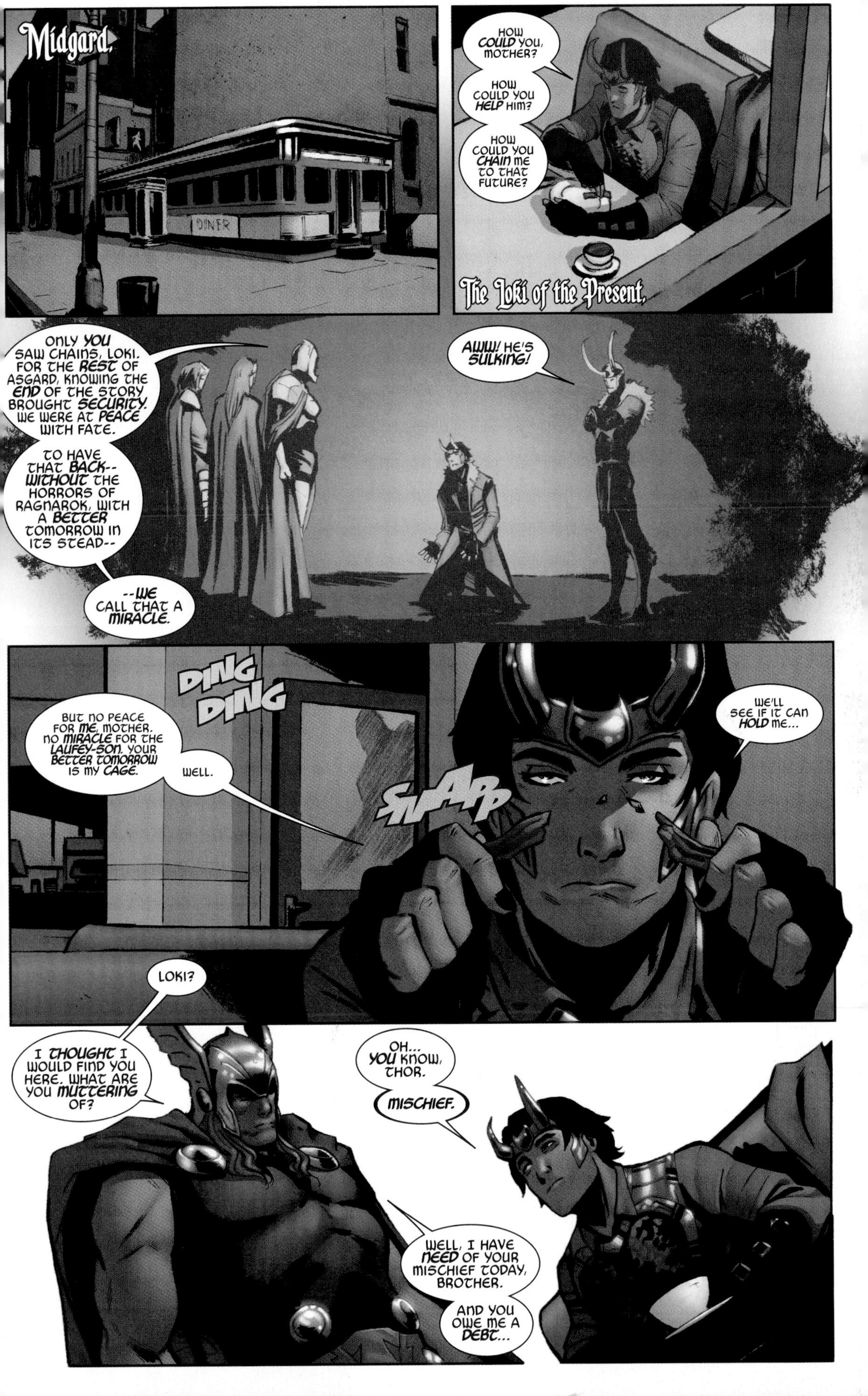
Midgard.
DINER
HOW COULD YOU, MOTHER?
HOW COULD YOU HELP HIM?
HOW COULD YOU CHAIN ME TO THAT FUTURE?
The Loki of the Present.
ONLY YOU SAW CHAINS, LOKI. FOR THE REST OF ASGARD, KNOWING THE END OF THE STORY BROUGHT SECURITY. WE WERE AT PEACE WITH FATE.
TO HAVE THAT BACK--WITHOUT THE HORRORS OF RAGNAROK, WITH A BETTER TOMORROW IN ITS STEAD--
--WE CALL THAT A MIRACLE.
AWW! HE'S SULKING!
DING DING
BUT NO PEACE FOR ME, MOTHER. NO MIRACLE FOR THE LAUFEY-SON. YOUR BETTER TOMORROW IS MY CAGE.
WELL.
SNAP
WE'LL SEE IF IT CAN HOLD ME...
LOKI?
I THOUGHT I WOULD FIND YOU HERE. WHAT ARE YOU MUTTERING OF?
OH... YOU KNOW, THOR.
MISCHIEF.
WELL, I HAVE NEED OF YOUR MISCHIEF TODAY, BROTHER.
AND YOU OWE ME A DEBT...

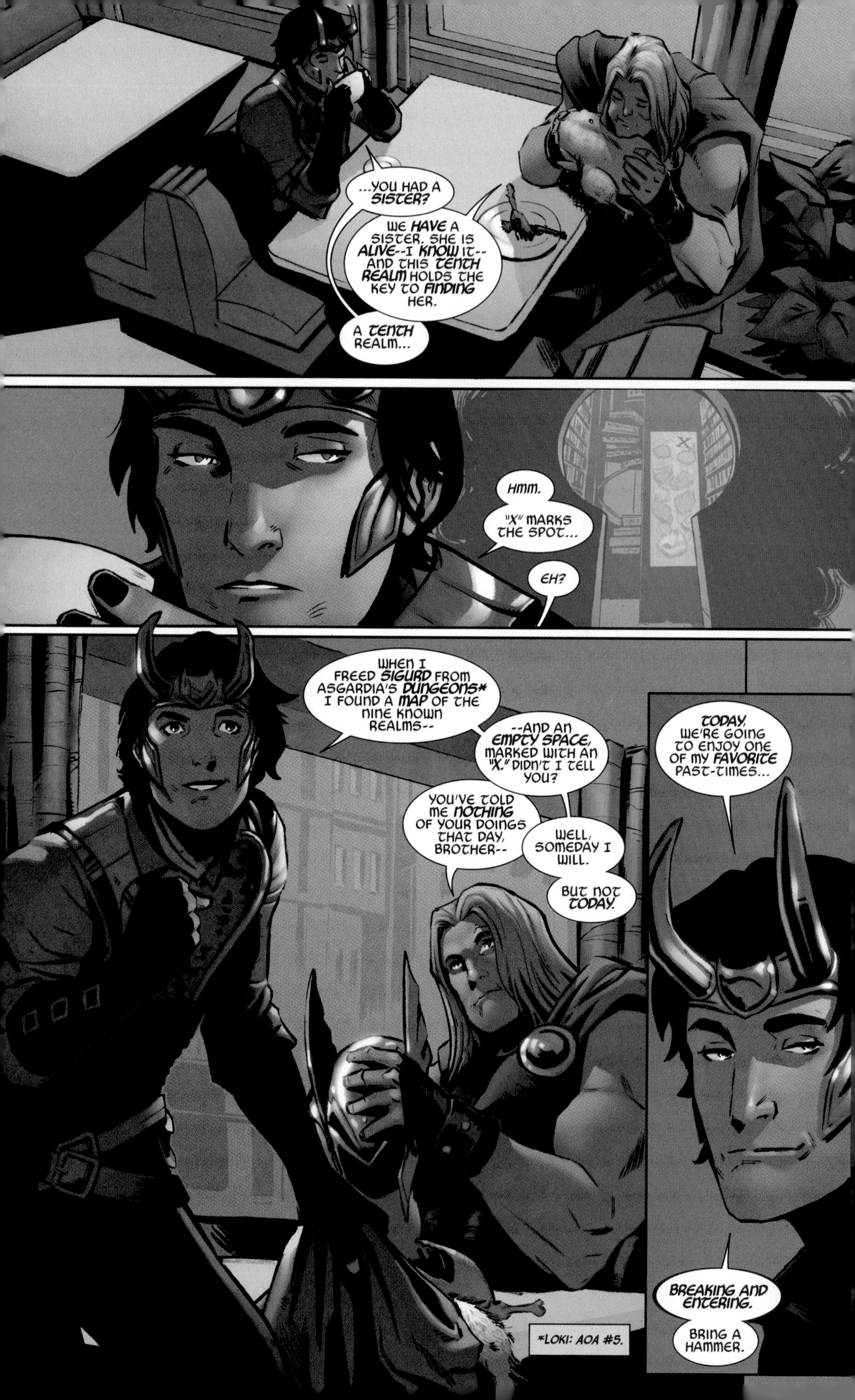
...YOU HAD A SISTER?
WE HAVE A SISTER. SHE IS ALIVE--I KNOW IT--AND THIS TENTH REALM HOLDS THE KEY TO FINDING HER.
A TENTH REALM...
HMM.
"X" MARKS THE SPOT...
EH?
WHEN I FREED SIGURD FROM ASGARDIA'S DUNGEONS* I FOUND A MAP OF THE NINE KNOWN REALMS--
--AND AN EMPTY SPACE, MARKED WITH AN "X." DIDN'T I TELL YOU?
YOU'VE TOLD ME NOTHING OF YOUR DOINGS THAT DAY, BROTHER--
WELL, SOMEDAY I WILL.
BUT NOT TODAY.
TODAY, WE'RE GOING TO ENJOY ONE OF MY FAVORITE PAST-TIMES...
BREAKING AND ENTERING.
BRING A HAMMER.
*LOKI: AOA #5.

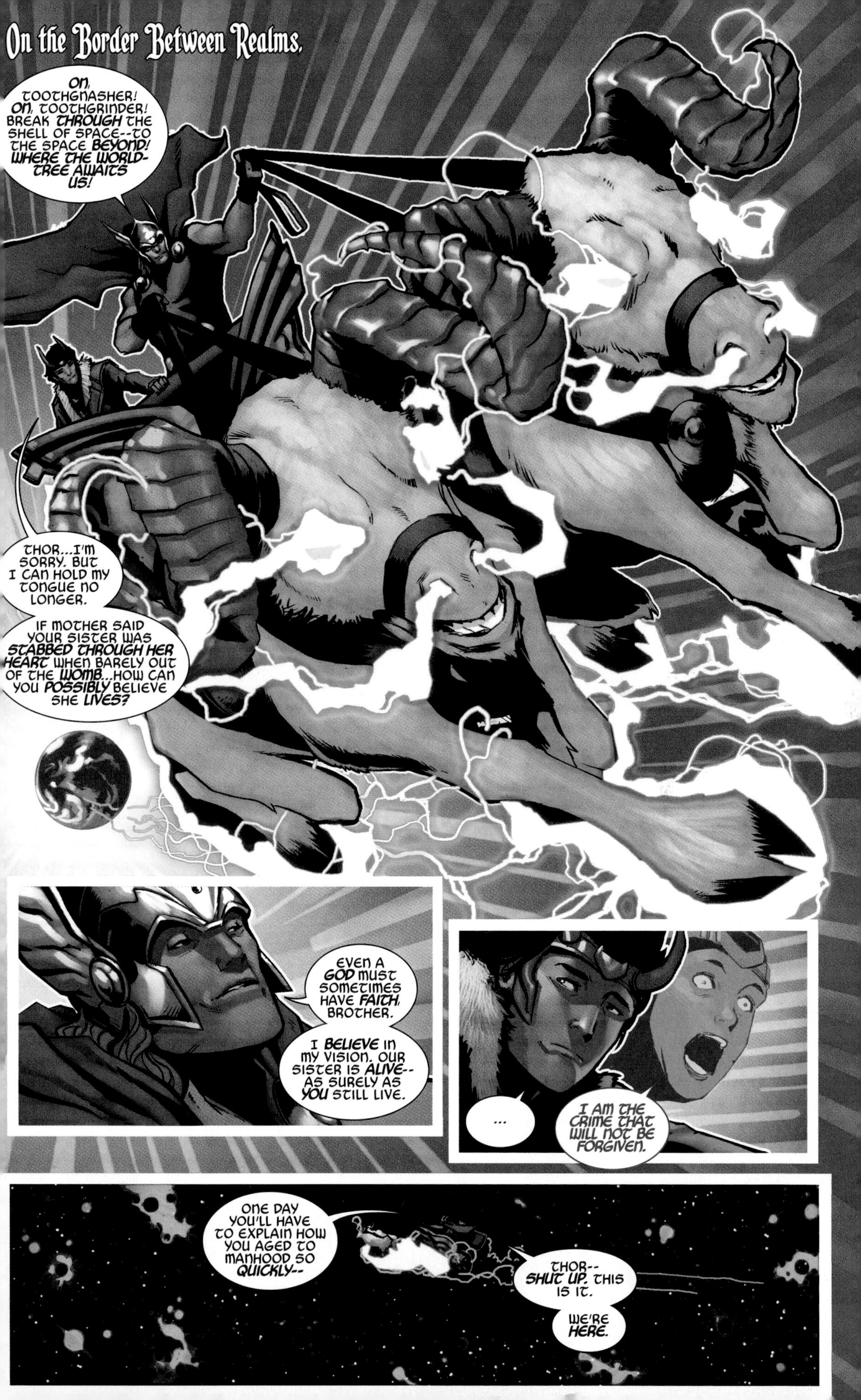
On the Border Between Realms.
ON, TOOTHGNASHER! ON, TOOTHGRINDER! BREAK THROUGH THE SHELL OF SPACE--TO THE SPACE BEYOND! WHERE THE WORLD-TREE AWAITS US!
THOR...I'M SORRY. BUT I CAN HOLD MY TONGUE NO LONGER.
IF MOTHER SAID YOUR SISTER WAS STABBED THROUGH HER HEART WHEN BARELY OUT OF THE WOMB...HOW CAN YOU POSSIBLY BELIEVE SHE LIVES?
EVEN A GOD MUST SOMETIMES HAVE FAITH, BROTHER.
I BELIEVE IN MY VISION. OUR SISTER IS ALIVE-- AS SURELY AS YOU STILL LIVE.
...
I AM THE CRIME THAT WILL NOT BE FORGIVEN.
ONE DAY YOU'LL HAVE TO EXPLAIN HOW YOU AGED TO MANHOOD SO QUICKLY--
THOR-- SHUT UP. THIS IS IT.
WE'RE HERE.

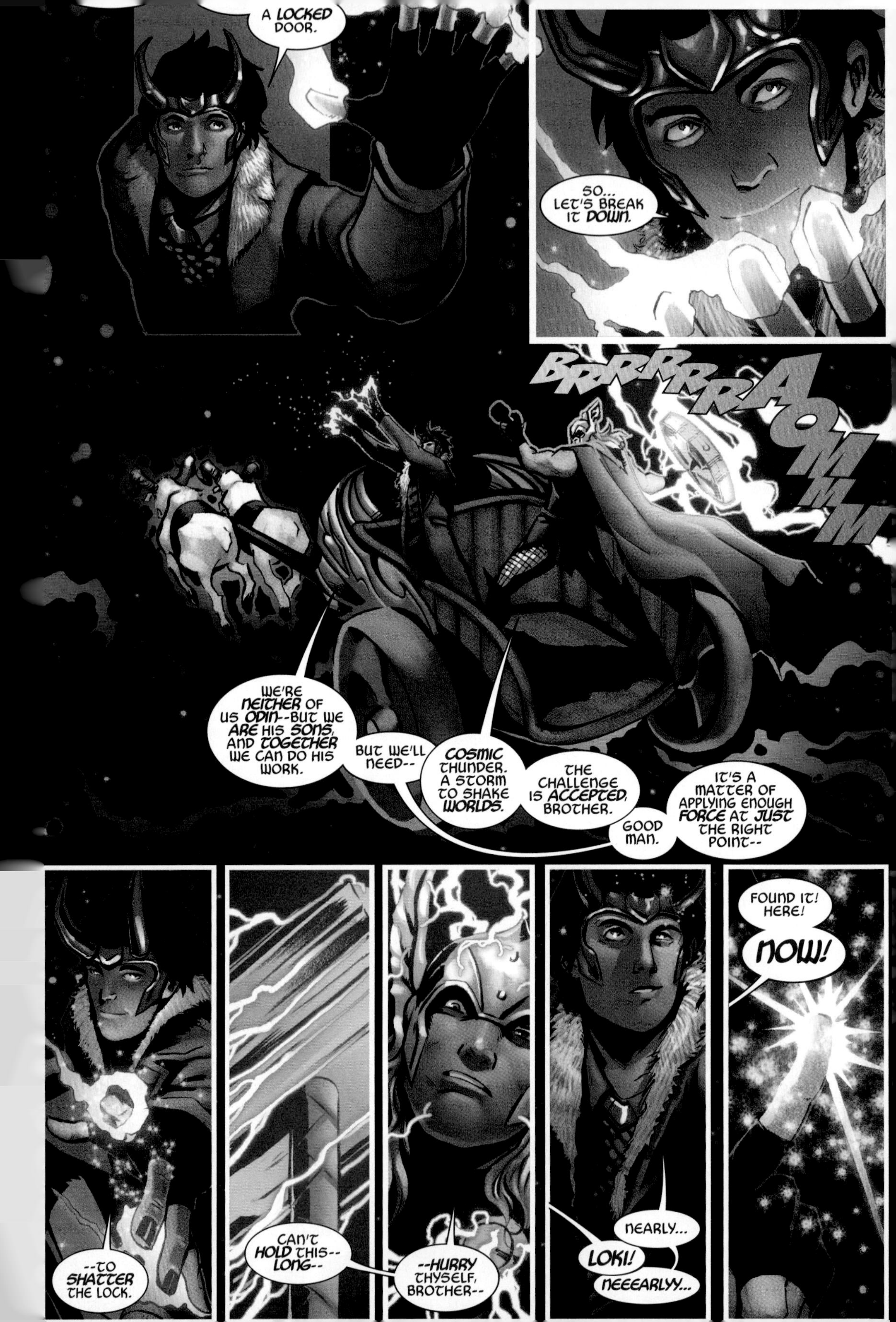

A LOCKED DOOR.
SO... LET'S BREAK IT DOWN.
BRRRRRRAOMMM
WE'RE NEITHER OF US ODIN--BUT WE ARE HIS SONS, AND TOGETHER WE CAN DO HIS WORK.
BUT WE'LL NEED--
COSMIC THUNDER. A STORM TO SHAKE WORLDS.
THE CHALLENGE IS ACCEPTED, BROTHER.
GOOD MAN.
IT'S A MATTER OF APPLYING ENOUGH FORCE AT JUST THE RIGHT POINT--
--TO SHATTER THE LOCK.
CAN'T HOLD THIS-- LONG--
--HURRY THYSELF, BROTHER--
NEARLY...
LOKI!
NEEEARLYY...
FOUND IT! HERE!
NOW!

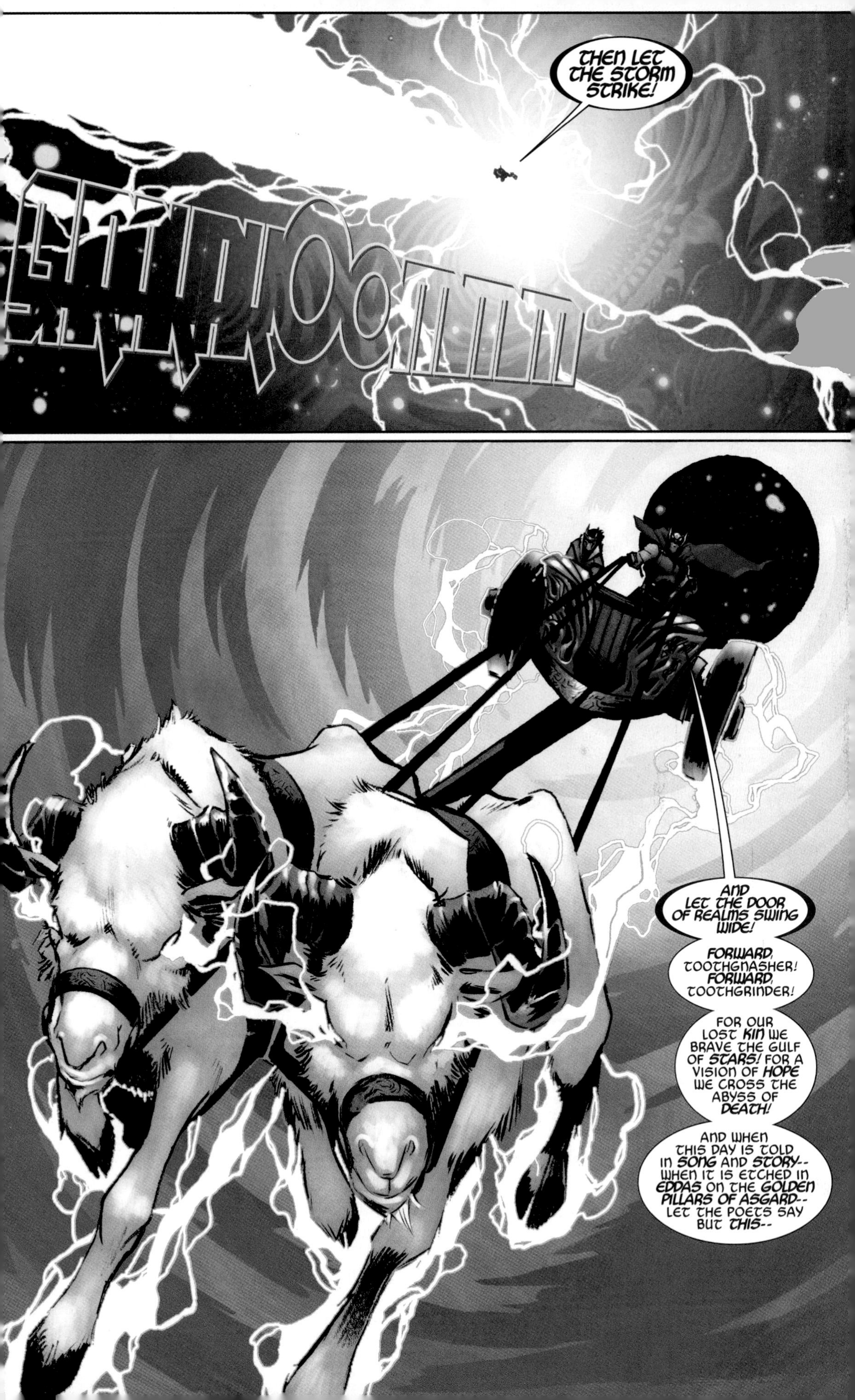
THEN LET THE STORM STRIKE!
AND LET THE DOOR OF REALMS SWING WIDE!
FORWARD, TOOTHGNASHER! FORWARD, TOOTHGRINDER!
FOR OUR LOST KIN WE BRAVE THE GULF OF STARS! FOR A VISION OF HOPE WE CROSS THE ABYSS OF DEATH!
AND WHEN THIS DAY IS TOLD IN SONG AND STORY-- WHEN IT IS ETCHED IN EDDAS ON THE GOLDEN PILLARS OF ASGARD-- LET THE POETS SAY BUT THIS--

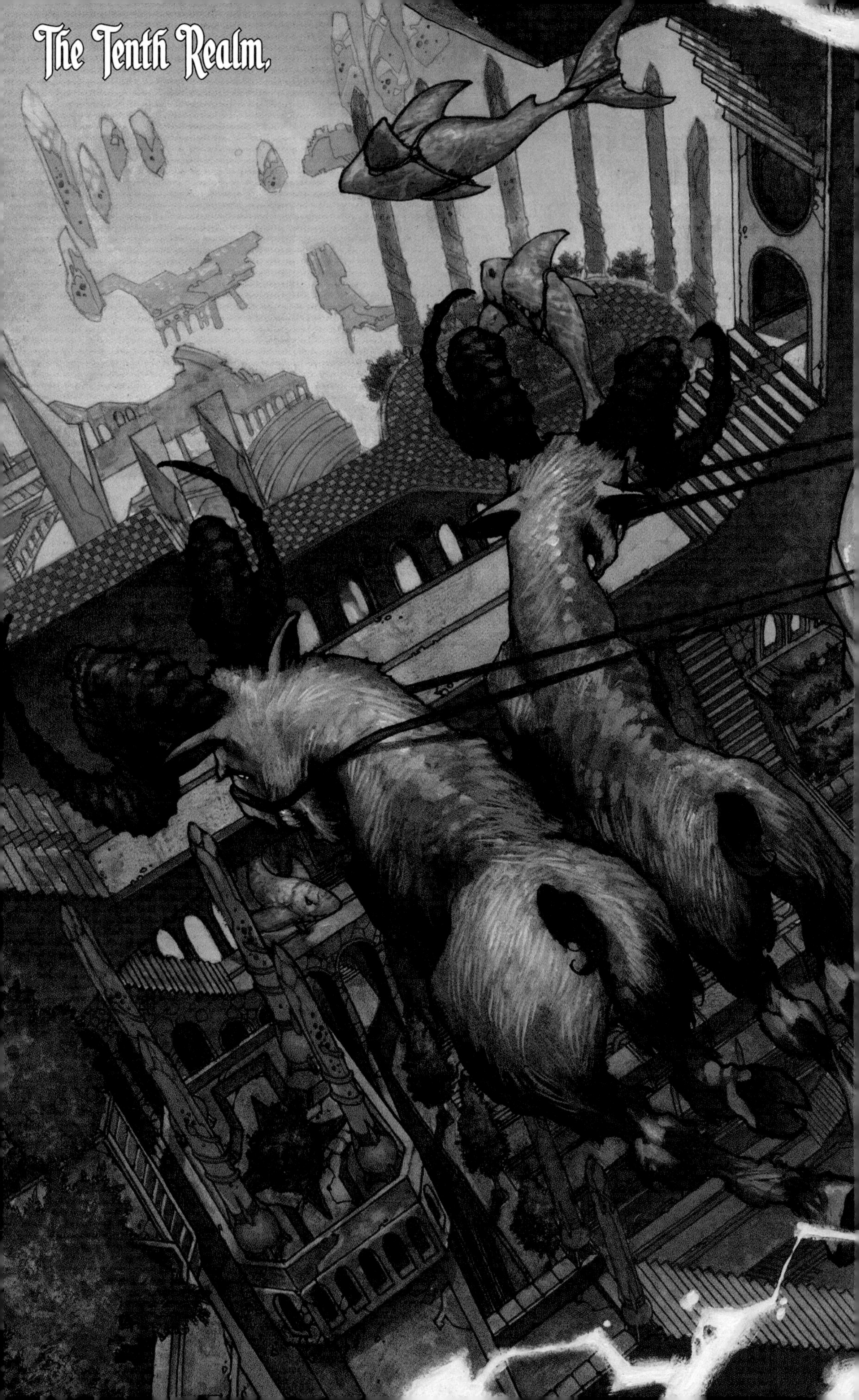
The Tenth Realm,

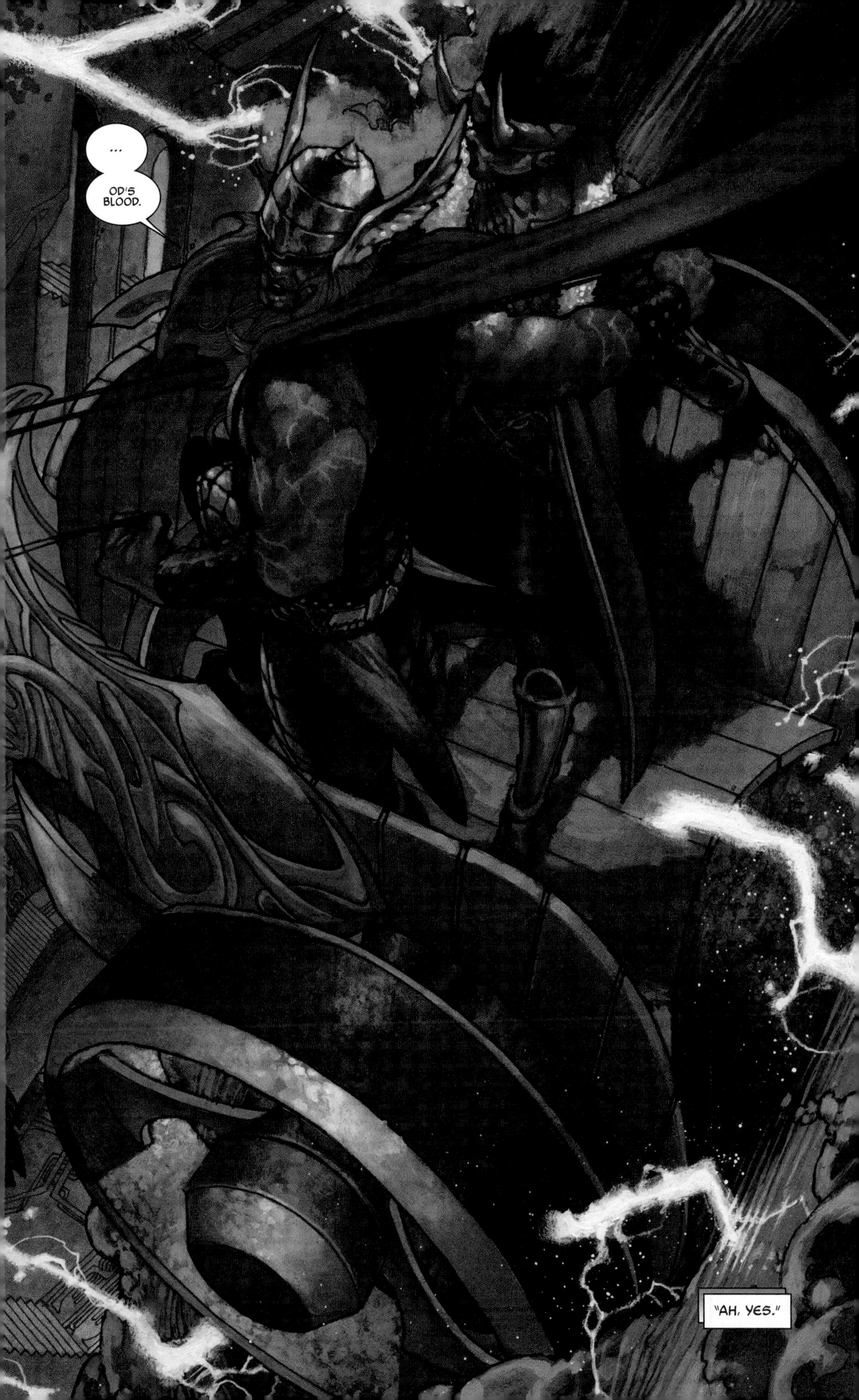
...
OD'S BLOOD.
"AH, YES."

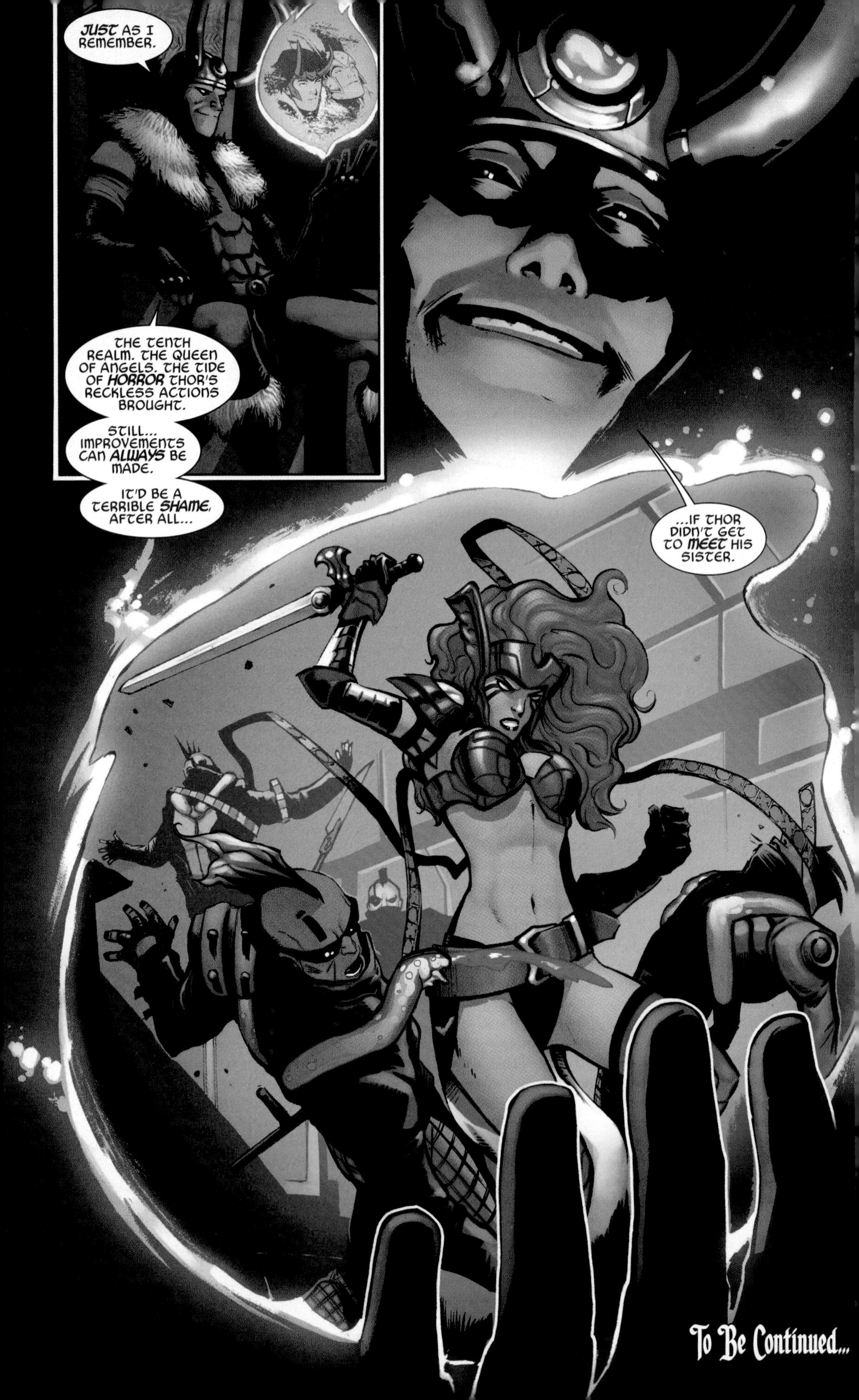
JUST AS I REMEMBER.
THE TENTH REALM. THE QUEEN OF ANGELS. THE TIDE OF HORROR THOR'S RECKLESS ACTIONS BROUGHT.
STILL... IMPROVEMENTS CAN ALWAYS BE MADE.
IT'D BE A TERRIBLE SHAME, AFTER ALL...
...IF THOR DIDN'T GET TO MEET HIS SISTER.
To Be Continued...

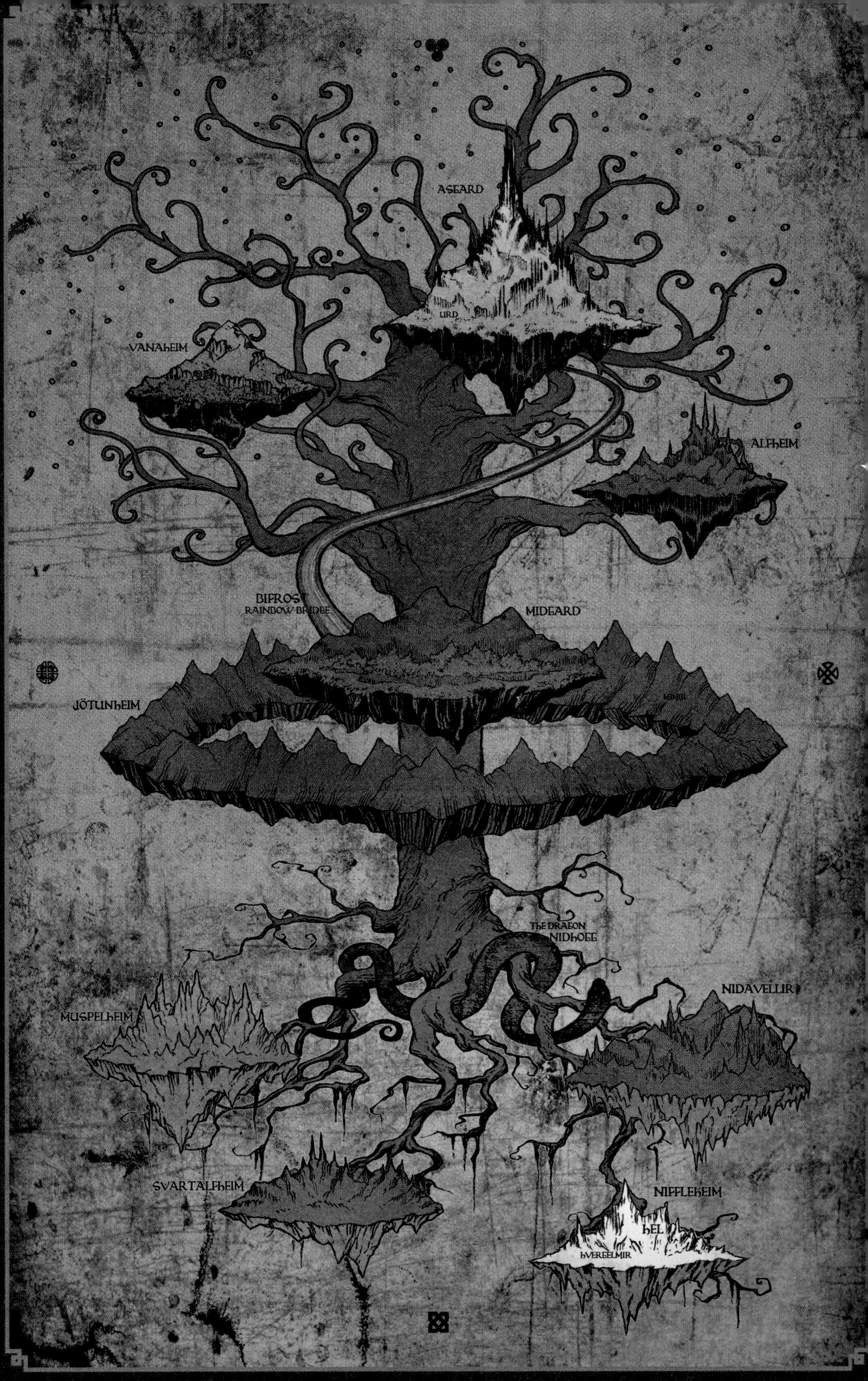
ASGARD
URD
VANAHEIM
ALFHEIM
BIFROST
RAINBOW BRIDGE
MIDGARD
JÖTUNHEIM
MIMIR
THE DRAGON
NIDHOGG
NIDAVELLIR
MUSPELHEIM
SVARTALFHEIM
NIFFLEHEIM
HEL
HVERGELMIR

MAP OF YGGDRASIL AND THE NINE REALMS, FROM ***LOKI (2010) #2***

(PUBLISHED BEFORE THE DISCOVERY OF THE TENTH REALM OF HEVEN)

PENCILER: **SEBASTIÁN FIUMARA** • INKER: **MICHEL LACOMBE** • COLORIST: **JOSÉ VILLARRUBIA**

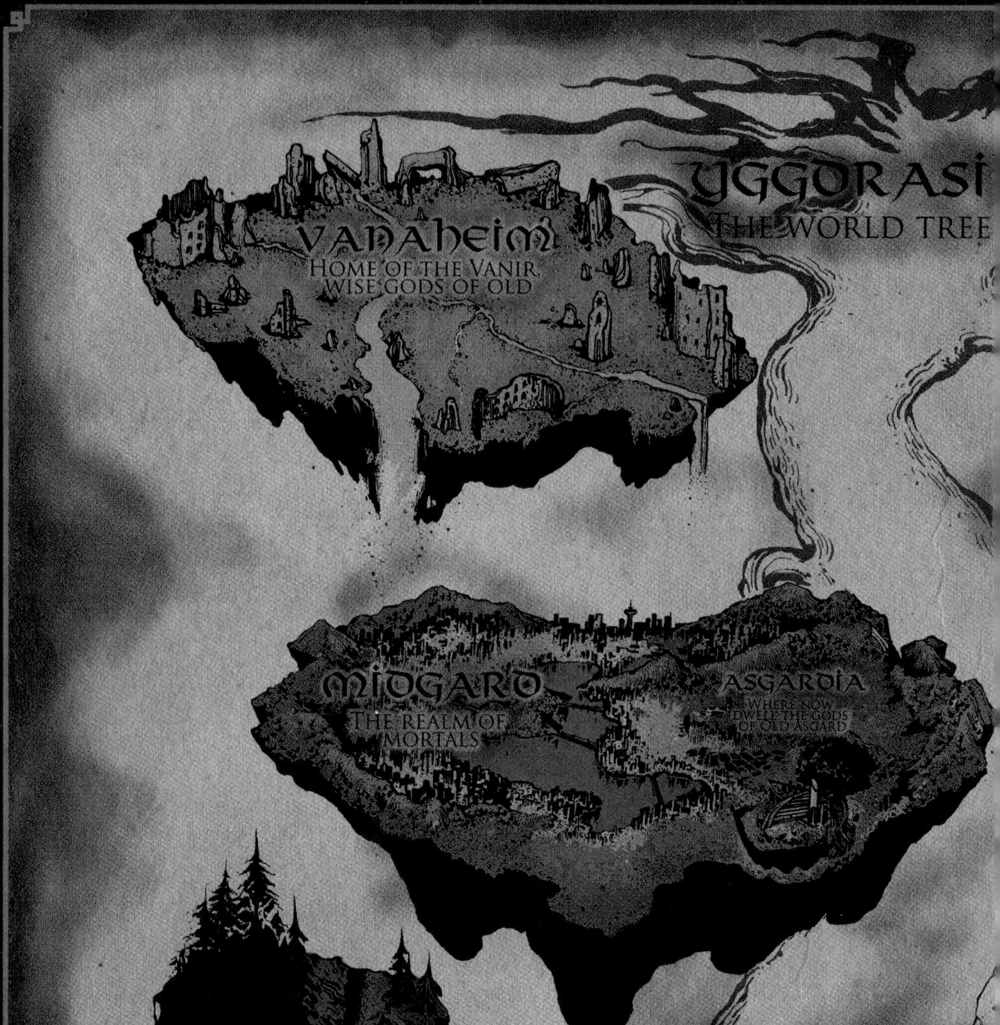
YGGDRASI
THE WORLD TREE
VANAHEIM
HOME OF THE VANIR, WISE GODS OF OLD
MIDGARD
THE REALM OF MORTALS
ASGARDIA
WHERE NOW DWELL THE GODS OF OLD ASGARD
NIFFLEHEIM
THE FROZEN UNDERWORLD
SVARTALFHEIM
THE DARK FAERIE REALM
THE NINE REALMS

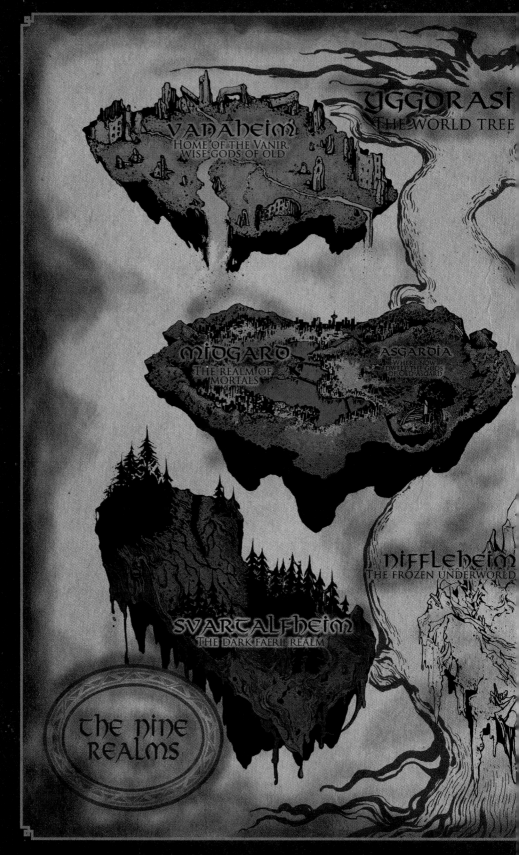

MAP OF YGGDRASIL AND THE NINE REALMS, FROM ***THOR: GOD OF THUNDER #13***
(PUBLISHED DURING A TIME WHEN THE ASGARDIANS HAD RELOCATED TO MIDGARD, BEFORE THE DISCOVERY OF THE TENTH REALM OF HEVEN)

ART BY **HAEMI JANG**

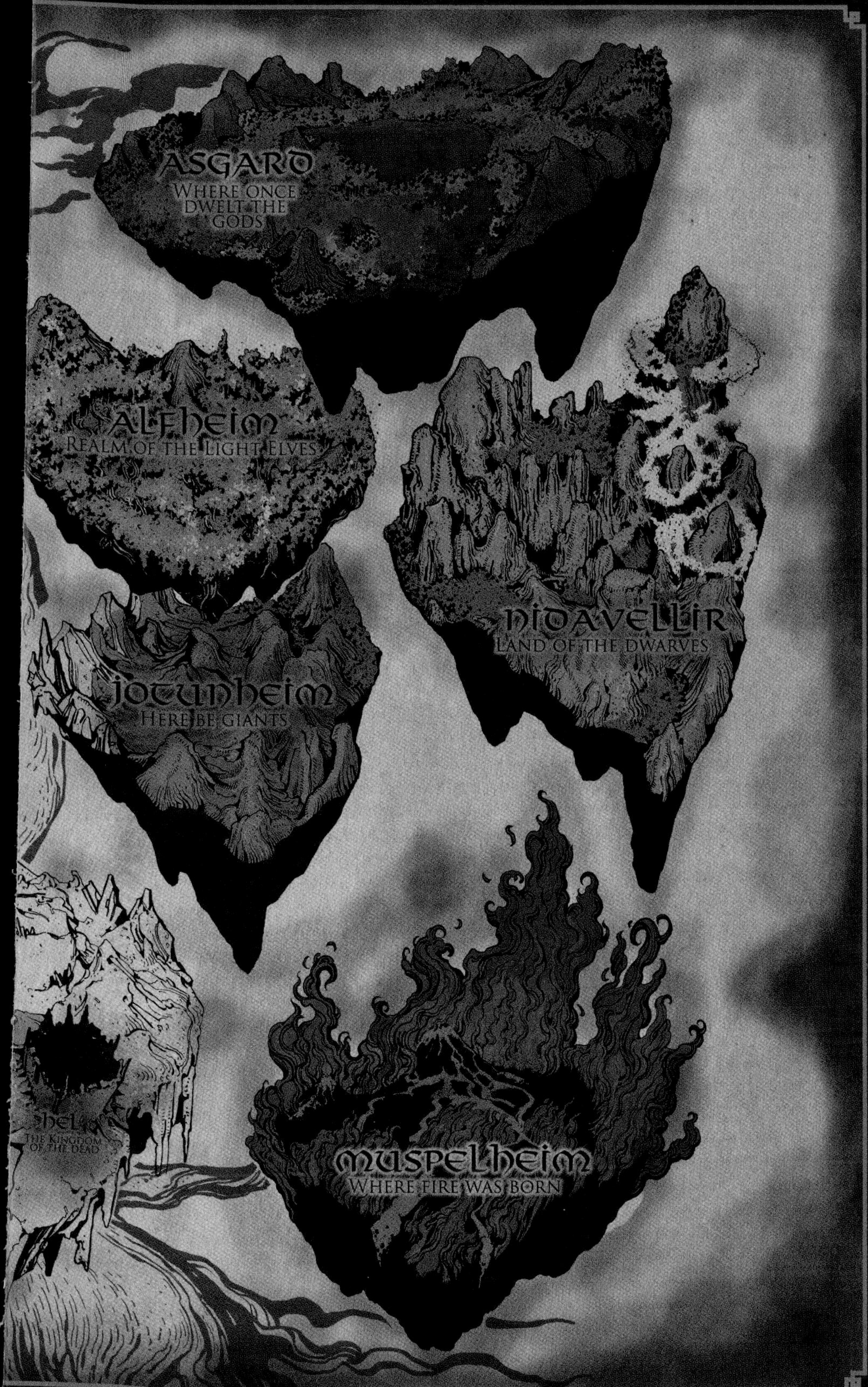
ASGARD
WHERE ONCE DWELT THE GODS
ALFHEIM
REALM OF THE LIGHT ELVES
NIDAVELLIR
LAND OF THE DWARVES
JOTUNHEIM
HERE BE GIANTS
HEL
THE KINGDOM OF THE DEAD
MUSPELHEIM
WHERE FIRE WAS BORN

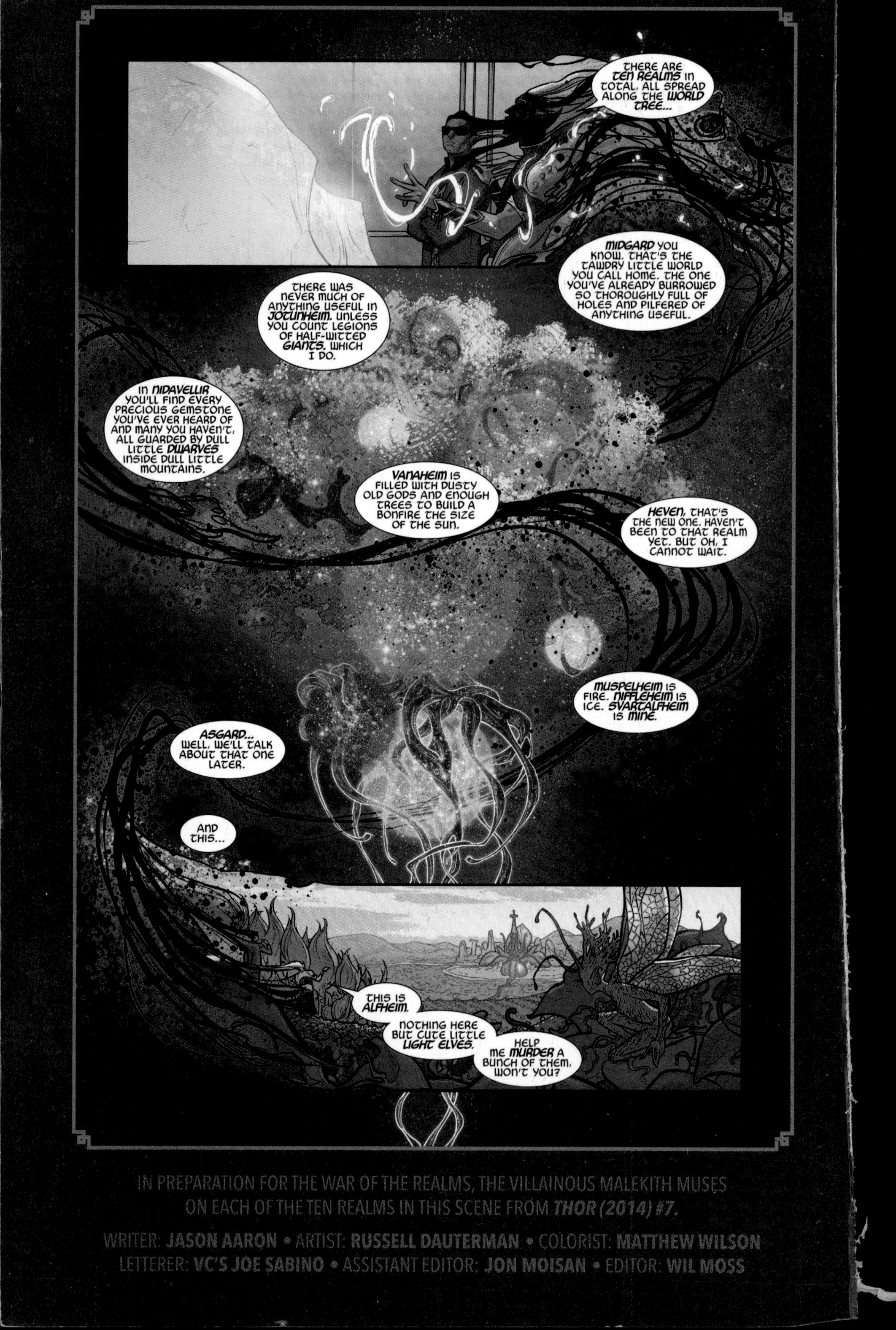
THERE ARE TEN REALMS IN TOTAL, ALL SPREAD ALONG THE WORLD TREE...
MIDGARD YOU KNOW. THAT'S THE TAWDRY LITTLE WORLD YOU CALL HOME. THE ONE YOU'VE ALREADY BURROWED SO THOROUGHLY FULL OF HOLES AND PILFERED OF ANYTHING USEFUL.
THERE WAS NEVER MUCH OF ANYTHING USEFUL IN JOTUNHEIM. UNLESS YOU COUNT LEGIONS OF HALF-WITTED GIANTS. WHICH I DO.
IN NIDAVELLIR YOU'LL FIND EVERY PRECIOUS GEMSTONE YOU'VE EVER HEARD OF AND MANY YOU HAVEN'T, ALL GUARDED BY DULL LITTLE DWARVES INSIDE DULL LITTLE MOUNTAINS.
VANAHEIM IS FILLED WITH DUSTY OLD GODS AND ENOUGH TREES TO BUILD A BONFIRE THE SIZE OF THE SUN.
HEVEN, THAT'S THE NEW ONE. HAVEN'T BEEN TO THAT REALM YET. BUT OH, I CANNOT WAIT.
MUSPELHEIM IS FIRE. NIFFLEHEIM IS ICE. SVARTALFHEIM IS MINE.
ASGARD... WELL, WE'LL TALK ABOUT THAT ONE LATER.
AND THIS...
THIS IS ALFHEIM.
NOTHING HERE BUT CUTE LITTLE LIGHT ELVES.
HELP ME MURDER A BUNCH OF THEM, WON'T YOU?

IN PREPARATION FOR THE WAR OF THE REALMS, THE VILLAINOUS MALEKITH MUSES ON EACH OF THE TEN REALMS IN THIS SCENE FROM *THOR (2014) #7.*

WRITER: **JASON AARON** • ARTIST: **RUSSELL DAUTERMAN** • COLORIST: **MATTHEW WILSON**
LETTERER: **VC'S JOE SABINO** • ASSISTANT EDITOR: **JON MOISAN** • EDITOR: **WIL MOSS**